The Brébeuf Hymnal

For both forms of the Roman Rite

Sophia Institute Press

SAINT JEAN DE BRÉBEUF HYMNAL

FOR BOTH FORMS OF THE ROMAN RITE

CATHOLIC CHURCH

Published with ecclesiastical approval.

Saint Jean de Brébeuf Hymnal

Printed & distributed by
Sophia Institute Press
SOPHIAINSTITUTE.COM

Printed in Belarus by Printcorp. Order 21048.

THREE Hurons escaped. Stricken with terror, they fled to the mission, where Brébeuf and Lalemant were just finishing the prayers after Mass. The priests heard the dreaded cry: "The Iroquois! They are at your gate!"

The two priests rose from their prayers and hurried out into the village. Stephen Annaotaha rushed up to them and exclaimed, "My brothers, save yourselves! Go now, while there is time!" Brébeuf and Lalemant knew they could escape, but they spurned the thought.

"No, Stephen," Brébeuf replied, "I am remaining to minister to my people to the end."

—From *The Life of Saint Jean de Brébeuf*

The Brébeuf Hymnal was created by and for choirmasters and priests working in real parishes across the globe; it is the antithesis of a theoretical exercise. Based upon the authentic Catholic liturgy, it neither mimics nor builds upon Protestant hymnals.

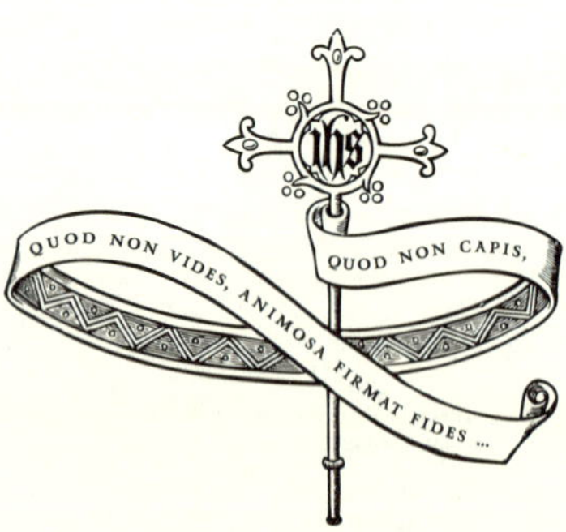

Our Guiding Principle: Excellence

BRÉBEUF and his companions wrote many letters to their superiors in France, which eventually formed the invaluable *Relations des Jésuites de la Nouvelle-France*. Considering the difficulties, it is a wonder that anything at all was written. Many of the Indians regarded writing as magic and feared that it might do them harm. That is why Father Chaumonot sometimes had to write in secluded places and carry his letters in his clothing. St. Isaac Jogues wrote some of his letters with a hand missing four fingers! Gunpowder was his ink; the earth, his table.

Today, Catholic musicians face *virtually the opposite* problem. There is so much available—of varying quality—it can be difficult to separate the wheat from the chaff.

> Our goal, therefore, was to include only
> the most excellent melodies,
> the most excellent texts, and
> the most excellent translations.

Abundance of Translations and Melodies

The ancient Latin hymns contain rich theology. For this reason, we have included *numerous translations*—since no single translation can fully capture the meaning.

To demonstrate the tradition of Catholic hymnody in the vernacular, we have printed extremely rare translations from Roman Catholic primers: 1599AD, 1685AD, 1706AD, and so forth. The admirable way our forefathers sought to faithfully translate the Latin is nothing short of remarkable. Because such ancient translations will not always be found suitable for today's congregations, we provide *modern translations* in addition to the historical specimens.

For many hymns, we provide *several tunes*, as singing a familiar text with a different melody forces one's mind to "consider again" the meaning—something conducive to intelligent prayer. We also provide the text alone, to which the thoughtful choirmaster can apply a melody already known by the congregation.

Traditional Catholic Hymnody

While our book certainly adds much that is new—in terms of texts and melodies—we had no interest in creating a "new" tradition of hymnody. The vast majority of our hymn selections (text and tune) were taken from outstanding Catholic hymnals, as will be observed from the sources provided at the bottom of each page.

NEXT TO the offering of the Eucharistical Sacrifice—which is the most sublime and the more essential act of divine worship—the singing of the praises of God and of the Lamb is unquestionably the noblest employment of a Christian. He who sings to God with a proper sense of devotion associates himself to the Choirs of Angels, and shares upon earth in the sweetest occupation of the blessed inhabitants of Heaven.

It cannot be doubted but that the most proper time for this holy exercise is when the faithful meet together in Church; and especially when the Lamb that was slain on the cross for the redemption of the world, comes down on our altars, and there continues to offer himself for us to his heavenly Father. [...]

Besides a variety of Spiritual Canticles, the Catholic reader will have the satisfaction of finding a translation in verse, as literal as this kind of composition could permit, of those ancient hymns, which have been sung in the Catholic Church on the various festivals of our Lord, of the Blessed Virgin and of the Saints, through the year, for upwards of fourteen centuries...

—From the Preface to *Hymns for the use of the Catholic Church in the United States of America* (Baltimore, 1807)

St. Jean de Brébeuf, SJ

Born, 1593; Ordained, 1622; Martyred, 1649.

"The history of the Jesuit Mission is connected with the origin of every celebrated town in the annals of French America. Not a cape was turned, not a river entered, but a Jesuit led the way." —*George Bancroft*

NOTHING IS MORE misunderstood by our current age than the virtue of humility. The Catholic understanding is simple: *humility is truth*. When we humble ourselves, it is merely a recognition that we deserve nothing and our Lord deserves everything. Ultimately, we sinful creatures do not have a "right" to anything:

(Lk 17.10) So you also, when you shall have done all these things that are commanded you, say: "We are unprofitable servants; we have done that which we ought to do."

The humility of Jean de Brébeuf made him feel utterly unworthy of the priesthood, prompting him to ask that he be a lay brother and no more, but the Master of Novices prevailed upon him to work toward the priesthood.[1] He would ultimately become—by the grace of God—a holy priest and one of the Church's greatest saints.

In 1617, Brébeuf made the decision to enter the Society of Jesus. The rigorous novitiate consisted of long hours of prayer, silence, fasting, and penance. Brébeuf's day—caged behind high walls in the heart of Rouen—was strictly broken up into half hours at the sound of an insistent bell, whereas before he had been free to follow his own ways in the open country, to arrange his own mode of life, and to make decisions for himself. In spite of the grinding routine, he was a model novice whose motto was, "I will be ground to powder rather than break a rule."

Very few have possessed Brébeuf's faith in God. He *volunteered* to become a missionary in New France (Canada). Leave aside for a moment his daily sufferings as a missionary—the wretched food, the constant annoyance of mosquitoes and gnats, the lack of any privacy, the unsanitary practices of the natives, the piercing cold, and so forth—which he suffered without complaint. Consider instead one solitary fact: Brébeuf willingly travelled thousands of miles on rivers (by canoe) and thousands of miles across the ocean (by ship)…yet he could not swim! This is true faith in God.

---

1 The biographical information about St. Jean de Brébeuf—as well as all quotations—come from *The First Martyrs of North America* (1953), by Rev. John Anthony O'Brien, SJ (d. 1980). Ordained in 1916, O'Brien earned a Ph.D. in psychology, wrote many books and pamphlets, and served as a professor at the University of Notre Dame. O'Brien's book is a summary of *Saint Among the Hurons* (1949) by Rev. Francis Xavier Talbot, SJ (d. 1953), who was the outstanding biographer of the Jesuit Martyrs of North America.

None but a fool would ask which of the Jesuit missionaries was the greatest. Even more foolish would be attempting to "rank" the torments they suffered, pitting one against the other. Nonetheless, due to the length of time he was in New France, the groundbreaking work he did, the native languages he deciphered, his towering physical size, and the fact that he served as superior, Brébeuf is considered the leader of the Jesuit martyrs of North America, and Fr. John A. O'Brien wrote as follows:

> Brébeuf was the only one of the eight canonized Jesuit martyrs of North America to exceed fifty years of age. All the others were born and died within the first half of the 17th century. He was among the first missionaries to enter Huronia and among the last to leave—and for years he was alone there. So much did he accomplish and so steadfastly did he labor, that it is scarcely too much to say that in a drama of surpassing characters he played the leading role.

We can learn about Brébeuf by studying the type of men he led.

Consider a short excerpt from the life of St. Isaac Jogues, one of Brébeuf's companions. Father Jogues had willingly given himself up to the Iroquois because he would not abandon his friends (in the same way Brébeuf would refuse to abandon his flock):

> In each village, the treatment was repeated, and their bodies were livid with bruises from head to foot. "Come," said an Iroquois chief, waving a knife, "let us caress these Frenchmen." The crowd surged up on the platform and beat and stabbed the prisoners. A sorcerer approached the priest and cried, "I hate this one most of all." With that, he commenced to gnaw his fingers. Next, he ordered a Christian Algonquin woman, a prisoner of the Iroquois, to saw off Jogues's left thumb with a jagged shell. She refused. The braves began to beat her and threatened to kill her. Trembling, she at last complied with reluctance. When the thumb fell to the floor, Jogues picked it up and, as he later wrote, "I presented it to Thee, O my God, in remembrance of the Sacrifices which—for the last seven years—I had offered on the altars of Thy Church and as an atonement for the want of love and reverence of which I have been guilty in touching Thy Sacred Body."
>
> In spite of his own piteous condition, Jogues never ceased to console the others. Kneeling at the side of William Coûture, an open sore from head to toe, he said: "Offer up all your pain to Almighty God, dear William. He will give you the strength to bear it and He will reward you a thousandfold."
>
> The Iroquois continued to torture the victims—cutting, stabbing, burning—till dusk fell. The prisoners then were placed in one of the houses, each of them stretched on his back, his limbs extended, his wrists and ankles bound fast to stakes driven into the earthen floor. It was time now for the children to amuse themselves. They placed live coals on the naked bodies. Sometimes the prisoners were able to shake off the coals. Like little demons, the youngsters chortled with glee when the victims were unable to dislodge the coals. On the three following days they were placed on the platform, where old and young, men and women, resumed their sport. In Tionontoguen, the children were adept and shameless in devising ways of tormenting the victims bound to the floor. "What things," exclaims Jogues, "what sort of things did they not do to us thus bound? What did they not do to my Huron brothers? What things, what sort of things, did they not attempt to do to me? But, again, I gave thanks to you, O my God, that always you have preserved me, your priest, pure from the impure hands of the savages."

Yes, these are the sort of men Brébeuf led. And that gut-wrenching description of the actions by Iroquois children is what caused us to make room in our book for hymns that will appeal to children in a special way.[2] May God grant that many children will sing these hymns, obtaining graces thereby, and may He eliminate cruelty from the hearts of

---

2 For example, hymn tunes like ZAHN and REGINALD, and hymn texts such as "Jesus, Lord And Savior, Hear Me As I Pray."

our children. May it be so. May it be so by the intercession of St. Isaac Jogues—who loved and forgave those who tortured him—and the intercession of St. Jean de Brébeuf, who had a special tenderness for children:

> As often as possible they gathered together the children of the village and sat them down in the cabin. Father Brébeuf would put on a surplice and biretta and chant the *Our Father*—which Father Daniel had translated into Huron rhymes—and the children would chant it after him. Next, he taught them the sign of the cross, the *Hail Mary*, the *Apostles' Creed*, and the Commandments.

We ask again: What type of men did Brébeuf lead? All the Jesuit martyrs were extremely intelligent, sophisticated men who had taught in the colleges of France. Consider St. Charles Garnier—a priest of noble birth—who repeatedly begged his superiors to grant him permission to serve as a missionary in New France. He was eventually allowed to do just that, travelling across the ocean to assist Brébeuf and the others:

> Father Francis Bressani (d. 1672), a Jesuit who had been tortured by the Iroquois in 1644—losing nine fingers in the process—relates that Garnier thought nothing of walking thirty or forty miles on the hottest summer day to baptize some dying Indian, when the woods were infested with Iroquois. On such errands he would sometimes pass the night alone in the forest in the dead of winter, reclining on pine branches. He sometimes carried sick people on his back (although he was not a strong man) for distances of up to six miles in order to gain the opportunity of baptizing them. Far from dreading an encounter with the Iroquois, Garnier "often told us," says Father Ragueneau, "that he would be quite content to fall into the hands of the Iroquois and remain their prisoner if, while they were torturing him, he at least had a chance of instructing them in the Catholic Faith as long as his torments lasted."

Father Garnier, in all his teaching activities, carefully noted the reactions of the Indians to the objects of devotion which the missionaries used to assist the catechumens in understanding the Faith, as shown by this letter to his superiors:

> I want a picture of Christ without a beard or with very little, as, for instance, when He was about eighteen years old. On the cross the figure must be very distinct, and with no one near Him, so as not to distract attention. Put a crown on the Blessed Virgin, a scepter in her hand, and have Our Lord standing on her knee. That quite takes the Indians' fancy. Do not use a halo; they will mistake it for a hat. In fact, the head must always be uncovered. Send me pictures of the Resurrection, and make the souls of the blessed as happy looking as possible. Avoid confusion in representing the General Judgment. In the resurrection of the dead the figures must stand out, and (if possible) let them be illuminated. The faces should not be in profile, but full and with the eyes wide open. The bodies should not be completely draped; at least a part should be bare. There must be no curly hair, and no saint should be bald. Beards also should be debarred, and birds or animals should be kept out of the picture. Our Lord and the Blessed Virgin must be very white, and with vivid-colored robes, red, blue, scarlet, but not green or brown. Let the saints coming down from Heaven be as white as snow, with bright garments, and with a happy, smiling countenance, looking affectionately on the spectators and pointing to a motto above: "The eye hath not seen," etc.

This letter by Garnier was quite important to our editorial team. Imitating Garnier, we meticulously examined each hymn text, fixing phrases which might be problematic—such as excessively archaic language, words whose connotations have changed, etc.—while always being careful to preserve the theology contained in these sacred texts. Brébeuf also inspired us in this arena, because of his work on *language*. He had become the world's leading linguist vis-à-vis languages spoken by the natives: Huron, Iroquois, Algonquin, and more. He never set out to be a linguist, but circumstances required it;

so he cheerfully spent countless hours creating dictionaries, devising equivalent phrases for theological concepts, and producing books (such as Ledesma's catechism, which he translated from Latin to Huron).

An interesting detail is mentioned by Father Paul Le Jeune (d. 1664), about St. Antoine Daniel, another of Brébeuf's companions:

> When we saw Father Daniel, our hearts began to melt. His face was wreathed in smiles but he was all spent. He was in his bare feet; he held a paddle in his hand, wore a ragged cassock, and his breviary was hanging by a string around his neck. His shirt was rotting on his back. He saluted all the chiefs and Frenchmen, and then we embraced. After adoring the Blessed Sacrament we all withdrew to my little room, where he told us how the Faith was progressing among the Hurons.

It would be interesting to know which version of the breviary was "hanging by a string around his neck," since this occurred in 1636, just five years after Pope Urban VIII rewrote all the breviary hymns. (We must forgive him for his ghastly mistake because it was he who gave Father Jogues special permission to celebrate Mass after the Iroquois had sliced off his fingers, making it impossible for him to follow the Mass rubrics.)

Speaking of the breviary, if anyone had an excuse to neglect their prayers, it would be the Jesuit missionaries—yet they never omitted a single devotion, no matter how exhausted they were. Fr. François du Péron was amazed to discover that in the missions:

> ...the daily prayers from the breviary are as well regulated as in our French colleges. At 4:00AM the rising bell rings; then follows the orison, at the end of which the Masses begin and continue until 8:00AM; during this period each one keeps silent, reads his spiritual book, and says his lesser hours.

Father Francis Xavier Talbot (d. 1953) wrote of Brébeuf:

> Just as he tried to divert attention from himself in the sacrifices he endured in helping others, so likewise Father Brébeuf concealed as best he could the penances he performed in private for his own sanctification. According to his spiritual director: "To the continual sufferings which are inseparable from the duties which he had in the Missions, on the journeys, in whatever place he was; and to those which charity caused him to embrace, often above his strength, although below his courage, he added many voluntary mortifications: disciplines every day, and often twice each day; very frequent fasts; haircloths and belts with iron points; vigils which advanced far into the night. And after all these, his heart could not be satiated with sufferings, and he believed that he had never endured aught."

Throughout Brébeuf's life, we constantly see his utter resignation to the will of God. Never did he ask God to take away the crosses sent to him. For this reason, we have included many hymns which focus on the Cross. Consider a letter Brébeuf wrote in 1637, when it seemed that he and his companions were about to be killed:

> Whatever conclusion they reach, and whatever treatment they accord us, we will try, by the Grace of Our Lord, to endure it patiently for His service. It is a singular favor that His Goodness gives us, to allow us to endure something for love of Him. Now it is that we consider ourselves as belonging truly to the Society. May He be forever blessed for having chosen us, from among so many others better than we and destined for this country, to aid Him in bearing His cross.

More than anything else, a music director working in today's environment must possess *equanimity*. The stress that accompanies the vocation of Church musician can at times seem insurmountable. Brébeuf truly is a special patron for Church musicians, as Father O'Brien explains:

> The other Jesuits had been daily witnesses to Brébeuf's piety, austerities, prayer prolonged far into the night in the blackness of the chapel, unfailing kindness, and selfless zeal. They valued especially his equanimity of temper, so important in a mission where vexations were daily and even hourly visitors. "His evenness of temper," wrote his later superior, Father Ragueneau, "seemed to be the virtue that outweighed all others. *Nothing* could upset him. During the twelve years I have known him, whether as superior or subject, I never saw him angry or even slightly indignant."

When a Huron village was captured by Iroquois, Brébeuf willingly surrendered—along with St. Gabriel Lalemant—even though he could have escaped. (He did this in order to strengthen the Huron captives.) Then began Brébeuf's martyrdom:

> Shivering from the bitterly cold March winds, the priests were driven with the Hurons into a huge cabin. Fires were burning about six torture posts. Brébeuf and Lalemant managed to speak words of consolation to the huddled Hurons, urging them to offer their sufferings to God. Each missionary listened to the other in confession and raised his hand in absolution. The Iroquois chose Brébeuf and some Hurons for the first torments. Leaping upon him as he prayed, they broke the bones of his hands and tore out his fingernails. When they dragged him to one of the posts, he embraced it and kissed it. Quickly they pulled back his arms and fastened his wrists to the post. They were determined to smash his courage and to make him cry for mercy. Placing burning sticks about his feet, they ran flaming torches up, down, and between his legs, around his neck, and under his armpits. Puzzled that he neither cried out nor winced, they held the firebrands closer till the skin frizzled, then they slashed his flesh with knives. Brébeuf thundered in a loud voice: "Jesus, have mercy on us!" This cry was re-echoed by the Christian Hurons.
>
> Greatly angered by his defiance, the Iroquois cut away his lower lip and thrust a red-hot iron down his throat. As the indomitable priest voiced no sound of pain, no plea for mercy, they tried other means. When Lalemant saw the burnt and bleeding body of his superior, aghast and trembling he spoke the words of St. Paul: "We are made a spectacle to the world, to angels and to men." Around Brébeuf's neck the Iroquois hung a collar of six red-hot hatchets that reached over his shoulders; when he stood erect, the irons burned him equally on front and back; if he leaned forward, three irons burned into his back, and if he leaned back, three irons ate into his stomach. "Jesus, have mercy on us!" was his only cry.
>
> Frantic at being unable to break his courage, the Iroquois fastened wood to his thighs and waist and kindled it until he was a living torch. They poured scalding hot water slowly over his head. They cut strips of flesh from his legs and arms and ate them before his eyes. "You told us," said a renegade Huron, as he stabbed Brébeuf repeatedly with a knife, "that the more one suffers on earth the happier he is in Heaven. We wish to make you happy; we torment you because we love you, and you ought to thank us for it." The priest spoke no word of reproof. He prayed for the forgiveness of his torturers and asked that through his agony the grace of faith might come to them.
>
> "Jesus, have mercy!" he cried, lifting his eyes to Heaven. They cut off his nose, sliced off his upper lip, and hacked off a piece of his tongue. They placed firebrands against his bleeding flesh and shoved one of them into his mouth. They even gouged out his eyes with a flaming stick. They hacked off his charred feet, tore off his scalp, and cut out his heart. This they devoured, and they drank his blood, thinking to imbibe some of his invincible courage. A chief raised his tomahawk over the head of Brébeuf and split the jaw in two. His four hours of torture were finished at 4:00 PM on 16 March 1649.

His wish had been granted, his vow fulfilled. Father Brébeuf had given his life for Christ and sanctified the soil of North America with his blood.

IN MARCH of 2018, a great theologian was asked why God has allowed the current crisis in the Catholic Church. He replied that these scandals are a type of test for true believers, to see whether we—being creatures—will respond with a simple prayer: "Lord, do with me what Thou wilt." Let us imitate St. Jean de Brébeuf, who exhibited a most remarkable resignation to Divine Providence throughout his life, in spite of unbelievable setbacks.

Brébeuf is considered the founder of the Huron Mission, which—from a worldly perspective—was a complete failure, because just as Christianity began to take hold, the Huron nation was destroyed by three scourges: (1) the relentless attacks of the Iroquois, armed with firearms sold to them by the Dutch; (2) famine; and (3) severe epidemics:

> The new year of 1650 brought the Hurons no new hope nor better prospects, but emphasized their state of desperation. Worse than the prowling Iroquois was the famine. The acorn supply was utterly exhausted. In their extremity, the Hurons dug up the carrion of dogs, foxes, and other animals. As more of the people died, the survivors ate their corpses. "They even devoured one another," reports Father Ragueneau, "but this in secret, and with horror. No longer did necessity recognize any law. Famished teeth no more discerned the nature of what they ate. Mothers fed upon their children. Children no longer recognized in a corpse him whom, while he lived, they had called their father."

The demise of the Hurons followed soon after the martyrdom of Brébeuf. Father Talbot has written: "By the providence of God, which none could understand and none could question, the Huron people and nations were brought to God and to death at the same time. Truly, the Huron Mission died with the death of him who had begun it."

But as Pope Pius IX reminds us: "He who does God's work does not do so in vain."

Saint Jean de Brébeuf now enjoys the eternal bliss of the Beatific Vision. He left for us an example *par excellence* of bravery, purity, Christian virtue, and total commitment to Jesus Christ. May he intercede for us.

Operam non perdit qui Deo laborat. (Pius IX)

Sixteen Instructions

1. Introducing new hymn tunes

Our book contains many beautiful melodies you will want to introduce to your congregation. However, we recommend beginning with tunes they already know. Play the new tune as an organ prelude, or improvise on it during the Offertory. Then have the choir alone sing it—in Latin or English—for a few Sundays, perhaps with just treble voices. These are ways a congregation can be taught "subliminally," so the introduction of a new melody causes no consternation.

2. Same tune, different text

Our hymnal deliberately uses the same melody for many texts. That makes it easy to expand your congregation's repertoire. Moreover, when it comes to feasts which occur only once each year (such as the Ascension), the director of music can easily choose tunes familiar to the congregation. No effort has been spared in this regard.

3. Same text, different tune

We have indicated possible tune pairings, but much will depend on which tunes your congregation knows. Two melodies worthy of special commendation are Eisenach and Gonfalon Royal, since both are compatible with ABAB or AABB rhyme schemes.

4. Pairings: Proceed with caution

Each congregation has its own sensitivities, and sometimes a particular melody has become strongly associated with a certain liturgical season. For example, Une Vaine Crainte, Tempus Adest Floridum, and Altona once had associations which have not fully faded in certain localities. Therefore, let each choirmaster pair according to what will be accepted by the congregation. If a suggestion made by us does not work, *skip over it and choose a different tune.*

5. Importance of the index

The indices are essential to this book, and have been placed in the center out of consideration for the musician. Whatever is used most frequently in a book belongs in its center. For the same reason, the Ordo Missae—*the part used most frequently*—is always located in the center of the Roman Missal. This tradition goes back a millennium.

6. Latin possibilities

For parishes wishing to incorporate Latin, as mandated by the Second Vatican Council (cf. *Sacrosanctum Concilium*, §36), we include many Latin hymns. They can be sung to metrical tunes or plainsong settings. Some believe plainsong hymnody is better performed by the choir alone, since large congregations often lack the requisite fluidity. When this is done, the congregation should utilize the "Assistance in comprehension," printed opposite the Latin. Plainsong settings do not belong in our book, since they are abundant in the *Liber Usualis, Cantus Selecti, Parish Book of Chant*, *Liber Hymnarius, Cantus Varii*, *Liber Antiphonarius*, and so on.

7. A comprehensive hymnal?

No publication could possibly contain every hymn, especially vis-à-vis Christmas hymns, which vary according to country. If a hymn is missing from our book, we recommend printing the text in your parish bulletin.

8. Unique treatment

Every text in our hymnal has been deliberately treated in a unique manner. Generally speaking, texts which are extremely ancient (or whose translations are particularly fine) are given more melodies than "normal" texts. In many instances—but not all—we print the text only, without musical notes, allowing choirmasters to assign their own melodies.

9. Notes at the bottom of the page

Footnotes have been formatted according to each text. If excessive notes would have cluttered the page, they are given as numbers/letters.[1] Our strong desire to make each page "self-contained" vis-à-vis footnotes necessitated an occasional inconsistency in layout, which we trust the reader will excuse.

10. Melodies for the choir only

Generally speaking, the tunes are very simple, but the alert choirmaster will notice a few melodies which would be better sung by the choir alone, such as Canon VIII. In such cases, the congregation participates the same way they participate in the homily: by listening.

11. "Last verses" collections

Footnotes reference two crucial Kevin Mayhew collections which provide colorful harmonizations for tunes: (a) *Last Verses for Manuals* by Richard Lloyd (1993); and (b) *400 Last Verses* by Noel Rawsthorne (2011).

1 The digit refers to the stanza, while the letter refers to the line of that stanza. So "5d" would refer to the fourth line of the fifth stanza.

12. A discovery has been made

Prior to being released, the melodies in this book were tested by real choirs, and a discovery has been made: American choirs are capable of singing hymns from the text only, just as English choirs do.[2] This applies to unison and SATB singing, if the hymn be of a reasonable length.

13. Stations of the Cross

Three versions of *The Way of the Cross* have been included so that priests will not have to worry about additional booklets during Lent. Catholics can also pray the Stations during visits to the Blessed Sacrament.

14. Urbanite or ancient?

Two obstacles prevented our indicating whether each translator used the ancient text or the Urbanite. First, some translators mix both versions. Second, differences were often so meager that such labels would have caused needless confusion. We, therefore, went with the ancient titles.

15. Capitalization conventions

In our hymnal, we honor the capitalization conventions of each author. Changing the poems to make them appear as if they were written by the same author would do violence to the artist's conception and is wholly unnecessary.[3]

16. Organization of hymnody

We avoid strict assignment of hymns to certain feasts or seasons because doing so improperly limits them. A few examples: *Ad Cenam Agni Providi* could easily be used as a Communion hymn; *Rex Sempiterne* touches on numerous themes of our Lord's life and, as Walpole points out, "is not especially suited" to Easter; *Jesu Nostra Redemptio* is in no way specific to the Ascension,[4] and so forth. Similar statements could be made about *Placare Christe Servulis*, *Pange Lingua* (Fortunatus), *Lux Alma*, and *Conditor Alme Siderum*. On the other hand, a Catholic sensibility would tend to limit certain hymns to specific seasons because of the associations which have developed over the centuries. Let common sense prevail.

---

2 Underlining is used to assist. For example, "earliest" would be sung with two syllables, not three.

3 Fortescue and Knox, for example, never capitalize pronouns referring to our Lord. On the other hand, certain publications—such as the *Laudate Hymnal* (1942)—do capitalize pronouns referring to our Lord, as well as many other words: *Jesus' holy Side; Gift Divine; the living Fountain, Fire and Love; before the throne of Grace does come; under Christ, our Head*; and so on. Each Roman Catholic primer also has its own radically different approach. Perhaps the most peculiar of all is Fr. Caswall, who capitalizes certain words when they refer to Christ—*Thou, Thee, Him, Heart*, etc.—yet does the opposite for other words referring to Christ such as *thy, his*, and *thine*.

4 Indeed, the official 1908 GRADUALE ROMANUM (p. 126*) assigns *Jesu Nostra Redemptio* and *Salutis Humanae Sator* (its Urbanite counterpart) as processional hymns for the feast of Corpus Christi.

Overview • Brébeuf Hymnal

Part I • Ancient Hymns of the Catholic Church

With literal translation, as well as numerous melodies and metrical translations.

Color Plates

Including facsimiles of Catholic hymnals with rhyming vernacular translations of breviary hymns reaching as far back as 1599AD.

Complete Indices

Located in the center of the book, immediately after the color pages.

Part II • Additional Hymns

Organized by the various seasons: Advent, Christmas, and so forth.

Stations of the Cross

ABECEDARIUS – The Life of Christ (5th century) 1

Alphabetical Hymn by Caelius Sedulius, Christian Poet

To sing in Latin,
use any 88 88 (LM) tune.

FROM the hinge of the sun's rising
to the boundary of the land,
let us sing Christ our Sovereign,
born of the Virgin Mary.

A SOLIS ortus cárdine
Ad usque terrae límitem,
Christum canámus Príncipem,
Natum María Vírgine.

2. The blessed Founder of the world
puts on the body of a slave:
that freeing their flesh with his flesh,
he might not lose those whom he fashioned.

BEÁTUS Auctor saéculi
Servíle corpus índuit:
Ut carne carnem líberans,
Ne pérderet quos cóndidit.

3. Heavenly grace enters
the body of the chaste Bearer:
the womb of the Maiden bears
secrets that she has not learned.

CASTAE Paréntis víscera
Caeléstis intrat grátia:
Venter puéllae bájulat
Secréta, quae non nóverat.

4. The house of a modest heart
suddenly becomes the temple of God:
one uncompromised, who knows not man,
conceives the Son in her womb.

DOMUS pudíci péctoris
Templum repénte fit Dei:
Intácta nésciens virum,
Concépit alvo Fílium.

5. The expectant Mother brings forth
him whom Gabriel foretold,
whom the Baptist perceived exulting,
enclosed in his mother's womb.

ENÍTITUR puérpera
Quem Gábriel praedíxerat,
Quem ventre matris géstiens
Baptísta clausum sénserat.

6. He submitted to lying in hay,
did not recoil from the manger:
and he by whom no bird goes hungry
was fed with a little milk.

FENO jacére pértulit,
Praesépe non abhórruit:
Parvóque lacte pastus est
Per quem nec ales ésurit.

7. The choir of heavenly ones rejoices,
and Angels sing to God;
and clearly known to shepherds becomes
the Shepherd and Creator of all.

GAUDET chorus caeléstium,
Et ángeli canunt Deo;
Palámque fit pastóribus
Pastor, Creátor ómnium.

8. O Herod, ungodly foe, why dost thou
fear that Christ should come? He who gives
heavenly kingdoms does not snatch away
those which are death-doomed.

HOSTIS Heródes ímpie,
Christum veníre quid times?
Non éripit mortália,
Qui regna dat caeléstia.

CAELIUS SEDULIUS lived in the fifth century, probably being born at Rome, and taught philosophy at Rome and in Achaia. It seems that he was converted by a certain Macedonius and that he then turned his talents to the cause of Christianity. Some state that he was always a layman, while others believe he was ordained a priest.

Abecedarius ... (cont'd)

Assistance for comprehension provided alongside the Latin

9. The Magi went, following
the guiding star they had seen:
by its light they seek the Light:
by their gifts they confess their God.

IBANT Magi, quam víderant,
Stellam sequéntes praéviam:
Lumen requírunt lúmine:
Deum faténtur múnere.

10. The band of mothers cries,
bewailing their children dashed together, *n1*
thousands of whom the tyrant
hallowed as victims for Christ.

KATÉRVA matrum pérsonat
conlísa deflens pígnora, *n1*
quorum tyránnus mília
Christo sacrávit víctimam.

11. The heavenly Lamb touched *n2*
the bath of pure water:
the sins that he did not bring
in cleansing us he took away.

LAVÁCRA puri gúrgitis *n2*
Caeléstis Agnus áttigit:
Peccáta, quae non détulit,
Nos abluéndo sústulit.

12. He gave assurance through miracles
that he had God as his Father,
healing sick bodies
and reviving corpses.

MIRÁCULIS dedit fidem
Habére se Deum patrem,
Infírma sanans córpora
Et súscitans cadávera.

13. A new kind of might:
the pots of water grow red:
and bidden to pour wine,
the liquid has changed its source. *n3*

NOVUM genus poténtiae:
Aquae rubéscunt hýdriae:
Vinúmque jussa fúndere,
Mutávit und*a* oríginem. *n3*

14. The centurion, kneeling,
prays for health for his slave,
the great fervor of the believer
has quenched the fires of fever. *cf. Mt 8.5-10*

ORAT salútem sérvulo
flexus genu centúrio,
credéntis ardor plúrimus
extínxit ignes fébrium.

15. Peter walked on the waves,
lifted by the right hand of Christ:
a path that nature refused
belief prepared. *cf. Mt 14.28-31*

PETRUS per undas ámbulat
Christi levátus déxtera:
natúra quam negáverat
fides parávit sémitam.

16. On the 4th day, already ill-smelling, *Jn 11.39*
Lazarus received life,
and free of the bonds of death
became a survivor of himself. *n4*

QUARTA die jam fétidus
vitam recépit Lázarus
mortísque liber vínculis
factus supérstes est sibi. *n4*

[1] "Pignora" means children by extension (lit. pledges, earnests).

[2] "Gurges" is a poetic term for water (lit. eddy, whirlpool).

[3] "Unda" is a poetic term for water (lit. wave, billow).

[4] I.e. "came to outlive himself."

Assistance for comprehension provided alongside the Latin

RIVOS cruóris tórridi
contácta vestis óbstruit,
fletu rigánte súpplicis
arent fluénta sánguinis. *n5*

17. His garment when touched stops up
the streams of parching gore: when the
weeping of the entreater waters them
the flows of blood go dry. *n5*

SOLÚTUS omni córpore
jussus repénte súrgere,
suis vicíssim gréssibus
aeger vehébat léctulum. *n6*

18. Slack in all his body,
bidden suddenly to rise,
by his own steps in turn
the sick man carried his stretcher. *n6*

TUNC ille Judas cárnifex
ausus magístrum trádere,
pacem ferébat ósculo,
quam non habébat péctore. *n7*

19. Then Judas, that butcher,
daring to betray his Master,
with a kiss bore him a peace
that he did not have in his heart. *n7*

VERAX datur fallácibus,
Pium flagéllat ímpius,
Crucíque fixus ínnocens
Conjúnctus est latrónibus.

20. The truthful one is given to the deceitful,
the ungodly one scourges the godly,
and the innocent one, nailed to a cross,
is put together with thieves.

XEROMÝRRAM post sábbatum
Quaedam vehébant cómpares,
Quas adlocútus ángelus
Vivum sepúlcro non tegi. *n8*

21. After the sabbath certain associates
were bringing dry myrrh,
and an Angel told them that the living one
was not sheltered in the tomb. *n8*

YMNIS, veníte, dúlcibus
omnes canámus súbditum
Christi triúmpho tártarum, *n9*
qui nos redémit vénditus.

22. Come ye, with sweet hymns
let us all sing hell made subject
by the victory of Christ, *n9*
who ransomed us when he was sold.

ZELUM dracónis ínvidi
et os leónis péssimi
calcávit únicus Dei
seséque caelis réddidit.

23. The only Son of God trampled
the jealousy of the malicious dragon
and the mouth of the most wicked lion
and returned himself to heaven.

[5] Mt 9.20, Mk 5.27, Lk 8.44.

[6] Cf. Mt 9.6-7, Mk 2.10-12, Lk 5.24-25, Jn 5.5-9.

[7] Cf. Mt 26.49, Lk 22.47, Mk 14.45.

[8] Cf. Mt 28.1-6, Mk 16.1-6, Lk 24.1-6.

[9] "Tartarus" is the hell of classical antiquity. Christ was sold by Judas (for 30 pieces of silver).

4 A Solis Ortus Cardine (5th century)

Caelius Sedulius, Christian Poet

To sing in Latin,
use any 88 88 (LM) tune.

A SOLIS ortus cárdine
Ad usque terrae límitem,
Christum canámus príncipem
Natum María Vírgine.

BEÁTUS Auctor saéculi
Servíle corpus índuit:
Ut carne carnem líberans,
Non pérderet quos cóndidit. *n1*

CASTAE Paréntis víscera
Caeléstis intrat grátia:
Venter puéllae bájulat
Secréta, quae non nóverat.

DOMUS pudíci péctoris
Templum repénte fit Dei;
Intácta nésciens virum,
Verbo concépit Fílium. *n2*

ENÍXA est Puérpera,
Quem Gábriel praedíxerat,
Quem matris alvo géstiens,
Clausus Joánnes sénserat.

FENO jacére pértulit,
Praesépe non abhórruit:
Parvóque lacte pastus est,
Per quem nec ales ésurit.

GAUDET chorus caeléstium,
Et Ángeli canunt Deo:
Palámque fit pastóribus
Pastor, Creátor ómnium.

† Glória tibi, Dómine,
Qui natus es de Vírgine,
Cum Patre et Sancto Spíritu,
In sempitérna saécula.

88 88 (LM)

Tune:
VARIOUS

CAELIUS SEDULIUS lived in the fifth century, probably being born at Rome, and taught philosophy at Rome and in Achaia. It seems that he was converted by a certain Macedonius and that he then turned his talents to the cause of Christianity. Some state that he was always a layman, while others believe he was ordained a priest.

Assistance for comprehension

FROM the hinge of the sun's rising
to the boundary of the land,
let us sing of Christ our sovereign,
born of the Virgin Mary.

2. The blessed Founder of the world
put on the body of a slave, *cf. Phil 2.7*
that freeing their flesh through his flesh,
he might not lose those whom he fashioned. *n1*

3. Heavenly grace enters
the body of the chaste Bearer:
the womb of a Maiden carries
secrets that she has not learned.

4. The house of a modest heart
suddenly becomes the temple of God;
one uncompromised, who did not know man, *cf. Lk 1.34*
conceived the Son through a word. *n2*

5. The expectant Mother brought forth
him whom Gabriel foretold,
whom John perceived exulting,
enclosed in his mother's womb. *cf. Lk 1.41*

6. He submitted to lying in hay,
did not recoil from the manger:
and he by whom no bird goes hungry *cf. Mt 6.26, Lk 12.24*
was fed with a little milk.

7. The choir of heavenly ones rejoices
and Angels sing to God:
and clearly known to shepherds becomes
the Shepherd and Creator of all. *cf. Lk 2.8-20*

8. Glory to thee, O Lord,
who wert born of the Virgin,
with the Father and Holy Spirit,
for ever and ever.

[1] "Lose" could also mean "destroy," i.e. damn.

[2] The word of the Annunciation (*Angelic Salutation*) brought about the Incarnation. On this, cf. *Quem Terra, Pontus, Aethera* (Fortunatus), the stanza beginning "Miréntur ergo saécula" and the third verse of *Agnoscat Omne Saeculum* (Fortunatus).

6 A Solis Ortus Cardine (5th century)

First Tune – *Trns: Fr. John Wilfrid Wallace, OSB (d. 1896)*

1. Now, from the ris - ing of the sun
2. The bless - èd Found - er of the World,
3. The splen - dor of ce - les - tial grace

Un - to the ut - most bounds of earth,
In form of guilt - y slave ar - rayed;
That bow - er fresh and fair il - lumes;

We sing the praise of Christ our King,
For flesh in flesh re - demp - tion wrought,
A Vir - gin's womb be - comes the shrine,

The Child of Mar - y's vir - gin - birth.
Lest they should per - ish whom He made.
Where God His hid - den throne as - sumes.

4. The chaste enclosure of that frame
Becomes a temple all divine;
In stainless purity she bore
The Son of God within that shrine.

5. The time fulfilled, she gave Him birth
Whom Gabriel had once foretold;
And whom, when yet within the womb,
Saint John exulted to behold.

6. A manger was His lowly bed,
Disdaining not on hay to lie;
And meager milk supported Him
Who feeds the ravens when they cry.

7. The choirs of heav'n exult with joy,
And angels sing before His throne;
The Shepherd of our souls supreme
To shepherds makes His Glory known.

8. O Jesus Virgin-born, to Thee
Eternal glory be confessed,
With Father and with Spirit, Lord
For ever in one Godhead blest.

* This melody at a lower key is on page 436.

88 88 (LM)

Tune:
Trinity College

Melody: John Bacchus Dykes (d. 1876).
M. Source: *Hymns Ancient and Modern* (1972) p. 64.
T. Source: *Hymns of the Church* (London: Burns & Oates, 1874) p. 66; the author is Fr. John Wallace, D.D., a secular priest who later became a Benedictine, taking the name "Wilfrid."

A Solis Ortus Cardine (5th century)

Second Tune – *Trns: Fr. John Wilfrid Wallace, OSB (d. 1896)*

4. The chaste enclosure of that frame
Becomes a temple all divine;
In stainless purity she bore
The Son of God within that shrine.

5. The time fulfilled, she gave Him birth
Whom Gabriel had once foretold;
And whom, when yet within the womb,
Saint John exulted to behold.

6. A manger was His lowly bed,
Disdaining not on hay to lie;
And meager milk supported Him
Who feeds the ravens when they cry.

7. The choirs of heav'n exult with joy,
And angels sing before His throne;
The Shepherd of our souls supreme
To shepherds makes His Glory known.

8. O Jesus Virgin-born, to Thee
Eternal glory be confessed,
With Father and with Spirit, Lord
For ever in one Godhead blest.

* This melody at a lower key is on page 864.

Melody: From a hymn book published by Fr. Melchior Ludolf Herold (d. 1810).
M. Source: *New Westminster Hymnal* (1939) p. 173.
T. Source: *Hymns of the Church* (London: Burns & Oates, 1874) p. 66; the author is Fr. John Wallace, D.D., a secular priest who later became a Benedictine, taking the name "Wilfrid."

88 88 (LM)

Tune: Bressani

8 A Solis Ortus Cardine (5th century)

Third Tune – *Trns: Fr. John Wilfrid Wallace, OSB (d. 1896)*

4. The chaste enclosure of that frame
Becomes a temple all divine;
In stainless purity she bore
The Son of God within that shrine.

5. The time fulfilled, she gave Him birth
Whom Gabriel had once foretold;
And whom, when yet within the womb,
Saint John exulted to behold.

6. A manger was His lowly bed,
Disdaining not on hay to lie;
And meager milk supported Him
Who feeds the ravens when they cry.

7. The choirs of heav'n exult with joy,
And angels sing before His throne;
The Shepherd of our souls supreme
To shepherds makes His Glory known.

8. O Jesus Virgin-born, to Thee
Eternal glory be confessed,
With Father and with Spirit, Lord
For ever in one Godhead blest.

88 88 (LM)

Tune:
O Invidenda Martyrum

Melody: Dijon Church melody.
M. Source: *New Westminster Hymnal* (1939) p. 42.
T. Source: *Hymns of the Church* (London: Burns & Oates, 1874) p. 66; the author is Fr. John Wallace, D.D., a secular priest who later became a Benedictine, taking the name "Wilfrid."

A Solis Ortus Cardine (5th century)

Fourth Tune – *Trns: Fr. John Wilfrid Wallace, OSB (d. 1896)*

4. The chaste enclosure of that frame
Becomes a temple all divine;
In stainless purity she bore
The Son of God within that shrine.

5. The time fulfilled, she gave Him birth
Whom Gabriel had once foretold;
And whom, when yet within the womb,
Saint John exulted to behold.

6. A manger was His lowly bed,
Disdaining not on hay to lie;
And meager milk supported Him
Who feeds the ravens when they cry.

7. The choirs of heav'n exult with joy,
And angels sing before His throne;
The Shepherd of our souls supreme
To shepherds makes His Glory known.

8. O Jesus Virgin-born, to Thee
Eternal glory be confessed,
With Father and with Spirit, Lord
For ever in one Godhead blest.

Final Verses: Richard Lloyd (1993) #158; Noel Rawsthorne (2011) #242.
Melody: Louis Bourgeois (d. 1561) based on a popular chanson. Bourgeois helped produce the *Genevan Psalter* and was once imprisoned (3 December 1551) for changing the melodies of well-known psalms "without a license." The tune was originally in the Tenor voice, but soon became its own melody; cf. Day's *Psalter* (1584) p. 272.
M. Source: *Hymns, Psalms, and Spiritual Canticles* (Marier, 1983) p. 361; *New Saint Basil Hymnal* (1958) p. 92.
T. Source: *Hymns of the Church* (London: Burns & Oates, 1874) p. 66; the author is Fr. John Wallace, D.D., a secular priest who later became a Benedictine, taking the name "Wilfrid."

88 88 (LM)
Tune: Old Hundredth

10 **A Solis Ortus Cardine** (5th century)

Fifth Tune – *Trns: Fr. John Wilfrid Wallace, OSB (d. 1896)*

4. The chaste enclosure of that frame
Becomes a temple all divine;
In stainless purity she bore
The Son of God within that shrine.

5. The time fulfilled, she gave Him birth
Whom Gabriel had once foretold;
And whom, when yet within the womb,
Saint John exulted to behold.

6. A manger was His lowly bed,
Disdaining not on hay to lie;
And meager milk supported Him
Who feeds the ravens when they cry.

7. The choirs of heav'n exult with joy,
And angels sing before His throne;
The Shepherd of our souls supreme
To shepherds makes His Glory known.

8. O Jesus Virgin-born, to Thee
Eternal glory be confessed,
With Father and with Spirit, Lord
For ever in one Godhead blest.

88 88 (LM)

Tune:
Whitehead

T. Source: *Hymns of the Church* (London: Burns & Oates, 1874) p. 66; the author is Fr. John Wallace, D.D., a secular priest who later became a Benedictine, taking the name "Wilfrid."
Melody: H. Whitehead, OP; about whom no information is available.
M. Source: *New Saint Basil Hymnal* (1958) p. 211.

A Solis Ortus Cardine (5th century)

Sixth Tune – *Trns: Fr. John Wilfrid Wallace, OSB (d. 1896)*

4. The chaste enclosure of that frame
Becomes a temple all divine;
In stainless purity she bore
The Son of God within that shrine.

5. The time fulfilled, she gave Him birth
Whom Gabriel had once foretold;
And whom, when yet within the womb,
Saint John exulted to behold.

6. A manger was His lowly bed,
Disdaining not on hay to lie;
And meager milk supported Him
Who feeds the ravens when they cry.

7. The choirs of heav'n exult with joy,
And angels sing before His throne;
The Shepherd of our souls supreme
To shepherds makes His Glory known.

8. O Jesus Virgin-born, to Thee
Eternal glory be confessed,
With Father and with Spirit, Lord
For ever in one Godhead blest.

Melody: Geoffrey Charles Edward Ryley (d. 1947); this tune can be sung as a Soprano-Tenor canon.
M. Source: *Hymns Ancient and Modern* (1972) p. 324.
T. Source: *Hymns of the Church* (London: Burns & Oates, 1874) p. 66; the author is Fr. John Wallace, D.D., a secular priest who later became a Benedictine, taking the name "Wilfrid."

88 88 (LM)

Tune: Canon VIII

A Solis Ortus Cardine (5th century)

Seventh Tune – *Trns: Fr. John Wilfrid Wallace, OSB (d. 1896)*

4. The chaste enclosure of that frame
Becomes a temple all divine;
In stainless purity she bore
The Son of God within that shrine.

5. The time fulfilled, she gave Him birth
Whom Gabriel had once foretold;
And whom, when yet within the womb,
Saint John exulted to behold.

6. A manger was His lowly bed,
Disdaining not on hay to lie;
And meager milk supported Him
Who feeds the ravens when they cry.

7. The choirs of heav'n exult with joy,
And angels sing before His throne;
The Shepherd of our souls supreme
To shepherds makes His Glory known.

8. O Jesus Virgin-born, to Thee
Eternal glory be confessed,
With Father and with Spirit, Lord
For ever in one Godhead blest.

88 88 (LM)

Tune:
Altona

Final Verses: Noel Rawsthorne (2011) #378; one note altered.
Melody: Schumann's *Geistliche Lieder* (1539); an adaptation by Fr. Stephan Lück (d. 1883) in his hymnal, *Gesang- und Gebetbuch für die Diözese Trier* (1847) p. 19. Called by various names (Vom Himmel Hoch, Erfurt, etc.) this melody has been set by such composers as Hassler, Gesius, Praetorius, and Bach.
M. Source: *Hosanna Catholic Hymn Book* (1914) p. 17; *New Westminster Hymnal* (1939) p. 8.
T. Source: *Hymns of the Church* (London: Burns & Oates, 1874) p. 66; the author is Fr. John Wallace, D.D., a secular priest who later became a Benedictine, taking the name "Wilfrid."

A Solis Ortus Cardine (5th century)

Trns: Fr. John Wilfrid Wallace, OSB (d. 1896)

Can be sung with any 88 88 meter: Hilderstone, Duguet, Breslau, Notre Dame, Melcombe, Wareham, Old Hundredth, Mein Seel O Gott, Trinity College, and so forth.

NOW, from the rising of the sun
Unto the utmost bounds of earth,
We sing the praise of Christ our King,
The Child of Mary's virgin-birth.

2. The blessèd Founder of the World,
In form of guilty slave arrayed;
For flesh in flesh redemption wrought,
Lest they should perish whom He made.

3. The splendor of celestial grace
That bower fresh and fair illumes;
A Virgin's womb becomes the shrine,
Where God His hidden throne assumes.

4. The chaste enclosure of that frame
Becomes a temple all divine;
In stainless purity she bore
The Son of God within that shrine.

5. The time fulfilled, she gave Him birth
Whom Gabriel had once foretold;
And whom, when yet within the womb,
Saint John exulted to behold.

6. A manger was His lowly bed,
Disdaining not on hay to lie;
And meager milk supported Him
Who feeds the ravens when they cry.

7. The choirs of heav'n exult with joy,
And angels sing before His throne;
The Shepherd of our souls supreme
To shepherds makes His Glory known.

8. O Jesus Virgin-born, to Thee
Eternal glory be confessed,
With Father and with Spirit, Lord
For ever in one Godhead blest.

88 88 (LM)

T. Source: *Hymns of the Church* (London: Burns & Oates, 1874) p. 66; the author is Fr. John Wallace, D.D., a secular priest who later became a Benedictine, taking the name "Wilfrid."

Tune: Various

14 Hostis Herodes Impie (5th century)

Caelius Sedulius, Christian Poet

To sing in Latin,
use any 88 88 (LM) tune.

HOSTIS Heródes ímpie,
Christum veníre quid times?
Non éripit mortália,
Qui regna dat caeléstia. *n1*

IBANT Magi, quam víderant,
Stellam sequéntes praéviam:
Lumen requírunt lúmine: *n2*
Deum faténtur múnere. *n3*

...

LAVÁCRA puri gúrgitis
Caeléstis Agnus áttigit:
Peccáta, quae non détulit,
Nos abluéndo sústulit.

...

NOVUM genus poténtiae:
Aquae rubéscunt hýdriae,
Vinúmque jussa fúndere,
Mutávit und*a* oríginem.

† Glória tibi, Dómine,
Qu*i* apparuísti hódie,
Cum Patr*e* et Sancto Spíritu,
In sempitérna saécula.

88 88 (LM)

Tune:
VARIOUS

This hymn is an excerpt from the ABECEDARIUS, just as *A Solis Ortus Cardine* was. After 1631, its title became *Crudelis Herodes Deum*, which does violence to the alphabetical progression of Sedulius. Several verses (i.e. "letters") were omitted in the Breviary to make it suitable for the EPIPHANY ("appearance" or "manifestation") which commemorates a three-fold manifestation: (1) to the Gentiles in the persons of the Magi (Mt 2.1-12); (2) to the Jews at the Baptism of Christ in the Jordan (Mk 1.9-11); and (3) to the apostles at the marriage feast (Jn 2.1-11). The doxology, needless to say, was not written by Sedulius—and "apparuisti" sounds the note characteristic of the Epiphany. Regarding the missing "letters," Msgr. Knox could not resist adding them.

Assistance for comprehension

O HEROD, ungodly foe, why dost thou
fear that Christ should come? He who gives
heavenly kingdoms does not snatch away
those which are death-doomed. *n1*

2. The Magi went, following
the guiding star they had seen:
by its light they seek the Light: *n2*
by their gifts they confess their God. *n3*

…

3. The heavenly Lamb touched
the bath of pure water:
the sins that he did not bring
in cleansing us he took away.

…

4. A new kind of might:
the pots of water grow red:
and bidden to pour wine,
the liquid has changed its source.

5. Glory to thee, O Lord,
who didst appear this day,
with the Father and Holy Spirit,
for ever and ever.

[1] "And I dispose to you, as my Father hath disposed to me, a kingdom…" (Lk 22.29).

[2] "A light of revelation to the Gentiles…" (Lk 2.32); cf. also Jn 8.12 and Is 60.3.

[3] The gifts of the Magi were expressive of their belief in Christ's royal generation, His divine nature, and His human nature. GOLD, the noblest of metals and hence suitable for a king, was symbolical of His royal generation. FRANKINCENSE, symbolical of prayer, was an acknowledgement of His divinity. MYRRH, used in embalming, was symbolical of their belief in His mortality as man.

16 Hostis Herodes Impie (5th century)

Trns: Msgr. Ronald A. Knox (d. 1957)

4. Lo, dipped in Jordan's cleansing stream,
   The Lamb of God would whiter seem;
   Yet 'twas our sins, in foul array,
   He bore, and bearing washed away.

5. Marvels the Pharisees refute
   That would his heav'nly birth dispute;
   The sick no more with fever burn,
   And at his voice the dead return.

6. New evidence of wondrous pow'r
   Behold in Cana's marriage-dow'r;
   Swift its own nature to resign,
   The water blushes into wine.

7. Jesus, to thee our praise we own,
   To Gentile pilgrims here made known;
   Praise to the Father endlessly
   And his life-giving Spirit be.

88 88 (LM)

Tune:
Gonfalon Royal

Final Verses: Richard Lloyd (1993) #80; Noel Rawsthorne (2011) #136.
T. Source: *New Westminster Hymnal* (1939) p. 11.
Melody: Sir Percy Carter Buck (d. 1947); first published in *Fourteen Hymn Tunes* (1913).
M. Source: *Catholic Hymn Book* (London Oratory, 1998) p. 140. The tune was originally paired with *Vexilla Regis* ("Flag of the King"). A *gonfalon* ("flag") was traditionally carried during Catholic processions.

Hostis Herodes Impie (5th century)

Trns: Msgr. Ronald A. Knox (d. 1957)

Can be sung with any 88 88 meter, such as EISENACH, ROGERS PARK, BRESSANI, LA ROCHELLE, KEMPEN, BESSEMER, TALLIS CANON, WINCHESTER NEW, etc.

HEROD, why thrills thy heart with fear?
The royal Child thou seekest here
Desires no earthly toys, for he
A heav'nly crown doth offer thee.

IN haste to Bethlehem that day
The wise men took their star-led way,
Their light to seek, where light doth show,
Gifts on the Giver to bestow.

KILLED at the tyrant's anxious call,
For Christ a thousand victims fall;
And mothers' hearts the piteous tale
Of murdered innocents bewail.

LO, dipped in Jordan's cleansing stream,
The Lamb of God would whiter seem;
Yet 'twas our sins, in foul array,
He bore, and bearing washed away.

MARVELS the Pharisees refute
That would his heav'nly birth dispute;
The sick no more with fever burn,
And at his voice the dead return.

NEW evidence of wondrous pow'r
Behold in Cana's marriage-dow'r;
Swift its own nature to resign,
The water blushes into wine.

† Jesus, to thee our praise we own,
To Gentile pilgrims here made known;
Praise to the Father endlessly
And his life-giving Spirit be.

88 88 (LM)

Tune: VARIOUS

T. Source: *New Westminster Hymnal* (1939) p. 11.

18 **Hostis Herodes Impie** (5th century)

Trns: Bishop Edward G. Bagshawe (d. 1915)

4. The water-jars blush rosy red,
New prodigy of Pow'r Divine!
The water its own nature changed,
When bidden to pour forth as wine.

5. Who to the Gentiles wast revealed,
O Christ, may glory be to Thee,
With Father and with Holy Ghost,
Now, and for all Eternity.

88 88 (LM)

Tune:
Altona

Final Verses: Noel Rawsthorne (2011) #378; one note altered.
T. Source: *Breviary Hymns and Missal Sequences* (London: Burns & Oates, 1900) p. 45; Father Bagshawe was a priest of the Oratory of St. Philip Neri until 1874, when he was consecrated bishop of the Catholic diocese of Nottingham.
Melody: Schumann's *Geistliche Lieder* (1539); an adaptation by Fr. Stephan Lück (d. 1883) in his hymnal, *Gesang- und Gebetbuch für die Diözese Trier* (1847) p. 19. Called by various names (Vom Himmel Hoch, Erfurt, etc.) this melody has been set by such composers as Hassler, Gesius, Praetorius, and Bach.
M. Source: *Hosanna Catholic Hymn Book* (1914) p. 17; *New Westminster Hymnal* (1939) p. 8.

Hostis Herodes Impie (5th century)

Trns: Bishop Edward G. Bagshawe (d. 1915)

Can be sung with any 88 88 meter, such as Hilderstone, Duguet, Breslau, Melcombe, Wareham, Old Hundredth, Mein Seel, Trinity College, etc.

THAT God Himself as King should come,
Why, cruel Herod, fearest thou?
He takes no earthly realms away,
Who doth with Heav'nly ones endow.

2. The Magi saw the star revealed,
And followed as it went before;
The true Light by its light they seek,
And as true God by gifts adore.

3. The pure and Heav'nly Lamb of God,
Into the limpid waters went,
And washed and cleansed us from our sins,
All pure Himself, and innocent.

4. The water-jars blush rosy red, *
New prodigy of Pow'r Divine!
The water its own nature changed,
When bidden to pour forth as wine.

5. Who to the Gentiles wast revealed,
O Christ, may glory be to Thee,
With Father and with Holy Ghost,
Now, and for all Eternity.

* The Catholic poet Crashaw beautifully refers to this miracle: "The modest water saw its God and blushed." When translating *Hostis Herodes*, many translators incorporate this language.

T. Source: *Breviary Hymns and Missal Sequences* (London: Burns & Oates, 1900) p. 45; Father Bagshawe was a priest of the Oratory of St. Philip Neri until 1874, when he was consecrated bishop of the Catholic diocese of Nottingham.

88 88 (LM)

Tune: Various

20 Hostis Herodes Impie (5th century)

Trns: Fr. Frederick C. Husenbeth (d. 1872)

4. Behold a new display of might,
As Cana's waters redden bright;
He spoke the word, and forth there flowed
A stream that nature ne'er bestowed.

5. To Christ, who did the Gentiles call,
Be endless glory paid by all;
To God the Father we repeat
The same, and to the Paraclete.

* This melody at a lower key is on page 436.

88 88 (LM)

Tune:
Trinity College

Melody: John Bacchus Dykes (d. 1876).
M. Source: *Hymns Ancient and Modern* (1972) p. 64.
T. Source: *Vespers Book for the Use of the Laity* (1841) p. 68; Rev. Frederick C. Husenbeth, a Catholic priest, also edited *The Roman Missal for the Use of the Laity* (1848). Several verses have been borrowed from other sources.

Hostis Herodes Impie (5th century)

Trns: Fr. Frederick C. Husenbeth (d. 1872)

Can be sung with any 88 88 meter, such as EISENACH, ROGERS PARK, BRESSANI, LA ROCHELLE, KEMPEN, BESSEMER, TALLIS CANON, WINCHESTER NEW, etc.

WHY, cruel Herod, dost thou fear,
Lest Christ, our God and King appear?
He who can heav'nly crowns bestow
Comes not to seize thy throne below.

2. The Wise Men, guided by the star,
Pursued their way from realms afar;
Lit by that light, the Light they seek;
Their gifts the present God bespeak.

3. Unto the pure and cleansing stream
Then came the Lamb, the Lord Supreme;
That He, to whom no sin was known,
Might cleanse His people from their own.

4. Behold a new display of might,
As Cana's waters redden bright;
He spoke the word, and forth there flowed
A stream that nature ne'er bestowed.

5. To Christ, who did the Gentiles call,
Be endless glory paid by all;
To God the Father we repeat
The same, and to the Paraclete.

88 88 (LM)

T. Source: *Vespers Book for the Use of the Laity* (1841) p. 68; Rev. Frederick C. Husenbeth, a Catholic priest, also edited *The Roman Missal for the Use of the Laity* (1848). Several verses have been borrowed from other sources.

Tune: VARIOUS

22 Hostis Herodes Impie (5th century)

1619AD – Historic Roman Catholic Translation

Can be sung with any 88 88 meter, such as HILDERSTONE, DUGUET, BRESLAU, MELCOMBE, WAREHAM, OLD HUNDREDTH, MEIN SEEL, TRINITY COLLEGE, etc.

O HEROD wicked enemy,
Why should Christ's coming thee afright?
He takes no mortal Sovereignty,
Who can to heav'nly Realms invite.

2. The sages went, e'en as their sight
Could note the star to go before,
They strive to find the light by light,
And him as God with gifts adore.

3. The Baptism of the river clear
Was hallow'd by the heav'nly Lamb;
He washing us, away did bear
Our sins, as without sin he came.

4. He shows new pow'r in actions strange,
The pitchers' waters ruddy grow;
That element doth nature change,
When forth in wine he bids it flow.

5. Glory (ô Lord) be giv'n to thee,
Who hast appear'd upon this day,
And Glory to the Father be,
And to the holy Ghost for aye.

Hostis Heródes ímpie,
Christum veníre quid times?
Non éripit mortália,
Qui regna dat caeléstia.

Ibant Magi, quam víderant,
Stellam sequéntes praéviam:
Lumen requírunt lúmine:
Deum faténtur múnere.

Lavácra puri gúrgitis
Caeléstis Agnus áttigit:
Peccáta, quae non détulit,
(Nos abluéndo) sústulit.

Novum genus poténtiae:
Aquae rubéscunt hýdriae:
Vinúmque jussa fúndere,
Mutávit und*a* oríginem.

Glória tibi, Dómine,
Qui apparuísti hódie,
Cum Patr*e* et Sancto Spíritu,
In sempitérna saécula.

88 88 (LM)

Tune: VARIOUS

T. Source: *The Primer, More ample, and in a new Order, containing The Three Offices of the B. Virgin Mary, In Latin and English, And all Offices and Dévotions, which were in former primers. In this last Edition the Hymns are in a better version and six Offices newly added: 1. Of the holy Trinity; 2. Of the B. Sacrament; 3. Of the holy name of Jesus, with a Letany; 4. Of the Immaculate Conception of our B. Lady, with a Letany; 5. Of the Angel-Guardian; 6. Of S. Joseph, and Sundry sweet Dévotions, and Instructions taken out of the holy Scripture for to live a devout Christian life. A large and short examen of conscience. To the calendar are annexed many English and Irish Saints.* (Rouen: Thomas Fitz Simon, 1684) p. 350.

Hostis Herodes Impie (Urbanite)

1719AD – Historic Roman Catholic Translation

Can be sung with any 88 88 meter, such as EISENACH, ROGERS PARK, BRESSANI, LA ROCHELLE, KEMPEN, BESSEMER, TALLIS CANON, WINCHESTER NEW, etc.

Crudélis Heródes, Deum
Regem veníre quid times?
Non éripit mortália,
Qui regna dat caeléstia.

Ibant Magi, quam víderant,
Stellam sequéntes praéviam:
Lumen requírunt lúmine:
Deum faténtur múnere.

Lavácra puri gúrgitis
Caeléstis Agnus áttigit:
Peccáta, quae non détulit,
Nos abluéndo sústulit.

Novum genus poténtiae:
Aquae rubéscunt hýdriae,
Vinúmque jussa fúndere,
Mutávit und*a* oríginem.

Jesu, tibi sit glória,
Qu*i* apparuísti Géntibus,
Cum Patr*e* et almo Spíritu,
In sempitérna saécula.

WHAT makes thee, cruel Herod, shake
For Fear that Christ thy Crown should take?
He will not seize an earthly Throne,
Who heav'nly Kingdoms makes our own.

2. The Sages coming from afar
Follow the new-appearing Star:
With Light they seek a better Light:
Their Gifts confess the God of Might.

3. The heav'nly Lamb in Jordan stood
To sanctify the crystal Flood:
Our Sins with that baptismal Dew
Were washed in him who Sin ne'er knew.

4. A strange unusual Pow'r is shown:
The Water-Pots are ruddy grown,
Whose Waters by Command Divine,
Their Nature change and run pure Wine.

5. To Christ who did the Gentiles call,
Be endless Glory giv'n by all,
To God the Father we repeat
The same, and to the Paraclete.

88 88 (LM)

T. Source: *The Evening-Office of the Church in Latin and English, containing the Vespers for all Sundays and Festivals of Obligation, with the Addition of the Old Hymns* (1719) p. 205.

Tune: VARIOUS

Ad Cenam Agni Providi (4th century)

Title after 1631AD: *"Ad Regias Agni Dapes"*

To sing in Latin, use any 88 88 (LM) tune.

AD CENAM Agni próvidi,
Et stolis albis cándidi,
Post tránsitum maris rubri,
Christo canámus Príncipi.

2. Cujus corpus sanctíssimum,
In ara crucis tórridum,
Cruóre ejus róseo
Gustándo vívimus Deo.

3. Protécti Paschae véspere
A devastánte Ángelo,
Erépti de duríssimo
Pharaónis império.

4. Jam Pascha nostrum Christus est,
Qui immolátus Agnus est,
Sinceritátis ázyma,
Caro ejus obláta est.

5. O vere digna hóstia,
Per quam fracta sunt tártara,
Redémpta plebs captiváta,
Réddita vitae praémia.

6. Consúrgit Christus túmulo,
Victor redit de bárathro,
Tyránnum trudens vínculo,
Et Paradísum réserans.

7. Quaésumus, Auctor ómnium,
In hoc Pascháli gáudio,
Ab omni mortis ímpetu
Tuum defénde pópulum.

8. Glória tibi, Dómine,
Qui surrexíst*i* a mórtuis,
Cum Patr*e* et Sancto Spíritu,
In sempitérna saécula.

Text: The author is not known. One possible use would be as a Communion hymn.
T. Source: *Hymni de Tempore et de Sanctis in Textu Antiquo et Novo* (Solesmes, 1885) p. 48.

88 88 (LM)

Tune:
VARIOUS

[1a] Cf. Ex 12.11; Ap 19.9.

[1b] Cf. baptismal garments; cf. Ap 7.9, 14.

[1c] Cf. Ex 14.29f.

Assistance for comprehension

AT the Lamb's supper watching,
and in white robes shining,
after the crossing of the Red Sea,
let us sing to Christ our Sovereign.

2. By the partaking of his most holy body,
which was parched on the altar of the cross,
with his rosy blood,
we live to God.

3. Shielded on the evening of the Pasch
from the Angel laying waste,
snatched from the harshest
control of the Pharao.

4. Now Christ is our Pasch,
he who is the sacrificed Lamb,
unleavened bread of guilelessness,
his flesh has been offered.

5. O victim truly worthy,
by which the infernal realms are vanquished,
the captive folk ransomed,
the boons of life restored!

6. Christ rises up from the burial mound,
the conqueror returns from the abyss,
thrusting the despot in fetters,
and unlocking Paradise.

7. We beseech thee, Founder of all,
with this Paschal joy,
from every assault of death
safeguard thy people.

8. Glory to thee, O Lord,
who didst arise from the dead,
with the Father, and the Holy Spirit,
for ages everlasting.

[2b] Parched with thirst, cf. Jn 19.28; and thus roasted like the Paschal lamb, cf. Ex 12.8f.

[2d] Cf. Rom 6.9-11.

[3a] *Vesper* can mean "evening meal" as well as "evening."

[3b] Cf. Ex 12.13, 23; I Cor 10.10.

[4b] Cf. I Cor 5.7: *Pascha* can refer to the Passover lamb in particular as well as the Passover in general.

[4c] Cf. Ex 12.8; I Cor 5.8.

[6a] Figurative inasmuch as Christ was not buried but entombed.

[6c] Cf. Heb 2.14; Ap 20.2.

Ad Cenam Agni Providi (4th century)

First Tune – *Trns: Fr. John Fitzpatrick, Oblate of Mary* (*d.* 1929)

1. As at the Lamb's high feast we sit,
2. To us, with char - i - ty di - vine,
3. Awed, by the door posts marked with blood,

And, clad in white, par - take_ of__ it,
He doth His Sa - cred Blood as - sign:
The dev - as - ta - ting An - gel__ stood;

Since we have passed the dark Red Sea, Our_
His hal - lowed Bod - y, as a priest, His__
The sea is part - ed, then it flows To -

hymns for_ Christ, our Lead - er, be. *A - men.*
love_ ap - points our host and feast.
geth - er,__ drown - ing Is - raël's foes.

4. The Christ is now our Pasch indeed:
   Our Victim He, for us to plead;
   And He, since pure with pure is fed,
   Sincerity's unleavened Bread.

5. O Thou true Victim in the skies,
   Before Thee, hell subjected lies,
   By Thee are loosened death's cold chains,
   Through Thee the soul life's guerdon gains.

6. Thou, Christ victorious o'er the grave
   Unfurl'st Thy banner, there to wave,
   And, op'ning Heav'n, dost in Thy might
   The Prince of darkness put to flight.

Verse 7 may be omitted outside of Paschal Time :

7. O Jesus, that Thou mayest thus
   Be endless Paschal joy to us,
   Keep us, who now new life begin,
   Free from the woeful death of sin.

8. To God the Father glory be,
   The Son, from death arisen free,
   The Paraclete, from day to day,
   While ageless ages pass away.

88 88 (LM)

Tune:
Gonfalon Royal

Final Verses: Richard Lloyd (1993) #80; Noel Rawsthorne (2011) #136.
T. Source: *The Breviary and Missal Hymns* (London: Sands & Co, 1931) p. 72.
Melody: Sir Percy Carter Buck (d. 1947); first published in *Fourteen Hymn Tunes* (1913).
M. Source: *Catholic Hymn Book* (London Oratory, 1998) p. 140. The tune was originally paired with *Vexilla Regis* ("Flag of the King"). A *gonfalon* ("flag") was traditionally carried during Catholic processions.

Ad Cenam Agni Providi (4th century)

Second Tune – *Trns: Fr. John Fitzpatrick, Oblate of Mary (d. 1929)*

4. The Christ is now our Pasch indeed:
Our Victim He, for us to plead;
And He, since pure with pure is fed,
Sincerity's unleavened Bread.

5. O Thou true Victim in the skies,
Before Thee, hell subjected lies,
By Thee are loosened death's cold chains,
Through Thee the soul life's guerdon gains.

6. Thou, Christ victorious o'er the grave
Unfurl'st Thy banner, there to wave,
And, op'ning Heav'n, dost in Thy might
The Prince of darkness put to flight.

Verse 7 may be omitted outside of Paschal Time :

7. O Jesus, that Thou mayest thus
Be endless Paschal joy to us,
Keep us, who now new life begin,
Free from the woeful death of sin.

8. To God the Father glory be,
The Son, from death arisen free,
The Paraclete, from day to day,
While ageless ages pass away.

Final Verses: Richard Lloyd (1993) #64; Noel Rawsthorne (2011) #108.
T. Source: *The Breviary and Missal Hymns* (London: Sands & Co, 1931) p. 72.
Melody: Bartholomäus Gesius (d. 1613); adapted by Johann H. Schein (d. 1630).
M. Source: *New Saint Basil Hymnal* (1958) p. 120; *The Catholic Vesper Hymn Book set to Music either for Unison or Four Voices with Accompaniment* (Charles Lewis, 1877) p. 34; *Pope Pius XII Hymnal* (Ohio: Gregorian Institute of America, 1959) p. 13.

88 88 (LM)

Tune: Eisenach

Ad Cenam Agni Providi (4th century)

THIRD TUNE – *Trns: Fr. John Fitzpatrick, Oblate of Mary (d. 1929)*

88 88 A

Tune:
LASST UNS ERFREUEN

Final Verses: Richard Lloyd (1993) #111; Noel Rawsthorne (2011) #178.
T. Source: *The Breviary and Missal Hymns* (London: Sands & Co, 1931) p. 72.
Melody: From a Jesuit collection (Cologne, 1623) entitled *Sacred Catholic Church Hymns, from Pentecost to Advent, Christmastide, Lenten Hymns, Paschal Hymns, Pilgrim songs, and all kinds to be sung throughout the whole year.* Two forms exist—placing "Alleluia" in various spots—and both are equally authentic.
M. Source: *Catholic Hymn Book* (1998) p. 478; *Hymns, Psalms, & Spiritual Canticles* (Marier, 1983) p. 328.

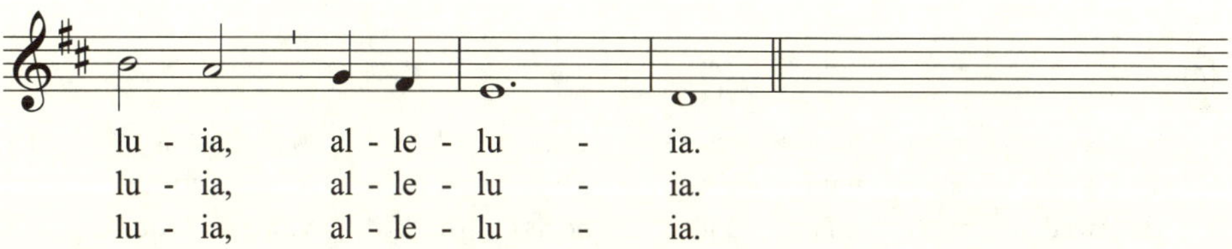

4. The Christ is now our Pasch indeed:
Our Victim He, for us to plead;
O praise Him! Alleluia!
And He, since pure with pure is fed,
Sincerity's unleavened Bread.

R. *Let us praise Him, let us praise Him,*
Alleluia, alleluia, alleluia.

5. O Thou true Victim in the skies,
Before Thee, hell subjected lies,
O praise Him! Alleluia!
By Thee are loosened death's cold chains,
Through Thee the soul life's guerdon gains. *R.*

6. Thou, Christ victorious o'er the grave
Unfurl'st Thy banner, there to wave,
O praise Him! Alleluia!
And, op'ning Heav'n, dost in Thy might
The Prince of darkness put to flight. *R.*

Verse 7 may be omitted outside of Paschal Time :

7. O Jesus, that Thou mayest thus
Be endless Paschal joy to us,
O praise Him! Alleluia!
Keep us, who now new life begin,
Free from the woeful death of sin. *R.*

8. To God the Father glory be,
The Son, from death arisen free,
O praise Him! Alleluia!
The Paraclete, from day to day,
While ageless ages pass away. *R.*

30 Ad Cenam Agni Providi (4th century)

FOURTH TUNE – *Trns: Fr. John Fitzpatrick, Oblate of Mary (d. 1929)*

4. The Christ is now our Pasch indeed:
   Our Victim He, for us to plead;
   And He, since pure with pure is fed,
   Sincerity's unleavened Bread.

5. O Thou true Victim in the skies,
   Before Thee, hell subjected lies,
   By Thee are loosened death's cold chains,
   Through Thee the soul life's guerdon gains.

6. Thou, Christ victorious o'er the grave
   Unfurl'st Thy banner, there to wave,
   And, op'ning Heav'n, dost in Thy might
   The Prince of darkness put to flight.

Verse 7 may be omitted outside of Paschal Time :

7. O Jesus, that Thou mayest thus
   Be endless Paschal joy to us,
   Keep us, who now new life begin,
   Free from the woeful death of sin.

8. To God the Father glory be,
   The Son, from death arisen free,
   The Paraclete, from day to day,
   While ageless ages pass away.

88 88 (LM)

Tune: ALTONA

Final Verses: Noel Rawsthorne (2011) #378; one note altered.
T. Source: *The Breviary and Missal Hymns* (London: Sands & Co, 1931) p. 72.
Melody: Schumann's *Geistliche Lieder* (1539); an adaptation by Fr. Stephan Lück (d. 1883) in his hymnal, *Gesang- und Gebetbuch für die Diözese Trier* (1847) p. 19. Called by various names (VOM HIMMEL HOCH, ERFURT, etc.) this melody has been set by such composers as Hassler, Gesius, Praetorius, and Bach.
M. Source: *Hosanna Catholic Hymn Book* (1914) p. 17; *New Westminster Hymnal* (1939) p. 8.

Ad Cenam Agni Providi (4th century)

Trns: Fr. John Fitzpatrick, Oblate of Mary (d. 1929)

Can be sung with any 88 88 meter: Eisenach, Bressani, Rogers Park, La Rochelle, Kempen, Bessemer, Tallis Canon, Winchester New, and so forth.

As at the Lamb's high feast we sit,
And, clad in white, partake of it,
Since we have passed the dark Red Sea,
Our hymns for Christ, our Leader, be.

2. To us, with charity divine,
He doth His Sacred Blood assign:
His hallowed Body, as a priest,
His love appoints our host and feast.

3. Awed, by the door posts marked with blood,
The devastating Angel stood;
The sea is parted, then it flows
Together, drowning Israël's foes.

4. The Christ is now our Pasch indeed:
Our Victim He, for us to plead;
And He, since pure with pure is fed,
Sincerity's unleavened Bread.

5. O Thou true Victim in the skies,
Before Thee, hell subjected lies,
By Thee are loosened death's cold chains,
Through Thee the soul life's guerdon gains.

6. Thou, Christ victorious o'er the grave
Unfurl'st Thy banner, there to wave,
And, op'ning Heav'n, dost in Thy might
The Prince of darkness put to flight.

Verse 7 may be omitted outside of Paschal Time :

7. O Jesus, that Thou mayest thus
Be endless Paschal joy to us,
Keep us, who now new life begin,
Free from the woeful death of sin.

8. To God the Father glory be,
The Son, from death arisen free,
The Paraclete, from day to day,
While ageless ages pass away.

88 88 (LM)

Tune: Various

T. Source: *The Breviary and Missal Hymns* (London: Sands & Co, 1931) p. 72.

Ad Cenam Agni Providi (4th century)

First Tune – *Trns: Fr. Frederick C. Husenbeth (d. 1872)*

4. Christ is the Pasch we sacrifice,
   Pure victim to the Father's eyes,
   Approaching with unsullied mind,
   May all his grace and mercy find.

5. Celestial victim, spotless, true,
   Who hell's dark victim overthrew,
   From chains of death our souls relieved,
   And life's perennial crown received.

6. Victor of hell, Christ ris'n displays
   His trophies bright with glory's rays,
   And op'ning heav'n, he binds his chain
   Around the king of hell's domain.

Verse 7 may be omitted outside of Paschal Time :

7. O Jesus! that our faithful mind
   In thee pure paschal joy may find,
   From deadly sin redeem us free,
   And grant us life renewed in thee.

8. To God the Father, to the Son,
   Who rose from death, his vict'ry won,
   And Holy Spirit, hymns of praise
   And glory sempiternal raise.

88 88 (LM)

Tune: Whitehall

Melody: Henry Lawes (d. 1662).
M. Source: *Saint Edmund Campion Missal and Hymnal* (2013) p. 888.
T. Source: *Vespers Book for the Use of the Laity* (1841) p. 93; Rev. Frederick C. Husenbeth, a Catholic priest, also edited *The Roman Missal for the Use of the Laity* (1848).

Ad Cenam Agni Providi (4th century)

Second Tune – *Trns: Fr. Frederick C. Husenbeth (d. 1872)*

4. Christ is the Pasch we sacrifice,
Pure victim to the Father's eyes,
Approaching with unsullied mind,
May all his grace and mercy find.

5. Celestial victim, spotless, true,
Who hell's dark victim overthrew,
From chains of death our souls relieved,
And life's perennial crown received.

6. Victor of hell, Christ ris'n displays
His trophies bright with glory's rays,
And op'ning heav'n, he binds his chain
Around the king of hell's domain.

Verse 7 may be omitted outside of Paschal Time :

7. O Jesus! that our faithful mind
In thee pure paschal joy may find,
From deadly sin redeem us free,
And grant us life renewed in thee.

8. To God the Father, to the Son,
Who rose from death, his vict'ry won,
And Holy Spirit, hymns of praise
And glory sempiternal raise.

Melody: Dieudonné Duguet (d. 1849), organist at the Catholic Cathedral in Liège, Belgium, and teacher of César Franck.

M. Source: *Mediator Dei Hymnal* (1955) p. 66; *New Saint Basil Hymnal* (1958) p. 93; *Arundel Catholic Hymnal* (1905) p. 26; *Hymnal and Vesperal* (Archdiocese of Baltimore, 1878) p. 168; *Catholic Vesper Hymn Book set to Music for Unison or Four Voices* (Charles Lewis, 1877) p. 6.

T. Source: *Vespers Book for the Use of the Laity* (1841) p. 93; Rev. Frederick C. Husenbeth, a Catholic priest, also edited *The Roman Missal for the Use of the Laity* (1848).

88 88 (LM)

Tune: Duguet

Ad Cenam Agni Providi (4th century)

Third Tune – *Trns: Fr. Frederick C. Husenbeth (d. 1872)*

4. Christ is the Pasch we sacrifice,
   Pure victim to the Father's eyes,
   Approaching with unsullied mind,
   May all his grace and mercy find.

5. Celestial victim, spotless, true,
   Who hell's dark victim overthrew,
   From chains of death our souls relieved,
   And life's perennial crown received.

6. Victor of hell, Christ ris'n displays
   His trophies bright with glory's rays,
   And op'ning heav'n, he binds his chain
   Around the king of hell's domain.

Verse 7 may be omitted outside of Paschal Time :

7. O Jesus! that our faithful mind
   In thee pure paschal joy may find,
   From deadly sin redeem us free,
   And grant us life renewed in thee.

8. To God the Father, to the Son,
   Who rose from death, his vict'ry won,
   And Holy Spirit, hymns of praise
   And glory sempiternal raise.

88 88 (LM)

Tune:
Melcombe

Final Verses: Richard Lloyd (1993) #133; Noel Rawsthorne (2011) #205.
T. Source: *Vespers Book for the Use of the Laity* (1841) p. 93; Rev. Frederick C. Husenbeth, a Catholic priest, also edited *The Roman Missal for the Use of the Laity* (1848).
Melody: Samuel Webbe, the elder (d. 1816).
M. Source: *Veritas Hymnal* (Dublin: Irish Church Music Association, 1974) p. 96; *Cantate Omnes: Hymnal of the Catholic Choirmasters' Guild* (1952) #78.

Ad Cenam Agni Providi (4th century)

Trns: Fr. Frederick C. Husenbeth (d. 1872)

Can be sung with any 88 88 meter: EISENACH, BRESSANI, ROGERS PARK, LA ROCHELLE, KEMPEN, BESSEMER, TALLIS CANON, WINCHESTER NEW, and so forth.

COME to the regal feast displayed
In robes of purest white arrayed,
The Red sea's threat'ning perils past,
And sing to Christ secure at last.

2. The Lamb's pure blood, the pledge of love,
Is freely giv'n us from above;
His body now in glorious state,
As priest, his love will immolate.

3. The doors which show the sanguine dye
Th'avenging angel passes by:
The waters of the deep divide:
The foe is whelmed beneath the tide.

4. Christ is the Pasch we sacrifice,
Pure victim to the Father's eyes,
Approaching with unsullied mind,
May all his grace and mercy find.

5. Celestial victim, spotless, true,
Who hell's dark victim overthrew,
From chains of death our souls relieved,
And life's perennial crown received.

6. Victor of hell, Christ ris'n displays
His trophies bright with glory's rays,
And op'ning heav'n, he binds his chain
Around the king of hell's domain.

Verse 7 may be omitted outside of Paschal Time :

7. O Jesus! that our faithful mind
In thee pure paschal joy may find,
From deadly sin redeem us free,
And grant us life renewed in thee.

8. To God the Father, to the Son,
Who rose from death, his vict'ry won,
And Holy Spirit, hymns of praise
And glory sempiternal raise.

88 88 (LM)

T. Source: *Vespers Book for the Use of the Laity* (1841) p. 93; Rev. Frederick C. Husenbeth, a Catholic priest, also edited *The Roman Missal for the Use of the Laity* (1848).

Tune: VARIOUS

Ad Cenam Agni Providi (4th century)

First Tune – *Trns: Robert Campbell of Skerrington (d. 1868)*

1. At the Lamb's high feast we sing Praise to our vic -
2. Where the Pas - chal blood is poured, Death's dark an - gel
3. Might - y Vic - tim from on high, Pow'rs of hell be -

to - rious King, Who hath washed us in the tide
sheathes his sword; Is - rael's hosts tri - um - phant go
neath thee lie; Death is con - quered in the fight;

Flow - ing from his pierc - èd side. Praise we him_ whose
Through the wave that drowns the foe. Christ, the Lamb, whose
Thou hast brought us life and light. Now thy ban - ner

love di - vine Gives the guests his blood for wine,
blood was shed, Pas - chal vic - tim, Pas - chal bread;
thou dost wave; Van - quished Sa - tan and the grave;

Gives his bod - y for the feast, Love the Vic - tim,
With sin - cer - i - ty and love Eat we man - na
An - gels join his praise to tell, See o'er - thrown the

Love the Priest.
from a - bove.
prince of hell.

4. Paschal triumph, Paschal joy,
Only sin can this destroy;
From the death of sin set free,
Souls re-born, dear Lord, in thee.
Hymns of glory, songs of praise,
Father, unto thee we raise;
Risen Lord, all praise to thee,
Ever with the Spirit be.

77 77 D

Tune:
Salzburg

Final Verses: Richard Lloyd (1993) #207; Noel Rawsthorne (2011) #325.
T. Source: *New Westminster Hymnal* (1939) p. 63.
Melody: Jacob Hintze (d. 1702), court musician to the Elector of Brandenburg at Berlin.
M. Source: *Catholic Hymn Book* (London Oratory, 1998) p. 116.

Ad Cenam Agni Providi (4th century)

Second Tune – *Trns: Robert Campbell of Skerrington (d. 1868)*

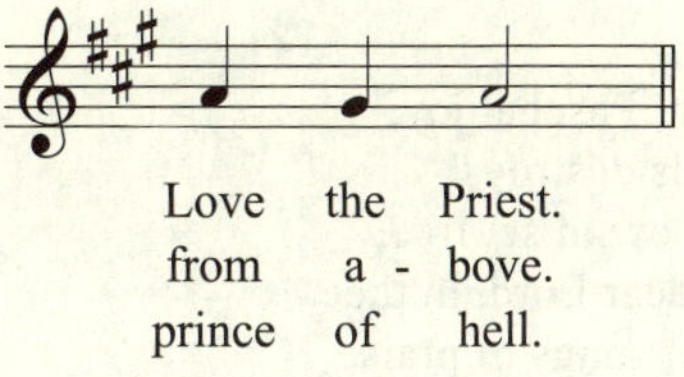

4. Paschal triumph, Paschal joy,
Only sin can this destroy;
From the death of sin set free,
Souls re-born, dear Lord, in thee.
Hymns of glory, songs of praise,
Father, unto thee we raise;
Risen Lord, all praise to thee,
Ever with the Spirit be.

77 77 D

T. Source: *New Westminster Hymnal* (1939) p. 63.
Melody: Würth's *Katholisches Gesangbuch* (1859).
M. Source: *Cantate Omnes: Hymnal of the Catholic Choirmasters' Guild* (1952) #46.

Tune:
Paschal Lamb

Ad Cenam Agni Providi (4th century)

Third Tune – *Trns: Robert Campbell of Skerrington (d. 1868)*

1. At the Lamb's high feast we sing Praise to our vic -
2. Where the Pas - chal blood is poured, Death's dark an - gel
3. Might - y Vic - tim from on high, Pow'rs of hell be -

to - rious King, Who hath washed us in the tide
sheathes his sword; Is - rael's hosts tri - um - phant go
neath thee lie; Death is con - quered in the fight;

Flow - ing from his pierc - èd side. Praise we him whose
Through the wave that drowns the foe. Christ, the Lamb, whose
Thou hast brought us life and light. Now thy ban - ner

love di - vine Gives the guests his blood for wine,
blood was shed, Pas - chal vic - tim, Pas - chal bread;
thou dost wave; Van - quished Sa - tan and the grave;

Gives his bod - y for the feast, Love the Vic - tim,
With sin - cer - i - ty and love Eat we man - na
An - gels join his praise to tell, See o'er - thrown the

Love the Priest.
from a - bove.
prince of hell.

4. Paschal triumph, Paschal joy,
Only sin can this destroy;
From the death of sin set free,
Souls re-born, dear Lord, in thee.
Hymns of glory, songs of praise,
Father, unto thee we raise;
Risen Lord, all praise to thee,
Ever with the Spirit be.

77 77 D

Tune:
St George

Final Verses: Richard Lloyd (1993) #197; Noel Rawsthorne (2011) #303.
Melody: George J. Elvey (d. 1893), organist at St George's Chapel at Windsor Castle.
M. Source: *Catholic Hymn Book* (1998) p. 120; *New Westminster Hymnal* (1939) p. 88; *Hymns, Psalms, and Spiritual Canticles* (Massachusetts: Theodore Marier, 1983) p. 230.
T. Source: *New Westminster Hymnal* (1939) p. 63.

Ad Cenam Agni Providi (4th century)

Fourth Tune – *Trns: Robert Campbell of Skerrington (d. 1868)*

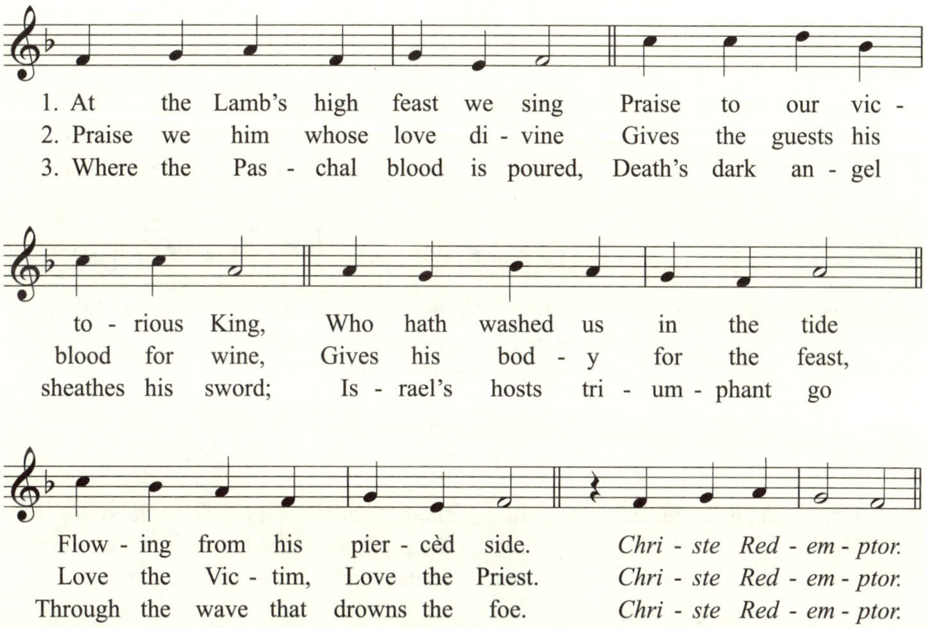

4. Christ, the Lamb, whose blood was shed,
Paschal victim, Paschal bread;
With sincerity and love
Eat we manna from above. *Christe Redemptor.*

5. Mighty Victim from on high,
Pow'rs of hell beneath thee lie;
Death is conquered in the fight;
Thou hast brought us life and light. *Christe Redemptor.*

6. Now thy banner thou dost wave;
Vanquished Satan and the grave;
Angels join his praise to tell,
See o'erthrown the prince of hell. *Christe Redemptor.*

7. Paschal triumph, Paschal joy,
Only sin can this destroy;
From the death of sin set free,
Souls re-born, dear Lord, in thee. *Christe Redemptor.*

8. Hymns of glory, songs of praise,
Father, unto thee we raise;
Risen Lord, all praise to thee,
Ever with the Spirit be. *Christe Redemptor.*

T. Source: *New Westminster Hymnal* (1939) p. 63.
Melody: *attr.* Pierre de Corbeil (d. 1222), Archbishop of Sens.
M. Source: *Mediator Dei Hymnal* (1955) #77; *American Catholic Hymnal according to the Motu Proprio of His Holiness Pope Pius X compiled by the Marist Brothers* (New York: Kenedy & Sons, 1913) p. 185.

77 77
Tune: Orientis Partibus

Ad Cenam Agni Providi (4th century)

Fifth Tune – *Trns: Robert Campbell of Skerrington (d. 1868)*

1. At the Lamb's high feast we_ sing Al - le - lu - ia.
2. Praise we him whose love di - vine Al - le - lu - ia.
3. Where the Pas - chal blood is__ poured, Al - le - lu - ia.

Praise to our vic - to - rious King, Al - le - lu - ia.
Gives the guests his blood for_ wine, Al - le - lu - ia.
Death's dark an - gel sheathes his_ sword; Al - le - lu - ia.

Who hath washed us in__ the__ tide Al - le - lu - ia.
Gives his bod - y for_ the__ feast, Al - le - lu - ia.
Is - rael's hosts tri - um - phant go Al - le - lu - ia.

Flow - ing from his pier - cèd_ side. Al - le - lu - ia.
Love the Vic - tim, Love the_ Priest. Al - le - lu - ia.
Through the wave that drowns the_ foe. Al - le - lu - ia.

The word "Alleluia" is sung after each line:

4. Christ, the Lamb, whose blood was shed,
Paschal victim, Paschal bread;
With sincerity and love
Eat we manna from above.

5. Mighty Victim from on high,
Pow'rs of hell beneath thee lie;
Death is conquered in the fight;
Thou hast brought us life and light.

6. Now thy banner thou dost wave;
Vanquished Satan and the grave;
Angels join his praise to tell,
See o'erthrown the prince of hell.

7. Paschal triumph, Paschal joy,
Only sin can this destroy;
From the death of sin set free,
Souls re-born, dear Lord, in thee.

8. Hymns of glory, songs of praise,
Father, unto thee we raise;
Risen Lord, all praise to thee,
Ever with the Spirit be.

77 77 A

Tune:
Llanfair

Final Verses: Lloyd (1993) #118; Noel Rawsthorne (2011) #186.
Melody: Robert Williams (d. 1821), a blind composer born in Wales.
M. Source: *Catholic Hymn Book* (London Oratory, 1998) p. 138.
T. Source: *New Westminster Hymnal* (1939) p. 63.

Ad Cenam Agni Providi (4th century)

Sixth Tune – *Trns: Robert Campbell of Skerrington (d. 1868)*

4. Christ, the Lamb, whose blood was shed,
Paschal victim, Paschal bread;
With sincerity and love
Eat we manna from above.

5. Mighty Victim from on high,
Pow'rs of hell beneath thee lie;
Death is conquered in the fight;
Thou hast brought us life and light.

6. Now thy banner thou dost wave;
Vanquished Satan and the grave;
Angels join his praise to tell,
See o'erthrown the prince of hell.

7. Paschal triumph, Paschal joy,
Only sin can this destroy;
From the death of sin set free,
Souls re-born, dear Lord, in thee.

8. Hymns of glory, songs of praise,
Father, unto thee we raise;
Risen Lord, all praise to thee,
Ever with the Spirit be.

Melody: Herrnhut *Choralbuch* (1735).
M. Source: *Catholic Hymn Book* (London Oratory, 1998) p. 459.
T. Source: *New Westminster Hymnal* (1939) p. 63.

77 77
Tune:
Savannah

Ad Cenam Agni Providi (4th century)

Seventh Tune – *Trns: Robert Campbell of Skerrington (d. 1868)*

4. Paschal triumph, Paschal joy, | Only sin can this destroy;
From the death of sin set free, | Souls re-born, dear Lord, in thee.
Hymns of glory, songs of praise, | Father, unto thee we raise;
Risen Lord, all praise to thee, | Ever with the Spirit be.

77 77 D

Tune:
Grosser Gott 7B

Final Verses: Richard Lloyd (1993) #99; Noel Rawsthorne (2011) #159.
T. Source: *New Westminster Hymnal* (1939) p. 63. Melody: *Katholisches Gesangbuch* (Vienna, 1774).
M. Source: *Arundel Catholic Hymnal* (1905) p. 151; this clever pairing of text and tune we owe to Charles Tindal Gatty (d. 1928) and Henry Howard, the Fifteenth Duke of Norfolk (d. 1917).

Ad Cenam Agni Providi (4th century)

First Tune – *Trns: Elizabeth Rundle Charles (d. 1896)*

4. For Christ our Passover is slain.
The Lamb is offered not in vain;
Sincerity's unleavened bread,
His flesh He gave, His blood He shed.

5. O Victim ever worthy, who
Didst all the bonds of hell undo,
Didst ransom captives from the foe
And life, thy gift, afresh bestow!

6. When Christ from out the tomb arose,
Victor o'er hell and all His foes,
The tyrant down in chains He threw,
And planted Paradise anew.

Final Verses: Noel Rawsthorne (2011) #323.
T. Source: *The Voice of Christian Life in Song* (1865) p. 103.
Melody: Paris *Antiphonale* (1681).
M. Source: *New Westminster Hymnal* (1939) p. 9; *Catholic Hymn Book* (London Oratory, 1998) p. 81.

88 88 (LM)
Tune:
St Venantius

44 Ad Cenam Agni Providi (4th century)

Second Tune – *Trns: Elizabeth Rundle Charles (d. 1896)*

4. For Christ our Passover is slain.
The Lamb is offered not in vain;
Sincerity's unleavened bread,
His flesh He gave, His blood He shed.

5. O Victim ever worthy, who
Didst all the bonds of hell undo,
Didst ransom captives from the foe
And life, thy gift, afresh bestow!

6. When Christ from out the tomb arose,
Victor o'er hell and all His foes,
The tyrant down in chains He threw,
And planted Paradise anew.

88 88 (LM)

Tune:
Devonshire

T. Source: *The Voice of Christian Life in Song* (1865) p. 103.
Melody: John Frederick Lampe (d. 1751).
M. Source: *Hymns Ancient and Modern* (1972) p. 83.

Ad Cenam Agni Providi (4th century) 45

Third Tune – *Trns: Elizabeth Rundle Charles (d. 1896)*

4. For Christ our Passover is slain.
The Lamb is offered not in vain;
Sincerity's unleavened bread,
His flesh He gave, His blood He shed.

5. O Victim ever worthy, who
Didst all the bonds of hell undo,
Didst ransom captives from the foe
And life, thy gift, afresh bestow!

6. When Christ from out the tomb arose,
Victor o'er hell and all His foes,
The tyrant down in chains He threw,
And planted Paradise anew.

T. Source: *The Voice of Christian Life in Song* (1865) p. 103.
Melody: Philip Hart (d. 1749), organist at St. Michael Church, Cornhill.
M. Source: *Hymns Ancient and Modern* (1972) p. 8; cf. *Church Hymns With Tunes* (1885) p. 230, edited by Sir Arthur Sullivan (d. 1900), organist at St. Peter Church, Kensington.

88 88 (LM)
Tune: Hilderstone

46 Ad Cenam Agni Providi (4th century)

Fourth Tune – *Trns: Elizabeth Rundle Charles (d. 1896)*

4. For Christ our Passover is slain.
   The Lamb is offered not in vain;
   Sincerity's unleavened bread,
   His flesh He gave, His blood He shed.

5. O Victim ever worthy, who
   Didst all the bonds of hell undo,
   Didst ransom captives from the foe
   And life, thy gift, afresh bestow!

6. When Christ from out the tomb arose,
   Victor o'er hell and all His foes,
   The tyrant down in chains He threw,
   And planted Paradise anew.

88 88 (LM)

Tune:
Kempen

Melody: Flor Peeters (d. 1986), organist at the Catholic Cathedral of Mechelen, Belgium, was made a Baron by King Baudouin.
M. Source: *People's Mass Book* (Omer Westendorf, 1964) p. 218.
T. Source: *The Voice of Christian Life in Song* (1865) p. 103.

Ad Cenam Agni Providi (4th century)

Trns: Elizabeth Rundle Charles (d. 1896)

Can be sung with any 88 88 meter, such as GONFALON ROYAL, TRINITY COLLEGE, ROGERS PARK, MELCOMBE, NOTRE DAME, BRESSANI, EISENACH, etc.

THE Supper of the Lamb to share,
We come in vesture white and fair,
The Red Sea crossed, our hymn we sing
To Christ, our Captain and our King.

2. His holy body on the cross,
Parched, on that altar hung for us;
Partaking of His sacred blood,
We live upon the living God.

3. Protected in the Paschal night
From the destroying angel's might,
And by a pow'rful hand set free
From Pharaoh's bitter slavery.

4. For Christ our Passover is slain.
The Lamb is offered not in vain;
Sincerity's unleavened bread,
His flesh He gave, His blood He shed.

5. O Victim ever worthy, who
Didst all the bonds of hell undo,
Didst ransom captives from the foe
And life, thy gift, afresh bestow!

6. When Christ from out the tomb arose,
Victor o'er hell and all His foes,
The tyrant down in chains He threw,
And planted Paradise anew.

88 88 (LM)

Tune:
VARIOUS

T. Source: *The Voice of Christian Life in Song* (1865) p. 103.

48 Ad Cenam Agni Providi (4th century)

1599AD – Historic Roman Catholic Translation

Can be sung with any 88 88 meter, such as HILDERSTONE, DUGUET, BRESLAU, MELCOMBE, WAREHAM, OLD HUNDREDTH, MEIN SEEL, TRINITY COLLEGE, etc.

AT supper of the Lamb prepar'd,
And with white vestures pure and chaste,
To Christ our prince let us sing praise,
The Red Sea's being overpast.

2. Whose corpse most holy did remain,
In torture on the cross distress'd,
By tasting of his blood so red,
Our life alone in God doth rest.

3. Protected on the paschal eve
From that same angel which destroys,
And we from Pharao freèd are
Of thraldom that the most annoys.

4. Our paschal Christ is now become
The Lamb he was and sacrific'd;
His flesh the bread both sweet and pure,
That for the off'ring hath suffic'd.

5. O worthy sacrifice and true,
Which didst the force of hell restrain,
And captive people didst redeem,
And yield rewards of life again.

6. Forth of his Tomb when Christ arose,
As conqueror from hell he came,
To bands he did the Tyrant bring,
And heaven's open passage frame.

7. We pray thee, author of us all,
During this joyful Easter tide,
Thou wilt vouchsafe from brunt of death
Thy people's safety to provide.

8. All glory be to thee o Lord,
Which from the death didst rise again,
With the Father, and holy Ghost,
That world without end may remain.

Ad cenam Agni próvidi,
Et stolis albis cándidi,
Post tránsitum maris rubri,
Christo canámus Príncipi.

Cujus corpus sanctíssimum,
In ara crucis tórridum,
Cruóre ejus róseo
Gustándo vívimus Deo.

Protécti Paschae véspere
A devastánte Ángelo,
Erépti de duríssimo
Pharaónis império.

Jam Pascha nostrum Christus est,
Qui immolátus Agnus est,
Sinceritátis ázyma,
Caro ejus obláta est.

O vere digna hóstia,
Per quam fracta sunt tártara,
Redémpta plebs captiváta,
Réddita vitae praémia.

Consúrgit Christus túmulo,
Victor redit de bárathro,
Tyránnum trudens vínculo,
Et Paradísum réserans.

Quaésumus, Auctor ómnium,
In hoc Pascháli gáudio,
Ab omni mortis ímpetu
Tuum defénde pópulum.

Glória tibi, Dómine,
Qui surrexíst*i* a mórtuis,
Cum Patr*e* et Sancto Spíritu,
In sempitérna saécula.

88 88 (LM)

Tune:
VARIOUS

T. Source: *Primer, or, Office of the Blessed Virgin Marie in Latin and English, according to the reformed Latin, and with Lyke Graces Privileged* (Antwerp, 1599) p. 11. The Catholic Encyclopedia of 1912 attributes the hymn translations to the book's editor, Richard Verstegan (d. 1636), a Catholic publisher. In the 1599 Preface, Verstegan says: "Notwithstanding the difficulty, these hymns have been so turned into English meter that they may be sung unto the same tunes in English that they bear in Latin." However, his accentual treatment is sometimes peculiar.

Ad Cenam Agni Providi (Urbanite)

1699AD – Historic Roman Catholic Translation

Can be sung with any 88 88 meter, such as EISENACH, ROGERS PARK, BRESSANI, LA ROCHELLE, KEMPEN, BESSEMER, TALLIS CANON, WINCHESTER NEW, etc.

Ad régias Agni dapes,
Stolis amícti cándidis,
Post tránsitum maris Rubri,
Christo canámus Príncipi.

Divína cujus Cháritas
Sacrum propínat sánguinem,
Almíque membra córporis
Amor sacérdos ímmolat.

Sparsum cruórem póstibus
Vastátor horret Ángelus;
Fugítque divísum mare:
Mergúntur hostes flúctibus.

Jam Pascha nostrum Christus est,
Paschális idem víctima:
Et pura puris méntibus
Sinceritátis ázyma.

O vera caéli víctima,
Subjécta cui sunt tártara,
Solúta mortis víncula,
Recépta vitae praémia.

Victor subáctis ínferis
Trophaéa Christus éxplicat,
Caelóque apérto, súbditum
Regem tenebrárum trahit.

Ut sis perénne méntibus
Paschále, Jesu, gáudium,
A morte dira críminum
Vitae renátos líbera.

Deo Patri sit glória,
Et Fílio, qu*i* a mórtuis
Surréxit, ac Paráclito,
In sempitérna saécula.

AT the Lamb's Regal Banquet, where
We must in Candid Robes appear,
After the Red Sea past, let's sing
A Hymn of Praise to Christ our King.

2. Whose Charity (Divinely Good)
Makes tender of his Sacred Blood,
While Love doth Sacrifice, as Priest,
The Body whereon Souls do Feast.

3. The striking Angel dreads the Gore
He sprinkled finds about the Door;
The yielding Sea divides his Waves:
The Foes there meet their Liquid Graves.

4. Now Christ our Pasch we rightly name,
Our Paschal Victim is the same;
Who is to Souls that purgèd be
Pure Azyme of Sincerity.

5. O Heav'nly Sacrifice! By whom
The Depths of Hell are overcome,
And Death's strong Bonds dissolved, for which
Life's Crown his Temples doth enrich!

6. Christ (Victor o'er Infernal Foes)
His Conquer'd Trophies does expose;
And, having Heav'n unlocked, enslaves
The King that rules hell's darksome caves.

7. That, Jesu, thou to Souls may'st be
A Paschal Joy Eternally,
Free from the Horrid Death of Sin
Us, who Regenerate have been.

8. Be God the Father Glorified
With Christ his Son, who for us Died
And Rose again; so likewise be
The Holy Ghost Eternally.

88 88 (LM)

Tune: VARIOUS

T. Source: *The Primer, or, Office of the Blessed Virgin Mary* (1699) p. 363.

50 Ad Preces Nostras Deitatis (10th century)

Medieval hymn for the holy season of Lent

To sing in Latin, use any 11 11 11 5 tune.

AD preces nostras Deitátis aures,
Deus, inclína pietáte sola,
Súpplicum vota súscipe, precámur
Fámuli tui.

2. Réspice clemens sólio de sancto
Vultu seréno, lámpades illústra
Lúmine tuo, ténebras depélle
Pectóre nostro.

3. Crímina laxa pietáte multa,
Áblue sordes, víncula disrúmpe,
Parce peccátis, réleva jacéntes
Déxtera tua.

4. Te sine tetro mérgimur profúndo,
Lábimur alta scéleris sub unda,
Bráchio tuo tráhimur ad clara
Sídera caeli.

5. Christe, lux vera, bónitas et vita,
Gáudium mundi, píetas imménsa,
Qui nos a morte róseo salvásti
Sánguine tuo.

6. Ínsere tuum, pétimus, amórem
Méntibus nostris, fídei refúnde
Lumen aetérnum, caritátis auge
Dilectiónem. *n1*

7. Tu nobis dona fontem lacrimárum,
Jejuniórum fórtia minístra,
Vítia carnis míllia retúnde
Frámea tua.

8. Procul a nobis pérfidus absístat
Satan, a tuis víribus confráctus,
Sanctus assístat Spíritus, a tua *n2*
Sede demíssus. *n3*

9. Glória Deo sit aetérno Patri,
Sit tibi semper Genitóris Nate,
Cum quo aequális Spíritus per cuncta
Saécula regnat.

11 11 11 5

Tune: Various

T. Source: *Liber Hymnarius* (Solesmes, 1983) p. 225; *Analecta Hymnica Medii Aevi, Volume 51* (Fr. Guido Dreves, 1908) p. 61. Alan G. McDougall called this hymn "one of the most beautiful examples of mediaeval hymnody," and many great composers have set it, such as Fr. Guillaume Du Fay (d. 1474) and Fr. Tomás Luis de Victoria (d. 1611).

Assistance for comprehension

TO our prayers, O God, bend the ears
of thy Godhead in thy singular tenderness,
welcome the vows of thine entreatants, we pray,
who are thy servants.

2. Look forth with mildness from thy holy seat
with a calm countenance, light our lamps *cf. Mt 25*
with thy light, drive away darkness
from our hearts.

3. Abate our misdeeds in thy great tenderness,
purge away our squalors, break our bonds asunder,
overlook our sins, raise up the fallen
with thy right hand.

4. Without thee we are plunged into the loathsome abyss,
we sink beneath the deep wave of wrongdoing,
by thine arm we are drawn
to the bright stars of heaven.

5. O Christ, true light, goodness and life,
joy of the world, unfathomable tenderness,
who hast saved us from death
through thy rosy blood.

6. Implant desire of thee, we beg,
in our minds, pour back
the eternal light of faith,
increase the love of charity. *n1*

7. Do thou grant us a spring of tears, *cf. Jer 9.1*
afford stamina in fasting,
subdue the myriad faults of the flesh
with thy sword. *cf. Eph 6.17; Heb 4.12*

8. Let Satan the faithless draw back
afar from us, broken by thy forces,
let the Holy Spirit draw nigh, *n2*
sent down from thy lodging. *n3*

9. Glory be to God the Father eternal,
and be it to thee, ever Son of the Father,
with whom the Spirit rules, their equal,
through all the ages.

[1] *Amor, Dilectio*, and *Caritas* might all be translated as "love."

[2] Notice the interplay of *Absistat* and *Assistat* ("draw back" and "draw nigh").

[3] *Sedes* ("lodging") may be translated as "seat," but cf. *Solium* in verse 2.

52 Ad Preces Nostras Deitatis (10th century)

1599AD – Historic Roman Catholic Translation

English translation can be sung with any 11 11 11 5 meter, such as Iste Confessor, Christe Sanctorum, Coelites Plaudant, Diva Servatrix, Herzliebster Jesu, etc.

TO our petitions the ears of thy Godhead,
O God incline thou merely of thy pity:
Thy plaintives' prayèrs, o let be accepted,
Thy servants pray thee.

2. From thy seat sacred, vouchsafe we be gracèd,
By thy mild visage our lamps do thou lighten:
With thy light, darkness, let from us be chasèd,
Our hearts to brighten.

3. Free by great pity the crimes of us wretched,
Wash clean our foulness break our bands asunder
Pardon offences raise with thy hand stretchèd
The casten under.

4. Unless thou help us in dark we lie drownèd,
In sinful water deëpest declining:
But we be raisèd by thine arm renownèd
To heav'n's clear shining.

5. O Christ the true light, life and goodness being,
The joy of this world, piety abounding,
By thy blood purple thou wroughtest our freeing,
From death's confounding.

6. Thy love in our hearts establish assurèd,
Pour in us of faith the light never-ceasing,
That fervor of love in us be procurèd,
Ever increasing.

7. A fountain of tears make from us fast flowing,
Force give that fasting by us be sustainèd,
All fleshly vices be from their up-growing,
By thee restrainèd.

8. False Satan from us far to make retire,
With thy force mighty let him be subjected:
Thy holy spirit for aid we require,
From thee directed.

9. To God the father glory be eternal,
To his son also ever so remaining:
And to the spirit with either co-equal
Endlessly reigning.

Ad preces nostras Deitátis aures,
Deus, inclína pietáte sola,
Súpplicum vota súscipe, precámur
Fámuli tui.

Réspice clemens sólio de sancto
Vultu seréno, lámpades illústra
Lúmine tuo, ténebras depélle
Pectóre nostro.

Crímina laxa pietáte multa,
Áblue sordes, víncula disrúmpe,
Parce peccátis, réleva jacéntes
Déxtera tua.

Te sine tetro mérgimur profúndo,
Lábimur alta scéleris sub unda,
Bráchio tuo tráhimur ad clara
Sídera caeli.

Christe, lux vera, bónitas et vita,
Gáudium mundi, píetas imménsa,
Qui nos a morte róseo salvásti
Sánguine tuo.

Ínsere tuum, pétimus, amórem
Méntibus nostris, fídei refúnde
Lumen aetérnum, caritátis auge
Dilectiónem.

Tu nobis dona fontem lacrimárum,
Jejuniórum fórtia minístra,
Vítia carnis míllia retúnde
Frámea tua.

Procul a nobis pérfidus absístat
Satan, a tuis víribus confráctus,
Sanctus assístat Spíritus, a tua
Sede demíssus.

Glória Deo sit aetérno Patri,
Sit tibi semper Genitóris Nate,
Cum quo aequális Spíritus per cuncta
Saécula regnat.

11 11 11 5

Tune:
Various

T. Source: *Primer, or, Office of the Blessed Virgin Marie in Latin and English, according to the reformed Latin, and with Lyke Graces Privileged* (Antwerp, 1599) p. 47. The Catholic Encyclopedia of 1912 attributes the hymn translations to the book's editor, Richard Verstegan (d. 1636), a Catholic publisher. In the 1599 Preface, Verstegan says: "Notwithstanding the difficulty, these hymns have been so turned into English meter that they may be sung unto the same tunes in English that they bear in Latin." However, his accentual treatment is sometimes peculiar.

Ad Preces Nostras Deitatis (10th century) 53

First Tune – *Trns: Alan Gordon McDougall (d. 1965)*

4. Reft of thy guiding we are lost in darkness,
Drowned in the great wide sea of sin we perish,
But we are led by thy strong hand to climb the | Ascents of heaven.

5. Christ, very light and goodness, life of all things,
Joy of the whole world, infinite in kindness,
Who by the crimson flowing of thy life-blood | From death hast saved us,

6. Plant, sweetest Jesus, at our supplication
Deep in our hearts thy charity: upon us
Faith's everlasting light be poured, and increase | Grant us of loving.

7. Grant to our souls a holy fount of weeping,
Grant to us strength to aid us in our fasting,
And all the thousand hosts of evil banish | Far from thy people.

8. Bruised by thine heel may Satan and his legions
Far from our minds be driven, that are guided
By the indwelling of the Holy Spirit | Sent from thy heaven.

9. Glory to God the Father everlasting, | Glory for ever to the Sole-begotten,
With whom the Holy Spirit through the ages | Reigneth coequal.

Melody: Johann Crüger (d. 1662), choirmaster of St. Nicholas' Church, Berlin.
M. Source: *Catholic Hymn Book* (London Oratory, 1998) p. 92.
T. Source: *Pange Lingua: Breviary Hymns of Old Uses* (1916) p. 19; *New Westminster Hymnal* (1939) p. 45.

11 11 11 5
Tune:
Herzliebster Jesu

54 Ad Preces Nostras Deitatis (10th century)

Second Tune – *Trns: Alan Gordon McDougall (d. 1965)*

4. Reft of thy guiding we are lost in darkness,
Drowned in the great wide sea of sin we perish,
But we are led by thy strong hand to climb the | Ascents of heaven.

5. Christ, very light and goodness, life of all things,
Joy of the whole world, infinite in kindness,
Who by the crimson flowing of thy life-blood | From death hast saved us,

6. Plant, sweetest Jesus, at our supplication
Deep in our hearts thy charity: upon us
Faith's everlasting light be poured, and increase | Grant us of loving.

7. Grant to our souls a holy fount of weeping,
Grant to us strength to aid us in our fasting,
And all the thousand hosts of evil banish | Far from thy people.

8. Bruised by thine heel may Satan and his legions
Far from our minds be driven, that are guided
By the indwelling of the Holy Spirit | Sent from thy heaven.

9. Glory to God the Father everlasting, | Glory for ever to the Sole-begotten,
With whom the Holy Spirit through the ages | Reigneth coequal.

11 11 11 5

Tune:
Iste Confessor

Final Verses: Richard Lloyd (1993) #106; Noel Rawsthorne (2011) #168.
Melody: *Vesperale* (Poitiers, 1746).
M. Source: *Catholic Hymn Book* (1998) p. 416; *Worship II Hymnal* (GIA, 1975) #221.
T. Source: *Pange Lingua: Breviary Hymns of Old Uses* (1916) p. 19; *New Westminster Hymnal* (1939) p. 45.

Ad Preces Nostras Deitatis (10th century)

Trns: Alan Gordon McDougall (d. 1965)

Can be sung with any 11 11 11 5 meter, such as ISTE CONFESSOR, LOBET DEN HERREN, CHRISTE SANCTORUM, COELITES PLAUDANT, DIVA SERVATRIX, HERZLIEBSTER JESU, etc.

GOD, of thy pity, unto us thy children
Bend down thine ear in thine own lovingkindness,
And all thy people's prayers and vows ascending
Hear, we beseech thee.

2. Look down in mercy from thy seat of glory,
Pour on our souls the radiance of thy presence,
Drive from our weary hearts the shades of darkness,
Lighten our footsteps.

3. Free us from sin by might of thy great loving,
Cleanse thou the sordid, loose the fettered spirit,
Spare every sinner, raise with thine own right hand
All who are fallen.

4. Christ, very light and goodness, life of all things,
Joy of the whole world, infinite in kindness,
Who by the crimson flowing of thy life-blood
Life hast restored us,

5. Plant, sweetest Jesus, at our supplication
Deep in our hearts thy charity: upon us
Faith's everlasting light be poured, and increase
Grant us of loving.

6. Grant to our souls a holy fount of weeping,
Grant to us strength to aid us in our fasting,
And all the thousand hosts of evil banish
Far from thy people.

7. Glory to God the Father everlasting,
Glory for ever to the Sole-begotten,
With whom the Holy Spirit through the ages
Reigneth coequal.

T. Source: *Pange Lingua: Breviary Hymns of Old Uses with an English Rendering by Alan G. McDougall and an Introduction by Adrian Fortescue* (London: Burns & Oates, 1916) p. 19; *New Westminster Hymnal* (1939) p. 45. Translators for this meter employ multifarious rhyme schemes. There is also a convention—which McDougall followed—to avoid rhyme in this meter.

11 11 11 5

Tune: VARIOUS

56 Adoro Te Devote, Latens Deitas (1264 AD)

St. Thomas Aquinas, Dominican Priest (d. 1274 AD)

ADÓRO te devóte, latens Déitas,
Quae sub his figúris vere látitas:
Tibi se cor meum totum súbjicit
Quia te contémplans totum déficit.

2. Visus, tactus, gustus in te fállitur,
Sed audítu solo tuto créditur:
Credo quidquid dixit Dei Fílius:
Nil hoc verbo Veritátis vérius.

3. In cruce latébat sola Déitas,
At hic latet simul et humánitas:
Ambo tamen credens atque cónfitens,
Peto quod petívit latro paénitens.

4. Plagas, sicut Thomas, non intúeor
Deum tamen meum te confíteor:
Fac me tibi semper magis crédere,
In te spem habére, te dilígere. *n1*

5. O memoriále mortis Dómini,
Panis vivus vitam praéstans hómini,
Praesta meae menti de te vívere,
Et te illi semper dulce sápere. *n2*

6. Pie pellicáne Jesu Dómine,
Me immúndum munda tuo sánguine,
Cujus una stilla salvum fácere
Totum mundum quit ab omni scélere.

7. Jesu, quem velátum nunc aspício,
Oro fiat illud quod tam sítio:
Ut te reveláta cernens fácie,
Visu sim beátus tuae glóriae. *n3*

T. Source: *Mass and Vespers with Gregorian Chant* (Solesmes Abbey, 1957) p. 1894. The first and second verse have irregularities of which the singers must be aware; apart from these, the meter is regular and the Latin text can be sung with any 65 65 D meter: ANIMA CHRISTI, LAUDES, CUDDESDON, FIORILLO, SWAHILI, UNE VAINE CRAINTE, ADORO TE (Plainsong), KING'S WESTON, ST RITA, etc.

65 65 D

Tune:
VARIOUS

[1] "Believe … hope … love" : prayer for increase in the theological virtues cf. I Cor 13.13.

[2] Literally: "grant to my mind to live from thee, and thee ever sweetly to bring flavor to it." *Sapere* means not only "have flavor" but also "have discernment."

Assistance for comprehension

I ADORE thee devotedly, Godhead lying hidden,
which truly art in hiding beneath these forms:
my heart submits itself to thee completely
because, considering thee, it founders completely.

2. In thee sight, touch and taste are deceived,
but by hearing alone does faith have assurance:
I believe whatever the Son of God has said:
there is nothing truer than this word of Truth.

3. On the cross the Godhead alone lay hidden,
but here likewise lies hidden the manhood:
yet believing and acknowledging both,
I seek that which the repentant thief sought.

4. I do not observe thy wounds, as Thomas did,
yet I acknowledge that thou art my God:
cause me ever more to believe in thee,
to hope in thee and to love thee. *n1*

5. O remembrance of the Lord's death,
living bread granting life to man,
grant to my mind that it may live by thee
and thou ever pleasantly flavor it. *n2*

6. Gracious pelican, Jesus Lord,
cleanse me (who am unclean) with thy blood,
one drop of which is able to make
the entire world secure from every wrong.

7. Jesus, now I look at thee veiled:
let that for which I thirst come about, I pray,
that beholding thee with face unveiled,
I may be made blissful by the sight of thy glory. *n3*

[3] The BEATIFIC VISION is the knowledge of God possessed by the angels and saints in heaven; glory is defined as "clear knowledge with praise" (*clara notitia cum laude*).

II Cor 3.18: "But we all beholding the glory of the Lord with open face [*revelata facie*], are transformed into the same image from glory to glory, as by the Spirit of the Lord." I Cor 13.12: "Then we shall see face to face."

I Jn 3.2: "We know, that, when he shall appear, we shall be like to him: because we shall see him as he is."

Adoro Te Devote, Latens Deitas (1264 AD)

First Tune – *Trns: Msgr. Hugh T. Henry (d. 1946)*

1. Tru - ly I a - dore Thee, hid - den De - i - ty,
2. Taste and touch and vi - sion are de - ceived in Thee,
3. On the cross was hid - den but the De - i - ty;

That be - neath these fig - ures hid - est ver - i - ly:
And the hear - ing on - ly can safe wit - ness be.
Nor is here the Man - hood e - ven ours to see:

Sub - ject is my spir - it whol - ly to Thy sway,
I be - lieve what - ev - er from the Lord is heard:
Yet these both con - fess - ing with the same be - lief,

For in con - tem - plat - ing Thee it faints a - way.
Noth - ing can be tru - er than Truth's ver - y word.
I will make pe - ti - tion like the dy - ing thief.

4. Though Thy wounds as Thomas saw, I see not now,
Thee my lips shall ever Lord and God avow.
Grant that I may ever more and more believe,
Hope in Thee and love Thee barring all reprieve.

5. O Memorial blessèd of the Savior's death,
O true Bread that giveth man his vital breath,
Let mine understanding live on Thee alone,
And let it forever but Thy sweetness own.

6. Pelican most tender, Jesus, Lord and God,
Wash my guilty spirit in Thy Precious Blood:
One sole drop availeth all the world to win
From its ban of bondage and its stain of sin.

7. Jesus, Whom but veilèd see I here below,
Cede the draft, I pray Thee, that I thirst for so—
That, the veil once riven, in Thy fond embrace
I may see Thy glory ever face to face.

65 65 D

Tune:
St Rita

Melody: Alfred Calabrese (b. 1961), choirmaster at Saint Rita Catholic Church in Dallas.
M. Source: *Saint Jean de Brébeuf Hymnal* (2018).
T. Source: *Eucharistica: Verse & Prose in Honor of the Hidden God* (Philadelphia: Dolphin Press, 1912) p. 59. Monsignor Hugh T. Henry, professor of homiletics at the Catholic University of America, also taught Gregorian chant at St. Charles Seminary (Overbrook, Pennsylvania).

Adoro Te Devote, Latens Deitas (1264 AD)

Second Tune – *Trns: Msgr. Hugh T. Henry (d. 1946)*

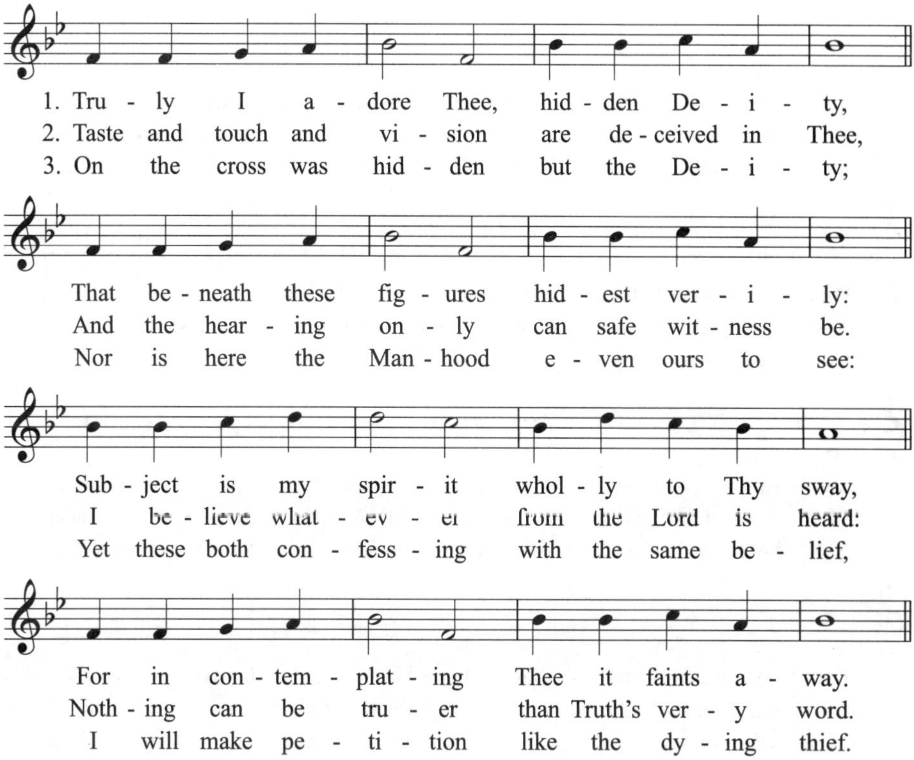

4. Though Thy wounds as Thomas saw, I see not now,
Thee my lips shall ever Lord and God avow.
Grant that I may ever more and more believe,
Hope in Thee and love Thee barring all reprieve.

5. O Memorial blessèd of the Savior's death,
O true Bread that giveth man his vital breath,
Let mine understanding live on Thee alone,
And let it forever but Thy sweetness own.

6. Pelican most tender, Jesus, Lord and God,
Wash my guilty spirit in Thy Precious Blood:
One sole drop availeth all the world to win
From its ban of bondage and its stain of sin.

7. Jesus, Whom but veilèd see I here below,
Cede the draft, I pray Thee, that I thirst for so—
That, the veil once riven, in Thy fond embrace
I may see Thy glory ever face to face.

Melody: Traditional French Noël.
M. Source: *Adoremus Hymnal* (1997) #540; *New Westminster Hymnal* (1939) p. 156.
T. Source: *Eucharistica: Verse & Prose in Honor of the Hidden God* (Philadelphia: Dolphin Press, 1912) p. 59. Monsignor Hugh T. Henry, professor of homiletics at the Catholic University of America, also taught Gregorian chant at St. Charles Seminary (Overbrook, Pennsylvania).

65 65 D

Tune: Une Vaine Crainte

60 Adoro Te Devote, Latens Deitas (1264 AD)

THIRD TUNE – *Trns: Msgr. Hugh T. Henry (d. 1946)*

4. Though Thy wounds as Thomas saw, I see not now,
Thee my lips shall ever Lord and God avow.
Grant that I may ever more and more believe,
Hope in Thee and love Thee barring all reprieve.

5. O Memorial blessèd of the Savior's death,
O true Bread that giveth man his vital breath,
Let mine understanding live on Thee alone,
And let it forever but Thy sweetness own.

6. Pelican most tender, Jesus, Lord and God,
Wash my guilty spirit in Thy Precious Blood:
One sole drop availeth all the world to win
From its ban of bondage and its stain of sin.

7. Jesus, Whom but veilèd see I here below,
Cede the draft, I pray Thee, that I thirst for so—
That, the veil once riven, in Thy fond embrace
I may see Thy glory ever face to face.

65 65 D

Tune:
CUDDESDON

Melody: William H. Ferguson (d. 1950), organist at Lancing College, Sussex; studied theology at Cuddesdon College.
M. Source: *New English Hymnal* (1986) p. 786; first published in 1919, this tune was marked to be sung in unison.
T. Source: *Eucharistica: Verse & Prose in Honor of the Hidden God* (Philadelphia: Dolphin Press, 1912) p. 59.
Monsignor Hugh T. Henry, professor of homiletics at the Catholic University of America, also taught Gregorian chant at St. Charles Seminary (Overbrook, Pennsylvania).

Adoro Te Devote, Latens Deitas (1264 AD)

Trns: Msgr. Hugh T. Henry (d. 1946)

Can be sung with any 65 65 D meter: ANIMA CHRISTI, LAUDES, CUDDESDON, FIORILLO, SWAHILI, UNE VAINE CRAINTE, ADORO TE (Plainsong), KING'S WESTON, ST RITA, etc.

TRULY I adore Thee, hidden Deity,
That beneath these figures hidest verily:
Subject is my spirit wholly to Thy sway,
For in contemplating Thee it faints away.

2. Taste and touch and vision are deceived in Thee,
And the hearing only can safe witness be.
I believe whatever from the Lord is heard:
Nothing can be truer than Truth's very word.

3. On the cross was hidden but the Deity;
Nor is here the Manhood even ours to see:
Yet these both confessing with the same belief,
I will make petition like the dying thief.

4. Though Thy wounds as Thomas saw, I see not now,
Thee my lips shall ever Lord and God avow.
Grant that I may ever more and more believe,
Hope in Thee and love Thee barring all reprieve.

5. O Memorial blessèd of the Savior's death,
O true Bread that giveth man his vital breath,
Let mine understanding live on Thee alone,
And let it forever but Thy sweetness own.

6. Pelican most tender, Jesus, Lord and God,
Wash my guilty spirit in Thy Precious Blood:
One sole drop availeth all the world to win
From its ban of bondage and its stain of sin.

7. Jesus, Whom but veilèd see I here below,
Cede the draft, I pray Thee, that I thirst for so—
That, the veil once riven, in Thy fond embrace
I may see Thy glory ever face to face.

T. Source: *Eucharistica: Verse & Prose in Honor of the Hidden God* (Philadelphia: Dolphin Press, 1912) p. 59. Monsignor Hugh T. Henry, professor of homiletics at the Catholic University of America, also taught Gregorian chant at St. Charles Seminary (Overbrook, Pennsylvania).

65 65 D

Tune: VARIOUS

Adoro Te Devote, Latens Deitas (1264 AD)

First Tune – *Trns: Bishop Edward G. Bagshawe (d. 1915)*

1. I wor - ship Thee de - vout - ly, who dost hide
2. Though sight, and taste, and touch, do fail in Thee,
3. Up - on the Cross the De - i - ty was hid,

With - in these fig - ures, Hid - den De - i - ty,
Yet may we trust to what from Thee we hear;
But here His Hu - man Na - ture lies con - cealed,

And ut - ter - ly sub - ject my heart to Thee,
I do be - lieve in what God's Son hath said,
Yet, both be - liev - ing, that I sup - pli - cate,

To com - pre - hend Thee, fail - ing ut - ter - ly.
Nought tru - er than that word of Truth most clear.
For which the Thief from off his cross ap - pealed.

4. Thy wounds, like Thomas, I do not behold,
Yet Thee, as God, I worship and adore,
O make me with more faith in Thee believe,
And hope in Thee, and love Thee, more and more.

5. I now behold Thee, hidden under veils,
O grant my prayer, that I Thy Face may see,
Revealed in glory, sight for which I thirst,
To make me blessèd for Eternity.

10 10 10 10

Tune:
Toulon

T. Source: *Breviary Hymns and Missal Sequences* (London: Burns & Oates, 1900) p. 92; Father Bagshawe was a priest of the Oratory of St. Philip Neri until 1874, when he was consecrated bishop of the Catholic diocese of Nottingham. In his translation of the *Adoro Te Devote*, he omitted the fifth and sixth verses.
Melody: Louis Bourgeois (d. 1559) in the *Genevan Psalter* (1551); also called "Old 124th."
M. Source: *People's Mass Book* (1964) p. 226; *New Saint Basil Hymnal* (1958) p. 80.

Adoro Te Devote, Latens Deitas (1264 AD)

Second Tune – *Trns: Bishop Edward G. Bagshawe (d. 1915)*

4. Thy wounds, like Thomas, I do not behold,
Yet Thee, as God, I worship and adore,
O make me with more faith in Thee believe,
And hope in Thee, and love Thee, more and more.

5. I now behold Thee, hidden under veils,
O grant my prayer, that I Thy Face may see,
Revealed in glory, sight for which I thirst,
To make me blessèd for Eternity.

Final Verses: Richard Lloyd (1993) #73; Noel Rawsthorne (2011) #123.
T. Source: *Breviary Hymns and Missal Sequences* (London: Burns & Oates, 1900) p. 92; Father Bagshawe was a priest of the Oratory of St. Philip Neri until 1874, when he was consecrated bishop of the Catholic diocese of Nottingham. In his translation of the *Adoro Te Devote*, he omitted the fifth and sixth verses.
Melody: Henry Lawes (d. 1662), whose compositions John Milton (d. 1674) praised in a famous sonnet.
M. Source: *New Westminster Hymnal* (1939) p. 234; *Catholic Hymn Book* (London Oratory, 1998) p. 250.

10 10 10 10
Tune:
Farley Castle

64 Adoro Te Devote, Latens Deitas (1264 AD)

Third Tune – *Trns: Bishop Edward G. Bagshawe (d. 1915)*

4. Thy wounds, like Thomas, I do not behold,
Yet Thee, as God, I worship and adore,
O make me with more faith in Thee believe,
And hope in Thee, and love Thee, more and more.

5. I now behold Thee, hidden under veils,
O grant my prayer, that I Thy Face may see,
Revealed in glory, sight for which I thirst,
To make me blessèd for Eternity.

10 10 10 10

Tune:
All Souls

T. Source: *Breviary Hymns and Missal Sequences* (London: Burns & Oates, 1900) p. 92; Father Bagshawe was a priest of the Oratory of St. Philip Neri until 1874, when he was consecrated bishop of the Catholic diocese of Nottingham. In his translation of the *Adoro Te Devote*, he omitted the fifth and sixth verses.
Melody: John Yoakley (d. 1932), organist at All Saints Church in Portsmouth.
M. Source: *New English Hymnal* (1986) p. 848; *Saint Edmund Campion Hymnal* (2013) p. 898.

Adoro Te Devote, Latens Deitas (1264 AD)

FOURTH TUNE – *Trns: Bishop Edward G. Bagshawe (d. 1915)*

4. Thy wounds, like Thomas, I do not behold,
Yet Thee, as God, I worship and adore,
O make me with more faith in Thee believe,
And hope in Thee, and love Thee, more and more.

5. I now behold Thee, hidden under veils,
O grant my prayer, that I Thy Face may see,
Revealed in glory, sight for which I thirst,
To make me blessèd for Eternity.

Final Verses: Noel Rawsthorne (2011) #341.

T. Source: *Breviary Hymns and Missal Sequences* (London: Burns & Oates, 1900) p. 92; Father Bagshawe was a priest of the Oratory of St. Philip Neri until 1874, when he was consecrated bishop of the Catholic diocese of Nottingham. In his translation of the *Adoro Te Devote*, he omitted the fifth and sixth verses.

Melody: Orlando Gibbons (d. 1625), organist at Westminster Abbey.

M. Source: *Catholic Hymn Book* (London Oratory, 1998) p. 189; cf. *The Hymnes and Songs of the Church* (1623) p. 77, originally used for "How sad and solitary now (alas!)" from the Lamentations of Jeremias.

10 10 10 10

Tune: SONG 24

Adoro Te Devote, Latens Deitas (1264 AD)

FIFTH TUNE – *Trns: Bishop Edward G. Bagshawe (d. 1915)*

4. Thy wounds, like Thomas, I do not behold,
Yet Thee, as God, I worship and adore,
O make me with more faith in Thee believe,
And hope in Thee, and love Thee, more and more.

5. I now behold Thee, hidden under veils,
O grant my prayer, that I Thy Face may see,
Revealed in glory, sight for which I thirst,
To make me blessèd for Eternity.

10 10 10 10

Tune:
EVENTIDE

T. Source: *Breviary Hymns and Missal Sequences* (London: Burns & Oates, 1900) p. 92; Father Bagshawe was a priest of the Oratory of St. Philip Neri until 1874, when he was consecrated bishop of the Catholic diocese of Nottingham. In his translation of the *Adoro Te Devote*, he omitted the fifth and sixth verses.
Melody: William H. Monk (d. 1889), organist at King's College London.
M. Source: *St. Mark's Hymnal for Use in the Catholic Church in the United States* (Peoria, Illinois: 1910) p. 184.

Adoro Te Devote, Latens Deitas (1264 AD)

Trns: Bishop Edward G. Bagshawe (d. 1915)

Can be sung with any 10 10 10 10 meter, such as OLD BATH, PAX DEI, BIRMINGHAM, etc.

I WORSHIP Thee devoutly, who dost hide
Within these figures, Hidden Deity,
And utterly subject my heart to Thee,
To comprehend Thee, failing utterly.

2. Though sight, and taste, and touch, do fail in Thee,
Yet may we trust to what from Thee we hear;
I do believe in what God's Son hath said,
Nought truer than that word of Truth most clear.

3. Upon the Cross the Deity was hid,
But here His Human Nature lies concealed,
Yet, both believing, that I supplicate,
For which the Thief from off his cross appealed.

4. Thy wounds, like Thomas, I do not behold,
Yet Thee, as God, I worship and adore,
O make me with more faith in Thee believe,
And hope in Thee, and love Thee, more and more.

5. I now behold Thee, hidden under veils,
O grant my prayer, that I Thy Face may see,
Revealed in glory, sight for which I thirst,
To make me blessèd for Eternity.

10 10 10 10

Tune: VARIOUS

T. Source: *Breviary Hymns and Missal Sequences* (London: Burns & Oates, 1900) p. 92; Father Bagshawe was a priest of the Oratory of St. Philip Neri until 1874, when he was consecrated bishop of the Catholic diocese of Nottingham. In his translation of the *Adoro Te Devote*, he omitted the fifth and sixth verses.

68 Adoro Te Devote, Latens Deitas (1264 AD)

Trns: Fr. Gerard Manley Hopkins, Society of Jesus (d. 1889)

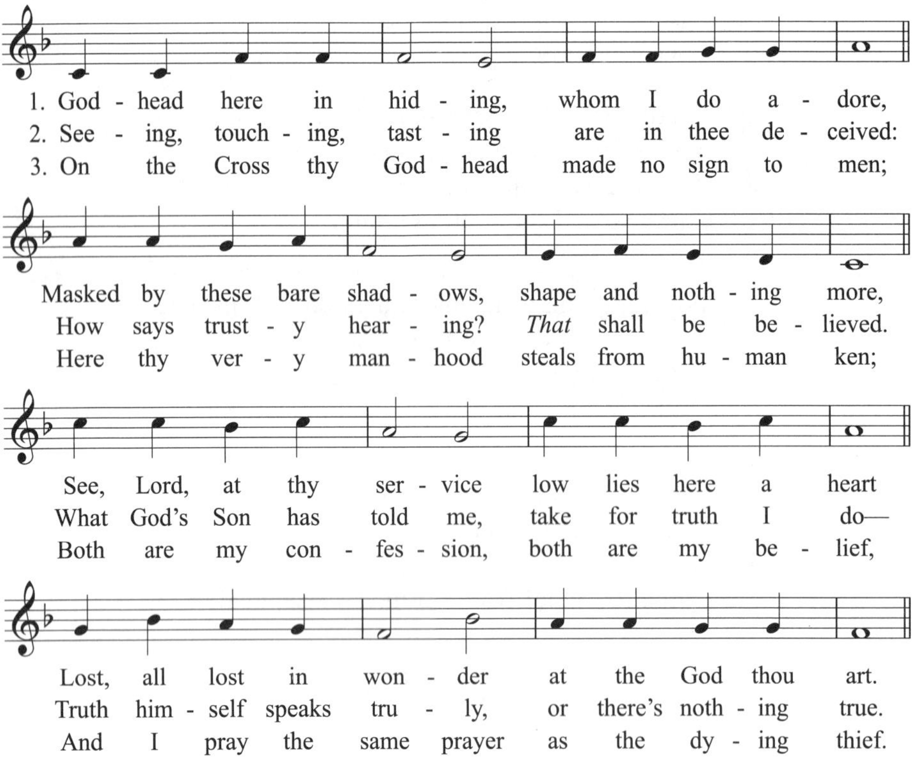

4. I am not like Thomas, wounds I cannot see,
But can plainly call thee Lord and God as he;
This faith each day deeper be my holding of,
Daily make me harder hope and dearer love.

5. O thou our reminder of Christ crucified,
Living Bread, the life of us for whom he died,
Lend this life to me then: feed and feast my mind,
There be thou the sweetness man was meant to find.

6. Bring the tender tale true of the Pelican,
Bathe me, Jesus Lord, in what thy bosom ran—
Blood that but one drop of has the worth to win
All the world forgiveness of its world of sin.

7. Jesus, whom I look at shrouded here below,
I beseech thee send me what I long for so,
Some day to gaze on thee face to face in light
And be blest for ever with thy glory's sight.

65 65 D

Tune:
ANIMA CHRISTI

Final Verses: Noel Rawsthorne (2011) #22.
Melody: Fr. William J. Maher (d. 1877), editor of Trappes's *Hymns for the Liturgical Year* (1865).
M. Source: *New Saint Basil Hymnal* (1958) p. 119; *Catholic Hymn Book* (1998) p. 215.
* Created circa 1882, this translation remained unpublished until Orby Shipley (d. 1916) provided it to the *Irish Monthly* (Dublin, 1903), p. 163. The original first lines were: "Godhead, I adore Thee, fast in hiding; Thou | God in these rare shapes, poor shadows, darkling now." We have substituted the version in the *New Westminster Hymnal* (1939) p. 97.

Adoro Te Devote, Latens Deitas (1264 AD)

Trns: Fr. Gerard Manley Hopkins, Society of Jesus (d. 1889)

Can be sung with any 65 65 D meter: ANIMA CHRISTI, LAUDES, CUDDESDON, FIORILLO, SWAHILI, UNE VAINE CRAINTE, ADORO TE (Plainsong), KING'S WESTON, ST RITA, etc.

GODHEAD here in hiding, whom I do adore,
Masked by these bare shadows, shape and nothing more,
See, Lord, at thy service low lies here a heart
Lost, all lost in wonder at the God thou art.

2. Seeing, touching, tasting are in thee deceived:
How says trusty hearing? *That* shall be believed.
What God's Son has told me, take for truth I do—
Truth himself speaks truly, or there's nothing true.

3. On the Cross thy Godhead made no sign to men;
Here thy very manhood steals from human ken;
Both are my confession, both are my belief,
And I pray the same prayer as the dying thief.

4. I am not like Thomas, wounds I cannot see,
But can plainly call thee Lord and God as he;
This faith each day deeper be my holding of,
Daily make me harder hope and dearer love.

5. O thou our reminder of Christ crucified,
Living Bread, the life of us for whom he died,
Lend this life to me then: feed and feast my mind,
There be thou the sweetness man was meant to find.

6. Bring the tender tale true of the Pelican,
Bathe me, Jesus Lord, in what thy bosom ran—
Blood that but one drop of has the worth to win
All the world forgiveness of its world of sin.

7. Jesus, whom I look at shrouded here below,
I beseech thee send me what I long for so,
Some day to gaze on thee face to face in light
And be blest for ever with thy glory's sight.

* Created circa 1882, this translation remained unpublished until Orby Shipley (d. 1916) provided it to the *Irish Monthly* (Dublin, 1903), p. 163. The original first lines were:

> "Godhead, I adore Thee, fast in hiding; Thou
> God in these rare shapes, poor shadows, darkling now."

We have substituted the version in the *New Westminster Hymnal* (1939) p. 97.

65 65 D

Tune: VARIOUS

Adoro Te Devote, Latens Deitas (1264 AD)

Trns: Charles Kegan Paul (d. 1902)

4. On Thy wounds, like Thomas, though I do not gaze,
Yet, my Lord, I know Thee, and confess always;
Give me in Thee ever faith all faiths above,
Give me hope increasing, give me greater love.

5. O Thou high memorial of my Lord who died,
Living Bread, for mortals Thou dost life provide;
Grant through Thee my soul's life never more may waste,
Give in it Thy savor sweetly to my taste.

6. Pelican of mercy, Jesus, Lord and God,
Cleanse me, wretched sinner, in Thy Precious Blood;
One drop, and one only, might avail to win
Pardon, full, abounding, for the whole world's sin.

7. Jesus, whom thus dimly under veils I see,
Grant the boon I thirst for, grant my prayer to me,
That, veils rent asunder, I may see by Grace,
Finally the glory of Thy very Face.

65 65 D

Tune: FIORILLO

Melody: Richard J. Clark (b. 1969), choirmaster at the Cathedral of the Holy Cross in Boston.
M. Source: *Saint Jean de Brébeuf Hymnal* (2018).
T. Source: *On the Way Side, Verses and Translations* (1899), by Charles Kegan Paul, who converted to Catholicism in 1890. For the first stanza, we have substituted a version by Dr. Neale, as printed in *A Treasury of Catholic Song, comprising some two hundred hymns from Catholic sources for congregational use* (Maryland: St. Mary's Catholic Church, 1915) #91. For verse 6, cf. Volume 29 of *Irish Monthly* (Dublin, 1901) p. 656.

Adoro Te Devote, Latens Deitas (1264 AD)

Trns: Charles Kegan Paul (d. 1902)

Can be sung with any 65 65 D meter: ANIMA CHRISTI, LAUDES, CUDDESDON, FIORILLO, SWAHILI, UNE VAINE CRAINTE, ADORO TE (Plainsong), KING'S WESTON, ST RITA, etc.

HUMBLY I adore Thee, Hidden Deity,
Who beneath these figures hidest verily:
Wholly in submission Thee my spirit hails,
For in contemplating Thee it wholly fails.

2. Seeing, tasting, touching are in Thee deceived,
And alone the hearing safely is believed:
All the Son of God said I accept and hold,
Truest truth that must be which the Truth has told.

3. Once 'twas Godhead only hidden on the Tree,
Now the Manhood also is not here to see;
Both I now believe, and vowing my belief,
Seek I what of old sought the repentant thief.

4. On Thy wounds, like Thomas, though I do not gaze,
Yet, my Lord, I know Thee, and confess always;
Give me in Thee ever faith all faiths above,
Give me hope increasing, give me greater love.

5. O Thou high memorial of my Lord who died,
Living Bread, for mortals Thou dost life provide;
Grant through Thee my soul's life never more may waste,
Give in it Thy savor sweetly to my taste.

6. Pelican of mercy, Jesus, Lord and God,
Cleanse me, wretched sinner, in Thy Precious Blood;
One drop, and one only, might avail to win
Pardon, full, abounding, for the whole world's sin.

7. Jesus, whom thus dimly under veils I see,
Grant the boon I thirst for, grant my prayer to me,
That, veils rent asunder, I may see by Grace,
Finally the glory of Thy very Face.

T. Source: *On the Way Side, Verses and Translations* (1899), by Charles Kegan Paul, who converted to Catholicism in 1890. For the first stanza, we have substituted a version by Dr. Neale, as printed in *A Treasury of Catholic Song, comprising some two hundred hymns from Catholic sources for congregational use* (Maryland: St. Mary's Catholic Church, 1915) #91. For verse 6, cf. Volume 29 of *Irish Monthly* (Dublin, 1901) p. 656.

65 65 D

Tune: VARIOUS

Agnoscat Omne Saeculum (6th century)

Venantius Fortunatus, Bishop of Poitiers (d. 609AD)

To sing in Latin,
use any 88 88 (LM) tune.

AGNÓSCAT omne saéculum
Venísse vitae praémium;
Post hostis ásperi jugum
Appáruit redémptio

2. Esaías quae praécinit
Compléta sunt in Vírgine;
Annuntiávit Ángelus,
Sanctus replévit Spíritus.

3. María ventre cóncipit *n1*
Verbi fidélis sémine:
Quem totus orbis non capit
Portant puéllae víscera.

4. Radix jam Jesse flóruit,
Et virga fructum édidit;
Fecúnda partum prótulit,
Et Virgo mater pérmanet.

5. Praesépe poni pértulit
Qui lucis auctor éxstitit,
Cum Patre caelos cóndidit,
Sub Matre pannos índuit.

6. Legem dedit qui saéculo,
Cujus decem praecépta sunt,
Dignándo factus est homo
Sub legis esse vínculo.

7. Adam vetus quod pólluit
Adam novus hoc ábluit:
Tumens quod ille dejécit
Humíllimus hic érigit.

8. Jam nata lux est et salus,
Fugáta nox et victa mors;
Veníte, gentes, crédite:
Deum María prótulit.

88 88 (LM)

Tune:
VARIOUS

T. Source: *The Liturgical Year by the Right Rev'd Dom Prosper Guéranger; Christmas—Volume II* (Stanbrook Abbey, 1904) p. 217.

Assistance in comprehension

LET all the world acknowledge
that the recompense of life has come,
that after the yoke of the savage foe
redemption has appeared.

2. The things that Isaias foretells
have been fulfilled in a Virgin; *cf. Is 7.14*
an Angel has brought tidings,
the Holy Spirit has replenished her. *cf. Lk 1.26-35*

3. Mary conceives in her womb *n1*
believing through the seed of the word: *cf. Lk 8.11; 1.45*
the one whom the whole world does not hold
the body of a maiden bears.

4. Now the root of Jesse has blossomed
and his rod has produced fruit: *cf. Is 11.1*
the fertile one has brought forth offspring,
and the Mother remains a Virgin.

5. He who was the Maker of light
accepts to be laid in a manger:
with the Father he established the heavens
subject to his Mother, he puts on swaddling.

6. He who gave the world the Law,
he whose the ten commandments are,
has become man, by deigning
to be under the bond of the Law. *cf. Gal 4.4*

7. The old Adam sullied
that which the new Adam has cleansed:
what the former, swelling with pride, cast down,
the latter, most lowly, has raised up.

8. Now light and salvation have been born,
night put to flight and death conquered;
come, ye nations, believe:
Mary has brought forth God.

[1] Fortunatus once again evokes the theme of conception through the word, or through the ear; cf. explanatory notes on QUEM TERRA, PONTUS, AETHERA for *Miréntur ergo saécula, quod ángelus fert sémina, quod aure virgo cóncipit et corde credens párturit.*

74 # Agnoscat Omne Saeculum (6th century)

"Virgin Mother of God, He whom the whole world cannot contain was enclosed in thy womb, and was made man."—Virgo Dei Genitrix, vl

4. There springs a branch from Jesse's root, | And lo, his rod puts forth its fruit:
The Mother, though she truly bore, | Abides a Virgin, as before.

5. He at whose wish the light was made, | Yet willingly in manger laid,
Who with his Father spread the skies, | Now swaddled by his Mother lies.

6. Commandments ten, the Law he gave, | A heedless world to teach and save,
Who, man become, a bondsman is | Of that same Law whose gift was his.

7. The latter Adam washes clear | Where once the former chose to smear:
That which the proud man forfeited | The lowliest upholds instead.

8. Now light is born and strength renewed, | The night dispelled and death subdued:
Come and believe, ye nations, then, | That Mary brings their God to men.

88 88 (LM)

Tune: FULDA

Final Verses: Richard Lloyd (1993) #75; Noel Rawsthorne (2011) #128.
ENGLISH TRANSLATION: Editors of the *Saint Jean de Brébeuf Hymnal* (2018).
Melody: William Gardiner (d. 1853) in *Sacred Melodies* (1815).
M. Source: *Catholic Hymn Book* (London Oratory, 1998) p. 334.

"Virgin Mother of God, He whom the whole world cannot contain was enclosed in thy womb, and was made man."—Virgo Dei Genitrix, vl

Can be sung with any 88 88 meter, such as Eisenach, Rogers Park, Bressani, La Rochelle, Kempen, Bessemer, Tallis Canon, Winchester New, etc.

HE who is life's reward draws near,
Let all the world confess him here:
The ruthless foeman's yoke is past,
Redemption hath appeared at last.

2. Fulfillment of Isaiah's strain
A Virgin merits to attain:
The same an Angel came to greet
The Holy Ghost hath left replete.

3. The blessèd Mary hath conceived
By that true word which she believed:
And he whom worlds cannot comprise
Within a maiden's body lies.

4. There springs a branch from Jesse's root,
And lo, his rod puts forth its fruit:
The Mother, though she truly bore,
Abides a Virgin, as before.

5. He at whose wish the light was made,
Yet willingly in manger laid,
Who with his Father spread the skies,
Now swaddled by his Mother lies.

6. Commandments ten, the Law he gave,
A heedless world to teach and save,
Who, man become, a bondsman is
Of that same Law whose gift was his.

7. The latter Adam washes clear
Where once the former chose to smear:
That which the proud man forfeited
The lowliest upholds instead.

8. Now light is born and strength renewed,
The night dispelled and death subdued:
Come and believe, ye nations, then,
That Mary brings their God to men.

88 88 (LM)

Tune: Various

English Translation: Editors of the *Saint Jean de Brébeuf Hymnal* (2018).

76 Auctor Beate Saeculi (18th century)

Hymn to the Most Sacred Heart of Jesus

To sing in Latin,
use any 88 88 (LM) tune.

AUCTOR beáte saéculi, *n1*
Christe Redémptor ómnium,
Lumen Patris de lúmine,
Deúsque verus de Deo.

2. Amor coégit te tuus
Mortále corpus súmere,
Ut novus Adam rédderes
Quod vetus ill*e* abstúlerat.

3. Ill*e* amor almus ártifex
Terrae marísqu*e* et síderum,
Erráta patrum míserans, *n2*
Et nostra rumpens víncula.

4. Non corde discédat tuo
Vis ill*a* amóris ínclyti:
Hoc fonte gentes háuriant
Remissiónis grátiam.

5. Percúss*um* ad hoc est láncea,
Passúmqu*e* ad hoc est vúlnera;
Ut nos laváret sórdibus
Unda fluént*e* et Sánguine. *n3*

6. Decus Parént*i* et Fílio,
Sanctóque sit Spirítui,
Quibus potéstas, glória,
Regnúmqu*e* in omn*e* est saéculum.

88 88 (LM)

Tune:
VARIOUS

Text: The author of this Latin hymn is not known, but it appears to be from the 18th century.
T. Source: *Hymnarium Vesperale* (London: John Lambert, 1851) p. 21.

Assistance for comprehension

O BLESSED Framer of the world, *n1*
Christ the Redeemer of all,
light from the Father's light
and true God from God.

2. Thy love compelled thee
to take on a death-bound body,
that thou as the new Adam mightest restore
that which the old one bore away.

3. That love was the bounteous crafter
of earth and sea and stars,
pitying the straying of our fathers, *n2*
and breaking our bonds.

4. Let not that force of illustrious love
depart from thy HEART :
from this spring let the nations draw
the grace of forgiveness.

5. For this IT was struck by the spear,
and for this IT suffered wounds:
that IT might cleanse us of our squalors
when ITS water and blood ran. *n3*

6. Honor be to the Father and the Son,
and to the Holy Spirit,
to whom belong might, glory,
and rule in every age.

[1] "Christ as Creator," cf. second footnote on page 421.

[2] "Fathers" in the sense of "forefathers."

[3] *Unda* is a poetic term for water (literally "wave, billow").

78 Auctor Beate Saeculi (18th century)

First Tune – *Trns: Fr. Dominic Popplewell (b. 1973)*

4. Let not that force of noble love
from out its proper seat depart:
and let the nations draw the grace
of pardon at that spring, thy Heart:

5. The which for this once suffered wounds,
and e'en for this the bitter spear:
ourselves, who were in filthy state,
while water ran with blood, to clear.

6. Let praise the Father, and the Son,
and Holy Ghost this day attend,
as glory, might and rule beseem
the same, nor evermore shall end.

88 88 (LM)

Tune:
Melcombe

Final Verses: Richard Lloyd (1993) #133; Noel Rawsthorne (2011) #205.
T. Source: *Saint Jean de Brébeuf Hymnal* (2018).
Melody: Samuel Webbe, the elder (d. 1816).
M. Source: *Veritas Hymnal* (Dublin: Irish Church Music Association, 1974) p. 96; *Cantate Omnes: Hymnal of the Catholic Choirmasters' Guild* (1952) #78.

Auctor Beate Saeculi (18th century)

Second Tune – *Trns: Fr. Dominic Popplewell (b. 1973)*

4. Let not that force of noble love
from out its proper seat depart:
and let the nations draw the grace
of pardon at that spring, thy Heart:

5. The which for this once suffered wounds,
and e'en for this the bitter spear:
ourselves, who were in filthy state,
while water ran with blood, to clear.

6. Let praise the Father, and the Son,
and Holy Ghost this day attend,
as glory, might and rule beseem
the same, nor evermore shall end.

Melody: Flor Peeters (d. 1986), organist at the Catholic Cathedral of Mechelen, Belgium, was made a Baron by King Baudouin.
M. Source: *People's Mass Book* (Omer Westendorf, 1964) p. 218.
T. Source: *Saint Jean de Brébeuf Hymnal* (2018).

88 88 (LM)

Tune: Kempen

80 Auctor Beate Saeculi (18th century)

Third Tune – *Trns: Fr. Dominic Popplewell (b. 1973)*

4. Let not that force of noble love
from out its proper seat depart:
and let the nations draw the grace
of pardon at that spring, thy Heart:

5. The which for this once suffered wounds,
and e'en for this the bitter spear:
ourselves, who were in filthy state,
while water ran with blood, to clear.

6. Let praise the Father, and the Son,
and Holy Ghost this day attend,
as glory, might and rule beseem
the same, nor evermore shall end.

88 88 (LM)

Tune:
Bessemer

Melody: Kevin Allen (b. 1965), choirmaster at the Monastery of the Holy Cross in Chicago.
M. Source: *Saint Edmund Campion Missal and Hymnal* (2013) p. 880.
T. Source: *Saint Jean de Brébeuf Hymnal* (2018).

Auctor Beate Saeculi (18th century) 81

FOURTH TUNE – *Trns: Fr. Dominic Popplewell (b. 1973)*

4. Let not that force of noble love
from out its proper seat depart:
and let the nations draw the grace
of pardon at that spring, thy Heart:

5. The which for this once suffered wounds,
and e'en for this the bitter spear:
ourselves, who were in filthy state,
while water ran with blood, to clear.

6. Let praise the Father, and the Son,
and Holy Ghost this day attend,
as glory, might and rule beseem
the same, nor evermore shall end.

Final Verses: Richard Lloyd (1993) #239; Noel Rawsthorne (2011) #382.
Melody: William Knapp (d. 1768), church organist for the town of Wareham, in Dorset.
M. Source: *Catholic Hymn Book* (London Oratory, 1998) p. 218; *Hymns, Psalms, and Spiritual Canticles* (Massachusetts: Theodore Marier, 1983) p. 488.
T. Source: *Saint Jean de Brébeuf Hymnal* (2018).

88 88 (LM)

Tune: WAREHAM

Auctor Beate Saeculi (18th century)

Fifth Tune – *Trns: Fr. Dominic Popplewell (b. 1973)*

4. Let not that force of noble love
from out its proper seat depart:
and let the nations draw the grace
of pardon at that spring, thy Heart:

5. The which for this once suffered wounds,
and e'en for this the bitter spear:
ourselves, who were in filthy state,
while water ran with blood, to clear.

6. Let praise the Father, and the Son,
and Holy Ghost this day attend,
as glory, might and rule beseem
the same, nor evermore shall end.

88 88 (LM)

Tune:
Winchester New

Final Verses: Richard Lloyd (1993) #244; Noel Rawsthorne (2011) #392.
Melody: Georg Wittwe's *Musikalisches Handbuch der Geistlichen Melodien* (Hamburg, 1690).
M. Source: *Episcopal Hymnal* (1940) ABAB #548; *New Saint Basil Hymnal* (1958) p. 1.
T. Source: *Saint Jean de Brébeuf Hymnal* (2018).

Auctor Beate Saeculi (18th century)

Trns: Fr. Dominic Popplewell (b. 1973)

Can be sung with any 88 88 meter, such as Hilderstone, Duguet, Breslau, Melcombe, Wareham, Old Hundredth, Mein Seel, Trinity College, etc.

O BLESSÈD Framer of the world,
O Christ, all things who dost redeem,
art very God of very God,
the gleaming of the Father's gleam:

2. Thy love it was did thee constrain
on thee to take our mortal clay,
the latter Adam, to restore
that which the former took away.

3. Thy love it was did earth, and sea,
and stars with bounteous crafting make,
took pity when our fathers strayed,
and did our own confinements break.

4. Let not that force of noble love
from out its proper seat depart:
and let the nations draw the grace
of pardon at that spring, thy Heart:

5. The which for this once suffered wounds,
and e'en for this the bitter spear:
ourselves, who were in filthy state,
while water ran with blood, to clear.

6. Let praise the Father, and the Son,
and Holy Ghost this day attend,
as glory, might and rule beseem
the same, which nevermore shall end.

88 88 (LM)

Tune: Various

T. Source: *Saint Jean de Brébeuf Hymnal* (2018).

84 Auctor Beate Saeculi (18th century)

Trns: Msgr. Hugh T. Henry (d. 1946)

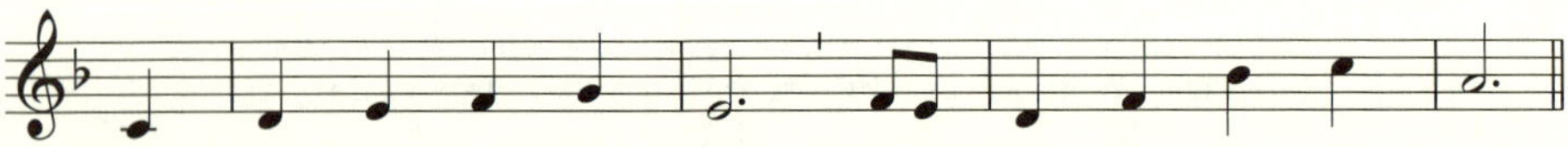

1. Blest Au - thor of the world, Re - deem - er of our race,
2. 'Twas love that bade Thee take Our frame of mor - tal clay,
3. Thy love that build - ed fair The earth, the sea, the stars;

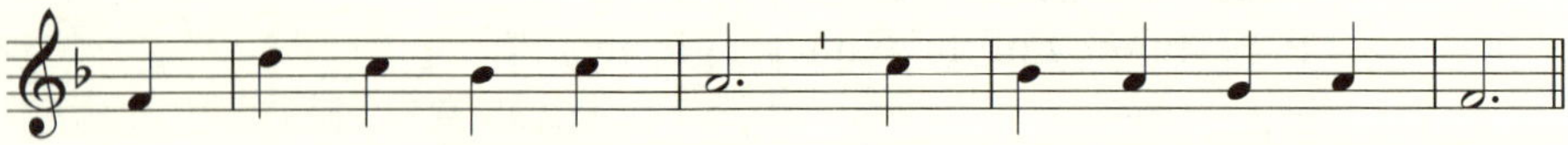

Thou ver - y God of God, Light of the Fa - ther's face:
New Ad - am for the Old, His thiev - ing to re - pay.
That pit - ied old - en faults, And broke our pris - on - bars:

4. O may Thy Heart retain
For e'er such wondrous love!
Let all approach the Fount,
And Thy sweet mercy prove.

5. For this alone the lance
Set free Its saving flood,
To wash our sins away
In water and in blood.

6. To Father and to Son
And Holy Spirit be
The kingdom and the pow'r
Through all eternity.

66 66 Iambic

Tune:
SEÁN

Melody: Richard J. Clark (b. 1969), choirmaster at the Cathedral of the Holy Cross in Boston.
M. Source: *Saint Jean de Brébeuf Hymnal* (2018).
T. Source: *Eucharistica: Verse & Prose in Honor of the Hidden God* (Philadelphia: Dolphin Press, 1912) p. 167. Monsignor Hugh T. Henry, professor of homiletics at the Catholic University of America, also taught Gregorian chant at St. Charles Seminary (Overbrook, Pennsylvania).

Trns: Msgr. Hugh T. Henry (d. 1946)

English translation can be sung with any 66 66 meter (iambic), such as CAMCOLT, QUAM DILECTA, ST CECILIA, IBSTONE, CLERMONT, SEÁN, etc.

BLEST Author of the world,
Redeemer of our race,
Thou very God of God,
Light of the Father's face:

2. 'Twas love that bade Thee take
Our frame of mortal clay,
New Adam for the Old,
His thieving to repay.

3. Thy love that builded fair
The earth, the sea, the stars;
That pitied olden faults,
And broke our prison-bars:

4. O may Thy Heart retain
For e'er such wondrous love!
Let all approach the Fount,
And Thy sweet mercy prove.

5. For this alone the lance
Set free Its saving flood,
To wash our sins away
In water and in blood.

6. To Father and to Son
And Holy Spirit be
The kingdom and the pow'r
Through all eternity.

T. Source: *Eucharistica: Verse & Prose in Honor of the Hidden God* (Philadelphia: Dolphin Press, 1912) p. 167. Monsignor Hugh T. Henry, professor of homiletics at the Catholic University of America, also taught Gregorian chant at St. Charles Seminary (Overbrook, Pennsylvania).

66 66 Iambic
Tune:
VARIOUS

86 Auctor Beate Saeculi (18th century)

Trns: Bishop Edward G. Bagshawe (d. 1915)

4. Let not that mighty noble Love,
To e'er depart from out Thy Heart ;
Let nations drink that pard'ning grace,
Which this sweet Fountain doth impart.

5. For this the lance did pierce It through,
For this Its wounds It did endure,
To cleanse us from our filthy stains,
It poured forth Blood and Water pure.

6. Glory to Father and to Son,
And to the Holy Spirit, be,
Let pow'r and honor be to Them,
And may They reign eternally.

* This melody at a lower key is on page 436.

88 88 (LM)

Tune: Trinity College

Melody: John Bacchus Dykes (d. 1876).
M. Source: *Hymns Ancient and Modern* (1972) p. 64.
T. Source: *Breviary Hymns and Missal Sequences* (London: Burns & Oates, 1900) p. 93; Father Bagshawe was a priest of the Oratory of St. Philip Neri until 1874, when he was consecrated bishop of the Catholic diocese of Nottingham.

Auctor Beate Saeculi (18th century)

Trns: Bishop Edward G. Bagshawe (d. 1915)

Can be sung with any 88 88 meter, such as HILDERSTONE, DUGUET, BRESLAU, MELCOMBE, WAREHAM, OLD HUNDREDTH, MEIN SEEL, TRINITY COLLEGE, etc.

O CHRIST, who didst the world create,
And man hast by redemption freed,
Light of the Father's Light art Thou,
True God from God Thou dost proceed.

2. A mortal body to assume,
Thy wondrous love didst Thee constrain,
To give what the old Adam took,
As the new Adam, back again.

3. That Love the maker was of earth
And sea and stars in olden time,
Our father's errors it forgave,
It breaks for us the bonds of crime.

4. Let not that mighty noble Love,
To e'er depart from out Thy HEART ;
Let nations drink that pard'ning grace,
Which this sweet Fountain doth impart.

5. For this the lance did pierce IT through,
For this ITS wounds IT did endure,
To cleanse us from our filthy stains,
IT poured forth Blood and Water pure.

6. Glory to Father and to Son,
And to the Holy Spirit, be,
Let pow'r and honor be to Them,
And may They reign eternally.

T. Source: *Breviary Hymns and Missal Sequences* (London: Burns & Oates, 1900) p. 93; Father Bagshawe was a priest of the Oratory of St. Philip Neri until 1874, when he was consecrated bishop of the Catholic diocese of Nottingham.

88 88 (LM)

Tune:
VARIOUS

88 Audi Benigne Conditor (6th century)

Pope Saint Gregory the Great (d. 604AD)

To sing in Latin,
use any 88 88 (LM) tune.

AUDI benígne Cónditor,
Nostras preces cum flétibus,
In hoc sacro jejúnio
Fusas quadragenário.

2. Scrutátor alme córdium, *n1*
Infírma tu scis vírium:
Ad te revérsis éxhibe
Remissiónis grátiam.

3. Multum quidem peccávimus,
Sed parce confiténtibus:
Ad laudem tui nóminis,
Confer medélam lánguidis.

4. Sic corpus extra cónteri
Dona per abstinéntiam,
Jejúnet ut mens sóbria
A labe prorsus críminum. *n2*

5. Praesta, beáta Trínitas,
Concéde, simplex Únitas,
Ut fructuósa sint tuis
Jejuniórum múnera. *n3*

88 88 (LM)

Tune:
VARIOUS

T. Source: *The Hymns of the Dominican Missal and Breviary* (Father Aquinas Byrnes: 1943) p. 85.

Assistance for comprehension

HEAR, O kind Creator,
our prayers, poured out
with tears during this
sacred forty-day fast.

2. O generous prover of hearts, *n1*
thou knowest the weakness of our power:
to those who have returned to thee
display the grace of thy forgiveness.

3. We have sinned much indeed,
but spare us, who confess:
for the praise of thy name,
bring remedy to the ailing.

4. Grant that we may so humble
our bodies outwardly by refraining,
that our minds, being temperate, fast
utterly from the downfall of misdeeds. *n2*

5. Grant, O blessed Trinity,
permit, O simple Unity,
that the duty of fasting be fruitful
for those who are thine own. *n3*

[1] "Prover": cf. Ps 7.10; Jer 11.20; Ap 2.23.

[2] Literally:

> *Grant the body so to be crushed*
> *outwardly by refraining,*
> *that the temperate mind may fast*
> *utterly from the downfall of misdeeds.*

[3] "Duty of fasting": literally, "duties of fasts."

90 Audi Benigne Conditor (6th century)

First Tune – *Trns: Fr. John Fitzpatrick, Oblate of Mary* (*d.* 1929)

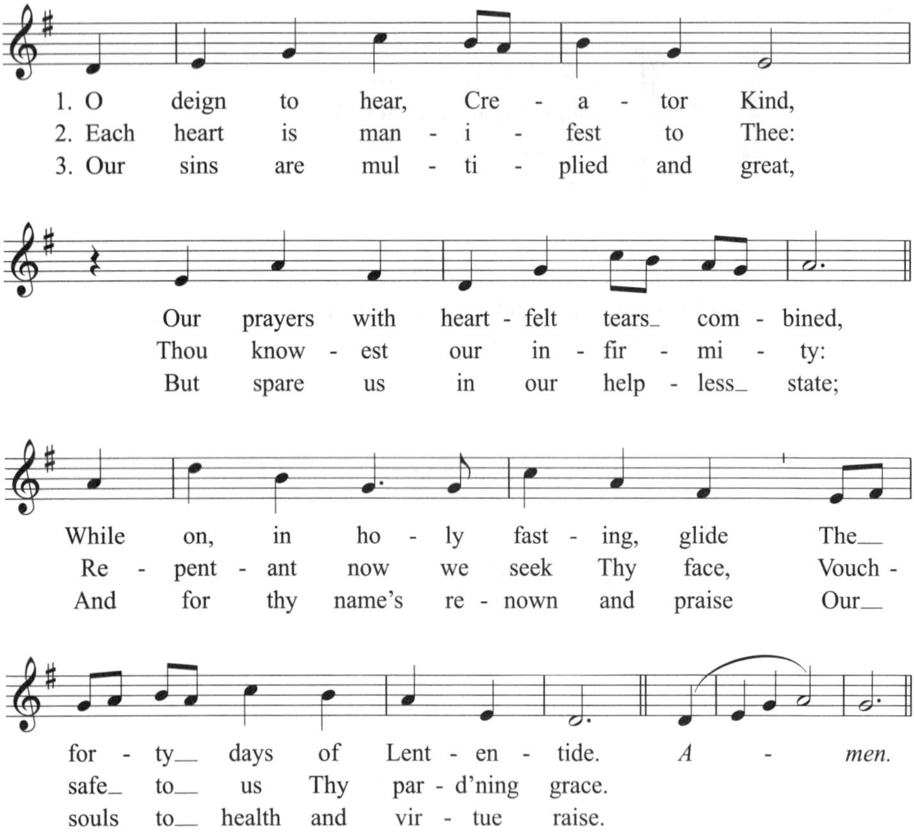

4. Grant that our body's every sense
May conquered be through abstinence,
That so our hearts, which fast from sin,
May find no food for fault therein.

5. This, Holy Trinity, who art
A perfect Unity, impart;
That they who are Thine own may see
How fruitful shall their fasting be.

88 88 (LM)

Tune:
Gonfalon Royal

Final Verses: Richard Lloyd (1993) #80; Noel Rawsthorne (2011) #136.
T. Source: *The Breviary and Missal Hymns* (London: Sands & Co, 1931) p. 57; alterations have been made to the original text by Fr. Fitzpatrick.
Melody: Sir Percy Carter Buck (d. 1947); first published in *Fourteen Hymn Tunes* (1913).
M. Source: *Catholic Hymn Book* (London Oratory, 1998) p. 140. The tune was originally paired with *Vexilla Regis* ("Flag of the King"). A *gonfalon* ("flag") was traditionally carried during Catholic processions.

Audi Benigne Conditor (6th century)

Second Tune – *Trns: Fr. John Fitzpatrick, Oblate of Mary (d. 1929)*

4. Grant that our body's every sense
May conquered be through abstinence,
That so our hearts, which fast from sin,
May find no food for fault therein.

5. This, Holy Trinity, who art
A perfect Unity, impart;
That they who are Thine own may see
How fruitful shall their fasting be.

Final Verses: Richard Lloyd (1993) #64; Noel Rawsthorne (2011) #108.
T. Source: *The Breviary and Missal Hymns* (London: Sands & Co, 1931) p. 57; alterations have been made to the original text by Fr. Fitzpatrick.
Melody: Bartholomäus Gesius (d. 1613); adapted by Johann H. Schein (d. 1630).
M. Source: *New Saint Basil Hymnal* (1958) p. 120; *The Catholic Vesper Hymn Book set to Music either for Unison or Four Voices with Accompaniment* (Charles Lewis, 1877) p. 34; *Pope Pius XII Hymnal* (Ohio: Gregorian Institute of America, 1959) p. 13.

88 88 (LM)

Tune:
Eisenach

Audi Benigne Conditor (6th century)

Third Tune – *Trns: Fr. John Fitzpatrick, Oblate of Mary (d. 1929)*

1. O deign to hear, Cre - a - tor Kind,
2. Each heart is man - i - fest to Thee:
3. Our sins are mul - ti - plied and great,

Our prayers with heart - felt tears com - bined,
Thou know - est our in - fir - mi - ty:
But spare us in our help - less state;

While on, in ho - ly fast - ing, glide
Re - pent - ant now we seek Thy face,
And for thy name's re - nown and praise

The for - ty days of Lent - en - tide.
Vouch - safe to us Thy par - d'ning grace.
Our souls to health and vir - tue raise.

4. Grant that our body's every sense
May conquered be through abstinence,
That so our hearts, which fast from sin,
May find no food for fault therein.

5. This, Holy Trinity, who art
A perfect Unity, impart;
That they who are Thine own may see
How fruitful shall their fasting be.

88 88 (LM)

Tune:
Melcombe

Final Verses: Richard Lloyd (1993) #133; Noel Rawsthorne (2011) #205.
T. Source: *The Breviary and Missal Hymns* (London: Sands & Co, 1931) p. 57; alterations have been made to the original text by Fr. Fitzpatrick.
Melody: Samuel Webbe, the elder (d. 1816).
M. Source: *Veritas Hymnal* (Dublin: Irish Church Music Association, 1974) p. 96; *Cantate Omnes: Hymnal of the Catholic Choirmasters' Guild* (1952) #78.

Audi Benigne Conditor (6th century) 93

Fourth Tune – *Trns: Fr. John Fitzpatrick, Oblate of Mary (d. 1929)*

4. Grant that our body's every sense
May conquered be through abstinence,
That so our hearts, which fast from sin,
May find no food for fault therein.

5. This, Holy Trinity, who art
A perfect Unity, impart;
That they who are Thine own may see
How fruitful shall their fasting be.

T. Source: *The Breviary and Missal Hymns* (London: Sands & Co, 1931) p. 57; alterations have been made to the original text by Fr. Fitzpatrick.
Melody: *Christliches Gesangbüchlein* (1568).
M. Source: *New Westminster Hymnal* (1939) p. 41.

88 88 (LM)
Tune: Saxony

94 Audi Benigne Conditor (6th century)

Fifth Tune – *Trns: Fr. John Fitzpatrick, Oblate of Mary (d. 1929)*

4. Grant that our body's every sense
May conquered be through abstinence,
That so our hearts, which fast from sin,
May find no food for fault therein.

5. This, Holy Trinity, who art
A perfect Unity, impart;
That they who are Thine own may see
How fruitful shall their fasting be.

88 88 (LM)

Tune:
Wareham

Final Verses: Richard Lloyd (1993) #239; Noel Rawsthorne (2011) #382.
Melody: William Knapp (d. 1768), church organist for the town of Wareham, in Dorset.
M. Source: *Catholic Hymn Book* (London Oratory, 1998) p. 218; *Hymns, Psalms, and Spiritual Canticles* (Massachusetts: Theodore Marier, 1983) p. 488.
T. Source: *The Breviary and Missal Hymns* (London: Sands & Co, 1931) p. 57; alterations have been made to the original text by Fr. Fitzpatrick.

Audi Benigne Conditor (6th century) 95

Sixth Tune – *Trns: Fr. John Fitzpatrick, Oblate of Mary (d. 1929)*

4. Grant that our body's every sense
May conquered be through abstinence,
That so our hearts, which fast from sin,
May find no food for fault therein.

5. This, Holy Trinity, who art
A perfect Unity, impart;
That they who are Thine own may see
How fruitful shall their fasting be.

T. Source: *The Breviary and Missal Hymns* (London: Sands & Co, 1931) p. 57;
alterations have been made to the original text by Fr. Fitzpatrick.
Melody: Traditional French air, sometimes sung with "O amor quam exstaticus."
M. Source: cf. *New Saint Basil Hymnal* (1958) p. 184; cf. *New Westminster Hymnal* (1939) p. 238.

88 88 (LM)
Tune:
Notre Dame

96 Audi Benigne Conditor (6th century)

Seventh Tune – *Trns: Fr. John Fitzpatrick, Oblate of Mary (d. 1929)*

4. Grant that our body's every sense
May conquered be through abstinence,
That so our hearts, which fast from sin,
May find no food for fault therein.

5. This, Holy Trinity, who art
A perfect Unity, impart;
That they who are Thine own may see
How fruitful shall their fasting be.

88 88 (LM)

Tune:
Alfreton

T. Source: *The Breviary and Missal Hymns* (London: Sands & Co, 1931) p. 57; alterations have been made to the original text by Fr. Fitzpatrick.
M. Source: *A Supplement to a New Version of the Psalms of David* (1708).

Audi Benigne Conditor (6th century)

Eighth Tune – *Trns: Fr. John Fitzpatrick, Oblate of Mary (d. 1929)*

4. Grant that our body's every sense
May conquered be through abstinence,
That so our hearts, which fast from sin,
May find no food for fault therein.

5. This, Holy Trinity, who art
A perfect Unity, impart;
That they who are Thine own may see
How fruitful shall their fasting be.

* This melody at a lower key is on page 864.

T. Source: *The Breviary and Missal Hymns* (London: Sands & Co, 1931) p. 57; alterations have been made to the original text by Fr. Fitzpatrick.
Melody: From a hymn book published by Fr. Melchior Ludolf Herold (d. 1810).
M. Source: *New Westminster Hymnal* (1939) p. 173.

88 88 (LM)

Tune: Bressani

98 Audi Benigne Conditor (6th century)

Ninth Tune – *Trns: Fr. John Fitzpatrick, Oblate of Mary (d. 1929)*

4. Grant that our body's every sense
May conquered be through abstinence,
That so our hearts, which fast from sin,
May find no food for fault therein.

5. This, Holy Trinity, who art
A perfect Unity, impart;
That they who are Thine own may see
How fruitful shall their fasting be.

88 88 (LM)

Tune:
Kempen

Melody: Flor Peeters (d. 1986), organist at the Catholic Cathedral of Mechelen, Belgium, was made a Baron by King Baudouin.
M. Source: *People's Mass Book* (Omer Westendorf, 1964) p. 218.
T. Source: *The Breviary and Missal Hymns* (London: Sands & Co, 1931) p. 57; alterations have been made to the original text by Fr. Fitzpatrick.

Audi Benigne Conditor (6th century) 99

Tenth Tune – *Trns: Fr. John Fitzpatrick, Oblate of Mary (d. 1929)*

4. Grant that our body's every sense
May conquered be through abstinence,
That so our hearts, which fast from sin,
May find no food for fault therein.

5. This, Holy Trinity, who art
A perfect Unity, impart;
That they who are Thine own may see
How fruitful shall their fasting be.

T. Source: *The Breviary and Missal Hymns* (London: Sands & Co, 1931) p. 57; alterations have been made to the original text by Fr. Fitzpatrick.
Melody: Philip Hart (d. 1749), organist at St. Michael Church, Cornhill.
M. Source: *Hymns Ancient and Modern* (1972) p. 8; cf. *Church Hymns With Tunes* (1885) p. 230, edited by Sir Arthur Sullivan (d. 1900), organist at St. Peter Church, Kensington.

88 88 (LM)

Tune: Hilderstone

100 Audi Benigne Conditor (6th century)

Eleventh Tune – *Trns: Fr. John Fitzpatrick, Oblate of Mary (d. 1929)*

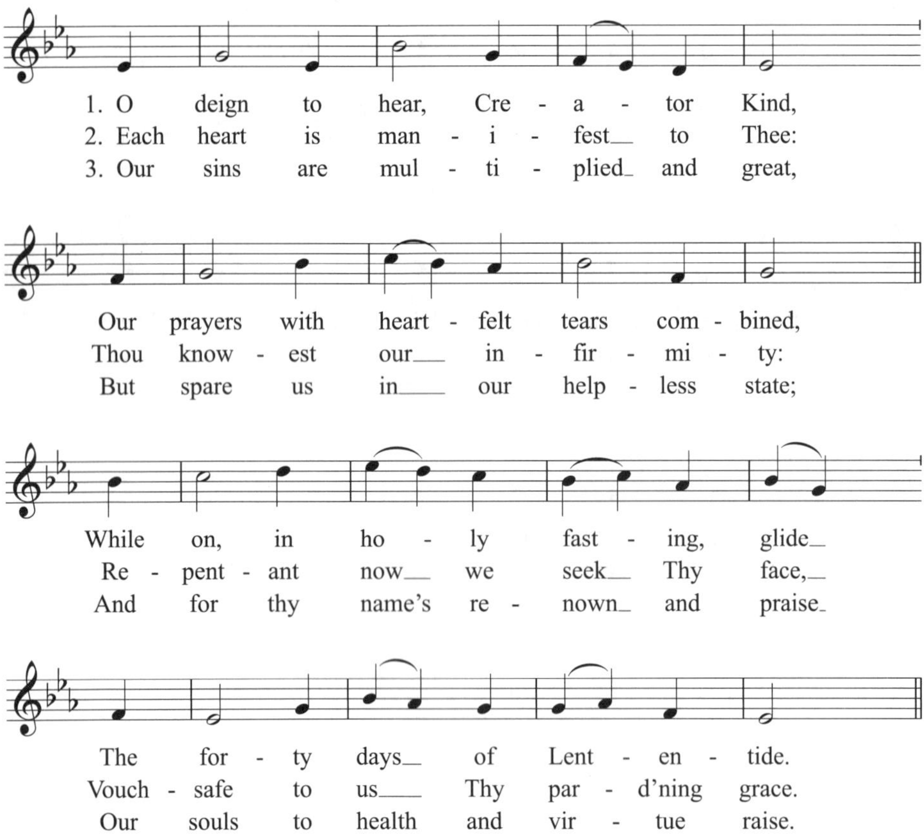

4. Grant that our body's every sense
May conquered be through abstinence,
That so our hearts, which fast from sin,
May find no food for fault therein.

5. This, Holy Trinity, who art
A perfect Unity, impart;
That they who are Thine own may see
How fruitful shall their fasting be.

* This melody at a lower key is on page 248.

88 88 (LM)

Tune:
Ioannes

T. Source: *The Breviary and Missal Hymns* (London: Sands & Co, 1931) p. 57; alterations have been made to the original text by Fr. Fitzpatrick.
M. Source: Cento from *The Parochial Hymn Book, Words and Melodies; containing Vespers, Compline, and all the Liturgical Hymns for the Year both in Latin and English* (London, 1883), edited by Fr. Anatole Police; Imprimatur by Henry Edward Cardinal Manning (d. 1892), who in 1851 converted from Anglicanism and was appointed Archbishop of Westminster in 1865.

Audi Benigne Conditor (6th century) 101

Twelfth Tune – *Trns: Fr. John Fitzpatrick, Oblate of Mary (d. 1929)*

4. Grant that our body's every sense
May conquered be through abstinence,
That so our hearts, which fast from sin,
May find no food for fault therein.

5. This, Holy Trinity, who art
A perfect Unity, impart;
That they who are Thine own may see
How fruitful shall their fasting be.

T. Source: *The Breviary and Missal Hymns* (London: Sands & Co, 1931) p. 57; alterations have been made to the original text by Fr. Fitzpatrick.
Melody: Kevin Allen (b. 1965), choirmaster at the Monastery of the Holy Cross in Chicago.
M. Source: *Saint Edmund Campion Missal and Hymnal* (2013) p. 880.

88 88 (LM)
Tune: Bessemer

102 Audi Benigne Conditor (6th century)

Thirteenth Tune – *Trns: Fr. Fitzpatrick, Oblate of Mary (d. 1929)*

4. Grant that our body's every sense
May conquered be through abstinence,
That so our hearts, which fast from sin,
May find no food for fault therein.

5. This, Holy Trinity, who art
A perfect Unity, impart;
That they who are Thine own may see
How fruitful shall their fasting be.

88 88 (LM)

Tune:
Whitehall

Melody: Henry Lawes (d. 1662).
M. Source: *Saint Edmund Campion Missal and Hymnal* (2013) p. 888.
T. Source: *The Breviary and Missal Hymns* (London: Sands & Co, 1931) p. 57; alterations have been made to the original text by Fr. Fitzpatrick.

Audi Benigne Conditor (6th century)

Trns: Fr. John Fitzpatrick, Oblate of Mary (d. 1929)

Can be sung with any 88 88 meter, such as Eisenach, Rogers Park, Bressani, La Rochelle, Kempen, Bessemer, Tallis Canon, Winchester New, etc.

O DEIGN to hear, Creator Kind,
Our prayers with heartfelt tears combined,
While on, in holy fasting, glide
The forty days of Lenten-tide.

2. Each heart is manifest to Thee:
Thou knowest our infirmity:
Repentant now we seek Thy face,
Vouchsafe to us Thy pard'ning grace.

3. Our sins are multiplied and great,
But spare us in our helpless state,
And for thy name's renown and praise
Our souls to health and virtue raise.

4. Grant that our body's every sense
May conquered be through abstinence,
That so our hearts, which fast from sin,
May find no food for fault therein.

5. This, Holy Trinity, who art
A perfect Unity, impart;
That they who are Thine own may see
How fruitful shall their fasting be.

88 88 (LM)

T. Source: *The Breviary and Missal Hymns* (London: Sands & Co, 1931) p. 57; alterations have been made to the original text by Fr. Fitzpatrick.

Tune: Various

104 Audi Benigne Conditor (6th century)

First Tune – *Trns: Fr. Thomas Joseph Potter (d. 1873)*

4. As saving fasts our flesh subdue,
May thy sweet grace our hearts renew,
That vice may thus unfed remain,
And we from sin and guilt abstain.

5. Grant us, O sacred Trinity,
Grant us, O perfect Unity,
That these our fasts may fruitful prove
Of endless bliss, in realms above.

88 88 (LM)

Tune:
Agincourt

Melody: From a 15th century English manuscript.
M. Source: *Hymns, Psalms, and Spiritual Canticles* (Massachusetts: Theodore Marier, 1983) p. 450.
T. Source: Orby Shipley's *Annus Sanctus: Hymns of the Church for the Ecclesiastical Year; Translated from the Sacred Offices by various Authors, with Modern, Original, and other Hymns, and an Appendix of Earlier Versions* (London: Burns and Oates, 1884) p. 73; with first verse altered.
Father Thomas Joseph Potter, who converted in 1847 and was ordained a Catholic priest in 1857, translated nearly all the Vespers hymns in *The Catholic Psalmist* (Dublin, 1858).

Audi Benigne Conditor (6th century)

Second Tune – *Trns: Fr. Thomas Joseph Potter (d. 1873)*

4. As saving fasts our flesh subdue,
May thy sweet grace our hearts renew,
That vice may thus unfed remain,
And we from sin and guilt abstain.

5. Grant us, O sacred Trinity,
Grant us, O perfect Unity,
That these our fasts may fruitful prove
Of endless bliss, in realms above.

* This melody at a lower key is on page 436.

Melody: John Bacchus Dykes (d. 1876).
M. Source: *Hymns Ancient and Modern* (1972) p. 64.
T. Source: Orby Shipley's *Annus Sanctus: Hymns of the Church for the Ecclesiastical Year; Translated from the Sacred Offices by various Authors, with Modern, Original, and other Hymns, and an Appendix of Earlier Versions* (London: Burns and Oates, 1884) p. 73; with first verse altered. Father Thomas Joseph Potter, who converted in 1847 and was ordained a Catholic priest in 1857, translated nearly all the Vespers hymns in *The Catholic Psalmist* (Dublin, 1858).

88 88 (LM)

Tune: Trinity College

106 Audi Benigne Conditor (6th century)

THIRD TUNE – *Trns: Fr. Thomas Joseph Potter (d. 1873)*

4. As saving fasts our flesh subdue,
May thy sweet grace our hearts renew,
That vice may thus unfed remain,
And we from sin and guilt abstain.

5. Grant us, O sacred Trinity,
Grant us, O perfect Unity,
That these our fasts may fruitful prove
Of endless bliss, in realms above.

88 88 (LM)

Tune:
ROGERS PARK

Melody: Kevin Allen (b. 1965), choirmaster at the Monastery of the Holy Cross in Chicago.
M. Source: *Saint Jean de Brébeuf Hymnal* (2018).
T. Source: Orby Shipley's *Annus Sanctus: Hymns of the Church for the Ecclesiastical Year; Translated from the Sacred Offices by various Authors, with Modern, Original, and other Hymns, and an Appendix of Earlier Versions* (London: Burns and Oates, 1884) p. 73; with first verse altered. Father Thomas Joseph Potter, who converted in 1847 and was ordained a Catholic priest in 1857, translated nearly all the Vespers hymns in *The Catholic Psalmist* (Dublin, 1858).

Audi Benigne Conditor (6th century)

FOURTH TUNE – *Trns: Fr. Thomas Joseph Potter (d. 1873)*

4. As saving fasts our flesh subdue,
May thy sweet grace our hearts renew,
That vice may thus unfed remain,
And we from sin and guilt abstain.

5. Grant us, O sacred Trinity,
Grant us, O perfect Unity,
That these our fasts may fruitful prove
Of endless bliss, in realms above.

Melody: Geoffrey Charles Edward Ryley (d. 1947); this tune can be sung as a Soprano-Tenor canon.
M. Source: *Hymns Ancient and Modern* (1972) p. 324.
T. Source: Orby Shipley's *Annus Sanctus: Hymns of the Church for the Ecclesiastical Year; Translated from the Sacred Offices by various Authors, with Modern, Original, and other Hymns, and an Appendix of Earlier Versions* (London: Burns and Oates, 1884) p. 73; with first verse altered.
Father Thomas Joseph Potter, who converted in 1847 and was ordained a Catholic priest in 1857, translated nearly all the Vespers hymns in *The Catholic Psalmist* (Dublin, 1858).

88 88 (LM)
Tune:
CANON VIII

108 Audi Benigne Conditor (6th century)

Fifth Tune – *Trns: Fr. Thomas Joseph Potter (d. 1873)*

1. Be - nign__ Cre - a - tor of the spheres,
2. Thy pierc - ing eye__ our hearts doth scan,
3. Much have__ we sinned, and to ex - cess,

Hear thou__ the prayers, be - hold__ the tears,
And mea - sure all__ the woes__ of man;
But spare__ us, Lord,__ who thus__ con - fess;

That in__ this ho - ly sea - son we
Whilst now,__ we sor - r'wing turn__ to thee,
And for__ the glo - ry of__ thy name,

With Lent - en fas - tings, pour to thee.
From sin's__ foul bur - den set us free.
Thy sav - ing mer - cy now pro - claim.

4. As saving fasts our flesh subdue,
May thy sweet grace our hearts renew,
That vice may thus unfed remain,
And we from sin and guilt abstain.

5. Grant us, O sacred Trinity,
Grant us, O perfect Unity,
That these our fasts may fruitful prove
Of endless bliss, in realms above.

88 88 (LM)

Tune: St Venantius

Final Verses: Noel Rawsthorne (2011) #323.
Melody: Paris *Antiphonale* (1681).
M. Source: *New Westminster Hymnal* (1939) p. 9; *Catholic Hymn Book* (London Oratory, 1998) p. 81.
T. Source: Orby Shipley's *Annus Sanctus: Hymns of the Church for the Ecclesiastical Year; Translated from the Sacred Offices by various Authors, with Modern, Original, and other Hymns, and an Appendix of Earlier Versions* (London: Burns and Oates, 1884) p. 73; with first verse altered.
Father Thomas Joseph Potter, who converted in 1847 and was ordained a Catholic priest in 1857, translated nearly all the Vespers hymns in *The Catholic Psalmist* (Dublin, 1858).

Audi Benigne Conditor (6th century) 109

Sixth Tune – *Trns: Fr. Thomas Joseph Potter (d. 1873)*

4. As saving fasts our flesh subdue,
May thy sweet grace our hearts renew,
That vice may thus unfed remain,
And we from sin and guilt abstain.

5. Grant us, O sacred Trinity,
Grant us, O perfect Unity,
That these our fasts may fruitful prove
Of endless bliss, in realms above.

Final Verses: Richard Lloyd (1993) #24; Noel Rawsthorne (2011) #50.
Melody: cf. Theme used by J.S. Bach (d. 1750) in "O Jesu Christ, meins Lebens Licht," BWV 118.
M. Source: *Pope Pius XII Hymnal* (Ohio: Gregorian Institute of America, 1959) p. 6.
T. Source: Orby Shipley's *Annus Sanctus: Hymns of the Church for the Ecclesiastical Year; Translated from the Sacred Offices by various Authors, with Modern, Original, and other Hymns, and an Appendix of Earlier Versions* (London: Burns and Oates, 1884) p. 73; with first verse altered. Father Thomas Joseph Potter, who converted in 1847 and was ordained a Catholic priest in 1857, translated nearly all the Vespers hymns in *The Catholic Psalmist* (Dublin, 1858).

88 88 (LM)

Tune: Breslau

Audi Benigne Conditor (6th century)

Seventh Tune – *Trns: Fr. Thomas Joseph Potter (d. 1873)*

1. Be - nign Cre - a - tor of the spheres,
2. Thy pierc - ing eye our hearts doth scan,
3. Much have we sinned, and to ex - cess,

Hear thou the prayers, be - hold the tears,
And mea - sure all the woes of man;
But spare us, Lord, who thus con - fess;

That in this ho - ly sea - son we____
Whilst now, we sor - r'wing turn to thee,____
And for the glo - ry of thy name,____

With Lent - en fas - tings, pour to thee.
From sin's foul bur - den set us free.
Thy sav - ing mer - cy now pro - claim.

4. As saving fasts our flesh subdue,
May thy sweet grace our hearts renew,
That vice may thus unfed remain,
And we from sin and guilt abstain.

5. Grant us, O sacred Trinity,
Grant us, O perfect Unity,
That these our fasts may fruitful prove
Of endless bliss, in realms above.

88 88 (LM)

Tune:
Jesu Dulcis Memoria

Plainsong Melody: *Mass and Vespers with Gregorian Chant* (Paris: Solesmes, 1957) p. 271.
M. Source: *Hymns, Psalms, and Spiritual Canticles* (Massachusetts: Theodore Marier, 1983) p. 367.
T. Source: Orby Shipley's *Annus Sanctus: Hymns of the Church for the Ecclesiastical Year; Translated from the Sacred Offices by various Authors, with Modern, Original, and other Hymns, and an Appendix of Earlier Versions* (London: Burns and Oates, 1884) p. 73; with first verse altered. Father Thomas Joseph Potter, who converted in 1847 and was ordained a Catholic priest in 1857, translated nearly all the Vespers hymns in *The Catholic Psalmist* (Dublin, 1858).

Audi Benigne Conditor (6th century)

Trns: Fr. Thomas Joseph Potter (d. 1873)

Can be sung with any 88 88 meter, such as EISENACH, ROGERS PARK, BRESSANI, LA ROCHELLE, KEMPEN, BESSEMER, TALLIS CANON, WINCHESTER NEW, etc.

BENIGN Creator of the spheres,
Hear thou the prayers, behold the tears,
That in this holy season we
With Lenten fastings, pour to thee.

2. Thy piercing eye our hearts doth scan,
And measure all the woes of man;
Whilst now, we sorr'wing turn to thee,
From sin's foul burden set us free.

3. Much have we sinned, and to excess,
But spare us, Lord, who thus confess;
And for the glory of thy name,
Thy saving mercy now proclaim.

4. As saving fasts our flesh subdue,
May thy sweet grace our hearts renew,
That vice may thus unfed remain,
And we from sin and guilt abstain.

5. Grant us, O sacred Trinity,
Grant us, O perfect Unity,
That these our fasts may fruitful prove
Of endless bliss, in realms above.

T. Source: Orby Shipley's *Annus Sanctus: Hymns of the Church for the Ecclesiastical Year; Translated from the Sacred Offices by various Authors, with Modern, Original, and other Hymns, and an Appendix of Earlier Versions* (London: Burns and Oates, 1884) p. 73; with first verse altered. Father Thomas Joseph Potter, who converted in 1847 and was ordained a Catholic priest in 1857, translated nearly all the Vespers hymns in *The Catholic Psalmist* (Dublin, 1858).

88 88 (LM)

Tune: VARIOUS

112 Audi Benigne Conditor (6th century)

1599AD – Historic Roman Catholic Translation

Can be sung with any 88 88 meter, such as Hilderstone, Duguet, Breslau, Melcombe, Wareham, Old Hundredth, Mein Seel, Trinity College, etc.

O THOU Creator most benign,
Unto the prayèrs bend thine ears,
Which in this fast of forty days,
We unto thee pour forth with tears.

2. O kindly searcher of the hearts,
Thou know'st the weakness of our strength;
Yield unto those that turn to thee,
Thy grace of pardon at the length.

3. We sinnèd have exceedingly,
Yet pardon those their faults confess;
And for the glory of thy name,
Unto the sick vouchsafe redress.

4. As outwardly the body pines,
By inward abstinence provide:
The sober mind be so restrained,
That there no blots of sin abide.

5. Grant that, O blessed Trinity,
Vouchsafe one only Unity:
The duties of this fasting may,
Unto thy servants fruitful be.

Audi benígne Cónditor,
Nostras preces cum flétibus,
In hoc sacro jejúnio
Fusas quadragenário.

Scrutátor alme córdium,
Infírma tu scis vírium:
Ad te revérsis éxhibe
Remissiónis grátiam.

Multum quidem peccávimus,
Sed parce confiténtibus:
Ad laudem tui nóminis,
Confer medélam lánguidis.

Sic corpus extra cónteri
Dona per abstinéntiam,
Jejúnet ut mens sóbria
A labe prorsus críminum.

Praesta, beáta Trínitas,
Concéde, simplex Únitas,
Ut fructuósa sint tuis
Jejuniórum múnera.

88 88 (LM)

Tune:
Various

T. Source: *Primer, or, Office of the Blessed Virgin Marie in Latin and English, according to the reformed Latin, and with Lyke Graces Privileged* (Antwerp, 1599) p. 8. The Catholic Encyclopedia of 1912 attributes the hymn translations to the book's editor, Richard Verstegan (d. 1636), a Catholic publisher. In the 1599 Preface, Verstegan says: "Notwithstanding the difficulty, these hymns have been so turned into English meter that they may be sung unto the same tunes in English that they bear in Latin." However, his accentual treatment is sometimes peculiar.

Audi Benigne Conditor (Urbanite)

1687 AD – Historic Roman Catholic Translation

Can be sung with any 88 88 meter, such as EISENACH, ROGERS PARK, BRESSANI, LA ROCHELLE, KEMPEN, BESSEMER, TALLIS CANON, WINCHESTER NEW, etc.

Audi benígne Cónditor,
Nostras preces cum flétibus,
In hoc sacro jejúnio
Fusas quadragenário.

Scrutátor alme córdium,
Infírma tu scis vírium:
Ad te revérsis éxhibe
Remissiónis grátiam.

Multum quidem peccávimus,
Sed parce confiténtibus:
Ad nóminis laudem tui
Confer medélam lánguidis.

Concéde nostrum cónteri
Corpus per abstinéntiam,
Culp*ae* ut relínquant pábulum
Jejúna corda críminum.

Praesta, beáta Trínitas,
Concéde simplex Únitas,
Ut fructuósa sint tuis
Jejuniórum múnera.

BENIGN Creator, lend thine ears
To Pray'rs accompanied with tears,
To celebrate this sacred Fast,
For forty days ordain'd to last.

2. Clear searcher of all hearts, 'tis known
To thee how weak our strength is grown;
The favour of remission deign,
To such as turn to thee again.

3. We have offended in excess,
Yet pardon who their faults confess;
Let those who languish, find in Thee
(To thy great praise) a Remedy.

4. Grant that our flesh by abstinence
May so be tamed, that from offence
Our souls may fast; nor e'er let in
The flood that's apt to nourish sin.

5. O blessed Trinity, afford,
O single Unity, accord,
The duties of this fast to be
Fruitful to those rely on thee.

T. Source: *The Office of the B. V. Mary in English; to which is added the Vespers in Latin and English, As it is Sung in the Catholic Church upon all Sundays and principal Holy-days throughout the whole Year* (Henry Hills, 1687) p. 135. The version above is a mixture, containing verses from a 1686 Primer, as well as *A Manuel of Prayers and Litanies distributed according to the Days of the Week with other Excellent Devotions* (1688) p. 467. The frequent changes to hymn texts in Catholic primers—even those published within a few months of one another—is astonishing, and demonstrates how seriously the publishers took English renderings.

88 88 (LM)

Tune: VARIOUS

Ave Maris Stella (7th century)

Ancient hymn to the Blessed Virgin Mary

To sing in Latin,
use 66 66 (trochaic)
such as St Martin, Ravenshaw,
Waltham Forest, Ave Radix, etc.

AVE maris stella, *n1*
Dei mater alma,
Atque semper virgo,
Felix caeli porta.

2. Sumens illud Ave,
Gabriélis ore,
Funda nos in pace,
Mutans Hevae nomen. *n2*

3. Solve vincla reis,
Profer lumen caecis,
Mala nostra pelle,
Bona cuncta posce.

4. Monstra t*e* esse matrem,
Sumat per te preces, *n3*
Qui pro nobis natus,
Tulit esse tuus.

5. Virgo singuláris,
Inter omnes mitis,
Nos culpis solútos,
Mites fac et castos.

6. Vitam praesta puram,
Iter para tutum,
Ut vidéntes Jesum,
Semper collaetémur. *n4*

7. Sit laus Deo Patri,
Summo Christo decus,
Spirítui Sancto,
Tribus honor unus.

66 66 Trochaic

Tune:
Various

[1] The meaning of the name "Mary" is uncertain. The Latin word *Mária* (with accent on first syllable) means "sea waters," and in Hebrew, the name Mary (*Miriam*) means "Star of the Sea." St. Bernard writes as follows: "Let us speak briefly of this name, which is said to mean star of the sea, and is so well and suitably applied to the Virgin Mother. Indeed most aptly is she compared to a star; for as a star sheds its beams without any decay on its part, so the Virgin brought forth her Son without any damage to her virginity. Neither does the beam lessen the brightness of the star, nor the Son the inviolateness of the Virgin." (*Roman Breviary*, 12 September, Lesson IV).

Assistance in comprehension

HAIL, O star of the sea, *n1*
bounteous Mother of God
and ever a Virgin,
happy gate of heaven.

2. Taking that Hail (*Ave*)
from the mouth of Gabriel,
establish us in peace,
changing the name of Eve (*Eva*). *n2*

3. Loose the bonds of the guilty,
bring light to the blind,
banish our ills,
beg all goods for us.

4. Show that thou art our mother:
by thee may he receive our prayers, *n3*
who, born for us,
accepted to be thine.

5. O unique Virgin,
meek among all others,
loosed from our guilt, make us
meek and chaste.

6. Provide a clean life to us,
ready a safe path for us,
that, seeing Jesus, we may be
glad altogether for ever. *n4*

7. Praise be to God the Father,
glory to Christ most high,
and to the Holy Spirit:
to the three one honor.

[2] AVE is EVA in reverse. The Angel Gabriel greeted Mary: "Ave gratia plena: Dominus tecum: benedicta tu in mulieribus" (Lk 1.28).

[3] That is, may he who was born for us and accepted to be thy Son receive our prayers.

[4] That is, help us to lead pure lives, and to take the "narrow way" (cf. Mt 7.14) to heaven, so that we may see Christ in the beatific vision and enjoy supernal bliss.

116 Ave Maris Stella (7th century)

Trns: Bishop Edward G. Bagshawe (d. 1915)

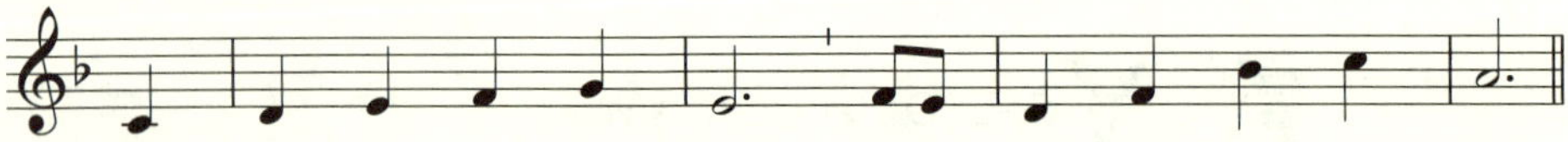

1. Hail, Star of o - cean, hail; God's Moth - er full of love,
2. Since from Saint Ga - briel's lips, To_ thee that "A - ve" came,
3. Un - loose the sin - ner's chains, Light to the blind re - store,

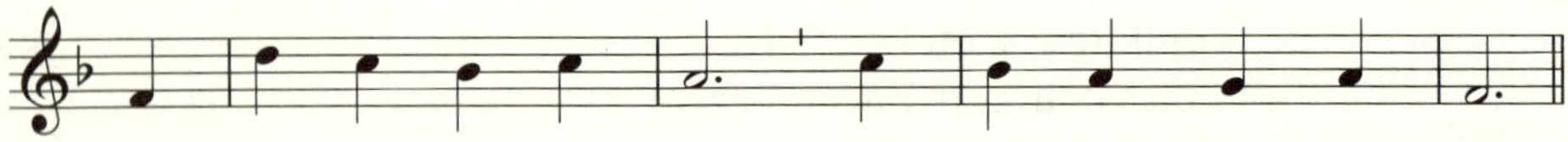

And ev - er Vir - gin pure, Blest Gate of Heav'n a - bove.
Es - tab - lish us in peace, Trans - pos - ing E - va's name.
Drive far a - way our ills, And all good things im - plore.

4. A Mother show thyself,
Through thee, our prayers may He
Accept, who born for us,
Deigned to be born of thee.

5. O all-excelling Maid,
With special meekness graced,
O free us from our sins,
And keep us always chaste.

6. Pure lives for us obtain,
And a safe way prepare,
That we may Jesus see,
And His joy ever share.

7. To God the Father praise,
And glory to the Son,
And to the Holy Ghost,
To Three be honor One.

66 66 Iambic

Tune:
Seán

T. Source: *Breviary Hymns and Missal Sequences* (London: Burns & Oates, 1900) p. 105; Father Bagshawe was a priest of the Oratory of St. Philip Neri until 1874, when he was consecrated bishop of the Catholic diocese of Nottingham.
Melody: Richard J. Clark (b. 1969), choirmaster at the Cathedral of the Holy Cross in Boston.
M. Source: *Saint Jean de Brébeuf Hymnal* (2018).

Ave Maris Stella (7th century)

Trns: Msgr. Ronald A. Knox (d. 1957)

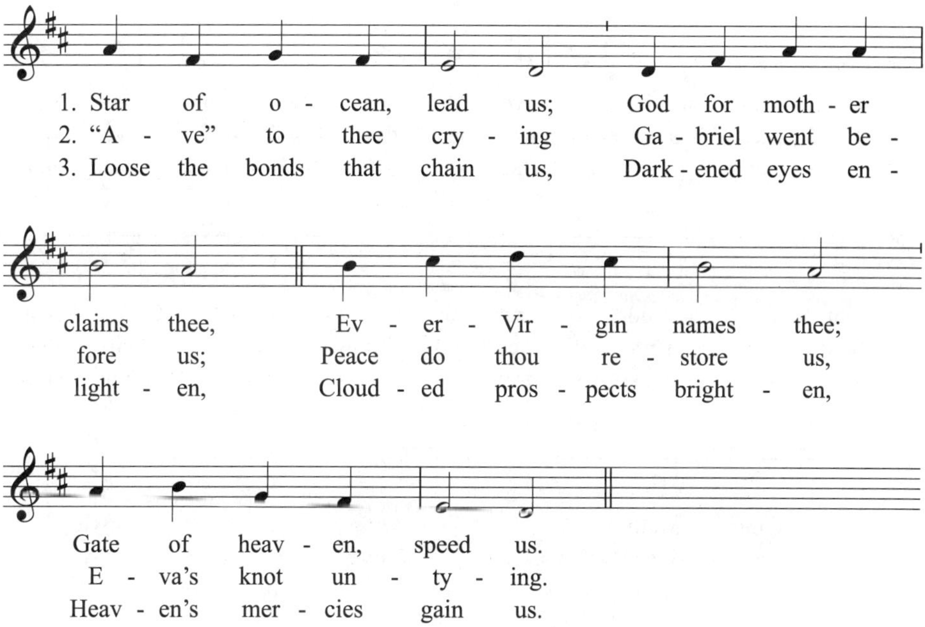

4. For thy sons thou carest;
Offer Christ our praying—
Still thy word obeying—
Whom on earth thou barest.

5. Purer, kinder maiden
God did never fashion;
Pureness and compassion
Grant to hearts sin-laden.

6. From that sin release us,
Shield us, heav'nward faring—
Heav'n, that is but sharing
In thy joy with Jesus.

7. Honor, praise and merit
To our God address we;
Three in One confess we,
Father, Son, and Spirit.

T. Source: *New Westminster Hymnal* (1939) p. 138.
Melody: Caspar Ett's *Cantica Sacra* (1840).
M. Source: *Arundel Catholic Hymnal* (1905) p. 326; *Catholic Hymn Book* (1998) p. 272; *Catholic Vesper Hymn Book set to Music either for Unison or Four Voices with Accompaniment* (Charles Lewis, 1877) p. 3.

66 66 Trochaic
Tune:
St Martin

Ave Maris Stella (7th century)

First Tune – *Trns: Fr. John Fitzpatrick, Oblate of Mary (d. 1929)*

76 76 D

Tune:
Ave Virgo Virginum

Final Verses: Richard Lloyd (1993) #15; Noel Rawsthorne (2011) #31.
T. Source: *The Breviary and Missal Hymns* (London: Sands & Co, 1931) p. 196.
Melody: Medieval melody arranged by Johann Roh (d. 1547).
M. Source: Printed in *Catholicum Hymnologium Germanicum* (Leisentritt, 1584).

Ave Maris Stella (7th century) 119

Second Tune – *Trns: Fr. John Fitzpatrick, Oblate of Mary (d. 1929)*

76 76 D

T. Source: *The Breviary and Missal Hymns* (London: Sands & Co, 1931) p. 196.
M. Source: 13th century Spring song, published in *Piae Cantiones* (Theodoric Petri, 1582); version as found in *The Hymnal* (1940) with a text for Martyrs.

Tune: Tempus Adest Floridum

120 Ave Maris Stella (7th century)

Third Tune – *Trns: Fr. John Fitzpatrick, Oblate of Mary (d. 1929)*

76 76 D

Tune:
Christus Christus Christus Ist

Melody: Peter Franck (d. 1675), first published in 1657.
M. Source: *Choral Harmony* (London: G. H. Davidson, 1854) #203.
T. Source: *The Breviary and Missal Hymns* (London: Sands & Co, 1931) p. 196.

Fourth Tune – *Trns: Fr. John Fitzpatrick, Oblate of Mary (d. 1929)*

76 76 D

Melody: Melchior Vulpius (d. 1615).
M. Source: *Songs of Syon* (Woodward, 1910) p. 567; cf. *Ein schön geistlich Gesangbuch* (1609).
T. Source: *The Breviary and Missal Hymns* (London: Sands & Co, 1931) p. 196.

Tune:
Jesu Leiden Pein Und Tod

122 Ave Maris Stella (7th century)

Fifth Tune – *Trns: Fr. John Fitzpatrick, Oblate of Mary (d. 1929)*

76 76 D

Tune:
Salzburg E6

Final Verses: Richard Lloyd (1993) #207; Noel Rawsthorne (2011) #325.
T. Source: *The Breviary and Missal Hymns* (London: Sands & Co, 1931) p. 196.
Melody: Jacob Hintze (d. 1702), court musician to the Elector of Brandenburg at Berlin.
M. Source: *Catholic Hymn Book* (London Oratory, 1998) p. 116.

Ave Maris Stella (7th century) 123

Sixth Tune – *Trns: Fr. John Fitzpatrick, Oblate of Mary (d. 1929)*

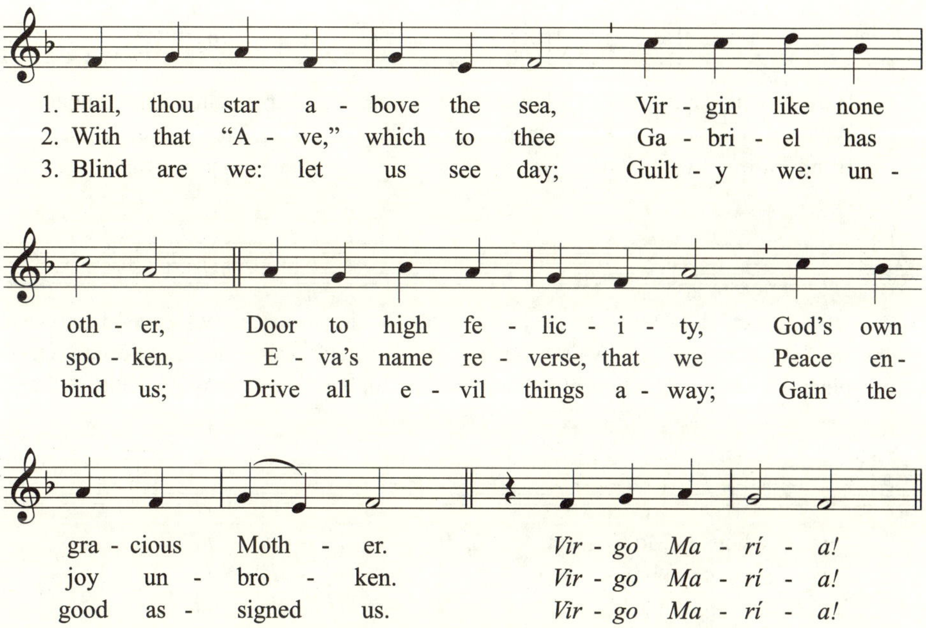

4. Prove thyself a mother thus;
Pray, at our petition,
Till He hears who, born for us,
Showed thee all submission. *Virgo María!*

5. First of virgins, who of all
Art most meek and lowly,
Make us, free of evil's pall,
Chaste and gentle wholly. *Virgo María!*

6. Let our lives grow pure apace,
Guide and guard our going,
Till, beholding Jesus' face,
Ours be bliss o'er flowing. *Virgo María!*

7. Glory to the Father be,
And the Christ supernal,
And the Spirit: to the Three
Equal praise eternal. *Virgo María!*

Melody: *attr.* Pierre de Corbeil (d. 1222), Archbishop of Sens.
M. Source: *Mediator Dei Hymnal* (1955) #77; *American Catholic Hymnal according to the Motu Proprio of His Holiness Pope Pius X compiled by the Marist Brothers* (New York: Kenedy & Sons, 1913) p. 185.
T. Source: *The Breviary and Missal Hymns* (London: Sands & Co, 1931) p. 196.

76 76
Tune:
Orientis Partibus E6

124 Ave Maris Stella (7th century)

Seventh Tune – *Trns: Fr. John Fitzpatrick, Oblate of Mary (d. 1929)*

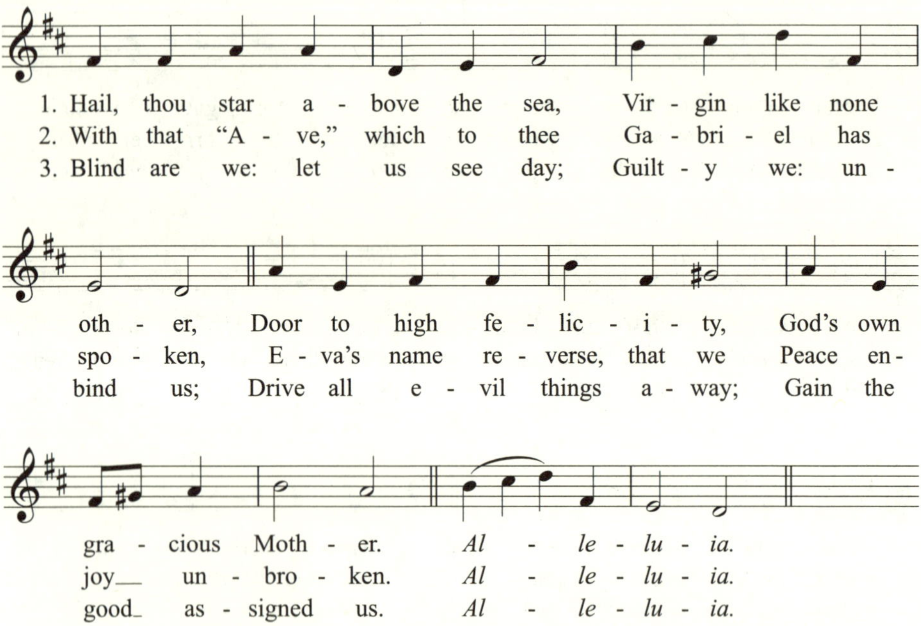

4. Prove thyself a mother thus;
Pray, at our petition,
Till He hears who, born for us,
Showed thee all submission. *Alleluia.*

5. First of virgins, who of all
Art most meek and lowly,
Make us, free of evil's pall,
Chaste and gentle wholly. *Alleluia.*

6. Let our lives grow pure apace,
Guide and guard our going,
Till, beholding Jesus' face,
Ours be bliss o'er flowing. *Alleluia.*

7. Glory to the Father be,
And the Christ supernal,
And the Spirit: to the Three
Equal praise eternal. *Alleluia.*

76 76 A

Tune:
Würtemburg E6

Melody: From *Hundert Arien* (Dresden, 1697), adapted by
William H. Monk (d. 1889), organist at King's College London.
M. Source: *Songs of Syon* (Woodward, 1910) p. 455; *New Westminster Hymnal* (1939) p. 80.
T. Source: *The Breviary and Missal Hymns* (London: Sands & Co, 1931) p. 196.

Ave Maris Stella (7th century) 125

Eighth Tune – *Trns: Fr. John Fitzpatrick, Oblate of Mary (d. 1929)*

4. Prove thyself a mother thus;
Pray, at our petition,
Till He hears who, born for us,
Showed thee all submission.

5. First of virgins, who of all
Art most meek and lowly,
Make us, free of evil's pall,
Chaste and gentle wholly.

6. Let our lives grow pure apace,
Guide and guard our going,
Till, beholding Jesus' face,
Ours be bliss o'er flowing.

7. Glory to the Father be,
And the Christ supernal,
And the Spirit: to the Three
Equal praise eternal.

Final Verses: Richard Lloyd (1993) #142; Noel Rawsthorne (2011) #216.
T. Source: *The Breviary and Missal Hymns* (London: Sands & Co, 1931) p. 196.
Melody: Johann A. Freylinghausen (d. 1739); adapted by John B. Wilkes (d. 1869), organist at the Monkland church, near Leominster.
M. Source: *Catholic Hymn Book* (London Oratory, 1998) p. 412.

76 76
Tune:
Monkland E6

Ave Maris Stella (7th century)

Ninth Tune – *Trns: Fr. John Fitzpatrick, Oblate of Mary (d. 1929)*

4. Prove thyself a mother thus;
Pray, at our petition,
Till He hears who, born for us,
Showed thee all submission.

5. First of virgins, who of all
Art most meek and lowly,
Make us, free of evil's pall,
Chaste and gentle wholly.

6. Let our lives grow pure apace,
Guide and guard our going,
Till, beholding Jesus' face,
Ours be bliss o'er flowing.

7. Glory to the Father be,
And the Christ supernal,
And the Spirit: to the Three
Equal praise eternal.

76 76

Tune:
Culbach E6

Final Verses: Richard Lloyd (1993) #49; Noel Rawsthorne (2011) #82.
T. Source: *The Breviary and Missal Hymns* (London: Sands & Co, 1931) p. 196.
Melody: From a Chorale in Johann Scheffler's *Heilige Seelenlust* (1657).
M. Source: *New Saint Basil Hymnal* (1958) p. 218; *Mediator Dei Hymnal* (1955) p. 83.

Ave Maris Stella (7th century) 127

Tenth Tune – *Trns: Fr. John Fitzpatrick, Oblate of Mary (d. 1929)*

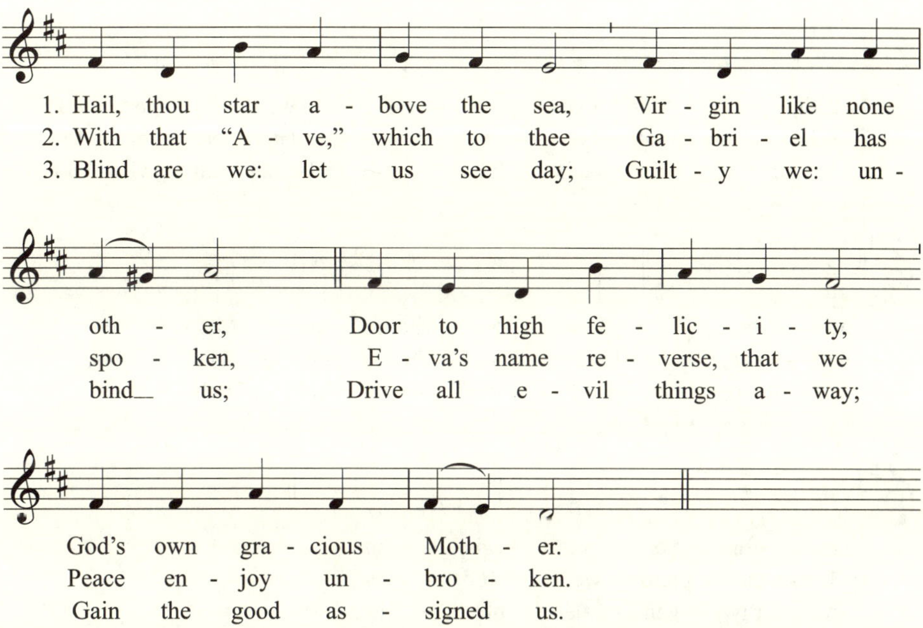

4. Prove thyself a mother thus;
Pray, at our petition,
Till He hears who, born for us,
Showed thee all submission.

5. First of virgins, who of all
Art most meek and lowly,
Make us, free of evil's pall,
Chaste and gentle wholly.

6. Let our lives grow pure apace,
Guide and guard our going,
Till, beholding Jesus' face,
Ours be bliss o'er flowing.

7. Glory to the Father be,
And the Christ supernal,
And the Spirit: to the Three
Equal praise eternal.

Final Verses: Richard Lloyd (1993) #233; Noel Rawsthorne (2011) #373.
T. Source: *The Breviary and Missal Hymns* (London: Sands & Co, 1931) p. 196.
Melody: Henry J. Gauntlett (d. 1876), organist at St. Olave's Church, London.
M. Source: *New English Hymnal* (1986) p. 916.

76 76
Tune:
University College E6

128 Ave Maris Stella (7th century)

First Tune – *Trns: John Athelstan Riley (d. 1945)*

4. Jesus' tender Mother,
Make thy supplication
Unto him who chose thee
At his Incarnation;

5. That, O matchless Virgin,
Passing meek and lowly,
Thy dear Son may make us
Blameless, chaste and holy.

6. So, as now we journey,
Aid our weak endeavor,
Till we gaze on Jesus,
And rejoice for ever.

7. Father, Son and Spirit,
Three in One confessing,
Give we equal glory,
Equal praise and blessing.

66 66 Trochaic

Tune:
St Martin

T. Source: *Hymnal for the Hours* (San Francisco: Benedict XVI Institute, 2014) p. 343.
Melody: Caspar Ett's *Cantica Sacra* (1840).
M. Source: *Arundel Catholic Hymnal* (1905) p. 326; *Catholic Hymn Book* (1998) p. 272; *Catholic Vesper Hymn Book set to Music either for Unison or Four Voices with Accompaniment* (Charles Lewis, 1877) p. 3.

Ave Maris Stella (7th century)

SECOND TUNE – *Trns: John Athelstan Riley (d. 1945)*

4. Jesus' tender Mother,
Make thy supplication
Unto him who chose thee
At his Incarnation;

5. That, O matchless Virgin,
Passing meek and lowly,
Thy dear Son may make us
Blameless, chaste and holy.

6. So, as now we journey,
Aid our weak endeavor,
Till we gaze on Jesus,
And rejoice for ever.

7. Father, Son and Spirit,
Three in One confessing,
Give we equal glory,
Equal praise and blessing.

Final Verses: Richard Lloyd (1993) #174; Noel Rawsthorne (2011) #264.
T. Source: *Hymnal for the Hours* (San Francisco: Benedict XVI Institute, 2014) p. 343.
Melody: Medieval German tune adapted by William H. Monk (d. 1889).
M. Source: *Arundel Catholic Hymnal* (1905) p. 335.

66 66 Trochaic
Tune: RAVENSHAW

130 Ave Maris Stella (7th century)

Third Tune – *Trns: John Athelstan Riley (d. 1945)*

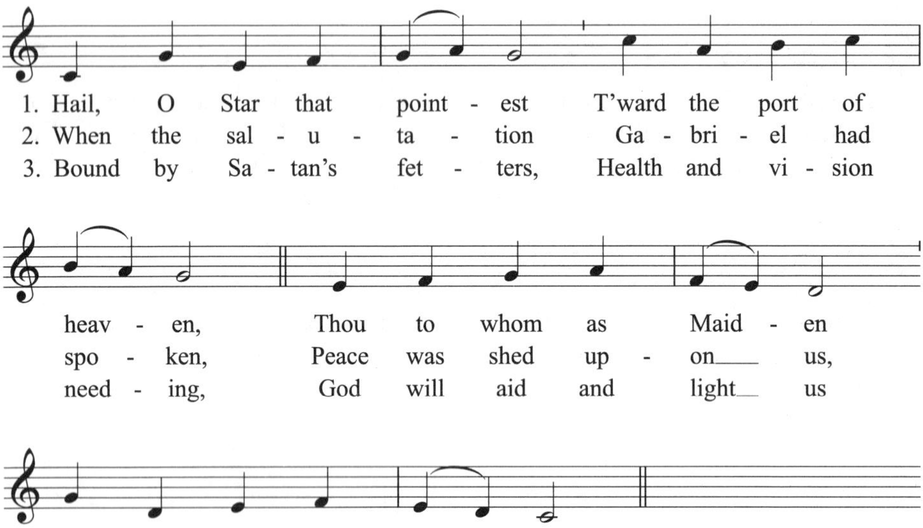

4. Jesus' tender Mother,
Make thy supplication
Unto him who chose thee
At his Incarnation;

5. That, O matchless Virgin,
Passing meek and lowly,
Thy dear Son may make us
Blameless, chaste and holy.

6. So, as now we journey,
Aid our weak endeavor,
Till we gaze on Jesus,
And rejoice for ever.

7. Father, Son and Spirit,
Three in One confessing,
Give we equal glory,
Equal praise and blessing.

66 66 Trochaic

Tune:
Ave Radix

T. Source: *Hymnal for the Hours* (San Francisco: Benedict XVI Institute, 2014) p. 343.
Melody: *Sens Processional* (1728).
M. Source: *Hymns Ancient and Modern* (1972) p. 285.

Ave Maris Stella (7th century)

FOURTH TUNE – *Trns: John Athelstan Riley (d. 1945)*

1. Hail, O Star that point - est T'ward the port of
2. When the sal - u - ta - tion Ga - bri - el— had
3. Bound by Sa - tan's fet - ters, Health and vi - sion

heav - en, Thou to whom as Maid - en
spo - ken, Peace was shed up - on us,
need - ing, God will aid and light us

God for Son was giv - en.
E - va's bonds were bro - ken.
At thy gen - tle plead - ing.

4. Jesus' tender Mother,
   Make thy supplication
   Unto him who chose thee
   At his Incarnation;

5. That, O matchless Virgin,
   Passing meek and lowly,
   Thy dear Son may make us
   Blameless, chaste and holy.

6. So, as now we journey,
   Aid our weak endeavor,
   Till we gaze on Jesus,
   And rejoice for ever.

7. Father, Son and Spirit,
   Three in One confessing,
   Give we equal glory,
   Equal praise and blessing.

T. Source: *Hymnal for the Hours* (San Francisco: Benedict XVI Institute, 2014) p. 343.
Melody: From an 18th century English Antiphonary.
M. Source: *Arundel Catholic Hymnal* (1905) p. 332; *New English Hymnal* (1986) p. 410.

66 66 Trochaic
Tune:
WALTHAM FOREST

132 Ave Maris Stella (7th century)

First Tune – *Trns: Catholic Hymnal for the United States (1807)*

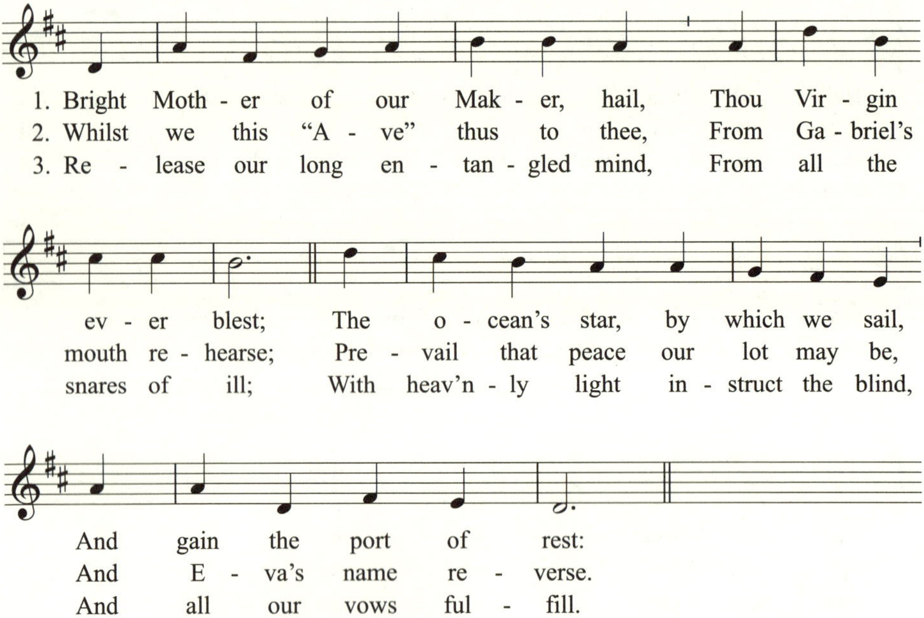

4. Exert for us a mother's care,
And us thy children own;
Prevail with Him to hear our pray'r,
Who chose to be thy son.

5. O spotless maid, whose virtues shine,
With brightest purity;
Each action of our lives refine,
And make us pure like thee.

6. Preserve our lives unstain'd with ill;
And guard us in our way;
That Christ one day our souls may fill
With joys that ne'er decay.

7. To God the Father, endless praise;
To God the Son, the same;
And, Holy Ghost, whose equal rays
One equal glory claim.

86 86 (CM)

Tune:
Song 67

Final Verses: Richard Lloyd (1993) #215.
T. Source: *Hymns for the Use of the Catholic Church in America* (Baltimore: John W. Butler, 1807) p. 80.
Melody: Orlando Gibbons (d. 1625), organist at Westminster Abbey.
M. Source: *Catholic Hymn Book* (London Oratory, 1998) p. 287.

Second Tune – *Trns: Catholic Hymnal for the United States (1807)*

1. Bright Moth - er of our Mak - er, hail, Thou Vir - gin
2. Whilst we this "A - ve" thus_ to thee, From Ga - briel's
3. Re - lease our long en - tan - gled mind, From all__ the

ev - er blest; The o - cean's star,_ by which we sail,
mouth_ re - hearse; Pre - vail_ that peace our lot__ may be,
snares_ of ill; With heav'n - ly light_ in - struct the blind,

And gain_ the port___ of rest:
And E - va's name___ re - verse.
And all___ our vows___ ful - fill.

4. Exert for us a mother's care,
And us thy children own;
Prevail with Him to hear our pray'r,
Who chose to be thy son.

5. O spotless maid, whose virtues shine,
With brightest purity;
Each action of our lives refine,
And make us pure like thee.

6. Preserve our lives unstain'd with ill;
And guard us in our way;
That Christ one day our souls may fill
With joys that ne'er decay.

7. To God the Father, endless praise;
To God the Son, the same;
And, Holy Ghost, whose equal rays
One equal glory claim.

Final Verses: Richard Lloyd (1993) #180; Noel Rawsthorne (2011) #272.
T. Source: *Hymns for the Use of the Catholic Church in America* (Baltimore: John W. Butler, 1807) p. 80.
Melody: Thomas Haweis (d. 1820); adapted by Samuel Webbe the younger (d. 1843).
M. Source: *Catholic Hymn Book* (London Oratory, 1998) p. 402.

86 86 (CM)

Tune: Richmond

 # Ave Maris Stella (7th century)

Third Tune – *Trns: Catholic Hymnal for the United States (1807)*

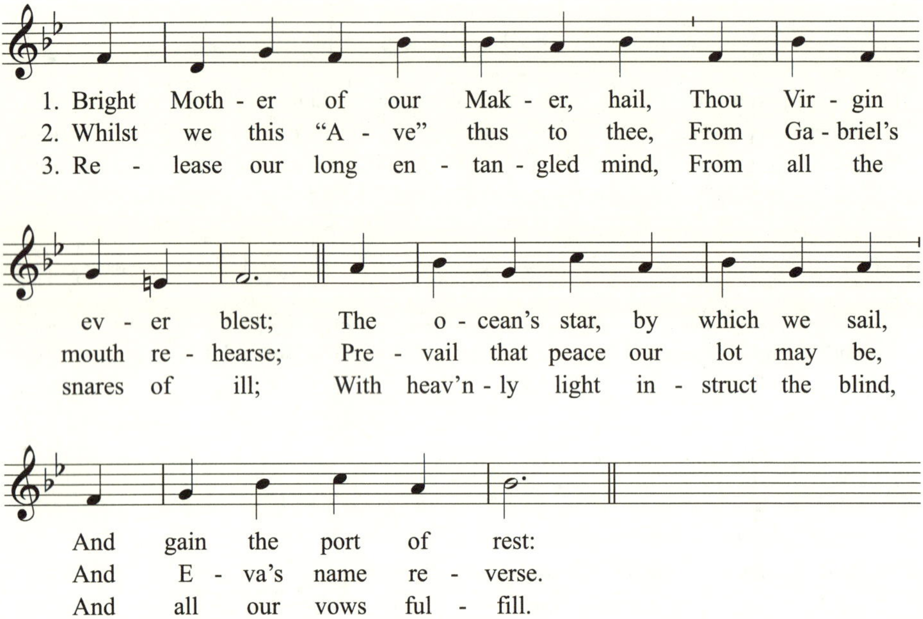

4. Exert for us a mother's care,
   And us thy children own;
   Prevail with Him to hear our pray'r,
   Who chose to be thy son.

5. O spotless maid, whose virtues shine,
   With brightest purity;
   Each action of our lives refine,
   And make us pure like thee.

6. Preserve our lives unstain'd with ill;
   And guard us in our way;
   That Christ one day our souls may fill
   With joys that ne'er decay.

7. To God the Father, endless praise;
   To God the Son, the same;
   And, Holy Ghost, whose equal rays
   One equal glory claim.

86 86 (CM)

Tune:
St Anne

Final Verses: Richard Lloyd (1993) #186; Noel Rawsthorne (2011) #282.
T. Source: *Hymns for the Use of the Catholic Church in America* (Baltimore: John W. Butler, 1807) p. 80.
Melody: William Croft (d. 1727), organist at Westminster Abbey.
M. Source: *Hymns, Psalms, and Spiritual Canticles* (Massachusetts: Theodore Marier, 1983) p. 507.

Trns: Catholic Hymnal for the United States (1807)

Can be sung with any 86 86 meter, such as St Magnus, Bedford, St Columba, Westminster, St Anne, St Hugh, Hereford, St Flavian, etc.

BRIGHT Mother of our Maker, hail,
Thou Virgin ever blest;
The ocean's star, by which we sail,
And gain the port of rest:

2. Whilst we this "Ave" thus to thee,
From Gabriel's mouth rehearse;
Prevail that peace our lot may be,
And Eva's name reverse.

3. Release our long entangled mind,
From all the snares of ill;
With heav'nly light instruct the blind,
And all our vows fulfill.

4. Exert for us a mother's care,
And us thy children own;
Prevail with Him to hear our pray'r,
Who chose to be thy son.

5. O spotless maid, whose virtues shine,
With brightest purity;
Each action of our lives refine,
And make us pure like thee.

6. Preserve our lives unstain'd with ill;
And guard us in our way;
That Christ one day our souls may fill
With joys that ne'er decay.

7. To God the Father, endless praise;
To God the Son, the same;
And, Holy Ghost, whose equal rays
One equal glory claim.

86 86 (CM)

Tune: Various

T. Source: *Hymns for the Use of the Catholic Church in America* (Baltimore: John W. Butler, 1807) p. 80.

Ave Maris Stella (7th century)

1599AD – Historic Roman Catholic Translation

English translation can be sung with any 66 66 meter (iambic), such as CAMCOLT, QUAM DILECTA, ST CECILIA, IBSTONE, CLERMONT, SEÁN, etc.

ALL hail, star of the sea, God's Mother clear and bright, The happy gate of bliss, And still in virgin's plight. *n1*	Ave maris stella, Dei mater alma, Atque semper virgo, Felix caeli porta.
2. Receiving that "all hail" Which Gabriel's mouth did give, Establish us in peace, Changing the name of Eve.	Sumens illud Ave, Gabriélis ore, Funda nos in pace, Mutans Hevae nomen.
3. The guilty's bonds unbind, Blind men their sight assure, Ill things from us expel, All good for us procure.	Solve vincla reis, Profer lumen caecis, Mala nostra pelle, Bona cuncta posce.
4. A mother show thyself: He take our plaints by thee *n2* That, being for us born, Vouchsafed thy Son to be.	Monstra t*e* esse matrem, Sumat per te preces, Qui pro nobis natus, Tulit esse tuus.
5. O rarest virgin pure, Of all that meekest wast, Dischargèd of our sin, Make thou us meek, and chaste.	Virgo singuláris, Inter omnes mitis, Nos culpis solútos, Mites fac et castos.
6. Grant that our life be pure, Make safe for us the way, That, while we Jesus see, Our joy may last for aye.	Vitam praesta puram, Iter para tutum, Ut vidéntes Jesum, Semper collaetémur.
7. To God the Father praise, To Christ high worship be, And to the Holy Ghost, One honor unto three.	Sit laus Deo Patri, Summo Christo decus, Spirítui Sancto, Tribus honor unus.

[1] "Plight" here means *state*; that is, Mary was Christ's mother, but lost not the status of virgin.

[2] Here "plaints" probably means *petitions*.

66 66 Iambic

Tune: VARIOUS

T. Source: *Primer, or, Office of the Blessed Virgin Marie in Latin and English, according to the reformed Latin, and with Lyke Graces Privileged* (Antwerp, 1599) p. 47. The Catholic Encyclopedia of 1912 attributes the hymn translations to the book's editor, Richard Verstegan (d. 1636), a Catholic publisher. In the 1599 Preface, Verstegan says: "Notwithstanding the difficulty, these hymns have been so turned into English meter that they may be sung unto the same tunes in English that they bear in Latin." However, his accentual treatment is sometimes peculiar.

Ave Maris Stella (7th century)

1669AD – Historic Roman Catholic Translation

English translation can be sung with any 66 66 meter (iambic), such as CAMCOLT, QUAM DILECTA, ST CECILIA, IBSTONE, CLERMONT, SEÁN, etc.

Ave maris stella, Dei mater alma, Atque semper virgo, Felix caeli porta.	HAIL you, the sea's bright star, who God's pure Mother are, a virgin still, and ev'n the happy gate of heav'n.
Sumens illud Ave, Gabriélis ore, Funda nos in pace, Mutans Hevae nomen.	2. Taking that Ave's song from th'Angel Gabriel's tongue, firm peace unto us give, changing the name of Eve.
Solve vincla reis, Profer lumen caecis, Mala nostra pelle, Bona cuncta posce.	3. Offenders' bonds unbind, give light unto the blind, our evils clean disband, all good for us demand.
Monstra te esse matrem, Sumat per te preces, Qui pro nobis natus, Tulit esse tuus.	4. Do, like a mother, bear our prayers up to his ear who, for us born, put on the title of thy Son.
Virgo singuláris, Inter omnes mitis, Nos culpis solútos, Mites fac et castos.	5. O singularly chaste, whose meekness all surpassed, our sins from us exiled, render us chaste and mild.
Vitam praesta puram, Iter para tutum, Ut vidéntes Jesum, Semper collaetémur.	6. Grant that our life be pure, prepare the way secure, that, seeing Jesus, we may joy eternally.
Sit laus Deo Patri, Summo Christo decus, Spirítui Sancto, Tribus honor unus.	7. Be God the Father praised, Christ's glory highly raised, the Holy Ghost the same, to three one honor frame.

T. Source: *The Primer more ample, and in a new Order, containing The Three Offices of the B. Virgin Mary, in Latin and English, and this last Edition of the Hymns are in a better verse, and six Offices newly added* (1669) p. 98.

66 66 Iambic

Tune: VARIOUS

138 Ave Vivens Hostia (13th century)

John Pecham, Archbishop of Canturbury (d. 1292)

AVE, vivens hóstia,
Véritas et vita,
In qua sacrifícia
Cuncta sunt finíta:
Per te Patri glória
Datur infiníta;
Per te stat Ecclésia
Júgiter muníta.

HAIL, O living victim,
truth and life,
in whom all other sacrifices
are brought to an end:
by thee endless glory
is given to the Father;
by thee the Church stands
constantly protected.

AVE, vas cleméntiae,
Scrínium dulcóris, *n1*
In quo sunt delíciae
Caélici sapóris,
Véritas substántiae
Tota Salvatóris,
Sacraméntum grátiae,
Pábulum amóris.

2. Hail, O vessel of compassion,
haven of sweetness, *n1*
in which are delicacies
of heavenly flavor,
entire truth
of the Savior's substance,
sacrament of grace,
sustenance of love.

AVE, manna caélicum
vérius legáli,
Datum in viáticum *n2*
Mísero mortáli,
Medicámen mýsticum
Morbo spirituáli,
Morte dans Cathólicum
Vitae immortáli.

3. Hail, O manna more truly from heaven
than that received under the Law,
given as a wayfaring provision *n2*
to the wretched and death-bound,
mystical remedy
for spiritual disease,
delivering the Catholic at his death
to a life undying.

AVE, corpus Dómini
et munus finále,
Corpus junctum Númini,
Nóbile jocále,
Quod relíquit hómini
In memoriále,
Cum fináli término
Mundo dixit vale.

4. Hail, O body of the Lord
and last gift,
body united to the Godhead,
noble jewel,
which he left to man
for his remembrance
when at his last extremity
he bade the world farewell.

76 76 D

Tune:
VARIOUS

T. Source: *Analecta Hymnica Medii Aevi* (Leipzig: 1898) Volume 31, p. 111. This mighty collection, edited by two Jesuit priests—Fr. Clemens Blume and Fr. Guido Maria Dreves—contains more than 10,000 ancient Catholic hymns, and was published in 55 volumes between 1886 and 1922.

To sing in Latin, use any 76 76 D (trochaic) tune: St John Damascene, St Kevin, Ave Virgo Virginum, Ave Fragrantissime, Tempus Adest Floridum, etc.

AVE, plenum gaúdium, Vita beatórum, Paúperum solátium, Salus miserórum; Grande privilégium Est hoc viatórum, Quorum sacrifícium Merces est caelórum.	5. Hail, O full joy, life of the blessed, consolation of the poor, salvation of the wretched; this is the great distinction of wayfarers, whose sacrifice is the wage of heaven.
AVE, virtus fórtium, Óbvians ruínae, Turris et praesídium Plebis peregrínae, Quam insúltus hóstium, Frángere non sine, Ne vi malignántium Péreat in fine.	6. Hail, O power of the strong, preventing destruction, tower and safeguard of a pilgrim people: permit not the affronts of their foes to fracture them, lest by dint of ill-willers they perish at the last.
HIC Jesus veráciter Duplex est natúra; *n3* Non est partiáliter Nec solum figúra: Sed essentiáliter Caro Christi pura Latet integráliter Brevi sub clausúra.	7. Here in truth is each of Jesus' two natures; *n3* nor is Christ's pure flesh present only in part or figuratively: but in its essence it lies hidden in completeness beneath a slight enclosure.
CAELO visibíliter Caro Christi sita: Forma panis áliter Latet hic vestíta; Solus novit quáliter, Hanc qui ponit ita: Potest hoc facíliter Virtus infiníta.	8. The flesh of Christ is stationed visibly in heaven: here, by contrast, it lies hidden, clothed with the appearance of bread; only he knows how who proposes thus: Boundless power can easily do this.

[1] *Scrinium*, literally a chest or casket, cf. "shrine."

[2] Cf. Jn 6.32 "wayfaring provision": viaticum.

[3] "Each…natures"; literally "the twofold nature of Jesus." God the Son possesses his divine nature from eternity and assumes his human nature in time.

SUMPTUM non consúmitur Corpus Salvatóris; Idem totus súmitur Ómnibus in horis; Forma panis frángitur Dente comestóris: Virtus carnis súgitur Mórsibus amóris.	9.	The Savior's body is not depleted when received; at all hours the same is received entire; the appearance of bread is fractured by the teeth of the consumer: the power of Christ's flesh is absorbed in morsels of love.
CHRISTUS nihil pátitur Hujus laesiónis: Forma panis sólvitur Vi digestiónis; Tunc si Christus quaéritur, Est in caeli thronis; Sicut vult, hinc tóllitur, Datis vitae donis.	10.	Christ suffers none of this injury: the appearance of bread is dispersed by dint of digestion; if Christ be sought then, he is on the throne of heaven: he is removed hence, as he wills, having delivered gifts of life.
HOC ardóris cálculo Veni nos igníre; Hoc amóris stímulo Frange motus irae; Et eódem férculo, Qui nos vis nutríre, Velis cordis vínculo Fórtiter uníre. *n4*	11.	With this dose of fervor come to fire us; with this goad of love fracture the stirrings of wrath; and through the same portion, thou who willest to nourish us, mayest thou strongly join us with heartfelt bonds. *n4*
MORIS est amántium Ínvicem sitíre, Ut arcána córdium Possint introíre: Sic vult Rex regnántium, Caritátis mirae, Cibándo fidélium Íntima subíre.	12.	It belongs to the manner of lovers to thirst after one other, that they may penetrate the secrets of their hearts: so wills the King of kings, of wondrous charity, in feeding those who believe to enter their inmost selves.

O JESU dulcíssime,
Cibus salutáris,
Qui sic nobis íntime
Tríbui dignáris:
Mala nostra déprime
Flétibus amáris,
Et afféctus ímprime
Quibus delectáris.

13. O sweetest Jesus,
saving food,
who vouchsafest thus to be
bestowed on us inwardly:
repress our ills
through our bitter tears,
and impress on us those attitudes
by which thou art delighted.

JESU, vivens hóstia,
Placa majestátem;
Sacraménti grátia
Confer sanitátem;
Paúperum substántia,
Da aeternitátem;
Dómini memória,
Fove caritátem.

14. O Jesus, living victim,
appease the divine majesty;
through the grace of this sacrament
bestow health;
O fortune of the poor,
grant us everlasting life;
O remembrance of the Lord,
foster our charity.

VANITÁTEM spérnere
Fac nos, consolátor;
Hostes dona víncere,
Christe, propugnátor;
Et quod doces crédere,
Jesu, reparátor,
Per te tandem cérnere
Da, remunerátor.

15. Cause us to scorn vainglory,
O thou, our consoler;
grant us to conquer our foes,
O Christ, our champion; and that
which thou teachest us to believe,
O Jesus, our restorer,
grant us at last to see
through thyself, our requiter.

[4] "Heartfelt bonds"; literally "a bond of the heart."

142 Ave Vivens Hostia (13th century)

First Tune – *Trns: Msgr. Ronald A. Knox (d. 1957)*

4. Jesus truly in this place | God and Man resideth;
Him no shadow doth replace, | Him no rent divideth,
Very flesh, although his face, | Glorified, he hideth;
Garnered in this little space | All of Christ abideth.

5. Seen in heav'n by blessèd eyes | This his body reigneth;
Form of bread, in other wise, | Here its scope containeth;—
Myst'ry he alone descries | Who the same ordaineth;
Well may he such thing devise | Whom no pow'r restraineth.

6. Plead, true Victim, in our stead | To the Father crying,
Thou, thy children's daily bread, | Daily health supplying;
Banquet for the exile spread, | Grant us life undying;
May our love from thine be fed, | Self and sense denying!

76 76 D

Tune:
Ave Virgo Virginum

Final Verses: Richard Lloyd (1993) #15; Noel Rawsthorne (2011) #31.
T. Source: *New Westminster Hymnal* (1939) p. 107.
Melody: Medieval melody arranged by Johann Roh (d. 1547).
M. Source: Printed in *Catholicum Hymnologium Germanicum* (Leisentritt, 1584).

Ave Vivens Hostia (13th century) 143

Second Tune – *Trns: Msgr. Ronald A. Knox (d. 1957)*

4. Jesus truly in this place | God and Man resideth;
Him no shadow doth replace, | Him no rent divideth,
Very flesh, although his face, | Glorified, he hideth;
Garnered in this little space | All of Christ abideth.

5. Seen in heav'n by blessèd eyes | This his body reigneth;
Form of bread, in other wise, | Here its scope containeth;—
Myst'ry he alone descries | Who the same ordaineth;
Well may he such thing devise | Whom no pow'r restraineth.

6. Plead, true Victim, in our stead | To the Father crying,
Thou, thy children's daily bread, | Daily health supplying;
Banquet for the exile spread, | Grant us life undying;
May our love from thine be fed, | Self and sense denying!

Final Verses: Richard Lloyd (1993) #207; Noel Rawsthorne (2011) #325.
T. Source: *New Westminster Hymnal* (1939) p. 107.
Melody: Jacob Hintze (d. 1702), court musician to the Elector of Brandenburg at Berlin.
M. Source: *Catholic Hymn Book* (London Oratory, 1998) p. 116.

76 76 D
Tune:
Salzburg E6

144 Ave Vivens Hostia (13th century)

Third Tune – *Trns: Msgr. Ronald A. Knox (d. 1957)*

4. Jesus truly in this place | God and Man resideth;
Him no shadow doth replace, | Him no rent divideth,
Very flesh, although his face, | Glorified, he hideth;
Garnered in this little space | All of Christ abideth.

5. Seen in heav'n by blessèd eyes | This his body reigneth;
Form of bread, in other wise, | Here its scope containeth;—
Myst'ry he alone descries | Who the same ordaineth;
Well may he such thing devise | Whom no pow'r restraineth.

6. Plead, true Victim, in our stead | To the Father crying,
Thou, thy children's daily bread, | Daily health supplying;
Banquet for the exile spread, | Grant us life undying;
May our love from thine be fed, | Self and sense denying!

N.B. This melody is excellent for use during Lent.

76 76 D

Tune:
Aus Der Tiefe E6

Final Verses: Richard Lloyd (1993) #13; Noel Rawsthorne (2011) #29.
T. Source: *New Westminster Hymnal* (1939) p. 107.
Melody: Martin Herbst (d. 1681); first published in *Nürnbergerisches Gesangbuch* (1676).
M. Source: *New Westminster Hymnal* (1939) p. 60; *Catholic Hymn Book* (London Oratory, 1998) p. 82.

Fourth Tune – *Trns: Msgr. Ronald A. Knox (d. 1957)*

4. Jesus truly in this place | God and Man resideth;
Him no shadow doth replace, | Him no rent divideth,
Very flesh, although his face, | Glorified, he hideth;
Garnered in this little space | All of Christ abideth.

5. Seen in heav'n by blessèd eyes | This his body reigneth;
Form of bread, in other wise, | Here its scope containeth;—
Myst'ry he alone descries | Who the same ordaineth;
Well may he such thing devise | Whom no pow'r restraineth.

6. Plead, true Victim, in our stead | To the Father crying,
Thou, thy children's daily bread, | Daily health supplying;
Banquet for the exile spread, | Grant us life undying;
May our love from thine be fed, | Self and sense denying!

N.B. This melody is excellent for use during Advent.

T. Source: *New Westminster Hymnal* (1939) p. 107.
Melody: Based on "Veni Redemptor Gentium"; for plainsong score, cf. *Liber Hymnarius* (1983) p. 11.
M. Source: *New Westminster Hymnal* (1939) p. 146; *Catholic Hymn Book* (1998) p. 278; *Summit Choirbook* (Dominican Monastery of Our Lady of the Rosary, 1983) #25; *Saint Andrew Hymnal, authorized by the Bishops of Scotland for use in the Scottish Dioceses* (1964) p. 203.

76 76 D
Tune:
Nun Komm E4

146 Ave Vivens Hostia (13th century)

Fifth Tune – *Trns: Msgr. Ronald A. Knox (d. 1957)*

1. Hail, true Vic - tim, life and light Un - to sin - ners
2. Hail, true Man - na from the sky— Is - rael nev - er
3. Hail, Christ's Bod - y— gift he made, His own death fore -

lend - ing— Ev - 'ry old - er form and rite Hath in
knew thee; Pil - grims, for the day's sup - ply, Dai - ly
show - ing, (God - head un - der earth - ly shade Like a

thee its end - ing— Spot - less in the Fa - ther's sight
hom - age do thee; When our souls in sick - ness lie,
jew - el glow - ing), Sa - cred mem - 'ries, ne'er to fade,

Ev - er - more as - cend - ing, Ho - ly church in bit - ter
Yields that sick - ness to thee; Chris - tians, when they come to
On his Church be - stow - ing, When to earth fare - well he

fight Ev - er - more be - friend - ing.
die, Live im - mor - tal through thee.
bade, To his Pas - sion go - ing.

4. Jesus truly in this place | God and Man resideth;
Him no shadow doth replace, | Him no rent divideth,
Very flesh, although his face, | Glorified, he hideth;
Garnered in this little space | All of Christ abideth.

5. Seen in heav'n by blessèd eyes | This his body reigneth;
Form of bread, in other wise, | Here its scope containeth;—
Myst'ry he alone descries | Who the same ordaineth;
Well may he such thing devise | Whom no pow'r restraineth.

6. Plead, true Victim, in our stead | To the Father crying,
Thou, thy children's daily bread, | Daily health supplying;
Banquet for the exile spread, | Grant us life undying;
May our love from thine be fed, | Self and sense denying!

76 76 D

Tune:
Christus Christus Christus Ist

Melody: Peter Franck (d. 1675), first published in 1657.
M. Source: *Choral Harmony* (London: G. H. Davidson, 1854) #203.
T. Source: *New Westminster Hymnal* (1939) p. 107.

Ave Vivens Hostia (13th century) 147

Sixth Tune – *Trns: Msgr. Ronald A. Knox (d. 1957)*

4. Jesus truly in this place | God and Man resideth;
Him no shadow doth replace, | Him no rent divideth,
Very flesh, although his face, | Glorified, he hideth;
Garnered in this little space | All of Christ abideth.

5. Seen in heav'n by blessèd eyes | This his body reigneth;
Form of bread, in other wise, | Here its scope containeth;—
Myst'ry he alone descries | Who the same ordaineth;
Well may he such thing devise | Whom no pow'r restraineth.

6. Plead, true Victim, in our stead | To the Father crying,
Thou, thy children's daily bread, | Daily health supplying;
Banquet for the exile spread, | Grant us life undying;
May our love from thine be fed, | Self and sense denying!

76 76 D

Melody: Melchior Vulpius (d. 1615).
M. Source: *Songs of Syon* (Woodward, 1910) p. 567; cf. *Ein schön geistlich Gesangbuch* (1609).
T. Source: *New Westminster Hymnal* (1939) p. 107.

Tune:
Jesu Leiden Pein Und Tod

148 Ave Vivens Hostia (13th century)

Seventh Tune – *Trns: Msgr. Ronald A. Knox (d. 1957)*

4. Jesus truly in this place | God and Man resideth;
Him no shadow doth replace, | Him no rent divideth,
Very flesh, although his face, | Glorified, he hideth;
Garnered in this little space | All of Christ abideth.

5. Seen in heav'n by blessèd eyes | This his body reigneth;
Form of bread, in other wise, | Here its scope containeth;—
Myst'ry he alone descries | Who the same ordaineth;
Well may he such thing devise | Whom no pow'r restraineth.

6. Plead, true Victim, in our stead | To the Father crying,
Thou, thy children's daily bread, | Daily health supplying;
Banquet for the exile spread, | Grant us life undying;
May our love from thine be fed, | Self and sense denying!

76 76 D

Tune:
Ach Wie Kurz

Melody: J. H. Reiman, first published in 1747.
M. Source: *New Westminster Hymnal* (1939) p. 81.
T. Source: *New Westminster Hymnal* (1939) p. 107.

Ave Vivens Hostia (13th century)

Trns: Msgr. Ronald A. Knox (d. 1957)

Can be sung with any 76 76 D (trochaic) meter, such as HATFIELD, ST KEVIN, SCHWING DICH AUF ZU DEINEM GOTT, TEMPUS ADEST FLORIDUM, etc.

Verse numbers correspond to the complete hymn (above) which has fifteen verses :

HAIL, true Victim, life and light | Unto sinners lending—
Ev'ry older form and rite | Hath in thee its ending—
Spotless in the Father's sight | Evermore ascending,
Holy church in bitter fight | Evermore befriending.

3. Hail, true Manna from the sky— | Israel never knew thee;
Pilgrims, for the day's supply, | Daily homage do thee;
When our souls in sickness lie, | Yields that sickness to thee;
Christians, when they come to die, | Live immortal through thee.

4. Hail, Christ's Body—gift he made, | His own death foreshowing,
(Godhead under earthly shade | Like a jewel glowing),
Sacred mem'ries, ne'er to fade, | On his Church bestowing,
When to earth farewell he bade, | To his Passion going.

7. Jesus truly in this place | God and Man resideth;
Him no shadow doth replace, | Him no rent divideth,
Very flesh, although his face, | Glorified, he hideth;
Garnered in this little space | All of Christ abideth.

8. Seen in heav'n by blessèd eyes | This his body reigneth;
Form of bread, in other wise, | Here its scope containeth;—
Myst'ry he alone descries | Who the same ordaineth;
Well may he such thing devise | Whom no pow'r restraineth.

14. Plead, true Victim, in our stead | To the Father crying,
Thou, thy children's daily bread, | Daily health supplying;
Banquet for the exile spread, | Grant us life undying;
May our love from thine be fed, | Self and sense denying!

76 76 D

Tune: VARIOUS

T. Source: *New Westminster Hymnal* (1939) p. 107.

150 Ave Vivens Hostia (13th century)

First Tune – *Trns: Msgr. Hugh T. Henry (d. 1946)*

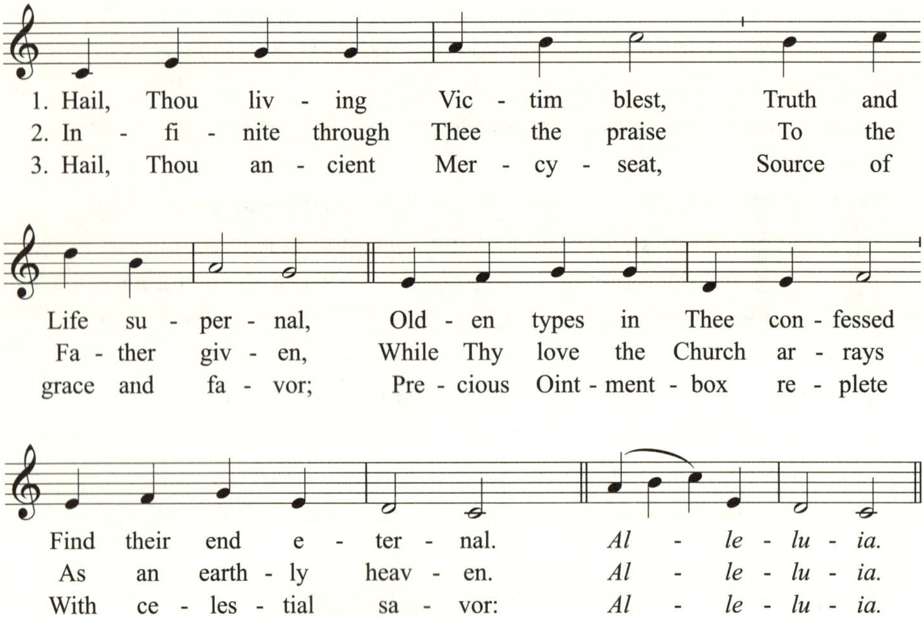

4. Thou the God-man truly art
In divine completeness:
Fed on Thee, the loving heart
Knows Thy raptured sweetness.
Alleluia.

5. Hail, Thou Manna from the skies,
Yet more truly given
To the pilgrim soul that sighs
For her promised Heaven:
Alleluia.

6. Mystic medicine Thou art
For the wounded spirit;
Healed by Thee, may every heart
Endless life inherit.
Alleluia.

76 76 A

Tune:
Gott Sei Dank E6

Final Verses: Richard Lloyd (1993) #83; Noel Rawsthorne (2011) #192.
Melody: Adapted by Johann Anastasius Freylinghausen (d. 1739) in his *Geist-reiches Gesang-Buch, den Kern alter und neuer Lieder* (Halle, 1704); also called Lübeck.
M. Source: *New Westminster Hymnal* (1939) p. 249; *New Saint Basil Hymnal* (1958) p. 229.
T. Source: *Eucharistica: Verse & Prose in Honor of the Hidden God* (Philadelphia: Dolphin Press, 1912) p. 95. Monsignor Hugh T. Henry, professor of homiletics at the Catholic University of America, also taught Gregorian chant at St. Charles Seminary (Overbrook, Pennsylvania).

SECOND TUNE – *Trns: Msgr. Hugh T. Henry (d. 1946)*

1. Hail, Thou liv - ing Vic - tim blest, Truth and Life su -
2. In - fi - nite through Thee the praise To the Fa - ther
3. Hail, Thou an - cient Mer - cy - seat, Source of grace and

per - nal, Old - en types in Thee con - fessed
giv - en, While Thy love the Church ar - rays
fa - vor; Pre - cious Oint - ment - box re - plete

Find their end e - ter - nal.
As an earth - ly heav - en.
With ce - les - tial sa - vor:

4. Thou the God-man truly art
In divine completeness:
Fed on Thee, the loving heart
Knows Thy raptured sweetness.

5. Hail, Thou Manna from the skies,
Yet more truly given
To the pilgrim soul that sighs
For her promised Heaven:

6. Mystic medicine Thou art
For the wounded spirit;
Healed by Thee, may every heart
Endless life inherit.

Final Verses: Richard Lloyd (1993) #233; Noel Rawsthorne (2011) #373.
T. Source: *Eucharistica: Verse & Prose in Honor of the Hidden God* (Philadelphia: Dolphin Press, 1912) p. 95. Monsignor Hugh T. Henry, professor of homiletics at the Catholic University of America, also taught Gregorian chant at St. Charles Seminary (Overbrook, Pennsylvania).
Melody: Henry J. Gauntlett (d. 1876), organist at St. Olave's Church, London.
M. Source: *New English Hymnal* (1986) p. 916.

76 76
Tune:
UNIVERSITY COLLEGE E6

152 Ave Vivens Hostia (13th century)

Third Tune – *Trns: Msgr. Hugh T. Henry (d. 1946)*

1. Hail, Thou liv - ing Vic - tim blest, Truth and Life su -
2. In - fi - nite through Thee the praise To the Fa - ther
3. Hail, Thou an - cient Mer - cy - seat, Source of grace and

per - nal, Old - en types in Thee con - fessed
giv - en, While Thy love the Church ar - rays
fa - vor; Pre - cious Oint - ment - box re - plete

Find their end e - ter - nal. *Je - su Sal - vá - tor!*
As an earth - ly heav - en. *Je - su Sal - vá - tor.*
With ce - les - tial sa - vor: *Je - su Sal - vá - tor.*

4. Thou the God-man truly art
In divine completeness:
Fed on Thee, the loving heart
Knows Thy raptured sweetness.
Jesu Salvátor.

5. Hail, Thou Manna from the skies,
Yet more truly given
To the pilgrim soul that sighs
For her promised Heaven:
Jesu Salvátor.

6. Mystic medicine Thou art
For the wounded spirit;
Healed by Thee, may every heart
Endless life inherit.
Jesu Salvátor.

76 76

Tune:
Orientis Partibus E6

Melody: *attr.* Pierre de Corbeil (d. 1222), Archbishop of Sens.
M. Source: *Mediator Dei Hymnal* (1955) #77; *American Catholic Hymnal according to the Motu Proprio of His Holiness Pope Pius X compiled by the Marist Brothers* (New York: Kenedy & Sons, 1913) p. 185.
T. Source: *Eucharistica: Verse & Prose in Honor of the Hidden God* (Philadelphia: Dolphin Press, 1912) p. 95. Monsignor Hugh T. Henry, professor of homiletics at the Catholic University of America, also taught Gregorian chant at St. Charles Seminary (Overbrook, Pennsylvania).

Trns: Msgr. Hugh T. Henry (d. 1946)

By doubling the verses, this text can be sung with any 76 76 D (trochaic) meter, such as TEMPUS ADEST FLORIDUM, ACH WIE KURZ, AVE VIRGO VIRGINUM, etc.

HAIL, Thou living Victim blest,
Truth and Life supernal,
Olden types in Thee confessed
Find their end eternal.

2. Infinite through Thee the praise
To the Father given,
While Thy love the Church arrays
As an earthly heaven.

3. Hail, Thou ancient Mercy-seat,
Source of grace and favor;
Precious Ointment-box replete
With celestial savor:

4. Thou the God-man truly art
In divine completeness:
Fed on Thee, the loving heart
Knows Thy raptured sweetness.

5. Hail, Thou Manna from the skies,
Yet more truly given
To the pilgrim soul that sighs
For her promised Heaven:

6. Mystic medicine Thou art
For the wounded spirit;
Healed by Thee, may every heart
Endless life inherit.

T. Source: *Eucharistica: Verse & Prose in Honor of the Hidden God* (Philadelphia: Dolphin Press, 1912) p. 95. Monsignor Hugh Thomas Henry, professor of homiletics at the Catholic University of America, also taught Gregorian chant at Saint Charles Borromeo Seminary (Overbrook, Pennsylvania).

76 76

Tune: VARIOUS

154 Christe Redemptor Omnium (9th century)

Rabanus Maurus, Archbishop of Mainz (d. 856AD)

To sing in Latin, use any 88 88 (LM) tune.

CHRISTE, Redémptor ómnium,
Consérva tuos fámulos,
Beátae semper Vírginis
Placátus sanctis précibus.

2. Beáta quoque ágmina
Caeléstium spiríctuum, *n1*
Praetérita, praeséntia,
Futúra mala péllite.

3. Vates aetérni Júdicis *n2*
Apostolíque Dómini,
Supplíciter expóscimus,
Salvári vestris précibus.

4. Mártyres Dei íncliti,
Confessorésque lúcidi,
Vestris oratiónibus
Nos ferte in caeléstibus.

5. Chori sanctárum Vírginum
Monachorúmque ómnium,
Simul cum Sanctis ómnibus
Consórtes Christi fácite.

6. Gentem auférte pérfidam *n3*
Credéntium de fínibus,
Ut Christo laudes débitas
Persolvámus alácriter.

7. Glória Patr*i* ingénito,
Ejúsque Unigénito,
Una cum Sancto Spíritu,
In sempitérna saécula.

88 88 (LM)

Tune:
VARIOUS

T. Source: *Hymni de Tempore et de Sanctis in Textu Antiquo et Novo* (Solesmes, 1885) p. 108.

[1] That is, *Angels*.

[2] That is, *Prophets*.

Assistance for comprehension

O CHRIST, Redeemer of all,
keep thy servants safe,
appeased by the holy prayers
of the blessed ever-Virgin.

2. And ye also, blessed hosts
of heavenly Spirits, *n1*
banish all ills: those past,
those present, and those to come.

3. Ye Oracles of the everlasting Judge, *n2*
and ye Apostles of the Lord,
we beg entreatingly
to be saved by your prayers.

4. Ye glorious Martyrs of God
and illustrious Confessors,
by your intercession
convey us to the heavenly realms.

5. Ye choirs of holy Virgins
and of all Monks,
together with all his Saints,
make us partakers with Christ.

6. Discard the faithless folk *n3*
from the borders of believers,
that we may joyfully render
to Christ the praises we owe him.

7. Glory to the unbegotten Father
and his only-begotten Son,
together with the Holy Spirit,
for ever and ever.

[3] When the celebration of All Saints was extended to the Frankish empire in 825AD, after having been observed in Rome for two centuries, this verse was added to the hymn with reference to the Normans and Saracens who were laying waste both the northwest of Gaul and the south of Italy; cf. *The Roman Breviary its Sources and History* (Dom Jules Baudot, OSB) p. 68.

156 Christe Redemptor Omnium (9th century)

First Tune – *Trns: Fr. John Fitzpatrick, Oblate of Mary (d. 1929)*

4. Ye Martyrs purple-clad, and all
Rewarded in the white-robed band
Who faith confessed, from exile call
Us onward to our native land. *Alleluia.*

5. O joyous choir of Virgins chaste,
With all whom earth has sent on high,
Once dwellers of the desert waste,
Supernal thrones to us supply. *Alleluia.*

6. Drive out the false and faithless race
From where the bounds of faith are set,
That there may be in every place
One Shepherd and one sheepfold yet. *Alleluia.*

88 88 A

Tune:
Erschienen Ist

Melody: Nikolaus Hermann (d. 1561), organist at Joachimsthal, Bohemia.
M. Source: *Hymns Ancient and Modern* (1972) p. 832; cf. "Erschienen ist der herrlich Tag" in *The Four-Part Chorals of J. S. Bach with the German Text of the Hymns and English Translations* (Charles Sanford Terry, 1964) p. 87.
T. Source: *The Breviary and Missal Hymns* (London: Sands & Co, 1931) p. 188.

Second Tune – *Trns: Fr. John Fitzpatrick, Oblate of Mary (d. 1929)*

1. O Christ, Thy ser - vants deign to spare,
2. Ye bless - èd hosts who are ar - rayed
3. Ye Proph - ets and A - pos - tles, plead

For whom their Vir - gin - Pa - tron speaks
In cir - cles nine of le - gions bright,
For us be - fore our Judge se - vere

Be - fore Thy bar of grace, and there
Who gave and give us time - ly aid:
To show us mer - cy, as in - deed

The Fa - ther's kind in - dul - gence seeks.
Our fu - ture let no e - vil blight.
We mourn our guilt with grief sin - cere.

4. Ye Martyrs purple-clad, and all
Rewarded in the white-robed band
Who faith confessed, from exile call
Us onward to our native land.

5. O joyous choir of Virgins chaste,
With all whom earth has sent on high,
Once dwellers of the desert waste,
Supernal thrones to us supply.

6. Drive out the false and faithless race
From where the bounds of faith are set,
That there may be in every place
One Shepherd and one sheepfold yet.

Final Verses: Richard Lloyd (1993) #158; Noel Rawsthorne (2011) #242.
T. Source: *The Breviary and Missal Hymns* (London: Sands & Co, 1931) p. 188.
Melody: Louis Bourgeois (d. 1561) based on a popular chanson. Bourgeois helped produce the *Genevan Psalter* and was once imprisoned (3 December 1551) for changing the melodies of well-known psalms "without a license." The tune was originally in the Tenor voice, but soon became its own melody; cf. Day's *Psalter* (1584) p. 272.
M. Source: *Hymns, Psalms, and Spiritual Canticles* (Marier, 1983) p. 361; *New Saint Basil Hymnal* (1958) p. 92.

88 88 (LM)
Tune: Old Hundredth

158 Christe Redemptor Omnium (9th century)

Third Tune – *Trns: Fr. John Fitzpatrick, Oblate of Mary (d. 1929)*

4. Ye Martyrs purple-clad, and all
Rewarded in the white-robed band
Who faith confessed, from exile call
Us onward to our native land.

5. O joyous choir of Virgins chaste,
With all whom earth has sent on high,
Once dwellers of the desert waste,
Supernal thrones to us supply.

6. Drive out the false and faithless race
From where the bounds of faith are set,
That there may be in every place
One Shepherd and one sheepfold yet.

88 88 (LM)

Tune:
Hilderstone

T. Source: *The Breviary and Missal Hymns* (London: Sands & Co, 1931) p. 188.
Melody: Philip Hart (d. 1749), organist at St. Michael Church, Cornhill.
M. Source: *Hymns Ancient and Modern* (1972) p. 8; cf. *Church Hymns With Tunes* (1885) p. 230, edited by Sir Arthur Sullivan (d. 1900), organist at St. Peter Church, Kensington.

Christe Redemptor Omnium (9th century) 159

Fourth Tune – *Trns: Fr. John Fitzpatrick, Oblate of Mary (d. 1929)*

4. Ye Martyrs purple-clad, and all
Rewarded in the white-robed band
Who faith confessed, from exile call
Us onward to our native land.

5. O joyous choir of Virgins chaste,
With all whom earth has sent on high,
Once dwellers of the desert waste,
Supernal thrones to us supply.

6. Drive out the false and faithless race
From where the bounds of faith are set,
That there may be in every place
One Shepherd and one sheepfold yet.

Final Verses: Richard Lloyd (1993) #80; Noel Rawsthorne (2011) #136.
T. Source: *The Breviary and Missal Hymns* (London: Sands & Co, 1931) p. 188.
Melody: Sir Percy Carter Buck (d. 1947); first published in *Fourteen Hymn Tunes* (1913).
M. Source: *Catholic Hymn Book* (London Oratory, 1998) p. 140. The tune was originally paired with *Vexilla Regis* ("Flag of the King"). A *gonfalon* ("flag") was traditionally carried during Catholic processions.

88 88 (LM)

Tune:
Gonfalon Royal

160 Christe Redemptor Omnium (9th century)

Fifth Tune – *Trns: Fr. John Fitzpatrick, Oblate of Mary (d. 1929)*

4. Ye Martyrs purple-clad, and all
Rewarded in the white-robed band
Who faith confessed, from exile call
Us onward to our native land.

5. O joyous choir of Virgins chaste,
With all whom earth has sent on high,
Once dwellers of the desert waste,
Supernal thrones to us supply.

6. Drive out the false and faithless race
From where the bounds of faith are set,
That there may be in every place
One Shepherd and one sheepfold yet.

88 88 (LM)

Tune:
Cromer

T. Source: *The Breviary and Missal Hymns* (London: Sands & Co, 1931) p. 188.
Melody: John Ambrose Lloyd (d. 1874), choirmaster at Chapel Salem, Brownlow.
M. Source: *New English Hymnal* (1986) p. 346.

Christe Redemptor Omnium (9th century)

Sixth Tune – *Trns: Fr. John Fitzpatrick, Oblate of Mary (d. 1929)*

4. Ye Martyrs purple-clad, and all
Rewarded in the white-robed band
Who faith confessed, from exile call
Us onward to our native land.

5. O joyous choir of Virgins chaste,
With all whom earth has sent on high,
Once dwellers of the desert waste,
Supernal thrones to us supply.

6. Drive out the false and faithless race
From where the bounds of faith are set,
That there may be in every place
One Shepherd and one sheepfold yet.

Final Verses: Richard Lloyd (1993) #181; Noel Rawsthorne (2011) #276.
T. Source: *The Breviary and Missal Hymns* (London: Sands & Co, 1931) p. 188.
Melody: Dr. Edward Miller (d. 1807), organist of Doncaster Parish Church; originally published in *Psalms of David for the Use of Parish Churches* (1790) p. 12; based on Tunbridge (an older tune).
M. Source: *Catholic Hymn Book* (London Oratory, 1998) p. 115; *Church Hymns with Tunes* (1885) p. 44.

88 88 (LM)

Tune: Rockingham

Christe Redemptor Omnium (9th century)

SEVENTH TUNE – *Trns: Fr. John Fitzpatrick, Oblate of Mary (d. 1929)*

4. Ye Martyrs purple-clad, and all
Rewarded in the white-robed band
Who faith confessed, from exile call
Us onward to our native land.

5. O joyous choir of Virgins chaste,
With all whom earth has sent on high,
Once dwellers of the desert waste,
Supernal thrones to us supply.

6. Drive out the false and faithless race
From where the bounds of faith are set,
That there may be in every place
One Shepherd and one sheepfold yet.

88 88 (LM)

Tune:
BRESLAU

Final Verses: Richard Lloyd (1993) #24; Noel Rawsthorne (2011) #50.
T. Source: *The Breviary and Missal Hymns* (London: Sands & Co, 1931) p. 188.
Melody: cf. Theme used by J.S. Bach (d. 1750) in "O Jesu Christ, meins Lebens Licht," BWV 118.
M. Source: *Pope Pius XII Hymnal* (Ohio: Gregorian Institute of America, 1959) p. 6.

Christe Redemptor Omnium (9th century) 163

Trns: Fr. John Fitzpatrick, Oblate of Mary (d. 1929)

Can be sung with any 88 88 meter, such as HILDERSTONE, DUGUET, BRESLAU, MELCOMBE, WAREHAM, OLD HUNDREDTH, MEIN SEEL, TRINITY COLLEGE, etc.

O CHRIST, Thy servants deign to spare,
For whom their Virgin-Patron speaks
Before Thy bar of grace, and there
The Father's kind indulgence seeks.

2. Ye blessèd hosts who are arrayed
In circles nine of legions bright,
Who gave and give us timely aid:
Our future let no evil blight.

3. Ye Prophets and Apostles, plead
For us before our Judge severe
To show us mercy, as indeed
We mourn our guilt with grief sincere.

4. Ye Martyrs purple-clad, and all
Rewarded in the white-robed band
Who faith confessed, from exile call
Us onward to our native land.

5. O joyous choir of Virgins chaste,
With all whom earth has sent on high,
Once dwellers of the desert waste,
Supernal thrones to us supply.

6. Drive out the false and faithless race
From where the bounds of faith are set,
That there may be in every place
One Shepherd and one sheepfold yet.

88 88 (LM)

Tune:
VARIOUS

T. Source: *The Breviary and Missal Hymns* (London: Sands & Co, 1931) p. 188.

164 Christe Redemptor Omnium (9th century)

First Tune – *Trns: Richard F. Littledale (d. 1890)*

4. God's Martyrs who have won renown,
Confessors all in bright array,
beseech for us to win the crown
and us to realms above convey.

5. Ye choirs of holy Virgins fine,
of Monks who lived by sacred vow,
with all the Saints in prayer combine,
a partnership with Christ endow.

6. Do ye all unbelief expel
from every land of Christian claim,
that we to Christ our praise may tell
in bounden tribute to his name.

7. The unbegotten Father praise,
and laud the sole-begotten Son;
to God the Holy Spirit raise
the same, as endless ages run.

88 88 (LM)

Tune:
St Peter Claver

Melody: Kevin Allen (b. 1965), choirmaster at the Monastery of the Holy Cross in Chicago.
M. Source: *Saint Edmund Campion Missal and Hymnal* (2013) p. 823.
T. Source: *Breviary Offices from Lauds to Compline Inclusive, Trnsl. from the Sarum Book, and Supplemented from Gallican and Monastic Uses* (London, 1874) p. 327; *The People's Hymnal* (London, 1877) p. 108.

Christe Redemptor Omnium (9th century)

Second Tune – *Trns: Richard F. Littledale (d. 1890)*

4. God's Martyrs who have won renown,
Confessors all in bright array,
beseech for us to win the crown
and us to realms above convey.

5. Ye choirs of holy Virgins fine,
of Monks who lived by sacred vow,
with all the Saints in prayer combine,
a partnership with Christ endow.

6. Do ye all unbelief expel
from every land of Christian claim,
that we to Christ our praise may tell
in bounden tribute to his name.

7. The unbegotten Father praise,
and laud the sole-begotten Son;
to God the Holy Spirit raise
the same, as endless ages run.

Melody: Dieudonné Duguet (d. 1849), organist at the Catholic Cathedral in Liège, Belgium, and teacher of César Franck.
M. Source: *Mediator Dei Hymnal* (1955) p. 66; *New Saint Basil Hymnal* (1958) p. 93; *Arundel Catholic Hymnal* (1905) p. 26; *Hymnal and Vesperal* (Archdiocese of Baltimore, 1878) p. 168; *Catholic Vesper Hymn Book set to Music for Unison or Four Voices* (Charles Lewis, 1877) p. 6.
T. Source: *Breviary Offices from Lauds to Compline Inclusive, Trnsl. from the Sarum Book, and Supplemented from Gallican and Monastic Uses* (London, 1874) p. 327; *The People's Hymnal* (London, 1877) p. 108.

88 88 (LM)

Tune: Duguet

166 Christe Redemptor Omnium (9th century)

Third Tune – *Trns: Richard F. Littledale (d. 1890)*

4. God's Martyrs who have won renown,
Confessors all in bright array,
beseech for us to win the crown
and us to realms above convey.

5. Ye choirs of holy Virgins fine,
of Monks who lived by sacred vow,
with all the Saints in prayer combine,
a partnership with Christ endow.

6. Do ye all unbelief expel
from every land of Christian claim,
that we to Christ our praise may tell
in bounden tribute to his name.

7. The unbegotten Father praise,
and laud the sole-begotten Son;
to God the Holy Spirit raise
the same, as endless ages run.

88 88 (LM)

Tune:
Whitehall

Melody: Henry Lawes (d. 1662).
M. Source: *Saint Edmund Campion Missal and Hymnal* (2013) p. 888.
T. Source: *Breviary Offices from Lauds to Compline Inclusive, Trnsl. from the Sarum Book, and Supplemented from Gallican and Monastic Uses* (London, 1874) p. 327; *The People's Hymnal* (London, 1877) p. 108.

Christe Redemptor Omnium (9th century)

Trns: Richard F. Littledale (d. 1890)

Can be sung with any 88 88 meter, such as HILDERSTONE, DUGUET, BRESLAU, MELCOMBE, WAREHAM, OLD HUNDREDTH, MEIN SEEL, TRINITY COLLEGE, etc.

O CHRIST, Redeemer of mankind,
thy servants here protect and spare,
who hearest with a loving mind
the blessèd ever-Virgin's prayer.

2. Ye blessèd hosts who see his face,
the Spirits of the heav'nly home,
away from us all evils chase,
the past and present, and to come.

3. O Prophets of the Judge eterne,
Apostles of the Lord most high,
deliverance, for which we yearn,
we beg your patronage supply.

4. God's Martyrs who have won renown,
Confessors all in bright array,
beseech for us to win the crown
and us to realms above convey.

5. Ye choirs of holy Virgins fine,
of Monks who lived by sacred vow,
with all the Saints in prayer combine,
a partnership with Christ endow.

6. Do ye all unbelief expel
from every land of Christian claim,
that we to Christ our praise may tell
in bounden tribute to his name.

7. The unbegotten Father praise,
and laud the sole-begotten Son;
to God the Holy Spirit raise
the same, as endless ages run.

T. Source: *Breviary Offices from Lauds to Compline Inclusive, Trnsl. from the Sarum Book, and Supplemented from Gallican and Monastic Uses* (London, 1874) p. 327; *The People's Hymnal* (London, 1877) p. 108.

88 88 (LM)

Tune: VARIOUS

168 Christe Redemptor Omnium (9th century)

First Tune – *Historic Roman Catholic Translation (1684AD)*

1. Of all Re - deem - er, Christ, be pleased
2. And you, O bless - èd com - pa - nies
3. Th'e - ter - nal Judge - 's Proph - ets blest,

thy ser - vants to pre - serve_ and aid,
of spir - its, which in heav - en dwell,
and you__ A - pos - tles of__ his choice,

by her most ho - ly prayers ap - peased
at hand and past ca - lam - i - ties,
O by your prayers do we re - quest

who ev - er was__ a spot - less Maid.
and all that are__ to come,_ re - pel.
to be pre - served, with hum - ble voice.

4. You Martyrs, whose renown is great, | of God, our Lord's Confessors bright,
your intercession we entreat | to raise us up to heav'nly light.

5. You holy Virgins' spotless choirs | and Monks that lived in willing pain,
and all you Saints, with joint desires | implore that we with Christ remain.

6. The wicked infidels away | do drive from grounds where faith doth grow,
that we with joy to Christ may pay | those praises which to him we owe.

7. To Father even as to Son, | unsired and sole-begotten, be
with Holy Ghost, all glory done | for ages everlastingly.

88 88 (LM)

Tune:
Kempen

Melody: Flor Peeters (d. 1986), organist at the Catholic Cathedral of Mechelen, Belgium, was made a Baron by King Baudouin.
M. Source: *People's Mass Book* (Omer Westendorf, 1964) p. 218.
T. Source: *The Primer Containing the Three Offices of the Blessed Virgin Mary in Latin and English ... to the Calendar are annexed many English and Irish Saints* (Rouen, 1684) p. 367.

Second Tune – *Historic Roman Catholic Translation (1684AD)*

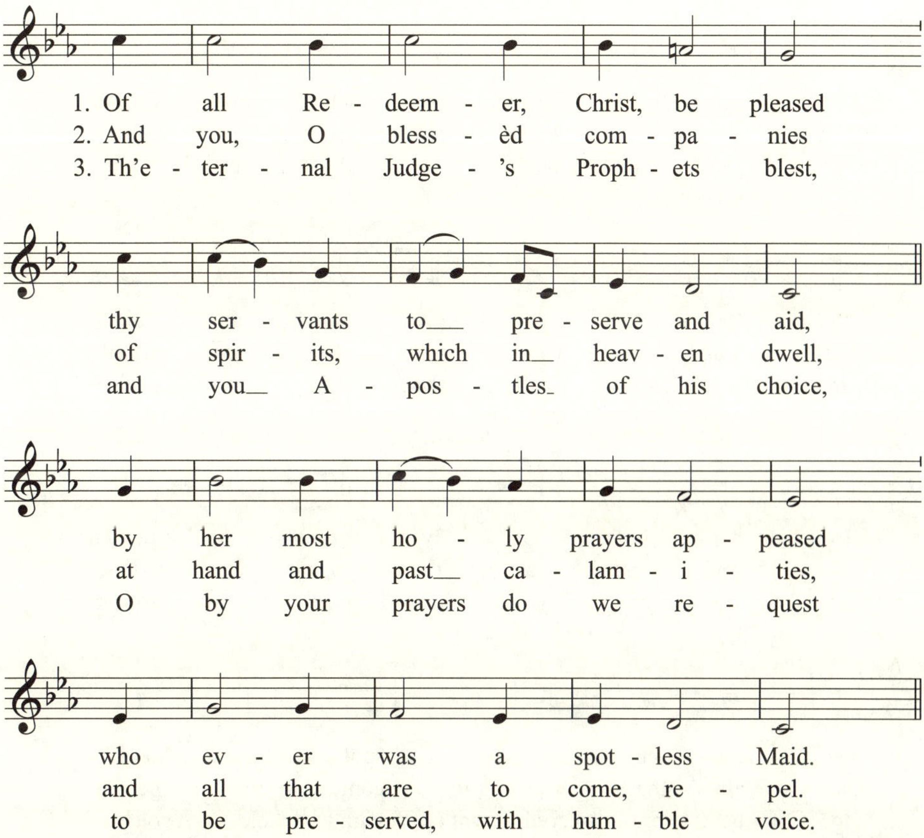

4. You Martyrs, whose renown is great, | of God, our Lord's Confessors bright,
your intercession we entreat | to raise us up to heav'nly light.

5. You holy Virgins' spotless choirs | and Monks that lived in willing pain,
and all you Saints, with joint desires | implore that we with Christ remain.

6. The wicked infidels away | do drive from grounds where faith doth grow,
that we with joy to Christ may pay | those praises which to him we owe.

7. To Father even as to Son, | unsired and sole-begotten, be
with Holy Ghost, all glory done | for ages everlastingly.

Melody: From a 15th century English manuscript.
M. Source: *Hymns, Psalms, and Spiritual Canticles* (Massachusetts: Theodore Marier, 1983) p. 450.
T. Source: *The Primer Containing the Three Offices of the Blessed Virgin Mary in Latin and English ... to the Calendar are annexed many English and Irish Saints* (Rouen, 1684) p. 367.

88 88 (LM)

Tune: Agincourt

170 Christe Redemptor Omnium (9th century)

THIRD TUNE – *Historic Roman Catholic Translation* (1684AD)

4. You Martyrs, whose renown is great, | of God, our Lord's Confessors bright,
your intercession we entreat | to raise us up to heav'nly light.

5. You holy Virgins' spotless choirs | and Monks that lived in willing pain,
and all you Saints, with joint desires | implore that we with Christ remain.

6. The wicked infidels away | do drive from grounds where faith doth grow,
that we with joy to Christ may pay | those praises which to him we owe.

7. To Father even as to Son, | unsired and sole-begotten, be
with Holy Ghost, all glory done | for ages everlastingly.

88 88 (LM)

Tune:
ALTONA

Final Verses: Noel Rawsthorne (2011) #378; one note altered.
T. Source: *The Primer Containing the Three Offices of the Blessed Virgin Mary in Latin and English ... to the Calendar are annexed many English and Irish Saints* (Rouen, 1684) p. 367.
Melody: Schumann's *Geistliche Lieder* (1539); an adaptation by Fr. Stephan Lück (d. 1883) in his hymnal, *Gesang- und Gebetbuch für die Diözese Trier* (1847) p. 19. Called by various names (VOM HIMMEL HOCH, ERFURT, etc.) this melody has been set by such composers as Hassler, Gesius, Praetorius, and Bach.
M. Source: *Hosanna Catholic Hymn Book* (1914) p. 17; *New Westminster Hymnal* (1939) p. 8.

Christe Redemptor Omnium (9th century)

Historic Roman Catholic Translation (1684AD)

Can be sung with any 88 88 meter, such as HILDERSTONE, DUGUET, BRESLAU, MELCOMBE, WAREHAM, OLD HUNDREDTH, MEIN SEEL, TRINITY COLLEGE, etc.

OF all Redeemer, Christ, be pleased
thy servants to preserve and aid,
by her most holy prayers appeased
who ever was a spotless Maid.

2. And you, O blessèd companies
of spirits, which in heaven dwell,
at hand and past calamities,
and all that are to come, repel.

3. Th'eternal Judge's Prophets blest,
and you Apostles of his choice,
O by your prayers do we request
to be preserved, with humble voice.

4. You Martyrs, whose renown is great,
of God, our Lord's Confessors bright,
your intercession we entreat
to raise us up to heav'nly light.

5. You holy Virgins' spotless choirs
and Monks that lived in willing pain,
and all you Saints, with joint desires
implore that we with Christ remain.

6. The wicked infidels away
do drive from grounds where faith doth grow,
that we with joy to Christ may pay
those praises which to him we owe.

7. To Father even as to Son,
unsired and sole-begotten, be
with Holy Ghost, all glory done
for ages everlastingly.

88 88 (LM)

T. Source: *The Primer Containing the Three Offices of the Blessed Virgin Mary in Latin and English ... to the Calendar are annexed many English and Irish Saints* (Rouen, 1684) p. 367.

Tune: VARIOUS

Christe Redemptor Omnium (9th century)

First Tune – *Trns: Bishop Edward G. Bagshawe (d. 1915)*

4. Ye Martyrs, purpled with your blood,
Confessors, all enrobed in white,
do us, in exile here below,
to seek our home on high invite.

5. O choir of Virgins fair and pure,
and ye who from the desert sand
attained the stars, for us obtain
with you a place in heaven's land.

6. Our foe deceitful deign to drive
from faithful dwellings far away,
that we may all, in one true fold,
one lawful Pastor's rule obey.

7. To God the Father glory be,
And to the Father's only Son,
And to the Holy Paraclete,
While everlasting ages run.

88 88 (LM)

Tune:
Eisenach

Final Verses: Richard Lloyd (1993) #64; Noel Rawsthorne (2011) #108.
T. Source: *Breviary Hymns and Missal Sequences* (London: Burns & Oates, 1900) p. 152; Father Bagshawe was a priest of the Oratory of St. Philip Neri until 1874, when he was consecrated bishop of the Catholic diocese of Nottingham.
Melody: Bartholomäus Gesius (d. 1613); adapted by Johann H. Schein (d. 1630).
M. Source: *New Saint Basil Hymnal* (1958) p. 120; *The Catholic Vesper Hymn Book set to Music either for Unison or Four Voices with Accompaniment* (Charles Lewis, 1877) p. 34; *Pope Pius XII Hymnal* (Ohio: Gregorian Institute of America, 1959) p. 13.

Christe Redemptor Omnium (9th century) 173

Second Tune – *Trns: Bishop Edward G. Bagshawe (d. 1915)*

4. Ye Martyrs, purpled with your blood,
Confessors, all enrobed in white,
do us, in exile here below,
to seek our home on high invite.

5. O choir of Virgins fair and pure,
and ye who from the desert sand
attained the stars, for us obtain
with you a place in heaven's land.

6. Our foe deceitful deign to drive
from faithful dwellings far away,
that we may all, in one true fold,
one lawful Pastor's rule obey.

7. To God the Father glory be,
And to the Father's only Son,
And to the Holy Paraclete,
While everlasting ages run.

Final Verses: Richard Lloyd (1993) #133; Noel Rawsthorne (2011) #205.
Melody: Samuel Webbe, the elder (d. 1816).
M. Source: *Veritas Hymnal* (Dublin: Irish Church Music Association, 1974) p. 96; *Cantate Omnes: Hymnal of the Catholic Choirmasters' Guild* (1952) #78.
T. Source: *Breviary Hymns and Missal Sequences* (London: Burns & Oates, 1900) p. 152; Father Bagshawe was a priest of the Oratory of St. Philip Neri until 1874, when he was consecrated bishop of the Catholic diocese of Nottingham.

88 88 (LM)

Tune: Melcombe

Christe Redemptor Omnium (9th century)

Third Tune – *Trns: Bishop Edward G. Bagshawe (d. 1915)*

4. Ye Martyrs, purpled with your blood,
Confessors, all enrobed in white,
do us, in exile here below,
to seek our home on high invite.

5. O choir of Virgins fair and pure,
and ye who from the desert sand
attained the stars, for us obtain
with you a place in heaven's land.

6. Our foe deceitful deign to drive
from faithful dwellings far away,
that we may all, in one true fold,
one lawful Pastor's rule obey.

7. To God the Father glory be,
And to the Father's only Son,
And to the Holy Paraclete,
While everlasting ages run.

88 88 (LM)

Tune:
Mein Seel O Gott

Melody: Michael Praetorius (d. 1621), a German organist and theorist.
M. Source: *New Westminster Hymnal* (1939) p. 205.
T. Source: *Breviary Hymns and Missal Sequences* (London: Burns & Oates, 1900) p. 152; Father Bagshawe was a priest of the Oratory of St. Philip Neri until 1874, when he was consecrated bishop of the Catholic diocese of Nottingham.

Christe Redemptor Omnium (9th century) 175

Fourth Tune – *Trns: Bishop Edward G. Bagshawe (d. 1915)*

4. Ye Martyrs, purpled with your blood,
Confessors, all enrobed in white,
do us, in exile here below,
to seek our home on high invite.

5. O choir of Virgins fair and pure,
and ye who from the desert sand
attained the stars, for us obtain
with you a place in heaven's land.

6. Our foe deceitful deign to drive
from faithful dwellings far away,
that we may all, in one true fold,
one lawful Pastor's rule obey.

7. To God the Father glory be,
And to the Father's only Son,
And to the Holy Paraclete,
While everlasting ages run.

Melody: Johann Sebastian Bach (d. 1750), the greatest composer of the Baroque.
M. Source: *New English Hymnal* (1986) p. 196; first published in Schemelli's *Gesangbuch* (1736).
T. Source: *Breviary Hymns and Missal Sequences* (London: Burns & Oates, 1900) p. 152;
Father Bagshawe was a priest of the Oratory of St. Philip Neri until 1874, when he was consecrated bishop of the Catholic diocese of Nottingham.

88 88 (LM)

Tune: Nürnberg

176 Christe Redemptor Omnium (9th century)

Fifth Tune – *Trns: Bishop Edward G. Bagshawe (d. 1915)*

4. Ye Martyrs, purpled with your blood,
Confessors, all enrobed in white,
do us, in exile here below,
to seek our home on high invite.

5. O choir of Virgins fair and pure,
and ye who from the desert sand
attained the stars, for us obtain
with you a place in heaven's land.

6. Our foe deceitful deign to drive
from faithful dwellings far away,
that we may all, in one true fold,
one lawful Pastor's rule obey.

7. To God the Father glory be,
And to the Father's only Son,
And to the Holy Paraclete,
While everlasting ages run.

88 88 (LM)

Tune:
Wareham

Final Verses: Richard Lloyd (1993) #239; Noel Rawsthorne (2011) #382.
Melody: William Knapp (d. 1768), church organist for the town of Wareham, in Dorset.
M. Source: *Catholic Hymn Book* (London Oratory, 1998) p. 218; *Hymns, Psalms, and Spiritual Canticles* (Massachusetts: Theodore Marier, 1983) p. 488.
T. Source: *Breviary Hymns and Missal Sequences* (London: Burns & Oates, 1900) p. 152; Father Bagshawe was a priest of the Oratory of St. Philip Neri until 1874, when he was consecrated bishop of the Catholic diocese of Nottingham.

Christe Redemptor Omnium (9th century)

Trns: Bishop Edward G. Bagshawe (d. 1915)

Can be sung with any 88 88 meter, such as Hilderstone, Duguet, Breslau, Melcombe, Wareham, Old Hundredth, Mein Seel, Trinity College, etc.

O CHRIST, thy gracious mercy be
to us, thy lowly servants, shown,
for whom a Virgin Patroness
is pleading at thy Father's throne.

2. Ye blessèd hosts in circles nine
of serried row and bright array,
our present harms, as those to come
or past, confront and chase away.

3. Apostles, too, and Prophets, bid
the Judge whom guile would never move
that seeing sinners' contrite tears,
he may to them his pity prove.

4. Ye Martyrs, purpled with your blood,
Confessors, all enrobed in white,
do us, in exile here below,
to seek our home on high invite.

5. O choir of Virgins fair and pure,
and ye who from the desert sand
attained the stars, for us obtain
with you a place in heaven's land.

6. Our foe deceitful deign to drive
from faithful dwellings far away,
that we may all, in one true fold,
one lawful Pastor's rule obey.

7. To God the Father glory be,
And to the Father's only Son,
And to the Holy Paraclete,
While everlasting ages run.

T. Source: *Breviary Hymns and Missal Sequences* (London: Burns & Oates, 1900) p. 152; Father Bagshawe was a priest of the Oratory of St. Philip Neri until 1874, when he was consecrated bishop of the Catholic diocese of Nottingham.

88 88 (LM)

Tune: Various

178 Christe Redemptor Omnium (9th century)

1599AD – Historic Roman Catholic Translation

Can be sung with any 88 88 meter, such as HILDERSTONE, DUGUET, BRESLAU, MELCOMBE, WAREHAM, OLD HUNDREDTH, MEIN SEEL, TRINITY COLLEGE, etc.

O CHRIST redeemer of us all,
Thy servants' safeties now provide:
Since of the Virgin ever-blest,
The prayers thee have pacified.

Christe, Redémptor ómnium,
Consérva tuos fámulos,
Beátae semper Vírginis
Placátus sanctis précibus.

2. And you the blessèd companies
Of Sp'rits celestial, we do pray:
All ill, past, present and to come,
From us vouchsafe to put away.

Beáta quoque ágmina
Caeléstium spiríttuum,
Praetérita, praeséntia,
Futúra mala péllite.

3. Ye Prophets of th'eternal judge,
And all our Lord's Apostles true,
By your good prayers to be safe
We intercession make to you.

Vates aetérni Júdicis
Apostolíque Dómini,
Supplíciter expóscimus,
Salvári vestris précibus.

4. Of God ye famous martyrs all,
And ye confessors shining bright:
By your good prayers us vouchsafe
To bring unto the heav'nly light.

Mártyres Dei íncliti,
Confessorésque lúcidi,
Vestris orationibus
Nos ferte in caeléstibus.

5. Ye choirs of holy virgins all,
And ye that solitude retain,
Make us with all the blessèd saints,
In fellowship with Christ to reign.

Chori sanctárum Vírginum
Monachorúmque ómnium,
Simul cum Sanctis ómnibus
Consórtes Christi fácite.

6. The false expel and put away,
From bounds of faithful men and true,
That with alacrity of heart,
We may to Christ yield praises due.

Gentem auférte pérfidam
Credéntium de fínibus,
Ut Christo laudes débitas
Persolvámus alácriter.

7. Unto the father unbegot,
And to his sole-begotten son,
Together with the holy ghost,
All glory endlessly be done.

Glória Patr*i* ingénito,
Ejúsque Unigénito,
Una cum Sancto Spíritu,
In sempitérna saécula.

88 88 (LM)

Tune: VARIOUS

T. Source: *Primer, or, Office of the Blessed Virgin Marie in Latin and English, according to the reformed Latin, and with Lyke Graces Privileged* (Antwerp, 1599) p. 19. The Catholic Encyclopedia of 1912 attributes the hymn translations to the book's editor, Richard Verstegan (d. 1636), a Catholic publisher. In the 1599 Preface, Verstegan says: "Notwithstanding the difficulty, these hymns have been so turned into English meter that they may be sung unto the same tunes in English that they bear in Latin." However, his accentual treatment is sometimes peculiar.

Christe Redemptor Omnium (Urbanite)

1687AD – Historic Roman Catholic Translation

Can be sung with any 88 88 meter, such as EISENACH, ROGERS PARK, BRESSANI, LA ROCHELLE, KEMPEN, BESSEMER, TALLIS CANON, WINCHESTER NEW, etc.

Placáre Christe sérvulis,
Quibus Patris cleméntiam,
Tu*ae* ad Tribúnal grátiae,
Patróna Virgo póstulat.

Et vos beáta per novem
Distíncta gyros ágmina,
Antíqua cum praeséntibus,
Futúra damna péllite.

Apóstoli cum Vátibus,
Apud sevérum Júdicem,
Veris reórum flétibus
Expóscit*e* indulgéntiam.

Vos purpuráti Mártyres,
Vos candidáti praémio
Confessiónis, éxsules
Vocáte nos in pátriam.

Choréa casta Vírginum,
Et quos erémus íncolas
Transmísit astris, caélitum
Locáte nos in sédibus.

Auférte gentem pérfidam
Credéntium de fínibus,
Ut unus omnes únicum
Ovíle nos pastor regat.

Deo Patri sit glória,
Natóque Patris único,
Sancto simul Paráclito,
In sempitérna saécula.

FORGIVE us, Christ, our faults, for whom
Thy Virgin-Mother is become
An Advocate, and sues to thee,
And to thy Father's clemency.

2. Next Her, O you Nine Sacred Choirs
Of Angels, favor our desires:
Past ills blot out, present destroy,
And let no future harm annoy.

3. You Prophets and Apostles, move
Th'offended Judge enthroned above,
That criminals' unfeignèd tears
May quit the score of sin's arrears.

4. Martyrs, who Royal Purple wear,
And you, who do in White appear,
Blest Confessors: obtain that we
With you in Heav'n may ever be.

5. Chaste Choir of Virgin Saints, and you
Whose souls to Heav'n from Deserts flew:
Let th'holy Gates of Paradise
Be open'd for us by your cries.

6. Drive wicked Infidels away
From faithful Realms, that so there may
O'er all, united in one Fold,
One Pastor jurisdiction hold.

7. Be Glory giv'n and Honor done,
To God the Father, and the Son,
And to the Holy Ghost on high,
From age to age eternally.

T. Source: *The Office of the B. V. Mary in English; To which is added the Vespers, in Latin and English; As it is Sung in the Catholic Church upon all Sundays and principal Holydays throughout the whole Year; With the Compline, Rosary, Hymn and Prayers that are sung at the Benediction of the B. Sacrament* (London: Henry Hills, 1687) p. 189.

88 88 (LM)

Tune: VARIOUS

180 Conditor Alme Siderum (7th century)

This hymn speaks of Christ as the Light of the World

To sing in Latin,
use any 88 88 (LM) tune.

CÓNDITOR alme síderum,
Aetérna lux credéntium,
Christe Redémptor ómnium,
Exáudi preces súpplicum.

2. Qui cóndolens intéritu
Mortis períre saéculum,
Salvásti mundum lánguidum,
Donans reis remédium:

3. Vergénte mundi véspere,
Uti sponsus de thálamo,
Egréssus honestíssima
Vírginis matris cláusula:

4. Cujus forti poténtiae
Genu curvántur ómnia,
Caeléstia, terréstria,
Nutu faténtur súbdita.

5. Te deprecámur, ágie,
Ventúre judex saéculi,
Consérva nos in témpore,
Hostis a telo pérfidi.

6. Laus, honor, virtus, glória
Deo Patri, et Filio,
Sancto simul Paráclito,
In saeculórum saécula.

88 88 (LM)

Tune:
VARIOUS

T. Source: *Hymni de Tempore et de Sanctis in Textu Antiquo et Novo* (Solesmes, 1885) p. 26.

The Advent hymns were greatly altered by the reform of Pope Urban VIII in 1631; for *Cónditor alme síderum*, only twelve words of the original hymn survived. Moreover, the change to *Creátor*—where the tonic accent is on the penult—does not make the hymn more "correct" or "classical" from the standpoint of poetry. Most ancient Latin hymns are *quantitative* (based on long and short syllables), although as the centuries elapsed, poets began to favor *qualitative* composition (based on stress-accent). Length is independent of stress-accent; the word *Páter*, for example, has the tonic accent on the "a," but that syllable is short. Not just the style was altered in 1631; consider the second verse as revised by Pope Urban: "Thou wert impelled by the power of love to become a remedy for the languid world, lest mankind should perish through the cunning of the devil."

For hundreds of years, ecclesiastical books have included accent marks, and the Church's wisdom is strikingly illustrated by this hymn, since *Cónditor* means "maker" whereas *Conditor* means "pickler."

Assistance for comprehension

O BOUNTEOUS Founder of the stars,
everlasting light of believers,
O Christ, Ransomer of all,
hear the prayers of thine entreaters:

2. Who, sorrowing that the world
should dissolve through the havoc of death,
didst save the fainting earth,
granting redress to the guilty:

3. Who, when the world's evening befell,
came forth, like a bridegroom from his chamber,
from the most honorable enclosure
of thy Maiden Mother:

4. To whose strong might
all things kneel, both heavenly and earthly,
and confess themselves to be
mastered by thy will:

5. Thee we beseech, Holy one,
the world's Judge to come,
keep us safe in time
from the dart of the wicked foe.

6. Praise, honor, power and glory
to God the Father and to the Son,
likewise to the holy Paraclete
for ever and ever.

[1a] *Conditor*. The external works of the Blessed Trinity are in common. Hence, the act of creation may be ascribed to Christ. "All things were made by Him, and without Him was made nothing that was made" (Jn 1.3); cf. also *Auctor beate saeculi,* first verse: "O Blessed Creator of the world, Christ, the Redeemer of all, Light of the Father's Light, and true God of God."

[1b] Christ is the "light that never faileth." Cf. Ecclus 24.6; Jn 1.9; Jn 8.12.

[1c] "Christ Jesus, who gave Himself a redemption for all" (I Tim 2.6).

[2b] *Mortis*. The ruin of spiritual death consequent upon original sin; "except the tree which brings knowledge of good and evil; if ever thou eatest of this, thy doom is death." (Gn 2.17).

[3b] "He hath set his tabernacle in the sun: and He, as a bridegroom coming out of His bride chamber, exults like some great runner who sees the track before Him" (Ps 18.6).

[4b] "Every knee shall be bowed to Me" (Is. 45.24); cf. Phil 2.10 and I Cor 15.27.

[5a] *Hagios* is from Greek, and this is the only time it is used in a Breviary hymn. "The Gentiles shall know that I am the Lord, the Holy One of Israel" (Ezech 39.7).

[5c] *Tempore* is simply "the time of the present life."

[5d] "Dart," cf. Eph 6.16. The translation by Monsignor Knox was altered for ease of singing; nevertheless, his original rendering is truly ingenious in its literalness:

Holiest of holy ones, from whom
Eternity receives its doom,
In this brief world of time, we pray,
Keep Satan's treach'rous darts at bay.

182 Conditor Alme Siderum (7th century)

First Tune – *Trns: Msgr. Ronald A. Knox (d. 1957)*

4. Such is Thy glory in its might
That, when Thy name in heaven's height
Is heard, or down in hell, to Thee
All bend alike on trembling knee.

5. O Christ, who at the latter day
Shalt be our Judge, we humbly pray,
Such arms of heav'nly grace to send,
As from our foes may us defend.

6. To God the Father, God the Son,
And God the Spirit, Three in One,
Laud, honor, might, and glory be
From age to age eternally.

N.B. This melody is excellent for use during Advent.

88 88 (LM)

Tune:
Creator Alme

T. Source: *New Westminster Hymnal* (1939) p. 1; with alterations.
Plainsong Melody: Cf. Abbot Joseph Pothier's *Liber Antiphonarius pro Vesperis et Completorio Officii Romani* (Solesmes, 1891) p. 57; cf. metrical adaptation by Fr. Stephan Lück (d. 1883) in his hymnal, *Gesang- und Gebetbuch für die Diözese Trier* (1847) p. 13.
M. Source: *Parochial Hymnal* (Rev. Carlo Rossini, 1951) p. 4; *New English Hymnal* (1986) p. 2.

Conditor Alme Siderum (7th century) 183

SECOND TUNE – *Trns: Msgr. Ronald A. Knox (d. 1957)*

4. Such is Thy glory in its might
That, when Thy name in heaven's height
Is heard, or down in hell, to Thee
All bend alike on trembling knee.

5. O Christ, who at the latter day
Shalt be our Judge, we humbly pray,
Such arms of heav'nly grace to send,
As from our foes may us defend.

6. To God the Father, God the Son,
And God the Spirit, Three in One,
Laud, honor, might, and glory be
From age to age eternally.

88 88 (LM)

Melody: Henry Lawes (d. 1662).
M. Source: *Saint Edmund Campion Missal and Hymnal* (2013) p. 888.
T. Source: *New Westminster Hymnal* (1939) p. 1; with alterations.

Tune: WHITEHALL

184 Conditor Alme Siderum (7th century)

THIRD TUNE – *Trns: Msgr. Ronald A. Knox (d. 1957)*

4. Such is Thy glory in its might
That, when Thy name in heaven's height
Is heard, or down in hell, to Thee
All bend alike on trembling knee.

5. O Christ, who at the latter day
Shalt be our Judge, we humbly pray,
Such arms of heav'nly grace to send,
As from our foes may us defend.

6. To God the Father, God the Son,
And God the Spirit, Three in One,
Laud, honor, might, and glory be
From age to age eternally.

88 88 (LM)

Tune:
JESU DULCIS MEMORIA

T. Source: *New Westminster Hymnal* (1939) p. 1; with alterations.
PLAINSONG MELODY: *Mass and Vespers with Gregorian Chant* (Paris: Solesmes, 1957) p. 271.
M. Source: *Hymns, Psalms, and Spiritual Canticles* (Massachusetts: Theodore Marier, 1983) p. 367.

Conditor Alme Siderum (7th century)

Fourth Tune – *Trns: Msgr. Ronald A. Knox (d. 1957)*

4. Such is Thy glory in its might
That, when Thy name in heaven's height
Is heard, or down in hell, to Thee
All bend alike on trembling knee.

5. O Christ, who at the latter day
Shalt be our Judge, we humbly pray,
Such arms of heav'nly grace to send,
As from our foes may us defend.

6. To God the Father, God the Son,
And God the Spirit, Three in One,
Laud, honor, might, and glory be
From age to age eternally.

* This melody at a lower key is on page 248.

T. Source: *New Westminster Hymnal* (1939) p. 1; with alterations.
M. Source: Cento from *The Parochial Hymn Book, Words and Melodies; containing Vespers, Compline, and all the Liturgical Hymns for the Year both in Latin and English* (London, 1883), edited by Fr. Anatole Police; Imprimatur by Henry Edward Cardinal Manning (d. 1892), who in 1851 converted from Anglicanism and was appointed Archbishop of Westminster in 1865.

88 88 (LM)

Tune: Ioannes

186 Conditor Alme Siderum (7th century)

Fifth Tune – *Trns: Msgr. Ronald A. Knox (d. 1957)*

4. Such is Thy glory in its might
That, when Thy name in heaven's height
Is heard, or down in hell, to Thee
All bend alike on trembling knee.

5. O Christ, who at the latter day
Shalt be our Judge, we humbly pray,
Such arms of heav'nly grace to send,
As from our foes may us defend.

6. To God the Father, God the Son,
And God the Spirit, Three in One,
Laud, honor, might, and glory be
From age to age eternally.

88 88 (LM)

Tune:
Kempen

Melody: Flor Peeters (d. 1986), organist at the Catholic Cathedral of Mechelen, Belgium, was made a Baron by King Baudouin.
M. Source: *People's Mass Book* (Omer Westendorf, 1964) p. 218.
T. Source: *New Westminster Hymnal* (1939) p. 1; with alterations.

Conditor Alme Siderum (7th century) 187

Sixth Tune – *Trns: Msgr. Ronald A. Knox (d. 1957)*

4. Such is Thy glory in its might
That, when Thy name in heaven's height
Is heard, or down in hell, to Thee
All bend alike on trembling knee.

5. O Christ, who at the latter day
Shalt be our Judge, we humbly pray,
Such arms of heav'nly grace to send,
As from our foes may us defend.

6. To God the Father, God the Son,
And God the Spirit, Three in One,
Laud, honor, might, and glory be
From age to age eternally.

Melody: James W. Elliott (d. 1915)
M. Source: *Hymns Ancient and Modern* (1972) p. 320.
T. Source: *New Westminster Hymnal* (1939) p. 1; with alterations.

88 88 (LM)

Tune:
La Rochelle

Conditor Alme Siderum (7th century)

Seventh Tune – *Trns: Msgr. Ronald A. Knox (d. 1957)*

4. Such is Thy glory in its might
That, when Thy name in heaven's height
Is heard, or down in hell, to Thee
All bend alike on trembling knee.

5. O Christ, who at the latter day
Shalt be our Judge, we humbly pray,
Such arms of heav'nly grace to send,
As from our foes may us defend.

6. To God the Father, God the Son,
And God the Spirit, Three in One,
Laud, honor, might, and glory be
From age to age eternally.

N.B. This melody is excellent for use during Advent.

88 88 (LM)

Tune:
O Heiland Reiss

T. Source: *New Westminster Hymnal* (1939) p. 1; with alterations.
Melody: *Rheinfelsisches Deutsches Catholisches Gesangbuch* (1666).
M. Source: *Gotteslob; Katholisches Gebet- und Gesangbuch Ausgabe für das Bistum Trier* (1975) p. 186; *The Parish Hymnal* (Sister Catherine Cecilia, 1957) p. 1; *Pope Pius XII Hymnal* (Ohio: Gregorian Institute of America, 1959) p. 10.

Conditor Alme Siderum (7th century)

Trns: Msgr. Ronald A. Knox (d. 1957)

Can be sung with any 88 88 meter, such as EISENACH, ROGERS PARK, BRESSANI, LA ROCHELLE, KEMPEN, BESSEMER, TALLIS CANON, WINCHESTER NEW, etc.

CREATOR of the starry height,
The faithful's everlasting light,
O Christ, Redeemer of mankind,
Our humble prayers vouchsafe to mind.

2. Thy love that pitied from on high
A guilty race foredoomed to die,
Was pleased that sentence to repeal,
Those failing energies to heal.

3. So, at the eventide of earth,
From that bridechamber of Thy birth
Our mortal flesh Thou didst assume,
Born of a spotless Virgin's womb.

4. Such is Thy glory in its might
That, when Thy name in heaven's height
Is heard, or down in hell, to Thee
All bend alike on trembling knee.

5. O Christ, who at the latter day
Shalt be our Judge, we humbly pray,
Such arms of heav'nly grace to send,
As from our foes may us defend.

6. To God the Father, God the Son,
And God the Spirit, Three in One,
Laud, honor, might, and glory be
From age to age eternally.

88 88 (LM)

Tune: VARIOUS

T. Source: *New Westminster Hymnal* (1939) p. 1; with alterations.

190 Conditor Alme Siderum (7th century)

First Tune – *Trns: Robert Campbell of Skerrington (d. 1868)*

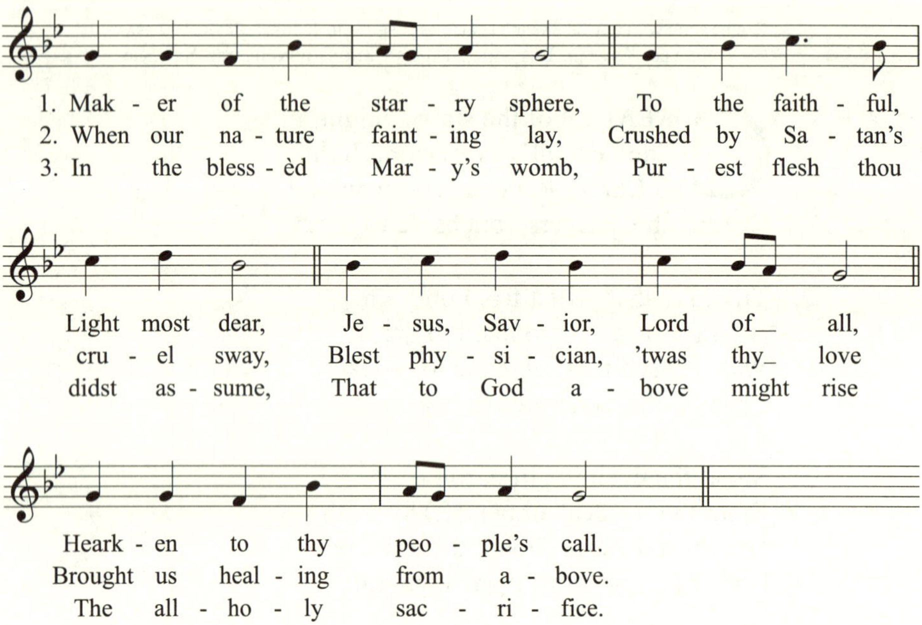

4. Unto heav'n exalted now,
At thy sacred name shall bow
All that on the earth do dwell,
All in heaven, all in hell.

5. Thou, who on the judgment-day
Our most secret thoughts shall weigh,
Shield us now with pitying care,
Guard us from temptation's snare.

6. Honor, glory, love and praise,
Be through never-ending days,
To the Father and the Son
And the Spirit, Three in One.

N.B. This melody is excellent for use during Advent.

77 77

Tune:
Nun Komm Der Heiden Heiland

T. Source: Orby Shipley's *Annus Sanctus: Hymns of the Church for the Ecclesiastical Year; Translated from the Sacred Offices by various Authors, with Modern, Original, and other Hymns, and an Appendix of Earlier Versions* (London: Burns and Oates, 1884) p. 13.
English Translation: Robert Campbell (d. 1868), who converted to the Catholic Church in 1852.
Melody: Based on "Veni Redemptor Gentium"; for plainsong score, cf. *Liber Hymnarius* (Solesmes: Saint Peter's Abbey, 1983) p. 11.
M. Source: *New Westminster Hymnal* (1939) p. 146; *Catholic Hymn Book* (1998) p. 278; *Summit Choirbook* (Dominican Monastery of Our Lady of the Rosary, 1983) #25; *Saint Andrew Hymnal, authorized by the Bishops of Scotland for use in the Scottish Dioceses* (1964) p. 203.

Conditor Alme Siderum (7th century) 191

Second Tune – *Trns: Robert Campbell of Skerrington (d. 1868)*

4. Unto heav'n exalted now,
At thy sacred name shall bow
All that on the earth do dwell,
All in heaven, all in hell.

5. Thou, who on the judgment-day
Our most secret thoughts shall weigh,
Shield us now with pitying care,
Guard us from temptation's snare.

6. Honor, glory, love and praise,
Be through never-ending days,
To the Father and the Son
And the Spirit, Three in One.

Final Verses: Richard Lloyd (1993) #142; Noel Rawsthorne (2011) #216.
Melody: Johann A. Freylinghausen (d. 1739); adapted by John B. Wilkes (d. 1869), organist at the Monkland church, near Leominster.
M. Source: *Catholic Hymn Book* (London Oratory, 1998) p. 412.
T. Source: Orby Shipley's *Annus Sanctus: Hymns of the Church for the Ecclesiastical Year; Translated from the Sacred Offices by various Authors, with Modern, Original, and other Hymns, and an Appendix of Earlier Versions* (London: Burns and Oates, 1884) p. 13.
English Translation: Robert Campbell (d. 1868), who converted to the Catholic Church in 1852.

77 77
Tune: Monkland

192 Conditor Alme Siderum (7th century)

Third Tune – *Trns: Robert Campbell of Skerrington (d. 1868)*

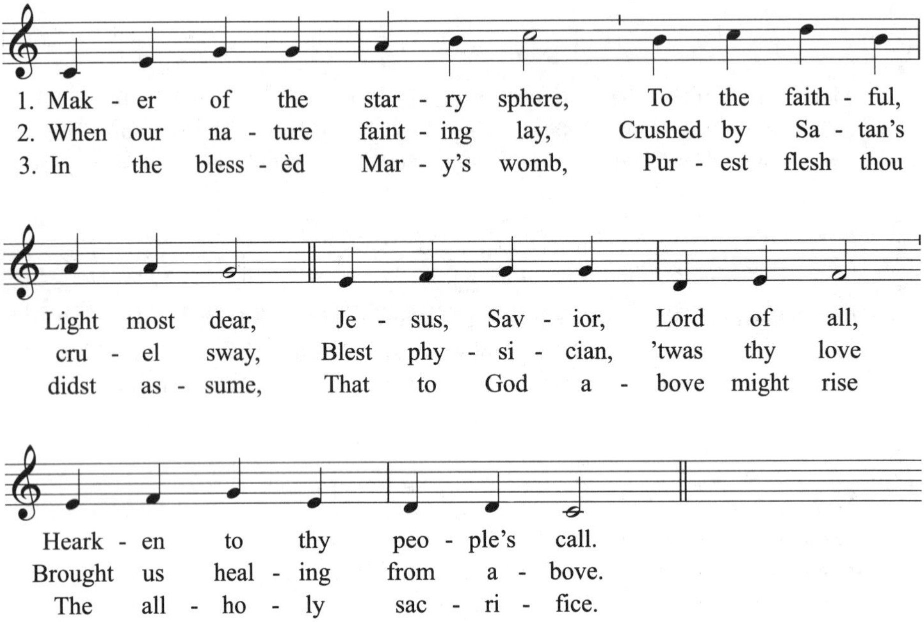

4. Unto heav'n exalted now,
At thy sacred name shall bow
All that on the earth do dwell,
All in heaven, all in hell.

5. Thou, who on the judgment-day
Our most secret thoughts shall weigh,
Shield us now with pitying care,
Guard us from temptation's snare.

6. Honor, glory, love and praise,
Be through never-ending days,
To the Father and the Son
And the Spirit, Three in One.

77 77

Tune:
Gott Sei Dank

Final Verses: Richard Lloyd (1993) #83; Noel Rawsthorne (2011) #192.
T. Source: Orby Shipley's *Annus Sanctus: Hymns of the Church for the Ecclesiastical Year; Translated from the Sacred Offices by various Authors, with Modern, Original, and other Hymns, and an Appendix of Earlier Versions* (London: Burns and Oates, 1884) p. 13.
English Translation: Robert Campbell (d. 1868), who converted to the Catholic Church in 1852.
Melody: Adapted by Johann Anastasius Freylinghausen (d. 1739) in his *Geist-reiches Gesang-Buch, den Kern alter und neuer Lieder* (Halle, 1704); also called Lübeck.
M. Source: *New Westminster Hymnal* (1939) p. 249; *New Saint Basil Hymnal* (1958) p. 229.

Conditor Alme Siderum (7th century)

Fourth Tune – *Trns: Robert Campbell of Skerrington (d. 1868)*

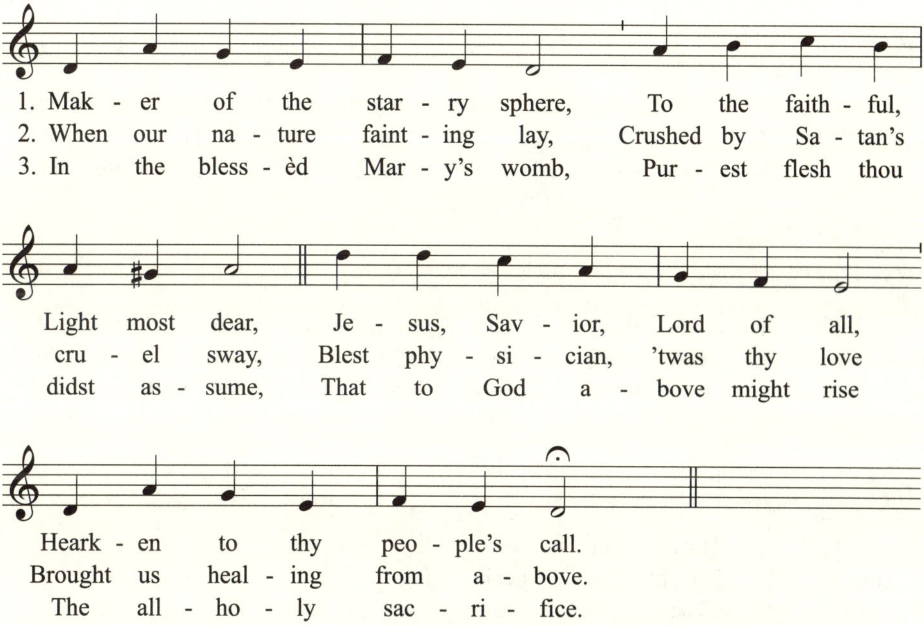

4. Unto heav'n exalted now,
At thy sacred name shall bow
All that on the earth do dwell,
All in heaven, all in hell.

5. Thou, who on the judgment-day
Our most secret thoughts shall weigh,
Shield us now with pitying care,
Guard us from temptation's snare.

6. Honor, glory, love and praise,
Be through never-ending days,
To the Father and the Son
And the Spirit, Three in One.

T. Source: Orby Shipley's *Annus Sanctus: Hymns of the Church for the Ecclesiastical Year; Translated from the Sacred Offices by various Authors, with Modern, Original, and other Hymns, and an Appendix of Earlier Versions* (London: Burns and Oates, 1884) p. 13.
English Translation: Robert Campbell (d. 1868), who converted to the Catholic Church in 1852.
Melody: *Kirchengeseng* (Böhmische Brüder, 1566).
M. Source: *Songs of Syon* (Woodward, 1910) p. 125.

77 77
Tune:
Als Christus Mit Seiner Lehr

194 Conditor Alme Siderum (7th century)

Fifth Tune – *Trns: Robert Campbell of Skerrington (d. 1868)*

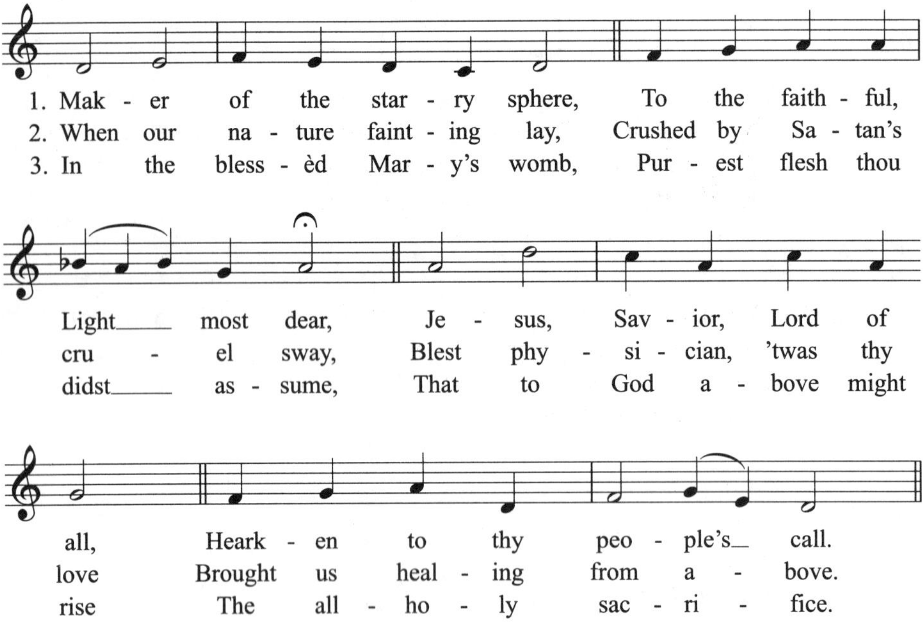

4. Unto heav'n exalted now,
At thy sacred name shall bow
All that on the earth do dwell,
All in heaven, all in hell.

5. Thou, who on the judgment-day
Our most secret thoughts shall weigh,
Shield us now with pitying care,
Guard us from temptation's snare.

6. Honor, glory, love and praise,
Be through never-ending days,
To the Father and the Son
And the Spirit, Three in One.

77 77

Tune:
Freuen Wir Uns All In Ein

T. Source: Orby Shipley's *Annus Sanctus: Hymns of the Church for the Ecclesiastical Year; Translated from the Sacred Offices by various Authors, with Modern, Original, and other Hymns, and an Appendix of Earlier Versions* (London: Burns and Oates, 1884) p. 13.
English Translation: Robert Campbell (d. 1868), who converted to the Catholic Church in 1852.
Melody: Bohemian melody adapted by Michael Weisse (d. 1534).
M. Source: *Songs of Syon* (Woodward, 1910) p. 459.

Conditor Alme Siderum (7th century) 195

Trns: Robert Campbell of Skerrington (d. 1868)

Can be sung with any 77 77 meter, such as SAVANNAH, UNIVERSITY COLLEGE, ORIENTIS PARTIBUS, LLANFAIR, CULBACH, MONKLAND, GOTT SEI DANK, etc.

MAKER of the starry sphere,
To the faithful, Light most dear,
Jesus, Savior, Lord of all,
Hearken to thy people's call.

2. When our nature fainting lay,
Crushed by Satan's cruel sway,
Blest physician, 'twas thy love
Brought us healing from above.

3. In the blessèd Mary's womb,
Purest flesh thou didst assume,
That to God above might rise
The all-holy sacrifice.

4. Unto heav'n exalted now,
At thy sacred name shall bow
All that on the earth do dwell,
All in heaven, all in hell.

5. Thou, who on the judgment-day
Our most secret thoughts shall weigh,
Shield us now with pitying care,
Guard us from temptation's snare.

6. Honor, glory, love and praise,
Be through never-ending days,
To the Father and the Son
And the Spirit, Three in One.

T. Source: Orby Shipley's *Annus Sanctus: Hymns of the Church for the Ecclesiastical Year; Translated from the Sacred Offices by various Authors, with Modern, Original, and other Hymns, and an Appendix of Earlier Versions* (London: Burns and Oates, 1884) p. 13.
ENGLISH TRANSLATION: Robert Campbell (d. 1868), who converted to the Catholic Church in 1852.

77 77
Tune:
VARIOUS

196 Conditor Alme Siderum (7th century)

1684AD – Historic Roman Catholic Translation

Can be sung with any 88 88 meter, such as HILDERSTONE, DUGUET, BRESLAU, MELCOMBE, WAREHAM, OLD HUNDREDTH, MEIN SEEL, TRINITY COLLEGE, etc.

BENIGN Creator of the stars,
Eternal light of faithful eyes,
Christ whose Redemption none debars,
Do not our humble prayers despise.

Cónditor alme síderum,
Aetérna lux credéntium,
Christe Redémptor ómnium,
Exáudi preces súpplicum.

2. Who for the state of man-kind grieved,
That it by death destroy'd should be,
Hast the diseasèd world relieved,
And giv'n the guilty remedy.

Qui cóndolens intéritu
Mortis períre saéculum,
Salvásti mundum lánguidum,
Donans reis remédium:

3. When th' evening of the world drew near,
Thou as a bridegroom deign'dst to come
Out of thy wedding chamber dear,
Thy virgin mother's purest womb.

Vergénte mundi véspere,
Uti sponsus de thálamo,
Egréssus honestíssima
Vírginis matris cláusula:

4. To the strong force of whose high reign,
All knees are bow'd with gesture low:
Creatures which earth or heav'n contain
With reverence their subjection show.

Cujus forti poténtiae
Genu curvántur ómnia,
Caeléstia, terréstria,
Nutu faténtur súbdita.

5. O holy Lord we thee desire,
Whom we expect to judge all faults,
Preserve us as the times require,
From our deceitful foe's assaults.

Te deprecámur, ágie,
Ventúre judex saéculi,
Consérva nos in témpore,
Hostis a telo pérfidi.

6. Praise, honor, strength and glory great,
To God the Father and the Son,
And to the holy Paraclete,
Whilst time lasts, and when time is done.

Laus, honor, virtus, glória
Deo Patri, et Filio,
Sancto simul Paráclito,
In saeculórum saécula.

88 88 (LM)

Tune:
VARIOUS

T. Source: *The Primer, More ample, and in a new Order, containing The Three Offices of the B. Virgin Mary, In Latin and English, And all Offices and Dévotions, which were in former primers. In this last Edition the Hymns are in a better version and six Offices newly added: 1. Of the holy Trinity; 2. Of the B. Sacrament; 3. Of the holy name of Jesus, with a Letany; 4. Of the Immaculate Conception of our B. Lady, with a Letany; 5. Of the Angel-Guardian; 6. Of S. Joseph, and Sundry sweet Dévotions, and Instructions taken out of the holy Scripture for to live a devout Christian life. A large and short examen of conscience. To the calendar are annexed many English and Irish Saints.* (Rouen: Thomas Fitz Simon, 1684) p. 347.

Conditor Alme Siderum (Urbanite)

1687AD – Historic Roman Catholic Translation

Can be sung with any 88 88 meter, such as EISENACH, ROGERS PARK, BRESSANI, LA ROCHELLE, KEMPEN, BESSEMER, TALLIS CANON, WINCHESTER NEW, etc.

Creátor alme síderum,
Aetérna lux credéntium,
Jesu Redémptor ómnium,
Inténde votis súpplicum:

MAKER of Heav'n, whose love imparts
Eternal light to faithful Hearts!
Jesus, the World's Deliverer,
In mercy to our Pray'rs give ear.

Qui daémonis ne fráudibus
Períret orbis, ímpetu
Amóris actus, lánguidi
Mundi medéla factus es.

2. O God, who, lest the powers of Death
Should rob us of our vital breath,
Compell'd by love to ruin'd Man;
Becam'st the World's Physician.

Commúne qui mundi nefas
Ut expiáres, ad Crucem
E Vírginis sacrário
Intácta prodis víctima.

3. Who from the Virgin's Womb didst pass
A spotless Victim to the Cross,
That there thou might'st our Ransom pay
And wash the stains of sin away.

Cujus potéstas glóriae,
Noménque cum primum sonat;
Et Coélites et ínferi
Treménte curvántur genu.

4. Such is thy Greatness, that thy Name
No sooner any voice can frame,
But all in Heav'n, in Earth, or Sea,
And ev'n in Hell, must bow the Knee.

Te deprecámur últimae
Magnum diéi Júdicem,
Armis supérnae grátiae
Defénde nos ab hóstibus.

5. O Christ, who at the last great Day
Shalt be our Judge, we humbly pray,
That now thou would'st that armor send,
As from our foes may us defend.

Virtus, honor, laus, glória
Deo Patri cum Fílio,
Sancto simul Paráclito,
In saeculórum saécula.

6. Be glory giv'n, and honor done,
To God the Father, and the Son,
And to the Holy Ghost on high,
From Age to Age, eternally.

T. Source: *The Office of the B. V. Mary in English; To which is added the Vespers, in Latin and English; As it is Sung in the Catholic Church upon all Sundays and principal Holydays throughout the whole Year; With the Compline, Rosary, Hymn and Prayers that are sung at the Benediction of the B. Sacrament* (London: Henry Hills, 1687) p. 133.

88 88 (LM)

Tune: VARIOUS

198 Die Parente Temporum (1745 AD)

Sunday Hymn from a French Breviary

To sing in Latin,
use any 88 88 (LM) tune.

DIE paránte témporum, *n1*
Quo, numen extra próferens,
Rerum Pater, fons ómnium,
Verbo fit orbis ártifex:

2. Quo, morte victa, Fílius
Se de sepúlchro súscitat,
Donísque mentes ígneis
Fecúndat almus Spíritus:

3. Adsit refúsa córdibus,
Qua ferveámus, cáritas,
Qua praedicémus, débitis
Vitae datórem cántibus.

4. Qui me suprémi Núminis,
Pater, creas imáginem,
Te mente tota cógitem,
Et corde toto díligam.

5. Tui simul fac fúneris,
Novaéque vitae párticeps,
Fili; tibi jam cónsecrer
Amóris igne víctima.

6. Auctor sacrórum múnerum,
Et ipse munus sánctius,
Sis fax perénnis, flámmeo
Qua te requíram péctore.

7. Tibi, Deus cordis mei,
Quem déprecor ter óptimum,
Totum modo me dévovens,
Totis amo te víribus.

8. Qui nos creávit, laus Patri;
Laus, qui redémit, Fílio;
Qui caritáte nos foves,
Sit par tibi laus, Spíritus.

88 88 (LM)

Tune:
VARIOUS

This hymn, which appeared in French local breviaries in the eighteenth century, is for use on Sundays (the "Lord's day"). It recalls the beginning of Creation, the Resurrection (beginning the "new creation"), and Pentecost—all of which occurred on Sunday. After a prayer for personal charity, the hymn addresses each person of the Holy Trinity, followed by an act of charity and final doxology. The version given here was printed in 1745 for the diocese of Carcassonne.

Assistance in comprehension

ON the day, originator of times, *n1*
on which, his will bringing forth outwardly,
the Father of things, spring of all,
becomes crafter of the earth:

2. On which, death overcome, the Son
rouses himself from the tomb,
and with fiery gifts the bounteous Spirit
makes minds fruitful:

3. In our hearts be found poured forth
the charity with which we should burn,
with which we should preach
the giver of life with due songs.

4. O Father, who createst me
an image of thy sovereign Deity,
with all my mind let me think thee,
and with all my heart let me love thee.

5. Even so make me partaker
of thy death and new life,
O Son; now let me be hallowed
a victim to thee through the fire of love.

6. O source of sacred gifts,
and thyself the gift most holy,
be thou a perpetual torch by which
I may seek thee with heart enflamed.

7. To thee, God of my heart,
thrice best, whom I beseech,
now vowing myself entirely,
with all my might do I love thee.

8. Praise to the Father, who created us;
praise to the Son, who redeemed us;
equal praise be to thee, O Spirit,
who dost foster us with thy charity.

[1] Sunday is the *parens temporum*, or "originator of times": the first day was the beginning of times and seasons.

200 Die Parente Temporum (1745 AD)

First Tune – *Trns: Henry Williams Baker (d. 1877)*

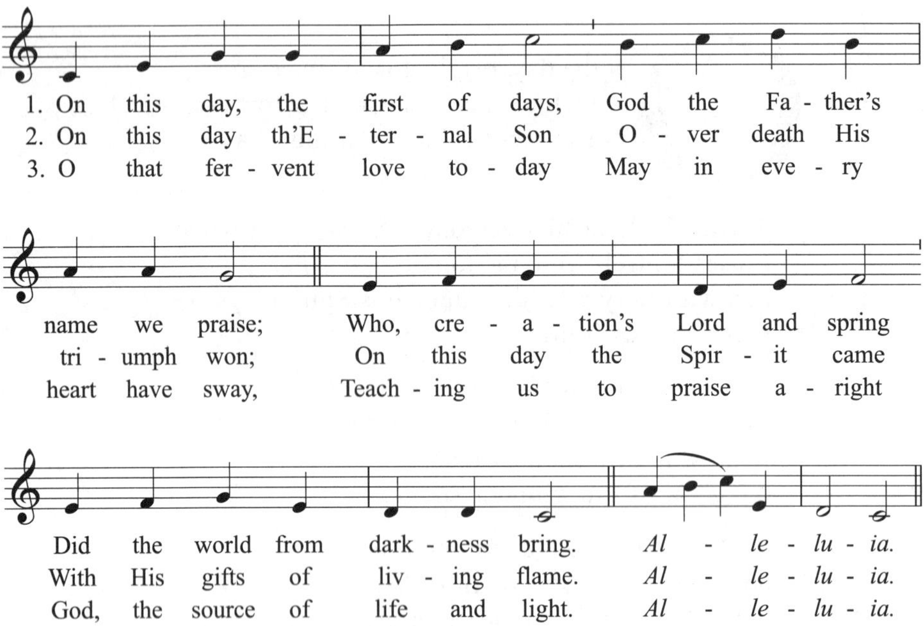

4. Father, who didst fashion me
Image of Thyself to be,
Fill me with Thy love divine,
Let my ev'ry thought be Thine.
Alleluia.

5. Holy Jesus, may I be
Dead and buried here with Thee;
And, by love inflamed, arise
Unto Thee a sacrifice.
Alleluia.

6. Thou, who dost all gifts impart,
Shine, sweet Spirit, in my heart;
Best of gifts Thyself bestow;
Make me burn Thy love to know.
Alleluia.

7. God, the blessèd Three in One,
Dwell within my heart alone;
Thou dost give Thyself to me;
May I give myself to Thee.
Alleluia.

8. Equal praise to Father, Son
And to Spirit now be done:
Who us made, and Who us bought,
Who by love is our support.
Alleluia.

77 77 A

Tune:
Gott Sei Dank

Final Verses: Richard Lloyd (1993) #83; Noel Rawsthorne (2011) #192.
T. Source: *Hymns Ancient and Modern* (1861) #21.
Melody: Adapted by Johann Anastasius Freylinghausen (d. 1739) in his *Geist-reiches Gesang-Buch, den Kern alter und neuer Lieder* (Halle, 1704); also called Lübeck.
M. Source: *New Westminster Hymnal* (1939) p. 249; *New Saint Basil Hymnal* (1958) p. 229.

Die Parente Temporum (1745 AD) 201

Second Tune – *Trns: Henry Williams Baker (d. 1877)*

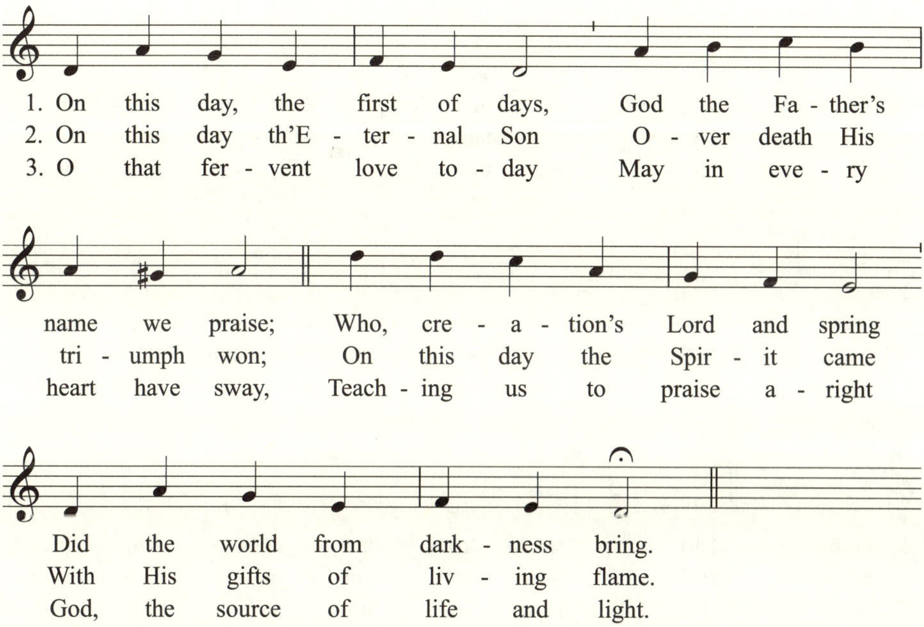

4. Father, who didst fashion me
Image of Thyself to be,
Fill me with Thy love divine,
Let my ev'ry thought be Thine.

5. Holy Jesus, may I be
Dead and buried here with Thee;
And, by love inflamed, arise
Unto Thee a sacrifice.

6. Thou, who dost all gifts impart,
Shine, sweet Spirit, in my heart;
Best of gifts Thyself bestow;
Make me burn Thy love to know.

7. God, the blessèd Three in One,
Dwell within my heart alone;
Thou dost give Thyself to me;
May I give myself to Thee.

8. Equal praise to Father, Son
And to Spirit now be done:
Who us made, and Who us bought,
Who by love is our support.

T. Source: *Hymns Ancient and Modern* (1861) #21.
Melody: *Kirchengeseng* (Böhmische Brüder, 1566).
M. Source: *Songs of Syon* (Woodward, 1910) p. 125.

77 77
Tune:
Als Christus Mit Seiner Lehr

Die Parente Temporum (1745 AD)

THIRD TUNE – *Trns: Henry Williams Baker (d. 1877)*

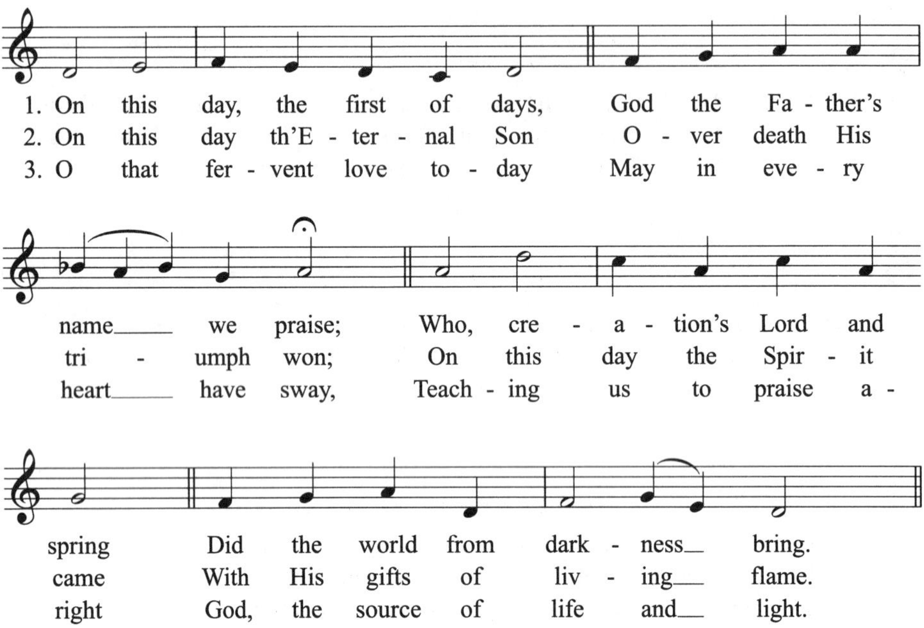

4. Father, who didst fashion me
Image of Thyself to be,
Fill me with Thy love divine,
Let my ev'ry thought be Thine.

5. Holy Jesus, may I be
Dead and buried here with Thee;
And, by love inflamed, arise
Unto Thee a sacrifice.

6. Thou, who dost all gifts impart,
Shine, sweet Spirit, in my heart;
Best of gifts Thyself bestow;
Make me burn Thy love to know.

7. God, the blessèd Three in One,
Dwell within my heart alone;
Thou dost give Thyself to me;
May I give myself to Thee.

8. Equal praise to Father, Son
And to Spirit now be done:
Who us made, and Who us bought,
Who by love is our support.

77 77

Tune:
FREUEN WIR UNS ALL IN EIN

T. Source: *Hymns Ancient and Modern* (1861) #21.
Melody: Bohemian melody adapted by Michael Weisse (d. 1534).
M. Source: *Songs of Syon* (Woodward, 1910) p. 459.

Die Parente Temporum (1745 AD) 203

FOURTH TUNE – *Trns: Henry Williams Baker (d. 1877)*

1. On this day, the first of days, God the Fa - ther's
2. On this day th'E - ter - nal Son O - ver death His
3. O that fer - vent love to - day May in eve - ry

name we praise; Who, cre - a - tion's Lord and spring
tri - umph won; On this day the Spir - it came
heart have sway, Teach - ing us to praise a - right

Did the__ world from dark - ness bring.
With His__ gifts of liv - ing flame.
God, the__ source of life and light.

4. Father, who didst fashion me
Image of Thyself to be,
Fill me with Thy love divine,
Let my ev'ry thought be Thine.

5. Holy Jesus, may I be
Dead and buried here with Thee;
And, by love inflamed, arise
Unto Thee a sacrifice.

6. Thou, who dost all gifts impart,
Shine, sweet Spirit, in my heart;
Best of gifts Thyself bestow;
Make me burn Thy love to know.

7. God, the blessèd Three in One,
Dwell within my heart alone;
Thou dost give Thyself to me;
May I give myself to Thee.

8. Equal praise to Father, Son
And to Spirit now be done:
Who us made, and Who us bought,
Who by love is our support.

Final Verses: Noel Rawsthorne (2011) #339.
T. Source: *Hymns Ancient and Modern* (1861) #21.
Melody: Orlando Gibbons (d. 1625), organist at Westminster Abbey.
M. Source: *Catholic Hymn Book* (1986) p. 223; *New Westminster Hymnal* (1939) p. 120.

77 77
Tune:
SONG 13

204 Die Parente Temporum (1745 AD)

Fifth Tune – *Trns: Henry Williams Baker (d. 1877)*

The word "Alleluia" is sung after each line:

4. Father, who didst fashion me
Image of Thyself to be,
Fill me with Thy love divine,
Let my ev'ry thought be Thine.

5. Holy Jesus, may I be
Dead and buried here with Thee;
And, by love inflamed, arise
Unto Thee a sacrifice.

6. Thou, who dost all gifts impart,
Shine, sweet Spirit, in my heart;
Best of gifts Thyself bestow;
Make me burn Thy love to know.

7. God, the blessèd Three in One,
Dwell within my heart alone;
Thou dost give Thyself to me;
May I give myself to Thee.

8. Equal praise to Father, Son
And to Spirit now be done:
Who us made, and Who us bought,
Who by love is our support.

77 77 A

Tune:
Llanfair

Final Verses: Lloyd (1993) #118; Noel Rawsthorne (2011) #186.
Melody: Robert Williams (d. 1821), a blind composer born in Wales.
M. Source: *Catholic Hymn Book* (London Oratory, 1998) p. 138.
T. Source: *Hymns Ancient and Modern* (1861) #21.

Die Parente Temporum (1745 AD) 205

Sixth Tune – *Trns: Henry Williams Baker (d. 1877)*

4. Father, who didst fashion me
Image of Thyself to be,
Fill me with Thy love divine,
Let my ev'ry thought be Thine.
Alleluia.

5. Holy Jesus, may I be
Dead and buried here with Thee;
And, by love inflamed, arise
Unto Thee a sacrifice.
Alleluia.

6. Thou, who dost all gifts impart,
Shine, sweet Spirit, in my heart;
Best of gifts Thyself bestow;
Make me burn Thy love to know.
Alleluia.

7. God, the blessèd Three in One,
Dwell within my heart alone;
Thou dost give Thyself to me;
May I give myself to Thee.
Alleluia.

8. Equal praise to Father, Son
And to Spirit now be done:
Who us made, and Who us bought,
Who by love is our support.
Alleluia.

T. Source: *Hymns Ancient and Modern* (1861) #21.
Melody: From *Hundert Arien* (Dresden, 1697), adapted by William H. Monk (d. 1889), organist at King's College London.
M. Source: *Songs of Syon* (Woodward, 1910) p. 455; *New Westminster Hymnal* (1939) p. 80.

77 77 A

Tune: Würtemburg

206 Die Parente Temporum (1745 AD)

Seventh Tune – *Trns: Henry Williams Baker (d. 1877)*

4. Father, who didst fashion me
Image of Thyself to be,
Fill me with Thy love divine,
Let my ev'ry thought be Thine,
Let my ev'ry thought be Thine.

5. Holy Jesus, may I be
Dead and buried here with Thee;
And, by love inflamed, arise
Unto Thee a sacrifice,
Unto Thee a sacrifice.

6. Thou, who dost all gifts impart,
Shine, sweet Spirit, in my heart;
Best of gifts Thyself bestow;
Make me burn Thy love to know,
Make me burn Thy love to know.

7. God, the blessèd Three in One,
Dwell within my heart alone;
Thou dost give Thyself to me;
May I give myself to Thee,
May I give myself to Thee.

8. Equal praise to Father, Son
And to Spirit now be done:
Who us made, and Who us bought,
Who by love is our support,
Who by love is our support.

77 77

Tune: T. Source: *Hymns Ancient and Modern* (1861) #21.
Zahn M. Source: Cento from *Die Melodien der deutschen evangelischen Kirchenlieder*, by Johannes Zahn (d. 1895).

Trns: Henry Williams Baker (d. 1877)

Can be sung with any 77 77 meter, such as Savannah, University College, Orientis Partibus, Llanfair, Culbach, Monkland, Gott Sei Dank, etc.

ON this day, the first of days,
God the Father's name we praise;
Who, creation's Lord and spring
Did the world from darkness bring.

2. On this day th'Eternal Son
Over death His triumph won;
On this day the Spirit came
With His gifts of living flame.

3. O that fervent love today
May in ev'ry heart have sway,
Teaching us to praise aright
God, the source of life and light.

4. Father, who didst fashion me
Image of Thyself to be,
Fill me with Thy love divine,
Let my ev'ry thought be Thine.

5. Holy Jesus, may I be
Dead and buried here with Thee;
And, by love inflamed, arise
Unto Thee a sacrifice.

6. Thou, who dost all gifts impart,
Shine, sweet Spirit, in my heart;
Best of gifts Thyself bestow;
Make me burn Thy love to know.

7. God, the blessèd Three in One,
Dwell within my heart alone;
Thou dost give Thyself to me;
May I give myself to Thee.

8. Equal praise to Father, Son
And to Spirit now be done:
Who us made, and Who us bought,
Who by love is our support.

77 77

* This text can also be sung with 77 77 D melodies: Paschal Lamb, Salzburg, Heustis, etc.

Tune: Various

T. Source: *Hymns Ancient and Modern* (1861) #21.

208 Die Parente Temporum (1745 AD)

First Tune – *Trns: William Cooke (d. 1894)*

4. O Father, in God's image Thou
In love didst fashion me;
Thee may I love with all my heart,
And meditate on Thee.

5. O Son, vouchsafe that I may die
With Thee, and with Thee rise;
For Thee, consumed by love, may be
A holy sacrifice.

6. O Holy Ghost, Thyself the best
Of gifts Thou dost bestow;
Burn, Fire of love, in me, that I
May burn Thy love to know.

7. God of my heart, Thrice Holy God,
Whose grace my prayers implore,
To Thee I vow myself; and Thee
Will love for evermore.

86 86 (CM)

Tune:
St Anne

Final Verses: Richard Lloyd (1993) #186; Noel Rawsthorne (2011) #282.
T. Source: *The Hymnary: A Book of Church Song* (London: Cooke & Webb, 1872) #9.
Melody: William Croft (d. 1727), organist at Westminster Abbey.
M. Source: *Hymns, Psalms, and Spiritual Canticles* (Massachusetts: Theodore Marier, 1983) p. 507.

Second Tune – *Trns: William Cooke (d. 1894)*

4. O Father, in God's image Thou
In love didst fashion me;
Thee may I love with all my heart,
And meditate on Thee.

5. O Son, vouchsafe that I may die
With Thee, and with Thee rise;
For Thee, consumed by love, may be
A holy sacrifice.

6. O Holy Ghost, Thyself the best
Of gifts Thou dost bestow;
Burn, Fire of love, in me, that I
May burn Thy love to know.

7. God of my heart, Thrice Holy God,
Whose grace my prayers implore,
To Thee I vow myself; and Thee
Will love for evermore.

Final Verses: Richard Lloyd (1993) #215.
T. Source: *The Hymnary: A Book of Church Song* (London: Cooke & Webb, 1872) #9.
Melody: Orlando Gibbons (d. 1625), organist at Westminster Abbey.
M. Source: *Catholic Hymn Book* (London Oratory, 1998) p. 287.

86 86 (CM)

Tune: Song 67

210 Die Parente Temporum (1745 AD)

THIRD TUNE – *Trns: William Cooke (d. 1894)*

4. O Father, in God's image Thou
In love didst fashion me;
Thee may I love with all my heart,
And meditate on Thee.

5. O Son, vouchsafe that I may die
With Thee, and with Thee rise;
For Thee, consumed by love, may be
A holy sacrifice.

6. O Holy Ghost, Thyself the best
Of gifts Thou dost bestow;
Burn, Fire of love, in me, that I
May burn Thy love to know.

7. God of my heart, Thrice Holy God,
Whose grace my prayers implore,
To Thee I vow myself; and Thee
Will love for evermore.

86 86 (CM)

Tune:
ST JAMES

Final Verses: Richard Lloyd (1993) #200; Noel Rawsthorne (2011) #307.
T. Source: *The Hymnary: A Book of Church Song* (London: Cooke & Webb, 1872) #9.
Melody: Raphael Courteville (d. 1772), organist at the church of St. James, Westminster.
M. Source: *New English Hymnal* (1986) p. 692.

Die Parente Temporum (1745 AD)

Trns: William Cooke (d. 1894)

Can be sung with any 86 86 meter, such as St Magnus, Bedford, St Columba, Westminster, St Anne, St Hugh, Hereford, St Flavian, etc.

THIS day the Father, Source of all,
Put forth creative might;
He spoke, and called the world He made
From darkness into light.

2. This day the Son triumphant left
The grave, and death o'ercame;
The Spirit came in human hearts
To sow His fruitful flame.

3. Let love inflame with fervent glow
Our hearts, this first of days;
That we to Him Who gives us life
May pay our debt of praise.

4. O Father, in God's image Thou
In love didst fashion me;
Thee may I love with all my heart,
And meditate on Thee.

5. O Son, vouchsafe that I may die
With Thee, and with Thee rise;
For Thee, consumed by love, may be
A holy sacrifice.

6. O Holy Ghost, Thyself the best
Of gifts Thou dost bestow;
Burn, Fire of love, in me, that I
May burn Thy love to know.

7. God of my heart, Thrice Holy God,
Whose grace my prayers implore,
To Thee I vow myself; and Thee
Will love for evermore.

86 86 (CM)

Tune: Various

T. Source: *The Hymnary: A Book of Church Song* (London: Cooke & Webb, 1872) #9.

212 Ex More Docti Mystico (6th century)

Pope Saint Gregory the Great (d. 604AD)

To sing in Latin, use any 88 88 (LM) tune.

EX more docti mýstico,
Servémus hoc jejúnium,
Deno diérum círculo *n1*
Ducto quater notíssimo.

2. Lex, et prophétae prímitus
Hoc praetulérunt, póstmodum
Christus sacrávit, ómnium
Rex, atque Factor témporum. *n2*

3. Utámur ergo párcius
Verbis, cibis, et pótibus,
Somno, jocis, et árctius
Perstémus in custódia. *n3*

4. Vitémus autem péssima,
Quae súbruunt mentes vagas,
Nullúmque demus cállidi
Hostis locum tyránnidi.

5. Dicámus omnes cérnui,
Clamémus atque sínguli,
Plorémus ante júdicem,
Flectámus iram víndicem.

6. Nostris malis offéndimus
Tuam, Deus, cleméntiam:
Effúnde nobis désuper
Remíssor indulgéntiam.

7. Meménto quod sumus tui,
Licet cadúci, plásmatis; *n4*
Ne des honórem nóminis
Tui, precámur, álteri.

8. Laxa malum quod fécimus,
Auge bonum quod póscimus;
Placére quo tandem tibi
Possímus hic, et pérpetim.

9. Praesta, beáta Trínitas,
Concéde simplex Únitas,
Ut fructuósa sint tuis
Jejuniórum múnera.

88 88 (LM)

Tune:
VARIOUS

T. Source: *Hymni de Tempore et de Sanctis in Textu Antiquo et Novo* (Solesmes, 1885) p. 37.

[1] "Denus" is an alternative form of "decnus."

[2] Literally "times" or "seasons."

[3] That is to say, "keeping watch over ourselves."

[4] In other words, we "have still been made by thee."

Assistance for comprehension

BEING taught by a mystical custom,
let us keep this fast,
in the well-known round *n1*
of ten days four times traversed.

2. The Law and Prophets
revealed it first, and later
Christ hallowed it, King of all
and Maker of time. *n2*

3. So let us make more sparing use
of words, food and drink,
of sleep and jests, and more closely
continue in vigilance. *n3*

4. And let us avoid the terrible things
that corrupt wandering thoughts,
nor let us cede any territory
to the tyranny of the cunning foe.

5. Prostrate, let all of us say,
and each of us cry;
let us weep before the judge,
let us soften his avenging wrath:

6. By our ills we have assailed,
O God, thy mildness:
From above pour out on us,
forgiver, thy pardon.

7. Remember that we, though fallen,
are yet of thy forming; *n4*
cede not the honor of thy name,
we pray thee, to another.

8. Undo the ill that we have done,
increase the good that we entreat,
and through it may we be able at last
to please thee here, and endlessly.

9. Accord, O blessèd Trinity,
grant, O single Unity,
that the duty of fasting
may be fruitful for those who are thine.

214 Ex More Docti Mystico (6th century)

First Tune – *Trns: Fr. John Fitzpatrick, Oblate of Mary (d. 1929)*

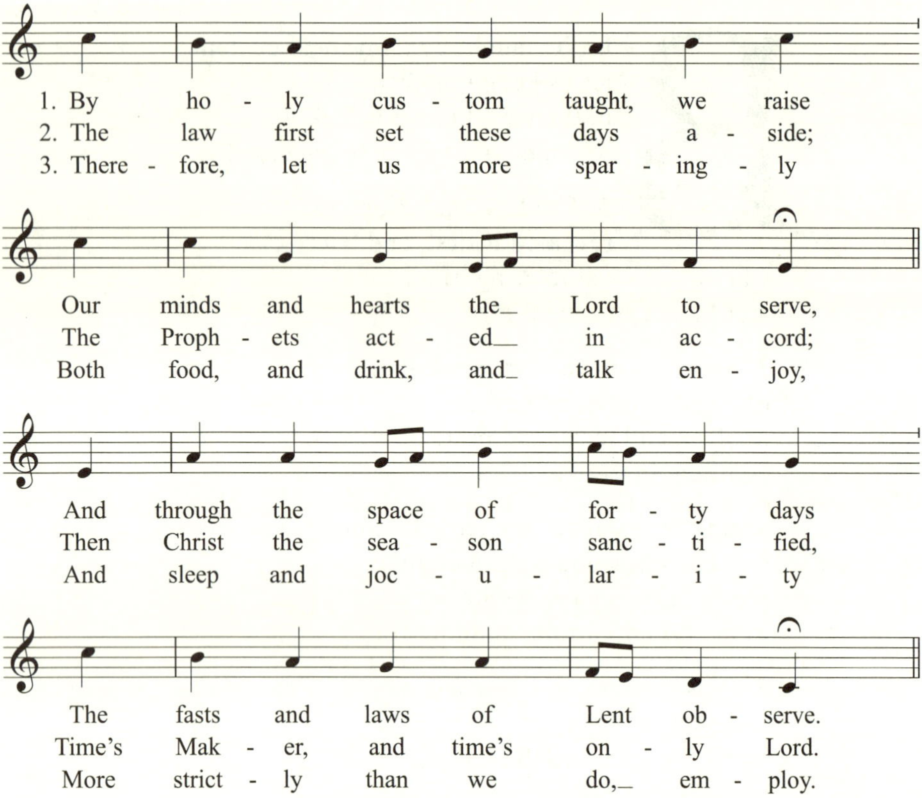

4. And let us shun each evil thought
That undermines the restless soul,
And bring the tempter's pow'r to naught
By spirits bound in close control.

5. We kneel before Thee, Lord, and weep;
Thine ire is just; our judge Thou art;
We cry with suppliant voice, and keep
Our hope in Thee, with humbled heart.

6. We often by our evil deeds,
O God, Thy clemency offend;
Forgiver, then, upon our needs
Pour down Thy mercies without end.

7. Remember that, though prone to fall,
From Thine own hands at first we came:
We beg Thee, let none take of all
The honor due to Thine own Name.

8. Forgive the evil we have done;
The blessing that we need, increase;
Inflame our hearts all sin to shun,
And keep our souls in endless peace.

9. Hear us, O Trinity sublime,
And undivided Unity;
So let this consecrated time
Bring forth Thy fruits abundantly.

88 88 (LM)

Tune:
Altona

Final Verses: Noel Rawsthorne (2011) #378; one note altered.

T. Source: *The Breviary and Missal Hymns* (London: Sands & Co, 1931) p. 58; this version employs several stanzas taken from Daniel J. Donahoe (d. 1933) and Msgr. Ronald A. Knox (d. 1957).

Melody: Schumann's *Geistliche Lieder* (1539); an adaptation by Fr. Stephan Lück (d. 1883) in his hymnal, *Gesang- und Gebetbuch für die Diözese Trier* (1847) p. 19. Called by various names (Vom Himmel Hoch, Erfurt, etc.) this melody has been set by such composers as Hassler, Gesius, Praetorius, and Bach.

M. Source: *Hosanna Catholic Hymn Book* (1914) p. 17; *New Westminster Hymnal* (1939) p. 8.

Ex More Docti Mystico (6th century) 215

Second Tune – *Trns: Fr. John Fitzpatrick, Oblate of Mary (d. 1929)*

4. And let us shun each evil thought
That undermines the restless soul,
And bring the tempter's pow'r to naught
By spirits bound in close control.

5. We kneel before Thee, Lord, and weep;
Thine ire is just; our judge Thou art;
We cry with suppliant voice, and keep
Our hope in Thee, with humbled heart.

6. We often by our evil deeds,
O God, Thy clemency offend;
Forgiver, then, upon our needs
Pour down Thy mercies without end.

7. Remember that, though prone to fall,
From Thine own hands at first we came:
We beg Thee, let none take of all
The honor due to Thine own Name.

8. Forgive the evil we have done;
The blessing that we need, increase;
Inflame our hearts all sin to shun,
And keep our souls in endless peace.

9. Hear us, O Trinity sublime,
And undivided Unity;
So let this consecrated time
Bring forth Thy fruits abundantly.

Melody: Christliches Gesangbüchlein (1568).
M. Source: *New Westminster Hymnal* (1939) p. 41.
T. Source: *The Breviary and Missal Hymns* (London: Sands & Co, 1931) p. 58; this version employs several stanzas taken from Daniel J. Donahoe (d. 1933) and Msgr. Ronald A. Knox (d. 1957).

88 88 (LM)

Tune: Saxony

Ex More Docti Mystico (6th century)

Third Tune – *Trns: Fr. John Fitzpatrick, Oblate of Mary (d. 1929)*

4. And let us shun each evil thought
That undermines the restless soul,
And bring the tempter's pow'r to naught
By spirits bound in close control.

5. We kneel before Thee, Lord, and weep;
Thine ire is just; our judge Thou art;
We cry with suppliant voice, and keep
Our hope in Thee, with humbled heart.

6. We often by our evil deeds,
O God, Thy clemency offend;
Forgiver, then, upon our needs
Pour down Thy mercies without end.

7. Remember that, though prone to fall,
From Thine own hands at first we came:
We beg Thee, let none take of all
The honor due to Thine own Name.

8. Forgive the evil we have done;
The blessing that we need, increase;
Inflame our hearts all sin to shun,
And keep our souls in endless peace.

9. Hear us, O Trinity sublime,
And undivided Unity;
So let this consecrated time
Bring forth Thy fruits abundantly.

88 88 (LM)

Tune: Eisenach

Final Verses: Richard Lloyd (1993) #64; Noel Rawsthorne (2011) #108.
T. Source: *The Breviary and Missal Hymns* (London: Sands & Co, 1931) p. 58; this version employs several stanzas taken from Daniel J. Donahoe (d. 1933) and Msgr. Ronald A. Knox (d. 1957).
Melody: Bartholomäus Gesius (d. 1613); adapted by Johann H. Schein (d. 1630)
M. Source: *New Saint Basil Hymnal* (1958) p. 120; *The Catholic Vesper Hymn Book set to Music either for Unison or Four Voices with Accompaniment* (Charles Lewis, 1877) p. 34; *Pope Pius XII Hymnal* (Ohio: Gregorian Institute of America, 1959) p. 13.

Ex More Docti Mystico (6th century) 217

Fourth Tune – *Trns: Fr. John Fitzpatrick, Oblate of Mary (d. 1929)*

4. And let us shun each evil thought
That undermines the restless soul,
And bring the tempter's pow'r to naught
By spirits bound in close control.

5. We kneel before Thee, Lord, and weep;
Thine ire is just; our judge Thou art;
We cry with suppliant voice, and keep
Our hope in Thee, with humbled heart.

6. We often by our evil deeds,
O God, Thy clemency offend;
Forgiver, then, upon our needs
Pour down Thy mercies without end.

7. Remember that, though prone to fall,
From Thine own hands at first we came:
We beg Thee, let none take of all
The honor due to Thine own Name.

8. Forgive the evil we have done;
The blessing that we need, increase;
Inflame our hearts all sin to shun,
And keep our souls in endless peace.

9. Hear us, O Trinity sublime,
And undivided Unity;
So let this consecrated time
Bring forth Thy fruits abundantly.

T. Source: *The Breviary and Missal Hymns* (London: Sands & Co, 1931) p. 58; this version employs several stanzas taken from Daniel J. Donahoe (d. 1933) and Msgr. Ronald A. Knox (d. 1957).
Melody: Traditional French air, sometimes sung with "O amor quam exstaticus."
M. Source: cf. *New Saint Basil Hymnal* (1958) p. 184; cf. *New Westminster Hymnal* (1939) p. 238.

88 88 (LM)
Tune:
Notre Dame

218 Ex More Docti Mystico (6th century)

Fifth Tune – *Trns: Fr. John Fitzpatrick, Oblate of Mary* (*d.* 1929)

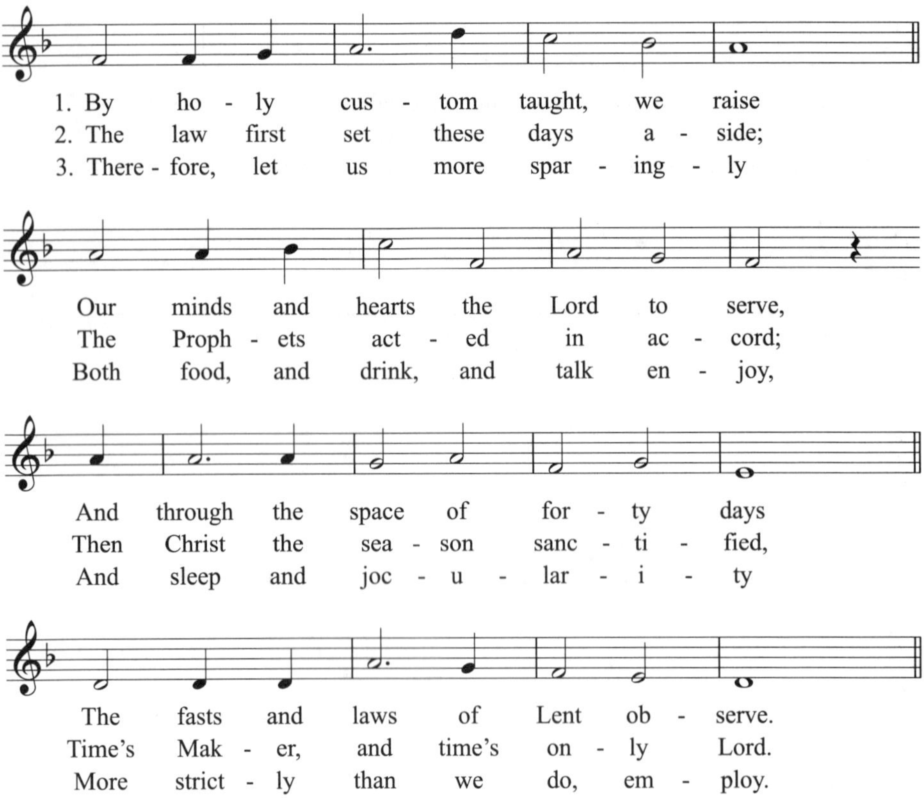

4. And let us shun each evil thought
That undermines the restless soul,
And bring the tempter's pow'r to naught
By spirits bound in close control.

5. We kneel before Thee, Lord, and weep;
Thine ire is just; our judge Thou art;
We cry with suppliant voice, and keep
Our hope in Thee, with humbled heart.

6. We often by our evil deeds,
O God, Thy clemency offend;
Forgiver, then, upon our needs
Pour down Thy mercies without end.

7. Remember that, though prone to fall,
From Thine own hands at first we came:
We beg Thee, let none take of all
The honor due to Thine own Name.

8. Forgive the evil we have done;
The blessing that we need, increase;
Inflame our hearts all sin to shun,
And keep our souls in endless peace.

9. Hear us, O Trinity sublime,
And undivided Unity;
So let this consecrated time
Bring forth Thy fruits abundantly.

88 88 (LM)

Tune:
St Cross

Final Verses: Richard Lloyd (1993) #64; Noel Rawsthorne (2011) #108.
T. Source: *The Breviary and Missal Hymns* (London: Sands & Co, 1931) p. 58; this version employs several stanzas taken from Daniel J. Donahoe (d. 1933) and Msgr. Ronald A. Knox (d. 1957).
Melody: John Bacchus Dykes (d. 1876).
M. Source: *Catholic Hymn Book* (London Oratory, 1998) p. 104.

Ex More Docti Mystico (6th century)

Sixth Tune – *Trns: Fr. John Fitzpatrick, Oblate of Mary (d. 1929)*

4. And let us shun each evil thought
That undermines the restless soul,
And bring the tempter's pow'r to naught
By spirits bound in close control.

5. We kneel before Thee, Lord, and weep;
Thine ire is just; our judge Thou art;
We cry with suppliant voice, and keep
Our hope in Thee, with humbled heart.

6. We often by our evil deeds,
O God, Thy clemency offend;
Forgiver, then, upon our needs
Pour down Thy mercies without end.

7. Remember that, though prone to fall,
From Thine own hands at first we came:
We beg Thee, let none take of all
The honor due to Thine own Name.

8. Forgive the evil we have done;
The blessing that we need, increase;
Inflame our hearts all sin to shun,
And keep our souls in endless peace.

9. Hear us, O Trinity sublime,
And undivided Unity;
So let this consecrated time
Bring forth Thy fruits abundantly.

Final Verses: Richard Lloyd (1993) #181; Noel Rawsthorne (2011) #276.
T. Source: *The Breviary and Missal Hymns* (London: Sands & Co, 1931) p. 58; this version employs several stanzas taken from Daniel J. Donahoe (d. 1933) and Msgr. Ronald A. Knox (d. 1957).
Melody: Dr. Edward Miller (d. 1807), organist of Doncaster Parish Church; originally published in *Psalms of David for the Use of Parish Churches* (1790) p. 12; based on Tunbridge (an older tune).
M. Source: *Catholic Hymn Book* (London Oratory, 1998) p. 115; *Church Hymns with Tunes* (1885) p. 44.

88 88 (LM)

Tune: Rockingham

220 Ex More Docti Mystico (6th century)

Seventh Tune – *Trns: Fr. John Fitzpatrick, Oblate of Mary (d. 1929)*

1. By ho - ly cus - tom taught, we raise
2. The law first set these days a - side;
3. There - fore, let us more spar - ing - ly

Our minds and hearts the Lord to serve,
The Proph - ets act - ed in ac - cord;
Both food, and drink, and talk en - joy,

And through the space of for - ty days
Then Christ the sea - son sanc - ti - fied,
And sleep and joc - u - lar - i - ty

The fasts and laws of Lent ob - serve.
Time's Mak - er, and time's on - ly Lord.
More strict - ly than we do, em - ploy.

4. And let us shun each evil thought
That undermines the restless soul,
And bring the tempter's pow'r to naught
By spirits bound in close control.

5. We kneel before Thee, Lord, and weep;
Thine ire is just; our judge Thou art;
We cry with suppliant voice, and keep
Our hope in Thee, with humbled heart.

6. We often by our evil deeds,
O God, Thy clemency offend;
Forgiver, then, upon our needs
Pour down Thy mercies without end.

7. Remember that, though prone to fall,
From Thine own hands at first we came:
We beg Thee, let none take of all
The honor due to Thine own Name.

8. Forgive the evil we have done;
The blessing that we need, increase;
Inflame our hearts all sin to shun,
And keep our souls in endless peace.

9. Hear us, O Trinity sublime,
And undivided Unity;
So let this consecrated time
Bring forth Thy fruits abundantly.

88 88 (LM)

Tune:
Song 34

Final Verses: Richard Lloyd (1993) #214; Noel Rawsthorne (2011) #342.
T. Source: *The Breviary and Missal Hymns* (London: Sands & Co, 1931) p. 58; this version employs several stanzas taken from Daniel J. Donahoe (d. 1933) and Msgr. Ronald A. Knox (d. 1957).
Melody: Orlando Gibbons (d. 1625), organist at Westminster Abbey.
M. Source: *The Hymnes and Songs of the Church* (1623) p. 114; originally sung to "Thus Angells sung, and thus sing we." We have adopted the most commonly used rhythm. Cf. *New Saint Basil Hymnal* (1958) p. 136.

Ex More Docti Mystico (6th century) 221

Eighth Tune – *Trns: Fr. John Fitzpatrick, Oblate of Mary (d. 1929)*

4. And let us shun each evil thought
That undermines the restless soul,
And bring the tempter's pow'r to naught
By spirits bound in close control.

5. We kneel before Thee, Lord, and weep;
Thine ire is just; our judge Thou art;
We cry with suppliant voice, and keep
Our hope in Thee, with humbled heart.

6. We often by our evil deeds,
O God, Thy clemency offend;
Forgiver, then, upon our needs
Pour down Thy mercies without end.

7. Remember that, though prone to fall,
From Thine own hands at first we came:
We beg Thee, let none take of all
The honor due to Thine own Name.

8. Forgive the evil we have done;
The blessing that we need, increase;
Inflame our hearts all sin to shun,
And keep our souls in endless peace.

9. Hear us, O Trinity sublime,
And undivided Unity;
So let this consecrated time
Bring forth Thy fruits abundantly.

Melody: From a hymn book published by Fr. Melchior Ludolf Herold (d. 1810).
M. Source: *New Westminster Hymnal* (1939) p. 173.
T. Source: *The Breviary and Missal Hymns* (London: Sands & Co, 1931) p. 58; this version employs several stanzas taken from Daniel J. Donahoe (d. 1933) and Msgr. Ronald A. Knox (d. 1957).

88 88 (LM)

Tune: Bressani

222 Ex More Docti Mystico (6th century)

Ninth Tune – *Trns: Fr. John Fitzpatrick, Oblate of Mary (d. 1929)*

4. And let us shun each evil thought
That undermines the restless soul,
And bring the tempter's pow'r to naught
By spirits bound in close control.

5. We kneel before Thee, Lord, and weep;
Thine ire is just; our judge Thou art;
We cry with suppliant voice, and keep
Our hope in Thee, with humbled heart.

6. We often by our evil deeds,
O God, Thy clemency offend;
Forgiver, then, upon our needs
Pour down Thy mercies without end.

7. Remember that, though prone to fall,
From Thine own hands at first we came:
We beg Thee, let none take of all
The honor due to Thine own Name.

8. Forgive the evil we have done;
The blessing that we need, increase;
Inflame our hearts all sin to shun,
And keep our souls in endless peace.

9. Hear us, O Trinity sublime,
And undivided Unity;
So let this consecrated time
Bring forth Thy fruits abundantly.

88 88 (LM)

Tune:
Gonfalon Royal

Final Verses: Richard Lloyd (1993) #80; Noel Rawsthorne (2011) #136.
T. Source: *The Breviary and Missal Hymns* (London: Sands & Co, 1931) p. 58; this version employs several stanzas taken from Daniel J. Donahoe (d. 1933) and Msgr. Ronald A. Knox (d. 1957).
Melody: Sir Percy Carter Buck (d. 1947); first published in *Fourteen Hymn Tunes* (1913).
M. Source: *Catholic Hymn Book* (London Oratory, 1998) p. 140. The tune was originally paired with *Vexilla Regis* ("Flag of the King"). A *gonfalon* ("flag") was traditionally carried during Catholic processions.

Ex More Docti Mystico (6th century)

Tenth Tune – *Trns: Fr. John Fitzpatrick, Oblate of Mary (d. 1929)*

4. And let us shun each evil thought
That undermines the restless soul,
And bring the tempter's pow'r to naught
By spirits bound in close control.

5. We kneel before Thee, Lord, and weep;
Thine ire is just; our judge Thou art;
We cry with suppliant voice, and keep
Our hope in Thee, with humbled heart.

6. We often by our evil deeds,
O God, Thy clemency offend;
Forgiver, then, upon our needs
Pour down Thy mercies without end.

7. Remember that, though prone to fall,
From Thine own hands at first we came:
We beg Thee, let none take of all
The honor due to Thine own Name.

8. Forgive the evil we have done;
The blessing that we need, increase;
Inflame our hearts all sin to shun,
And keep our souls in endless peace.

9. Hear us, O Trinity sublime,
And undivided Unity;
So let this consecrated time
Bring forth Thy fruits abundantly.

Final Verses: Richard Lloyd (1993) #133; Noel Rawsthorne (2011) #205.
Melody: Samuel Webbe, the elder (d. 1816).
M. Source: *Veritas Hymnal* (Dublin: Irish Church Music Association, 1974) p. 96;
Cantate Omnes: Hymnal of the Catholic Choirmasters' Guild (1952) #78.
T. Source: *The Breviary and Missal Hymns* (London: Sands & Co, 1931) p. 58; this version employs several stanzas taken from Daniel J. Donahoe (d. 1933) and Msgr. Ronald A. Knox (d. 1957).

88 88 (LM)

Tune: Melcombe

224 Ex More Docti Mystico (6th century)

Eleventh Tune – *Trns: Fr. John Fitzpatrick, Oblate of Mary (d. 1929)*

4. And let us shun each evil thought
That undermines the restless soul,
And bring the tempter's pow'r to naught
By spirits bound in close control.

5. We kneel before Thee, Lord, and weep;
Thine ire is just; our judge Thou art;
We cry with suppliant voice, and keep
Our hope in Thee, with humbled heart.

6. We often by our evil deeds,
O God, Thy clemency offend;
Forgiver, then, upon our needs
Pour down Thy mercies without end.

7. Remember that, though prone to fall,
From Thine own hands at first we came:
We beg Thee, let none take of all
The honor due to Thine own Name.

8. Forgive the evil we have done;
The blessing that we need, increase;
Inflame our hearts all sin to shun,
And keep our souls in endless peace.

9. Hear us, O Trinity sublime,
And undivided Unity;
So let this consecrated time
Bring forth Thy fruits abundantly.

* This melody at a lower key is on page 436.

88 88 (LM)

Tune: Trinity College

Melody: John Bacchus Dykes (d. 1876).
M. Source: *Hymns Ancient and Modern* (1972) p. 64.
T. Source: *The Breviary and Missal Hymns* (London: Sands & Co, 1931) p. 58; this version employs several stanzas taken from Daniel J. Donahoe (d. 1933) and Msgr. Ronald A. Knox (d. 1957).

Ex More Docti Mystico (6th century)

Trns: Fr. John Fitzpatrick, Oblate of Mary (d. 1929)

Can be sung with any 88 88 meter: HILDERSTONE, DUGUET, BRESLAU, NOTRE DAME, MELCOMBE, WAREHAM, OLD HUNDREDTH, MEIN SEEL O GOTT, TRINITY COLLEGE, and so forth.

BY holy custom taught, we raise
Our minds and hearts the Lord to serve,
And through the space of forty days
The fasts and laws of Lent observe.

2. The law first set these days aside;
The Prophets acted in accord;
Then Christ the season sanctified,
Time's Maker, and time's only Lord.

3. Therefore, let us more sparingly
Both food, and drink, and talk enjoy,
And sleep and jocularity
More strictly than we do, employ.

4. And let us shun each evil thought
That undermines the restless soul,
And bring the tempter's pow'r to naught
By spirits bound in close control.

5. We kneel before Thee, Lord, and weep;
Thine ire is just; our judge Thou art;
We cry with suppliant voice, and keep
Our hope in Thee, with humbled heart.

6. We often by our evil deeds,
O God, Thy clemency offend;
Forgiver, then, upon our needs
Pour down Thy mercies without end.

7. Remember that, though prone to fall,
From Thine own hands at first we came:
We beg Thee, let none take of all
The honor due to Thine own Name.

8. Forgive the evil we have done;
The blessing that we need, increase;
Inflame our hearts all sin to shun,
And keep our souls in endless peace.

9. Hear us, O Trinity sublime,
And undivided Unity;
So let this consecrated time
Bring forth Thy fruits abundantly.

88 88 (LM)

T. Source: *The Breviary and Missal Hymns* (London: Sands & Co, 1931) p. 58; this version employs several stanzas taken from Daniel J. Donahoe (d. 1933) and Msgr. Ronald A. Knox (d. 1957).

Tune: VARIOUS

226 Hoste Dum Victo Triumphans (17th century)

Jean-Baptiste de Santeul, Canon Regular of St Victor (d. 1697)

To sing in Latin,
use any 87 87 87 tune.

HOSTE dum victo triúmphans
Ábraham revértitur,
óbvius fit magnus illi
rex Salem Melchísedech,
vina qui, tamquam sacérdos,
atque panem prótulit.

2. Quam vetus signábat umbra
clara lucet véritas:
Póntifex novus, secúndum
órdinem Melchísedech,
pane sub vinóque corpus
dat suum cum sánguine.

3. Quo creáta cuncta Verbo
mira fit mutátio,
panis in carnem, merúmque
in cruórem vértitur:
déficit senus, sed alta
róborat mentem fides.

4. Qui semel Patri cruéntam
óbtulit se víctimam,
síngulis idem diébus,
per ministrórum manus,
rite nostris incruéntus
se sub aris ímmolat.

5. Ipsa quin astans sacrátis
sancta plebs altáribus,
máximo Christum Parénti
seque cum Christo litat,
carne posthac, quam litávit,
et cruóre pascitur.

6. Summa laus Deo Parénti,
qui creávit ómnia,
summa sit Nato, redémit
qui suo nos sánguine,
Flámini par, cujus almo
confovémur hálitu.

87 87 87

Tune:
VARIOUS

T. Source: *Breviarium Monasticum Ad Usum Sacri Ordinis Cluniacensis* (Paris, 1686) p. 557.

Assistance for comprehension

WHEN, the foe being conquered,
victorious, Abraham returned,
there came to meet him the great
king of Salem, Melchisedech,
who, as a priest, brought forth
wine and bread.

2. The truth that the ancient shadow
betokened now shines bright:
a new High Priest,
in the line of Melchisedech,
gives his body with his blood
under the appearance of bread and wine.

3. A wondrous change comes about by the Word
through whom all things were created,
bread is turned into flesh,
and wine into blood:
sensation fails, but lofty faith
reinforces understanding.

4. The same one who once
offered himself to the Father
as a bloody victim,
each day duly sacrifices himself
unbloody by the hands
of his servants on our altars.

5. Indeed the holy people
that stand by the hallowed altars
offer Christ to the supreme Father,
and themselves with Christ,
afterwards are fed with the flesh
and blood that they have offered.

6. Highest praise to God the Father,
who created all things,
highest praise to his Son,
who ransomed us with his blood,
equal praise to the Spirit, by whose
bounteous breath we are nurtured.

228 Hoste Dum Victo Triumphans (17th century)

First Tune – *Trns: Fr. Edward Caswall, Oratorian (d. 1878)*

4. He who once to die a Victim
On the Cross, did not refuse,
Day by day, upon our altars,
That same Sacrifice renews;
Through His holy Priesthood's hands,
Faithful to His last commands.

5. While the people all uniting
In the Sacrifice sublime,
Offer Christ to His high Father,
Offer up themselves with Him;
Then together with the Priest
On the living Victim feast.

87 87 77

Tune:
All Saints

Final Verses: Richard Lloyd (1993) #7; Noel Rawsthorne (2011) #13.
T. Source: *Masque of Mary* (1858) p. 307; the original title was "The Most Holy Sacrifice of the Mass."
Melody: *Geistreiches Gesangbuch* (Darmstadt, 1698).
M. Source: *New Saint Basil Hymnal* (1958) p. 203; *Catholic Hymn Book* (London Oratory, 1998) p. 290.

Second Tune – *Trns: Fr. Edward Caswall, Oratorian (d. 1878)*

1. When the Pa - triarch was re - turn - ing Crown'd with
2. On the truth thus dim - ly shad - ow'd Lat - er
3. Wond - 'rous gift! The Word who fash - ion'd All things

tri - umph from the fray, Him the peace - ful king of
days a lus - ter shed; When the great High - Priest e -
by His might di - vine, Bread in - to His Bod - y

Sa - lem Came to meet up - on his way; Meek - ly
ter - nal, Un - der forms of Wine and Bread, For the
chang - es, In - to His own Blood the wine; What though

bear - ing Bread and Wine, Ho - ly Priest- hood's aw - ful sign.
world's im - mor - tal food Gave His Flesh and gave His Blood.
sense no change per- ceives, Faith ad - mires, a - dores, be - lieves.

4. He who once to die a Victim
On the Cross, did not refuse,
Day by day, upon our altars,
That same Sacrifice renews;
Through His holy Priesthood's hands,
Faithful to His last commands.

5. While the people all uniting
In the Sacrifice sublime,
Offer Christ to His high Father,
Offer up themselves with Him;
Then together with the Priest
On the living Victim feast.

87 87 77

Melody: From Bremen, in North Germany (1680).
M. Source: *New Westminster Hymnal* (1939) p. 102.
T. Source: *Masque of Mary* (1858) p. 307; the original title was "The Most Holy Sacrifice of the Mass."

Tune: Coblenz

230 Hoste Dum Victo Triumphans (17th century)

THIRD TUNE – *Trns: Fr. Edward Caswall, Oratorian (d. 1878)*

4. He who once to die a Victim
On the Cross, did not refuse,
Day by day, upon our altars,
That same Sacrifice renews;
Through His holy Priesthood's hands,
Faithful to His last commands.

5. While the people all uniting
In the Sacrifice sublime,
Offer Christ to His high Father,
Offer up themselves with Him;
Then together with the Priest
On the living Victim feast.

87 87 77

Tune:
WESTMINSTER ABBEY F7

Melody: Henry Purcell (d. 1695), organist at Westminster Abbey.
M. Source: cf. Final "Hallelujah" section of an anthem (1681), *O God, Thou Art My God.* Like many other hymn tunes (BRESLAU, OLD HUNDREDTH, BEDFORD, PUER NOBIS NASCITUR, etc.) this melody can be sung in triple or quadruple meter; however, when sung in triple, it should follow Purcell's original rhythm and not what is commonly found in 20th century hymnals. For the "F7" melody, cf. *The New Office Hymn Book: Introits for the Sundays and Festivals,* Part III (John Frederick Watkinson Bullock, 1907) p. 155.
T. Source: *Masque of Mary* (1858) p. 307; the original title was "The Most Holy Sacrifice of the Mass."

Hoste Dum Victo Triumphans (17th century)

Fourth Tune – *Trns: Fr. Edward Caswall, Oratorian (d. 1878)*

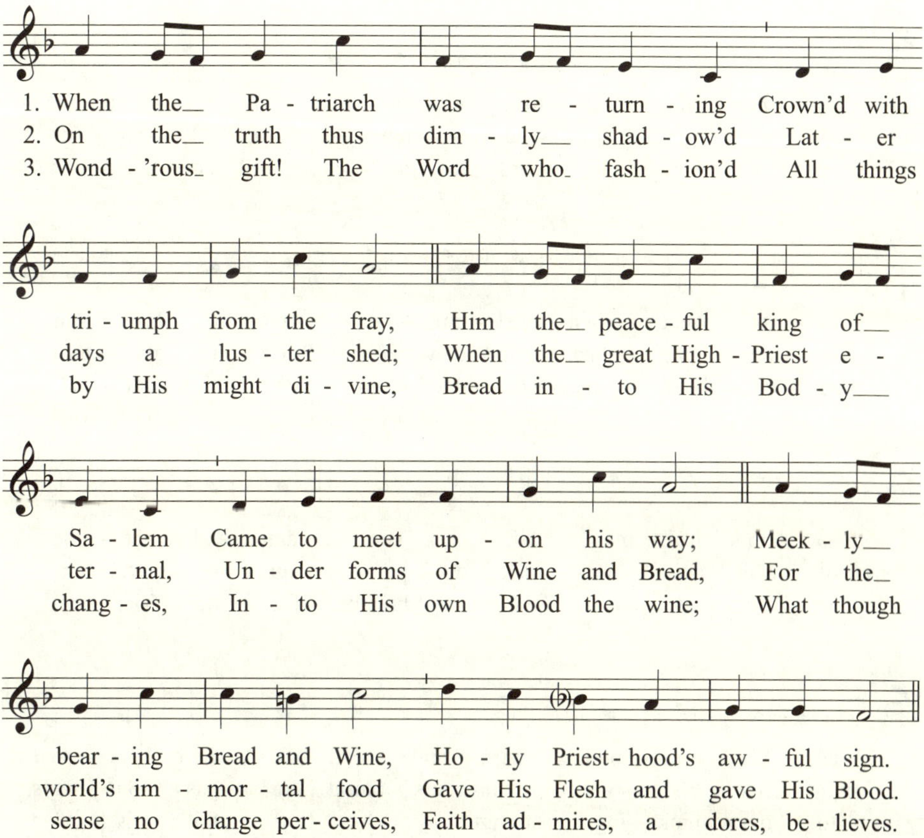

4. He who once to die a Victim
On the Cross, did not refuse,
Day by day, upon our altars,
That same Sacrifice renews;
Through His holy Priesthood's hands,
Faithful to His last commands.

5. While the people all uniting
In the Sacrifice sublime,
Offer Christ to His high Father,
Offer up themselves with Him;
Then together with the Priest
On the living Victim feast.

T. Source: *Masque of Mary* (1858) p. 307; the orig. title was "The Most Holy Sacrifice of the Mass."
Melody: Johann Christoph Bach (d. 1703); some hymnals erroneously attribute this tune, as his name resembles that of J.S. Bach's fifth son—Johann Christoph Friedrich Bach—as well as his youngest son, Johann Christian Bach (d. 1782), who became a Catholic and was admired by Mozart.
M. Source: *Meiningen Gesangbuch* (1693); this melody has multiple names (e.g. Komm O Komm Du Geist Des Lebens); cf. *New Saint Basil Hymnal* (1958) p. 71; cf. *The New Office Hymn Book: Introits for the Sundays and Festivals* (John Frederick Watkinson Bullock, 1907) pp. 134, 259, 338.

87 87 77

Tune:
Ich Begehr Nicht Mehr

232 Hoste Dum Victo Triumphans (17th century)

Trns: Fr. Dominic Popplewell (b. 1973)

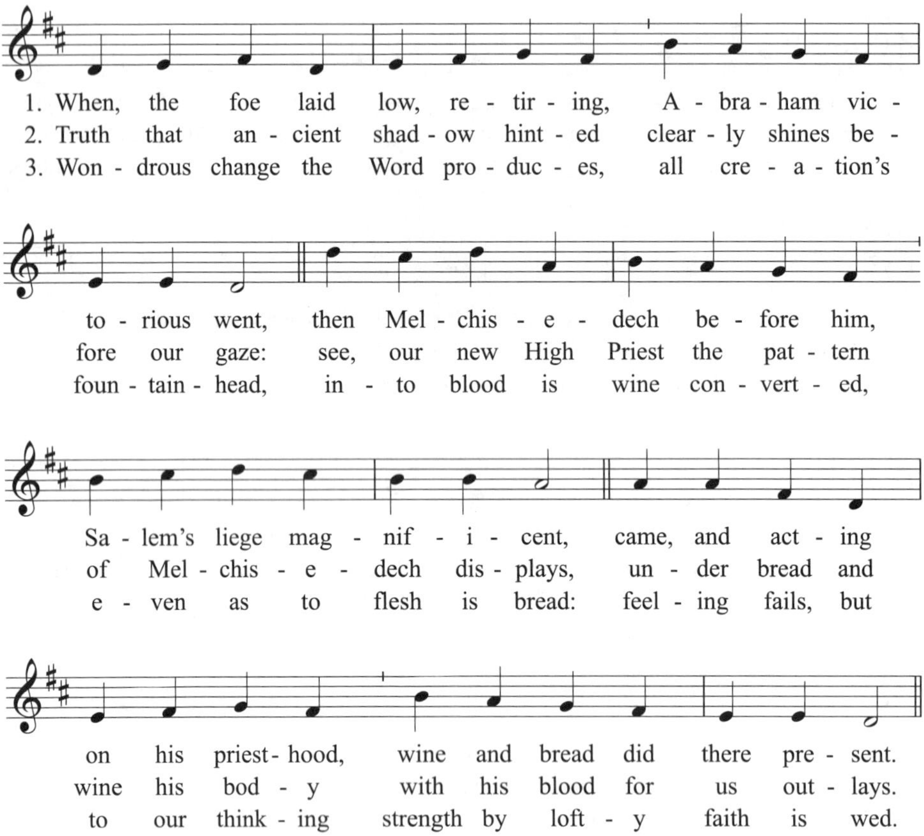

4. As in gory wise he offered
to the Father once of yore,
so himself he duly renders
daily, victim as before,
by the hands of those who serve him,
on our altars, without gore.

5. Drawing nigh the hallowed precincts,
there the holy people stand,
Christ unto the sovereign Father
and themselves with Christ remand,
by his flesh and blood thus yielded
feed then from a shepherd's hand.

6. Highest praise to God the Father,
who has made all things of naught,
highest praise be to his Offspring,
who us with his blood has bought,
to the Spirit, by whose bounteous
breath we thrive, the same be wrought.

87 87 87

Tune:
ST THOMAS (Webbe)

T. Source: *Saint Jean de Brébeuf Hymnal* (2018).
Melody: Samuel Webbe, the Elder (d. 1816), choirmaster of the Chapel of the Portuguese Embassy in Lincoln's Inn Fields (a public square), the only place in London where the Catholic liturgy could be publicly celebrated.
M. Source: Fr. Joseph Mohr's *Psälterlein* (Regensburg: Pustet, 1889) p. 542; *Hosanna Catholic Hymn Book* (St. Louis: Fr. Ludwig Bonvin, 1914) #187.

Hoste Dum Victo Triumphans (17th century)

Trns: Fr. Dominic Popplewell (b. 1973)

Sing with any 87 87 87 meter: RUNNELLS, MANNHEIM, DULCE CARMEN, REGENT SQUARE, LAUDA ANIMA, ST LEONARD, GAUFESTRE, PICARDY, BRETON, DAVOST, and so forth.

WHEN, the foe laid low, retiring,
Abraham victorious went,
then Melchisedech before him,
Salem's liege magnificent,
came, and acting on his priesthood,
wine and bread did there present.

2. Truth that ancient shadow hinted
clearly shines before our gaze:
see, our new High Priest the pattern
of Melchisedech displays,
under bread and wine his body
with his blood for us outlays.

3. Wondrous change the Word produces,
all creation's fountainhead,
into blood is wine converted,
even as to flesh is bread:
feeling fails, but to our thinking
strength by lofty faith is wed.

4. As in gory wise he offered
to the Father once of yore,
so himself he duly renders
daily, victim as before,
by the hands of those who serve him,
on our altars, without gore.

5. Drawing nigh the hallowed precincts,
there the holy people stand,
Christ unto the sovereign Father
and themselves with Christ remand,
by his flesh and blood thus yielded
feed then from a shepherd's hand.

6. Highest praise to God the Father,
who has made all things of naught,
highest praise be to his Offspring,
who us with his blood has bought,
to the Spirit, by whose bounteous
breath we thrive, the same be wrought.

87 87 87

Tune: VARIOUS

T. Source: *Saint Jean de Brébeuf Hymnal* (2018).

234 Jam Christe Sol Justitiae (6th century)

"Behold, now is the acceptable time; now is the day of salvation"

To sing in Latin,
use any 88 88 (LM) tune.

JAM Christe sol justítiae,
Mentis diéscant ténebrae,
Virtútum ut lux rédeat, *n1*
Terris diem cum réparas.

2. Dans tempus acceptábile
Et paénitens cor tríbue,
Convértat ut benígnitas,
Quos longa suffert píetas.

3. Quiddámque paeniténtiae
Da ferre, quamvis grávium,
Majóre tuo múnere,
Quo démptio fit críminum.

4. Dies venit, dies tua,
In qua reflórent omnia: *n2*
Laetémur in hac ad tuam
Per hanc redúcti grátiam.

5. Te rerum univérsitas,
Clemens, adóret, Trínitas,
Et nos novi per véniam
Novum canámus cánticum.

88 88 (LM)

Tune:
VARIOUS

T. Source: *Hymni de Tempore et de Sanctis in Textu Antiquo et Novo* (Solesmes, 1885) p. 38; the author is not known. In 1631, Pope Urban VIII changed the title to *O Sol Salutis Intimis*.

Assistance for comprehension

NOW, O Christ, sun of righteousness, *cf. Mal 4.2*
let the darkness of our thought turn to day,
that the light of virtue may return *n1*
when thou restorest day to the lands.

2. Granting us an acceptable time, *cf. II Cor 6.2*
accord us also a penitent heart,
that thy kindness may transform those
whom thy prolonged graciousness tolerates. *cf. Ps 102.8*

3. And grant that they undergo
something of repentance
through thy very great gift, by which comes about
the removal of wrongs, however great.

4. The day comes, thy day,
on which all things bloom again: *n2*
let us be glad on it, *cf. Ps 117.24*
led back by it to thy grace.

5. Let the generality of things
adore thee, O merciful Trinity,
and let us, made new by thy pardon,
sing a new canticle. *cf. Ps 32.3, 143.9, 149.1; Ap 5.9, 14.3*

[1] Literally "virtues."

[2] The physical spring of the northern hemisphere is an analogy for the spiritual rebirth which the Resurrection of Christ inaugurates.

236 Jam Christe Sol Justitiae (6th century)

First Tune – *Trns: Judge Daniel Joseph Donahoe (d. 1933)*

4. Thy day of glory comes; the glow
Shall every hollow fill and height;
And we rejoicing, Lord, shall go
In safety, guided by thy light.

5. Benignant Trinity, to thee
The world shall bow; the weak and strong
Shall call upon thy name; and we,
Renewed in grace, lift up the song.

88 88 (LM)

Tune:
Breslau

Final Verses: Richard Lloyd (1993) #24; Noel Rawsthorne (2011) #50.
T. Source: *Early Christian Hymns* (New York: The Grafton Press, 1908) p. 96.
Melody: cf. Theme used by J.S. Bach (d. 1750) in "O Jesu Christ, meins Lebens Licht," BWV 118.
M. Source: *Pope Pius XII Hymnal* (Ohio: Gregorian Institute of America, 1959) p. 6.

Second Tune – *Trns: Judge Daniel Joseph Donahoe (d. 1933)*

4. Thy day of glory comes; the glow
Shall every hollow fill and height;
And we rejoicing, Lord, shall go
In safety, guided by thy light.

5. Benignant Trinity, to thee
The world shall bow; the weak and strong
Shall call upon thy name; and we,
Renewed in grace, lift up the song.

Final Verses: Richard Lloyd (1993) #181; Noel Rawsthorne (2011) #276.
T. Source: *Early Christian Hymns* (New York: The Grafton Press, 1908) p. 96.
Melody: Dr. Edward Miller (d. 1807), organist of Doncaster Parish Church; originally published in *Psalms of David for the Use of Parish Churches* (1790) p. 12; based on Tunbridge (an older tune).
M. Source: *Catholic Hymn Book* (London Oratory, 1998) p. 115; *Church Hymns with Tunes* (1885) p. 44.

88 88 (LM)
Tune:
Rockingham

238 Jam Christe Sol Justitiae (6th century)

Third Tune – *Trns: Judge Daniel Joseph Donahoe (d. 1933)*

4. Thy day of glory comes; the glow
Shall every hollow fill and height;
And we rejoicing, Lord, shall go
In safety, guided by thy light.

5. Benignant Trinity, to thee
The world shall bow; the weak and strong
Shall call upon thy name; and we,
Renewed in grace, lift up the song.

88 88 (LM)

Tune:
Cromer

T. Source: *Early Christian Hymns* (New York: The Grafton Press, 1908) p. 96.
Melody: John Ambrose Lloyd (d. 1874), choirmaster at Chapel Salem, Brownlow.
M. Source: *New English Hymnal* (1986) p. 346.

Jam Christe Sol Justitiae (6th century) 239

Fourth Tune – *Trns: Judge Daniel Joseph Donahoe (d. 1933)*

4. Thy day of glory comes; the glow
Shall every hollow fill and height;
And we rejoicing, Lord, shall go
In safety, guided by thy light.

5. Benignant Trinity, to thee
The world shall bow; the weak and strong
Shall call upon thy name; and we,
Renewed in grace, lift up the song.

T. Source: *Early Christian Hymns* (New York: The Grafton Press, 1908) p. 96.
Melody: Philip Hart (d. 1749), organist at St. Michael Church, Cornhill.
M. Source: *Hymns Ancient and Modern* (1972) p. 8; cf. *Church Hymns With Tunes* (1885) p. 230, edited by Sir Arthur Sullivan (d. 1900), organist at St. Peter Church, Kensington.

88 88 (LM)

Tune: Hilderstone

240 Jam Christe Sol Justitiae (6th century)

Fifth Tune – *Trns: Judge Daniel Joseph Donahoe (d. 1933)*

1. O Sun of our sal - va - tion, rise,
2. Grant that we may with stream - ing tears
3. Seal up the fount of sin, and bring

Il - lume our souls with light di - vine;
Wash from the heart all stain of sin,
The sigh of sor - row and the smart;

Drive night and dark - ness from the skies,
And freed from world - ly joys and fears,
So shall the rod of pen - ance wring

And let thy day of mer - cy shine.
Kin - dle the fire of love there - in.
With soft'n - ing grief the har - dened heart.

4. Thy day of glory comes; the glow
Shall every hollow fill and height;
And we rejoicing, Lord, shall go
In safety, guided by thy light.

5. Benignant Trinity, to thee
The world shall bow; the weak and strong
Shall call upon thy name; and we,
Renewed in grace, lift up the song.

88 88 (LM)

Tune:
Song 34

Final Verses: Richard Lloyd (1993) #214; Noel Rawsthorne (2011) #342.
T. Source: *Early Christian Hymns* (New York: The Grafton Press, 1908) p. 96.
Melody: Orlando Gibbons (d. 1625), organist at Westminster Abbey.
M. Source: *The Hymnes and Songs of the Church* (1623) p. 114; originally sung to "Thus Angells sung, and thus sing we." We have adopted the most commonly used rhythm. Cf. *New Saint Basil Hymnal* (1958) p. 136.

1706AD – Historic Roman Catholic Translation

Can be sung with any 88 88 meter, such as EISENACH, ROGERS PARK, BRESSANI, LA ROCHELLE, KEMPEN, BESSEMER, TALLIS CANON, WINCHESTER NEW, etc.

O sol salútis, íntimis
Jesu refúlge méntibus,
Dum nocte pulsa grátior
Orbi dies renáscitur.

O SOV'REIGN Sun, diffuse thy Light,
And clear our inmost Minds of Night;
Thy Beams drive all that's dark away,
And give the World a better Day.

Dans tempus acceptábile,
Da lacrimárum rívulis
Laváre cordis víctimam,
Quam laet*a* adúrat cáritas.

2. Now days of Grace with mercy Flow,
O Lord, the gift of Tears bestow,
To wash our Stains in ev'ry part,
Whilst heav'nly fire consumes the Heart.

Quo fonte manávit nefas,
Fluent perénnes lácrimae,
Si virga paeniténtiae
Cordis rigórem cónterat.

3. Rise, crystal Tears, from that same source
From whence our sins derive their course;
Nor cease, till harden'd Hearts relent,
And soften'd by your Streams, repent.

Dies venit, dies tua,
In qua reflórent ómnia:
Laetémur et nos in viam
Tua redúcti déxtera.

4. Behold, the happy Days return,
The Days of Joy for them that Mourn;
May we of their Indulgence share,
And Bless the God that grants our Pray'r.

Te prona mundi máchina,
Clemens adóret Trínitas,
Et nos novi per grátiam,
Novum canámus cánticum.

5. May Heav'n and Earth aloud proclaim
The Trinity's Almighty Fame,
And we, restor'd to Grace, rejoice
In newness both of Hearts and Voice.

* In *Hymns of the Roman Liturgy* (1955), Fr. Joseph Connelly says the ancient version of this hymn (*Jam Christe Sol Justitiae*) "has many difficulties." Indeed, no Catholic has ever translated the ancient version into metrical English—possibly because many localities used *Ad Preces Nostras Deitatis* instead, as Alan G. McDougall, writing in 1916, reminds us:

> "Found in ante-Tridentine Roman Breviaries, *Ad Preces Nostras Deitatis* has now been superseded by *O Sol Salutis Intimis*. Its loss is much to be regretted, as it is one of the most beautiful examples of mediaeval hymnody."

We have included *Ad Preces Nostras Deitatis* on page 50.

T. Source: *The Primer, or, Office of the B. Virgin Mary, Revis'd; With a New and Approv'd Version of the Church-Hymns Throughout the Year; To which Are Added the Remaining Hymns of the Roman Breviary* (1706) p. 372. This translation may have been written by John Dryden (d. 1700), a famous poet and Catholic convert.

88 88 (LM)

Tune: VARIOUS

242 Jam Christe Sol Justitiae (6th century)

First Tune – *Trns: John David Chambers (d. 1893)*

4. Thy Day draws near, that Day of bliss,
When teeming Nature blooms afresh;
May we rejoice therein, O Lord,
To Thy sweet favor then restored.

5. Kind Trinity, for evermore
Let all Thy creatures Thee adore,
As, new by pardon, Thee we raise
A new-made canticle of praise.

88 88 (LM)

Tune:
Gonfalon Royal

Final Verses: Richard Lloyd (1993) #80; Noel Rawsthorne (2011) #136.
T. Source: *Lauda Syon: Ancient Latin Hymns* (London, 1857) p. 129.
Melody: Sir Percy Carter Buck (d. 1947); first published in *Fourteen Hymn Tunes* (1913).
M. Source: *Catholic Hymn Book* (London Oratory, 1998) p. 140. The tune was originally paired with *Vexilla Regis* ("Flag of the King"). A *gonfalon* ("flag") was traditionally carried during Catholic processions.

Second Tune – *Trns: John David Chambers (d. 1893)*

4. Thy Day draws near, that Day of bliss,
When teeming Nature blooms afresh;
May we rejoice therein, O Lord,
To Thy sweet favor then restored.

5. Kind Trinity, for evermore
Let all Thy creatures Thee adore,
As, new by pardon, Thee we raise
A new-made canticle of praise.

T. Source: *Lauda Syon: Ancient Latin Hymns* (London, 1857) p. 129.
Melody: Kevin Allen (b. 1965), choirmaster at the Monastery of the Holy Cross in Chicago.
M. Source: *Saint Jean de Brébeuf Hymnal* (2018).

88 88 (LM)
Tune: Rogers Park

244 Jam Christe Sol Justitiae (6th century)

THIRD TUNE – *Trns: John David Chambers (d. 1893)*

4. Thy Day draws near, that Day of bliss,
When teeming Nature blooms afresh;
May we rejoice therein, O Lord,
To Thy sweet favor then restored.

5. Kind Trinity, for evermore
Let all Thy creatures Thee adore,
As, new by pardon, Thee we raise
A new-made canticle of praise.

88 88 (LM)

Tune:
EISENACH

Final Verses: Richard Lloyd (1993) #64; Noel Rawsthorne (2011) #108.
T. Source: *Lauda Syon: Ancient Latin Hymns* (London, 1857) p. 129.
Melody: Bartholomäus Gesius (d. 1613); adapted by Johann H. Schein (d. 1630).
M. Source: *New Saint Basil Hymnal* (1958) p. 120; *The Catholic Vesper Hymn Book set to Music either for Unison or Four Voices with Accompaniment* (Charles Lewis, 1877) p. 34; *Pope Pius XII Hymnal* (Ohio: Gregorian Institute of America, 1959) p. 13.

Jam Christe Sol Justitiae (6th century)

Fourth Tune – *Trns: John David Chambers (d. 1893)*

4. Thy Day draws near, that Day of bliss,
When teeming Nature blooms afresh;
May we rejoice therein, O Lord,
To Thy sweet favor then restored.

5. Kind Trinity, for evermore
Let all Thy creatures Thee adore,
As, new by pardon, Thee we raise
A new-made canticle of praise.

Melody: Flor Peeters (d. 1986), organist at the Catholic Cathedral of Mechelen, Belgium, was made a Baron by King Baudouin.
M. Source: *People's Mass Book* (Omer Westendorf, 1964) p. 218.
T. Source: *Lauda Syon: Ancient Latin Hymns* (London, 1857) p. 129.

88 88 (LM)

Tune: Kempen

246 Jam Christe Sol Justitiae (6th century)

Fifth Tune – *Trns: John David Chambers (d. 1893)*

4. Thy Day draws near, that Day of bliss,
When teeming Nature blooms afresh;
May we rejoice therein, O Lord,
To Thy sweet favor then restored.

5. Kind Trinity, for evermore
Let all Thy creatures Thee adore,
As, new by pardon, Thee we raise
A new-made canticle of praise.

88 88 (LM)

Tune:
Agincourt

T. Source: *Lauda Syon: Ancient Latin Hymns* (London, 1857) p. 129.
Melody: From a 15th century English manuscript.
M. Source: *Hymns, Psalms, and Spiritual Canticles* (Massachusetts: Theodore Marier, 1983) p. 450.

Sixth Tune – *Trns: John David Chambers (d. 1893)*

4. Thy Day draws near, that Day of bliss,
When teeming Nature blooms afresh;
May we rejoice therein, O Lord,
To Thy sweet favor then restored.

5. Kind Trinity, for evermore
Let all Thy creatures Thee adore,
As, new by pardon, Thee we raise
A new-made canticle of praise.

88 88 (LM)

T. Source: *Lauda Syon: Ancient Latin Hymns* (London, 1857) p. 129.
M. Source: *A Supplement to a New Version of the Psalms of David* (1708).

Tune: Alfreton

248 Jam Christe Sol Justitiae (6th century)

Seventh Tune – *Trns: John David Chambers (d. 1893)*

4. Thy Day draws near, that Day of bliss,
When teeming Nature blooms afresh;
May we rejoice therein, O Lord,
To Thy sweet favor then restored.

5. Kind Trinity, for evermore
Let all Thy creatures Thee adore,
As, new by pardon, Thee we raise
A new-made canticle of praise.

88 88 (LM)

Tune:
Ioannes

T. Source: *Lauda Syon: Ancient Latin Hymns* (London, 1857) p. 129.
M. Source: Cento from *The Parochial Hymn Book, Words and Melodies; containing Vespers, Compline, and all the Liturgical Hymns for the Year both in Latin and English* (London, 1883), edited by Fr. Anatole Police; Imprimatur by Henry Edward Cardinal Manning (d. 1892), who in 1851 converted from Anglicanism and was appointed Archbishop of Westminster in 1865.

Jam Christe Sol Justitiae (6th century)

Trns: John David Chambers (d. 1893)

Can be sung with any 88 88 meter, such as EISENACH, ROGERS PARK, BRESSANI, LA ROCHELLE, KEMPEN, BESSEMER, TALLIS CANON, WINCHESTER NEW, etc.

THY rays, O Sun of Justice, send
and all our sinful shadows rend;
With virtue light our souls once more,
And unto earth Thy day restore.

2. The time acceptable is here;
Make our repentant hearts sincere;
Convert us with Thy kindly care,
Whom Thy long-suff'ring mercies spare.

3. Grant that for all our deep offense
We offer Thee meet penitence;
That Thy benign and sovereign grace
May these our grievous sins efface.

4. Thy Day draws near, that Day of bliss,
When teeming Nature blooms afresh;
May we rejoice therein, O Lord,
To Thy sweet favor then restored.

5. Kind Trinity, for evermore
Let all Thy creatures Thee adore,
As, new by pardon, Thee we raise
A new-made canticle of praise.

88 88 (LM)

T. Source: *Lauda Syon: Ancient Latin Hymns* (London, 1857) p. 129.

Tune: VARIOUS

250 Jam Christe Sol Justitiae (6th century)

Trns: Bishop Edward G. Bagshawe (d. 1915)

4. The day will come, Thy day, when all
Thou wilt in freshest bloom renew;
Then our glad souls let Thy right hand
Lead back, and with true life endue.

5. May all the world before Thee fall
And worship, Trinity Divine,
May we new songs of worship sing,
And with new graces ever shine.

88 88 (LM)

Tune:
ALTONA

Final Verses: Noel Rawsthorne (2011) #378; one note altered.
T. Source: *Breviary Hymns and Missal Sequences* (London: Burns & Oates, 1900) p. 7; Father Bagshawe was a priest of the Oratory of St. Philip Neri until 1874, when he was consecrated bishop of the Catholic diocese of Nottingham.
Melody: Schumann's *Geistliche Lieder* (1539); an adaptation by Fr. Stephan Lück (d. 1883) in his hymnal, *Gesang- und Gebetbuch für die Diözese Trier* (1847) p. 19. Called by various names (VOM HIMMEL HOCH, ERFURT, etc.) this melody has been set by such composers as Hassler, Gesius, Praetorius, and Bach.
M. Source: *Hosanna Catholic Hymn Book* (1914) p. 17; *New Westminster Hymnal* (1939) p. 8.

Jam Christe Sol Justitiae (6th century)

Trns: Bishop Edward G. Bagshawe (d. 1915)

Can be sung with any 88 88 meter, such as HILDERSTONE, DUGUET, BRESLAU, MELCOMBE, WAREHAM, OLD HUNDREDTH, MEIN SEEL, TRINITY COLLEGE, etc.

O JESUS, our salvation's Sun,
Shine Thou our inmost hearts within,
Dispel the night; let brighter day
Now for the darkened world begin.

2. Grant in this time acceptable
That we with tears may cleanse for Thee
The victim of our heart, and then
Burn it with gladsome charity.

3. The very source that poured forth guilt,
Shall with incessant weeping flow,
If hardened heart be made to melt
By rod of penitential woe.

4. The day will come, Thy day, when all
Thou wilt in freshest bloom renew;
Then our glad souls let Thy right hand
Lead back, and with true life endue.

5. May all the world before Thee fall
And worship, Trinity Divine,
May we new songs of worship sing,
And with new graces ever shine.

88 88 (LM)

Tune:
VARIOUS

T. Source: *Breviary Hymns and Missal Sequences* (London: Burns & Oates, 1900) p. 7; Father Bagshawe was a priest of the Oratory of St. Philip Neri until 1874, when he was consecrated bishop of the Catholic diocese of Nottingham.

252 Jam Desinant Suspiria (1736 AD)

Fr. Charles Coffin (d. 1749)

To sing in Latin,
use any 88 88 (LM) tune.

JAM désinant suspíria;
Audívit ex alto Deus:
Caeli patéscunt; en adest
Promíssa pax mortálibus.

2. Profúnda noctis ótia
Caeléstis abrúmpit chorus;
Natúmque festo cármine
Annúntiat terris Deum.

3. Specum sacrátam pérvigil
Dum turba pastórum subit,
Eámus, et castis pia
Cunis ferámus óscula.

4. At quale nobis pánditur
Intrántibus spectáculum!
Praesépe, foenum, fásciae,
Parens inops, infans puer.

5. Tu-n*e* ille, Christe, Fílius
Et splendor aetérni Patris?
Illum-ne cerno qui levi
Orbem pugíllo sústinet?

6. Sic est: verénda queis lates,
Fides penétrat núbila:
Agnósco quem proni vident,
Tremunt, adórant Ángeli.

7. Agis magístrum vel tacens:
Ex hac cathédra nos doces
Vitáre quod carni placet,
Caro quod horret pérpeti.

8. Castos amóres nútriens,
Sanans tuméntes spíritus,
Divíne, nostris, ô Puer,
Praecórdiis innáscere.

88 88 (LM)

Tune:
VARIOUS

T. Source: Bl. John Henry Cardinal Newman's *Hymni Ecclesiae* (London, 1865), p. 32; *Breviarium Sanctae Lugdunensis Ecclesiae*(Paris, 1780) p. 247; *Breviarium Ebroicense* (Paris, 1737) p. 209.

Assistance for comprehension

LET sighs now cease;
God on high has heard:
the heavens stretch wide; lo,
the peace pledged to mortals is at hand.

2. A heavenly choir breaks
the deep rest of the night;
and with celebratory chant
declares God born on earth.

3. As the wakeful host of shepherds
nears the hallowed cavern,
let us go, and bear devout kisses
to the chaste cradle.

4. But what manner of pageant
is unfolded to us as we enter?
A manger, hay, swaddling,
a poor Mother, an infant Child!

5. Art thou not, O Christ, the Son
and brightness of the Father everlasting?
Do I not behold him who bears
the globe with an easy hand?

6. It is so: faith pierces the dreadful clouds
by which thou art concealed:
I recognize him whom prostrate Angels see,
who tremble before him, and adore.

7. Even unspeaking thou dost act as our Master:
thou teachest us from this chair
to flee that which pleases the flesh,
to abide that at which the flesh quails.

8. Fostering chaste loves,
healing spirits swollen with pride,
O Child divine, come to birth
within our hearts!

254 **Jam Desinant Suspiria** (1736 AD)

Trns: Robert Campbell of Skerrington (d. 1868)

1. Ye peo - ple, cease from tears, Your prayers are
2. O'er Ju - dah's si - lent plains, An - gel - ic
3. The faith - ful shep - herds hear, And haste the

heard a - bove; And from his throne in heav'n ap - pears
voic - es sing, An - nounc - ing in tri - um - phant strains
Babe to greet; Let us like them with joy draw near,

The God of peace and love.
The birth - day of our king.
And wor - ship at his feet.

4. But, full of strange surprise,
What spectacle is seen?
An Infant in the manger lies,
His parents poor and mean.

5. Do not we here behold
The Son of God most high,
Who doth within his hand enfold
The earth and sea and sky?

6. Faith penetrates the veil,
And through the cloud drawn o'er,
Sees him whom angels trembling hail,
The God whom they adore.

7. O Babe, thy birth despised
And lowly manger tell,
To flee from all below that's prized,
And with the meek to dwell.

8. From sinful shame and pride
Guard us, thou Child divine;
Then wilt thou in our hearts abide,
Thy cradle and thy shrine.

* The word "mean" here denotes "lowly, humble, modest."

66 86 (SM)

Tune:
POTSDAM

ENGLISH TRANSLATION: Robert Campbell, a Scottish attorney who published *Hymns and Anthems for Use in the Holy Service of the Church* (1850). He converted to the Catholic Church in 1852, but was never a priest—despite the claim made in the *American Catholic Hymnal according to the Motu Proprio of His Holiness Pope Pius X* (1913) on page 251.
T. Source: Orby Shipley's *Annus Sanctus: Hymns of the Church for the Ecclesiastical Year; Translated from the Sacred Offices by various Authors, with Modern, Original, and other Hymns, and an Appendix of Earlier Versions* (London: Burns and Oates, 1884) p. 30.
Melody: Based on the magnificent Fugue in E, *Well-tempered Clavier*, Part II, No. 9, by J. S. Bach (d. 1750).
M. Source: *Adoremus Hymnal* (1997) #471; *Songs of Syon* (Woodward, 1910) p. 51.

Trns: Robert Campbell of Skerrington (d. 1868)

Can be sung with any 66 86 meter: FESTAL SONG, ALLINGTON, SEÁN 8M, DOMINICA, SOUTHWELL, ST MICHAEL, SONG 20, POTSDAM, etc.

YE people, cease from tears,
Your prayers are heard above;
And from his throne in heav'n appears
The God of peace and love.

2. O'er Judah's silent plains,
Angelic voices sing,
Announcing in triumphant strains
The birth-day of our king.

3. The faithful shepherds hear,
And haste the Babe to greet;
Let us like them with joy draw near,
And worship at his feet.

4. But, full of strange surprise,
What spectacle is seen?
An Infant in the manger lies,
His parents poor and mean.

5. Do not we here behold
The Son of God most high,
Who doth within his hand enfold
The earth and sea and sky?

6. Faith penetrates the veil,
And through the cloud drawn o'er,
Sees him whom angels trembling hail,
The God whom they adore.

7. O Babe, thy birth despised
And lowly manger tell,
To flee from all below that's prized,
And with the meek to dwell.

8. From sinful shame and pride
Guard us, thou Child divine;
Then wilt thou in our hearts abide,
Thy cradle and thy shrine.

ENGLISH TRANSLATION: Robert Campbell of Skerrington (d. 1868); cf. Orby Shipley's *Annus Sanctus: Hymns of the Church for the Ecclesiastical Year; Translated from the Sacred Offices by various Authors, with Modern, Original, and other Hymns, and an Appendix of Earlier Versions* (1884) p. 30.

88 88 (LM)

Tune: VARIOUS

256 Jesu Nostra Redemptio (7th century)

Title after 1631AD: *"Salutis Humanae Sator"*

To sing in Latin,
use any 88 88 (LM) tune.

JESU nostra redémptio,
Amor et desidérium,
Deus Creátor ómnium, *n1*
Homo in fine témporum. *n2*

2. Quae te vicit cleméntia,
Ut ferres nostra crímina,
Crudélem mortem pátiens,
Ut nos a morte tólleres?

3. Inférni claustra pénetrans,
Tuos captívos rédimens, *n3*
Victor triúmpho nóbili
Ad dextram Patris résidens.

4. Ipsa te cogat píetas
Ut mala nostra súperes
Parcénd*o* et voti cómpotes
Nos tuo vultu sáties. *n4*

5. Tu esto nostrum gáudium,
Qui es futúrus praémium,
Sit nostra in te glória,
Per cuncta semper saécula.

88 88 (LM)

Tune:
VARIOUS

T. Source: *Hymni de Tempore et de Sanctis in Textu Antiquo et Novo* (Solesmes, 1885) p. 49; the author of this hymn is not known.

Assistance for comprehension

O JESUS, our ransoming,
love and longing,
God, the Creator of all things, *n1*
man at the end of time. *n2*

2. What mercy conquered thee,
so as to bear our misdeeds,
suffering a cruel death,
so as to lift us from death?

3. Piercing the dungeons of hell,
ransoming thy hostages, *n3*
conqueror in a famous victory,
enthroned at the Father's right.

4. Let that tenderness impel thee
to overcome our ills
by sparing us, and sate us,
who share the desire, with thy face. *n4*

5. Be our joy,
thou who art to be our reward,
in thee be our glory
ever through all the ages.

[1] "Christ as Creator," cf. second footnote on page 421.

[2] "End of time" cf. Gal 4.4.

[3] "Thy hostages": captured by Satan, redeemed by Christ, and hence "his" hostages.

[4] "That tenderness": cf. verse 2; "by sparing": to destroy our sins by forgiving them "and sate us ... thy face" seems to mean: "Satisfy our longing to see thy face (through the beatific vision)."

258 Jesu Nostra Redemptio (7th century)

First Tune – *Trns: Fr. John Fitzpatrick, Oblate of Mary (d. 1929)*

4. Compelled by pity, let Thy grace
Our losses and our ills repair;
And may the vision of Thy face
With us its blessèd radiance share.

5. Our guide to Heaven and the road,
Be Thou the goal to which we tend;
Our joy in this our sad abode,
Our life's reward which ne'er shall end.

88 88 (LM)

Tune:
La Rochelle

Melody: James W. Elliott (d. 1915)
M. Source: *Hymns Ancient and Modern* (1972) p. 320.
T. Source: *The Breviary and Missal Hymns* (London: Sands & Co, 1931) p. 79.

Jesu Nostra Redemptio (7th century) 259

Second Tune – *Trns: Fr. John Fitzpatrick, Oblate of Mary (d. 1929)*

1. Re - deem - er of our fall - en state,
2. What clem - en - cy Thy heart o'er - came,
3. Thou dost the gates of hell with - stand,

Thou, Je - sus, joy of eve - ry heart,
That Thou wouldst bear our load of sin?
Its cap - tives from their fet - ters free,

Who didst Thy ran - somed world cre - ate,
And, sin - less, die a death of shame,
As vic - tor sit at God's right hand,

Pure light to faith - ful souls Thou art.
From death and hell our souls to win?
And reign with Him tri - um - phant - ly.

4. Compelled by pity, let Thy grace
Our losses and our ills repair;
And may the vision of Thy face
With us its blessèd radiance share.

5. Our guide to Heaven and the road,
Be Thou the goal to which we tend;
Our joy in this our sad abode,
Our life's reward which ne'er shall end.

Melody: Kevin Allen (b. 1965), choirmaster at the Monastery of the Holy Cross in Chicago.
M. Source: *Saint Jean de Brébeuf Hymnal* (2018).
T. Source: *The Breviary and Missal Hymns* (London: Sands & Co, 1931) p. 79.

88 88 (LM)
Tune:
Rogers Park

260 Jesu Nostra Redemptio (7th century)

THIRD TUNE – *Trns: Fr. John Fitzpatrick, Oblate of Mary* (*d. 1929*)

4. Compelled by pity, let Thy grace
Our losses and our ills repair;
And may the vision of Thy face
With us its blessèd radiance share.

5. Our guide to Heaven and the road,
Be Thou the goal to which we tend;
Our joy in this our sad abode,
Our life's reward which ne'er shall end.

88 88 (LM)

Tune:
BRESSANI

Melody: From a hymn book published by Fr. Melchior Ludolf Herold (d. 1810).
M. Source: *New Westminster Hymnal* (1939) p. 173.
T. Source: *The Breviary and Missal Hymns* (London: Sands & Co, 1931) p. 79.

Jesu Nostra Redemptio (7th century)

Trns: Fr. John Fitzpatrick, Oblate of Mary (d. 1929)

Can be sung with any 88 88 meter, such as HILDERSTONE, DUGUET, BRESLAU, MELCOMBE, WAREHAM, OLD HUNDREDTH, MEIN SEEL, TRINITY COLLEGE, etc.

REDEEMER of our fallen state,
Thou, Jesus, joy of every heart,
Who didst Thy ransomed world create,
Pure light to faithful souls Thou art.

2. What clemency Thy heart o'ercame,
That Thou wouldst bear our load of sin?
And, sinless, die a death of shame,
From death and hell our souls to win?

3. Thou dost the gates of hell withstand,
Its captives from their fetters free,
As victor sit at God's right hand,
And reign with Him triumphantly.

4. Compelled by pity, let Thy grace
Our losses and our ills repair;
And may the vision of Thy face
With us its blessèd radiance share.

5. Our guide to Heaven and the road,
Be Thou the goal to which we tend;
Our joy in this our sad abode,
Our life's reward which ne'er shall end.

88 88 (LM)

Tune: VARIOUS

T. Source: *The Breviary and Missal Hymns* (London: Sands & Co, 1931) p. 79.

262 Jesu Nostra Redemptio (7th century)

1599AD – Historic Roman Catholic Translation

Can be sung with any 88 88 meter, such as Hilderstone, Duguet, Breslau, Melcombe, Wareham, Old Hundredth, Mein Seel, Trinity College, etc.

O OUR redemption Jesus Christ,
Our love and our desire always:
O God that every thing did'st make,
And man became in later days.

Jesu nostra redémptio,
Amor et desidérium,
Deus Creátor ómnium,
Homo in fine témporum.

2. What clemency subdued thee so,
That thou wouldst take our sins on thee:
For us to suffer cruel death,
Thereby from death to set us free?

Quae te vicit cleméntia,
Ut ferres nostra crímina,
Crudélem mortem pátiens,
Ut nos a morte tólleres?

3. And piercing through the gates of hell,
Thine to redeem that were distrest,
As conqueror with triumph great,
On thy father's right hand to rest.

Inférni claustra pénetrans,
Tuos captívos rédimens,
Victor triúmpho nóbili
Ad dextram Patris résidens.

4. Let pity of itself thee urge,
That thou our evils do subdue,
And sparing us, with filled desire,
Of thy sweet face to take the view.

Ipsa te cogat píetas
Ut mala nostra súperes
Parcénd*o* et voti cómpotes
Nos tuo vultu sáties.

5. Our joy therefore vouchsafe to be,
Which art the hire that we attend,
Let all our glory rest in thee,
And that it never have an end.

Tu esto nostrum gáudium,
Qui es futúrus praémium,
Sit nostra in te glória,
Per cuncta semper saécula.

88 88 (LM)

Tune: Various

T. Source: *Primer, or, Office of the Blessed Virgin Marie in Latin and English, according to the reformed Latin, and with Lyke Graces Privileged* (Antwerp, 1599) p. 12. The Catholic Encyclopedia of 1912 attributes the hymn translations to the book's editor, Richard Verstegan (d. 1636), a Catholic publisher. In the 1599 Preface, Verstegan says: "Notwithstanding the difficulty, these hymns have been so turned into English meter that they may be sung unto the same tunes in English that they bear in Latin." However, his accentual treatment is sometimes peculiar.

1807AD – Historic Roman Catholic Translation

Can be sung with any 88 88 meter, such as EISENACH, ROGERS PARK, BRESSANI, LA ROCHELLE, KEMPEN, BESSEMER, TALLIS CANON, WINCHESTER NEW, etc.

Salútis humánae Sator, Jesu volúptas córdium, Orbis redémpti Cónditor, Et casta lux amántium.	O JESUS, Savior of mankind, Delight of ev'ry pious mind; Restorer of man's fallen race, And purest source of light and grace!
Qua victus es cleméntia, Ut nostra ferres crímina, Mortem subíres ínnocens, A morte nos ut tólleres?	2. O boundless love! O matchless grace! Thou, guiltless, tak'st the guilty's place; And, to make wretchèd sinners live, Thou, spotless Lamb! thy life would'st give.
Perrúmpis inférnum chaos, Vinctis caténas détrahis: Victor triúmpho nóbili, Ad déxteram Patris sedes.	3 Th' infernal gates are forc'd by thee, Hell's captives from their chains set free; And thou, with this triumphant train, Ascend'st on God's right hand to reign.
Te cogat indulgéntia, Ut damna nostra sárcias, Tuíque vultus cómpotes, Dites beáto lúmine.	4. Let now kind mercy plead our cause; Heal thou our wounds, repair our loss; And call us to enjoy thy sight, In realms of everlasting light.
Tu Dux ad astr*a* et sémita, Sis meta nostris córdibus, Sis lacrymárum gáudium, Sis dulce vitae praémium.	5. O Jesus, whilst on earth we stay, Guide thou our footsteps in thy way; And soothe our sorrows with thy love, Until we reign with thee above.

T. Source: *Hymns for the Use of the Catholic Church in America* (Baltimore: John W. Butler, 1807) p. 61. The Preface to this remarkable collection begins:

> Next to the offering of the Eucharistical Sacrifice, which is the most sublime and the more essential act of divine worship, the singing of the praises of God and of the Lamb is unquestionably the noblest employment of a Christian. He who sings to God with a proper sense of devotion associates himself to the Choirs of Angels, and shares upon earth in the sweetest occupation of the blessed inhabitants of Heaven.
>
> It cannot be doubted but that the most proper time for this holy exercise is when the faithful meet together in Church; and especially when the Lamb that was slain on the cross for the redemption of the world, comes down on our altars, and there continues to offer himself for us to his heavenly Father. […]
>
> Besides a variety of Spiritual Canticles, the Catholic reader will have the satisfaction of finding a translation in verse, as literal as this kind of composition could permit, of those ancient hymns, which have been sung in the Catholic Church on the various festivals of our Lord, of the Blessed Virgin and of the Saints, through the year, for upwards of fourteen centuries…

Such words could easily have been written today; yet—to give historical context—they appeared two years before Pope Pius VII was taken prisoner by Napoléon Bonaparte, not being released until 1814.

88 88 (LM)

Tune: VARIOUS

264 Jesu Redemptor Omnium (6th century)

Title before 1631AD: *"Christe Redemptor Omnium"*

To sing in Latin, use any 88 88 (LM) tune.

CHRISTE Redémptor ómnium,
Ex Patre Patris único,
Solus ante princípium *n1*
Natus ineffabíliter.

2. Tu lumen, tu splendor Patris, *n2*
Tu spes perénnis ómnium,
Inténde quas fundunt preces,
Tui per orbem fámuli.

3. Meménto salútis Auctor,
Quod nostri quondam córporis,
Ex illibáta Vírgine
Nascéndo, formam súmpseris.

4. Sic praesens testátur dies,
Currens per anni círculum,
Quod solus a sede Patris
Mundi salus advéneris.

5. Hunc caelum, terra, hunc mare,
Hunc omne quod in eis est,
Auctórem advéntus tui,
Laudans exsúltat cántico.

6. Nos quoque, qui sancto tuo
Redémpti Sánguine sumus, *n3*
Ob diem natális tui,
Hymnum novum concínimus. *n4*

7. Glória tibi, Dómine,
Qui natus es de Vírgine,
Cum Patr*e* et Sancto Spíritu,
In sempitérna saécula.

88 88 (LM)

Tune:
VARIOUS

T. Source: *Hymni de Tempore et de Sanctis in Textu Antiquo et Novo* (Solesmes, 1885) p. 30. The Urbanite title (*Jesu Redemptor Omnium*) is used throughout our book to avoid confusion with the 9th-century hymn by Rabanus Maurus, the Archbishop of Mainz, also called *Christe Redemptor Omnium*.

[1] "With thee is the principality in the day of thy strength: in the brightness of the saints: from the womb before the day star I begot thee." (Ps 109.3).

Assistance for comprehension

O CHRIST, Redeemer of all,
Only-begotten of the Father,
alone born of the Father *n1*
inexpressibly and before the beginning:

2. Thou light, thou radiance of the Father, *n2*
thou undying hope of all,
pay heed to the prayers that thy servants
pour forth throughout the earth.

3. Recall, O Founder of salvation,
that thou didst once take on
the cast of our body
through birth of a flawless virgin.

4. Thus does this day bear witness,
as it courses on a yearly orbit,
that thou, who alone art the world's salvation,
camest nigh from the Father's throne.

5. The sky, the land, the sea,
and everything that is in them,
revel in song as they praise
this day, the founder of thy coming.

6. We too, who have been redeemed
with thy holy blood, *n3*
meeting the day of thy birth,
sing together a new hymn. *n4*

7. Glory to thee, O Lord,
who wast born of the Virgin,
with the Father and the Holy Spirit,
forever and ever.

[2] Heb 1.3: "Who being the brightness of his glory, and the figure of his substance, and upholding all things by the word of his power, making purgation of sins, sitteth on the right hand of the majesty on high." Cf. also Wis 7.26; I Jn 1.5.

[3] "Knowing that you were not redeemed with corruptible things; but with the precious blood of Christ…" (I Pet 1.18).

[4] "And they sang a new canticle, saying: Thou art worthy, O Lord…because thou wast slain, and hast redeemed us to God, in thy blood…" (Apocalypse 5.9); "Sing to him a new canticle, sing well unto him with a loud noise" (Ps 32.3); "Sing ye to the Lord a new canticle: because he hath done wonderful things" (Ps 97.1); "Sing ye to the Lord a new canticle: let his praise be in the church of the saints" (Ps 149.1); "And they sang as it were a new canticle, before the throne…" (Jdth 16.15); "Let us sing a hymn to the Lord, let us sing a new hymn to our God" (Apocalypse 14.3).

266 Jesu Redemptor Omnium (6th century)

First Tune – *Trns: Msgr. Ronald A. Knox (d. 1957)*

4. Each waning year doth testify
That from thy Father's throne on high
Thou, and no other, on this morn
Didst come to save a world forlorn.

5. Earth, sea, and sky, thy three-fold plan,
And all that heaven's vault doth span,
Echo thy praise in mute accord
To greet the advent of their Lord.

6. And we in turn, whose life to save
That hallowed blood redemption gave,
On this, the birth day of our King
New songs of salutation bring.

7. Jesus, of Virgin Mother born,
Praise be to thee this holy morn;
Praise to the Father endlessly
And his life-giving Spirit be.

88 88 (LM)

Tune:
Song 34

Final Verses: Richard Lloyd (1993) #214; Noel Rawsthorne (2011) #342.
T. Source: *The New Westminster Hymnal* (1939) p. 9.
Melody: Orlando Gibbons (d. 1625), organist at Westminster Abbey.
M. Source: *The Hymnes and Songs of the Church* (1623) p. 114; originally sung to "Thus Angells sung, and thus sing we." We have adopted the most commonly used rhythm. Cf. *New Saint Basil Hymnal* (1958) p. 136.

Jesu Redemptor Omnium (6th century) 267

SECOND TUNE – *Trns: Msgr. Ronald A. Knox (d. 1957)*

4. Each waning year doth testify
That from thy Father's throne on high
Thou, and no other, on this morn
Didst come to save a world forlorn.

5. Earth, sea, and sky, thy three-fold plan,
And all that heaven's vault doth span,
Echo thy praise in mute accord
To greet the advent of their Lord.

6. And we in turn, whose life to save
That hallowed blood redemption gave,
On this, the birth day of our King
New songs of salutation bring.

7. Jesus, of Virgin Mother born,
Praise be to thee this holy morn;
Praise to the Father endlessly
And his life-giving Spirit be.

Final Verses: Richard Lloyd (1993) #75; Noel Rawsthorne (2011) #128.
T. Source: *The New Westminster Hymnal* (1939) p. 9.
Melody: William Gardiner (d. 1853) in *Sacred Melodies* (1815).
M. Source: *Catholic Hymn Book* (London Oratory, 1998) p. 334.

88 88 (LM)
Tune:
FULDA

268 Jesu Redemptor Omnium (6th century)

THIRD TUNE – *Trns: Msgr. Ronald A. Knox (d. 1957)*

4. Each waning year doth testify
That from thy Father's throne on high
Thou, and no other, on this morn
Didst come to save a world forlorn.

5. Earth, sea, and sky, thy three-fold plan,
And all that heaven's vault doth span,
Echo thy praise in mute accord
To greet the advent of their Lord.

6. And we in turn, whose life to save
That hallowed blood redemption gave,
On this, the birth day of our King
New songs of salutation bring.

7. Jesus, of Virgin Mother born,
Praise be to thee this holy morn;
Praise to the Father endlessly
And his life-giving Spirit be.

88 88 (LM)

Tune:
MEIN SEEL O GOTT

Melody: Michael Praetorius (d. 1621), a German organist and theorist.
M. Source: *New Westminster Hymnal* (1939) p. 205.
T. Source: *The New Westminster Hymnal* (1939) p. 9.

Jesu Redemptor Omnium (6th century) 269

FOURTH TUNE – *Trns: Msgr. Ronald A. Knox (d. 1957)*

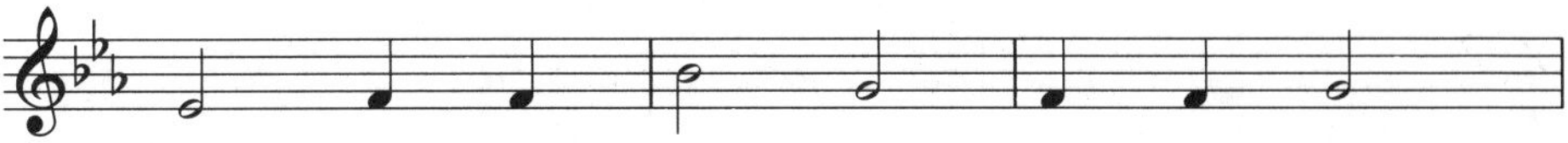

1. Sav - ior of all, for ev - er One
2. Splen - dor and light of his own fire,
3. Au - thor of life, re - mem - ber still

With God the Fa - ther; on - ly Son,
E - ter - nal hope of man's de - sire,
In for - mer times thy lov - ing will,

Whom he a - lone, when time was not,
Look down and hear the prayers that we
Our mor - tal na - ture to as - sume,

Past our im - ag - in - ing, be - got,
In world - wide hom - age make to thee.
Born of a spot - less Vir - gin's womb.

4. Each waning year doth testify
That from thy Father's throne on high
Thou, and no other, on this morn
Didst come to save a world forlorn.

5. Earth, sea, and sky, thy three-fold plan,
And all that heaven's vault doth span,
Echo thy praise in mute accord
To greet the advent of their Lord.

6. And we in turn, whose life to save
That hallowed blood redemption gave,
On this, the birth day of our King
New songs of salutation bring.

7. Jesus, of Virgin Mother born,
Praise be to thee this holy morn;
Praise to the Father endlessly
And his life-giving Spirit be.

88 88 (LM)

Melody: Kevin Allen (b. 1965), choirmaster at the Monastery of the Holy Cross in Chicago.
M. Source: *Saint Edmund Campion Missal and Hymnal* (2013) p. 882.
T. Source: *The New Westminster Hymnal* (1939) p. 9.

Tune: CUPERTINO

270 Jesu Redemptor Omnium (6th century)

Fifth Tune – *Trns: Msgr. Ronald A. Knox (d. 1957)*

1. Sav - ior of all, for ev - er__ One
2. Splen - dor and light of his own_ fire,
3. Au - thor of life, re - mem - ber__ still

With God the Fa - ther; on - ly__ Son,
E - ter - nal hope of man's de - sire,
In for - mer times thy lov - ing__ will,

Whom he a - lone, when time was_ not,
Look down and hear the prayers that_ we
Our mor - tal na - ture to as - sume,

Past our im - ag - in - ing, be - got,
In world - wide hom - age make to thee.
Born of a spot - less Vir - gin's womb.

4. Each waning year doth testify
That from thy Father's throne on high
Thou, and no other, on this morn
Didst come to save a world forlorn.

5. Earth, sea, and sky, thy three-fold plan,
And all that heaven's vault doth span,
Echo thy praise in mute accord
To greet the advent of their Lord.

6. And we in turn, whose life to save
That hallowed blood redemption gave,
On this, the birth day of our King
New songs of salutation bring.

7. Jesus, of Virgin Mother born,
Praise be to thee this holy morn;
Praise to the Father endlessly
And his life-giving Spirit be.

88 88 (LM)

Tune:
Symphoniacae

T. Source: *The New Westminster Hymnal* (1939) p. 9.
Melody: *Katholischen Kirchengesangbuch* (1625).
M. Source: *Episcopal Hymnal* (1940) #56; *Songs of Syon* (Woodward, 1910) p. 576.

Jesu Redemptor Omnium (6th century)

Trns: Msgr. Ronald A. Knox (d. 1957)

Can be sung with any 88 88 meter, such as EISENACH, ROGERS PARK, BRESSANI, LA ROCHELLE, KEMPEN, BESSEMER, TALLIS CANON, WINCHESTER NEW, etc.

SAVIOR of all, for ever One
With God the Father; only Son,
Whom he alone, when time was not,
Past our imagining, begot,

2. Splendor and light of his own fire,
Eternal hope of man's desire,
Look down and hear the prayers that we
In world-wide homage make to thee.

3. Author of life, remember still
In former times thy loving will,
Our mortal nature to assume,
Born of a spotless Virgin's womb.

4. Each waning year doth testify
That from thy Father's throne on high
Thou, and no other, on this morn
Didst come to save a world forlorn.

5. Earth, sea, and sky, thy three-fold plan,
And all that heaven's vault doth span,
Echo thy praise in mute accord
To greet the advent of their Lord.

6. And we in turn, whose life to save
That hallowed blood redemption gave,
On this, the birth day of our King
New songs of salutation bring.

7. Jesus, of Virgin Mother born,
Praise be to thee this holy morn;
Praise to the Father endlessly
And his life-giving Spirit be.

88 88 (LM)

Tune: VARIOUS

T. Source: *The New Westminster Hymnal* (1939) p. 9.

272 Jesu Redemptor Omnium (6th century)

Trns: Fr. Edward Caswall, Oratorian (d. 1878)

4. This day to that divine event
Doth year by year its witness bear:
Thou madest, by Thy Father sent,
The world's redemption Thine own care.

5. O Day! to which the seas and sky,
And earth and Heaven welcome sing;
O Day! which heal'd our misery,
And brought on earth salvation's King.

6. We too, whose souls Thy Precious Blood,
Hath cleansèd from their sinful stain,
A tribute to Thy birth day pay,
Raising our hymn with joyous strain.

7. Jesus, the Virgin's only Son,
Be praise and glory giv'n to Thee,
With Father and with Spirit one,
In time and in eternity.

88 88 (LM)

Tune: Altona

Final Verses: Noel Rawsthorne (2011) #378; one note altered.
Melody: Schumann's *Geistliche Lieder* (1539); an adaptation by Fr. Stephan Lück (d. 1883) in his hymnal, *Gesang- und Gebetbuch für die Diözese Trier* (1847) p. 19. Called by various names (Vom Himmel Hoch, Erfurt, etc.) this melody has been set by such composers as Hassler, Gesius, Praetorius, and Bach.
M. Source: *Hosanna Catholic Hymn Book* (1914) p. 17; *New Westminster Hymnal* (1939) p. 8.
T. Source: *Day Hours of the Church; According to the reforms of Pope Pius X, with a parallel English version edited by the Benedictine Nuns of the Abbey of Our Lady of Consolation at Stanbrook in Worcestershire with an Introduction by the Right Reverend Fernard Cabrol OSB, Lord Abbot of Farnborough in Hampshire* (London, 1921) p. 350.

Jesu Redemptor Omnium (6th century)

Trns: Fr. Edward Caswall, Oratorian (d. 1878)

Can be sung with any 88 88 meter, such as HILDERSTONE, DUGUET, BRESLAU, MELCOMBE, WAREHAM, OLD HUNDREDTH, MEIN SEEL, TRINITY COLLEGE, etc.

O CHRIST, Redeemer of the world,
Before the earliest dawn of light
From everlasting ages born,
Immense in glory as in might.

2. Immortal Hope of all mankind,
In whom the Father's face we see;
Hear Thou the prayers thy people pour
This day throughout the world to Thee.

3. Remember, O Creator Lord,
That in the Virgin's sacred womb
Thou wast conceiv'd, and of her flesh
Didst our mortality assume.

4. This day to that divine event
Doth year by year its witness bear:
Thou madest, by Thy Father sent,
The world's redemption Thine own care.

5. O Day! to which the seas and sky,
And earth and Heaven welcome sing;
O Day! which heal'd our misery,
And brought on earth salvation's King.

6. We too, whose souls Thy Precious Blood,
Hath cleansèd from their sinful stain,
A tribute to Thy birth day pay,
Raising our hymn with joyous strain.

7. Jesus, the Virgin's only Son,
Be praise and glory giv'n to Thee,
With Father and with Spirit one,
In time and in eternity.

T. Source: *Day Hours of the Church; According to the reforms of Pope Pius X, with a parallel English version edited by the Benedictine Nuns of the Abbey of Our Lady of Consolation at Stanbrook in Worcestershire with an Introduction by the Right Reverend Fernard Cabrol OSB, Lord Abbot of Farnborough in Hampshire* (London, 1921) p. 350.

88 88 (LM)
Tune: VARIOUS

274 Jesu Redemptor Omnium (6th century)

First Tune – *Trns: Robert Campbell of Skerrington (d. 1868)*

77 77 D

Tune:
St George

Final Verses: Richard Lloyd (1993) #197; Noel Rawsthorne (2011) #303.
Melody: George J. Elvey (d. 1893), organist at St George's Chapel at Windsor Castle.
M. Source: *Catholic Hymn Book* (1998) p. 120; *New Westminster Hymnal* (1939) p. 88; *Hymns, Psalms, and Spiritual Canticles* (Massachusetts: Theodore Marier, 1983) p. 230.
T. Source: Orby Shipley's *Annus Sanctus: Hymns of the Church for the Ecclesiastical Year; Translated from the Sacred Offices by various Authors, with Modern, Original, and other Hymns, and an Appendix of Earlier Versions* (London: Burns and Oates, 1884) p. 29.

Second Tune – *Trns: Robert Campbell of Skerrington (d. 1868)*

Melody: Würth's *Katholisches Gesangbuch* (1859).
M. Source: *Cantate Omnes: Hymnal of the Catholic Choirmasters' Guild* (1952) #46.
T. Source: Orby Shipley's *Annus Sanctus: Hymns of the Church for the Ecclesiastical Year; Translated from the Sacred Offices by various Authors, with Modern, Original, and other Hymns, and an Appendix of Earlier Versions* (London: Burns and Oates, 1884) p. 29.

77 77 D
Tune:
Paschal Lamb

276 Jesu Redemptor Omnium (6th century)

Third Tune – *Trns: Robert Campbell of Skerrington (d. 1868)*

77 77 D

Tune:
Heustis

Melody: Kevin Allen (b. 1965), choirmaster at the Monastery of the Holy Cross in Chicago.
M. Source: *Saint Jean de Brébeuf Hymnal* (2018).
T. Source: Orby Shipley's *Annus Sanctus: Hymns of the Church for the Ecclesiastical Year; Translated from the Sacred Offices by various Authors, with Modern, Original, and other Hymns, and an Appendix of Earlier Versions* (London: Burns and Oates, 1884) p. 29.

Jesu Redemptor Omnium (6th century)

Trns: Robert Campbell of Skerrington (d. 1868)

Can be sung with any 77 77 meter, such as SAVANNAH, UNIVERSITY COLLEGE, ORIENTIS PARTIBUS, LLANFAIR, CULBACH, MONKLAND, GOTT SEI DANK, etc.

LAMB, whose blood for all men streamed,
Light, that shone ere morning beamed,
God and God's eternal Son,
Ever with the Father one;

2. Splendor of the Father's light,
Star of hope for ever bright,
Hearken to the prayers that flow
From thy servants here below.

3. Lord, remember that for love
Thou didst leave thy throne above,
Man's frail nature to assume
In the holy Virgin's womb.

4. Now thy Church, each circling year,
Celebrates that love so dear;
Love that brought thee here alone,
For the guilty to atone.

5. Let not earth alone rejoice,
Seas and skies unite their voice
In a new song, to the morn
When the Lord of life was born.

6. Ransomed by the holy tide
Shed from thy most precious side,
Joyful let us hail the morn
When the Lord of life was born.

7. Virgin born, to thee be praise,
Now and through eternal days;
Father, equal praise to thee,
With the Spirit, ever be.

T. Source: Orby Shipley's *Annus Sanctus: Hymns of the Church for the Ecclesiastical Year; Translated from the Sacred Offices by various Authors, with Modern, Original, and other Hymns, and an Appendix of Earlier Versions* (London: Burns and Oates, 1884) p. 29.

77 77
Tune:
VARIOUS

278 Jesu Redemptor Omnium (6th century)

*1599*AD *– Historic Roman Catholic Translation*

Can be sung with any 88 88 meter, such as HILDERSTONE, DUGUET, BRESLAU, MELCOMBE, WAREHAM, OLD HUNDREDTH, MEIN SEEL, TRINITY COLLEGE, etc.

O CHRIST redeemer of us all,
And of the father only son,
Thy birth alone unspeakably,
Before beginning, was begun.

2. The father's light, and brightness both,
The lasting hope thou art of all:
Attend unto thy servants' plaints,
Throughout the earth on thee that call.

3. Be mindful author of our health,
That thou some-time didst take on thee,
Of a pure Virgin being born,
The form of our humanity.

4. And so this day doth witness well,
By yearly course as it doth pass:
That only from thy father's seat,
This world to save, thy coming was.

5. This day the heav'n, the earth, and sea,
This day within them all that live,
As cause that thou to us art come,
With songs rejoice and praises give.

6. And we which thy most holy blood,
Did freely to redemption bring,
In honor of thy day of birth,
A new song unto thee do sing.

7. Glory be unto thee o Lord,
The which the blessed Virgin bore,
With the father and holy ghost,
From this time forth for evermore.

Christe Redémptor ómnium,
Ex Patre Patris única,
Solus ante princípium
Natus ineffabíliter.

Tu lumen, tu splendor Patris,
Tu spes perénnis ómnium,
Inténde quas fundunt preces,
Tui per orbem fámuli.

Meménto salútis Auctor,
Quod nostri quondam córporis,
Ex illibáta Vírgine
Nascéndo, formam súmpseris.

Sic praesens testátur dies,
Currens per anni círculum,
Quod solus a sede Patris
Mundi salus advéneris.

Hunc caelum, terra, hunc mare,
Hunc omne quod in eis est,
Auctórem advéntus tui,
Laudans exsúltat cántico.

Nos quoque, qui sancto tuo
Redémpti Sánguine sumus,
Ob diem natális tui,
Hymnum novum concínimus.

Glória tibi, Dómine,
Qui natus es de Vírgine,
Cum Patr*e* et Sancto Spíritu,
In sempitérna saécula.

[1a] The Urbanite title (*Jesu Redemptor Omnium*) is used throughout our book in order to avoid confusion with the 9th-century hymn by Rabanus Maurus, the Archbishop of Mainz, also called *Christe Redemptor Omnium*.
[2c] "Plaints" here means "petitions."

88 88 (LM)

Tune: VARIOUS

T. Source: *Primer, or, Office of the Blessed Virgin Marie in Latin and English, according to the reformed Latin, and with Lyke Graces Privileged* (Antwerp, 1599) p. 2. The Catholic Encyclopedia of 1912 attributes the hymn translations to the book's editor, Richard Verstegan (d. 1636), a Catholic publisher. In the 1599 Preface, Verstegan says: "Notwithstanding the difficulty, these hymns have been so turned into English meter that they may be sung unto the same tunes in English that they bear in Latin." However, his accentual treatment is sometimes peculiar.

1778AD – Historic Roman Catholic Translation

Can be sung with any 88 88 meter, such as Eisenach, Rogers Park, Bressani, La Rochelle, Kempen, Bessemer, Tallis Canon, Winchester New, etc.

Jesu Redémptor ómnium,
Quem lucis ant*e* oríginem,
Parem Patérnae glóriae
Pater suprémus édidit:

Tu lumen et splendor Patris
Tu spes perénnis ómnium,
Inténde quas fundunt preces
Tui per orbem sérvuli.

Meménto, rerum Cónditor
Nostri quod olim córporis,
Sacrát*a* ab alvo Vírginis
Nascéndo, formam súmpseris.

Testátur hoc praesens dies,
Currens per anni círculum,
Quod solus e sinu Patris
Mundi salus advéneris.

Hunc astra, tellus, aéquora,
Hunc omne quod caelo subest
Salútis Auctórem novae
Novo salútat cántico.

Et nos, beáta quos sacri
Rigávit unda Sánguinis,
Natális ob diem tui
Hymni tribútum sólvimus.

Jesu, tibi sit glória,
Qui natus es de Virgine,
Cum Patr*e* et almo Spíritu,
In sempitérna saécula.

JESUS, the Ransomer of man.
Who, ere created light began,
Didst from the supreme Father spring,
His heav'nly glory equalling;

2. Thou Father's light and splendor art,
Th' eternal hope of ev'ry heart;
With gracious ear those prayers attend
Which thro' the world to thee ascend.

3. Divine Creator bear in mind,
That thou of our corporeal kind,
The form assumed'st heretofore,
When thee a sacred virgin bore.

4. This day which we now celebrate,
Does to our memories relate
That from thy Father's sacred throne,
To save the world thou camest down.

5. The stars, the seas, and the firm ground,
And what e'er else the heav'ns surround;
All offer a new song to thee,
Who bring'st us this new liberty.

6. And we presume too, who have been
Cleans'd by thy sacred blood from sin,
The Tribute of an hymn to pay
In honor of this joyful day.

7. To Jesus, from a Virgin sprung,
Be glory giv'n, and praises sung,
The like to God the Father be,
And holy Ghost eternally.

[1a] The Urbanite title (*Jesu Redemptor Omnium*) is used throughout our book in order to avoid confusion with the 9th-century hymn by Rabanus Maurus, the Archbishop of Mainz, also called *Christe Redemptor Omnium*.

[3a] Notice the 1631 revision (*Rerum Cónditor* vs. *Salutis Auctor*);
For more on "Christ as Creator," cf. second footnote on page 421.

T. Source: *The Evening-office of the Church, according to the Roman Breviary: Containing the Vespers for All Sundays and Festivals Throughout the Year in Latin and English* (1778) p. 178.

88 88 (LM)

Tune: Various

280 Mundus Effusis Redemptus (1686 AD)

Priests and Sacrifices of the Old Law are now obsolete

To sing in Latin, use any 87 87 87 tune.

MUNDUS effúsis redémptus
Júbilet jam gaúdiis;
Intrat ecce Sancta Christus,
Póntifex et hóstia;
Ut suo quem sponte fudit,
Cuncta mundet sánguine.

2. Désinat legis sacérdos,
Pro reis orans reus;
Víctimae cessent inánes,
Túrtures, hirci, boves;
Non Deus placátur istis,
Non piántur crímina.

3. Ecce quem vetus figúris
Lex adumbrávit suis;
Labis expers en Sacérdos,
Quem Deus non réspuat;
Quae Deum placáre possit,
En Deo par hóstia.

4. Spíritu sancto perúnctus,
Christus unde dícitur,
Quam sibi finxit paréntis
Vírginis carnem sinu,
Hanc crucis lubens sub ara,
Ímmolat Deo Deus.

5. Nésciens illi minístrat
Ipse tortórum furor;
Sánguinem fundunt, lavátur
Omne quo mundi scelus.
Hóstiam flagrans adúrit
Offeréntis cáritas.

6. Summa laus Deo Parénti,
Qui creávit ómnia;
Summa sit Nato, redémit
Qui suo nos sánguine;
Flámini par, cujus almo
Confovémur hálitu.

87 87 87

Tune:
VARIOUS

T. Source: *Breviarium Monasticum Ad Usum Sacri Ordinis Cluniacensis* (Paris, 1686) p. 556.

Assistance for comprehension

LET a world redeemed
now exult with joys poured forth;
behold, Christ enters the hallows, *cf. Heb 9.12*
High priest and victim;
that he may cleanse all things
with his blood, which he freely shed.

2. Let the priest of the old Law,
a guilty man who prays for the guilty, have done;
let the futile victims desist,
the turtledoves, bucks and bulls;
through these God is not appeased,
nor are misdeeds expiated. *cf. Heb 9.13-14*

3. Behold him whom the old Law
foreshadowed through its types;
lo, a Priest without shortcoming, *cf. Heb 7.26*
whom God would not spurn,
lo, a Victim fit for God,
and which can appease God.

4. Anointed with the Holy Spirit, *cf. Acts 10.38*
wherefore he is called the Christ,
the flesh that he fashioned for himself
in the womb of the Virgin, his Bearer,
he, who is God, sacrifices to God
readily on the altar of the cross. *cf. Is 53.7*

5. The very rage of his tormentors
unknowingly serves him; *cf. Jn 19.11*
they shed his blood, and every villainy,
wherever it be in the world, is purged.
The burning charity of the Offerer
consumes the Victim.

6. Highest praise to God the Father,
who created all things,
highest praise to his Son,
who ransomed us with his blood,
equal praise to the Spirit, by whose
bounteous breath we are nurtured.

282 Mundus Effusis Redemptus (1686 AD)

Trns: Fr. Dominic Popplewell (b. 1973) after Caswall

4. With the Holy Ghost anointed,
Thou the name of Christ dost bear,
God that flesh dost freely furnish
Which thou didst thyself prepare,
On the altar of the rood,
God and Virgin-Mother's brood.

5. Those who thee in fury torment
Yield thee service unawares;
As thy blood they shed, it cleanses
All the world, its crime repairs.
Love consumes that thou dost bring,
While it prompts the offering.

6. Highest praise to God the Father,
Who hath made all things of naught;
Highest praise his Son attribute,
Who us with his blood hath bought;
Equal praise, thou Breath divine
Whence we live and move, be thine!

87 87 77

Tune:
ALL SAINTS

Final Verses: Richard Lloyd (1993) #7; Noel Rawsthorne (2011) #13.
Melody: *Geistreiches Gesangbuch* (Darmstadt, 1698).
M. Source: *New Saint Basil Hymnal* (1958) p. 203; *Catholic Hymn Book* (London Oratory, 1998) p. 290.
ENGLISH TRANSLATION: The original translation by Fr. Caswall can be found on page 157 of *Hymns and Poems, Original and Translated* (London: Burns and Oates, 1873). The Latin text itself comes from a Cluniac Breviary published in 1686.

Mundus Effusis Redemptus (1686 AD)

Trns: Fr. Dominic Popplewell (b. 1973) after Caswall

Sing with any 87 87 77 meter, such as COBLENZ, WESTMINSTER ABBEY F7, ICH BEGEHR NICHT MEHR, IRBY, COELESTIA, etc.

SING, O earth, for thy redemption!
Lo, his race of sorrow run,
Christ the Sanctuary enters,
Priest and victim both in one,
There to make our peace with God,
By oblation of his blood.

2. Priest beneath the Law, and guilty,
For the guilty cease to plead!
Goats and oxen, shadows empty,
Of the which is no more need:
None so frail as these could win
Peace with God, could pardon sin.

3. Hail to thee, High Priest eternal,
Holy, infinite, divine:
Mystic figures once enshrouded
Thee, all sinless who dost shine!
Thou art he whose blood alone
Can for guilty man atone.

4. With the Holy Ghost anointed,
Thou the name of Christ dost bear,
God that flesh dost freely furnish
Which thou didst thyself prepare,
On the altar of the rood,
God and Virgin-Mother's brood.

5. Those who thee in fury torment
Yield thee service unawares;
As thy blood they shed, it cleanses
All the world, its crime repairs.
Love consumes that thou dost bring,
While it prompts the offering.

6. Highest praise to God the Father,
Who hath made all things of naught;
Highest praise his Son attribute,
Who us with his blood hath bought;
Equal praise, thou Breath divine
Whence we live and move, be thine!

ENGLISH TRANSLATION: The original translation by Fr. Caswall can be found on page 157 of *Hymns and Poems, Original and Translated* (London: Burns and Oates, 1873). The Latin text itself comes from a Cluniac Breviary published in 1686.

87 87 77

Tune: VARIOUS

284 Non Abluunt Lymphae Deum (1686 AD)

The Baptism of the Lord at the River Jordan

To sing in Latin,
use any 88 88 (LM) tune.

NON ábluunt lymphae Deum,
Sed ábluit lymphas Deus;
Carnísque contáctu sacrae
Vim dat lavándi críminis.

2. Promíssus ecce jam patet
Fons abluéndis córdibus.
Res mira! tíngitur caro,
Mentísque labes tóllitur. *n1*

3. His tincta nam canálibus
Regis suprémi púrpura
Tinctos cruéntat, et nivis
Instar dat esse cándidos. *n2*

4. Fecúnda sancto Spíritu
Virgo Deum nobis parit:
Fecúnda sancto Spíritu
Nunc unda nos parit Deo. *n3*

5. Mundi scelus qui díluis,
Jesu, tibi sit glória
Cum Patr*e* et almo Spíritu,
In sempitérna saécula.

88 88 (LM)

Tune:
VARIOUS

T. Source: Bl. John Henry Cardinal Newman's *Hymni Ecclesiae* (London, 1865), p. 53; *Breviarium Sanctae Ambianensis Ecclesiae* (1746) p. 375. The author of this hymn is not known; it was simply signed "NTPR" in a 1686 Cluniac breviary. Some versions begin with the "L" stanza (*Lavacra Puri Gurgitis*) from the ABECEDARIUS of Sedulius.

Assistance for comprehension

THE waters do not cleanse God,
but God cleanses the waters;
and through the touch of his hallowed flesh
he grants the power of purging wrong.

2. Lo, accessible now is the spring
pledged for the cleansing of hearts.
Wondrous thing: the flesh is moistened,
and the mind's failing is taken away! *n1*

3. Moistening through these runnels,
the scarlet of the highest King
imbrues those moistened, and grants them
to be as white as snow. *n2*

4. Fruitful through the Holy Spirit,
a Virgin delivers God for us:
fruitful through the Holy Spirit,
water now delivers us for God. *n3*

5. Thou who washest the world's villainy away,
Jesus, to thee be glory,
with the Father and bounteous Spirit,
to everlasting ages.

[1] The baptismal water touches the body, but grace attains the soul.

[2] The blood of Christ cleanses through the baptismal water, and makes them not crimson, but white: cf. Ap 22.14; Is 1.18.

[3] The sacred font is the womb from which the Church, our holy mother, brings forth new progeny.

286 Non Abluunt Lymphae Deum (1686 AD)

Trns: Robert Campbell of Skerrington (d. 1868)

4. Filled with the Holy Ghost, on Earth
The Virgin to our God gave birth!
Filled with the Holy Ghost are we
New-born in water, Christ, to Thee!

5. O Christ, to thee all praise we pay,
For thou hast washed our sins away;
The Father equally adore,
And Holy Spirit evermore.

88 88 (LM)

Tune:
Winchester New

Final Verses: Richard Lloyd (1993) #244; Noel Rawsthorne (2011) #392.
Melody: Georg Wittwe's *Musikalisches Handbuch der Geistlichen Melodien* (Hamburg, 1690).
M. Source: *Episcopal Hymnal* (1940) ABAB #548; *New Saint Basil Hymnal* (1958) p. 1.
T. Source: Orby Shipley's *Annus Sanctus: Hymns of the Church for the Ecclesiastical Year; Translated from the Sacred Offices by various Authors, with Modern, Original, and other Hymns, and an Appendix of Earlier Versions* (London: Burns and Oates, 1884) p. 55.

Non Abluunt Lymphae Deum (1686 AD)

Trns: Robert Campbell of Skerrington (d. 1868)

Can be sung with any 88 88 meter, such as EISENACH, ROGERS PARK, BRESSANI, LA ROCHELLE, KEMPEN, BESSEMER, TALLIS CANON, WINCHESTER NEW, etc.

GOD needeth not the cleansing wave,
But giveth it the pow'r to save;
His sinless flesh, baptized therein,
Hath hallowed it to cleanse from sin.

2. The sacred fountain long foretold
For all uncleanness here behold;
For thus the Lord his death applies,
And with his blood the spirit dyes.

3. For bathed in that baptismal flood,
The soul is dyed with Jesus' blood;
And clothed in robes which brightly glow,
Surpassing far the purest snow.

4. Filled with the Holy Ghost, on Earth
The Virgin to our God gave birth!
Filled with the Holy Ghost are we
New-born in water, Christ, to Thee!

5. O Christ, to thee all praise we pay,
For thou hast washed our sins away;
The Father equally adore,
And Holy Spirit evermore.

T. Source: Orby Shipley's *Annus Sanctus: Hymns of the Church for the Ecclesiastical Year; Translated from the Sacred Offices by various Authors, with Modern, Original, and other Hymns, and an Appendix of Earlier Versions* (London: Burns and Oates, 1884) p. 55.

88 88 (LM)

Tune: VARIOUS

288 O Sola Magnarum Urbium (4th century)

Aurelius Prudentius (d. 413AD), Christian Poet

To sing in Latin,
use any 88 88 (LM) tune.

O SOLA magnár*um* úrbium
Major Béthl*e*hem, cui cóntigit
Ducem salútis caélitus
Incorporátum gígnere:

2. Quem stella, quae solis rotam
Vincit decór*e* ac lúmine, *n1*
Venísse terris núntiat
Cum carne terréstri Deum:

3. Vidére postqu*am* illum Magi,
Eóa promunt múnera:
Stratíque votis ófferunt
Thus, myrrh*am* et aurum régium.

4. Regem Deúmqu*e* annúntiant
Thesáurus, et fragrans odor
Thuris Sabaé*i*, ac mýrrheus
Pulvis sepúlchrum praédocet. *n2*

5. Jesu, tibi sit glória,
Qu*i* apparuísti géntibus,
Cum Patr*e* et almo Spíritu,
In sempitérna saécula.

T. Source: *Hymni de Tempore et de Sanctis in Textu Antiquo et Novo* (Solesmes, 1885) p. 35.

Aurelius Clemens Prudentius (348-413), born in northern Spain, was successively an advocate, judge, and holder of an important military position at court. At the age of fifty-seven he retired from active life and devoted the remainder of his days to the service of God and to the writing of sacred poetry. He has been called the "Virgil and Horace of the Christians." Erasmus said of him *unum inter Christianos vere facundum poetam*. The two pervading influences in his work were the example of his contemporary, St. Ambrose, and the Christian art of the Catacombs.

This hymn is a Cento from the twelfth poem in the *Cathemerinon* of Prudentius. It was introduced by Pope Pius V (d. 1572) into the office of the Epiphany and assigned to Lauds. The Roman Breviary changes the second strophe's opening words, "Haec stella," to "Quem stella." Individual sections of his long poems were later adopted as hymns for the sacred liturgy, e.g. "Corde Natus Ex Parentis."

88 88 (LM)

Tune:
Various

Assistance for comprehension

O BETHLEHEM, of great cities
alone the greatest, whose lot was
to host, embodied from heaven,
the Captain of salvation:

2. The one whom a star, which in beauty
and light conquers the disc of the sun, *n1*
declares to have come to earth,
even God, in earthly flesh:

3. After the Magi have seen him,
they bring forth gifts from the East:
and prostrate they offer with their vows
frankincense, myrrh and kingly gold.

4. The treasure and sweet-smelling
perfume of Sabean frankincense
declare the king and God, and the powder
of myrrh forewarns the tomb. *n2*

5. O Jesus, glory be to thee
who hast appeared to the nations,
with the Father and bounteous Spirit,
for everlasting ages.

On this, see the second chapter of Saint Matthew:

> When Jesus therefore was born in Bethlehem of Juda,
> in the days of king Herod, behold,
> there came wise men from the east to Jerusalem, saying,
> "Where is he that is born king of the Jews?
> For we have seen his star in the east,
> and are come to adore him."
>
> And king Herod, hearing this, was troubled—and all Jerusalem with him.
> And assembling together all the chief priests and the scribes of the people,
> he inquired of them where Christ should be born. But they said to him:
> "In Bethlehem of Juda. For so it is written by the prophet:
> And thou Bethlehem the land of Juda art not the least among the princes of Juda:
> for out of thee shall come forth the captain that shall rule my people Israel." (cf. Micheas 5.2)

[1] "Vincit" is here used to indicate that the miraculous star "surpassed the sun in beauty and in splendor"; cf. Fr. Matthew Britt, *The Hymns of the Breviary and Missal* (New York: Benziger Brothers, 1922) p. 116.

[2] The gifts of the Magi were expressive of their belief in Christ's royal generation, His divine nature, and His human nature. GOLD, the noblest of metals and hence suitable for a king, was symbolical of His royal generation. FRANKINCENSE, symbolical of prayer, was an acknowledgement of His divinity. MYRRH, used in embalming, was symbolical of their belief in His mortality as man.

290 O Sola Magnarum Urbium (4th century)

First Tune – *Trns: Fr. John Fitzpatrick, Oblate of Mary (d. 1929)*

4. His Godhead and His Sov'reignty,
The incense and the gold reveal,
The dust of myrrh foretells the tomb,
Which shall His mortal form conceal.

5. Be glory, Jesus, unto Thee
Revealed for Gentile eyes to greet,
Be likewise praised eternally
The Father and the Paraclete.

88 88 (LM)

Tune:
Altona

Final Verses: Noel Rawsthorne (2011) #378; one note altered.
Melody: Schumann's *Geistliche Lieder* (1539); an adaptation by Fr. Stephan Lück (d. 1883) in his hymnal, *Gesang- und Gebetbuch für die Diözese Trier* (1847) p. 19. Called by various names (Vom Himmel Hoch, Erfurt, etc.) this melody has been set by such composers as Hassler, Gesius, Praetorius, and Bach.
M. Source: *Hosanna Catholic Hymn Book* (1914) p. 17; *New Westminster Hymnal* (1939) p. 8.
T. Source: *The Breviary and Missal Hymns* (London: Sands & Co, 1931) p. 63; v1 alterations based on *Hymns of the Church* (London: Burns & Oates, 1874) p. 69; that collection's author is Fr. John Wallace, D.D., who later became a Benedictine, taking the name "Wilfrid"; v4 alterations based on Most Rev. Edward Bagshawe, Bishop of Nottingham (d. 1915) in his *Breviary Hymns and Missal Sequences* (London: Burns & Oates, 1900) p. 47.

O Sola Magnarum Urbium (4th century) 291

Second Tune – *Trns: Fr. John Fitzpatrick, Oblate of Mary* (d. 1929)

4. His Godhead and His Sov'reignty,
The incense and the gold reveal,
The dust of myrrh foretells the tomb,
Which shall His mortal form conceal.

5. Be glory, Jesus, unto Thee
Revealed for Gentile eyes to greet,
Be likewise praised eternally
The Father and the Paraclete.

Final Verses: Richard Lloyd (1993) #244; Noel Rawsthorne (2011) #392.
Melody: Georg Wittwe's *Musikalisches Handbuch der Geistlichen Melodien* (Hamburg, 1690).
M. Source: *Episcopal Hymnal* (1940) ABAB #548; *New Saint Basil Hymnal* (1958) p. 1.
T. Source: *The Breviary and Missal Hymns* (London: Sands & Co, 1931) p. 63; v1 alterations based on *Hymns of the Church* (London: Burns & Oates, 1874) p.69; that collection's author is Fr. John Wallace, D.D., who later became a Benedictine, taking the name "Wilfrid"; v4 alterations based on Most Rev. Edward Bagshawe, Bishop of Nottingham (d. 1915) in his *Breviary Hymns and Missal Sequences* (London: Burns & Oates, 1900) p. 47.

88 88 (LM)

Tune: Winchester New

292 O Sola Magnarum Urbium (4th century)

THIRD TUNE – *Trns: Fr. John Fitzpatrick, Oblate of Mary (d. 1929)*

1. O Beth - le - hem, thou_ dost sur - pass
2. A star, out - shin - ing_ in its light
3. The Ma - gi, who His_ face be - hold,

All oth - er cit - ies_ in re - nown;
And beau - ty the re - volv - ing sun,
for Him their East - ern_ gifts have spread;

Thy priv - i - lege a - lone it was
Pro - claims to earth the_ God of might,
In in - cense, myrrh and_ roy - al gold,

To call from Heav'n our_ Sav - ior down.
Who now His mor - tal_ course will run.
They, pros - trate, all their vows have said.

4. His Godhead and His Sov'reignty,
The incense and the gold reveal,
The dust of myrrh foretells the tomb,
Which shall His mortal form conceal.

5. Be glory, Jesus, unto Thee
Revealed for Gentile eyes to greet,
Be likewise praised eternally
The Father and the Paraclete.

88 88 (LM)

Tune: STARRY

Melody: *Collection of Hymn Tunes; Selected from British and Foreign Sources with Harmonies* (London: Novello, 1872) p. 8; published by Samuel Sebastian Wesley (d. 1876).

M. Source: *New Westminster Hymnal* (1939) p. 141.

T. Source: *The Breviary and Missal Hymns* (London: Sands & Co, 1931) p. 63; v1 alterations based on *Hymns of the Church* (London: Burns & Oates, 1874) p.69; that collection's author is Fr. John Wallace, D.D., who later became a Benedictine, taking the name "Wilfrid"; v4 alterations based on Most Rev. Edward Bagshawe, Bishop of Nottingham (d. 1915) in his *Breviary Hymns and Missal Sequences* (London: Burns & Oates, 1900) p. 47.

O Sola Magnarum Urbium (4th century) 293

Fourth Tune – *Trns: Fr. John Fitzpatrick, Oblate of Mary (d. 1929)*

4. His Godhead and His Sov'reignty,
The incense and the gold reveal,
The dust of myrrh foretells the tomb,
Which shall His mortal form conceal.

5. Be glory, Jesus, unto Thee
Revealed for Gentile eyes to greet,
Be likewise praised eternally
The Father and the Paraclete.

Melody: William Crowfoot (d. 1783), parish organist in Beccles, England.
M. Source: *Hymns Ancient and Modern* (1972) p. 550; first published in William Crisp's *Divine Harmony, or the Psalm-Singer Instructed* (1755).
T. Source: *The Breviary and Missal Hymns* (London: Sands & Co, 1931) p. 63; v1 alterations based on *Hymns of the Church* (London: Burns & Oates, 1874) p.69; that collection's author is Fr. John Wallace, D.D., who later became a Benedictine, taking the name "Wilfrid"; v4 alterations based on Most Rev. Edward Bagshawe, Bishop of Nottingham (d. 1915) in his *Breviary Hymns and Missal Sequences* (London: Burns & Oates, 1900) p. 47.

88 88 (LM)

Tune: St Mark

294 O Sola Magnarum Urbium (4th century)

FIFTH TUNE – *Trns: Fr. John Fitzpatrick, Oblate of Mary (d. 1929)*

1. O Beth - le - hem, thou dost sur - pass
2. A star, out - shin - ing in its light
3. The Ma - gi, who His face be - hold,

All oth - er cit - ies in re - nown;
And beau - ty the re - volv - ing sun,
for Him their East - ern gifts have spread;

Thy priv - i - lege a - lone it was
Pro - claims to earth the God of might,
In in - cense, myrrh and roy - al gold,

To call from Heav'n our Sav - ior down.
Who now His mor - tal course will run.
They, pros - trate, all their vows have said.

4. His Godhead and His Sov'reignty,
The incense and the gold reveal,
The dust of myrrh foretells the tomb,
Which shall His mortal form conceal.

5. Be glory, Jesus, unto Thee
Revealed for Gentile eyes to greet,
Be likewise praised eternally
The Father and the Paraclete.

* This melody at a lower key is on page 436.

88 88 (LM)

Tune:
TRINITY COLLEGE

Melody: John Bacchus Dykes (d. 1876).
M. Source: *Hymns Ancient and Modern* (1972) p. 64.
T. Source: *The Breviary and Missal Hymns* (London: Sands & Co, 1931) p. 63; v1 alterations based on *Hymns of the Church* (London: Burns & Oates, 1874) p.69; that collection's author is Fr. John Wallace, D.D., who later became a Benedictine, taking the name "Wilfrid"; v4 alterations based on Most Rev. Edward Bagshawe, Bishop of Nottingham (d. 1915) in his *Breviary Hymns and Missal Sequences* (London: Burns & Oates, 1900) p. 47.

O Sola Magnarum Urbium (4th century)

Trns: Fr. John Fitzpatrick, Oblate of Mary (d. 1929)

Can be sung with any 88 88 meter, such as HILDERSTONE, DUGUET, BRESLAU, MELCOMBE, WAREHAM, OLD HUNDREDTH, MEIN SEEL, TRINITY COLLEGE, etc.

O BETHLEHEM, thou dost surpass
All other cities in renown;
Thy privilege alone it was
To call from Heav'n our Savior down.

2. A star, outshining in its light
And beauty the revolving sun,
Proclaims to earth the God of might,
Who now His mortal course will run.

3. The Magi, who His face behold,
for Him their Eastern gifts have spread;
In incense, myrrh and royal gold,
They, prostrate, all their vows have said.

4. His Godhead and His Sov'reignty,
The incense and the gold reveal,
The dust of myrrh foretells the tomb,
Which shall His mortal form conceal.

5. Be glory, Jesus, unto Thee
Revealed for Gentile eyes to greet,
Be likewise praised eternally
The Father and the Paraclete.

T. Source: *The Breviary and Missal Hymns* (London: Sands & Co, 1931) p. 63; v1 alterations based on *Hymns of the Church* (London: Burns & Oates, 1874) p.69; that collection's author is Fr. John Wallace, D.D., who later became a Benedictine, taking the name "Wilfrid"; v4 alterations based on Most Rev. Edward Bagshawe, Bishop of Nottingham (d. 1915) in his *Breviary Hymns and Missal Sequences* (London: Burns & Oates, 1900) p. 47.

88 88 (LM)

Tune: VARIOUS

296 O Sola Magnarum Urbium (4th century)

First Tune – *Trns: Fr. Edward Caswall, Oratorian (d. 1878)*

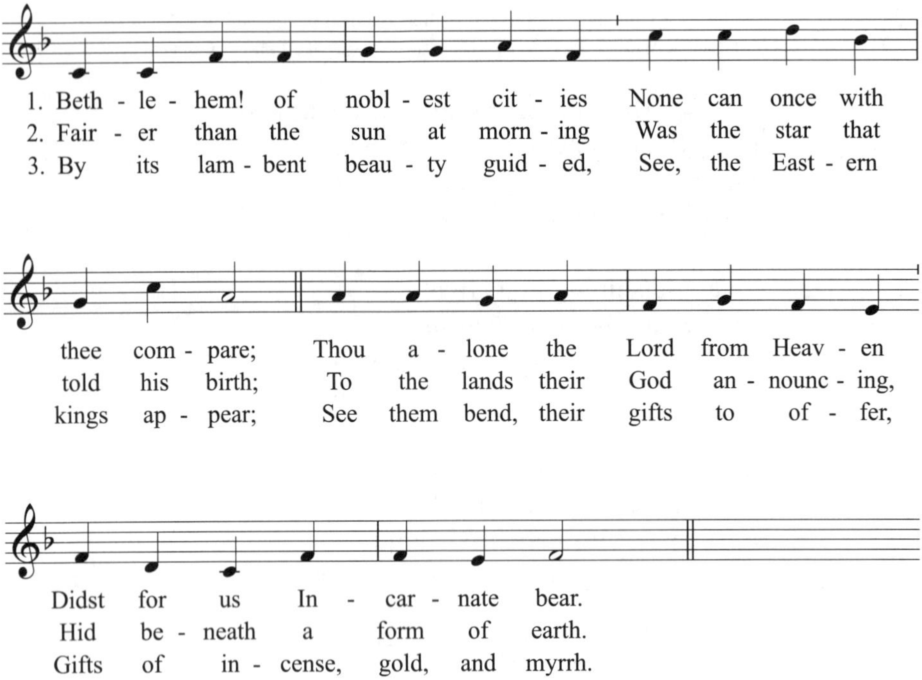

4. Offerings of hidden meaning:
Incense doth the God disclose;
Gold a royal child proclaimeth;
Myrrh a future tomb foreshows.

5. Holy Jesus, in thy brightness
To the Gentile world display'd,
With the Father, and the Spirit,
Endless praise to Thee be paid.

87 87

Tune: Stuttgart

Final Verses: Richard Lloyd (1993) #221; Noel Rawsthorne (2011) #353.
Melody: German tune adapted by Christian Friedrich Witt (d. 1716).
M. Source: *Mediator Dei Hymnal* (1955) #20; *New Saint Basil Hymnal* (1958) p. 28.
T. Source: *Lyra Catholica: Containing All the Hymns of the Roman Breviary and Missal* (New York, 1851) p. 100.

O Sola Magnarum Urbium (4th century)

SECOND TUNE – *Trns: Fr. Edward Caswall, Oratorian (d. 1878)*

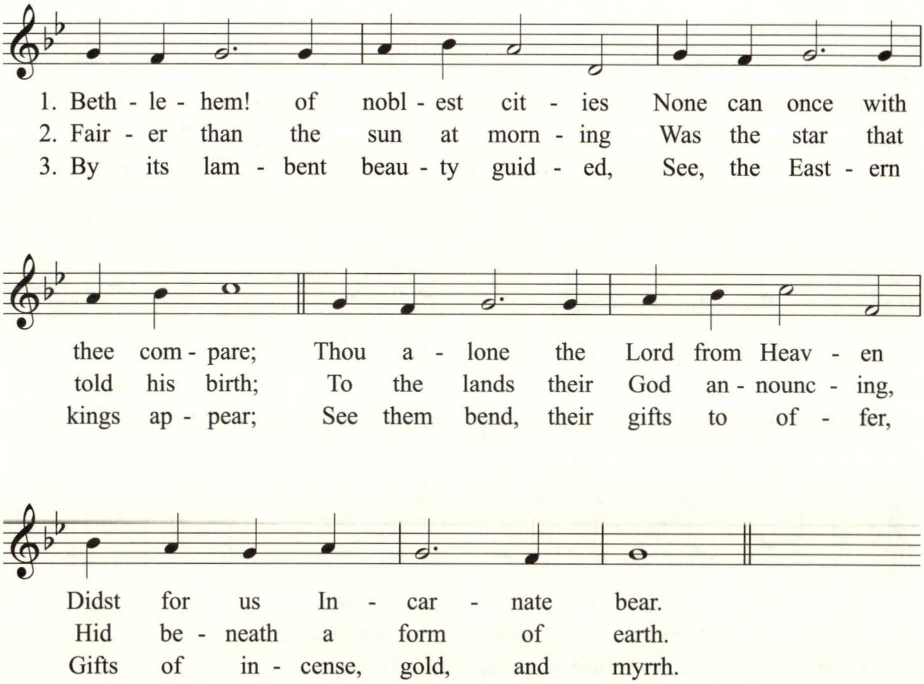

4. Offerings of hidden meaning:
Incense doth the God disclose;
Gold a royal child proclaimeth;
Myrrh a future tomb foreshows.

5. Holy Jesus, in thy brightness
To the Gentile world display'd,
With the Father, and the Spirit,
Endless praise to Thee be paid.

Melody: Kevin Allen (b. 1965), choirmaster at the Monastery of the Holy Cross in Chicago.
M. Source: *Saint Edmund Campion Missal and Hymnal* (2013) p. 823.
T. Source: *Lyra Catholica: Containing All the Hymns of the Roman Breviary and Missal* (New York, 1851) p. 100.

87 87

Tune: BRONZEVILLE

298 O Sola Magnarum Urbium (4th century)

THIRD TUNE – *Trns: Fr. Edward Caswall, Oratorian* (*d. 1878*)

1. Beth - le - hem! of nobl - est cit - ies None can once with
2. Fair - er than the sun at morn - ing Was the star_ that
3. By its lam - bent beau - ty guid - ed, See, the East - ern

thee com - pare;_ Thou a - lone the Lord from Heav - en
told his birth;_ To the lands their God an - nounc - ing,
kings ap - pear;_ See them bend, their gifts to of - fer,

Didst for us___ In - car - nate bear.
Hid be - neath_ a form of earth.
Gifts of in - cense, gold, and myrrh.

4. Offerings of hidden meaning:
   Incense doth the God disclose;
   Gold a royal child proclaimeth;
   Myrrh a future tomb foreshows.

5. Holy Jesus, in thy brightness
   To the Gentile world display'd,
   With the Father, and the Spirit,
   Endless praise to Thee be paid.

87 87

Tune:
CROSS OF JESUS

Final Verses: Richard Lloyd (1993) #47; Noel Rawsthorne (2011) #80.
Melody: John Stainer (d. 1901), organist at Magdalen College, Oxford, and St. Paul's Cathedral, London.
M. Source: *Catholic Hymn Book* (London Oratory, 1998) p. 98.
T. Source: *Lyra Catholica: Containing All the Hymns of the Roman Breviary and Missal* (New York, 1851) p. 100.

O Sola Magnarum Urbium (4th century)

Fourth Tune – *Trns: Fr. Edward Caswall, Oratorian (d. 1878)*

4. Offerings of hidden meaning:
Incense doth the God disclose;
Gold a royal child proclaimeth;
Myrrh a future tomb foreshows.

5. Holy Jesus, in thy brightness
To the Gentile world display'd,
With the Father, and the Spirit,
Endless praise to Thee be paid.

Final Verses: Richard Lloyd (1993) #82; Noel Rawsthorne (2011) #381.
Melody: Heinrich Albert (d. 1651) adapted by Charles Steggall (d. 1905).
M. Source: *New English Hymnal* (1986) #298; *Hymns Ancient and Modern* (1972) p. 876.
T. Source: *Lyra Catholica: Containing All the Hymns of the Roman Breviary and Missal* (New York, 1851) p. 100.

87 87

Tune: Waltham

300 O Sola Magnarum Urbium (4th century)

Fifth Tune – *Trns: Fr. Edward Caswall, Oratorian (d. 1878)*

1. Beth - le - hem! of nobl - est cit - ies None can once with
2. Fair - er than the sun at morn - ing Was the star that
3. By its lam - bent beau - ty guid - ed, See, the East - ern

thee com - pare; Thou a - lone the Lord from Heav - en
told his birth; To the lands their God an - nounc - ing,
kings ap - pear; See them bend, their gifts to of - fer,

Didst for us In - car - nate bear.
Hid be - neath a form of earth.
Gifts of in - cense, gold, and myrrh.

4. Offerings of hidden meaning:
   Incense doth the God disclose;
   Gold a royal child proclaimeth;
   Myrrh a future tomb foreshows.

5. Holy Jesus, in thy brightness
   To the Gentile world display'd,
   With the Father, and the Spirit,
   Endless praise to Thee be paid.

87 87

Tune:
Merton

Final Verses: Richard Lloyd (1993) #138; Noel Rawsthorne (2011) #210.
Melody: William H. Monk (d. 1889), organist at King's College London.
M. Source: *Hymns, Psalms, and Spiritual Canticles* (1983) p. 278; *New Westminster Hymnal* (1939) p. 3.
T. Source: *Lyra Catholica: Containing All the Hymns of the Roman Breviary and Missal* (New York, 1851) p. 100.

Trns: Fr. Edward Caswall, Oratorian (d. 1878)

Can be sung with any 87 87 meter: STUTTGART, HALTON HOLGATE, REDHEAD #46, BATTY, WALTHAM, VATICAN, MERTON, CROSS OF JESUS, MARCHING, BRONZEVILLE, etc.

BETHLEHEM! of noblest cities
None can once with thee compare;
Thou alone the Lord from Heaven
Didst for us Incarnate bear.

2. Fairer than the sun at morning
Was the star that told his birth;
To the lands their God announcing,
Hid beneath a form of earth.

3. By its lambent beauty guided,
See, the Eastern kings appear;
See them bend, their gifts to offer,
Gifts of incense, gold, and myrrh.

4. Offerings of hidden meaning:
Incense doth the God disclose;
Gold a royal child proclaimeth;
Myrrh a future tomb foreshows. .

5. Holy Jesus, in thy brightness
To the Gentile world display'd,
With the Father, and the Spirit,
Endless praise to Thee be paid.

87 87

T. Source: *Lyra Catholica: Containing All the Hymns of the Roman Breviary and Missal* (New York, 1851) p. 100.

Tune: VARIOUS

302 O Sola Magnarum Urbium (4th century)

1706AD – Historic Roman Catholic Translation

Can be sung with any 88 88 meter, such as EISENACH, ROGERS PARK, BRESSANI, LA ROCHELLE, KEMPEN, BESSEMER, TALLIS CANON, WINCHESTER NEW, etc.

LET other Cities strive, which most
Can of their Strength or Heroes boast:
Bethlem alone is chose to be
The Seat of Heav'n-born Majesty.

2. Here while our God Incarnate lay
Th' Officious Stars their Homage pay:
A Sun-like Meteor quits its Sphere,
To show the Sun of Justice here.

3. Hither the faithful Sages ran,
To own their King, both God and Man:
And with their Incense, Myrr, and Gold
The Myst'ries of their Vows unfold.

4. To God the Censer's Smoke ascends;
The Gold the Sov'reign King attends:
In Myrr the bitter Type we see
Of Suff'ring and Mortality.

5. Glory to thee, O Christ, whose rays
Illustrated the Gentiles' Ways;
Whilst equal Praises still repeat
The Father, and the Paraclete.

O sola magnár*um* úrbium
Major Bethlem, cui cóntigit
Ducem salútis caélitus
Incorporátum gígnere:

Quem stella, quae solis rotam
Vincit decór*e* ac lúmine,
Venísse terris núntiat
Cum carne terréstri Deum:

Vidére postqu*am* illum Magi,
Eóa promunt múnera:
Stratíque votis ófferunt
Thus, myrrh*am* et aurum régium.

Regem Deúmq*ue* annúntiant
Thesáurus, et fragrans odor
Thuris Sabaé*i,* ac mýrrheus
Pulvis sepúlchrum praédocet.

Jesu, tibi sit glória,
Qu*i* apparuísti géntibus,
Cum Patr*e* et almo Spíritu,
In sempitérna saécula.

88 88 (LM)

Tune:
VARIOUS

T. Source: *The Primer, or, Office of the B. Virgin Mary, Revis'd; With a New and Approv'd Version of the Church-Hymns Throughout the Year; To which Are Added the Remaining Hymns of the Roman Breviary* (1706) p. 351. This translation may have been written by John Dryden (d. 1700), a famous poet and Catholic convert.

O Sola Magnarum Urbium (4th century)

First Tune – *Trns: Judge Daniel Joseph Donahoe (d. 1933)*

4. Unto the King the golden hoard,
As tribute they prefer; *
The incense to the deathless Lord,
To mortal man the myrrh.

5. To thee, O Christ, be glory meet;
Thy name all lands adore;
Unto the Sire and Paraclete
Like glory evermore.

---

* The word "hoard" here denotes *treasure*;
the word "prefer" here means *present*.

Final Verses: Richard Lloyd (1993) #187; Noel Rawsthorne (2011) #289.
Melody: "Tochter Sion" (Cologne, 1741); adapted by John Richardson (d. 1879), a Catholic organist.
M. Source: *Mediator Dei Hymnal* (1955) p. 62; *Catholic Hymn Book* (London Oratory, 1998) p. 222.
T. Source: *Early Christian Hymns* (New York: The Grafton Press, 1908) p. 57.

86 86 (CM)

Tune:
St Bernard

304 O Sola Magnarum Urbium (4th century)

Second Tune – *Trns: Judge Daniel Joseph Donahoe (d. 1933)*

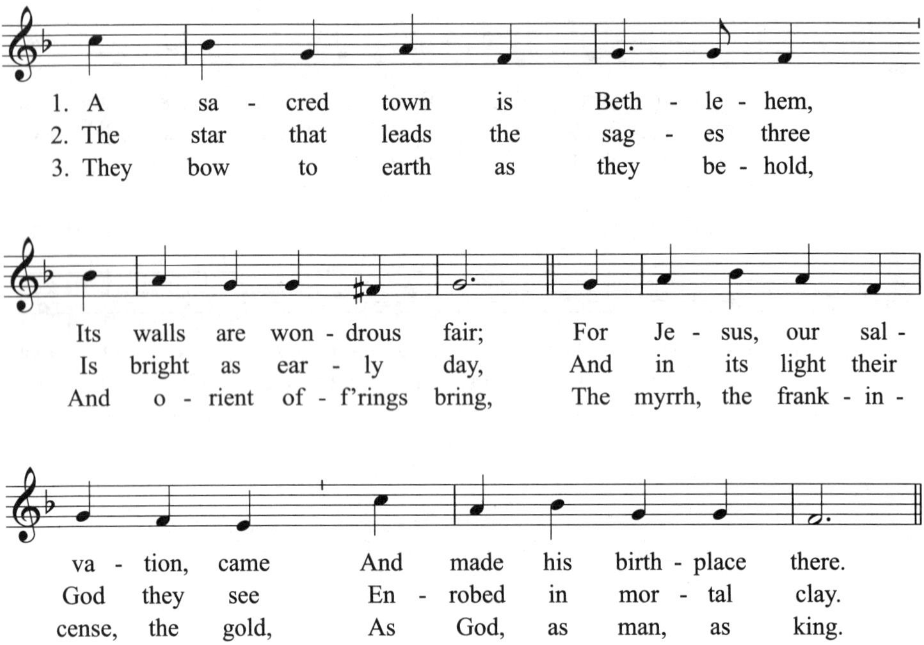

4. Unto the King the golden hoard,
As tribute they prefer; *
The incense to the deathless Lord,
To mortal man the myrrh.

5. To thee, O Christ, be glory meet;
Thy name all lands adore;
Unto the Sire and Paraclete
Like glory evermore.

---

* The word "hoard" here denotes *treasure*;
the word "prefer" here means *present*.

86 86 (CM)

Tune:
Bristol

Final Verses: Richard Lloyd (1993) #25; Noel Rawsthorne (2011) #51.
T. Source: *Early Christian Hymns* (New York: The Grafton Press, 1908) p. 57.
Melody: Thomas Ravenscroft (d. 1635), who also composed secular tunes, e.g. "Three Blind Mice." The melody of this tune can be sung in the Tenor.
M. Source: *Catholic Hymn Book* (London Oratory, 1998) p. 7.

O Sola Magnarum Urbium (4th century)

Trns: Judge Daniel Joseph Donahoe (d. 1933)

Can be sung with any 86 86 meter, such as St Magnus, Bedford, St Columba, Westminster, St Anne, St Hugh, Hereford, St Flavian, etc.

A SACRED town is Bethlehem,
Its walls are wondrous fair;
For Jesus, our salvation, came
And made his birthplace there.

2. The star that leads the sages three
Is bright as early day,
And in its light their God they see
Enrobed in mortal clay.

3. They bow to earth as they behold,
And orient off'rings bring,
The myrrh, the frankincense, the gold,
As God, as man, as king.

4. Unto the King the golden hoard,
As tribute they prefer; *
The incense to the deathless Lord,
To mortal man the myrrh.

5. To thee, O Christ, be glory meet;
Thy name all lands adore;
Unto the Sire and Paraclete
Like glory evermore.

---

* The word "hoard" here denotes *treasure*;
the word "prefer" here means *present*.

86 86 (CM)

Tune: Various

T. Source: *Early Christian Hymns* (New York: The Grafton Press, 1908) p. 57.

306 O Sola Magnarum Urbium (4th century)

Trns: Henry Trend (d. 1869)

4. Nor vain their mystic Offering:
The Incense owned the Child as God;
The Gold did homage to the King;
The Myrrh His Death and Burial showed.
Alleluia.

5. Who to the Gentiles wast revealed,
All glory, Jesus, be to Thee,
With Father and with Holy Ghost,
Now, and for all Eternity.
Alleluia.

88 88 A

Tune:
Erschienen Ist

Melody: Nikolaus Hermann (d. 1561), organist at Joachimsthal, Bohemia.
M. Source: *Hymns Ancient and Modern* (1972) p. 832; cf. "Erschienen ist der herrlich Tag" in *The Four-Part Chorals of J. S. Bach with the German Text of the Hymns and English Translations* (Charles Sanford Terry, 1964) p. 87.
T. Source: Orby Shipley's *Lyra Messianica: Hymns and Verses on the Life of Christ* (London, 1864) p. 161.

O Sola Magnarum Urbium (4th century)

Trns: Henry Trend (d. 1869)

Can be sung with any 88 88 meter, such as HILDERSTONE, DUGUET, BRESLAU, MELCOMBE, WAREHAM, OLD HUNDREDTH, MEIN SEEL, TRINITY COLLEGE, etc.

THE noblest cities on the earth
Must yield, O Bethlehem, to thee;
'Twas thine to give mysterious Birth
To Christ, th' Incarnate Deity.

2. More glorious than the Sun at morn,
Thy Herald-star its rays unfurled,
Proclaiming that the Babe was born,
Whose Pow'r should save a dying world.

3. Drawn by its guiding light from far,
The Sages at His Cradle meet,
With Gold, and Frankincense, and Myrrh,
To worship at His sacred Feet.

4. Nor vain their mystic Offering:
The Incense owned the Child as God;
The Gold did homage to the King;
The Myrrh His Death and Burial showed.

5. Who to the Gentiles wast revealed,
All glory, Jesus, be to Thee,
With Father and with Holy Ghost,
Now, and for all Eternity.

88 88 (LM)

T. Source: Orby Shipley's *Lyra Messianica: Hymns and Verses on the Life of Christ* (London, 1864) p. 161.

Tune: VARIOUS

308 Pange Lingua Gloriosi (6th century)

Venantius Fortunatus, Bishop of Poitiers (d. 609AD)

To sing in Latin,
use any 87 87 87 tune.

PANGE lingua gloriósi
Praélium certáminis,
Et super Crucis trophaéum
Dic triúmphum nóbilem:
Quáliter Redémptor orbis
Immolátus vícerit.

2. De paréntis protoplásti
Fraude Factor cóndolens,
Quando pomi noxiális
Mor*su* in mortem córruit:
Ipse lignum tunc notávit,
Damna lig*ni* ut sólveret. *n1*

3. Hoc opus nostrae salútis
Ordo depopóscerat,
Multifórmis proditóris
Ars ut artem fálleret, *n2*
Et medélam ferret inde,
Hostis unde laéserat.

4. Quando venit ergo sacri
Plenitúdo témporis,
Missus est ab arce Patris
Natus, orbis Cónditor;
Atque ventre virgináli
Caro factus pródiit.

5. Vagit infans inter arcta
Cónditus praesépia:
Membra pannis involúta
Virgo Mater álligat;
Et manus pedés*que* et crura
Stricta cingit fáscia.

T. Source: *Römisches Gradualbuch* (Düsseldorf: Schwann, 1917) p. 121.

87 87 87

Tune:
VARIOUS

[1] There is a marvelous symmetry in the fact that the fall of man came through a tree (the tree of knowledge), and the redemption of man also came through a tree (the tree of the Cross). Cf. Preface of the Holy Cross: *salutem humani generis in ligno Crucis constituisti: ut unde mors oriebatur, inde vita resurgeret: et qui in ligno vincebat, in ligno quoque vinceretur;* "Thou didst establish mankind's salvation by the wood of the Cross: that life might spring anew from that site from which death would arise: and that the one who conquered by wood might also be conquered by wood."

Assistance in comprehension

PUBLISH, O tongue, the battle
of a glorious campaign,
and tell a famous victory
on the monument of the Cross:
how the earth's Redeemer,
sacrificed, conquered.

2. For our first-formed father's
deception grieving,
when he fell down into death
through a bite of the harmful fruit,
our Maker then marked the wood
to clear the damages of the wood. *n1*

3. This work the scheme
of our salvation required;
that the shape-shifting betrayer's craft
its craft might beguile, *n2*
and bring a cure from that site
from which the foe had struck.

4. So when came the fullness
of the hallowed time, *Gal 4.4*
from the Father's fortress was sent
the Son, earth's Founder;
and from a virgin's womb,
made flesh, he went forth. *Jn 1.14*

5. He wails, a babe
stowed within confining stall:
his limbs, wrapped in swaddling,
his Virgin Mother binds, *Lk 2.7, 12*
and his hands and feet and legs
a tight-drawn band encircles.

[2] Holy Scripture teaches that Satan transforms himself into an angel of light (cf. II Cor 14.11), and when he deceived our first parents he appeared in the guise of a serpent (cf. Gn 3.1); Christ in the Gospel names him the father of lies (cf. Jn 8.44), and the Apocalypse reveals the serpent tempting Eve to be the dragon leading the whole world astray (cf. Ap 12.9); nevertheless all the guile and cunning of the enemy is no match for the power and wisdom of God, the word of the Cross, which seems foolish to those who perish (cf. I Cor 1.18).

310 Pange Lingua Gloriosi (6th century)

Concluding verses of the foregoing hymn

To sing in Latin,
use any 87 87 87 tune.

LUSTRIS sex qui jam peráctis,
Tempus implens córporis,
Se volénte natus ad hoc,
Passióni déditus,
Agnus in Crucis levátur
Immolándus stípite.

7. Hic acétum, fel, arúndo,
Sputa, clavi, láncea:
Mite corpus perforátur,
Sanguis, unda prófluit:
Terra, pontus, astra, mundus,
Quo lavántur flúmine! *n3*

8. Crux fidélis, inter omnes
Arbor una nóbilis:
Nulla silva talem profert
Fronde, flore, gérmine:
Dulce lignum, dulces clavos,
Dulce pondus sústinet.

9. Flecte ramos, arbor alta,
Tensa laxa víscera,
Et rigor lentéscat ille,
Quem dedit natívitas;
Ut supérni membra Regis
Miti tendas stípite.

10. Sola digna tu fuísti
Ferre saecli prétium,
Atque portum praeparáre
Nauta mundo náufrago:
Quem sacer cruor perúnxit,
Fusus Agni córpore. *n4*

T. Source: *Römisches Gradualbuch* (Düsseldorf: Schwann, 1917) p. 123.

87 87 87

Tune:
VARIOUS

[3] Along with the True Cross, the faithful venerate the other relics of the Passion, such as the nails that fastened our Lord's hands and feet, the spear that pierced His side, His crown of thorns and the winding-sheet that shrouded His body. The blood and water flowing from Jesus' side washes and purifies all creation: it has the power to do so because it belongs to God incarnate, who "wondrously founded the dignity of man's substance" and, having become man Himself, "yet more wondrously reformed it" (cf. Order of Mass, blessing of water at the offertory).

Assistance in comprehension

WHEN thirty years had already passed,
reaching the term of his bodily life,
of his own will, born for this, *Is 53.7, Jn 18.39*
intent on his suffering,
he, the Lamb, is raised up to be sacrificed
on the trunk of the Cross.

7. Here are the vinegar, gall, reed,
spittle, nails, spear;
his tender body is pierced through:
blood and water stream forth:
land, sea, stars, the world
are washed in that stream! *n3*

8. Cross of faith, among all
the one famous tree:
no woodland brings forth thy match
in bloom, foliage or seed:
the sweet wood, the sweet nails
and sweet burden upholds.

9. Bend thy branches, lofty tree,
slacken thy strained innards,
and may that stiffness soften
which thy birth gave thee;
that the limbs of the sovereign King
thou mayest spread on tender trunk!

10. Only thou wert worthy
to bear the ransom of humanity
and ready a harbor
for a shipwrecked world, mariner
whom the hallowed gore anointed,
poured from the Lamb's body. *n4*

[4] The last three verses directly address the Cross. It is hailed as the most celebrated and best of trees, since it had the privilege of bearing Christ. It is bidden to accommodate itself to Him, so that His passion may be less painful. Finally, it is described as a navigator— consecrated by the blood of Christ the Lamb—bringing the world to a safe haven. This last image recalls how the Israelites applied the blood of the lamb to the posts and lintels of their houses in order to shield them from destruction, and that redemption comes by the precious blood "as of a lamb unspotted and undefiled" (cf. I Pt 1.18-20).

312 Pange Lingua Gloriosi (6th century)

First Tune – *Trns: Fr. Edward Caswall, Oratorian (d. 1878)*

4. So, when now at length the fullness
Of the sacred time drew nigh,
Then the Son, the world's Creator,
Left his Father's throne on high;
From a Virgin's womb appearing,
Cloth'd in our mortality.

5. All within a lowly manger,
Lo, a tender babe he lies;
See his gentle Virgin mother
Lull to sleep his infant cries;
While the limbs of God Incarnate
Round with swathing bands she ties.

87 87 87

Tune:
Runnells

T. Source: *Lyra Catholica: Containing all the hymns of the Roman Breviary and Missal* (1851) p. 91; except for the eighth verse, which was not translated by Fr. Caswall.
Melody: Kevin Allen (b. 1965), choirmaster at the Monastery of the Holy Cross in Chicago.
M. Source: *Saint Jean de Brébeuf Hymnal* (2018).

Pange Lingua Gloriosi (6th century)

The concluding verses may form a separate hymn

9. Lofty tree, bend down thy branches,
To embrace thy sacred load;
Oh, relax the native tension
Of that all too rigid wood;
Gently, gently bear the members
Of thy dying King and God.

Verse 9 may be used as an SATB choral REFRAIN, especially on penitential days.

10. Tree, which solely wast found worthy
Earth's great Victim to sustain;
Harbor from the raging tempest,
Ark, that saved the world again,
Tree, with sacred Blood anointed
Of the Lamb for sinners slain.

87 87 87

Tune:
RUNNELLS

314 Pange Lingua Gloriosi (6th century)

Second Tune – *Trns: Fr. Edward Caswall, Oratorian (d. 1878)*

4. So, when now at length the fullness
Of the sacred time drew nigh,
Then the Son, the world's Creator,
Left his Father's throne on high;
From a Virgin's womb appearing,
Cloth'd in our mortality.

5. All within a lowly manger,
Lo, a tender babe he lies;
See his gentle Virgin mother
Lull to sleep his infant cries;
While the limbs of God Incarnate
Round with swathing bands she ties.

87 87 87

Tune: Breton

T. Source: *Lyra Catholica: Containing all the hymns of the Roman Breviary and Missal* (1851) p. 91; except for the eighth verse, which was not translated by Fr. Caswall.
Melody: Metrical Cento; cf. "Dum staret Abraham" (*Antiphonaire Monastique,* 13th century).
M. Source: *Paléographie musicale* (Volume XII), folio 81; *Cantus Selecti* (Solesmes, 1957) p. 245.

Pange Lingua Gloriosi (6th century) 315

The concluding verses may form a separate hymn

9. Lofty tree, bend down thy branches,
To embrace thy sacred load;
Oh, relax the native tension
Of that all too rigid wood;
Gently, gently bear the members
Of thy dying King and God.

Verse 9 may be used as an SATB choral Refrain, especially on penitential days.

10. Tree, which solely wast found worthy
Earth's great Victim to sustain;
Harbor from the raging tempest,
Ark, that saved the world again,
Tree, with sacred Blood anointed
Of the Lamb for sinners slain.

87 87 87

Tune:
Breton

316 Pange Lingua Gloriosi (6th century)

First Tune – *Trns: Fr. John Fitzpatrick, Oblate of Mary (d. 1929)*

4. Therefore, in its destined fullness
When the blessèd time befell,
Came the world's own Maker, sent us
From His Father's citadel:
Born in flesh He came, proceeding
From an ever-virgin cell.

5. Lying in a narrow manger,
Hark! His infant cries entreat;
Limb by limb the Virgin-Mother
Clothes her new-born Baby sweet,
With her swaddling bands enclosing
Of our God the hands and feet.

87 87 87

Tune:
Ad Perennis Vitae Fontem

T. Source: *The Breviary and Missal Hymns* (London: Sands & Co, 1931) p. 63.
Melody: *Tours Breviary* (1781), based on a 16th century French tune.
M. Source: *Songs of Syon* (1910) p. 106; *New English Hymnal* (1986) p. 712.

The concluding verses may form a separate hymn

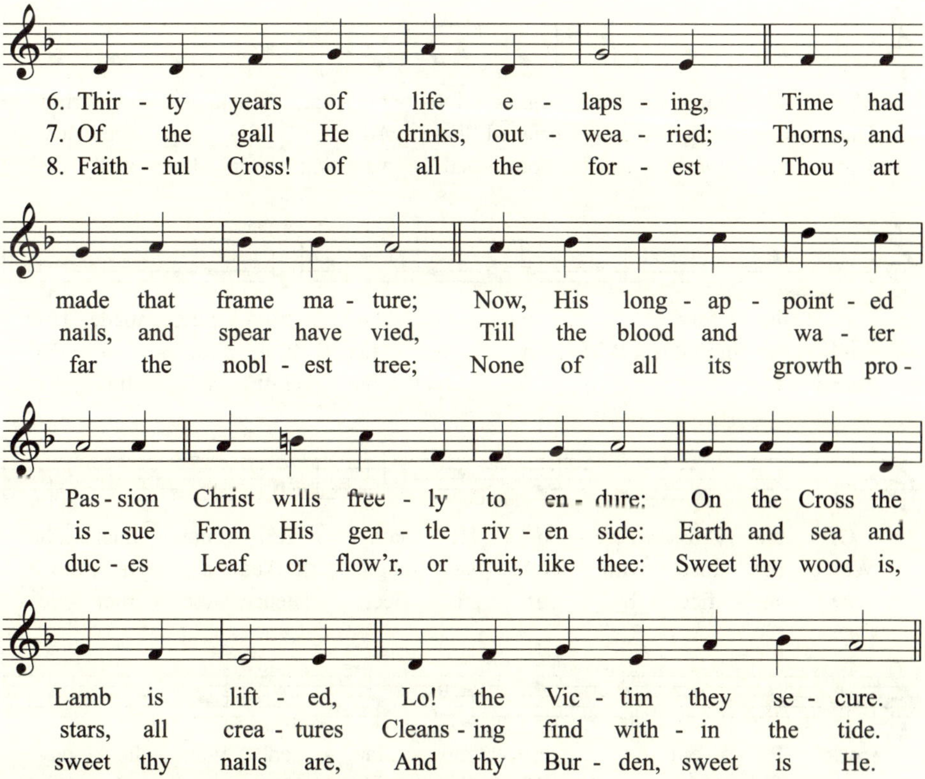

9. Bend thy branches, tree so lofty;
Let thy stubborn heart relent:
Henceforth softer be and pliant,
Conquering thy nature's bent;
That the King may stretch His members
On thy tender trunk's extent.

Verse 9 may be used as an SATB choral Refrain, especially on penitential days.

10. Thou, to bear the world's one Victim,
Wert the only worthy bed;
When we, shipwrecked, had no haven,
Like the Ark wert thou instead,
With the Sacred Blood anointed
By the Lamb's pure Body shed.

11. Sempiternal praise be given
Unto God, the One in Three;
To the Father, Son, and Spirit,
Equal glory rendered be;
Let the Triune Name be hallowed
Everywhere, eternally.

87 87 87

Tune:
Ad Perennis Vitae Fontem

318 Pange Lingua Gloriosi (6th century)

Second Tune – *Trns: Fr. John Fitzpatrick, Oblate of Mary* (*d.* 1929)

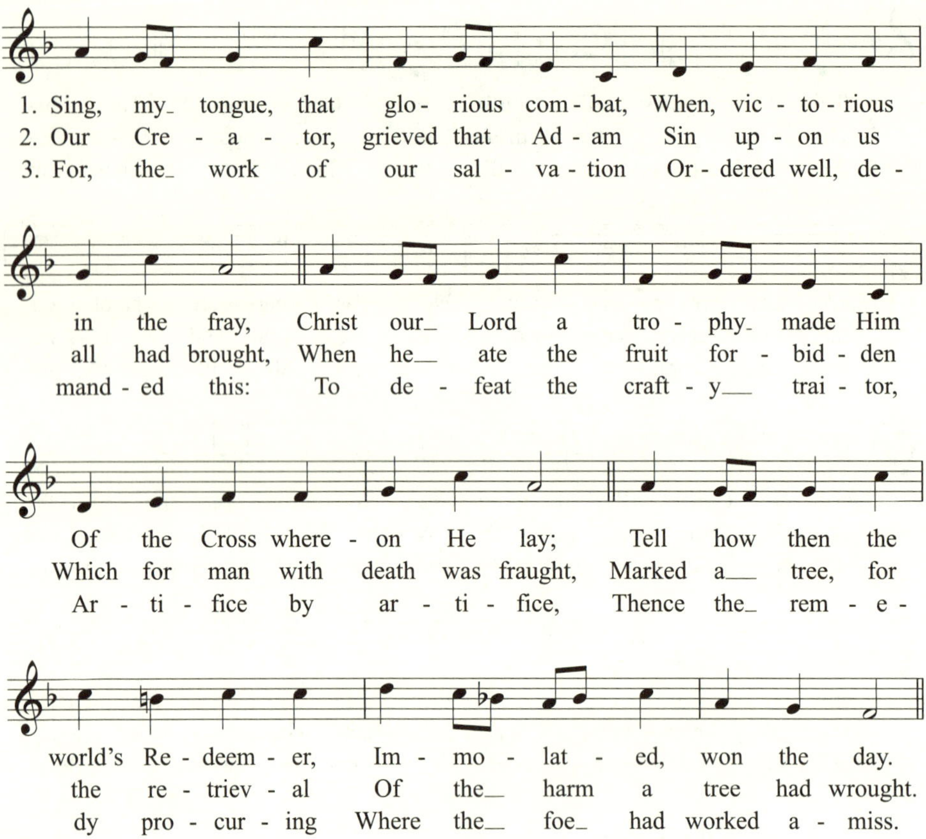

4. Therefore, in its destined fullness
When the blessèd time befell,
Came the world's own Maker, sent us
From His Father's citadel:
Born in flesh He came, proceeding
From an ever-virgin cell.

5. Lying in a narrow manger,
Hark! His infant cries entreat;
Limb by limb the Virgin-Mother
Clothes her new-born Baby sweet,
With her swaddling bands enclosing
Of our God the hands and feet.

87 87 87

Tune:
St Leonard

T. Source: *The Breviary and Missal Hymns* (London: Sands & Co, 1931) p. 63.
Melody: Johann Christoph Bach (d. 1703); some hymnals erroneously attribute this tune, as his name resembles that of J.S. Bach's fifth son—Johann Christoph Friedrich Bach—as well as his youngest son, Johann Christian Bach (d. 1782), who became a Catholic and was admired by Mozart.
M. Source: *Meiningen Gesangbuch* (1693); this melody has multiple names (e.g. Komm O Komm Du Geist Des Lebens) and is sometimes used for 87 87 77; cf. *New Saint Basil Hymnal* (1958) p. 71.

Pange Lingua Gloriosi (6th century)

The concluding verses may form a separate hymn

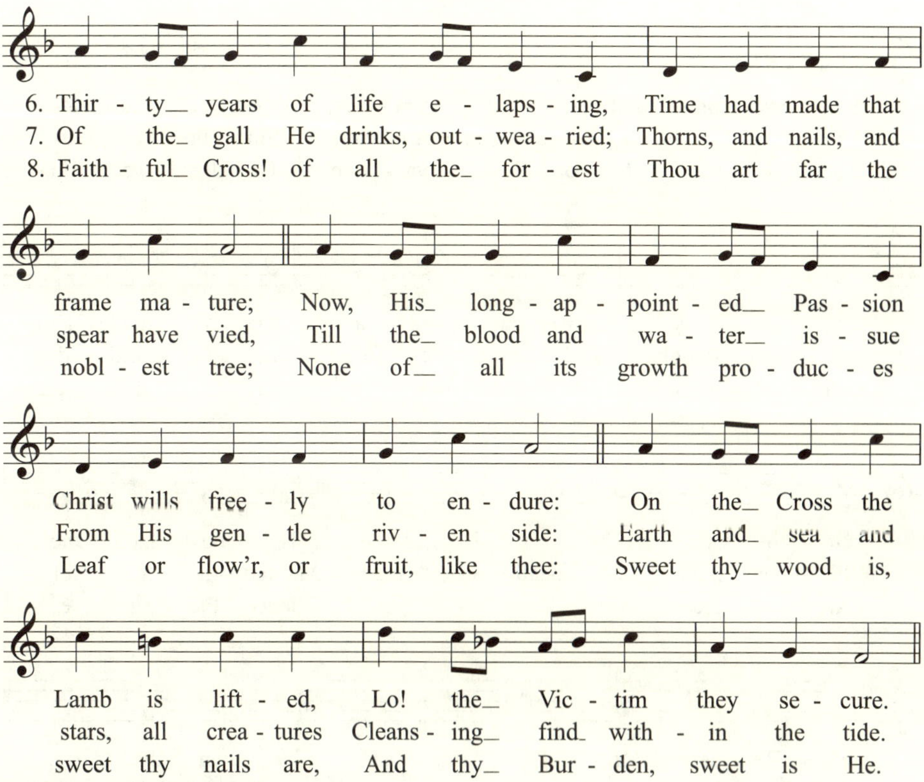

9. Bend thy branches, tree so lofty;
Let thy stubborn heart relent:
Henceforth softer be and pliant,
Conquering thy nature's bent;
That the King may stretch His members
On thy tender trunk's extent.

Verse 9 may be used as an SATB choral REFRAIN, especially on penitential days.

10. Thou, to bear the world's one Victim,
Wert the only worthy bed;
When we, shipwrecked, had no haven,
Like the Ark wert thou instead,
With the Sacred Blood anointed
By the Lamb's pure Body shed.

11. Sempiternal praise be given
Unto God, the One in Three;
To the Father, Son, and Spirit,
Equal glory rendered be;
Let the Triune Name be hallowed
Everywhere, eternally.

87 87 87

Tune:
ST LEONARD

320 Pange Lingua Gloriosi (6th century)

THIRD TUNE – *Trns: Fr. John Fitzpatrick, Oblate of Mary* (*d.* 1929)

4. Therefore, in its destined fullness
When the blessèd time befell,
Came the world's own Maker, sent us
From His Father's citadel:
Born in flesh He came, proceeding
From an ever-virgin cell.

5. Lying in a narrow manger,
Hark! His infant cries entreat;
Limb by limb the Virgin-Mother
Clothes her new-born Baby sweet,
With her swaddling bands enclosing
Of our God the hands and feet.

87 87 87

Tune:
ORIEL

Final Verses: Richard Lloyd (1993) #162; Noel Rawsthorne (2011) #248.
T. Source: *The Breviary and Missal Hymns* (London: Sands & Co, 1931) p. 63.
Melody: Caspar Ett (d. 1847), Catholic composer and organist at St. Michael's in Munich.
M. Source: *Cantica Sacra Catholica* (Freiburg: Leopoldo Lumpp, 1859), p. 22;
Saint Basil's Hymnal (1918) p. 281.

Pange Lingua Gloriosi (6th century) 321

The concluding verses may form a separate hymn

9. Bend thy branches, tree so lofty;
Let thy stubborn heart relent:
Henceforth softer be and pliant,
Conquering thy nature's bent;
That the King may stretch His members
On thy tender trunk's extent.

Verse 9 may be used as an SATB choral Refrain, especially on penitential days.

10. Thou, to bear the world's one Victim,
Wert the only worthy bed;
When we, shipwrecked, had no haven,
Like the Ark wert thou instead,
With the Sacred Blood anointed
By the Lamb's pure Body shed.

11. Sempiternal praise be given
Unto God, the One in Three;
To the Father, Son, and Spirit,
Equal glory rendered be;
Let the Triune Name be hallowed
Everywhere, eternally.

87 87 87

Tune: Oriel

322 Pange Lingua Gloriosi (6th century)

First Tune – *Adaptation by Fr. Dylan Schrader (b. 1985)*

4. When the ages reached their fullness,
From his throne above the sky
He came down amid our weakness,
Born to suffer and to die;
Mary first with joy embraced him,
In the flesh the Son most high.

5. Living with us, God almighty,
Comes of age and manhood's strength.
Hands and arms, once swaddled tightly,
Now embrace the Cross's weight.
He, the Lamb, a costly Victim,
Climbs the mount of sacrifice.

6. See the gall, the nails, the spitting,
Terrible and blessèd rood!
Mary, too, in sorrow watching
As her Son is crucified;
Gentle body, pierced and bleeding,
Springs of life where Life has died.

7. All the universe is mourning:
Darkness falls, the planets shake,
Till that radiant Easter morning
Sees the living Lord awake:
Glory be to Christ the Victor,
Glory to our risen King!

87 87 87

Tune:
Regent Square

Final Verses: Richard Lloyd (1993) #175; Noel Rawsthorne (2011) #265.
T. Source: *Saint Jean de Brébeuf Hymnal* (2018).
Melody: Henry Smart (d. 1879), organist at St. Philip's in London.
M. Source: *Catholic Hymn Book* (1998) p. 280; *Hymns, Psalms, and Spiritual Canticles* (1983) p. 213.

Pange Lingua Gloriosi (6th century) 323

Second Tune – *Adaptation by Fr. Dylan Schrader (b. 1985)*

4. When the ages reached their fullness,
From his throne above the sky
He came down amid our weakness,
Born to suffer and to die;
Mary first with joy embraced him,
In the flesh the Son most high.

5. Living with us, God almighty,
Comes of age and manhood's strength.
Hands and arms, once swaddled tightly,
Now embrace the Cross's weight.
He, the Lamb, a costly Victim,
Climbs the mount of sacrifice.

6. See the gall, the nails, the spitting,
Terrible and blessèd rood!
Mary, too, in sorrow watching
As her Son is crucified;
Gentle body, pierced and bleeding,
Springs of life where Life has died.

7. All the universe is mourning:
Darkness falls, the planets shake,
Till that radiant Easter morning
Sees the living Lord awake:
Glory be to Christ the Victor,
Glory to our risen King!

T. Source: *Saint Jean de Brébeuf Hymnal* (2018).
Melody: Fr. Jules de Verneuil (d. 1938).
M. Source: Fr. Anatole Police, *The Parochial Hymn Book* (London: Burns & Oates, 1897).

87 87 87
Tune: Davost

324 Pange Lingua Gloriosi (6th century)

Third Tune – *Adaptation by Fr. Dylan Schrader (b. 1985)*

1. Let our tongues sing out the sto - ry: Fear- some bat - tle,
2. God, our Mak - er, griev - ing with us At our fa - ther's
3. Yet our Fa - ther deigned to save us, Mark - ing out_ that

des - p'rate war! Laud the Cross, the pre - cious tro - phy
treach - er - y: Ad - am, made in his own im - age,
fate - ful wood, In a plan of res - cue won - drous

Of the Sav - ior of the world, Tell of sac - ri -
Ate of that_ for - bid - den tree; Duped by Sa - tan,
Foiled the cun - ning of our foe, From our bane a

fice and glo - ry, Praise the tri - umph of the Lord.
man would per - ish, Dead - ly fruit its fruit would see.
cure he gave us, From great e - vil, great - est good!

4. When the ages reached their fullness,
From his throne above the sky
He came down amid our weakness,
Born to suffer and to die;
Mary first with joy embraced him,
In the flesh the Son most high.

5. Living with us, God almighty,
Comes of age and manhood's strength.
Hands and arms, once swaddled tightly,
Now embrace the Cross's weight.
He, the Lamb, a costly Victim,
Climbs the mount of sacrifice.

6. See the gall, the nails, the spitting,
Terrible and blessèd rood!
Mary, too, in sorrow watching
As her Son is crucified;
Gentle body, pierced and bleeding,
Springs of life where Life has died.

7. All the universe is mourning:
Darkness falls, the planets shake,
Till that radiant Easter morning
Sees the living Lord awake:
Glory be to Christ the Victor,
Glory to our risen King!

87 87 87

Tune:
Westminster Abbey F

Melody: Henry Purcell (d. 1695), organist at Westminster Abbey.
M. Source: cf. Final "Hallelujah" section of an anthem (1681), *O God, Thou Art My God.* Like many hymn tunes (Breslau, Old Hundredth, Bedford, Puer Nobis Nascitur, etc.) this melody can be sung in triple or quadruple meter; however, when sung in triple, it should follow Purcell's original rhythm and not what is commonly found in 20th century hymnals.
T. Source: *Saint Jean de Brébeuf Hymnal* (2018).

Pange Lingua Gloriosi (6th century)

Fourth Tune – *Adaptation by Fr. Dylan Schrader (b. 1985)*

4. When the ages reached their fullness,
From his throne above the sky
He came down amid our weakness,
Born to suffer and to die;
Mary first with joy embraced him,
In the flesh the Son most high.

5. Living with us, God almighty,
Comes of age and manhood's strength.
Hands and arms, once swaddled tightly,
Now embrace the Cross's weight.
He, the Lamb, a costly Victim,
Climbs the mount of sacrifice.

6. See the gall, the nails, the spitting,
Terrible and blessèd rood!
Mary, too, in sorrow watching
As her Son is crucified;
Gentle body, pierced and bleeding,
Springs of life where Life has died.

7. All the universe is mourning:
Darkness falls, the planets shake,
Till that radiant Easter morning
Sees the living Lord awake:
Glory be to Christ the Victor,
Glory to our risen King!

Final Verses: Richard Lloyd (1993) #169; Noel Rawsthorne (2011) #258.
Melody: John Goss (d. 1880), Professor of Harmony at the Royal Academy of Music.
M. Source: *New Saint Basil Hymnal* (1958) p. 202; *Hymns, Psalms, and Spiritual Canticles* (1983) p. 294.
T. Source: *Saint Jean de Brébeuf Hymnal* (2018).

87 87 87
Tune:
Lauda Anima

326 Pange Lingua Gloriosi (Urbanite)

1717AD – Historic Roman Catholic Translation

English translation can be sung with any 88 88 88 meter, such as COLCHESTER, REGINA CAELORUM, ST MATTHIAS, SUSSEX CAROL, ST CHRYSOSTOM, etc.

SING, O my Tongue, the glorious Crown,
Which Christ, the God of Battles won:
How on the Cross thy God on high
Triumphs in Pomp and Victory;
And yields for us his saving Breath
At once to die and vanquish Death.

2. A kind Compassion made him take
Such Measures for his Creatures' Sake;
That fatal Wood, where Adam found
Sad Means to give the general Wound;
Should now contribute to restore
Our Life, that caus'd our Death before.

3. This Method, Providence decreed
For Christ to crush the Serpent's Head:
Art meets with Art, and countermines
The wily Foe's conceal'd Designs:
Defeats his Bane, and then applies,
Against the Poison, Remedies.

4. Thus when the sacred Period came,
Behold the World's redeeming Lamb
From God's Paternal Bosom sent,
Came down to human Banishment,
And taking Flesh of Mary's Womb
Stept forth to save the World from Doom.

5. Here God and Man an Infant lies,
The narrow Crib augments his Cries:
Those Hands by which the Lightning's hurl'd,
And Arms that grasp the bulky World,
In swathing Bands are wrapt and bound
With Poverty encompass'd round.

6. May all this praise, and honor Thee,
One undivided Trinity,
The Father, and Co-equal Son,
And Holy Spirit, Three in One,
Whose equal Pow'r and goodness claim
One Equal Everlasting Fame.

Pange, lingua, gloriósi
Láuream certáminis,
Et super Crucis trophaéo
Dic triúmphum nóbilem:
Quáliter Redémptor orbis
Immolátus vícerit.

De Paréntis protoplásti
Fraude Factor cóndolens,
Quando pomi noxiális
In necem morsu ruit:
Ipse lignum tunc notávit,
Damna lign*i* ut sólveret.

Hoc opus nostrae salútis
Ordo depopóscerat;
Multifórmis proditóris
Ars ut artem fálleret,
Et medélam ferret inde
Hostis unde laéserat.

Quando venit ergo sacri
Plenitúdo témporis,
Missus est ab arce Patris
Natus, orbis Cónditor:
Atque ventre Virginláli
Carn*e* amíctus pródiit.

Vagit infans inter arcta
Cónditus praesépia:
Membra pannis involúta
Virgo Mater álligat:
Et Dei manus pedésque
Stricta cingit fáscia.

Sempitérna sit beátae
Trinitáti glória:
Aequa Patri Filióque,
Par decus Paráclito :
Unius Triníque nomen
Laudet univérsitas.

88 88 88

Tune:
VARIOUS

T. Source: *The Primer, or, Office of the B. Virgin Mary, Revis'd; With a New and Approv'd Version of the Church-Hymns Throughout the Year; To which Are Added the Remaining Hymns of the Roman Breviary* (1717) p. 374. This translation may have been written by John Dryden (d. 1700), a famous poet and Catholic convert.

The concluding verses may form a separate hymn

English translation can be sung with any 88 88 88 meter, such as Colchester, Regina Caelorum, St Matthias, Sussex Carol, St Chrysostom, etc.

Lustra sex qui jam perégit
Tempus implens córporis,
Sponte líbera Redémptor
Passióni déditus,
Agnus in Crucis levátur
Immolándus stípite.

SIX Lustra's past, * the Sabbath came
On which the World-redeeming Lamb,
As freely he that Term decreed,
So freely chose for us to bleed,
And on the Cross's Altar laid,
The solemn Expiation made.

Felle potus ecce languet:
Spina, clavi, láncea
Mite corpus perforárunt:
Unda manat, et cruor:
Terra, pontus, astra, mundus
Quo lavántur flúmine!

8. Gall was his Drink: his Flesh they tear
With Thorns and Nails; the bolder Spear
His Side laid ope, and once again
Heav'n's Cataracts were seen to rain
Another Deluge; but the Flood
Was Water mix'd with saving Blood.

Crux fidélis, inter omnes
Arbor una nóbilis:
Silva talem nulla profert
Fronde, flore, gérmine :
Dulce ferrum, dulce lignum,
Dulce pondus sústinent.

9. O tow'ring Tree! whose branching Head
Like Heav'n is both sublime and spread:
No Citron groves, nor Myrtle Bowers
Can boast such Blossoms, Fruits or Flow'rs:
Since Christ's redeeming Arms display'd,
Create the Sweetness of thy Shade.

Flecte ramos, arbor alta,
Tensa laxa víscera,
Et rigor lentéscat ille,
Quem dedit natívitas;
Et supérni membra Regis
Tende miti stípite!

10. Tall Cedar rais'd to mate the Sky!
Hard as thou art, now mollify,
And teach Men how to treat their God:
Bow gently down beneath thy Load,
That unrelenting Man may learn
To change his Heart and feel Concern.

Sola digna tu fuísti
Ferre mundi víctimam;
Atque portum praeparáre
Arca mundo náufrago,
Quam sacer cruor perúnxit
Fusus Agni córpore.

11. Thou when the Shipwreck'd World was toss'd
On raging Seas, and Nature lost;
Besprinkled with the Savior's Gore,
Alone wert fit to waft us o'er
To that calm Port of endless Bliss;
Where future Storms and Dangers cease.

Sempitérna sit beátae
Trinitáti glória,
Aequa Patri Filióque,
Par decus Paráclito:
Unívs Triníque nomen,
Laudet univérsitas.

12. May all this praise, and honor Thee,
One undivided Trinity,
The Father, and Co-equal Son,
And Holy Spirit, Three in One,
Whose equal Pow'r and goodness claim
One Equal Everlasting Fame.

88 88 88

Tune:
Various

* The 1717 Primer includes a footnote about *Lustrum*, saying:
"A Period Signifying the Revolution of 5 years."

328 Pange Lingua Gloriosi (6th century)

First Tune – *Trns: Msgr. Ronald A. Knox (d. 1957)*

4. Therefore, when that hallowed hour
Time to its fulfillment brought,
From his Father's heav'nly tower
Came he, who the worlds had wrought,
From his Mother's secret bower,
Clothed in flesh, and welcome sought.

5. See a helpless infant crying,
Whom a manger doth enfold;
See his Virgin Mother tying
Rags about him in the cold;
Bound both hand and feet, and lying
'Mid the beasts, your God behold!

87 87 87

Tune: Mannheim

Final Verses: Richard Lloyd (1993) #129; Noel Rawsthorne (2011) #200.
T. Source: *New Westminster Hymnal* (1939) p. 48.
Melody: Friedrich Filitz (d. 1876) in *Vierstimmiges Choralbuch* (1847).
M. Source: *Catholic Hymn Book* (London Oratory, 1998) p. 410; *New Westminster Hymnal* (1939) p. 48; due to the considerable involvement Msgr. Knox had in the creation of the *New Westminster Hymnal*, it can be assumed that he preferred this tune.

Pange Lingua Gloriosi (6th century) 329

The concluding verses may form a separate hymn

9. Bend thy branches down to meet him,
Bend that stubborn heart of thine;
Let thy native force, to greet him,
All its ruggedness resign;
Gently let thy wood entreat him,
Royal suff'rer, and divine.

Verse 9 may be used as an SATB choral REFRAIN, especially on penitential days.

10. Victim of our race, he deignèd
On thy arms to lay his head;
Thou the ark, whose refuge gainèd,
Sinful man no more may dread;
Ark, whose planks are deeply stainèd
With the blood the Lamb hath shed.

11. Honor, glory, might and merit
To th'eternal Trinity,
Father, Son, and Holy Spirit,
Throned in heaven equally;
All that doth the world inherit,
Praise one God in Persons three.

87 87 87

Tune: MANNHEIM

330 Pange Lingua Gloriosi (6th century)

Second Tune – *Trns: Msgr. Ronald A. Knox (d. 1957)*

4. Therefore, when that hallowed hour
Time to its fulfillment brought,
From his Father's heav'nly tower
Came he, who the worlds had wrought,
From his Mother's secret bower,
Clothed in flesh, and welcome sought.

5. See a helpless infant crying,
Whom a manger doth enfold;
See his Virgin Mother tying
Rags about him in the cold;
Bound both hand and feet, and lying
'Mid the beasts, your God behold!

87 87 87

Tune:
Picardy

Final Verses: Richard Lloyd (1993) #168; Noel Rawsthorne (2011) #257.
T. Source: *New Westminster Hymnal* (1939) p. 48.
M. Source: *New English Hymnal* (1986) p. 1124.
Melody: 17th century French carol; cf. *Mélodies populaires des Provinces de France* (1848) #5, entitled *La Ballade de Jésus-Christ*. The name "Picardy" comes from the province of France from which it is believed to originate.

Pange Lingua Gloriosi (6th century) 331

The concluding verses may form a separate hymn

9. Bend thy branches down to meet him,
Bend that stubborn heart of thine;
Let thy native force, to greet him,
All its ruggedness resign;
Gently let thy wood entreat him,
Royal suff'rer, and divine.

Verse 9 may be used as an SATB choral Refrain, especially on penitential days.

10. Victim of our race, he deignèd
On thy arms to lay his head;
Thou the ark, whose refuge gainèd,
Sinful man no more may dread;
Ark, whose planks are deeply stainèd
With the blood the Lamb hath shed.

11. Honor, glory, might and merit
To th'eternal Trinity,
Father, Son, and Holy Spirit,
Throned in heaven equally;
All that doth the world inherit,
Praise one God in Persons three.

87 87 87

Tune: Picardy

332 Pange Lingua Gloriosi (6th century)

Trns: Dr. Hamilton M. Macgill (d. 1880)

4. At the time afore appointed,
Coming in His Father's name,
In the womb of Virgin Mother
Clothed in flesh, with feeble frame;
Born a man, the world's Creator
From the throne of glory came.

5. Hark, and see, the wailing Infant
In a manger mean is found:
Child all lowly, God all holy,
Whom no robes of light surround,
But who by a blessed Virgin
Close in swaddling has been bound.

87 87 87

Tune:
Dulce Carmen

T. Source: *Songs of the Christian Creed and Life* (London: Pickering, 1876) #36.
Melody: Samuel Webbe, the Elder (d. 1816), choirmaster of the Chapel of the Portuguese Embassy in Lincoln's Inn Fields (a public square), the only place in London where the Catholic liturgy could be publicly celebrated.
M. Source: *Essay on Church Plain-chant* (1782); *Mediator Dei Hymnal* (1955) #16; *St. Basil's Hymnal* (1918) p. 280; *St. Mark's Hymnal for Use in the Catholic Church in the United States* (Peoria, Illinois: 1910) pp. 23, 66.

The concluding verses may form a separate hymn

9. Tree of awful beauty, bend thee.
Bend; thy stubborn branches bring
Softly round the form thou bearest;
O'er His head thy shadow fling;
Gently in thine arms uphold Him,
For of glory He is King.

Verse 9 may be used as an SATB choral Refrain, especially on penitential days.

10. Worthy Thou to bear the ransom
Of a shipwreck'd world art found,
And to be our Ark of safety,
For celestial harbor bound;
Sacred, hence, that blood has made thee,
As it flowed and wrapt thee round.

11. Glory, glory, everlasting,
To the blessed Trinity,
Praise to Thee, Eternal Father,
Praise, Eternal Son, to Thee,
Praise to Thee, Eternal Spirit,
Three in One, and One in Three!

87 87 87

Tune: Dulce Carmen

Verse 6 • On this sentiment, cf. the Dies Irae, tenth stanza: *Quaérens me, sedísti lássus: Redemísti Crúcem pássus: Tántus lábor non sit cássus*; "It was me You were seeking out when, exhausted, You sat by the well; me that You redeemed when You suffered on the cross. Do not allow such toil to have been in vain."

334 Pange Lingua Gloriosi (6th century)

Historic Translation (1670AD) by Sir William K. Blount (d. 1717)

4. When the blest time was fully come,
The Father from His glorious home
Sent His eternal Son:
He that created heav'n and earth,
Of a poor Virgin took His birth,
And our frail flesh put on.

5. The tender Infant, as He lies
In the cold manger, shrinks and cries
As little children use:
While His chaste Mother binds His hands,
His feet, His legs in swathing bands;
Nor does He worse refuse.

886 D

Tune: INNSBRUCK M8

ENGLISH TRANSLATION: Sir William Kirkham Blount (d. 1717), printed in *The Office of the Holy Week according to the Missal and Roman Breviary* (1670).
Melody: Heinrich Isaac (d. 1527); adapted by Sir Richard R. Terry (d. 1938) in the *Westminster Hymnal* (1912) p. 38. It occurs famously in J.S. Bach's *St. Matthew Passion* (1727).
M. Source: This text and tune were paired in the *Book of Hymns with Tunes* (1910) p. 54, edited by Samuel Gregory Ould (d. 1939), a Benedictine priest.

Pange Lingua Gloriosi (6th century) 335

The concluding verses may form a separate hymn

6. Christ does not on - ly not re - fuse, But_ out of
7. Be - hold the gall_ and vin - e - gar, The_ mock - ing
8. Hail, ho - ly Cross, to thee we bow, To_ whose blest

pure love free - ly choose Death on this bit - ter Cross;
reed and cru - el spear, Their hate, His love dis - play:
Fruit our lives we owe; Our earth bears no such tree:

Where He, the sin - less Lamb, was slain, E - ter - nal
Be - hold the Bod - y cold and wan, Whence streams of
Dear are the nails, and dear the wood On_ which our

life for us to gain, And so_ re - pair our loss.
blood and wa - ter ran To wash_ our stains a - way.
dear Lord shed his blood 'Twas heav'n that plant - ed thee.

9. Bend, gentle tree, O quickly bend
Thy softened branches, and suspend
Thy native stubborn heart:
O give at least this small relief
To God of heav'n, but Man of grief,
At least abate His smart.

Verse 9 may be used as an SATB choral Refrain, especially on penitential days.

10. 'Twas thou alone wert worthy thought
To bear Him, Who our ransom brought
And on thee paid it down:
'Twas He alone and His dear Blood
That saved us from the common flood,
Which else the world would drown.

11. All glory to the sacred Three,
One undivided Deity,
All honor, bliss and praise!
O may we still adore Thy name,
Thy pow'r and goodness still proclaim
Beyond the end of days.

886 D

Tune:
Innsbruck M8

St. Robert Southwell, SJ

Heroic Martyr of Jesus Christ

ST. ROBERT SOUTHWELL (d. 1595), a Jesuit priest, was a renowned poet whose works were admired by Shakespeare. His crowning achievement was his martyrdom at the young age of 33, by which he left an example of unshakable loyalty to Jesus Christ.

Having been arrested for ministering to Catholics in England, Southwell was tortured so cruelly that he was never allowed to rest except when he seemed to be dying. Then they would take him down from the rack and "bring him to, by remedies." He would often vomit a quantity of blood, after which he was hung up again. During all this, he was so patient, and the expression of his countenance so sweet, that even the servant who watched him began to look upon him as a saint. His only exclamations were *Deus meus et omnia* ("My God and my all") and *Deus tibi Se, tu te Deo* ("God gave Himself to thee; give thyself to God"). [1]

Cecil, President of the Council at that time, during a conversation concerning the tortures exercised upon Southwell, is reported to have expressed himself thus:

> Let antiquity boast of its Roman heroes, and the patience of captives in torments; our own age is not inferior to it, nor do the minds of the English cede to the Romans. There is at present confined one Southwell, a Jesuit, who, thirteen times most cruelly tortured, cannot be induced to confess anything, not even the colour of the horse whereon on a certain day he rode, lest from such indication his adversaries might conjecture in what house, or in company of what Catholics, he that day was.

Southwell's perseverance is illustrated by a small anecdote apropos his three-year imprisonment in the tower. Father Garnett, who recovered from Southwell's jailer a breviary:

> … in turning over page after page found that the martyr had pricked with the point of a needle his favourite words—*Deus meus et omnia* and *Deus tibi Se, tu te Illi*—from which Father Garnett gathered that he had not been able to procure writing materials in prison.

1 The life of St. Robert Southwell has been treated by many competent authors. An outstanding contribution is Fr. Henry Foley's *Records of the English Province of the Society of Jesus* (London: Burns & Oates, 1877).

THE HEADER for St. Robert Southwell's magnificent hymn is: "On the Blessed Sacrament of the Altar." The full work comprises 770 words—and due to its length, our singable version below omits seven stanzas. The Blessed Sacrament was announced in the sixth chapter of St. John's Gospel, in which Our Lord and Master declares: "You can have no life in yourselves, unless you eat the flesh of the Son of Man, and drink his blood."

The Jews, who knew that God had forbidden (Lev 17.14) the drinking of blood, erroneously pictured a cannibalistic eating of raw human flesh and drinking of human blood; but Christ did not intend to be received in such a way. According to Catholic doctrine, Christ's body is ascended into heaven. But by its substance, independently of all the laws of space which affect substance through accidental qualities, this body is present in the Eucharist under the forms of bread and wine.

> (Jn 6.53) Then the Jews fell to disputing with one another,
> "How can this man give us his flesh to eat?"

> (Jn 6:61) And there were many of his disciples who said, when they heard it,
> "This is strange talk; who can be expected to listen to it?"

Fr. Leslie A. Rumble (d. 1975) explains Christ's message as follows: [2]

> You will not be asked to eat my flesh in the horrible and natural way you imagine, for my body as you see it with your eyes will be gone from this earth. Yet I shall leave my flesh and blood in another and supernatural way which your natural and carnal minds cannot understand. [...] It is the spirit of faith which will enable you to believe, not your natural judgment.

Archbishop Sheen reminds us that "the announcement of the Eucharist produced one of the greatest crises" in our Lord's life, where *crisis* means *judgment* : [3]

> (Jn 6.67) After this, many of his disciples went back to their old ways,
> and walked no more in his company.

Southwell's hymn does not attempt to "rationalize" the Eucharistic mystery, about which St. Thomas Aquinas (d. 1274) famously wrote:

Tantum ergo sacramentum	Let us therefore humbly reverence
veneremur cernui,	so great a sacrament.
Et antiquum documentum	Let the old types depart
novo cedat ritui;	and give way to the new rite.
Praestet fides supplementum	Let faith provide her help
sensuum defectui.	where all the senses fail.

Southwell makes this explicit in his ninth stanza:

---

2 Dr. Rumble went on to explicitly address those who insist our Savior intended cannibalism: "Christ is not present in the Eucharist under a form in which cannibalism could be possible. His body is really and substantially present, but not in a natural way. It is an entirely supernatural mode of presence which you may not believe, but which at least excludes all notions of cannibalism." (Radio address, 1940)

3 Fulton Sheen, *Life of Christ* (New York: McGraw-Hill, 1958) p. 144. For the Greek understanding of the word "crisis," see Fulton Sheen, *Treasure in Clay* (New York: Doubleday, 1980) p. 172.

> God's power our proofs, His works our wit exceed,
> Proud reason oft to fatal lapse doth lead.

According to Msgr. Hugh T. Henry (d. 1946), Southwell was the first to attempt an English translation of the (Eucharistic) *Lauda Sion* Sequence:

> While acting as chaplain and confessor of the Countess of Arundel (1590-1592) he composed the volume of poetry which has given him an honorable place in English literature, and rendered into English verse "Saint Thomas of Aquines Hyme Read on Corpus Christy Daye."

Although Alexander B. Grosart (d. 1899) gave no source for his assertion that *Lauda Sion* was Southwell's "favourite hymn," *On The Blessed Sacrament Of The Altar* is without question linked to it—and we will have more to say about this. Southwell's twelfth stanza (omitted for the reasons given above) demonstrates well this connection:

> Whole may His body be in smallest breadd,
> Whole in the whole, yea whole in every crumme;
> With which be one or be tenn thowsand fedd,
> All to ech one, to all but one doth cumme;
> And though ech one as much as all receive,
> Not one too much, nor all too little have.

Compare this to the *Lauda Sion*, translated by Southwell himself:

Fracto demum Sacramento	When the priest the host divideth,
Ne vacilles, sed memento,	Know that in each part abideth
Tantum esse sub fragmento,	All that the whole host covered.
Quantum toto tegitur.	Form of bread,
Nulla rei fit scissura:	not Christ is broken,
Signi tantum fit fractura:	Not of Christ,
Qua nec status, nec statura	but of His token,
Signati minuitur.	Is state or stature altered.

LITERARY SCHOLARSHIP has identified St. Robert Southwell as a forerunner of the Metaphysical poets, writers of the English Baroque. His verse is never profane, but reads like rhymed meditation, both discursive and affective, on Christian truths: no doubt showing the influence of the "Spiritual Exercises" of St. Ignatius Loyola, founder of the Society of Jesus, to which Southwell belonged.

Like other Metaphysicals, Southwell's work abounds in paradoxical "conceits," which he uses to move and edify the reader rather than to produce an effect for its own sake. In the following lines, he draws attention to the paradox that Christ at the Last Supper held Himself in his own hands, and was Himself that which he offered; and even though they saw Him truly and visibly before them, through Eucharistic communion He was also invisibly and truly present within His Apostles:

> That which He gave He was; O peerless gift:
> Both God and man He was, and both He gave!
> He in his hands Himself did truly lift,
> Far off they see whom in themselves they have.

Because of the centuries separating Southwell's age from our own, we make bold to reflect upon several rich stanzas for the benefit of today's Christians:

1. In Paschal feast, the end of ancient rite
An entrance was to never-ending grace:
Types yield to truth, dim glimpses to the light,
Performing deed presaging signs did chase;
Christ's final meal was fountain of our good,
For mortal fare He gave immortal food.

Reflection: The end of the Old Testament observances was the beginning of the New Covenant and justifying grace; Christ's offering is the antitype of the ancient sacrifices, and fulfills them; the Lord's Supper is the source of salvation; the Eucharist is the "medicine of immortality." Cf. *Lauda Sion:*

In hac mensa novi Regis,	At this table of the new King,
Novum Pascha novae legis	the new Pasch of the new law
Phase vetus terminat:	concludes the ancient passover:
Vetustatem novitas,	the new supplants the old,
Umbram fugat veritas,	truth puts to flight shadow,
Noctem lux eliminat.	light expels night.

The second stanza in our version is the third stanza in the original:

2. They saw, they heard, they felt Him sitting near,
Unseen, unfelt, unheard, they Him receiv'd:
No different thing, though different it appear,
Though senses fail, yet faith is not deceiv'd;
And if the wonder of the work be new,
Believe the worker, for his word is true.

Reflection: Christ was present in two ways: (1.) in His mortal body, by which He was visible, audible, palpable, etc. (2.) in the Eucharist, where He was invisible, inaudible, impalpable, etc. Yet one and the same Christ was present, as faith, rather than sensation, tells us. Although it is a marvel, Christ teaches us; and He cannot deceive. Cf. *Pange lingua* of St. Thomas Aquinas:

Et si sensus deficit,	And if sense fails,
Ad firmandum cor sincerum	faith by itself is enough
Sola fides sufficit.	to assure the guileless heart.

Cf. the Sequence for Corpus Christi (*Dogma datur Christianis*, etc.):

> Christ's followers know by faith that bread is changed into His flesh and wine into His blood. Man cannot understand this, cannot perceive it; but a lively faith affirms that the change—which is outside the natural course of things—takes place.

The third in our version is the eighth in the original:

3. Though blind men see no light, the sun doth shine,
Sweet is the sweet, though fever'd taste deny,

Pearls precious are, though trodden on by swine: (cf. Mt 7.6)
All truths are true, though not all men them try;
The best unto the bad doth work the worst,
Instead of blessing, make the more accurs'd. (cf. I Cor 11.27)

Reflection: Blindness and fever affect their subject, other objects remain as they are; perception is subjective, reality objective; the extrinsic value of a thing does not affect its intrinsic worth; truth depends on objective reality, not subjective perception; the wicked derive no benefit from receiving the Eucharist, but increase their guilt.

Cf. the Sequence for Corpus Christi:

Sumunt boni, sumunt mali:	The good receive, the bad receive:
Sorte tamen inaequali,	yet with a divergent fate,
Vitae vel interitus.	of life or of destruction.
Mors est malis, vita bonis:	It is death to the bad, life to the good:
Vide paris sumptionis	behold how unlike may be
Quam sit dispar exitus.	the fruit of a like reception.

The fourth in our version is the ninth in the original:

4. The angels' eyes, whom veils cannot deceive,
Might best disclose what best they did discern:
Men must, with meek and silent faith, receive
More than they can by sense or reason learn;
God's pow'r our proofs, His works our wit exceed,
Proud reason oft to fatal lapse doth lead.

Reflection: The blessed Angels enjoy the beatific vision of God (cf. Mt 18.10), and see all that they see through it; as pure spirits, their "sight" is the understanding of things in their essence. While angels know things in their causes, men come to know by reasoning; they can only attain to the knowledge of that which surpasses reason by virtue of faith, submitting to divine authority; God is as incomprehensible as His power is infinite; the fact that God can do anything is sufficient cause for Him to do whatever He wills. One variant reads: "The doer's might the reason of His deed." (cf. Ps 113.11; 134.6) As Msgr. Ronald Knox wrote: "A miracle cannot be probable or improbable; it is either possible or impossible."

The fifth in our version is the eleventh in the original:

5. The God of hosts in slender host doth dwell,
Yea, God and man, with all to either due:
The God who rules the heav'ns and rifled hell,
The man whose death did us to life renew;
The God and man who is the angels' bliss
In form of bread and wine our nurture is.

Reflection: The limitless God becomes present under the limited form of bread; and man too, since Christ is the Word made flesh; He is the celestial King who conquered the empire of death; by His assumed humanity, He died to save us; He is the joy of angels; He is our nourishment under the appearances of bread and wine. On *the angels' bliss*, cf. *Jesu, gaudium Angelorum* (Litany of the holy Name).

The sixth in our version is the thirteenth in the original:

6. One soul in man is all in ev'ry part,
One face at once in many mirrors shines,
One fearful noise doth make a thousand start,
One eye at once of countless things defines:
If nature proofs of one in many frame,
In stronger sort may God perform the same.

Reflection: A spirit is where it acts: thus a soul is coextensive with its body; a form may be visibly multiplied yet remain one; many ears can hear one sound; a single eye can see several things simultaneously; if the natural order exhibits such, much more may the supernatural order. With regard to "If nature of one…" : That which the lesser can do, the greater can also do: argument *a fortiori*.

The seventh in our version is the fourteenth in the original:

7. God is at hand at once in ev'ry place,
Yet God in ev'ry place is ever one:
So may there be, by supernat'ral grace,
One man in many spaces, filling none;
Since angels may effects of bodies show,
On bodies God may angels' gifts bestow.

Reflection: Again, a spirit is where it acts: God acts and is everywhere, yet there is only one God; God may endow a body with spiritual properties, so that it does not displace as a body but acts like a pure spirit; vice versa, pure spirits can assume bodily properties, as when angels become visible. Cf. the Sequence for Corpus Christi:

Fracto demum Sacramento	When the sacrament is at length
Ne vacilles, sed memento,	divided, do not waver, but recall
Tantum esse sub fragmento,	that there is as much in a division
Quantum toto tegitur.	as is harbored in the whole.
Nulla rei fit scissura:	No rending of the reality occurs: there
Signi tantum fit fractura:	occurs only a dividing of the symbol:
Qua nec status, nec statura	by which neither the state nor the stature
Signati minuitur.	of the one symbolized is lessened.

The eighth in our version is the fifteenth in the original:

8. What God as author made, He alter may,
No change so hard as making all of naught:
If Adam fashion'd were of earthly clay, (cf. Gn 2.7)
To sacred flesh of Christ may bread be wrought;
This may he do who made, by strength divine,
A snake of Moses' wand, of water wine. (cf. Ex 4.2-3; Jn 2.7-9)

Reflection: If God created everything, He may change anything; the power to create is sufficient to convert; if God made man from the slime of the earth, He can make bread into the body of Christ; He showed His power when He turned Moses' rod into a snake, and water into wine.

342 On The Blessed Sacrament

First Tune – *St. Robert Southwell, Martyr of Jesus Christ (d. 1595)*

4. The angels' eyes, whom veils cannot deceive,
Might best disclose what best they did discern:
Men must, with meek and silent faith, receive
More than they can by sense or reason learn;
God's pow'r our proofs, His works our wit exceed,
Proud reason oft to fatal lapse doth lead.

10 10 10 10 10 10

Tune:
Song 1

Final Verses: Richard Lloyd (1993) #212; Noel Rawsthorne (2011) #338.
T. Source: *Arundel Catholic Hymnal* (1905) p. 236.
Melody: Orlando Gibbons (d. 1625), organist at Westminster Abbey.
M. Source: *The Hymnes and Songs of the Church* (1623) p. 4.

The concluding verses may form a separate hymn

5. The God of hosts in slender host doth dwell,
6. One soul in man is all in every part,
7. God is at hand at once in every place,

Yea, God and man, with all to either due:
One face at once in many mirrors shines,
Yet God in every place is ever one:

The God who rules the heav'ns and rifled hell,
One fearful noise doth make a thousand start,
So may there be, by super-nat'ral grace,

The man whose death did us to life renew;
One eye at once of countless things defines:
One man in many spaces, filling none;

The God and man who is the angels' bliss
If nature proofs of one in many frame,
Since angels may effects of bodies show,

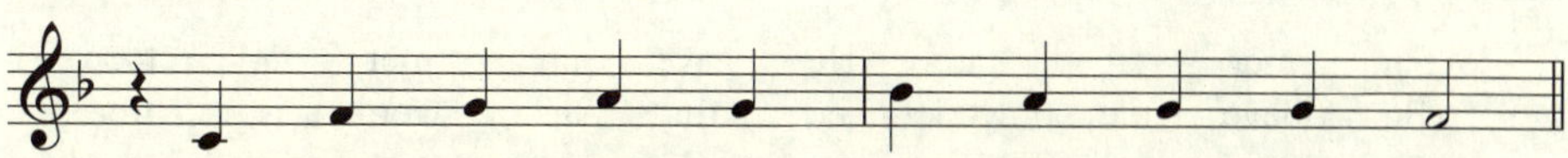

In form of bread and wine our nurture is.
In stronger sort may God perform the same.
On bodies God may angels' gifts bestow.

8. What God as author made, He alter may,
No change so hard as making all of naught:
If Adam fashion'd were of earthly clay,
To sacred flesh of Christ may bread be wrought;
This may he do who made, by strength divine,
A snake of Moses' wand, of water wine.

10 10 10 10 10 10

Tune:
SONG 1

344 On The Blessed Sacrament

Second Tune – *St. Robert Southwell, Martyr of Jesus Christ (d. 1595)*

4. The angels' eyes, whom veils cannot deceive,
Might best disclose what best they did discern:
Men must, with meek and silent faith, receive
More than they can by sense or reason learn;
God's pow'r our proofs, His works our wit exceed,
Proud reason oft to fatal lapse doth lead.

10 10 10 10 10 10

Tune:
Enemond

T. Source: *Arundel Catholic Hymnal* (1905) p. 236.
Melody: Kevin Allen (b. 1965), choirmaster at the Monastery of the Holy Cross in Chicago.
M. Source: *Saint Jean de Brébeuf Hymnal* (2018).

The concluding verses may form a separate hymn

8. What God as author made, He alter may,
No change so hard as making all of naught:
If Adam fashion'd were of earthly clay,
To sacred flesh of Christ may bread be wrought;
This may he do who made, by strength divine,
A snake of Moses' wand, of water wine.

10 10 10 10 10 10

Tune:
ENEMOND

346 Pange Lingua Gloriosi (1264 AD)

St. Thomas Aquinas, Dominican Priest (d. 1274 AD)

PANGE lingua gloriósi
Córporis mystérium
Sanguinísque pretiósi,
Quem in mundi prétium
Fructus ventris generósi,
Rex effúdit géntium.

2. Nobis datus, nobis natus
Ex intácta Vírgine,
Et in mundo conversátus, *n1*
Sparso verbi sémine,
Sui moras incolátus
Miro clausit órdine. *n2*

3. In suprémae nocte cenae
Recúmbens cum frátribus,
Observáta lege plene
Cibis in legálibus, *n3*
Cibum turbae duodénae
Se dat suis mánibus.

4. Verbum caro, panem verum
Verbo carnem éfficit,
Fitque sanguis Christi merum,
Et si sensus déficit,
Ad firmándum cor sincérum
Sola fides súfficit.

TANTUM ergo Sacraméntum
Venerémur cérnui:
Et antíquum documéntum
Novo cedat rítui:
Praestet fides suppleméntum
Sénsuum deféctui.

6. Genitóri, Genitóque
Laus et jubilátio,
Salus, honor, virtus quoque
Sit et benedíctio:
Procedénti ab utróque *n4*
Compar sit laudátio.

87 87 87

Tune:
VARIOUS

[1] "Having lived" : *conversari* also means "interact with others."

[2] *Miro clausit ordine* : on "scheme," cf. *Pange lingua* of Fortunatus, verse 3: *Hoc opus nostrae salutis ordo depoposcerat* ("This work the scheme of our salvation required"). The common Jewish name for the Paschal supper is "Seder" (*Ordo*).

Assistance for comprehension

PUBLISH, O tongue, the mystery
of the glorious Body
and the precious Blood
that, as the cost of the world,
he who was the fruit of a noble womb,
the King of the nations, poured forth.

2. Given for us, born for us
of a Virgin unblemished,
and having lived in the world, *n1*
strewing the seed of the word,
he closed the periods of his abiding
with a wondrous scheme. *n2*

3. On the night of that paramount supper
reclining with his brethren,
having kept the Law fully
through the foods of the Law, *n3*
with his own hands he gives himself
as food to the host of twelve.

4. The Word who is flesh, makes true bread
to be flesh through his word,
and wine becomes the blood of Christ,
and if sense fails,
faith by itself is enough
to assure the guileless heart.

THEREFORE let us reverence
a Sacrament so great:
and let the ancient injunction
yield to the new observance:
let faith furnish support
to the inadequacy of the senses.

6. To the Begetter, and the Begotten
be praise and triumph,
salvation, worship, and power
and blessing also be:
to the one proceeding from each of them *n4*
be equivalent praising.

[3] "Foods of the Law" : pre-eminently the Paschal lamb, but also the other ritual foods of the Seder.

[4] "Proceeding from each" : cf. Nicene creed, "who proceeds from the Father and the Son." The double procession of the Holy Spirit is denied by the schismatic Greeks; St. Thomas Aquinas died *en route* to the Second Council of Lyon (1274), where the Greek bishops embraced this doctrine and returned to Catholic unity; but later they reneged.

Pange Lingua Gloriosi (1264 AD)

St. Thomas Aquinas, Dominican Priest (d. 1274 AD)

Mode III

P Ange lingua glori-ósi Córporis my-

Sing my-tongue the-glorious Body's

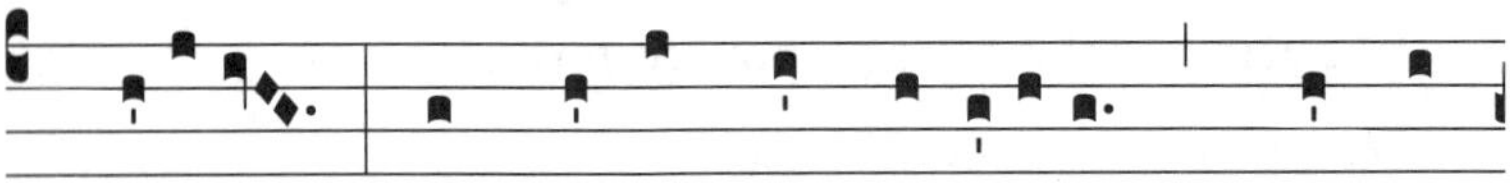

stéri-um, Sangui-nísque pre-ti-ósi, Quem in

mystery, And-of-the-Blood most-precious, Which for

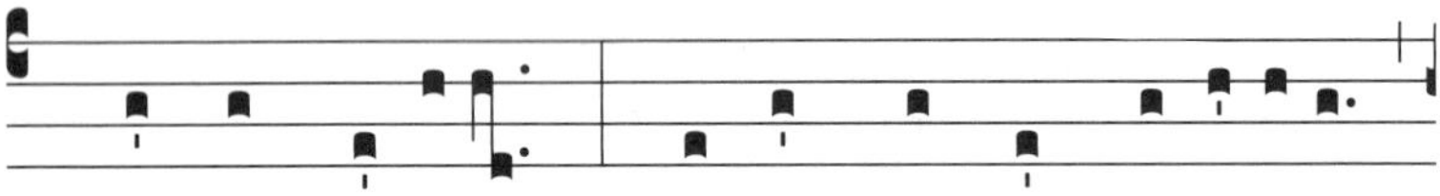

mundi pré-ti- um Fructus ventris generósi

the-world's ransom The-fruit of-a-womb most-generous

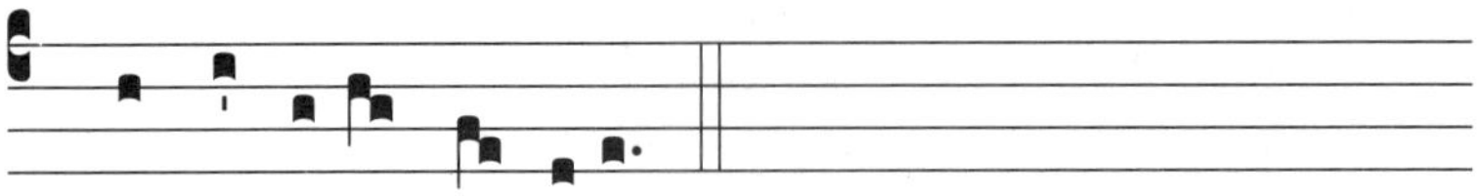

Rex effúdit génti-um.

The-King has-shed, the-King-of-nations.

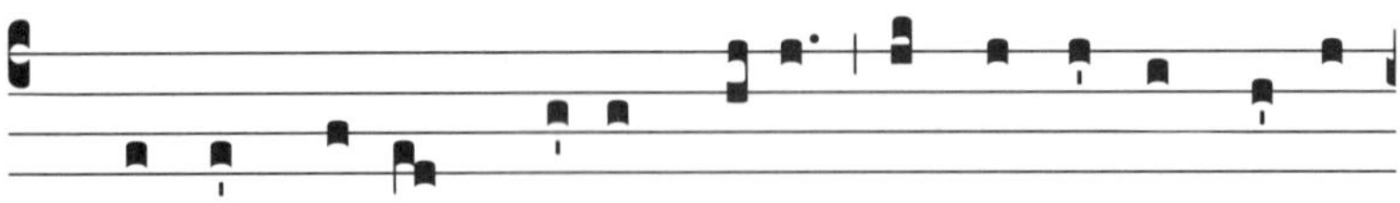

2. Nobis da-tus, nobis natus Ex intácta Vírgi-

To-us given, for-us born Of a-spotless Virgin,

ne, Et in mundo conversátus, Sparso verbi

And in the-world dwelling, Scattering the-word's

sémi-ne, Su-i moras incolátus Mi-ro clausit

seed, His course of-life-on-earth Wondrously He-closed

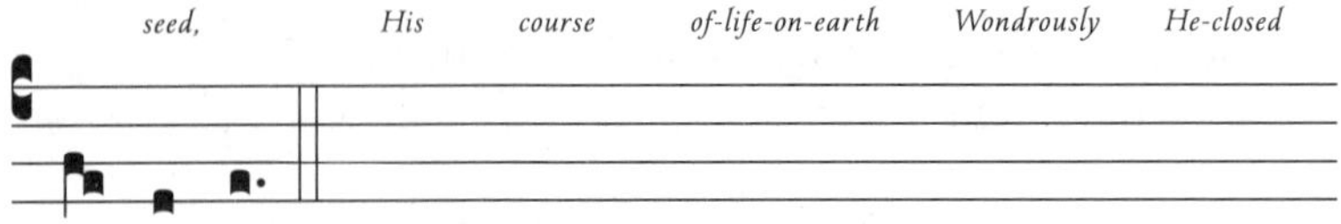

órdi-ne.

in-its-order.

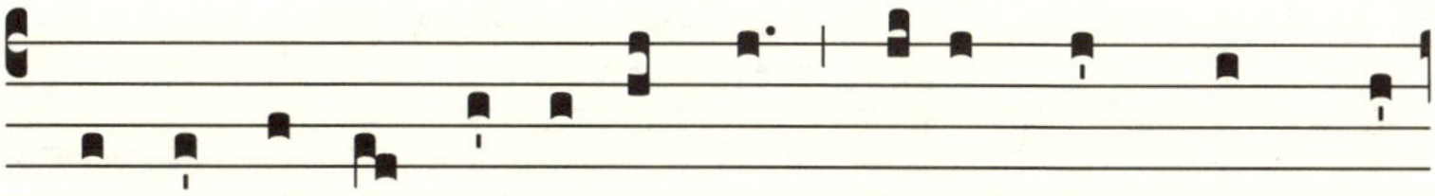

3. In suprémae nocte cœnae Recúmbens cum frá-

On [the night of His Last Supper] Reclining with

tri-bus, Observáta lege plene Ci-bis in legá-

His-brethren, Observing-the Law fully With-food by law-

li-bus, Ci-bum turbae du-odénae Se dat su-

prescribed, As-food-to-the company of-twelve [Himself He-gives]

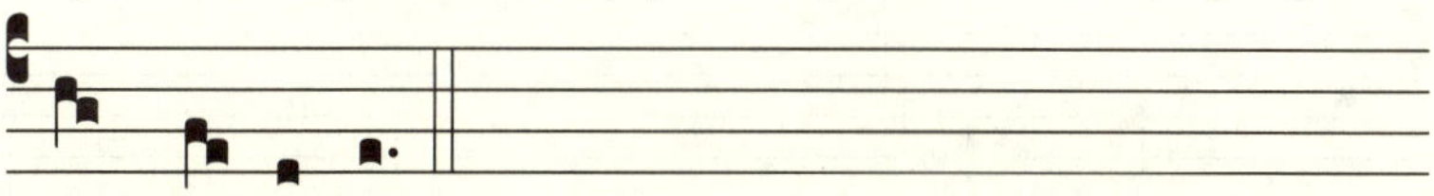

is má-ni-bus.

by-His-own-hands.

4. Verbum caro, panem verum Verbo carnem éf-

The-Word made-flesh, bread truly By-His-word to-His-flesh

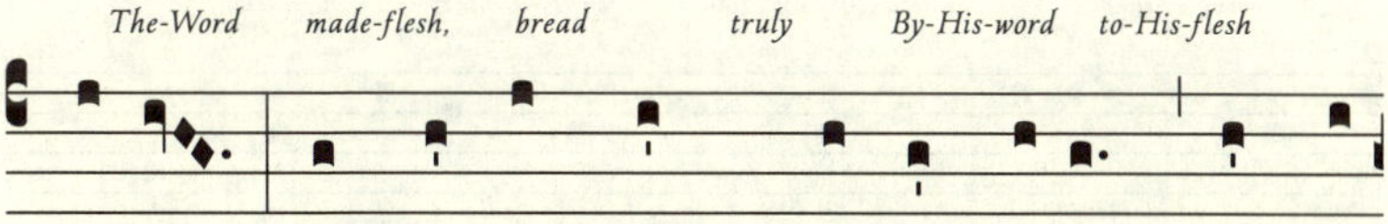

fi-cit: Fitque sanguis Chri-sti merum, Et si

He-changes: And-turned to-blood of-Christ is-wine, And if

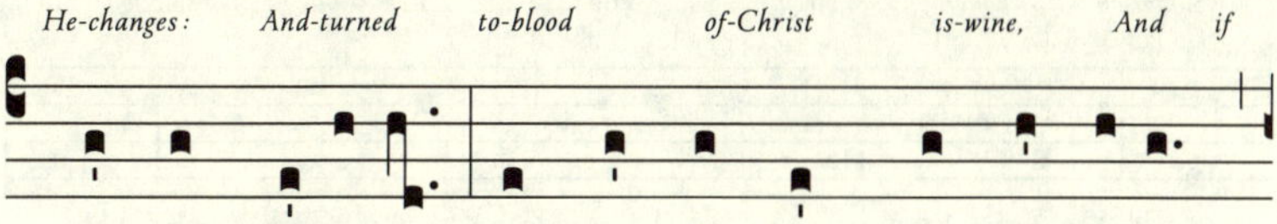

sensus dé-fi-cit, Ad firmándum cor sincérum

our-sense fails-us To confirm-the heart which-is-sincere,

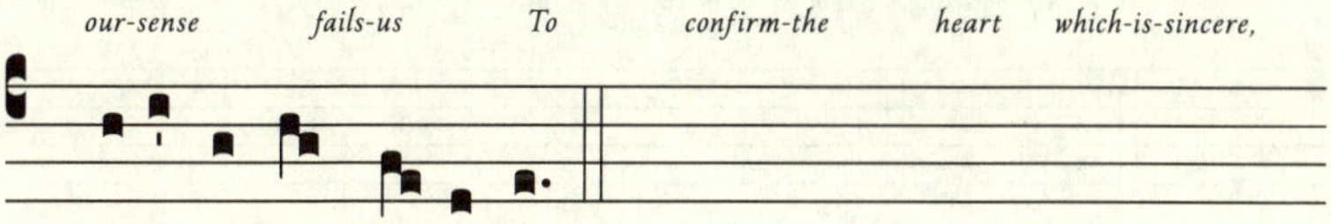

Sola fi-des súffi-cit.

Alone, faith suffices.

5. Tantum ergo Sacraméntum Venerémur cérnu-
So-great, therefore, this-Sacrament, Let-us-adore-It bending-low:
i: Et antí-quum documéntum Novo cedat
And the-ancient covenant To-the-New shall-yield
rí-tu- i: Praestet fi-des suppleméntum Sénsu-
to-this-rite: Provide-may faith a-supplement For-our-senses'
um de-fé-ctu-i.
deficiency.
6. Geni-tó-ri, Geni-tóque Laus et jubi-lá-ti-o,
To-the-Father and-to-the-Son Praise and jubilation,
Salus, honor, virtus quoque Sit et benedí-cti-
Salvation, honor, virtue also Be, and benediction:
o: Procedénti ab utróque Compar sit laudá-
To-Him-proceeding from both Equal be our-praising
ti-o. A- men.
So-be-it.

Trns: Fr. Edward Caswall, Oratorian (d. 1878)

Can be sung with any 87 87 87 meter: Picardy, Runnells, Mannheim, Gaufestre, Davost, Breton, Obiit, Neander, Lauda Anima, Dulce Carmen, St Leonard, Regent Square, and so forth.

SING, my tongue, the Savior's glory,
Of his Flesh the myst'ry sing;
Of the Blood, all price exceeding,
Shed by our immortal King,
Destin'd, for the world's redemption,
From a noble womb to spring.

2. Of a pure and spotless Virgin
Born for us on earth below,
He, as Man with man conversing,
Stay'd, the seeds of truth to sow;
Then He clos'd in solemn order
Wondrously his life of woe.

3. On the night of that Last Supper,
Seated with his chosen band,
He the paschal victim eating,
First fulfils the Law's command;
Then, as Food to all his brethren
Gives Himself with his own hand.

4. The Incarnate Word now changes
Bread to flesh at His command,
And the wine becomes His lifeblood.
Senses fail to understand;
But the heart that is in earnest
Can by faith its doubt withstand.

DOWN IN ADORATION FALLING,
THIS GREAT SACRAMENT WE HAIL;
Over ancient forms of worship
Newer rites of grace prevail;
Faith reminds us Christ is present
When our feeble senses fail.

6. To the Everlasting Father,
And the Son who reigns on high,
With the Holy Ghost proceeding
Forth from Each eternally,
Be salvation, honor, blessing,
Might, and endless majesty.

87 87 87

Tune: Various

T. Source: *Lyra Catholica: Containing all the hymns of the Roman Breviary and Missal* (1848) p. 111.

352 Pange Lingua (St. Thomas Aquinas)

First Tune – *Trns: Fr. Edward Caswall, Oratorian (d. 1878)*

4. The Incarnate Word now changes
Bread to flesh at His command,
And the wine becomes His lifeblood.
Senses fail to understand;
But the heart that is in earnest
Can by faith its doubt withstand.

5. Down in adoration falling,
This great Sacrament we hail;
Over ancient forms of worship
Newer rites of grace prevail;
Faith reminds us Christ is present
When our feeble senses fail.

6. To the Everlasting Father,
And the Son who reigns on high,
With the Holy Ghost proceeding
Forth from Each eternally,
Be salvation, honor, blessing,
Might, and endless majesty.

87 87 87

Tune:
St Thomas (Webbe)

T. Source: *Lyra Catholica: Containing all the hymns of the Roman Breviary and Missal* (1848) p. 111.
Melody: Samuel Webbe, the Elder (d. 1816), choirmaster of the Chapel of the Portuguese Embassy in Lincoln's Inn Fields (a public square), the only place in London where the Catholic liturgy could be publicly celebrated.
M. Source: Fr. Joseph Mohr's *Psälterlein* (Regensburg: Pustet, 1889) p. 542; *Hosanna Catholic Hymn Book* (St. Louis: Fr. Ludwig Bonvin, 1914) #187.

Pange Lingua (St. Thomas Aquinas)

SECOND TUNE – *Trns: Fr. Edward Caswall, Oratorian (d. 1878)*

1. Sing, my tongue, the Sav - ior's glo - ry, Of his Flesh the
2. Of a pure and spot - less Vir - gin Born for us on
3. On the night of that Last Sup - per, Seat - ed with his

mys - t'ry sing; Of the Blood, all price ex - ceed - ing,
earth___ be - low, He, as Man with man con - vers - ing,
cho - sen band, He the pas - chal vic - tim eat - ing,

Shed by our im - mor - tal King, Des - tin'd, for the
Stay'd, the seeds of truth___ to sow; Then He clos'd in
First ful - fils the Law's___ com - mand; Then, as Food to

world's re - demp - tion, From a no - ble womb to spring.
sol - emn or - der Won - drous - ly his life of woe.
all his breth - ren Gives Him - self with his own hand.

4. The Incarnate Word now changes
Bread to flesh at His command,
And the wine becomes His lifeblood.
Senses fail to understand;
But the heart that is in earnest
Can by faith its doubt withstand.

5. DOWN IN ADORATION FALLING,
This great Sacrament we hail;
Over ancient forms of worship
Newer rites of grace prevail;
Faith reminds us Christ is present
When our feeble senses fail.

6. To the Everlasting Father,
And the Son who reigns on high,
With the Holy Ghost proceeding
Forth from Each eternally,
Be salvation, honor, blessing,
Might, and endless majesty.

87 87 87

T. Source: *Lyra Catholica: Containing all the hymns of the Roman Breviary and Missal* (1848) p. 111.
Melody: Kevin Allen (b. 1965), choirmaster at the Monastery of the Holy Cross in Chicago.
M. Source: *Saint Jean de Brébeuf Hymnal* (2018).

Tune: RUNNELLS

354 Pange Lingua (St. Thomas Aquinas)

Third Tune – *Trns: Fr. Edward Caswall, Oratorian* (*d.* 1878)

4. The Incarnate Word now changes
Bread to flesh at His command,
And the wine becomes His lifeblood.
Senses fail to understand;
But the heart that is in earnest
Can by faith its doubt withstand.

5. Down in adoration falling,
This great Sacrament we hail;
Over ancient forms of worship
Newer rites of grace prevail;
Faith reminds us Christ is present
When our feeble senses fail.

6. To the Everlasting Father,
And the Son who reigns on high,
With the Holy Ghost proceeding
Forth from Each eternally,
Be salvation, honor, blessing,
Might, and endless majesty.

87 87 87

Tune:
Picardy

Final Verses: Richard Lloyd (1993) #168; Noel Rawsthorne (2011) #257.
M. Source: *New English Hymnal* (1986) p. 1124.
Melody: 17th century French carol; cf. *Mélodies populaires des Provinces de France* (1848) #5, entitled *La Ballade de Jésus-Christ.* The name "Picardy" comes from the province of France from which it is believed to originate.
T. Source: *Lyra Catholica: Containing all the hymns of the Roman Breviary and Missal* (1848) p. 111.

Fourth Tune – *Trns: Fr. Edward Caswall, Oratorian (d. 1878)*

4. The Incarnate Word now changes
Bread to flesh at His command,
And the wine becomes His lifeblood.
Senses fail to understand;
But the heart that is in earnest
Can by faith its doubt withstand.

5. Down in adoration falling,
This great Sacrament we hail;
Over ancient forms of worship
Newer rites of grace prevail;
Faith reminds us Christ is present
When our feeble senses fail.

6. To the Everlasting Father,
And the Son who reigns on high,
With the Holy Ghost proceeding
Forth from Each eternally,
Be salvation, honor, blessing,
Might, and endless majesty.

Melody: Fr. Jules de Verneuil (d. 1938).
M. Source: Fr. Anatole Police, *The Parochial Hymn Book* (London: Burns & Oates, 1897).
T. Source: *Lyra Catholica: Containing all the hymns of the Roman Breviary and Missal* (1848) p. 111.

87 87 87
Tune: Davost

356 Pange Lingua (St. Thomas Aquinas)

FIFTH TUNE – *Trns: Fr. Edward Caswall, Oratorian (d. 1878)*

4. The Incarnate Word now changes
Bread to flesh at His command,
And the wine becomes His lifeblood.
Senses fail to understand;
But the heart that is in earnest
Can by faith its doubt withstand.

5. DOWN IN ADORATION FALLING,
This great Sacrament we hail;
Over ancient forms of worship
Newer rites of grace prevail;
Faith reminds us Christ is present
When our feeble senses fail.

6. To the Everlasting Father,
And the Son who reigns on high,
With the Holy Ghost proceeding
Forth from Each eternally,
Be salvation, honor, blessing,
Might, and endless majesty.

87 87 87

Tune:
WESTMINSTER ABBEY F

Melody: Henry Purcell (d. 1695), organist at Westminster Abbey.
M. Source: cf. Final "Hallelujah" section of an anthem (1681), *O God, Thou Art My God.* Like many hymn tunes (BRESLAU, OLD HUNDREDTH, BEDFORD, PUER NOBIS NASCITUR, etc.) this melody can be sung in triple or quadruple meter; however, when sung in triple, it should follow Purcell's original rhythm and not what is commonly found in 20th century hymnals.
T. Source: *Lyra Catholica: Containing all the hymns of the Roman Breviary and Missal* (1848) p. 111.

Pange Lingua (St. Thomas Aquinas) 357

Sixth Tune – *Trns: Fr. Edward Caswall, Oratorian (d. 1878)*

4. The Incarnate Word now changes
Bread to flesh at His command,
And the wine becomes His lifeblood.
Senses fail to understand;
But the heart that is in earnest
Can by faith its doubt withstand.

5. Down in adoration falling,
This great Sacrament we hail;
Over ancient forms of worship
Newer rites of grace prevail;
Faith reminds us Christ is present
When our feeble senses fail.

6. To the Everlasting Father,
And the Son who reigns on high,
With the Holy Ghost proceeding
Forth from Each eternally,
Be salvation, honor, blessing,
Might, and endless majesty.

87 87 87

T. Source: *Lyra Catholica: Containing all the hymns of the Roman Breviary and Missal* (1848) p. 111.
Melody: Metrical Cento; cf. "Dum staret Abraham" (*Antiphonaire Monastique,* 13th century).
M. Source: *Paléographie musicale* (Volume XII), folio 81; *Cantus Selecti* (Solesmes, 1957) p. 245.

Tune: Breton

358 Pange Lingua (St. Thomas Aquinas)

First Tune – *Trns: Robert Campbell of Skerrington (d. 1868)*

4. Earthly things to things of heaven | Changed by God's incarnate Word,
Flesh and blood in myst'ry given, | We believe with faith assured;
As the Word hath said it, even | Be that word believed, adored.

5. Then before His altar bowing, | Let our hearts the Lord revere;
Faith her aid to vision lending, | Tells that He unseen is near;
Ancient types and shadows ending, | Christ our paschal Lamb is here.

6. To the Trinity be glory | Everlasting, as is meet:
Equal to the Father, equal | To the Son and Paraclete:
Blessèd Unity, whose praises | All created things repeat.

English Translation: Robert Campbell, a Scottish attorney who published *Hymns and Anthems for Use in the Holy Service of the Church* (1850). He converted to the Catholic Church in 1852, but was never a priest—despite the claim made in the *American Catholic Hymnal according to the Motu Proprio of His Holiness Pope Pius X* (1913) on page 251.
T. Source: Orby Shipley's *Annus Sanctus: Hymns of the Church for the Ecclesiastical Year; Translated from the Sacred Offices by various Authors, with Modern, Original, and other Hymns, and an Appendix of Earlier Versions* (1884) p. 185.
Melody: Kevin Allen (b. 1965), choirmaster at the Monastery of the Holy Cross in Chicago.
M. Source: *Saint Jean de Brébeuf Hymnal* (2018).

87 87 87

Tune:
Runnells

First Tune – *Textus originalis Latinus*

4. Verbum caro, panem verum | Verbo carnem éfficit,
Fitque sanguis Christi merum, | Et si sensus déficit,
Ad firmándum cor sincérum | Sola fides súfficit.

TANTUM ERGO SACRAMÉNTUM | Venerémur cérnui:
Et antíquum documéntum | Novo cedat rítui:
Praestet fides suppleméntum | Sénsuum deféctui.

6. Genitóri, Genitóque | Laus et jubilátio,
Salus, honor, virtus quoque | Sit et benedíctio:
Procedénti ab utróque | Compar sit laudátio.

T. Source: *Hymni de Tempore et de Sanctis in Textu Antiquo et Novo* (Solesmes, 1885) p. 59.
Melody: Kevin Allen (b. 1965), choirmaster at the Monastery of the Holy Cross in Chicago.
M. Source: *Saint Jean de Brébeuf Hymnal* (2018).

87 87 87
Tune:
RUNNELLS

360 Pange Lingua (St. Thomas Aquinas)

Second Tune – *Trns: Robert Campbell of Skerrington (d. 1868)*

4. Earthly things to things of heaven | Changed by God's incarnate Word,
Flesh and blood in myst'ry given, | We believe with faith assured;
As the Word hath said it, even | Be that word believed, adored.

5. Then before His altar bowing, | Let our hearts the Lord revere;
Faith her aid to vision lending, | Tells that He unseen is near;
Ancient types and shadows ending, | Christ our paschal Lamb is here.

6. To the Trinity be glory | Everlasting, as is meet:
Equal to the Father, equal | To the Son and Paraclete:
Blessèd Unity, whose praises | All created things repeat.

87 87 87

Tune:
Gaufestre

English Translation: Robert Campbell, a Scottish attorney who published *Hymns and Anthems for Use in the Holy Service of the Church* (1850). He converted to the Catholic Church in 1852, but was never a priest—despite the claim made in the *American Catholic Hymnal according to the Motu Proprio of His Holiness Pope Pius X* (1913) on page 251.
T. Source: Orby Shipley's *Annus Sanctus: Hymns of the Church for the Ecclesiastical Year; Translated from the Sacred Offices by various Authors, with Modern, Original, and other Hymns, and an Appendix of Earlier Versions* (1884) p. 185.
Melody: Anonymous Trappist Monk (Abbey of Gethsemani, KY). M. Source: *New Saint Basil Hymnal* (1958) p. 118.

Pange Lingua (St. Thomas Aquinas) 361

Second Tune – *Textus originalis Latinus*

4. Verbum caro, panem verum | Verbo carnem éfficit,
Fitque sanguis Christi merum, | Et si sensus déficit,
Ad firmándum cor sincérum | Sola fides súfficit.

TANTUM ERGO SACRAMÉNTUM | Venerémur cérnui:
Et antíquum documéntum | Novo cedat rítui:
Praestet fides suppleméntum | Sénsuum deféctui.

6. Genitóri, Genitóque | Laus et jubilátio,
Salus, honor, virtus quoque | Sit et benedíctio:
Procedénti ab utróque | Compar sit laudátio.

T. Source: *Hymni de Tempore et de Sanctis in Textu Antiquo et Novo* (Solesmes, 1885) p. 59.
Melody: Anonymous Trappist Monk (Abbey of Gethsemani, KY).
M. Source: *New Saint Basil Hymnal* (1958) p. 118.

87 87 87
Tune:
GAUFESTRE

362 Pange Lingua (St. Thomas Aquinas)

Third Tune – *Trns: Robert Campbell of Skerrington (d. 1868)*

4. Earthly things to things of heaven | Changed by God's incarnate Word,
Flesh and blood in myst'ry given, | We believe with faith assured;
As the Word hath said it, even | Be that word believed, adored.

5. Then before His altar bowing, | Let our hearts the Lord revere;
Faith her aid to vision lending, | Tells that He unseen is near;
Ancient types and shadows ending, | Christ our paschal Lamb is here.

6. To the Trinity be glory | Everlasting, as is meet:
Equal to the Father, equal | To the Son and Paraclete:
Blessèd Unity, whose praises | All created things repeat.

87 87 87

Tune:
Ad Perennis Vitae Fontem

Melody: *Tours Breviary* (1781), based on a 16th century French tune.
M. Source: *Songs of Syon* (1910) p. 106; *New English Hymnal* (1986) p. 712.
English Translation: Robert Campbell, a Scottish attorney who published *Hymns and Anthems for Use in the Holy Service of the Church* (1850). He converted to the Catholic Church in 1852, but was never a priest—despite the claim made in the *American Catholic Hymnal according to the Motu Proprio of His Holiness Pope Pius X* (1913) on page 251.
T. Source: Orby Shipley's *Annus Sanctus: Hymns of the Church for the Ecclesiastical Year; Translated from the Sacred Offices by various Authors, with Modern, Original, and other Hymns, and an Appendix of Earlier Versions* (1884) p. 185.

Pange Lingua (St. Thomas Aquinas) 363

FOURTH TUNE – *Trns: Robert Campbell of Skerrington (d. 1868)*

1. Hail, the_ bod - y bright and_ glo - rious, Mys - ter - y of
2. Born for_ us and to us_ giv - en Of a Vir - gin
3. On the_ night be - fore His_ Pas - sion, Seat - ed with His

love di - vine; Hail, the_ blood that flows vic - to - rious
pure as snow— He, as_ man, with man con - vers - ing,
cho - sen band, Je - sus,_ with the Law com - ply - ing,

From the true, the liv - ing vine; Hail, our_ ran - som
Stay'd, the seeds of truth to sow; Then at_ length in
Keeps the feast its rites de - mand; Then, more pre - cious

mer - i - to - rious, Flow'r and_ root_ of Da - vid's line.
won - drous or - der, Closed His_ so - journ here be - low.
food sup - ply - ing, Gives Him - self_ with His own hand.

4. Earthly things to things of heaven | Changed by God's incarnate Word,
Flesh and blood in myst'ry given, | We believe with faith assured;
As the Word hath said it, even | Be that word believed, adored.

5. THEN BEFORE HIS ALTAR BOWING, | Let our hearts the Lord revere;
Faith her aid to vision lending, | Tells that He unseen is near;
Ancient types and shadows ending, | Christ our paschal Lamb is here.

6. To the Trinity be glory | Everlasting, as is meet:
Equal to the Father, equal | To the Son and Paraclete:
Blessèd Unity, whose praises | All created things repeat.

ENGLISH TRANSLATION: Robert Campbell, a Scottish attorney who published *Hymns and Anthems for Use in the Holy Service of the Church* (1850). He converted to the Catholic Church in 1852, but was never a priest—despite the claim made in the *American Catholic Hymnal according to the Motu Proprio of His Holiness Pope Pius X* (1913) on page 251.
T. Source: Orby Shipley's *Annus Sanctus: Hymns of the Church for the Ecclesiastical Year; Translated from the Sacred Offices by various Authors, with Modern, Original, and other Hymns, and an Appendix of Earlier Versions* (1884) p. 185.
Melody: Johann Christoph Bach (d. 1703); some hymnals erroneously attribute this tune, since his name resembles that of J.S. Bach's fifth son—Johann Christoph Friedrich Bach—as well as his youngest son, Johann Christian Bach (d. 1782), who became a Catholic and was admired by Mozart.
M. Source: *Meiningen Gesangbuch* (1693); this melody has multiple names (e.g. KOMM O KOMM DU GEIST DES LEBENS) and is sometimes used for 87 87 77; cf. *New Saint Basil Hymnal* (1958) p. 71.

87 87 87
Tune: ST LEONARD

364 Pange Lingua (St. Thomas Aquinas)

Fifth Tune – *Trns: Robert Campbell of Skerrington (d. 1868)*

4. Earthly things to things of heaven | Changed by God's incarnate Word,
Flesh and blood in myst'ry given, | We believe with faith assured;
As the Word hath said it, even | Be that word believed, adored.

5. Then before His altar bowing, | Let our hearts the Lord revere;
Faith her aid to vision lending, | Tells that He unseen is near;
Ancient types and shadows ending, | Christ our paschal Lamb is here.

6. To the Trinity be glory | Everlasting, as is meet:
Equal to the Father, equal | To the Son and Paraclete:
Blessèd Unity, whose praises | All created things repeat.

87 87 87

Tune:
Lauda Anima

Final Verses: Richard Lloyd (1993) #169; Noel Rawsthorne (2011) #258.
Melody: John Goss (d. 1880), Professor of Harmony at the Royal Academy of Music.
M. Source: *New Saint Basil Hymnal* (1958) p. 202; *Hymns, Psalms, and Spiritual Canticles* (1983) p. 294.
English Translation: Robert Campbell, a Scottish attorney who published *Hymns and Anthems for Use in the Holy Service of the Church* (1850). He converted to the Catholic Church in 1852, but was never a priest—despite the claim made in the *American Catholic Hymnal according to the Motu Proprio of His Holiness Pope Pius X* (1913) on page 251.
T. Source: Orby Shipley's *Annus Sanctus: Hymns of the Church for the Ecclesiastical Year; Translated from the Sacred Offices by various Authors, with Modern, Original, and other Hymns, and an Appendix of Earlier Versions* (1884) p. 185.

Pange Lingua (St. Thomas Aquinas) 365

Sixth Tune – *Trns: Robert Campbell of Skerrington (d. 1868)*

4. Earthly things to things of heaven | Changed by God's incarnate Word,
Flesh and blood in myst'ry given, | We believe with faith assured;
As the Word hath said it, even | Be that word believed, adored.

5. Then before His altar bowing, | Let our hearts the Lord revere;
Faith her aid to vision lending, | Tells that He unseen is near;
Ancient types and shadows ending, | Christ our paschal Lamb is here.

6. To the Trinity be glory | Everlasting, as is meet:
Equal to the Father, equal | To the Son and Paraclete:
Blessèd Unity, whose praises | All created things repeat.

Final Verses: Richard Lloyd (1993) #162; Noel Rawsthorne (2011) #248.
Melody: Caspar Ett (d. 1847), Catholic composer and organist at St. Michael's in Munich.
M. Source: *Cantica Sacra Catholica* (Freiburg: Leopoldo Lumpp, 1859), p. 22; *Saint Basil's Hymnal* (1918) p. 281.
English Translation: Robert Campbell, a Scottish attorney who published *Hymns and Anthems for Use in the Holy Service of the Church* (1850). He converted to the Catholic Church in 1852, but was never a priest—despite the claim made in the *American Catholic Hymnal according to the Motu Proprio of His Holiness Pope Pius X* (1913) on page 251.
T. Source: Orby Shipley's *Annus Sanctus: Hymns of the Church for the Ecclesiastical Year; Translated from the Sacred Offices by various Authors, with Modern, Original, and other Hymns, and an Appendix of Earlier Versions* (1884) p. 185.

87 87 87

Tune: Oriel

366 Pange Lingua (St. Thomas Aquinas)

Seventh Tune – *Trns: Robert Campbell of Skerrington (d. 1868)*

4. Earthly things to things of heaven | Changed by God's incarnate Word,
Flesh and blood in myst'ry given, | We believe with faith assured;
As the Word hath said it, even | Be that word believed, adored.

5. Then before His altar bowing, | Let our hearts the Lord revere;
Faith her aid to vision lending, | Tells that He unseen is near;
Ancient types and shadows ending, | Christ our paschal Lamb is here.

6. To the Trinity be glory | Everlasting, as is meet:
Equal to the Father, equal | To the Son and Paraclete:
Blessèd Unity, whose praises | All created things repeat.

87 87 87

Tune:
Hyfrydol B7

Final Verses: Richard Lloyd (1993) #100; Noel Rawsthorne (2011) #160. (Eliminate repeat sign.)
Melody: Richard H. Pritchard (d. 1887); the tune name means "cheerful" in Welsh.
M. Source: *Catholic Hymn Book* (1998) p. 182; *Hymns, Psalms, and Spiritual Canticles* (Marier, 1983) pp. 192, 226, 404.
English Translation: Robert Campbell, a Scottish attorney who published *Hymns and Anthems for Use in the Holy Service of the Church* (1850). He converted to the Catholic Church in 1852, but was never a priest—despite the claim made in the *American Catholic Hymnal according to the Motu Proprio of His Holiness Pope Pius X* (1913) on page 251.
T. Source: Orby Shipley's *Annus Sanctus: Hymns of the Church for the Ecclesiastical Year; Translated from the Sacred Offices by various Authors, with Modern, Original, and other Hymns, and an Appendix of Earlier Versions* (1884) p. 185.

Pange Lingua (St. Thomas Aquinas) 367

Eighth Tune – *Trns: Robert Campbell of Skerrington (d. 1868)*

4. Earthly things to things of heaven | Changed by God's incarnate Word,
Flesh and blood in myst'ry given, | We believe with faith assured;
As the Word hath said it, even | Be that word believed, adored.

5. Then before His altar bowing, | Let our hearts the Lord revere;
Faith her aid to vision lending, | Tells that He unseen is near;
Ancient types and shadows ending, | Christ our paschal Lamb is here.

6. To the Trinity be glory | Everlasting, as is meet:
Equal to the Father, equal | To the Son and Paraclete:
Blessèd Unity, whose praises | All created things repeat.

Final Verses: Richard Lloyd (1993) #14; Noel Rawsthorne (2011) #30.
Melody: Franz Joseph Haydn (d. 1809), a Catholic who often prayed the rosary when he encountered difficulties composing. The tune is based on "Stal se jesem," a Croatian folk song. The title of Haydn's version: "Gott erhalte Franz den Kaiser."
M. Source: *Saint Basil's Hymnal* (1918) p. 280; *Catholic Hymn Book* (1998) p. 453.
English Translation: Robert Campbell, a Scottish attorney who published *Hymns and Anthems for Use in the Holy Service of the Church* (1850). He converted to the Catholic Church in 1852, but was never a priest—despite the claim made in the *American Catholic Hymnal according to the Motu Proprio of His Holiness Pope Pius X* (1913) on page 251.
T. Source: Orby Shipley's *Annus Sanctus: Hymns of the Church for the Ecclesiastical Year; Translated from the Sacred Offices by various Authors, with Modern, Original, and other Hymns, and an Appendix of Earlier Versions* (1884) p. 185.

87 87 87

Tune: Austria B7

368 Pange Lingua (St. Thomas Aquinas)

Ninth Tune – *Trns: Robert Campbell of Skerrington (d. 1868)*

4. Earthly things to things of heaven | Changed by God's incarnate Word,
Flesh and blood in myst'ry given, | We believe with faith assured;
As the Word hath said it, even | Be that word believed, adored.

5. Then before His altar bowing, | Let our hearts the Lord revere;
Faith her aid to vision lending, | Tells that He unseen is near;
Ancient types and shadows ending, | Christ our paschal Lamb is here.

6. To the Trinity be glory | Everlasting, as is meet:
Equal to the Father, equal | To the Son and Paraclete:
Blessèd Unity, whose praises | All created things repeat.

87 87 87

Tune: Picardy

Final Verses: R. Lloyd (1993) #168; N. Rawsthorne (2011) #257. M. Source: *New English Hymnal* (1986) p. 1124.
Melody: 17th century French carol; cf. *Mélodies populaires des Provinces de France* (1848) #5, entitled *La Ballade de Jésus-Christ*. The name "Picardy" comes from the province of France from which it is believed to originate.
English Translation: Robert Campbell, a Scottish attorney who published *Hymns and Anthems for Use in the Holy Service of the Church* (1850). He converted to the Catholic Church in 1852, but was never a priest—despite the claim made in the *American Catholic Hymnal according to the Motu Proprio of His Holiness Pope Pius X* (1913) on page 251.
T. Source: Orby Shipley's *Annus Sanctus: Hymns of the Church for the Ecclesiastical Year; Translated from the Sacred Offices by various Authors, with Modern, Original, and other Hymns, and an Appendix of Earlier Versions* (1884) p. 185.

Pange Lingua (St. Thomas Aquinas) 369

Tenth Tune – *Trns: Robert Campbell of Skerrington (d. 1868)*

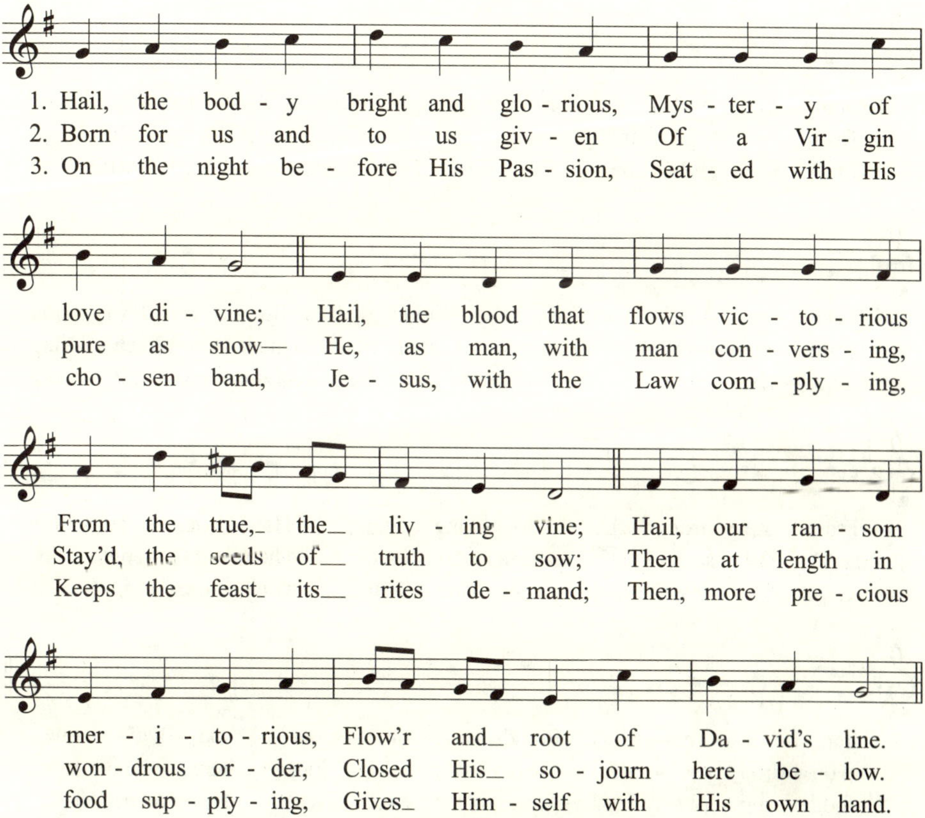

4. Earthly things to things of heaven | Changed by God's incarnate Word,
Flesh and blood in myst'ry given, | We believe with faith assured;
As the Word hath said it, even | Be that word believed, adored.

5. Then before His altar bowing, | Let our hearts the Lord revere;
Faith her aid to vision lending, | Tells that He unseen is near;
Ancient types and shadows ending, | Christ our paschal Lamb is here.

6. To the Trinity be glory | Everlasting, as is meet:
Equal to the Father, equal | To the Son and Paraclete:
Blessèd Unity, whose praises | All created things repeat.

Melody: Samuel Webbe, the Elder (d. 1816), choirmaster of the Chapel of the Portuguese Embassy in Lincoln's Inn Fields (a public square), the only place in London where the Catholic liturgy could be publicly celebrated.
M. Source: *Essay on Church Plain-chant* (1782); *Mediator Dei Hymnal* (1955) #16; *St. Basil's Hymnal* (1918) p. 280; *St. Mark's Hymnal for Use in the Catholic Church in the United States* (Peoria, Illinois: 1910) p. 23, 66.
English Translation: Robert Campbell, a Scottish attorney who published *Hymns and Anthems for Use in the Holy Service of the Church* (1850). He converted to the Catholic Church in 1852, but was never a priest—despite the claim made in the *American Catholic Hymnal according to the Motu Proprio of His Holiness Pope Pius X* (1913) on page 251.
T. Source: Orby Shipley's *Annus Sanctus: Hymns of the Church for the Ecclesiastical Year; Translated from the Sacred Offices by various Authors, with Modern, Original, and other Hymns, and an Appendix of Earlier Versions* (1884) p. 185.

87 87 87
Tune: Dulce Carmen

370 Pange Lingua (St. Thomas Aquinas)

Eleventh Tune – *Trns: Robert Campbell of Skerrington* (*d. 1868*)

4. Earthly things to things of heaven | Changed by God's incarnate Word,
Flesh and blood in myst'ry given, | We believe with faith assured;
As the Word hath said it, even | Be that word believed, adored.

5. Then before His altar bowing, | Let our hearts the Lord revere;
Faith her aid to vision lending, | Tells that He unseen is near;
Ancient types and shadows ending, | Christ our paschal Lamb is here.

6. To the Trinity be glory | Everlasting, as is meet:
Equal to the Father, equal | To the Son and Paraclete:
Blessèd Unity, whose praises | All created things repeat.

87 87 87

Tune: Regent Square

Final Verses: Richard Lloyd (1993) #175; Noel Rawsthorne (2011) #265.
Melody: Henry Smart (d. 1879), organist at St. Philip's in London.
M. Source: *Catholic Hymn Book* (1998) p. 280; *Hymns, Psalms, and Spiritual Canticles* (1983) p. 213.
English Translation: Robert Campbell, a Scottish attorney who published *Hymns and Anthems for Use in the Holy Service of the Church* (1850). He converted to the Catholic Church in 1852, but was never a priest—despite the claim made in the *American Catholic Hymnal according to the Motu Proprio of His Holiness Pope Pius X* (1913) on page 251.
T. Source: Orby Shipley's *Annus Sanctus: Hymns of the Church for the Ecclesiastical Year; Translated from the Sacred Offices by various Authors, with Modern, Original, and other Hymns, and an Appendix of Earlier Versions* (1884) p. 185.

Pange Lingua (St. Thomas Aquinas) 371

Twelfth Tune – *Trns: Robert Campbell of Skerrington (d. 1868)*

1. Hail, the bod - y__ bright and glo - rious, Mys - ter - y of
2. Born for us and_ to us giv - en Of a__ Vir - gin
3. On the night be - fore His Pas - sion, Seat - ed_ with His

love di - vine; Hail, the blood that flows vic - to - rious
pure as snow— He, as man, with man con - vers - ing,
cho - sen band, Je - sus, with the Law com - ply - ing,

From the_ true, the liv - ing vine; Hail, our ran - som_
Stay'd, the_ seeds of truth to sow; Then at length in__
Keeps the_ feast its rites de - mand; Then, more pre - cious

mer - i - to - rious, Flow'r and root_ of Da - vid's line.
won - drous or - der, Closed His so - journ here be - low.
food sup - ply - ing, Gives Him - self_ with His own hand.

4. Earthly things to things of heaven | Changed by God's incarnate Word,
Flesh and blood in myst'ry given, | We believe with faith assured;
As the Word hath said it, even | Be that word believed, adored.

5. Then before His altar bowing, | Let our hearts the Lord revere;
Faith her aid to vision lending, | Tells that He unseen is near;
Ancient types and shadows ending, | Christ our paschal Lamb is here.

6. To the Trinity be glory | Everlasting, as is meet:
Equal to the Father, equal | To the Son and Paraclete:
Blessèd Unity, whose praises | All created things repeat.

Melody: Metrical Cento; cf. "Dum staret Abraham" (*Antiphonaire Monastique,* 13th century).
M. Source: *Paléographie musicale* (Volume XII), folio 81; *Cantus Selecti* (Solesmes, 1957) p. 245.
English Translation: Robert Campbell, a Scottish attorney who published *Hymns and Anthems for Use in the Holy Service of the Church* (1850). He converted to the Catholic Church in 1852, but was never a priest—despite the claim made in the *American Catholic Hymnal according to the Motu Proprio of His Holiness Pope Pius X* (1913) on page 251.
T. Source: Orby Shipley's *Annus Sanctus: Hymns of the Church for the Ecclesiastical Year; Translated from the Sacred Offices by various Authors, with Modern, Original, and other Hymns, and an Appendix of Earlier Versions* (1884) p. 185.

87 87 87

Tune: Breton

372 Pange Lingua (St. Thomas Aquinas)

1599AD – Historic Roman Catholic Translation

This translation, although 87 87 87, is more suited to plainsong, owing to the placement of accents. The same can be said about some of the other 1599AD translations.

OF Christ, his body glorious,
Sing my tongue the mystery,
And also of his precious blood,
Which the world's price to be,
The king of nations did shed forth,
Fruit of noble womb was he.

2. On us bestowed and for us born
Of a Maid untouched indeed,
Conversant upon the èarth,
Sowing of his word the seed,
And of his time of being here,
Strangely he the end decreed.

3. The night he with his brethren sat,
And his supper last did make,
In full observance of the law,
Law-assignèd meats did take,
Himself food to th'Apostles twelve,
With his hands he did betake.

4. The Word now being flesh become,
So *very* bread flesh by the word,
And wine the blood of Christ is made,
Though our sense it not afford,
But this in heart sincere to fix,
Faith sufficeth to accord.

5. Wherefore a Sacrament so great
Humbly prostrate we adore,
And unto rites begun of late,
Laws must yield that were before,
And where our sense is seen to fail,
There must faith supply restore.

6. Unto the Father and the Son,
Joy and praise ascribèd be,
And saving health, honor and pow'r,
As also b*ene*dicite:
And to him that from both proceeds,
Praises like acknowledge we.

Pange lingua gloriósi
Córporis mystérium
Sanguinísque pretiósi,
Quem in mundi prétium
Fructus ventris generósi,
Rex effúdit géntium.

Nobis datus, nobis natus
Ex intácta Vírgine,
Et in mundo conversátus,
Sparso verbi sémine,
Sui moras incolátus
Miro clausit órdine.

In suprémae nocte cenae
Recúmbens cum frátribus,
Observáta lege plene
Cibis in legálibus,
Cibum turbae duodénae
Se dat suis mánibus.

Verbum caro, panem verum
Verbo carnem éfficit,
Fitque sanguis Christi merum,
Et si sensus déficit,
Ad firmándum cor sincérum
Sola fides súfficit.

Tantum ergo Sacraméntum
Venerémur cérnui:
Et antíquum documéntum
Novo cedat rítui:
Praestet fides suppleméntum
Sénsuum deféctui.

Genitóri, Genitóque
Laus et jubilátio,
Salus, honor, virtus quoque
Sit et benedíctio:
Procedénti ab utróque
Compar sit laudátio.

87 87 87

Tune:
VARIOUS

T. Source: *Primer, or, Office of the Blessed Virgin Marie in Latin and English, according to the reformed Latin, and with Lyke Graces Privileged* (Antwerp, 1599) p. 14. The Catholic Encyclopedia of 1912 attributes the hymn translations to the book's editor, Richard Verstegan (d. 1636), a Catholic publisher. In the 1599 Preface, Verstegan says: "Notwithstanding the difficulty, these hymns have been so turned into English meter that they may be sung unto the same tunes in English that they bear in Latin." However, his accentual treatment is sometimes peculiar.

1687AD – Historic Roman Catholic Translation

English translation can be sung with any 88 88 88 meter, such as Colchester, Regina Caelorum, St Matthias, Sussex Carol, St Chrysostom, etc.

Pange lingua gloriósi
Córporis mystérium
Sanguinísque pretiósi,
Quem in mundi prétium
Fructus ventris generósi,
Rex effúdit géntium.

SING, O my Tongue, devoutly sing
The glorious Body's Mystery:
And of that precious Blood, the King
Of Nations pourèd forth, to free
The World from a disastrous Doom:
O blessèd Fruit of noblest Womb!

Nobis datus, nobis natus
Ex intácta Vírgine,
Et in mundo conversátus,
Sparso verbi sémine,
Sui moras incolátus
Miro clausit órdine.

2. On us bestow'd, for us by birth
He from a Virgin did proceed,
And, being conversant on Earth,
Till he had sow'n the Gospel's Seed,
Among us to prolong his stay
His Love invented this strange way.

In suprémae nocte cenae
Recúmbens cum frátribus,
Observáta lege plene
Cibis in legálibus,
Cibum turbae duodénae
Se dat suis mánibus.

3. He on the Final Supper-Night,
With his dear Brethren taking Seat,
Observing well the ancient Rite
Touching the Law's prescribèd Meat,
Gave to the twelve (his chosen Band)
Himself for Food with his own Hand.

Verbum caro, panem verum
Verbo carnem éfficit,
Fitque sanguis Christi merum,
Et si sensus déficit,
Ad firmándum cor sincérum
Sola fides súfficit.

4. The Word made Flesh, by th'Word he said,
Turns into Flesh, substantial Bread;
And Wine the Blood of Christ was made,
Though sense finds nothing alterèd:
This to confirm in Hearts sincere,
There needs no more, if Faith be there.

Tantum ergo Sacraméntum
Venerémur cérnui:
Et antíquum documéntum
Novo cedat rítui:
Praestet fides suppleméntum
Sénsuum deféctui.

5. Let's then this Sacrament adore,
And prostrate give the worship due;
And may the ancient Rite no more
Take place, but yield it to the new:
Let faith in Jesus Christ supply
The Senses insufficiency.

Genitóri, Genitóque
Laus et jubilátio,
Salus, honor, virtus quoque
Sit et benedíctio:
Procedénti ab utróque
Compar sit laudátio.

6. To Father and the Son let's bring
Triumphant Praises; let's aspire,
Their honor, pow'r and bliss to sing,
While Benedictions fill the Quire;
And He an equal Praise receives,
Who from them comes, and with them lives.

T. Source: *The Office of the B. V. Mary in English; To which is added the Vespers, in Latin and English; As it is Sung in the Catholic Church upon all Sundays and principal Holydays throughout the whole Year; With the Compline, Rosary, Hymn and Prayers that are sung at the Benediction of the B. Sacrament* (London: Henry Hills, 1687) p. 175.

88 88 88
Tune: Various

374 Quem Terra, Pontus, Aethera (6th century)

Venantius Fortunatus, Bishop of Poitiers (d. 609AD)

To sing in Latin,
use any 88 88 (LM) tune.

QUEM terra, pontus, aéthera,
Colunt, adórant, praédicant,
Trinam regéntem máchinam
Claustrum Maríae bájulat.

2. Cui luna, sol, et ómnia
Desérviunt per témpora,
Perfúsa caeli grátia,
Gestant Puéllae víscera. *n1*

E. *Miréntur ergo saécula,*
Quod Ángelus fert sémina, *n2*
Quod aure virgo cóncipit
Et corde credens párturit.

3. Beáta Mater múnere,
Cujus, supérnus Ártifex,
Mundum pugíllo cóntinens,
Ventris sub arca clausus est.

4. Beáta caeli núntio,
Fecúnda Sancto Spíritu,
Desiderátus Géntibus,
Cujus per alvum fusus est. *n3*

5. Glória tibi, Dómine,
Qui natus es de Vírgine,
Cum Patre et Sancto Spíritu,
In sempitérna saécula.

88 88 (LM)

Tune:
VARIOUS

T. Source: *Hymni de Tempore et de Sanctis in Textu Antiquo et Novo* (Solesmes, 1885) p. 140.

Assistance for comprehension

THE one whom the earth, sea and atmosphere
worship, adore and proclaim,
who governs their threefold system,
Mary's enclosure carries.

2. The one whom the moon, the sun
and all things serve in season,
when heaven's grace has flooded her,
the body of a Maiden conveys. *n1*

E. *So let the ages marvel*
that an Angel brings progeny, *n2*
that a maiden conceives through her ear
and, believing, bears from her heart.

3. Blessed is the Mother
through whose calling the sovereign Craftsman,
who holds the world in his hand,
is enclosed in the coffer of a womb.

4. Blessed through heaven's messenger,
fruitful through the Holy Spirit,
by whose womb the one desired
by the nations has been poured forth. *n3*

5. Glory to thee, O Lord,
who wert born of a Virgin,
with the Father and the Holy Spirit,
for everlasting ages.

[1] Literally "innards."

[2] Literally "seeds." Our Lady conceived by obeying—that is, hearing and heeding—the invitation of God brought to her ear by the Angel Gabriel (cf. Lk 1.45). Our Lady bore the word of God in her heart before she bore the divine Word in her body.

[3] Cf. Gen 49.10, Agg 2.8

376 Quem Terra, Pontus, Aethera (6th century)

First Tune – *Trns: Very Rev'd Dominic Aylward, OP (d. 1872)*

4. Blest by the herald-angel's tongue,
O'er thee God's shad'wing Spirit hung
And filled thy womb—whence issued forth
The Long-desir'd of all the earth.

5. O Mary, Mother of all Grace
And Mercy to our sinful race,
Drive back the foe; and to thy Son
Lead thou our souls when life is done.

6. All glory be to thee, O Lord,
A Virgin's Son, by all adored;
And equal praise for ever greet
The Father and the Paraclete.

88 88 (LM)

Tune:
Eisenach

Final Verses: Richard Lloyd (1993) #64; Noel Rawsthorne (2011) #108.
T. Source: *Carmina Mariana* (Orby Shipley, 1893) p. 41.
Melody: Bartholomäus Gesius (d. 1613); adapted by Johann H. Schein (d. 1630)
M. Source: *New Saint Basil Hymnal* (1958) p. 120; *The Catholic Vesper Hymn Book set to Music either for Unison or Four Voices with Accompaniment* (Charles Lewis, 1877) p. 34; *Pope Pius XII Hymnal* (Ohio: Gregorian Institute of America, 1959) p. 13.

Quem Terra, Pontus, Aethera (6th century) 377

Second Tune – *Trns: Very Rev'd Dominic Aylward, OP (d. 1872)*

1. Whom earth and sea and sky pro - claim
2. Her womb, the seat of eve - ry grace,
3. O hap - py Moth - er that thou art,

The Rul - er of their tri - ple frame,
Is now the Lord's a - bid - ing place;
Close un - der - neath thy beat - ing heart

He, un - to whom their prais - es__ rise,
That Lord to whom the sun by__ day,
Lies the Cre - a - tor - God, who planned

With - in the womb of Mar - y lies.
The moon by night, their hom - age pay.
The world he holds with - in his hand.

4. Blest by the herald-angel's tongue,
O'er thee God's shad'wing Spirit hung
And filled thy womb—whence issued forth
The Long-desir'd of all the earth.

5. O Mary, Mother of all Grace
And Mercy to our sinful race,
Drive back the foe; and to thy Son
Lead thou our souls when life is done.

6. All glory be to thee, O Lord,
A Virgin's Son, by all adored;
And equal praise for ever greet
The Father and the Paraclete.

T. Source: *Carmina Mariana* (Orby Shipley, 1893) p. 41.
Melody: Dieudonné Duguet (d. 1849), organist at the Catholic Cathedral in Liège, Belgium, and teacher of César Franck.
M. Source: *Mediator Dei Hymnal* (1955) p. 66; *New Saint Basil Hymnal* (1958) p. 93; *Arundel Catholic Hymnal* (1905) p. 26; *Hymnal and Vesperal* (Archdiocese of Baltimore, 1878) p. 168; *Catholic Vesper Hymn Book set to Music for Unison or Four Voices* (Charles Lewis, 1877) p. 6.

88 88 (LM)

Tune: Duguet

378 Quem Terra, Pontus, Aethera (6th century)

Third Tune – *Trns: Very Rev'd Dominic Aylward, OP* (*d. 1872*)

4. Blest by the herald-angel's tongue,
O'er thee God's shad'wing Spirit hung
And filled thy womb—whence issued forth
The Long-desir'd of all the earth.

5. O Mary, Mother of all Grace
And Mercy to our sinful race,
Drive back the foe; and to thy Son
Lead thou our souls when life is done.

6. All glory be to thee, O Lord,
A Virgin's Son, by all adored;
And equal praise for ever greet
The Father and the Paraclete.

88 88 (LM)

Tune:
Whitehall

Melody: Henry Lawes (d. 1662).
M. Source: *Saint Edmund Campion Missal and Hymnal* (2013) p. 888.
T. Source: *Carmina Mariana* (Orby Shipley, 1893) p. 41.

Quem Terra, Pontus, Aethera (6th century) 379

Fourth Tune – *Trns: Very Rev'd Dominic Aylward, OP (d. 1872)*

1. Whom earth and sea and sky pro - claim
2. Her womb, the seat of eve - ry grace,
3. O hap - py Moth - er that thou art,

The Rul - er of their tri - ple frame,
Is now the Lord's a - bid - ing place;
Close un - der - neath thy beat - ing heart

He, un - to whom their prais - es rise,
That Lord to whom the sun by day,
Lies the Cre - a - tor - God, who planned

With - in the womb of Mar - y lies.
The moon by night, their hom - age pay.
The world he holds with - in his hand.

4. Blest by the herald-angel's tongue,
O'er thee God's shad'wing Spirit hung
And filled thy womb—whence issued forth
The Long-desir'd of all the earth.

5. O Mary, Mother of all Grace
And Mercy to our sinful race,
Drive back the foe; and to thy Son
Lead thou our souls when life is done.

6. All glory be to thee, O Lord,
A Virgin's Son, by all adored;
And equal praise for ever greet
The Father and the Paraclete.

Final Verses: Richard Lloyd (1993) #133; Noel Rawsthorne (2011) #205.
T. Source: *Carmina Mariana* (Orby Shipley, 1893) p. 41.
Melody: Samuel Webbe, the elder (d. 1816).
M. Source: *Veritas Hymnal* (Dublin: Irish Church Music Association, 1974) p. 96; *Cantate Omnes: Hymnal of the Catholic Choirmasters' Guild* (1952) #78.

88 88 (LM)

Tune: Melcombe

380 Quem Terra, Pontus, Aethera (6th century)

Fifth Tune – *Trns: Very Rev'd Dominic Aylward, OP (d. 1872)*

4. Blest by the herald-angel's tongue,
O'er thee God's shad'wing Spirit hung
And filled thy womb—whence issued forth
The Long-desir'd of all the earth.

5. O Mary, Mother of all Grace
And Mercy to our sinful race,
Drive back the foe; and to thy Son
Lead thou our souls when life is done.

6. All glory be to thee, O Lord,
A Virgin's Son, by all adored;
And equal praise for ever greet
The Father and the Paraclete.

88 88 (LM)

Tune:
Kempen

Melody: Flor Peeters (d. 1986), organist at the Catholic Cathedral of Mechelen, Belgium, was made a Baron by King Baudouin.
M. Source: *People's Mass Book* (Omer Westendorf, 1964) p. 218.
T. Source: *Carmina Mariana* (Orby Shipley, 1893) p. 41.

Quem Terra, Pontus, Aethera (6th century)

Trns: Very Rev'd Dominic Aylward, OP (d. 1872)

Can be sung with any 88 88 meter, such as Eisenach, Rogers Park, Bressani, La Rochelle, Kempen, Bessemer, Tallis Canon, Winchester New, etc.

WHOM earth and sea and sky proclaim
The Ruler of their triple frame,
He, unto whom their praises rise,
within the womb of Mary lies.

2. Her womb, the seat of every grace,
Is now the Lord's abiding place;
That Lord to whom the sun by day,
The moon by night, their homage pay.

3. O happy Mother that thou art,
Close underneath thy beating heart
Lies the Creator-God, who planned
The world he holds within his hand.

4. Blest by the herald-angel's tongue,
O'er thee God's shad'wing Spirit hung
And filled thy womb—whence issued forth
The Long-desir'd of all the earth.

5. O Mary, Mother of all Grace
And Mercy to our sinful race,
Drive back the foe; and to thy Son
Lead thou our souls when life is done.

6. All glory be to thee, O Lord,
A Virgin's Son, by all adored;
And equal praise for ever greet
The Father and the Paraclete.

88 88 (LM)

Tune: Various

T. Source: *Carmina Mariana* (Orby Shipley, 1893) p. 41; written in 1845 by Very Rev'd Fr. James Ambrose Dominic Aylward, OP (d. 1872), first Prior of Woodchester. Most of Aylward's Latin hymn translations first appeared in *The Catholic Weekly Instructor*. His *Lauda Sion* translation achieved great fame.

382 Quem Terra, Pontus, Aethera (6th century)

First Tune – *Trns: Fr. John Fitzpatrick, Oblate of Mary (d. 1929)*

4. Blessèd by God's own message made,
And fruitful 'neath His spirit's shade
She was, of whom conceived came He,
Whom all the nations longed to see.

5. Jesus the Virgin's only Son,
With Father and with spirit One,
Be praise and glory giv'n to Thee
In time and in eternity.

88 88 (LM)

Tune:
Gonfalon Royal

Final Verses: Richard Lloyd (1993) #80; Noel Rawsthorne (2011) #136.
T. Source: *The Breviary and Missal Hymns* (London: Sands & Co, 1931) p. 198.
Melody: Sir Percy Carter Buck (d. 1947); first published in *Fourteen Hymn Tunes* (1913).
M. Source: *Catholic Hymn Book* (London Oratory, 1998) p. 140. The tune was originally paired with *Vexilla Regis* ("Flag of the King"). A *gonfalon* ("flag") was traditionally carried during Catholic processions.

Second Tune – *Trns: Fr. John Fitzpatrick, Oblate of Mary (d. 1929)*

4. Blessèd by God's own message made,
And fruitful 'neath His spirit's shade
She was, of whom conceived came He,
Whom all the nations longed to see.

5. Jesus the Virgin's only Son,
With Father and with spirit One,
Be praise and glory giv'n to Thee
In time and in eternity.

* This melody at a lower key is on page 436.

Melody: John Bacchus Dykes (d. 1876).
M. Source: *Hymns Ancient and Modern* (1972) p. 64.
T. Source: *The Breviary and Missal Hymns* (London: Sands & Co, 1931) p. 198.

88 88 (LM)
Tune:
Trinity College

384 Quem Terra, Pontus, Aethera (6th century)

THIRD TUNE – *Trns: Fr. John Fitzpatrick, Oblate of Mary (d. 1929)*

4. Blessèd by God's own message made,
And fruitful 'neath His spirit's shade
She was, of whom conceived came He,
Whom all the nations longed to see.

5. Jesus the Virgin's only Son,
With Father and with spirit One,
Be praise and glory giv'n to Thee
In time and in eternity.

88 88 (LM)

Tune:
ROCKINGHAM

Final Verses: Richard Lloyd (1993) #181; Noel Rawsthorne (2011) #276.
T. Source: *The Breviary and Missal Hymns* (London: Sands & Co, 1931) p. 198.
Melody: Dr. Edward Miller (d. 1807), organist of Doncaster Parish Church; originally published in *Psalms of David for the Use of Parish Churches* (1790) p. 12; based on TUNBRIDGE (an older tune).
M. Source: *Catholic Hymn Book* (London Oratory, 1998) p. 115; *Church Hymns with Tunes* (1885) p. 44.

Quem Terra, Pontus, Aethera (6th century) 385

Fourth Tune – *Trns: Fr. John Fitzpatrick, Oblate of Mary (d. 1929)*

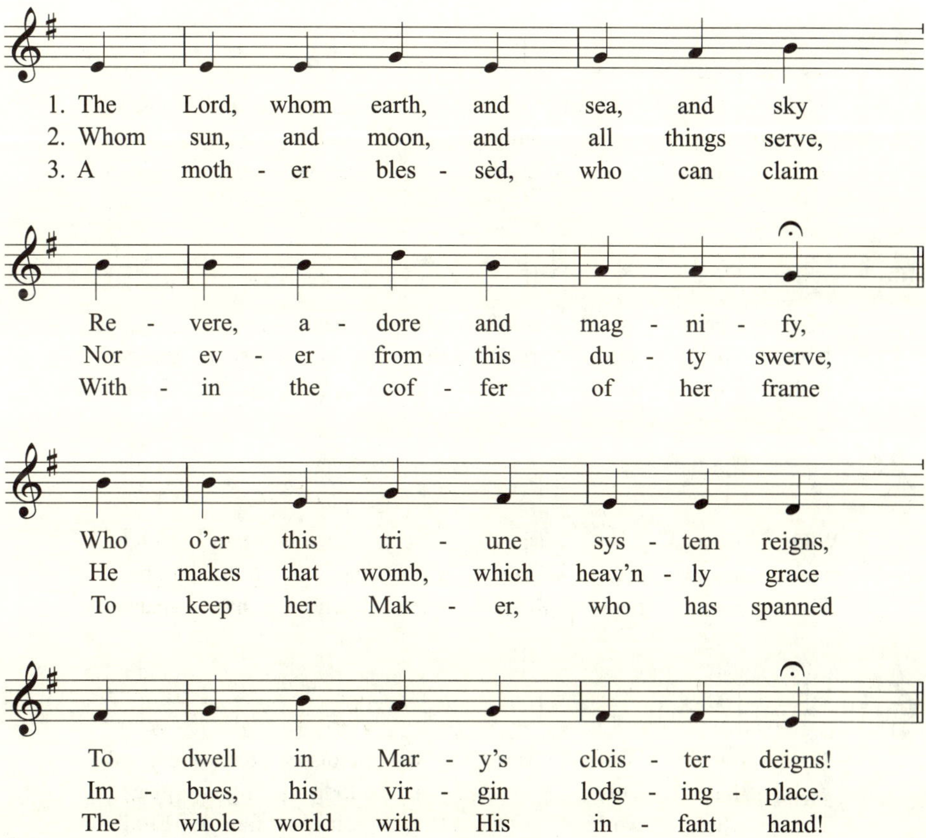

4. Blessèd by God's own message made,
And fruitful 'neath His spirit's shade
She was, of whom conceived came He,
Whom all the nations longed to see.

5. Jesus the Virgin's only Son,
With Father and with spirit One,
Be praise and glory giv'n to Thee
In time and in eternity.

88 88 (LM)

T. Source: *The Breviary and Missal Hymns* (London: Sands & Co, 1931) p. 198.
Melody: Christliches Gesangbüchlein (1568). M. Source: *New Westminster Hymnal* (1939) p. 41.

Tune: Saxony

386 Quem Terra, Pontus, Aethera (6th century)

FIFTH TUNE – *Trns: Fr. John Fitzpatrick, Oblate of Mary (d. 1929)*

4. Blessèd by God's own message made,
And fruitful 'neath His spirit's shade
She was, of whom conceived came He,
Whom all the nations longed to see.

5. Jesus the Virgin's only Son,
With Father and with spirit One,
Be praise and glory giv'n to Thee
In time and in eternity.

88 88 (LM)

Tune:
PUER NOBIS NASCITUR

Final Verses: Richard Lloyd (1993) #170; Noel Rawsthorne (2011) #259.
T. Source: *The Breviary and Missal Hymns* (London: Sands & Co, 1931) p. 198.
Melody: Michael Praetorius (d. 1621), a German organist and theorist.
M. Source: *Hymns, Psalms, and Spiritual Canticles* (1983) p. 224. *Catholic Hymn Book* (1998) p. 30.

Quem Terra, Pontus, Aethera (6th century) 387

Trns: Fr. John Fitzpatrick, Oblate of Mary (d. 1929)

Can be sung with any 88 88 meter, such as EISENACH, ROGERS PARK, BRESSANI, LA ROCHELLE, KEMPEN, BESSEMER, TALLIS CANON, WINCHESTER NEW, etc.

THE Lord, whom earth, and sea, and sky
Revere, adore and magnify,
Who o'er this triune system reigns,
To dwell in Mary's cloister deigns!

2. Whom sun, and moon, and all things serve,
Nor ever from this duty swerve,
He makes that womb, which heav'nly grace
Imbues, his virgin lodging-place.

3. A mother blessèd, who can claim
Within the coffer of her frame
To keep her Maker, who has spanned
The whole world with His infant hand!

4. Blessèd by God's own message made,
And fruitful 'neath His spirit's shade
She was, of whom conceived came He,
Whom all the nations longed to see.

5. Jesus the Virgin's only Son,
With Father and with spirit One,
Be praise and glory giv'n to Thee
In time and in eternity.

88 88 (LM)

Tune: VARIOUS

T. Source: *The Breviary and Missal Hymns* (London: Sands & Co, 1931) p. 198.

388 Quem Terra, Pontus, Aethera (6th century)

First Tune – *This version is suitable for Christmas*

4. Blest by Angel's salutation,
   Fruitful by the Spirit's might,
   Christ, the hope of every nation,
   God and man, she brought to light
   At the providential tide,
   Him for whom the ages sighed.

5. Hark, the heav'nly host rejoices
   With exultant hymns of praise:
   Let our grateful hearts and voices
   Add their burden to those lays,
   With that multitude to cry
   Peace to men from God on high!

87 87 77

Tune:
All Saints

Final Verses: Richard Lloyd (1993) #7; Noel Rawsthorne (2011) #13.
T. Source: *Sentence of Kaïres* (London: Longmans & Green, 1867) p. 161; adapted for Christmastide in *A Selection of Carols, Pieces, and Anthems Suitable for Christmas* (Penzance: F. Rodda, 1872).
Melody: *Geistreiches Gesangbuch* (Darmstadt, 1698).
M. Source: *New Saint Basil Hymnal* (1958) p. 203; *Catholic Hymn Book* (London Oratory, 1998) p. 290.

Quem Terra, Pontus, Aethera (6th century) 389

Second Tune – *This version is suitable for Christmas*

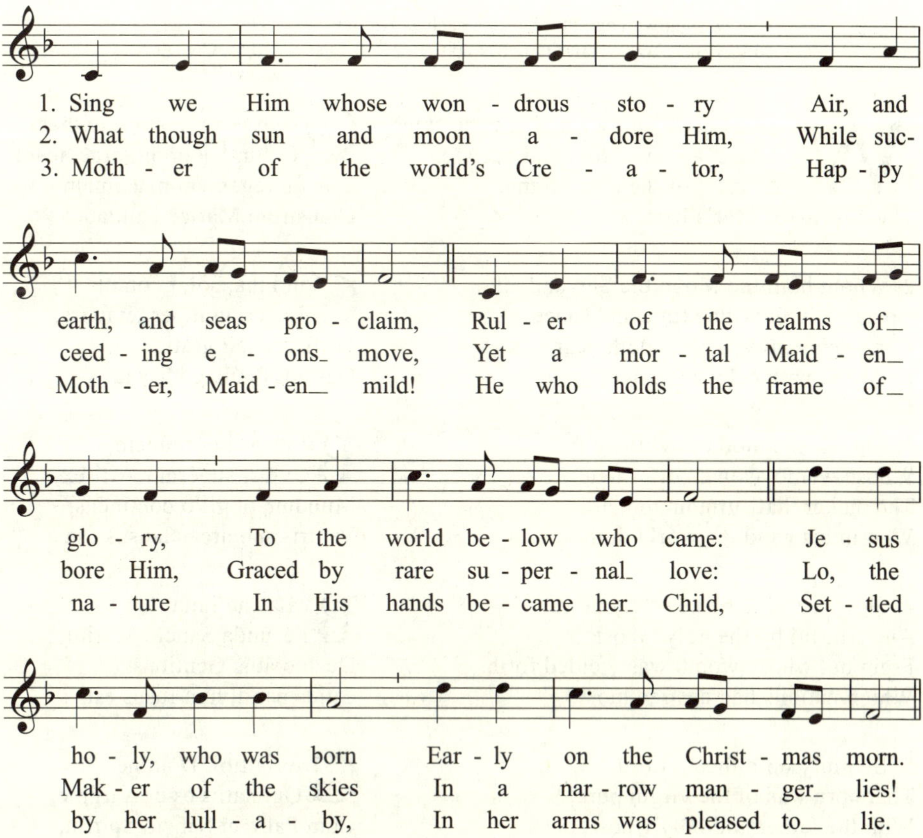

4. Blest by Angel's salutation,
Fruitful by the Spirit's might,
Christ, the hope of every nation,
God and man, she brought to light
At the providential tide,
Him for whom the ages sighed.

5. Hark, the heav'nly host rejoices
With exultant hymns of praise:
Let our grateful hearts and voices
Add their burden to those lays,
With that multitude to cry
Peace to men from God on high!

Final Verses: Richard Lloyd (1993) #104; Noel Rawsthorne (2011) #166.
T. Source: *Sentence of Kaïres* (London: Longmans & Green, 1867) p. 161; adapted for Christmastide in *A Selection of Carols, Pieces, and Anthems Suitable for Christmas* (Penzance: F. Rodda, 1872).
Melody: Henry J. Gauntlett (d. 1876), organist at St. Olave's Church, London.
M. Source: *Catholic Hymn Book* (1998) p. 290; *Hymns, Psalms, and Spiritual Canticles* (1983) p. 390.

87 87 77

Tune: Irby

390 Quem Terra, Pontus, Aethera (6th century)

1599AD – Historic Roman Catholic Translation

Can be sung with any 88 88 meter, such as Hilderstone, Duguet, Breslau, Melcombe, Wareham, Old Hundredth, Mein Seel, Trinity College, etc.

WHOM earth and sea and eke the skies,
Adore, and worship, and declare,
As ruler of the triple frame,
The closure of Maria bare. *n1*

2. Whom both the Moon the Sun and all,
Do serve in their due time and space,
A maiden's inward parts doth bear,
Bedewèd with celestial grace.

3. Blest is the mother by this gift,
Whose womb as in a coffer held,
The maker that surmounteth all,
Who in his hand the world doth weld.

4. She blessèd is by heav'nly news,
And fruitful by the holy Ghost,
From out whose womb was yielded forth,
Whom nations had desirèd most.

5. Be glory unto thee o Lord,
That born was of the virgin pure,
With the father and holy Ghost,
All ages ever to endure.

Quem terra, pontus, aéthera,
Colunt, adórant, praédicant,
Trinam regéntem máchinam
Claustrum Maríae bájulat.

Cui luna, sol, et ómnia
Desérviunt per témpora,
Perfúsa caeli grátia,
Gestant Puéllae víscera.

Beáta Mater múnere,
Cujus, supérnus Ártifex,
Mundum pugíllo cóntinens,
Ventris sub arca clausus est.

Beáta caeli núntio,
Fecúnda Sancto Spíritu,
Desiderátus Géntibus,
Cujus per alvum fusus est.

Glória tibi, Dómine,
Qui natus es de Vírgine,
Cum Patre et Sancto Spíritu,
In sempitérna saécula.

[1] "Eke" is an archaic word meaning *also*, *even*, or *moreover*. "Bare" is an archaic word meaning "bore" or "carried."

T. Source: *Primer, or, Office of the Blessed Virgin Marie in Latin and English, according to the reformed Latin, and with Lyke Graces Privileged* (Antwerp, 1599) p. 3. The Catholic Encyclopedia of 1912 attributes the hymn translations to the book's editor, Richard Verstegan (d. 1636), a Catholic publisher. In the 1599 Preface, Verstegan says: "Notwithstanding the difficulty, these hymns have been so turned into English meter that they may be sung unto the same tunes in English that they bear in Latin." However, his accentual treatment is sometimes peculiar.

88 88 (LM)

Tune:
Various

Quem Terra, Pontus, Aethera (Urbanite)

1651AD – Historic Roman Catholic Translation

Can be sung with any 88 88 meter, such as EISENACH, ROGERS PARK, BRESSANI, LA ROCHELLE, KEMPEN, BESSEMER, TALLIS CANON, WINCHESTER NEW, etc.

Quem terra, pontus, sídera,
Colunt, adórant, praédicant,
Trinam regéntem máchinam
Claustrum Maríae bájulat.

Cui luna, sol, et ómnia
Desérviunt per témpora,
Perfúsa caeli grátia,
Gestant puéllae víscera.

Beáta Mater, múnere,
Cujus supérnus Ártifex,
Mundum pugíllo cóntinens,
Ventris sub arca clausus est.

Beáta caeli núntio,
Fecúnda Sancto Spíritu,
Desiderátus géntibus,
Cujus per alvum fusus est.

Jesu tibi sit glória,
Qui natus es de Vírgine,
Cum Patre et almo Spíritu,
In sempitérna saécula.

HE whom the Land, the Sea, the Sky,
Worship, adore, and magnify,
As Ruler of the Triple Frame,
Is cloist'red in the Virgin Dame.

2. Whom Sun and Moon, and ev'ry thing,
Serve as their Times and Seasons spring,
Him doth a Maiden's Womb include,
Being with celestial Grace bedew'd.

3. Blest Mother, who by Gift Divine,
Within thy bowells did'st inshrine
The Framer of the World's vast Ball,
Whose pow'rfull Hand sustains it all.

4. Blest with the news of th'Angel Post,
And pregnant by the Holy Ghost,
Thy fruitfull Womb did to us bring
Of Nations the desirèd King.

5. Jesu, be Glory to thy Name,
Born of a Virgin; and the same
To th'Holy Ghost and Father be
Through Ages to Eternity.

88 88 (LM)

T. Source: *The Primer or Office of the Blessed Virgin Mary In English: Exactly revised, and the new Hymnes and Prayers added, according to the Reformation of Pope Urban VIII* (1651) p. 4.

Tune: VARIOUS

392 Quem Terra, Pontus, Aethera (6th century)

First Tune – *Trns: Catholic Hymnal for the United States (1807)*

4. An angel brings the happy news;
The Holy Ghost, thy heav’nly spouse,
Thee covers with his fruitful shade,
And Christ’s blest Mother thou art made.

5. O Mary, full of grace divine,
Thy glories now the stars outshine;
Lo! thy Creator and thy God
Draws from thy body life and food.

6. O gracious Mother of mankind,
What Eve had lost, in thee we find;
The way to heav’n is now by thee
To mourning sinners open’d free.

7. Thou art the gate of heav’nly light,
Thru which the conqu’ring Prince of might
Comes, captive mankind to redeem;
Ye, Nations, sound the glorious theme.

8. May age to age forever sing
The Virgin’s Son and angels’ King;
And praise with the celestial host,
The Father, Son and Holy Ghost.

Verses 5-7 are from *O gloriosa femina*, which was originally the second half of *Quem Terra, Pontus, Aethera.*

88 88 (LM)

Tune: Brockham

Final Verses: Richard Lloyd (1993) #26; Noel Rawsthorne (2011) #52.
T. Source: *Hymns for the Use of the Catholic Church in America* (Baltimore: John W. Butler, 1807) p. 81.
Melody: Jeremiah Clarke (d. 1707), organist at St Paul’s Cathedral, London.
M. Source: *Catholic Hymn Book* (London Oratory, 1998) p. 288.

Quem Terra, Pontus, Aethera (6th century) 393

Second Tune – *Trns: Catholic Hymnal for the United States (1807)*

4. An angel brings the happy news;
The Holy Ghost, thy heav'nly spouse,
Thee covers with his fruitful shade,
And Christ's blest Mother thou art made.

5. O Mary, full of grace divine,
Thy glories now the stars outshine;
Lo! thy Creator and thy God
Draws from thy body life and food.

6. O gracious Mother of mankind,
What Eve had lost, in thee we find;
The way to heav'n is now by thee
To mourning sinners open'd free.

7. Thou art the gate of heav'nly light,
Thru which the conqu'ring Prince of might
Comes, captive mankind to redeem;
Ye, Nations, sound the glorious theme.

8. May age to age forever sing
The Virgin's Son and angels' King;
And praise with the celestial host,
The Father, Son and Holy Ghost.

Verses 5-7 are from *O gloriosa femina*, which was originally the second half of *Quem Terra, Pontus, Aethera*.

Melody: James W. Elliott (d. 1915)
M. Source: *Hymns Ancient and Modern* (1972) p. 320.
T. Source: *Hymns for the Use of the Catholic Church in America* (Baltimore: John W. Butler, 1807) p. 81.

88 88 (LM)
Tune:
La Rochelle

394 Quem Terra, Pontus, Aethera (6th century)

Third Tune – *Trns: Catholic Hymnal for the United States (1807)*

4. An angel brings the happy news;
The Holy Ghost, thy heav'nly spouse,
Thee covers with his fruitful shade,
And Christ's blest Mother thou art made.

5. O Mary, full of grace divine,
Thy glories now the stars outshine;
Lo! thy Creator and thy God
Draws from thy body life and food.

6. O gracious Mother of mankind,
What Eve had lost, in thee we find;
The way to heav'n is now by thee
To mourning sinners open'd free.

7. Thou art the gate of heav'nly light,
Thru which the conqu'ring Prince of might
Comes, captive mankind to redeem;
Ye, Nations, sound the glorious theme.

8. May age to age forever sing
The Virgin's Son and angels' King;
And praise with the celestial host,
The Father, Son and Holy Ghost.

Verses 5-7 are from *O gloriosa femina*, which was originally the second half of *Quem Terra, Pontus, Aethera.*

88 88 (LM)

Tune:
Altona

Final Verses: Noel Rawsthorne (2011) #378; one note altered.
T. Source: *Hymns for the Use of the Catholic Church in America* (Baltimore: John W. Butler, 1807) p. 81.
Melody: Schumann's *Geistliche Lieder* (1539); an adaptation by Fr. Stephan Lück (d. 1883) in his hymnal, *Gesang- und Gebetbuch für die Diözese Trier* (1847) p. 19. Called by various names (Vom Himmel Hoch, Erfurt, etc.) this melody has been set by such composers as Hassler, Gesius, Praetorius, and Bach.
M. Source: *Hosanna Catholic Hymn Book* (1914) p. 17; *New Westminster Hymnal* (1939) p. 8.

Quem Terra, Pontus, Aethera (6th century) 395

Trns: Catholic Hymnal for the United States (1807)

Can be sung with any 88 88 meter: Eisenach, Bressani, Rogers Park, La Rochelle, Kempen, Bessemer, Tallis Canon, Winchester New, and so forth.

THE Sov'reign God whose hands sustain
The heav'nly orbs, the earth, the main;
Whose generation none can tell,
In thee, O Mary, chose to dwell.

2. He, whom the sun and moon obey,
To whom all creatures homage pay,
The mighty Ruler of the skies,
In thee conceal'd, an infant lies.

3. Thrice happy Maid, whom Heaven's choice
Has made the source of all our joys;
Since he, by whom we move and live,
From thee would life and food receive.

4. An angel brings the happy news;
The Holy Ghost, thy heav'nly spouse,
Thee covers with his fruitful shade,
And Christ's blest Mother thou art made.

5. O Mary, full of grace divine,
Thy glories now the stars outshine;
Lo, God thy Maker from thy frame
Is pleased His life and food to claim.

6. O gracious Mother of mankind,
What Eve had lost, in thee we find;
The way to heav'n is now by thee
To mourning sinners open'd free.

7. Thou art the gate of heav'nly light,
Through which the conqu'ring Prince of might
Comes, captive mankind to redeem;
Ye, Nations, sound the glorious theme.

8. May age to age forever sing
The Virgin's Son and angels' King;
And praise with the celestial host,
The Father, Son and Holy Ghost.

88 88 (LM)

T. Source: *Hymns for the Use of the Catholic Church in America* (Baltimore: John W. Butler, 1807) p. 81.
Verses 5-7 are from *O gloriosa femina*, which was originally the second half of *Quem Terra, Pontus, Aethera.*

Tune: Various

396 Quem Terra, Pontus, Aethera (6th century)

Trns: Fr. Edward Caswall, Oratorian (d. 1878)

4. Yea blest, to whom an angel spoke,
Who through the Holy Spirit bore,
Whose womb the nations' long-desired
In wondrous fashion would outpour!

5. O Jesus, born of Virgin bright,
Immortal glory be to Thee;
Praise to the Father infinite,
And Paraclete eternally.

88 88 (LM)

Tune:
HILDERSTONE

Melody: Philip Hart (d. 1749), organist at St. Michael Church, Cornhill.
M. Source: *Hymns Ancient and Modern* (1972) p. 8; cf. *Church Hymns With Tunes* (1885) p. 230, edited by Sir Arthur Sullivan (d. 1900), organist at St. Peter Church, Kensington.
T. Source: *Lyra Catholica: Containing all the hymns of the Roman Breviary and Missal* (1851) p. 199.

Quem Terra, Pontus, Aethera (6th century) 397

Trns: Fr. Edward Caswall, Oratorian (d. 1878)

Can be sung with any 88 88 meter, such as HILDERSTONE, DUGUET, BRESLAU, MELCOMBE, WAREHAM, OLD HUNDREDTH, MEIN SEEL, TRINITY COLLEGE, etc.

THE Lord, whom earth, and sea, and sky
With one adoring voice proclaim;
Who rules them all in majesty;
Enclos'd Himself in Mary's frame.

2. Lo! in a humble Virgin's womb,
O'ershadowed by Almighty pow'r;
He whom the stars, and sun, and moon,
Each serve in their appointed hour.

3. O Mother blest, to whom was giv'n
Within thy body to contain
The Architect of earth and Heav'n,
Whose hands the universe sustain.

4. Yea blest, to whom an angel spoke,
Who through the Holy Spirit bore,
Whose womb the nations' long-desired
In wondrous fashion would outpour!

5. O Jesus, born of Virgin bright,
Immortal glory be to Thee;
Praise to the Father infinite,
And Paraclete eternally.

88 88 (LM)

Tune:
VARIOUS

T. Source: *Lyra Catholica: Containing all the hymns of the Roman Breviary and Missal* (1851) p. 199.

398 Mary, The Mother Of God (Catholic Doctrine)

Objections Answered by Fr. Leslie A. Rumble (d. 1975)

You teach that the Holy Ghost proceeds from the Son, yet is responsible for the birth of that Son.

Answer : The eternal Son of God, in becoming man, took a human nature from the Virgin Mary. Thus was born a being who was both God and man. As God, this Second Person of the Holy Trinity always existed, and from Him in eternity the Holy Ghost always proceeds, as from the Father also. In this sense the Holy Ghost does not give being to the Son. But the human nature, which began in time, was due to the operation of the Holy Ghost, and was assumed by the Son. There is no inconsistency in this doctrine. (#645)

How could Mary be the mother of the One who created her?

Answer : Mary owed her being, of course, to God, but this under the aspect of His eternal Nature. Subsequent to her creation that human nature was born of her which the Son of God had assumed to Himself. She was, therefore, the mother of Christ. But Christ was one Divine Person existing in two natures, one eternal and divine; the other temporal and human. Mary necessarily gave birth to a being with one Personality and that Divine, and she is rightly called the Mother of God. (#762)

Why pray to Mary at all?

Answer : Because God wills that we should do so, and because such prayers to her are of the utmost value. God often wills to give certain favors only on condition that we go to some secondary agent. Sodom was to be spared through the intercession of Abraham; Naaman, the leper, was to be cured only through the waters of the Jordan. Now Mary is, and must ever remain, the mother of Christ. She still has a mother's rights and privileges, and is able to obtain for us many graces. But let us view things reasonably. If I desire to pray, I can certainly pray to God directly. Yet would you blame me if, at times, I were to ask my own earthly mother to pray for me also? Such a request is really a prayer to her that she may intercede for me with God. Certainly, if I met the mother of Christ on earth, I would ask her to pray for me, and she would do so. And in her more perfect state with Christ in heaven she is not less able to help me. (#1408)

But a prayer to God directly must be more efficacious than a prayer to Mary.

Answer : Not necessarily. It might well be that God intends to honor Our Lady by granting the favor I seek through her intercession in a particular way. In that case the grace is to be given through her provided I honor her by addressing myself to her. Again, every prayer to Mary is in reality the asking of a favor from God even as the mother of Christ is requested to ask the same favor also. It is often better to ask God for a favor and to have someone else praying to God with one for the same favor. Two prayers are better than one. And above all, when the other one praying is Christ's own mother. (#1409)

It is unscriptural to attribute power to Mary.

Answer : That is a very unscriptural statement. At His mother's request Jesus changed water into wine at Cana, though He had said, "My time is not yet come." St. James tells us that "the prayer of a just man availeth much." *James 5.16*. How much more the prayer of Mary! (#1411)

Does the Bible sanction such prayers to Mary?

Answer : Yes. All through the Bible you will find God conferring favors through the prayers of others. In the Old Testament we read of the prayers of Abraham, Moses, and of the various prophets. In the New Testament, St. James tells us to "pray for one another," in the text I have just quoted. If we must always pray directly to God and may not ask the prayers of others, why did St. Paul write to the Thessalonians, "Pray for us that we may be delivered from importunate and evil men?" *II Thessalonians 3.2*. Why did he not ask that directly of God, instead of asking the prayers of the Thessalonians? Or would you be more scriptural than the New Testament itself? (#1412)

There is but one mediator; there is no place for Mary.

Answer : Christ is the principal mediator in His own right. Mary is a secondary mediatrix, through, with, and in Christ. Without Him she would have no power, and therefore He is the source of all mediation with God on behalf of men. (#1413)

Source: *Radio Replies*, with 1938 Imprimatur by
Archbishop John G. Murray (Saint Paul, Minnesota)

Quem Terra, Pontus, Aethera (6th century) 399

Trns: Dr. John M. Neale (d. 1866)

4. All honor, laud, and glory be,
O Jesus, Virgin-born, to thee!
All glory, as is ever meet,
To Father and to Paraclete.

Can be sung with any 88 88 meter, such as GONFALON ROYAL, DUGUET, etc.

THE God whom earth and sea and sky
Adore and laud and magnify,
Whose might they own, whose praise they tell,
In Mary's body deigned to dwell.

2. O Mother blest, the chosen shrine
Wherein the Architect divine,
Whose hand contains the earth and sky,
Vouchsafed, as in his ark, to lie!

3. Blest in the message Gabriel brought;
Blest by the work the Spirit wrought:
From whom the great Desire of earth
Took human flesh and human birth.

4. All honor, laud, and glory be,
O Jesus, Virgin-born, to thee!
All glory, as is ever meet,
To Father and to Paraclete.

Final Verses: Richard Lloyd (1993) #64; Noel Rawsthorne (2011) #108.
T. Source: CENTO based on a translation by Dr. John Mason Neale (d. 1866); cf. *Hymns Ancient and Modern* (1972) p. 689; cf. *New Westminster Hymnal* (1939) p. 140; cf. *Hymnal for the Hours* (San Francisco: Benedict XVI Institute, 2014) p. 341.
Melody: Bartholomäus Gesius (d. 1613); adapted by Johann H. Schein (d. 1630). M. Source: *Pius XII Hymnal* (1959) p. 13.

88 88 (LM)
Tune: EISENACH

400 Rebus Creatis Nil Egens (1736 AD)

Fr. Charles Coffin (d. 1749)

To sing in Latin, use any 88 88 (LM) tune.

REBUS creátis nil egens,
Temet beátus, nunc tuo
Prodis ab arcáno, Deus,
Mundóque das primórdia.

2. Tu cuncta quae non sunt vocas,
Et illa se sistunt tibi;
Miróque concéntu suo
Dant Conditóri gloriam.

3. At mundus e sinu tuo
Dum prodit adspectábilis;
Augustiórem cógitas
Mundum, Creátor, álterum. *n1*

4. Illum Redémptor ártifex
Virtútibus condet suis,
Sparsóque terris ómnibus *n2*
Verbi poténtis sémine.

5. Illum, peráctis séculis,
Caelo locábit; et throni
Mensaéque consórtem suae
Deo redonábit Patri.

6. Utríque mundo qui praees, *n3*
Utrúmque consérva, Pater:
Utrúmque, Fili, dírige:
Utrúmque, Flamen, cónsecra.

88 88 (LM)

Tune:
VARIOUS

T. Source: Bl. John Henry Cardinal Newman's *Hymni Ecclesiae* (London, 1865), p. 60.

Assistance for comprehension

NEEDING nothing from created things,
in thyself blessèd, now from thy secret store
thou bringest forth, O God,
and layest foundations for the world.

2. Thou callest all things, which had no being, *cf. Rom 4.17*
and they present themselves before thee;
and with their wondrous harmony
they give glory to their Founder.

3. Yet while from thy heart
the visible world comes forth,
thou conceivest, O Creator
another world more venerable. *n1*

4. The Redeemer-craftsman
will found it with his virtues,
and when the seed of the mighty Word *n2*
has been scattered all through the lands.

5. At the ending of the ages,
he will settle it in heaven; and as
the partner of his throne and table
present it again to God the Father.

6. Thou who presidest over each of the worlds, *n3*
O Father, each one maintain,
O Son, each one guide,
O Spirit, each one hallow.

[1] Cf. 4th Lateran Council (1215 AD):

> [... *Deus est*] *unum universorum principium: creator omnium visibilium et invisibilium, spiritualium et corporalium: qui sua omnipotenti virtute simul ab initio temporis utramque de nihilo condidit creaturam, spiritualem et corporalem, angelicam videlicet et mundanam* [...]

> [... God is] the one principle of all things: the creator of all things visible and invisible, spiritual and corporeal: who by his own almighty power founded together at the beginning of time the spiritual and corporeal creations, namely, the angelic and the earthly [...]

[2] Cf. *Pange lingua ... Corporis: sparso verbi semine;* cf. Lk 8.11.

[3] God preserves heaven by willing its ongoing existence (if he withdrew his will, it would cease to exist); he directs heaven because he is its king; and he sanctifies it because he is the origin of all holiness.

402 Rebus Creatis Nil Egens (1736 AD)

FIRST TUNE — *"We have new heavens and a new earth to look forward to, the dwelling-place of holiness; that is what he has promised."—II Peter 3.13*

4. For Thou didst will that Christ should frame
A new creation by His Name;
Its seed, the living word of grace
He scatters wide in every place;

5. Its home, when time shall be no more,
In heav'n with Thee for evermore;
Accepted in Thy boundless love
To share His throne and joy above.

6. O Father, Son, and Spirit blest,
One God in heav'n and earth confessed,
Preserve, direct, and sanctify
Thy realm below, Thy realm on high.

88 88 (LM)

Tune:
GONFALON ROYAL

Final Verses: Richard Lloyd (1993) #80; Noel Rawsthorne (2011) #136.
ENGLISH TRANSLATION: Based on John David Chambers (d. 1893) in *Lauda Syon: Ancient Latin Hymns of the English and Other Churches* (London, 1857) p. 121.
Melody: Sir Percy Carter Buck (d. 1947); first published in *Fourteen Hymn Tunes* (1913).
M. Source: *Catholic Hymn Book* (London Oratory, 1998) p. 140. The tune was originally paired with *Vexilla Regis* ("Flag of the King"). A *gonfalon* ("flag") was traditionally carried during Catholic processions.

Rebus Creatis Nil Egens (1736 AD) 403

Second Tune — *"We have new heavens and a new earth to look forward to, the dwelling-place of holiness; that is what he has promised."—II Peter 3.13*

4. For Thou didst will that Christ should frame
A new creation by His Name;
Its seed, the living word of grace
He scatters wide in every place;

5. Its home, when time shall be no more,
In heav'n with Thee for evermore;
Accepted in Thy boundless love
To share His throne and joy above.

6. O Father, Son, and Spirit blest,
One God in heav'n and earth confessed,
Preserve, direct, and sanctify
Thy realm below, Thy realm on high.

* This melody at a lower key is on page 864.

English Translation: Based on John David Chambers (d. 1893) in *Lauda Syon: Ancient Latin Hymns of the English and Other Churches* (London, 1857) p. 121.
Melody: From a hymn book published by Fr. Melchior Ludolf Herold (d. 1810).
M. Source: *New Westminster Hymnal* (1939) p. 173.

88 88 (LM)

Tune: Bressani

404 Rebus Creatis Nil Egens (1736 AD)

Third Tune — *"We have new heavens and a new earth to look forward to, the dwelling-place of holiness; that is what he has promised."—II Peter 3.13*

4. For Thou didst will that Christ should frame
A new creation by His Name;
Its seed, the living word of grace
He scatters wide in every place;

5. Its home, when time shall be no more,
In heav'n with Thee for evermore;
Accepted in Thy boundless love
To share His throne and joy above.

6. O Father, Son, and Spirit blest,
One God in heav'n and earth confessed,
Preserve, direct, and sanctify
Thy realm below, Thy realm on high.

* This melody at a lower key is on page 436.

88 88 (LM)

Tune:
Trinity College

English Translation: Based on John David Chambers (d. 1893) in *Lauda Syon: Ancient Latin Hymns of the English and Other Churches* (London, 1857) p. 121.
Melody: John Bacchus Dykes (d. 1876).
M. Source: *Hymns Ancient and Modern* (1972) p. 64.

FOURTH TUNE — *"We have new heavens and a new earth to look forward to, the dwelling-place of holiness; that is what he has promised."—II Peter 3.13*

4. For Thou didst will that Christ should frame
A new creation by His Name;
Its seed, the living word of grace
He scatters wide in every place;

5. Its home, when time shall be no more,
In heav'n with Thee for evermore;
Accepted in Thy boundless love
To share His throne and joy above.

6. O Father, Son, and Spirit blest,
One God in heav'n and earth confessed,
Preserve, direct, and sanctify
Thy realm below, Thy realm on high.

ENGLISH TRANSLATION: Based on John David Chambers (d. 1893) in *Lauda Syon: Ancient Latin Hymns of the English and Other Churches* (London, 1857) p. 121.
Melody: Kevin Allen (b. 1965), choirmaster at the Monastery of the Holy Cross in Chicago.
M. Source: *Saint Edmund Campion Missal and Hymnal* (2013) p. 880.

88 88 (LM)
Tune: BESSEMER

406 Rebus Creatis Nil Egens (1736 AD)

Fifth Tune — *"We have new heavens and a new earth to look forward to, the dwelling-place of holiness; that is what he has promised."—II Peter 3.13*

4. For Thou didst will that Christ should frame
A new creation by His Name;
Its seed, the living word of grace
He scatters wide in every place;

5. Its home, when time shall be no more,
In heav'n with Thee for evermore;
Accepted in Thy boundless love
To share His throne and joy above.

6. O Father, Son, and Spirit blest,
One God in heav'n and earth confessed,
Preserve, direct, and sanctify
Thy realm below, Thy realm on high.

88 88 (LM)

Tune:
Whitehall

English Translation: Based on John David Chambers (d. 1893) in *Lauda Syon: Ancient Latin Hymns of the English and Other Churches* (London, 1857) p. 121.
Melody: Henry Lawes (d. 1662).
M. Source: *Saint Edmund Campion Missal and Hymnal* (2013) p. 888.

Sixth Tune — *"We have new heavens and a new earth to look forward to, the dwelling-place of holiness; that is what he has promised."—II Peter 3.13*

1. O Lord, in per - fect bliss_ a - bove
2. Things that were not, at Thy_ com - mand,
3. But e - ven while the world came forth

Thou couldst not need_ cre - at - ed love;
In per - fect bliss_ be - fore Thee stand;
In all the beau - ty of its birth,

And yet Thou didst_ Thy pow'r_ dis - play,_
And all to their_ Cre - a - tor raise_
In Thy deep thought Thou didst_ be - hold_

And earth's foun - da - tions firm - ly lay.
A won - drous har - mo - ny_ of praise.
An - oth - er world of nobl - er mold.

4. For Thou didst will that Christ should frame
A new creation by His Name;
Its seed, the living word of grace
He scatters wide in every place;

5. Its home, when time shall be no more,
In heav'n with Thee for evermore;
Accepted in Thy boundless love
To share His throne and joy above.

6. O Father, Son, and Spirit blest,
One God in heav'n and earth confessed,
Preserve, direct, and sanctify
Thy realm below, Thy realm on high.

* This melody at a lower key is on page 248.

English Translation: Based on John David Chambers (d. 1893) in *Lauda Syon: Ancient Latin Hymns of the English and Other Churches* (London, 1857) p. 121.

M. Source: Cento from *The Parochial Hymn Book, Words and Melodies; containing Vespers, Compline, and all the Liturgical Hymns for the Year both in Latin and English* (London, 1883), edited by Fr. Anatole Police; Imprimatur by Henry Edward Cardinal Manning (d. 1892), who in 1851 converted from Anglicanism and was appointed Archbishop of Westminster in 1865.

88 88 (LM)

Tune: Ioannes

408 Rebus Creatis Nil Egens (1736 AD)

Seventh Tune — *"We have new heavens and a new earth to look forward to, the dwelling-place of holiness; that is what he has promised."—II Peter 3.13*

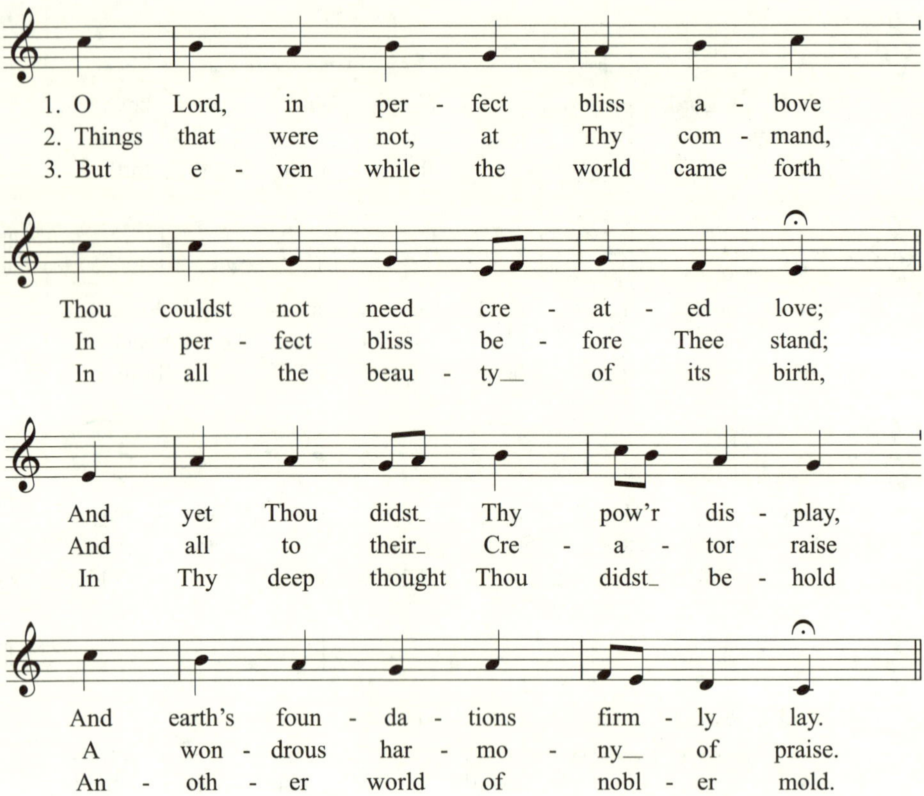

4. For Thou didst will that Christ should frame
A new creation by His Name;
Its seed, the living word of grace
He scatters wide in every place;

5. Its home, when time shall be no more,
In heav'n with Thee for evermore;
Accepted in Thy boundless love
To share His throne and joy above.

6. O Father, Son, and Spirit blest,
One God in heav'n and earth confessed,
Preserve, direct, and sanctify
Thy realm below, Thy realm on high.

88 88 (LM)

Tune:
Altona

Final Verses: Noel Rawsthorne (2011) #378; one note altered.
English Translation: Based on John David Chambers (d. 1893) in *Lauda Syon: Ancient Latin Hymns of the English and Other Churches* (London, 1857) p. 121.
Melody: Schumann's *Geistliche Lieder* (1539); an adaptation by Fr. Stephan Lück (d. 1883) in his hymnal, *Gesang- und Gebetbuch für die Diözese Trier* (1847) p. 19. Called by various names (Vom Himmel Hoch, Erfurt, etc.) this melody has been set by such composers as Hassler, Gesius, Praetorius, and Bach.
M. Source: *Hosanna Catholic Hymn Book* (1914) p. 17; *New Westminster Hymnal* (1939) p. 8.

"We have new heavens and a new earth to look forward to, the dwelling-place of holiness; that is what he has promised."—II Peter 3.13

Can be sung with any 88 88 meter, such as EISENACH, ROGERS PARK, BRESSANI, LA ROCHELLE, KEMPEN, BESSEMER, TALLIS CANON, WINCHESTER NEW, etc.

O LORD, in perfect bliss above
Thou couldst not need created love;
And yet Thou didst Thy pow'r display,
And earth's foundations firmly lay.

2. Things that were not, at Thy command,
In perfect bliss before Thee stand;
And all to their Creator raise
A wondrous harmony of praise.

3. But even while the world came forth
In all the beauty of its birth,
In Thy deep thought Thou didst behold
Another world of nobler mold.

4. For Thou didst will that Christ should frame
A new creation by His Name;
Its seed, the living word of grace
He scatters wide in every place;

5. Its home, when time shall be no more,
In heav'n with Thee for evermore;
Accepted in Thy boundless love
To share His throne and joy above.

6. O Father, Son, and Spirit blest,
One God in heav'n and earth confessed,
Preserve, direct, and sanctify
Thy realm below, Thy realm on high.

[6c] God preserves heaven by willing its ongoing existence (if he withdrew his will it would cease to exist); he directs heaven because he is its king; and he sanctifies it because he is the origin of all holiness.

ENGLISH TRANSLATION: Based on John David Chambers (d. 1893) in *Lauda Syon: Ancient Latin Hymns of the English and Other Churches* (London, 1857) p. 121.

88 88 (LM)

Tune: VARIOUS

Rebus Creatis Nil Egens (1736 AD)

First Tune – *Trns: Robert Campbell of Skerrington (d. 1868)*

4. Its Maker Christ, our Lord and God,
Its frame His truth and grace,
And, far as foot of man hath trod,
It finds a resting place.

5. And when the course of time has run
His loving call will ring,
And it will rise, e'er with the Son
To dwell, the sov'reign King.

6. Thy new creation, Lord, direct,
Till fixed above secure;
O Father, from its foes protect;
O, cleanse it, Spirit Pure.

86 86 (CM)

Tune:
Bristol

Final Verses: Richard Lloyd (1993) #25; Noel Rawsthorne (2011) #51.
English Translation: Robert Campbell (d. 1868), who converted to the Catholic Church in 1852.
T. Source: *Hymnal for the Scottish Church* (1857) p. 39.
Melody: Thomas Ravenscroft (d. 1635), who also composed secular tunes,
e.g. "Three Blind Mice." The melody of this tune can be sung in the Tenor.
M. Source: *Catholic Hymn Book* (London Oratory, 1998) p. 7.

Rebus Creatis Nil Egens (1736 AD)

SECOND TUNE – *Trns: Robert Campbell of Skerrington (d. 1868)*

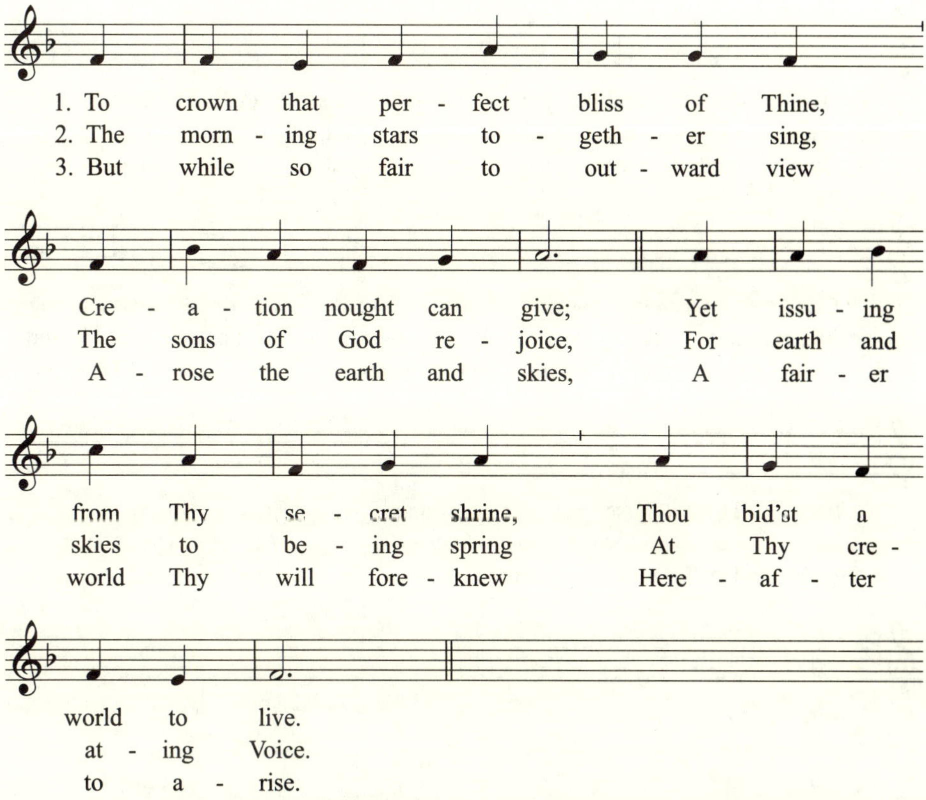

4. Its Maker Christ, our Lord and God,
Its frame His truth and grace,
And, far as foot of man hath trod,
It finds a resting place.

5. And when the course of time has run
His loving call will ring,
And it will rise, e'er with the Son
To dwell, the sov'reign King.

6. Thy new creation, Lord, direct,
Till fixed above secure;
O Father, from its foes protect;
O, cleanse it, Spirit Pure.

Final Verses: Richard Lloyd (1993) #194; Noel Rawsthorne (2011) #125.
ENGLISH TRANSLATION: Robert Campbell (d. 1868), who converted to the Catholic Church in 1852.
T. Source: *Hymnal for the Scottish Church* (1857) p. 39.
Melody: *The Whole Booke of Psalmes collected into Englishe metre* (London: John Daye, 1584) p. 367. The texts for this book were composed by Thomas Sternhold (d. 1549), a special servant to King Henry VIII, in charge of bringing forward ceremonial clothing during the monarch's coronation.
M. Source: *New Westminster Hymnal* (1939) p. 93; *Adoremus Hymnal* (1997) #360; A version from 1621 has the melody in the Tenor voice; cf. *Hymns Ancient and Modern* (1972) p. 202.

86 86 (CM)

Tune: ST FLAVIAN

412 Rebus Creatis Nil Egens (1736 AD)

Third Tune – *Trns: Robert Campbell of Skerrington (d. 1868)*

4. Its Maker Christ, our Lord and God,
Its frame His truth and grace,
And, far as foot of man hath trod,
It finds a resting place.

5. And when the course of time has run
His loving call will ring,
And it will rise, e'er with the Son
To dwell, the sov'reign King.

6. Thy new creation, Lord, direct,
Till fixed above secure;
O Father, from its foes protect;
O, cleanse it, Spirit Pure.

86 86 (CM)

Tune: Horsley

Final Verses: Richard Lloyd (1993) #97; Noel Rawsthorne (2011) #156.
English Translation: Robert Campbell (d. 1868), who converted to the Catholic Church in 1852.
T. Source: *Hymnal for the Scottish Church* (1857) p. 39.
Melody: William Horsley (d. 1858), organist at Ely Chapel, Holborn.
M. Source: *Catholic Hymn Book* (London Oratory, 1998) p. 114.

Fourth Tune – *Trns: Robert Campbell of Skerrington (d. 1868)*

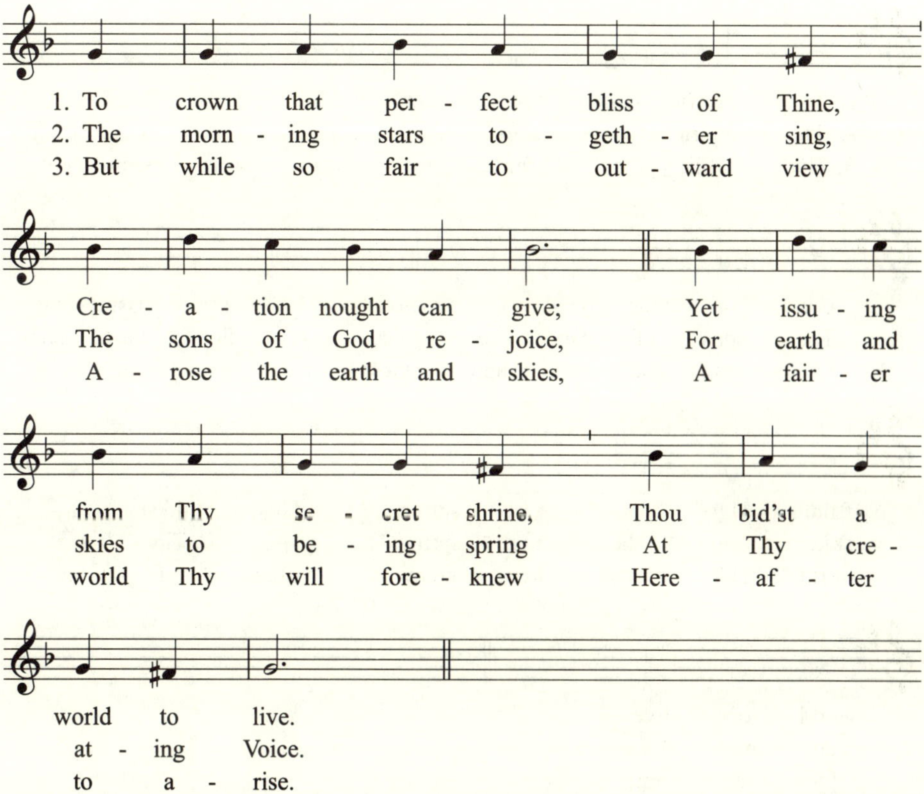

4. Its Maker Christ, our Lord and God,
Its frame His truth and grace,
And, far as foot of man hath trod,
It finds a resting place.

5. And when the course of time has run
His loving call will ring,
And it will rise, e'er with the Son
To dwell, the sov'reign King.

6. Thy new creation, Lord, direct,
Till fixed above secure;
O Father, from its foes protect;
O, cleanse it, Spirit Pure.

English Translation: Robert Campbell (d. 1868), who converted to the Catholic Church in 1852.
T. Source: *Hymnal for the Scottish Church* (1857) p. 39.
Melody: *The former Booke of the Musicke of M. William Damon, late one of her Majesties Musitions, containing all the tunes of David's Psalms, as they are ordinarily soung in the Church: most excellently by him composed into 4 partes* (1591).
M. Source: *Hymns Ancient and Modern* (1972) p. 443.

86 86 (CM)

Tune: Windsor

Rebus Creatis Nil Egens (1736 AD)

Fifth Tune – *Trns: Robert Campbell of Skerrington (d. 1868)*

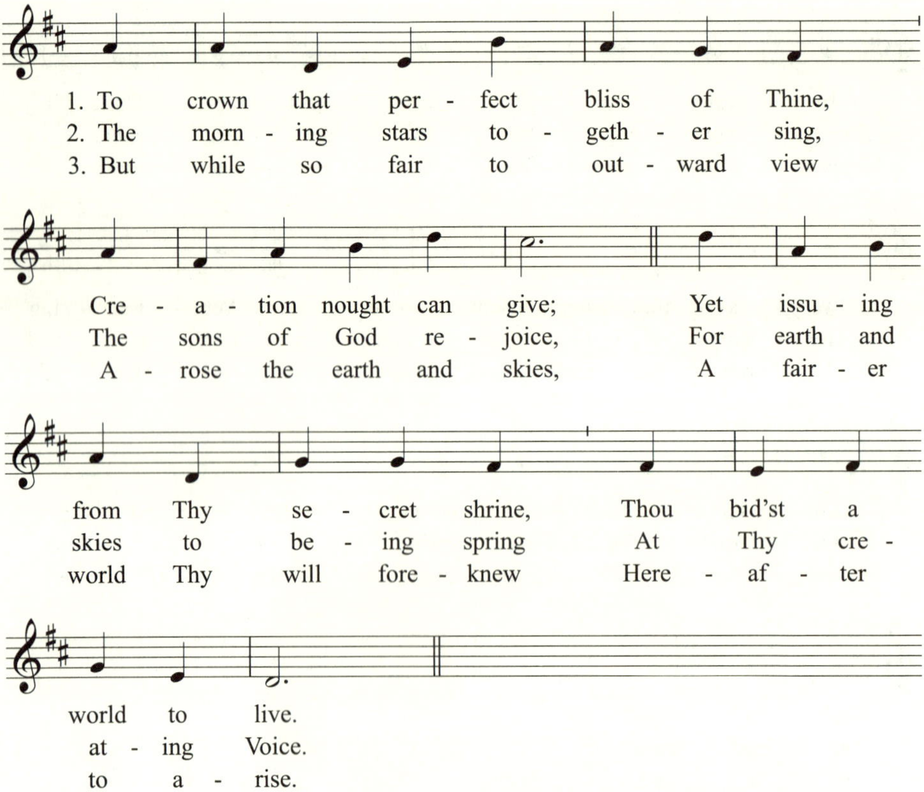

4. Its Maker Christ, our Lord and God,
   Its frame His truth and grace,
   And, far as foot of man hath trod,
   It finds a resting place.

5. And when the course of time has run
   His loving call will ring,
   And it will rise, e'er with the Son
   To dwell, the sov'reign King.

6. Thy new creation, Lord, direct,
   Till fixed above secure;
   O Father, from its foes protect;
   O, cleanse it, Spirit Pure.

86 86 (CM)

Tune:
St Fulbert

Final Verses: Richard Lloyd (1993) #196.
Melody: Henry J. Gauntlett (d. 1876), organist at St. Olave's Church, London.
M. Source: *New Westminster Hymnal* (1939) p. 76; *Catholic Hymn Book* (London Oratory, 1998) p. 134.
English Translation: Robert Campbell (d. 1868), who converted to the Catholic Church in 1852.
T. Source: *Hymnal for the Scottish Church* (1857) p. 39.

Rebus Creatis Nil Egens (1736 AD)

Sixth Tune – *Trns: Robert Campbell of Skerrington (d. 1868)*

4. Its Maker Christ, our Lord and God,
Its frame His truth and grace,
And, far as foot of man hath trod,
It finds a resting place.

5. And when the course of time has run
His loving call will ring,
And it will rise, e'er with the Son
To dwell, the sov'reign King.

6. Thy new creation, Lord, direct,
Till fixed above secure;
O Father, from its foes protect;
O, cleanse it, Spirit Pure.

Final Verses: Richard Lloyd (1993) #245; Noel Rawsthorne (2011) #393.
English Translation: Robert Campbell (d. 1868), who converted to the Catholic Church in 1852.
T. Source: *Hymnal for the Scottish Church* (1857) p. 39.
Melody: Christopher Tye (d. 1573), choirmaster at Ely Cathedral. This famous tune—found in Chapter VIII ("Meane" voice) of his *Acts of the Apostles* (1553)—was adapted by George Kirbye (d. 1634) for *The Whole Book of Psalms, with Their Wonted Tunes Harmonized in Four Parts* (1592), published by Thomas Este (d. 1609), William Byrd's friend and printer. The tune can be sung in the Tenor, and the *New English Hymnal* (1986) contains a descant for it.
M. Source: *Catholic Hymn Book* (London Oratory, 1998) p. 69.

86 86 (CM)

Tune:
Winchester Old

Rebus Creatis Nil Egens (1736 AD)

Seventh Tune – *Trns: Robert Campbell of Skerrington (d. 1868)*

4. Its Maker Christ, our Lord and God,
Its frame His truth and grace,
And, far as foot of man hath trod,
It finds a resting place.

5. And when the course of time has run
His loving call will ring,
And it will rise, e'er with the Son
To dwell, the sov'reign King.

6. Thy new creation, Lord, direct,
Till fixed above secure;
O Father, from its foes protect;
O, cleanse it, Spirit Pure.

86 86 (CM)

Tune:
St Anne

Final Verses: Richard Lloyd (1993) #186; Noel Rawsthorne (2011) #282.
English Translation: Robert Campbell (d. 1868), who converted to the Catholic Church in 1852.
T. Source: *Hymnal for the Scottish Church* (1857) p. 39.
Melody: William Croft (d. 1727), organist at Westminster Abbey.
M. Source: *Hymns, Psalms, and Spiritual Canticles* (Massachusetts: Theodore Marier, 1983) p. 507.

Rebus Creatis Nil Egens (1736 AD)

Trns: Robert Campbell of Skerrington (d. 1868)

Can be sung with any 86 86 meter, such as ST MAGNUS, BEDFORD, ST COLUMBA, WESTMINSTER, ST ANNE, ST HUGH, HEREFORD, ST FLAVIAN, etc.

TO crown that perfect bliss of Thine,
Creation nought can give;
Yet issuing from Thy secret shrine,
Thou bid'st a world to live.

2. The morning stars together sing,
The sons of God rejoice,
For earth and skies to being spring
At Thy creating Voice.

3. But while so fair to outward view
Arose the earth and skies,
A fairer world Thy will foreknew
Hereafter to arise.

4. Its Maker Christ, our Lord and God,
Its frame His truth and grace,
And, far as foot of man hath trod,
It finds a resting place.

5. And when the course of time has run
His loving call will ring,
And it will rise, e'er with the Son
To dwell, the sov'reign King.

6. Thy new creation, Lord, direct,
Till fixed above secure;
O Father, from its foes protect;
O, cleanse it, Spirit Pure.

[6c] God preserves heaven by willing its ongoing existence (if he withdrew his will it would cease to exist); he directs heaven because he is its king; and he sanctifies it because he is the origin of all holiness.
ENGLISH TRANSLATION: Robert Campbell (d. 1868), who converted to the Catholic Church in 1852.
T. Source: *Hymnal for the Scottish Church* (1857) p. 39.

86 86 (CM)
Tune: VARIOUS

418 Rex Sempiterne Domine (5th century)

Title after 1631AD: *"Rex Sempiterne Caelitum"*

To sing in Latin, use any 88 88 (LM) tune.
Several verses break the meter (e.g. 17a), owing to this hymn's antiquity.

REX sempitérne Dómine, Rerum Creátor ómnium, Qui eras ante saécula Semper cum Patre Fílius.	1. Everlasting King and Lord, Creator of all things, Son who before the ages wast always with the Father.
2. Qui mundi in primórdio Adam plasmásti hóminem: Cui tuae imágini Vultum dedísti símilem.	2. Thou who at the commencement of the world didst mold the man Adam, to whom thou gavest a countenance like to thine own image.
3. Quem diábolus decéperat Hostis humáni géneris: Cujus tu formam córporis Assúmere dignátus es.	3. He whom the devil, mankind's foe, had led astray, the shape of whose body thou vouchsafedst to adopt.
4. Ut hóminem redímeres, Quem ante jam plasmáveras: Et nos Deo conjúngeres Per carnis contubérnium.	4. That thou mightest ransom man, whom thou hadst molded long since, and wed us to God by barracking with us in flesh.
5. Quem éditum ex Vírgine Pavéscit omnis ánima: Per quem et nos resúrgere, Devóta mente crédimus.	5. When a Maiden brings thee forth every soul grows fearful: and with devout conviction we believe that by thee we may rise again.
6. Qui nobis per baptísmata Donásti indulgéntiam, Qui tenebámur vínculis Ligáti consciéntiae.	6. Thou who by baptism hast granted pardon to us who were held bound with the shackles of conscience.
7. Qui crucem propter hóminem Suscípere dignátus es: Dedísti tuum sánguinem, Nostrae salútis prétium.	7. Thou who for man's sake vouchsafedst to take up the cross, and gavest thy blood, the cost of our salvation.
8. Nam velum templi scissum est Et omnis terra trémuit. Tu multos dormiéntium Resuscitásti, Dómine.	8. For the temple's veil was torn and all the land quaked; thou, Lord, didst rouse again many of those who slept.

88 88 (LM)

Tune:
VARIOUS

The cadre of Pope Urban VIII "corrected" this hymn with such severity—leaving only one line untouched—that we have provided a literal translation of the corrected version as well, including important information regarding both versions of this hymn; cf. *Rex Sempiterne Caelitum*.

Mr. Arthur Sumner Walpole (d. 1922) wrote: "The first thing that strikes us in this ancient hymn is the number of lines defective in metre." Walpole then notes how curious it is that Bede the Venerable praised this hymn for its excellence. Cf. *Early Latin Hymns* (1922) p. 211.

Assistance for comprehension provided alongside the Latin

9. Tu hostis ántiqui vires
Per crucem mortis cónterens,
Qua nos signáti fróntibus
Vexíllum fídei férimus.

9. Thou crushest the ancient foe's
forces by the death of the cross; marked
with that cross on our foreheads,
we bear the standard of faith.

10. Tu illum a nobis semper
Repéllere dignáveris,
Ne umquam possit laédere
Redémptos tuo sánguine.

10. Do thou vouchsafe always
to drive him away from us,
lest he ever avail to injure
those ransomed with thy blood.

11. Qui propter nos ad ínferos
Descéndere dignátus es,
Ut mortis debitóribus
Vitae donáres múnera.

11. Thou who for our sake
didst vouchsafe to go down to hell,
that thou mightest give life's gifts
to those in debt to death.

12. Tibi noctúrno témpore
Hymnum defléntes cánimus:
Ignósce nobis, Dómine,
Ignósce confiténtibus,

12. To thee at night-time
we sing a hymn, lamenting:
Forgive us, Lord,
forgive us who confess to thee.

13. Quia tu testis et judex es,
Quem nemo potest fállere,
Secréta consciéntiae
Nostrae videns vestígia.

13. Because thou art the witness
and judge whom none can deceive,
who seest the concealed traces
of our conscience.

14. Tu qui nostrórum péctorum
Solus investigátor es,
Tu vúlnerum laténtium
Bonus assístis médicus.

14. Thou art the only
tracer of our hearts,
thou dost attend us,
good physician of hidden wounds.

15. Tu es, qui certo témpore
Datúrus finem saéculi,
Tu pro cunctórum méritis
Justus remunerátor es.

15. Thou art he who at a sure time
will bring an end to the world,
thou art the righteous requiter
of every man's deserts.

16. Te ergo, sancte, quaésumus,
Ut nostra cures vúlnera,
Qui es cum Patre, Fílius,
Semper cum Sancto Spíritu.

16. So, holy one, we beseech thee
to heal our wounds,
O Son, who art always with the Father
and with the Holy Spirit.

17. Glória tibi, Pater,
Glória Unigénito
Una cum Sancto Spíritu
In sempitérna saécula.

17. Glory to thee, O Father,
glory to the Only-begotten,
together with the Holy Spirit,
for everlasting ages.

This ancient hymn has many variants; where possible, we have chosen those which facilitate its singing. Cf. *Liber Responsorialis Pro Festis I. Classis Et Communi Sanctorum* (Solesmes, 1895) p. 82; *Breviarium Monasticum Pauli V. ac Urbani VIII. Summorum Pontificum Auctoritate Recognitum* (Venice, 1770) p. 414.

420 Rex Sempiterne Caelitum (Urbanite)

This hymn speaks of Christ as Creator and Redeemer

To sing in Latin, use any 88 88 (LM) tune.

REX sempitérne Caélitum, *n1*
Rerum Creátor ómnium, *n2*
Aequális ante saécula
Semper Paŕenti Fílius:

2. Nascénte qui mundo Faber
Imáginem vultus tui
Tradens Adámo, nóbilem
Limo jugásti spíritum:

3. Cum livor et fraus daémonis
Foedásset humánum genus,
Tu, carn*e* amíctus, pérditam
Formam refórmas ártifex.

4. Qui natus ol*im* e Vírgine,
Nunc e sepúlcro násceris:
Tecúmque nos a mórtuis
Jubes sepúltos súrgere. *n3*

5. Qui Pastor aetérnus grégem
Aqua lavas baptísmatis:
Haec est lavácrum méntium:
Haec est sepúlcrum críminum.

6. Nobis diu qui débitae
Redémptor affíxus Cruci,
Nostrae dedísti pródigus
Prétium salútis sánguinem. *n4*

T. Source: *Hymni de Tempore et de Sanctis in Textu Antiquo et Novo* (Solesmes, 1885) p. 46.

[1] This hymn in its unaltered form is extremely ancient, being mentioned by such authors as CAESARIUS (d. 543) and AURELIAN (d. 555). The original title "Rex Aeterne Domine" was from a time when *aeterne* would have been pronounced as four syllables. (The 1568 revision has "Rex semipterne Domine.") Pope Urban VIII's Jesuit cadre altered every line of this hymn except one in their 1631 reform, which hymnologists have universally condemned. However, in this instance, Abbé Pimont admits that Urban's team was "never, perhaps, better inspired."

Nothing in the revised version—and certainly nothing in the original—in any way limits this hymn to Eastertide; cf. page 212 of Walpole's *Early Latin Hymns* (London: Cambridge University Press, 1922): "Originally it was written to commemorate the whole redeeming work of Christ; but from the 10th century onwards the first seven stanzas were taken by themselves to form an Easter hymn, for which purpose they are not especially suited."

88 88 (LM)

Tune:
VARIOUS

Assistance for comprehension

EVERLASTING King of the heavenly realms, *n1*
CREATOR of all things, *n2*
Son ever equal to the Father
before the ages:

2. SHAPER who, when the world was born,
conferring the likeness
of thy countenance on Adam, yoked
a noble spirit to clay:

3. When the envy and guile of the devil
had corrupted mankind,
thou, CRAFTSMAN, clothed with flesh,
formest the lost form again.

4. Thou who wast once born of the Virgin,
art now born of the tomb:
and biddest us, entombed,
to rise from the dead with thee. *n3*

5. Thou who art an eternal SHEPHERD
washest the flock with the water of baptism:
this is the bath of thoughts:
this is the tomb of misdeeds.

6. Thou who art the REDEEMER,
nailed to a Cross long due to ourselves,
lavishly gavest thy blood
as the cost of our salvation. *n4*

[2] The word "Christ," which comes via Latin from Greek, is equivalent to the Hebrew MESSIAH, "Anointed," and thus the title of the promised Son of David, Savior of the Jews. The New Testament reveals Christ as Savior not only of the Jews, but of the whole world (Jn 4.42, I Jn 4.14). The bearer of this title, Jesus the Son of Mary, (Mk 6.3, cf. Mt 13.55) is not just a mere man, but rather the God-man, whose humanity is personally joined to his divinity. This "hypostatic union" permits the "sharing of the properties" (*communicatio idiomata*) that belong to either nature with the other. Thus one may call Christ the CREATOR as well as the Son of Mary (and, by extension, one may call Christ's Mother the Mother of God).

CHRIST AS CREATOR: The breviary hymns constantly mention Christ as Creator—Cf. *Auctor Beate Saeculi* (v. 1); *Jesu Redemptor Omnium* (v. 3); *Creator Alme Siderum* (v. 1); *Jesu Nostra Redemptio* (v. 1); *Vexilla Regis Prodeunt*: "Quo carne carnis Conditor"; *Corde Natus Ex Parentis*: "Ipse jussit et creata, dixit ipse et facta sunt, etc."; *Pange Lingua* translation (Roman Catholic Primer of 1706) : "How Christ…left mankind the blood that paid the ransom for the souls he made"; *A Solis Ortus Cardine* (v. 2).

[3] "In our baptism, we have been buried with him, died like him, so that—just as Christ was raised up by his Father's power from the dead—we too might live and move in a new kind of existence." (Rom 6.4)

[4] The following verse— taken verbatim from *Ad Cenam Agni*—was added in the 1631 Breviary revisions:

Urbanite revision: *Ut sis perénne méntibus | Paschále, Jesu, gáudium, | A morte dira críminum | Vitae renátos líbera.*
Original version: *Quaésumus, Auctor ómnium, | In hoc Pascháli gáudio, | Ab omni mortis ímpetu | Tuum defénde pópulum.*

422 Rex Sempiterne Domine (5th century)

First Tune – *Trns: Fr. John Fitzpatrick, Oblate of Mary (d. 1929)*

4. Now born again from out the tomb,
As once, from Mary's virgin womb,
Thou biddest us ourselves bestir
And quit with Thee the sepulchre.

5. Eternal Shepherd, who dost purge
The flock in Thy baptismal surge:
This is the bath from which arise
Pure thoughts, and where sin buried lies.

6. Redeemer, on the Cross upraised,
Long owing to ourselves, be praised
That there Thy Blood salvation's price
Paid lavishly in sacrifice.

7. May endless worlds the glories tell
Of Christ, who vanquished death and hell;
And one eternal praise repeat
The Father and the Paraclete.

88 88 (LM)

Tune: Alfreton

M. Source: *A Supplement to a New Version of the Psalms of David* (1708).
T. Source: *The Breviary and Missal Hymns* (London: Sands & Co, 1931) p. 74.

Rex Sempiterne Domine (5th century) 423

Second Tune – *Trns: Fr. John Fitzpatrick, Oblate of Mary (d. 1929)*

4. Now born again from out the tomb,
As once, from Mary's virgin womb,
Thou biddest us ourselves bestir
And quit with Thee the sepulchre.
Alleluia.

5. Eternal Shepherd, who dost purge
The flock in Thy baptismal surge:
This is the bath from which arise
Pure thoughts, and where sin buried lies.
Alleluia.

6. Redeemer, on the Cross upraised,
Long owing to ourselves, be praised
That there Thy Blood salvation's price
Paid lavishly in sacrifice.
Alleluia.

7. May endless worlds the glories tell
Of Christ, who vanquished death and hell;
And one eternal praise repeat
The Father and the Paraclete.
Alleluia.

Melody: Nikolaus Hermann (d. 1561), organist at Joachimsthal, Bohemia.
M. Source: *Hymns Ancient and Modern* (1972) p. 832; cf. "Erschienen ist der herrlich Tag" in *The Four-Part Chorals of J. S. Bach with the German Text of the Hymns and English Translations* (Charles Sanford Terry, 1964) p. 87.
T. Source: *The Breviary and Missal Hymns* (London: Sands & Co, 1931) p. 74.

88 88 A
Tune:
Erschienen Ist

424 Rex Sempiterne Domine (5th century)

THIRD TUNE – *Trns: Fr. John Fitzpatrick, Oblate of Mary (d. 1929)*

4. Now born again from out the tomb,
As once, from Mary's virgin womb,
Thou biddest us ourselves bestir
And quit with Thee the sepulchre.

5. Eternal Shepherd, who dost purge
The flock in Thy baptismal surge:
This is the bath from which arise
Pure thoughts, and where sin buried lies.

6. Redeemer, on the Cross upraised,
Long owing to ourselves, be praised
That there Thy Blood salvation's price
Paid lavishly in sacrifice.

7. May endless worlds the glories tell
Of Christ, who vanquished death and hell;
And one eternal praise repeat
The Father and the Paraclete.

88 88 (LM)

Tune:
GRÉLON

T. Source: *The Breviary and Missal Hymns* (London: Sands & Co, 1931) p. 74.
M. Source: Based on a melody by Dom Andrew G. Murray, OSB (d. 1992), a student of Sir Richard Runciman Terry (d. 1938). Cf. *New Westminster Hymnal* (1939) p. 125.

Rex Sempiterne Domine (5th century) 425

Fourth Tune – *Trns: Fr. John Fitzpatrick, Oblate of Mary (d. 1929)*

4. Now born again from out the tomb,
As once, from Mary's virgin womb,
Thou biddest us ourselves bestir
And quit with Thee the sepulchre.

5. Eternal Shepherd, who dost purge
The flock in Thy baptismal surge:
This is the bath from which arise
Pure thoughts, and where sin buried lies.

6. Redeemer, on the Cross upraised,
Long owing to ourselves, be praised
That there Thy Blood salvation's price
Paid lavishly in sacrifice.

7. May endless worlds the glories tell
Of Christ, who vanquished death and hell;
And one eternal praise repeat
The Father and the Paraclete.

Final Verses: Richard Lloyd (1993) #53; Noel Rawsthorne (2011) #93.
T. Source: *The Breviary and Missal Hymns* (London: Sands & Co, 1931) p. 74.
Melody: Grenoble Antiphonale (1753).
M. Source: *Catholic Hymn Book* (London Oratory, 1998) p. 238;
New Saint Basil Hymnal (1958) p. 59.

88 88 (LM)

Tune:
Deus Tuorum Militum

426 Rex Sempiterne Domine (5th century)

Fifth Tune – *Trns: Fr. John Fitzpatrick, Oblate of Mary (d. 1929)*

4. Now born again from out the tomb,
   As once, from Mary's virgin womb,
   Thou biddest us ourselves bestir
   And quit with Thee the sepulchre.

5. Eternal Shepherd, who dost purge
   The flock in Thy baptismal surge:
   This is the bath from which arise
   Pure thoughts, and where sin buried lies.

6. Redeemer, on the Cross upraised,
   Long owing to ourselves, be praised
   That there Thy Blood salvation's price
   Paid lavishly in sacrifice.

7. May endless worlds the glories tell
   Of Christ, who vanquished death and hell;
   And one eternal praise repeat
   The Father and the Paraclete.

88 88 (LM)

Tune:
Kempen

Melody: Flor Peeters (d. 1986), organist at the Catholic Cathedral of Mechelen, Belgium, was made a Baron by King Baudouin.
M. Source: *People's Mass Book* (Omer Westendorf, 1964) p. 218.
T. Source: *The Breviary and Missal Hymns* (London: Sands & Co, 1931) p. 74.

Rex Sempiterne Domine (5th century)

Sixth Tune – *Trns: Fr. John Fitzpatrick, Oblate of Mary (d. 1929)*

4. Now born again from out the tomb,
As once, from Mary's virgin womb,
Thou biddest us ourselves bestir
And quit with Thee the sepulchre.

5. Eternal Shepherd, who dost purge
The flock in Thy baptismal surge:
This is the bath from which arise
Pure thoughts, and where sin buried lies.

6. Redeemer, on the Cross upraised,
Long owing to ourselves, be praised
That there Thy Blood salvation's price
Paid lavishly in sacrifice.

7. May endless worlds the glories tell
Of Christ, who vanquished death and hell;
And one eternal praise repeat
The Father and the Paraclete.

T. Source: *The Breviary and Missal Hymns* (London: Sands & Co, 1931) p. 74.
Melody: Geoffrey Charles Edward Ryley (d. 1947); this tune can be sung as a Soprano-Tenor canon.
M. Source: *Hymns Ancient and Modern* (1972) p. 324.

88 88 (LM)

Tune: Canon VIII

428 Rex Sempiterne Domine (5th century)

Seventh Tune – *Trns: Fr. John Fitzpatrick, Oblate of Mary (d. 1929)*

4. Now born again from out the tomb,
As once, from Mary's virgin womb,
Thou biddest us ourselves bestir
And quit with Thee the sepulchre.

5. Eternal Shepherd, who dost purge
The flock in Thy baptismal surge:
This is the bath from which arise
Pure thoughts, and where sin buried lies.

6. Redeemer, on the Cross upraised,
Long owing to ourselves, be praised
That there Thy Blood salvation's price
Paid lavishly in sacrifice.

7. May endless worlds the glories tell
Of Christ, who vanquished death and hell;
And one eternal praise repeat
The Father and the Paraclete.

88 88 (LM)

Tune:
Gonfalon Royal

Final Verses: Richard Lloyd (1993) #80; Noel Rawsthorne (2011) #136.
T. Source: *The Breviary and Missal Hymns* (London: Sands & Co, 1931) p. 74.
Melody: Sir Percy Carter Buck (d. 1947); first published in *Fourteen Hymn Tunes* (1913).
M. Source: *Catholic Hymn Book* (London Oratory, 1998) p. 140. The tune was originally paired with *Vexilla Regis* ("Flag of the King"). A *gonfalon* ("flag") was traditionally carried during Catholic processions.

Rex Sempiterne Domine (5th century)

Trns: Fr. John Fitzpatrick, Oblate of Mary (d. 1929)

Can be sung with any 88 88 meter, such as EISENACH, ROGERS PARK, BRESSANI, LA ROCHELLE, KEMPEN, BESSEMER, TALLIS CANON, WINCHESTER NEW, etc.

TO Thee, O everlasting King,
And Maker of the worlds, we sing,
Who, with the Father ever one,
Wert ever His co-equal Son.

2. Creator who, when earth began,
To Thine own image madest man,
Thou didst, in Adam, wed to clay
A spirit noble ev'ry way.

3. And when, with envy many-wiled,
The devil had our race defiled,
Made Man, man's likeness unto Thee
Thou didst restore with mastery.

4. Now born again from out the tomb,
As once, from Mary's virgin womb,
Thou biddest us ourselves bestir
And quit with Thee the sepulchre.

5. Eternal Shepherd, who dost purge
The flock in Thy baptismal surge:
This is the bath from which arise
Pure thoughts, and where sin buried lies.

6. Redeemer, on the Cross upraised,
Long owing to ourselves, be praised
That there Thy Blood salvation's price
Paid lavishly in sacrifice.

7. May endless worlds the glories tell
Of Christ, who vanquished death and hell;
And one eternal praise repeat
The Father and the Paraclete.

88 88 (LM)

Tune: VARIOUS

T. Source: *The Breviary and Missal Hymns* (London: Sands & Co, 1931) p. 74.

430 Rex Sempiterne Domine (5th century)

First Tune – *Trns: Bishop Edward G. Bagshawe (d. 1915)*

4. Thou, who wast once of Virgin born,
Now from the tomb art born again,
And our poor dead and buried race,
To bid to rise with Thee dost deign.

5. Eternal Shepherd, thou thy sheep
Dost in baptismal waters dye;
Here let our hearts their nature steep,
Here let our vices buried lie.

6. Thou—though to us the Cross was due—
Wast nailed upon its sacred wood,
And for salvation's price didst give,
Unsparingly Thy Precious Blood.

7. Be God the Father glorified,
And He who rose, from death, His Son,
And Thou, the Holy Paraclete,
While everlasting ages run.

88 88 (LM)

Tune:
Melcombe

Final Verses: Richard Lloyd (1993) #133; Noel Rawsthorne (2011) #205.
Melody: Samuel Webbe, the elder (d. 1816).
M. Source: *Veritas Hymnal* (Dublin: Irish Church Music Association, 1974) p. 96; *Cantate Omnes: Hymnal of the Catholic Choirmasters' Guild* (1952) #78.
T. Source: *Breviary Hymns and Missal Sequences* (London: Burns & Oates, 1900) p. 78; Father Bagshawe was a priest of the Oratory of St. Philip Neri until 1874, when he was consecrated bishop of the Catholic diocese of Nottingham.

Second Tune – *Trns: Bishop Edward G. Bagshawe (d. 1915)*

1. E - ter - nal King of Heav - en's hosts,
2. Thou gav - est when the earth was new,
3. And, when man's race had been de - filed,

Who didst the U - ni - verse cre - ate,
To Ad - am's race Thine im - age bright;
By Sa - tan's en - vious fraud and hate,

Who ev - er e - qual art with Him,
His bas - er clay Thou didst en - due
Thou didst as - sume man's flesh, and man

From whom Thou dost o - rig - i - nate:
With spir - it breath - ing love and light.
In his lost beau - ty re - in - state.

4. Thou, who wast once of Virgin born,
Now from the tomb art born again,
And our poor dead and buried race,
To bid to rise with Thee dost deign.

5. Eternal Shepherd, thou thy sheep
Dost in baptismal waters dye;
Here let our hearts their nature steep,
Here let our vices buried lie.

6. Thou—though to us the Cross was due—
Wast nailed upon its sacred wood,
And for salvation's price didst give,
Unsparingly Thy Precious Blood.

7. Be God the Father glorified,
And He who rose, from death, His Son,
And Thou, the Holy Paraclete,
While everlasting ages run.

Melody: Dieudonné Duguet (d. 1849), organist at the Catholic Cathedral in Liège, Belgium, and teacher of César Franck.
M. Source: *Mediator Dei Hymnal* (1955) p. 66; *New Saint Basil Hymnal* (1958) p. 93; *Arundel Catholic Hymnal* (1905) p. 26; *Hymnal and Vesperal* (Archdiocese of Baltimore, 1878) p. 168; *Catholic Vesper Hymn Book set to Music for Unison or Four Voices* (Charles Lewis, 1877) p. 6.
T. Source: *Breviary Hymns and Missal Sequences* (London: Burns & Oates, 1900) p. 78;
Father Bagshawe was a priest of the Oratory of St. Philip Neri until 1874, when he was consecrated bishop of the Catholic diocese of Nottingham.

88 88 (LM)

Tune:
Duguet

432 Rex Sempiterne Domine (5th century)

THIRD TUNE – *Trns: Bishop Edward G. Bagshawe (d. 1915)*

4. Thou, who wast once of Virgin born,
Now from the tomb art born again,
And our poor dead and buried race,
To bid to rise with Thee dost deign.

5. Eternal Shepherd, thou thy sheep
Dost in baptismal waters dye;
Here let our hearts their nature steep,
Here let our vices buried lie.

6. Thou—though to us the Cross was due—
Wast nailed upon its sacred wood,
And for salvation's price didst give,
Unsparingly Thy Precious Blood.

7. Be God the Father glorified,
And He who rose, from death, His Son,
And Thou, the Holy Paraclete,
While everlasting ages run.

* This melody at a lower key is on page 864.

88 88 (LM)

Tune:
BRESSANI

Melody: From a hymn book published by Fr. Melchior Ludolf Herold (d. 1810).
M. Source: *New Westminster Hymnal* (1939) p. 173.
T. Source: *Breviary Hymns and Missal Sequences* (London: Burns & Oates, 1900) p. 78; Father Bagshawe was a priest of the Oratory of St. Philip Neri until 1874, when he was consecrated bishop of the Catholic diocese of Nottingham.

Rex Sempiterne Domine (5th century) 433

Fourth Tune – *Trns: Bishop Edward G. Bagshawe (d. 1915)*

4. Thou, who wast once of Virgin born,
Now from the tomb art born again,
And our poor dead and buried race,
To bid to rise with Thee dost deign.

5. Eternal Shepherd, thou thy sheep
Dost in baptismal waters dye;
Here let our hearts their nature steep,
Here let our vices buried lie.

6. Thou—though to us the Cross was due—
Wast nailed upon its sacred wood,
And for salvation's price didst give,
Unsparingly Thy Precious Blood.

7. Be God the Father glorified,
And He who rose, from death, His Son,
And Thou, the Holy Paraclete,
While everlasting ages run.

Melody: Philip Hart (d. 1749), organist at St. Michael Church, Cornhill.
M. Source: *Hymns Ancient and Modern* (1972) p. 8; cf. *Church Hymns With Tunes* (1885) p. 230, edited by Sir Arthur Sullivan (d. 1900), organist at St. Peter Church, Kensington.
T. Source: *Breviary Hymns and Missal Sequences* (London: Burns & Oates, 1900) p. 78; Father Bagshawe was a priest of the Oratory of St. Philip Neri until 1874, when he was consecrated bishop of the Catholic diocese of Nottingham.

88 88 (LM)

Tune: Hilderstone

434 Rex Sempiterne Domine (5th century)

Fifth Tune – *Trns: Bishop Edward G. Bagshawe (d. 1915)*

4. Thou, who wast once of Virgin born,
Now from the tomb art born again,
And our poor dead and buried race,
To bid to rise with Thee dost deign.

5. Eternal Shepherd, thou thy sheep
Dost in baptismal waters dye;
Here let our hearts their nature steep,
Here let our vices buried lie.

6. Thou—though to us the Cross was due—
Wast nailed upon its sacred wood,
And for salvation's price didst give,
Unsparingly Thy Precious Blood.

7. Be God the Father glorified,
And He who rose, from death, His Son,
And Thou, the Holy Paraclete,
While everlasting ages run.

88 88 (LM)

Tune:
Notre Dame

Melody: Traditional French air, sometimes sung with "O amor quam exstaticus."
M. Source: cf. *New Saint Basil Hymnal* (1958) p. 184; cf. *New Westminster Hymnal* (1939) p. 238.
T. Source: *Breviary Hymns and Missal Sequences* (London: Burns & Oates, 1900) p. 78;
Father Bagshawe was a priest of the Oratory of St. Philip Neri until 1874, when he was consecrated bishop of the Catholic diocese of Nottingham.

Rex Sempiterne Domine (5th century) 435

Sixth Tune – *Trns: Bishop Edward G. Bagshawe (d. 1915)*

4. Thou, who wast once of Virgin born,
Now from the tomb art born again,
And our poor dead and buried race,
To bid to rise with Thee dost deign.

5. Eternal Shepherd, thou thy sheep
Dost in baptismal waters dye;
Here let our hearts their nature steep,
Here let our vices buried lie.

6. Thou—though to us the Cross was due—
Wast nailed upon its sacred wood,
And for salvation's price didst give,
Unsparingly Thy Precious Blood.

7. Be God the Father glorified,
And He who rose, from death, His Son,
And Thou, the Holy Paraclete,
While everlasting ages run.

Final Verses: Richard Lloyd (1993) #64; Noel Rawsthorne (2011) #108.
Melody: Bartholomäus Gesius (d. 1613); adapted by Johann H. Schein (d. 1630)
M. Source: *New Saint Basil Hymnal* (1958) p. 120; *The Catholic Vesper Hymn Book set to Music either for Unison or Four Voices with Accompaniment* (Charles Lewis, 1877) p. 34; *Pope Pius XII Hymnal* (Ohio: Gregorian Institute of America, 1959) p. 13.
T. Source: *Breviary Hymns and Missal Sequences* (London: Burns & Oates, 1900) p. 78; Father Bagshawe was a priest of the Oratory of St. Philip Neri until 1874, when he was consecrated bishop of the Catholic diocese of Nottingham.

88 88 (LM)

Tune: Eisenach

436 Rex Sempiterne Domine (5th century)

Seventh Tune – *Trns: Bishop Edward G. Bagshawe (d. 1915)*

4. Thou, who wast once of Virgin born,
Now from the tomb art born again,
And our poor dead and buried race,
To bid to rise with Thee dost deign.

5. Eternal Shepherd, thou thy sheep
Dost in baptismal waters dye;
Here let our hearts their nature steep,
Here let our vices buried lie.

6. Thou—though to us the Cross was due—
Wast nailed upon its sacred wood,
And for salvation's price didst give,
Unsparingly Thy Precious Blood.

7. Be God the Father glorified,
And He who rose, from death, His Son,
And Thou, the Holy Paraclete,
While everlasting ages run.

88 88 (LM)

Tune:
Trinity College

Melody: John Bacchus Dykes (d. 1876).
M. Source: *Hymns Ancient and Modern* (1972) p. 64.
T. Source: *Breviary Hymns and Missal Sequences* (London: Burns & Oates, 1900) p. 78; Father Bagshawe was a priest of the Oratory of St. Philip Neri until 1874, when he was consecrated bishop of the Catholic diocese of Nottingham.

Trns: Bishop Edward G. Bagshawe (d. 1915)

Can be sung with any 88 88 meter, such as HILDERSTONE, DUGUET, BRESLAU, MELCOMBE, WAREHAM, OLD HUNDREDTH, MEIN SEEL, TRINITY COLLEGE, etc.

ETERNAL King of Heaven's hosts,
Who didst the Universe create,
Who ever equal art with Him,
From whom Thou dost originate:

2. Thou gavest when the earth was new,
To Adam's race Thine image bright;
His baser clay Thou didst endue
With spirit breathing love and light.

3. And, when man's race had been defiled,
By Satan's envious fraud and hate,
Thou didst assume man's flesh, and man
In his lost beauty reinstate.

4. Thou, who wast once of Virgin born,
Now from the tomb art born again,
And our poor dead and buried race,
To bid to rise with Thee dost deign.

5. Eternal Shepherd, thou thy sheep
Dost in baptismal waters dye;
Here let our hearts their nature steep,
Here let our vices buried lie.

6. Thou—though to us the Cross was due—
Wast nailed upon its sacred wood,
And for salvation's price didst give,
Unsparingly Thy Precious Blood.

7. Be God the Father glorified,
And He who rose, from death, His Son,
And Thou, the Holy Paraclete,
While everlasting ages run.

T. Source: *Breviary Hymns and Missal Sequences* (London: Burns & Oates, 1900) p. 78; Father Bagshawe was a priest of the Oratory of St. Philip Neri until 1874, when he was consecrated bishop of the Catholic diocese of Nottingham.

88 88 (LM)

Tune: VARIOUS

438 Salve Caput Cruentatum (The Holy Face)

attr. St. Bernard of Clairvaux (d. 1153)

SALVE, caput cruentátum,
totum spinis coronátum,
conquassátum, vulnerátum,
harúndine verberátum,
fácie sputis íllita.

2. Salve, cujus dulcis vultus,
immutátus et incúltus,
immutávit suum florem,
totus versus in pallórem,
quem tremit caeli cúria.

3. Omnis vigor atque viror
hinc recéssit, non admíror:
mors appáret in aspéctu,
totus pendens in deféctu,
attrítus aegra mácie.

4. Sic affέctus, sic despéctus,
propter me sic interféctus:
peccatóri tam indígno
cum amóris intersígno
appáre clara fácie.

5. In hac tua passióne,
me agnósce, pastor bone,
cujus sumpsi mel ex ore,
haustum lactis cum dulcóre,
prae ómnibus delíciis.

6. Non me reum aspernéris,
nec indígnum dedignéris:
morte tibi jam vicína,
tuum caput hic inclína,
in meis pausa bráchiis.

7. Tuae sanctae passióni
me gaudérem interpóni,
in hac cruce tecum mori:
praesta crucis amatóri
sub cruce tua móriar.

HAIL, O bloodstained head,
entirely crowned with thorns,
shaken, wounded,
struck with a reed,
with a face smeared with spittle.

2. Hail, thou whose sweet look,
altered and ungroomed,
has altered its beauty,
entirely turned to paleness,
at which the court of heaven trembles.

3. All liveliness and freshness have withdrawn
from there, and I am not astonished:
death appears in thy countenance,
entirely drooping with weakness,
worn away with sick leanness.

4. Thus impaired, thus disdained,
for me thus killed:
to a sinner so unworthy
with a token of love
appear with a bright face.

5. In this thy passion,
recognize me, O good shepherd,
from whose mouth I have received honey,
a draft of milk with sweetness,
beyond every delicacy.

6. Mayest thou not reject me as guilty,
nor refuse me as unworthy:
with death already near thee,
bow thy head here,
rest in my arms.

7. I should rejoice were I introduced
to thy holy passion,
to die with thee on this cross:
grant to a lover of the cross
that I may die beneath thy cross.

88 88 8

Tune:
VARIOUS

[2c] "Florem" literally means "flower" and denotes utter purity.

T. Source: *Deutsches Lesebuch: Proben der deutschen Poesie seit dem XVI Jahrhundert* (Schweighauserische Verlagsbuchhandlung, 1836) p. 1581; *Latin Hymns with English Notes* (New York: Harper Brothers, 1874) p. 116.

Assistance for comprehension provided alongside the Latin

8. Morti tuae tam amárae grates ago, Jesu care: qui es clemens, pie Deus, fac quod petit tuus reus, ut absque te non fíniar.	8. For thy death so bitter I thank thee, dear Jesus: thou who art God, gracious and tender, accomplish that which thy guilty one seeks, that I may not end without thee.
9. Dum me mori est necésse, noli mihi tunc deésse: in treménda mortis hora veni, Jesu, absque mora, tuére me et líbera.	9. When it is needful that I should die, then do not be lacking from me: at the dread hour of death come, O Jesus, without delay, protect and free me.
10. Cum me jubes emigráre, Jesu care, tunc appáre: o amátor amplecténde, temetípsum tunc osténde in cruce salutífera.	10. When thou commandest me to depart, dear Jesus, appear then: O loving one to be embraced, then show thyself with the salvation-bearing cross.

SALVE CAPUT CRUENTATUM is the concluding section of a much longer work (*Salve Mundi Salutare*) attributed to St. Bernard of Clairvaux (d. 1153). Catholics know it as "O Sacred Head Surrounded," an English translation by Sir Henry W. Baker (d. 1877). In addition to Baker's, we have included translations by Msgr. Ronald Knox and Fr. Dominic Popplewell. The latter is noteworthy in that it matches the original meter, while Knox and Baker do not.

Baker's famous rendering is rather free, but does correspond to the original:

Verse 1 ("O Sacred Head") conveys vv. 1-2, whose final words rhyme (*íllita, cúria*).
Verse 2 ("I see Thy strength") conveys vv. 3-4, whose final words rhyme (*mácie, fácie*).
Verse 3 ("In this Thy bitter Passion") conveys vv. 5-6, whose final words rhyme (*delíciis, bráchiis*).

Protestant hymnals favor translations of "O Haupt voll Blut und Wunden," a German version of *Salve Caput Cruentatum* by Lutheran minister Paul Gerhardt (d. 1676). Catholic hymnals, on the other hand, favor Baker's version—which translates the original Latin—and this hymn is almost never omitted, as demonstrated by a few examples:

Hosanna Catholic Hymn Book (Fr. Bonvin, 1914) p. 58
Parochial Hymnal (Fr. Rossini 1936) p. 23
Mount Mary Hymnal (Sister Gisela, 1937) p. 39
Daily Hymn Book (Society of St. John the Evangelist, 1948) p. 72
Cantate Omnes (Catholic Choirmasters' Guild, 1952) #33
Catholic Hymns (Fr. Selner, 1954) p. 65
Mediator Dei Hymnal (1955) p. 26
Christ the King Hymnal (Fr. Knauff, 1955) p. 42
Parish Hymnal (Sisters of St. Joseph, 1957) p. 9
New Saint Basil Hymnal (1958) p. 41
Hymns, Psalms, and Spiritual Canticles (Dr. Marier, 1983) p. 364
Catholic Hymn Book (London Oratory, 1998) p. 106

440 Salve Caput Cruentatum (The Holy Face)

Trns: Msgr. Ronald A. Knox (d. 1957)

4. In this thy sacred Passion
O that some share had I!
O may thy Cross's fashion
O'erlook me when I die!
For these dear pains that rack thee
A sinner's thanks receive;
O, lest in death I lack thee,
A sinner's care relieve.

5. Since death must be my ending,
In that dread hour of need,
My friendless cause befriending,
Lord, to my rescue speed;
Thyself, dear Jesus, trace me
That passage to the grave,
And from thy Cross embrace me
With arms outstretched to save.

76 76 D

Tune:
Passion Chorale

Final Verses: Noel Rawsthorne (2011) #252.
Text: *attr.* St. Bernard of Clairvaux (d. 1153).
T. Source: *New Westminster Hymnal* (1939) p. 57.
English Translation: Msgr. Ronald A. Knox (d. 1957); due to the considerable involvement Knox had in the creation of the *New Westminster Hymnal*, it can be assumed that he preferred this melody for his text.
Melody: Hans Leo Hassler (d. 1612), a student of Andrea Gabrieli (d. 1585).
M. Source: *Accompaniment to the Music of Holy Week* (Lapierre, 1957) p. 82; *Pius XII Hymnal* (1959) p. 19.

Salve Caput Cruentatum (The Holy Face) 441

Trns: Sir Henry Williams Baker (d. 1877)

1. O Sa - cred Head, sur - round - ed By crown of pierc - ing thorn,
2. I see Thy strength and vig - or All fad - ing in_ the strife,
3. In this Thy bit - ter Pas - sion, Good Shep-herd, think of me

O Bleed - ing Head, so wound - ed, Re - viled, and put_ to scorn,
And Death, with cru - el ri - gor, Be - reav - ing Thee of life;
With Thy most sweet com - pas - sion, Un - wor - thy though I be:

Death's pal - lid hue comes o'er Thee, The glow of life de - cays,
O ag - o - ny of dy - ing, O love to sin - ners free;
Be - neath Thy Cross a - bid - ing For - ev - er would I rest,

Yet An - gel hosts a - dore Thee, And trem - ble as they gaze.
Je - sus,_ all grace sup - ply - ing, O turn Thy Face on me.
In Thy_ dear love con - fid - ing, And with Thy Pres - ence blest.

4. O Jesus, I adore Thee,
My thorn-crowned Lord and King;
I bow my heart before Thee,
Thy gracious Name I sing:
Thy Name that brought salvation,
Thy Name, in life my stay,
My hope and consolation
When life shall fade away.

Final Verses: Noel Rawsthorne (2011) #252.
Text: *attr.* St. Bernard of Clairvaux (d. 1153).
T. Source: *Cantate Omnes: Hymnal of the Catholic Choirmasters' Guild* (1952) #33.
English Translation: Sir Henry Williams Baker (d. 1877), who was the driving force behind *Hymns Ancient and Modern*, which appeared in 1861. Baker was not Catholic, but was sympathetic to Catholic theology. He came under attack from Protestants because of his inclusion of hymns honoring Our Lady and the Sanctissimum. The fourth verse, not by Baker, is only loosely based on *Salve Caput Cruentatum*.
Melody: Hans Leo Hassler (d. 1612), a student of Andrea Gabrieli (d. 1585).
M. Source: *Accompaniment to the Music of Holy Week* (Lapierre, 1957) p. 82; *Pius XII Hymnal* (1959) p. 19.

76 76 D

Tune:
Passion Chorale

442 Salve Caput Cruentatum (The Holy Face)

Textus originalis Latinus

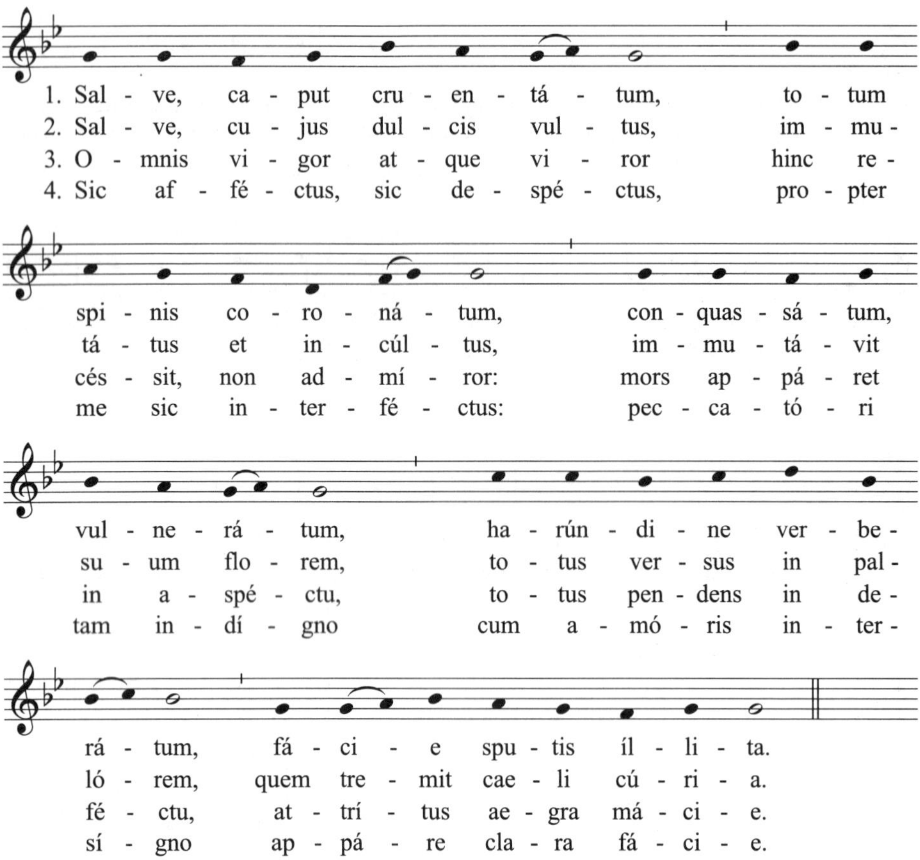

5. In hac tua passióne,
me agnósce, pastor bone,
cujus sumpsi mel ex ore,
haustum lactis cum dulcóre,
prae ómnibus delíciis.

6. Non me reum aspernéris,
nec indígnum dedignéris:
morte tibi jam vicína,
tuum caput hic inclína,
in meis pausa bráchiis.

7. Tuae sanctae passióni
me gaudérem interpóni,
in hac cruce tecum mori:
praesta crucis amatóri
sub cruce tua móriar.

8. Morti tuae tam amárae
grates ago, Jesu care:
qui es clemens, pie Deus,
fac quod petit tuus reus,
ut absque te non fíniar.

9. Dum me mori est necésse,
noli mihi tunc deésse:
in treménda mortis hora
veni, Jesu, absque mora,
tuére me et líbera.

10. Cum me jubes emigráre,
Jesu care, tunc appáre:
o amátor amplecténde,
temetípsum tunc osténde
in cruce salutífera.

88 88 8

Tune:
SILLERY

Text: *attr.* St. Bernard of Clairvaux (d. 1153).
Melody: Peter Lejeune (b. 1991), organist at Saint John Vianney Catholic Church in Springfield.
M. Source: *Saint Jean de Brébeuf Hymnal* (2018).

Salve Caput Cruentatum (The Holy Face) 443

Trns: Fr. Dominic Popplewell (b. 1973)

1. Hail, O head whose gore pours down thee, bear - ing
2. Hail, whose face, ere cheer be - stow - ing, strange now
3. All the bloom and fresh - ness yon - der has re -
4. Thus as - sailed, thus cheap - ly rat - ed, thus for

thorns that ful - ly crown thee, buf - fet - ed, which
and un - kempt is grow - ing, now its flour - ish -
moved, nor do I won - der: for that mien is
me to slaugh - ter freight - ed: to this sin - ner

wounds have bit - ten, hav - ing with a reed been
ing es - trang - ing, all there - in to wan - ness
death un - veil - ing, droop - ing full where it is
ill com - mend - ed, proof of love with - al ex -

smit - ten, be - grimed whose vis - age spit - tle makes.
chang - ing, at which the court of heav - en quakes.
fail - ing, by sick - ly wast - ing worn a - way.
tend - ed, thy vis - age bright, thy - self dis - play.

5. While thy passion occupies thee,
pray, good shepherd, recognize me,
honey from thy mouth once taking,
drawing milk, with sweetness slaking
that delicacies all surpassed.

6. Nor to spurn a culprit stir thee,
nor to scorn me, though unworthy:
death already nigh thee winging,
bow thy head, it hither bringing,
in mine arms rest before the last.

7. In thy holy passion planted
were I, this were joy me granted,
on yon cross with thee expiring:
suffer me, the cross desiring,
beneath thy cross from life to wend.

8. Jesu dear, whose death would bite thee
so, with thanks do I requite thee:
gracious God who art and tender,
what thy culprit craves me render,
without thee lest I come to end.

9. Dying, when it is my burden,
lack of thee be not my guerdon:
at the hour of death dismaying,
Jesu, come without delaying,
yea, watch thou me and save from loss.

10. Jesu dear, when thou hast bidden
me depart, remain not hidden,
loving one, how worth embracing,
then thyself before me placing,
arrayed upon the healing cross.

88 88 8

Text: *attr.* St. Bernard of Clairvaux (d. 1153). T. Source: *Saint Jean de Brébeuf Hymnal* (2018).
Melody: Peter Lejeune (b. 1991), organist at Saint John Vianney Catholic Church in Springfield.
M. Source: *Saint Jean de Brébeuf Hymnal* (2018).

Tune: SILLERY

444 Sancti Venite, Christi Corpus Sumite (640AD)

The oldest known Latin Eucharistic Hymn

SANCTI veníte,
Christi corpus súmite,
sanctum bibéntes,
quo redémpti sánguinem.

2. Salváti Christi
córpore et sánguine,
a quo reffécti
laudes dicámus Deo.

E. *Hoc sacraménto
córporis et sánguinis
omnes exúti
ab inférni fáucibus.* n1

3. Dator salútis,
Christus Fílius Dei,
mundum salvávit
per crucem et sánguinem.

4. Pro univérsis
immolátus Dóminus
ipse sacérdos
exístit et hóstia.

5. Lege praecéptum
immolári hóstias,
qua adumbrántur
divína mystéria. n2

6. Lucis indúltor
et salvátor ómnium
praecláram sanctis
largítus est grátiam.

YE HOLY, come,
take the body of Christ,
drinking the holy blood
by which you were ransomed.

2. Saved through the body
and blood of Christ,
refreshed by him,
let us sing praises to God.

E. *Through this sacrament
of his body and blood
all of us have been snatched
from the jaws of hell.* n1

3. The giver of salvation,
Christ the Son of God,
saved the world
by his cross and blood.

4. The Lord, offered
in sacrifice for all,
himself became
their priest and victim.

5. For victims to be sacrificed
is a command in the Law,
through which are foreshadowed
the divine mysteries. n2

6. The bestower of light
and Savior of all
has lavished resplendent grace
on his holy ones.

57 57

Tune:
VARIOUS

T. Source: *Bangor Antiphonale*, which was composed at Bangor Abbey, an Irish monastery founded in 552AD.

Assistance for comprehension provided alongside the Latin

7. Accédant omnes pura mente créduli, sumant aetérnam salútis custódiam.	7. Let all believers whose thought is clean draw nigh; let them take the everlasting safeguard of salvation.
8. Sanctórum custos, rector quoque Dóminus vitam perénnem largítur credéntibus.	8. The Lord, the guardian and governor of the holy, lavishes life unending on those who believe.
9. Caeléstem panem dat esuriéntibus; de fonte vivo praebet sitiéntibus.	9. Heavenly bread he gives to the hungry; from a living spring he provides for the thirsty.
10. Alph*a* et Ómega ipse Christus Dóminus venit ventúrus judicáre hómines.	10. The Alpha and Omega, *cf. Ap 1.8* even Christ the Lord, comes: he who is to come to judge men.

To sing in Latin,
use any 57 57 tune.

[1] Some sources omit this "extra" verse.

[2] The sacrifices of the Old Covenant prefigure the sacrament of the Eucharist, which is the sacrifice of Christ and his Church; the blessed Sacrament was anciently called "the Mysteries" (cf. the acts of St. Tarcisius).

446 Sancti Venite, Christi Corpus Sumite (640AD)

First Tune – *Trns: Fr. Adrian Fortescue (d. 1923)*

1. Come all ye ho - ly, take the bod - y of your Lord,
2. Christ our sal - va - tion, he who is the Son of God,
3. God to our fa - thers or - dered sac - ri - fice of old;

Drink of his chal - ice, take the blood for you out - poured.
Pur - chased our ran - som by his cross and pre - cious blood.
So he in sym - bols Christ the vic - tim true fore - told.

Saved by his bod - y, by his sa - cred blood, we raise
Dy - ing for all men, he the Lord pre - pared this feast,
Source of all bright - ness, sole Re - deem - er of our race,

Grate - ful our voic - es un - to God in hymns of praise.
Of - fered as vic - tim, of - fer - ing him - self as priest.
He___ to his ho - ly ser - vants gives a - bun - dant grace.

4. Come, who with pure hearts
in the Savior's word believe;
Come, and partaking
saving grace from him receive.
God our defender,
guardian sure in this our strife,
Gives to his faithful
after death eternal life.

5. Bread come from heaven
gives he to the hungering,
As for the thirsty
opens he the living spring.
Christ, source of all things,
who here feeds us sinful men,
When this great day dawns,
judge of all, will come again.

57 57
Tune:
Fortescue

T. Source: *Hymnal for the Church of Saint Hugh* (Letchworth: Fr. Adrian Fortescue, 1913) pp. 70-73.
Melody: Peter Lejeune (b. 1991), organist at Saint John Vianney Catholic Church in Springfield.
M. Source: *Saint Jean de Brébeuf Hymnal* (2018).

Sancti Venite, Christi Corpus Sumite (640AD) 447

First Tune – *Textus originalis Latinus*

4. Accédant omnes
pura mente créduli,
sumant aetérnam
salútis custódiam.
Sanctórum custos,
rector quoque Dóminus
vitam perénnem
largítur credéntibus.

5. Caeléstem panem
dat esuriéntibus;
de fonte vivo
praebet sitiéntibus.
Alph*a* et Ómega
ipse Christus Dóminus
venit ventúrus
judicáre hómines.

T. Source: *Hymnal for the Church of Saint Hugh* (Letchworth: Fr. Adrian Fortescue, 1913) pp. 70-73.
Melody: Peter Lejeune (b. 1991), organist at Saint John Vianney Catholic Church in Springfield.
M. Source: *Saint Jean de Brébeuf Hymnal* (2018).

57 57
Tune:
Fortescue

448 Sancti Venite, Christi Corpus Sumite (640AD)

Second Tune – *Trns: Fr. Adrian Fortescue (d. 1923)*

1. Come all ye ho - ly, take the bod - y of your Lord,
2. Saved by his bod - y, by his sa - cred blood, we raise
3. Christ our sal - va - tion, he who is the Son of God,

Drink of his chal - ice, take the blood for you out - poured.
Grate - ful our voic - es un - to God in hymns of praise.
Pur - chased our ran - som by his cross and pre - cious blood.

4. Dying for all men,
he the Lord prepared this feast,
Offered as victim,
offering himself as priest.

5. God to our fathers
ordered sacrifice of old;
So he in symbols
Christ the victim true foretold.

6. Source of all brightness,
sole Redeemer of our race,
He to his holy
servants gives abundant grace.

7. Come, who with pure hearts
in the Savior's word believe;
Come, and partaking
saving grace from him receive.

8. God our defender,
guardian sure in this our strife,
Gives to his faithful
after death eternal life.

9. Bread come from heaven
gives he to the hungering,
As for the thirsty
opens he the living spring.

10. Christ, source of all things,
who here feeds us sinful men,
When this great day dawns,
judge of all, will come again.

57 57

Tune:
Mankato

T. Source: *Hymnal for the Church of Saint Hugh* (Letchworth: Fr. Adrian Fortescue, 1913) pp. 70-73.
Melody: Kevin Allen (b. 1965), choirmaster at the Monastery of the Holy Cross in Chicago.
M. Source: *Saint Jean de Brébeuf Hymnal* (2018).

Sancti Venite, Christi Corpus Sumite (640AD) 449

Second Tune – *Textus originalis Latinus*

1. San - cti ve - ní - te, Chri - sti cor - pus sú - mi - te,
2. Sal - vá - ti Chri - sti cór - po - re et sán - gui - ne,
3. Da - tor sa - lú - tis, Chri - stus Fí - li - us De - i,

san - ctum bi - bén - tes, quo red - ém - pti sán - gui - nem.
a quo re - fé - cti lau - des di - cá - mus De - o.
mun - dum sal - vá - vit per cru - cem et sán - gui - nem.

4. Pro univérsis
immolátus Dóminus
ipse sacérdos
exístit et hóstia.

5. Lege praecéptum
immolári hóstias,
qua adumbrántur
divína mystéria.

6. Lucis indúltor
et salvátor ómnium
praecláram sanctis
largítus est grátiam.

7. Accédant omnes
pura mente créduli,
sumant aetérnam
salútis custódiam.

8. Sanctórum custos,
rector quoque Dóminus
vitam perénnem
largítur credéntibus.

9. Caeléstem panem
dat esuriéntibus;
de fonte vivo
praebet sitiéntibus.

10. Alph*a* et Ómega
ipse Christus Dóminus
venit ventúrus
judicáre hómines.

T. Source: *Hymnal for the Church of Saint Hugh* (Letchworth: Fr. Adrian Fortescue, 1913) pp. 70-73.
Melody: Kevin Allen (b. 1965), choirmaster at the Monastery of the Holy Cross in Chicago.
M. Source: *Saint Jean de Brébeuf Hymnal* (2018).

57 57
Tune:
Mankato

450 Sancti Venite, Christi Corpus Sumite (640AD)

THIRD TUNE – *Trns: Fr. Adrian Fortescue (d. 1923)*

1. Come all ye ho - ly, take the bod - y of your
2. Saved by his bod - y, by his sa - cred blood, we
3. Christ our sal - va - tion, he who is the Son of

Lord, Drink__ of his chal - ice, take the blood for
raise Grate - ful our voic - es un - to God in
God, Pur - chased our ran - som by his cross and

you out - poured. *Al - le - lu - ia.*
hymns of praise. *Al - le - lu - ia.*
pre - cious blood. *Al - le - lu - ia.*

4. Dying for all men,
he the Lord prepared this feast,
Offered as victim,
offering himself as priest.
Alleluia.

5. God to our fathers
ordered sacrifice of old;
So he in symbols
Christ the victim true foretold.
Alleluia.

6. Source of all brightness,
sole Redeemer of our race,
He to his holy
servants gives abundant grace.
Alleluia.

7. Come, who with pure hearts
in the Savior's word believe;
Come, and partaking
saving grace from him receive.
Alleluia.

8. God our defender,
guardian sure in this our strife,
Gives to his faithful
after death eternal life.
Alleluia.

9. Bread come from heaven
gives he to the hungering,
As for the thirsty
opens he the living spring.
Alleluia.

10. Christ, source of all things,
who here feeds us sinful men,
When this great day dawns,
judge of all, will come again.
Alleluia.

57 57 A

Tune:
COELESTEM PANEM 5B

Melody: Peter Lejeune (b. 1991), after "Louez Dieu tout hautement."
M. Source: *Saint Jean de Brébeuf Hymnal* (2018).
T. Source: *Hymnal for the Church of Saint Hugh* (Letchworth: Fr. Adrian Fortescue, 1913) pp. 70-73.

Sancti Venite, Christi Corpus Sumite (640AD) 451

THIRD TUNE – *Textus originalis Latinus*

4. Pro univérsis
immolátus Dóminus
ipse sacérdos
exístit et hóstia.
Alleluia.

5. Lege praecéptum
immolári hóstias,
qua adumbrántur
divína mystéria.
Alleluia.

6. Lucis indúltor
et salvátor ómnium
praecláram sanctis
largítus est grátiam.
Alleluia.

7. Accédant omnes
pura mente créduli,
sumant aetérnam
salútis custódiam.
Alleluia.

8. Sanctórum custos,
rector quoque Dóminus
vitam perénnem
largítur credéntibus.
Alleluia.

9. Caeléstem panem
dat esuriéntibus;
de fonte vivo
praebet sitiéntibus.
Alleluia.

10. Alph*a* et Ómega
ipse Christus Dóminus
venit ventúrus
judicáre hómines.
Alleluia.

57 57 A

Melody: Peter Lejeune (b. 1991), after "Louez Dieu tout hautement."
M. Source: *Saint Jean de Brébeuf Hymnal* (2018).
T. Source: *Hymnal for the Church of Saint Hugh* (Letchworth: Fr. Adrian Fortescue, 1913) pp. 70-73.

Tune:
COELESTEM PANEM 5B

452 Sancti Venite, Christi Corpus Sumite (640AD)

FOURTH TUNE – *Trns: Fr. Adrian Fortescue (d. 1923)*

1. Come_ all ye ho - ly, take the bod - y of your
2. Saved_ by his bod - y, by his sa - cred blood, we
3. Christ_ our sal - va - tion, he who is the Son of

Lord, Drink_ of his chal - ice, take the blood for
raise Grate - ful our voic - es un - to God in
God, Pur - chased our ran - som by his cross and

you out - poured. *Al - le - lu - ia.*
hymns of praise. *Al - le - lu - ia.*
pre - cious blood. *Al - le - lu - ia.*

4. Dying for all men,
he the Lord prepared this feast,
Offered as victim,
offering himself as priest.
Alleluia.

5. God to our fathers
ordered sacrifice of old;
So he in symbols
Christ the victim true foretold.
Alleluia.

6. Source of all brightness,
sole Redeemer of our race,
He to his holy
servants gives abundant grace.
Alleluia.

7. Come, who with pure hearts
in the Savior's word believe;
Come, and partaking
saving grace from him receive.
Alleluia.

8. God our defender,
guardian sure in this our strife,
Gives to his faithful
after death eternal life.
Alleluia.

9. Bread come from heaven
gives he to the hungering,
As for the thirsty
opens he the living spring.
Alleluia.

10. Christ, source of all things,
who here feeds us sinful men,
When this great day dawns,
judge of all, will come again.
Alleluia.

57 57 A

Tune:
GOTT SEI DANK 5B

Final Verses: Richard Lloyd (1993) #83; Noel Rawsthorne (2011) #192.
T. Source: *Hymnal for the Church of Saint Hugh* (Letchworth: Fr. Adrian Fortescue, 1913) pp. 70-73.
Melody: Adapted by Johann Anastasius Freylinghausen (d. 1739) in his *Geist-reiches Gesang-Buch, den Kern alter und neuer Lieder* (Halle, 1704); also called LÜBECK.
M. Source: *New Westminster Hymnal* (1939) p. 249; *New Saint Basil Hymnal* (1958) p. 229.

Sancti Venite, Christi Corpus Sumite (640AD) 453

Fourth Tune – *Textus originalis Latinus*

4. Pro univérsis
immolátus Dóminus
ipse sacérdos
exístit et hóstia. *Alleluia.*

5. Lege praecéptum
immolári hóstias,
qua adumbrántur
divína mystéria. *Alleluia.*

6. Lucis indúltor
et salvátor ómnium
praecláram sanctis
largítus est grátiam. *Alleluia.*

7. Accédant omnes
pura mente créduli,
sumant aetérnam
salútis custódiam. *Alleluia.*

8. Sanctórum custos,
rector quoque Dóminus
vitam perénnem
largítur credéntibus. *Alleluia.*

9. Caeléstem panem
dat esuriéntibus;
de fonte vivo
praebet sitiéntibus. *Alleluia.*

10. Alph*a* et Ómega
ipse Christus Dóminus
venit ventúrus
judicáre hómines. *Alleluia.*

Final Verses: Richard Lloyd (1993) #83; Noel Rawsthorne (2011) #192.
T. Source: *Hymnal for the Church of Saint Hugh* (Letchworth: Fr. Adrian Fortescue, 1913) pp. 70-73.
Melody: Adapted by Johann Anastasius Freylinghausen (d. 1739) in his *Geist-reiches Gesang-Buch, den Kern alter und neuer Lieder* (Halle, 1704); also called Lübeck.
M. Source: *New Westminster Hymnal* (1939) p. 249; *New Saint Basil Hymnal* (1958) p. 229.

57 57 A
Tune:
Gott Sei Dank 5B

454 Sancti Venite, Christi Corpus Sumite (640AD)

Fifth Tune – *Trns: Fr. Adrian Fortescue (d. 1923)*

4. Dying for all men,
he the Lord prepared this feast,
Offered as victim,
offering himself as priest. *R.*

5. God to our fathers
ordered sacrifice of old;
So he in symbols
Christ the victim true foretold. *R.*

6. Source of all brightness,
sole Redeemer of our race,
He to his holy
servants gives abundant grace. *R.*

7. Come, who with pure hearts
in the Savior's word believe;
Come, and partaking
saving grace from him receive. *R.*

8. God our defender,
guardian sure in this our strife,
Gives to his faithful
after death eternal life. *R.*

9. Bread come from heaven
gives he to the hungering,
As for the thirsty
opens he the living spring. *R.*

10. Christ, source of all things,
who here feeds us sinful men,
When this great day dawns,
judge of all, will come again. *R.*

57 57

Tune: Zahn 5B

T. Source: *Hymnal for the Church of Saint Hugh* (Letchworth: Fr. Adrian Fortescue, 1913) pp. 70-73.
M. Source: Cento from *Die Melodien der deutschen evangelischen Kirchenlieder*, by Johannes Zahn (d. 1895).

Sancti Venite, Christi Corpus Sumite (640AD) 455

Fifth Tune – *Textus originalis Latinus*

4. Pro univérsis
immolátus Dóminus
ipse sacérdos
exístit et hóstia. *R.*

5. Lege praecéptum
immolári hóstias,
qua adumbrántur
divína mystéria. *R.*

6. Lucis indúltor
et salvátor ómnium
praecláram sanctis
largítus est grátiam. *R.*

7. Accédant omnes
pura mente créduli,
sumant aetérnam
salútis custódiam. *R.*

8. Sanctórum custos,
rector quoque Dóminus
vitam perénnem
largítur credéntibus. *R.*

9. Caeléstem panem
dat esuriéntibus;
de fonte vivo
praebet sitiéntibus. *R.*

10. Alph*a* et Ómega
ipse Christus Dóminus
venit ventúrus
judicáre hómines. *R.*

57 57

T. Source: *Hymnal for the Church of Saint Hugh* (Letchworth: Fr. Adrian Fortescue, 1913) pp. 70-73.
M. Source: Cento from *Die Melodien der deutschen evangelischen Kirchenlieder*, by Johannes Zahn (d. 1895).

Tune: Zahn 5B

456 Sancti Venite, Christi Corpus Sumite (640AD)

Sixth Tune – *Trns: Fr. Adrian Fortescue (d. 1923)*

1. Come_ all ye ho - ly, take the bod - y
2. Saved_ by his bod - y, by his sa - cred
3. Christ_ our sal - va - tion, he who is the

of your Lord, Drink_ of his chal - ice,
blood, we raise Grate - ful our voic - es
Son of God, Pur - chased our ran - som

take the blood for you out - poured.
un - to God in hymns of praise.
by his cross and pre - cious blood.

4. Dying for all men,
he the Lord prepared this feast,
Offered as victim,
offering himself as priest.

5. God to our fathers
ordered sacrifice of old;
So he in symbols
Christ the victim true foretold.

6. Source of all brightness,
sole Redeemer of our race,
He to his holy
servants gives abundant grace.

7. Come, who with pure hearts
in the Savior's word believe;
Come, and partaking
saving grace from him receive.

8. God our defender,
guardian sure in this our strife,
Gives to his faithful
after death eternal life.

9. Bread come from heaven
gives he to the hungering,
As for the thirsty
opens he the living spring.

10. Christ, source of all things,
who here feeds us sinful men,
When this great day dawns,
judge of all, will come again.

57 57

Tune:
Culbach 5B

Final Verses: Richard Lloyd (1993) #49; Noel Rawsthorne (2011) #82.
T. Source: *Hymnal for the Church of Saint Hugh* (Letchworth: Fr. Adrian Fortescue, 1913) pp. 70-73.
Melody: From a Chorale in Johann Scheffler's *Heilige Seelenlust* (1657).
M. Source: *New Saint Basil Hymnal* (1958) p. 218; *Mediator Dei Hymnal* (1955) p. 83.

Sancti Venite, Christi Corpus Sumite (640AD) 457

Sixth Tune – *Textus originalis Latinus*

4. Pro univérsis
immolátus Dóminus
ipse sacérdos
exístit et hóstia.

5. Lege praecéptum
immolári hóstias,
qua adumbrántur
divína mystéria.

6. Lucis indúltor
et salvátor ómnium
praecláram sanctis
largítus est grátiam.

7. Accédant omnes
pura mente créduli,
sumant aetérnam
salútis custódiam.

8. Sanctórum custos,
rector quoque Dóminus
vitam perénnem
largítur credéntibus.

9. Caeléstem panem
dat esuriéntibus;
de fonte vivo
praebet sitiéntibus.

10. Alph*a* et Ómega
ipse Christus Dóminus
venit ventúrus
judicáre hómines.

Final Verses: Richard Lloyd (1993) #49; Noel Rawsthorne (2011) #82.
T. Source: *Hymnal for the Church of Saint Hugh* (Letchworth: Fr. Adrian Fortescue, 1913) pp. 70-73.
Melody: From a Chorale in Johann Scheffler's *Heilige Seelenlust* (1657).
M. Source: *New Saint Basil Hymnal* (1958) p. 218; *Mediator Dei Hymnal* (1955) p. 83.

57 57
Tune:
Culbach 5B

458 Sancti Venite, Christi Corpus Sumite (640AD)

Seventh Tune – *Trns: Fr. Adrian Fortescue (d. 1923)*

1. Come all ye ho - ly, take the bod - y__
2. Saved by his bod - y, by his sa - cred
3. Christ our sal - va - tion, he who is the_

of__ your Lord, Drink of his chal - ice,
blood,_ we raise Grate - ful our voic - es
Son__ of God, Pur - chased our ran - som

take the blood for you out - poured.
un - to God in hymns of praise.
by his cross and pre - cious blood.

4. Dying for all men,
he the Lord prepared this feast,
Offered as victim,
offering himself as priest.

5. God to our fathers
ordered sacrifice of old;
So he in symbols
Christ the victim true foretold.

6. Source of all brightness,
sole Redeemer of our race,
He to his holy
servants gives abundant grace.

7. Come, who with pure hearts
in the Savior's word believe;
Come, and partaking
saving grace from him receive.

8. God our defender,
guardian sure in this our strife,
Gives to his faithful
after death eternal life.

9. Bread come from heaven
gives he to the hungering,
As for the thirsty
opens he the living spring.

10. Christ, source of all things,
who here feeds us sinful men,
When this great day dawns,
judge of all, will come again.

57 57
Tune:
Hartford 5B

T. Source: *Hymnal for the Church of Saint Hugh* (Letchworth: Fr. Adrian Fortescue, 1913) pp. 70-73.
Melody: Benjamin Milgrove (d. 1810), organist at a chapel in Somerset (South West England).
M. Source: *Songs of Syon* (1910) p. 40; *New English Hymnal* (1986) p. 494.

SEVENTH TUNE – *Textus originalis Latinus*

1. San - cti ve - ní - te, Chri - sti cor - pus_
2. Sal - vá - ti Chri - sti cór - po - re et__
3. Da - tor sa - lú - tis, Chri - stus Fí - li -

sú - mi - te, san - ctum bi - bén - tes,
sán - gui - ne, a quo re - fé - cti
us__ De - i, mun - dum sal - vá - vit

quo red - ém - pti sán - gui - nem.
lau - des di - cá - mus De - o.
per cru - cem et sán - gui - nem.

4. Pro univérsis
immolátus Dóminus
ipse sacérdos
exístit et hóstia.

5. Lege praecéptum
immolári hóstias,
qua adumbrántur
divína mystéria.

6. Lucis indúltor
et salvátor ómnium
praecláram sanctis
largítus est grátiam.

7. Accédant omnes
pura mente créduli,
sumant aetérnam
salútis custódiam.

8. Sanctórum custos,
rector quoque Dóminus
vitam perénnem
largítur credéntibus.

9. Caeléstem panem
dat esuriéntibus;
de fonte vivo
praebet sitiéntibus.

10. Alph*a* et Ómega
ipse Christus Dóminus
venit ventúrus
judicáre hómines.

57 57

T. Source: *Hymnal for the Church of Saint Hugh* (Letchworth: Fr. Adrian Fortescue, 1913) pp. 70-73.
Melody: Benjamin Milgrove (d. 1810), organist at a chapel in Somerset (South West England).
M. Source: *Songs of Syon* (1910) p. 40; *New English Hymnal* (1986) p. 494.

Tune:
HARTFORD 5B

460 Sancti Venite, Christi Corpus Sumite (640AD)

Eighth Tune – *Trns: Fr. Adrian Fortescue (d. 1923)*

4. Dying for all men,
he the Lord prepared this feast,
Offered as victim,
offering himself as priest.

5. God to our fathers
ordered sacrifice of old;
So he in symbols
Christ the victim true foretold.

6. Source of all brightness,
sole Redeemer of our race,
He to his holy
servants gives abundant grace.

7. Come, who with pure hearts
in the Savior's word believe;
Come, and partaking
saving grace from him receive.

8. God our defender,
guardian sure in this our strife,
Gives to his faithful
after death eternal life.

9. Bread come from heaven
gives he to the hungering,
As for the thirsty
opens he the living spring.

10. Christ, source of all things,
who here feeds us sinful men,
When this great day dawns,
judge of all, will come again.

57 57

Tune:
Heart of Sorrow 5B

T. Source: *Hymnal for the Church of Saint Hugh* (Letchworth: Fr. Adrian Fortescue, 1913) pp. 70-73.
Melody: *Gesang- und Gebetbuch für die Diözese Trier* (1847).
M. Source: *Mediator Dei Hymnal* (1955) p. 48.

Sancti Venite, Christi Corpus Sumite (640AD) 461

Eighth Tune – *Textus originalis Latinus*

4. Pro univérsis
immolátus Dóminus
ipse sacérdos
exístit et hóstia.

5. Lege praecéptum
immolári hóstias,
qua adumbrántur
divína mystéria.

6. Lucis indúltor
et salvátor ómnium
praecláram sanctis
largítus est grátiam.

7. Accédant omnes
pura mente créduli,
sumant aetérnam
salútis custódiam.

8. Sanctórum custos,
rector quoque Dóminus
vitam perénnem
largítur credéntibus.

9. Caeléstem panem
dat esuriéntibus;
de fonte vivo
praebet sitiéntibus.

10. Alph*a* et Ómega
ipse Christus Dóminus
venit ventúrus
judicáre hómines.

T. Source: *Hymnal for the Church of Saint Hugh* (Letchworth: Fr. Adrian Fortescue, 1913) pp. 70-73.
Melody: *Gesang- und Gebetbuch für die Diözese Trier* (1847).
M. Source: *Mediator Dei Hymnal* (1955) p. 48.

57 57
Tune:
Heart of Sorrow 5B

462 Sancti Venite, Christi Corpus Sumite (640AD)

Ninth Tune – *Trns: Fr. Adrian Fortescue (d. 1923)*

4. Dying for all men,
he the Lord prepared this feast,
Offered as victim,
offering himself as priest.
Alleluia.

5. God to our fathers
ordered sacrifice of old;
So he in symbols
Christ the victim true foretold.
Alleluia.

6. Source of all brightness,
sole Redeemer of our race,
He to his holy
servants gives abundant grace.
Alleluia.

7. Come, who with pure hearts
in the Savior's word believe;
Come, and partaking
saving grace from him receive.
Alleluia.

8. God our defender,
guardian sure in this our strife,
Gives to his faithful
after death eternal life.
Alleluia.

9. Bread come from heaven
gives he to the hungering,
As for the thirsty
opens he the living spring.
Alleluia.

10. Christ, source of all things,
who here feeds us sinful men,
When this great day dawns,
judge of all, will come again.
Alleluia.

57 57 A

Tune:
Würtemburg 5B

Melody: From *Hundert Arien* (Dresden, 1697), adapted by William H. Monk (d. 1889), organist at King's College London.
M. Source: *Songs of Syon* (Woodward, 1910) p. 455; *New Westminster Hymnal* (1939) p. 80.
T. Source: *Hymnal for the Church of Saint Hugh* (Letchworth: Fr. Adrian Fortescue, 1913) pp. 70-73.

NINTH TUNE – *Textus originalis Latinus*

4. Pro univérsis
immolátus Dóminus
ipse sacérdos
exístit et hóstia.
Alleluia.

5. Lege praecéptum
immolári hóstias,
qua adumbrántur
divína mystéria.
Alleluia.

6. Lucis indúltor
et salvátor ómnium
praecláram sanctis
largítus est grátiam.
Alleluia.

7. Accédant omnes
pura mente créduli,
sumant aetérnam
salútis custódiam.
Alleluia.

8. Sanctórum custos,
rector quoque Dóminus
vitam perénnem
largítur credéntibus.
Alleluia.

9. Caeléstem panem
dat esuriéntibus;
de fonte vivo
praebet sitiéntibus.
Alleluia.

10. Alph*a* et Ómega
ipse Christus Dóminus
venit ventúrus
judicáre hómines.
Alleluia.

Melody: From *Hundert Arien* (Dresden, 1697), adapted by William H. Monk (d. 1889), organist at King's College London.
M. Source: *Songs of Syon* (Woodward, 1910) p. 455; *New Westminster Hymnal* (1939) p. 80.
T. Source: *Hymnal for the Church of Saint Hugh* (Letchworth: Fr. Adrian Fortescue, 1913) pp. 70-73.

57 57 A
Tune: WÜRTEMBURG 5B

464 Sancti Venite, Christi Corpus Sumite (640AD)

Tenth Tune – *Trns: Fr. Adrian Fortescue (d. 1923)*

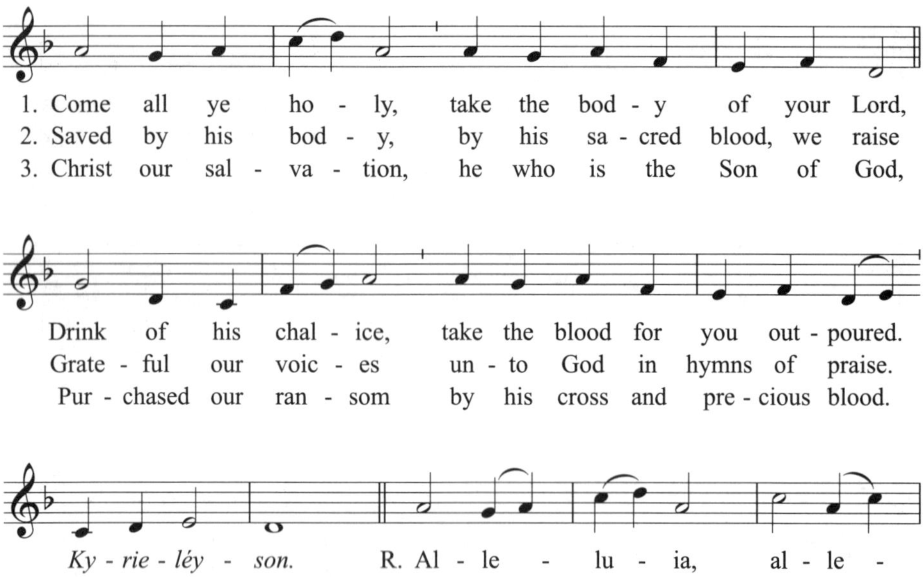

This melody is excellent for use during Eastertide.

4. Dying for all men, | he the Lord prepared this feast,
Offered as victim, | offering himself as priest. *Ky-rie-léy-son.* R.

5. God to our fathers | ordered sacrifice of old;
So he in symbols | Christ the victim true foretold. *Ky-rie-léy-son.* R.

6. Source of all brightness, | sole Redeemer of our race,
He to his holy | servants gives abundant grace. *Ky-rie-léy-son.* R.

7. Come, who with pure hearts | in the Savior's word believe;
Come, and partaking | saving grace from him receive. *Ky-rie-léy-son.* R.

8. God our defender, | guardian sure in this our strife,
Gives to his faithful | after death eternal life. *Ky-rie-léy-son.* R.

9. Bread come from heaven | gives he to the hungering,
As for the thirsty | opens he the living spring. *Ky-rie-léy-son.* R.

10. Christ, source of all things, | who here feeds us sinful men,
When this great day dawns, | judge of all, will come again. *Ky-rie-léy-son.* R.

57 57

Tune:
Christ Ist Erstanden

T. Source: *Hymnal for the Church of Saint Hugh* (Letchworth: Fr. Adrian Fortescue, 1913) pp. 70-73.
Melody: *Christ ist erstanden*, dating from the 12th century, is the oldest known Easter hymn in the vernacular. The melody is based on the *Victimae Paschali* (an 11th century Sequence) and was often inserted into it, thereby mixing German with Latin. It was set by famous composers throughout history, such as Heinrich Isaac (d. 1517), Orlando de Lassus (d. 1594), and Johann Sebastian Bach (d. 1750). We have paired it with a text which more faithfully matches the original neumes. Cf. *Divini Cultus Studium* (Altötting: Fr. Robert Skeris, 1990) p. 129.

Sancti Venite, Christi Corpus Sumite (640AD) 465

Tenth Tune – *Textus originalis Latinus*

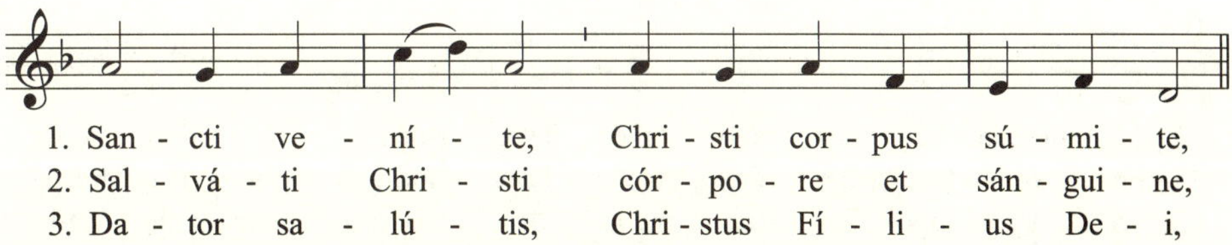

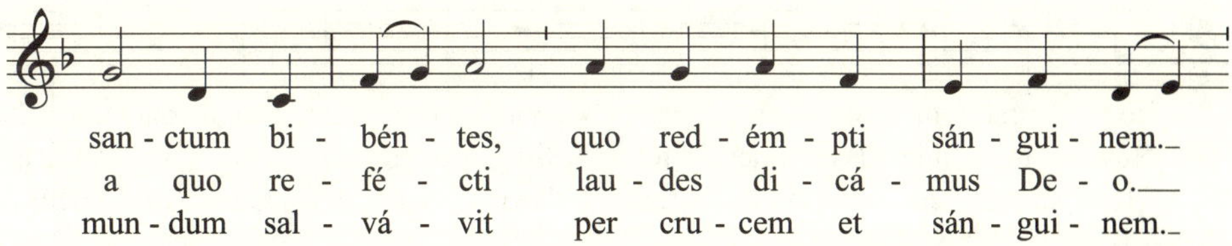

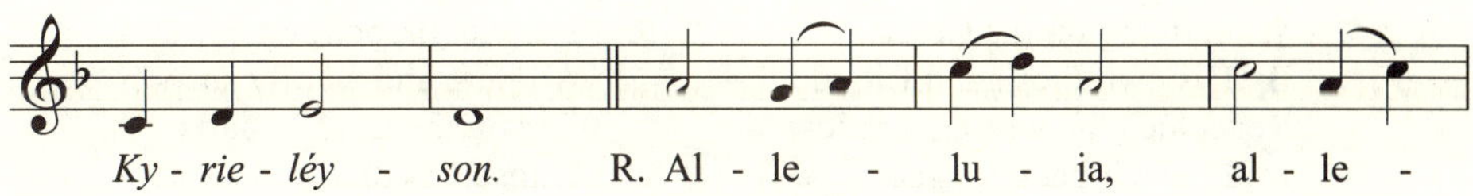

This melody is excellent for use during Eastertide.

4. Pro univérsis | immolátus Dóminus
ipse sacérdos | exístit et hóstia. *Ky-rie-léy-son.* R.

5. Lege praecéptum | immolári hóstias,
qua adumbrántur | divína mystéria. *Ky-rie-léy-son.* R.

6. Lucis indúltor | et salvátor ómnium
praecláram sanctis | largítus est grátiam. *Ky-rie-léy-son.* R.

7. Accédant omnes | pura mente créduli,
sumant aetérnam | salútis custódiam. *Ky-rie-léy-son.* R.

8. Sanctórum custos, | rector quoque Dóminus
vitam perénnem | largítur credéntibus. *Ky-rie-léy-son.* R.

9. Caeléstem panem | dat esuriéntibus;
de fonte vivo | praebet sitiéntibus. *Ky-rie-léy-son.* R.

10. Alph*a* et Ómega | ipse Christus Dóminus
venit ventúrus | judicáre hómines. *Ky-rie-léy-son.* R.

T. Source: *Hymnal for the Church of Saint Hugh* (Letchworth: Fr. Adrian Fortescue, 1913) pp. 70-73.
M. Source: Great variation exists for this ancient melody as it appears in Catholic hymnals. Frequently the English texts paired to it are unsatisfactory. Cf. *Cantate Omnes: Hymnal of the Catholic Choirmasters' Guild* (1952) #47; *Hosanna Catholic Hymn Book* (St. Louis: Fr. Ludwig Bonvin, 1914) #55; *Summit Choirbook* (Dominican Monastery of Our Lady of the Rosary, 1983) #98; *Pope Pius XII Hymnal* (Ohio: Gregorian Institute of America, 1959) p. 8.

57 57
Tune:
Christ Ist Erstanden

466 Sancti Venite, Christi Corpus Sumite (640AD)

First Tune – *Trns: Msgr. Hugh T. Henry (d. 1946)*

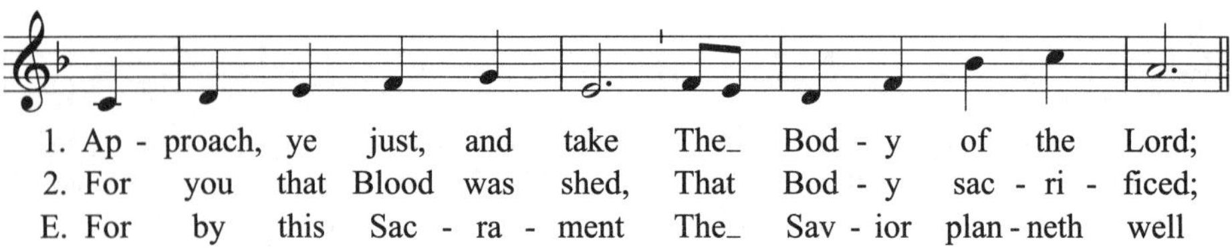

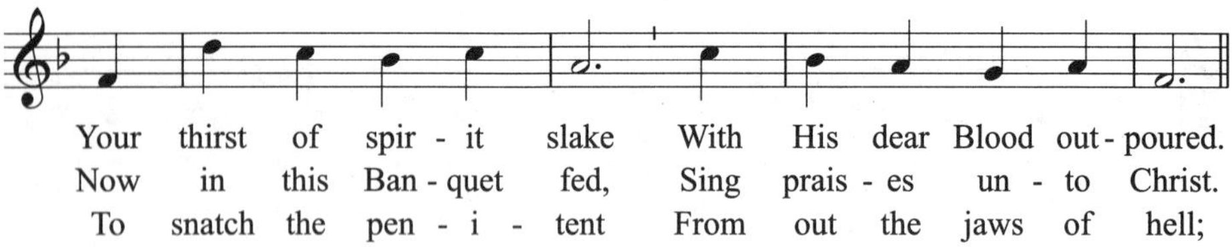

3. Who, dying on the Cross,
By His own Flesh and Blood
Redeemed the world from loss
And gave it back to God.

4. For all on Calv'ry slain,
He Victim was, and Priest,
And still He doth remain
Both, in this Sacred Feast.

5. When in the Ancient Law
A priest the victim slew,
In type the prophets saw
The Myst'ries of the New.

6. The Savior and the Light
Of all the human race
Gives, in this Holy Rite,
A fount of endless grace.

7. Draw nigh, believing hearts,
All pure and wholly shriv'n:
To you the Lord imparts
Himself as pledge of heav'n.

8. By whom all creatures live,
The Lord of life and death,
Eternal life shall give
To men of humble faith,

9. And shall their hunger quench
With living, heav'nly Bread,
Their thirsting spirit drench
With living fountains fed.

10. Alpha-Omega, when
The course of time is sped,
Shall surely come again
To judge the quick and dead.

66 66 Iambic

Tune:
Seán

Melody: Richard J. Clark (b. 1969), choirmaster at the Cathedral of the Holy Cross in Boston.
M. Source: *Saint Jean de Brébeuf Hymnal* (2018).
T. Source: *Eucharistica: Verse & Prose in Honor of the Hidden God* (Philadelphia: Dolphin Press, 1912) pp. 76-79. Monsignor Hugh T. Henry, professor of homiletics at the Catholic University of America, also taught Gregorian chant at St. Charles Seminary (Overbrook, Pennsylvania).

Sancti Venite, Christi Corpus Sumite (640AD) 467

Second Tune – *Trns: Msgr. Hugh T. Henry (d. 1946)*

1. Ap - proach, ye just, and take The Bod - y of the Lord;
2. For you that Blood was shed, That Bod - y sac - ri - ficed;
E. For by this Sac - ra - ment The Sav - ior plan - neth well

Your thirst of spir - it slake With His_ dear Blood out - poured.
Now in this Ban - quet fed, Sing prais - es__ un - to Christ.
To snatch the pen - i - tent From out_ the_ jaws of hell;

3. Who, dying on the Cross,
By His own Flesh and Blood
Redeemed the world from loss
And gave it back to God.

4. For all on Calv'ry slain,
He Victim was, and Priest,
And still He doth remain
Both, in this Sacred Feast.

5. When in the Ancient Law
A priest the victim slew,
In type the prophets saw
The Myst'ries of the New.

6. The Savior and the Light
Of all the human race
Gives, in this Holy Rite,
A fount of endless grace.

7. Draw nigh, believing hearts,
All pure and wholly shriv'n:
To you the Lord imparts
Himself as pledge of heav'n.

8. By whom all creatures live,
The Lord of life and death,
Eternal life shall give
To men of humble faith,

9. And shall their hunger quench
With living, heav'nly Bread,
Their thirsting spirit drench
With living fountains fed.

10. Alpha-Omega, when
The course of time is sped,
Shall surely come again
To judge the quick and dead.

Melody: Kevin Allen (b. 1965), choirmaster at the Monastery of the Holy Cross in Chicago.
M. Source: *Saint Jean de Brébeuf Hymnal* (2018).
T. Source: *Eucharistica: Verse & Prose in Honor of the Hidden God* (Philadelphia: Dolphin Press, 1912) pp. 76-79. Monsignor Hugh T. Henry, professor of homiletics at the Catholic University of America, also taught Gregorian chant at St. Charles Seminary (Overbrook, Pennsylvania).

66 66 Iambic
Tune:
Camcolt

468 Sancti Venite, Christi Corpus Sumite (640AD)

THIRD TUNE – *Trns: Msgr. Hugh T. Henry (d. 1946)*

1. Ap - proach, ye just, and take The Bod - y of the Lord;
2. For you that Blood was shed, That Bod - y sac - ri - ficed;
E. For by this Sac - ra - ment The Sav - ior plan - neth well

Your thirst of spir - it slake With His dear Blood out - poured.
Now in this Ban - quet fed, Sing prais - es un - to Christ.
To snatch the pen - i - tent From out the jaws of hell;

3. Who, dying on the Cross,
By His own Flesh and Blood
Redeemed the world from loss
And gave it back to God.

4. For all on Calv'ry slain,
He Victim was, and Priest,
And still He doth remain
Both, in this Sacred Feast.

5. When in the Ancient Law
A priest the victim slew,
In type the prophets saw
The Myst'ries of the New.

6. The Savior and the Light
Of all the human race
Gives, in this Holy Rite,
A fount of endless grace.

7. Draw nigh, believing hearts,
All pure and wholly shriv'n:
To you the Lord imparts
Himself as pledge of heav'n.

8. By whom all creatures live,
The Lord of life and death,
Eternal life shall give
To men of humble faith,

9. And shall their hunger quench
With living, heav'nly Bread,
Their thirsting spirit drench
With living fountains fed.

10. Alpha-Omega, when
The course of time is sped,
Shall surely come again
To judge the quick and dead.

66 66 Iambic

Tune:
CLERMONT

Melody: Alfred Calabrese (b. 1961), choirmaster at Saint Rita Catholic Church in Dallas.
M. Source: *Saint Jean de Brébeuf Hymnal* (2018).
T. Source: *Eucharistica: Verse & Prose in Honor of the Hidden God* (Philadelphia: Dolphin Press, 1912) pp. 76-79. Monsignor Hugh T. Henry, professor of homiletics at the Catholic University of America, also taught Gregorian chant at St. Charles Seminary (Overbrook, Pennsylvania).

Sancti Venite, Christi Corpus Sumite (640AD) 469

Trns: Msgr. Hugh T. Henry (d. 1946)

English translation can be sung with any 66 66 meter (iambic), such as CAMCOLT, QUAM DILECTA, ST CECILIA, IBSTONE, CLERMONT, SEÁN, etc.

APPROACH, ye just, and take
The Body of the Lord;
Your thirst of spirit slake
With His dear Blood outpoured.

2. For you that Blood was shed,
That Body sacrificed;
Now in this Banquet fed,
Sing praises unto Christ.

E. For by this Sacrament
The Savior planneth well
To snatch the penitent
From out the jaws of hell;

3. Who, dying on the Cross,
By His own Flesh and Blood
Redeemed the world from loss
And gave it back to God.

4. For all on Calv'ry slain,
He Victim was, and Priest,
And still He doth remain
Both, in this Sacred Feast.

5. When in the Ancient Law
A priest the victim slew,
In type the prophets saw
The Myst'ries of the New.

6. The Savior and the Light
Of all the human race
Gives, in this Holy Rite,
A fount of endless grace.

7. Draw nigh, believing hearts,
All pure and wholly shriv'n:
To you the Lord imparts
Himself as pledge of heav'n.

8. By whom all creatures live,
The Lord of life and death,
Eternal life shall give
To men of humble faith,

9. And shall their hunger quench
With living, heav'nly Bread,
Their thirsting spirit drench
With living fountains fed.

10. Alpha-Omega, when
The course of time is sped,
Shall surely come again
To judge the quick and dead.

T. Source: *Eucharistica: Verse & Prose in Honor of the Hidden God* (Philadelphia: Dolphin Press, 1912) pp. 76-79. Monsignor Hugh T. Henry, professor of homiletics at the Catholic University of America, also taught Gregorian chant at St. Charles Seminary (Overbrook, Pennsylvania).

66 66 Iambic
Tune:
VARIOUS

470 Sancti Venite, Christi Corpus Sumite (640AD)

First Tune – *Trns: Fr. Herbert Thurston (d. 1939) after Neale*

4. Approach ye then with faithful hearts sincere,
And take the safeguard of salvation here.
He that His saints in this world rules and shields
To all believers life eternal yields.

5. He feeds the hungry with the Bread of Heav'n,
And living streams to those who thirst are giv'n.
Alpha and Omega—to whom shall bow
All nations at the Doom—is with us now.

10 10 10 10

Tune:
All Souls

* The first line in Thurston's version was "Come saints and take the Body of the Lord," which is more faithful to the Latin original, to which he added: "By the word *saints*, as used in the first line and twice afterwards, the Celtic writer probably meant no more than *faithful Christians*. It is important to remember this in reading early Celtic documents."
English Translation: *The early cultus of the Blessed Sacrament* in *The Month* (1907) v. 109, p. 377; Fr. Thurston acknowledges his version's debt to Dr. Neale's translation in *Mediaeval Hymns and Sequences* (1851) p. 13.
Melody: John Yoakley (d. 1932), organist at All Saints Church in Portsmouth.
M. Source: *New English Hymnal* (1986) p. 848; *Saint Edmund Campion Hymnal* (2013) p. 898.

Sancti Venite, Christi Corpus Sumite (640AD)

Second Tune – *Trns: Fr. Herbert Thurston (d. 1939) after Neale*

4. Approach ye then with faithful hearts sincere,
   And take the safeguard of salvation here.
   He that His saints in this world rules and shields
   To all believers life eternal yields.

5. He feeds the hungry with the Bread of Heav'n,
   And living streams to those who thirst are giv'n.
   Alpha and Omega—to whom shall bow
   All nations at the Doom—is with us now.

Final Verses: Noel Rawsthorne (2011) #22.

* The first line in Thurston's version was "Come saints and take the Body of the Lord," which is more faithful to the Latin original, to which he added: "By the word *saints*, as used in the first line and twice afterwards, the Celtic writer probably meant no more than *faithful Christians*. It is important to remember this in reading early Celtic documents."

English Translation: *The early cultus of the Blessed Sacrament* in *The Month* (1907) v. 109, p. 377; Fr. Thurston acknowledges his version's debt to Dr. Neale's translation in *Mediaeval Hymns and Sequences* (1851) p. 13.

Melody: William J. Maher, SJ (d. 1877) in *Liturgical Hymns for the Chief Festivals of the Year selected from the Office of the Catholic Church and so translated into English as to be adapted to Old and New Music* (London, 1865), for which Fr. Maher edited the music and Fr. Francis Trappes the texts.

M. Source: *New Saint Basil Hymnal* (1958) p. 119; *Catholic Hymn Book* (London Oratory, 1998) p. 215.

10 10 10 10

Tune: Anima Christi 10A

472 Sancti Venite, Christi Corpus Sumite (640AD)

Third Tune – *Trns: Fr. Herbert Thurston (d. 1939) after Neale*

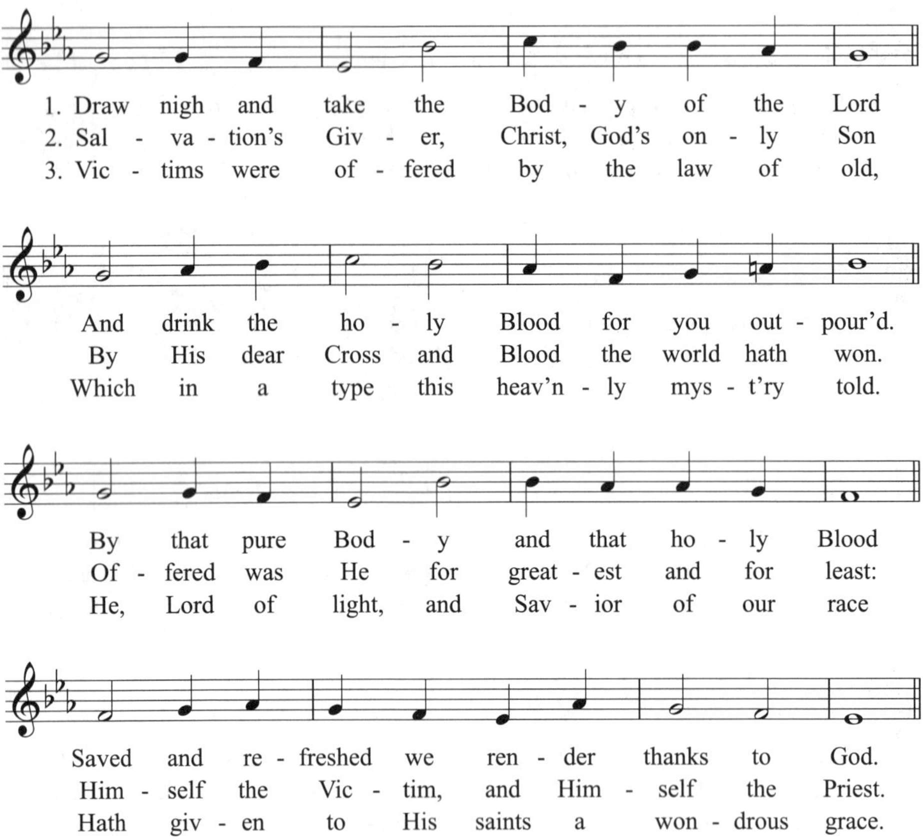

4. Approach ye then with faithful hearts sincere,
And take the safeguard of salvation here.
He that His saints in this world rules and shields
To all believers life eternal yields.

5. He feeds the hungry with the Bread of Heav'n,
And living streams to those who thirst are giv'n.
Alpha and Omega—to whom shall bow
All nations at the Doom—is with us now.

10 10 10 10

Tune:
Eventide

* The first line in Thurston's version was "Come saints and take the Body of the Lord," which is more faithful to the Latin original, to which he added: "By the word *saints*, as used in the first line and twice afterwards, the Celtic writer probably meant no more than *faithful Christians*. It is important to remember this in reading early Celtic documents."
English Translation: *The early cultus of the Blessed Sacrament* in *The Month* (1907) v. 109, p. 377; Fr. Thurston acknowledges his version's debt to Dr. Neale's translation in *Mediaeval Hymns and Sequences* (1851) p. 13.
Melody: William H. Monk (d. 1889), organist at King's College London.
M. Source: *St. Mark's Hymnal for Use in the Catholic Church in the United States* (Peoria, Illinois: 1910) p. 184.

Sancti Venite, Christi Corpus Sumite (640AD)

Fourth Tune – *Trns: Fr. Herbert Thurston (d. 1939) after Neale*

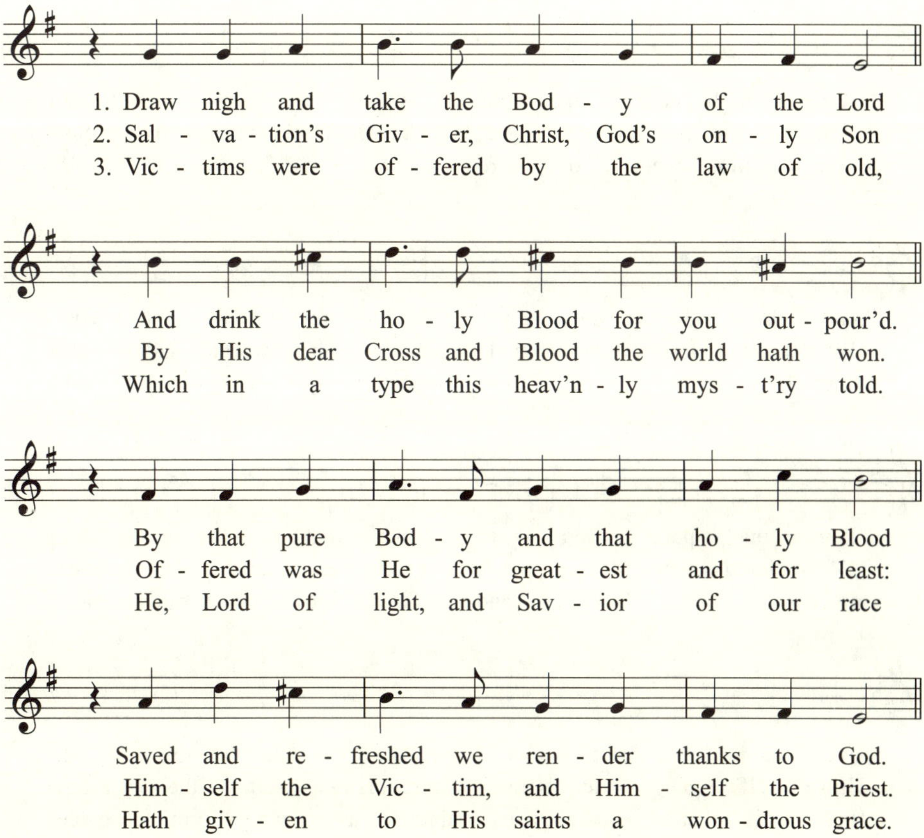

4. Approach ye then with faithful hearts sincere,
And take the safeguard of salvation here.
He that His saints in this world rules and shields
To all believers life eternal yields.

5. He feeds the hungry with the Bread of Heav'n,
And living streams to those who thirst are giv'n.
Alpha and Omega—to whom shall bow
All nations at the Doom—is with us now.

Final Verses: Noel Rawsthorne (2011) #341.

* The first line in Thurston's version was "Come saints and take the Body of the Lord," which is more faithful to the Latin original, to which he added: "By the word *saints*, as used in the first line and twice afterwards, the Celtic writer probably meant no more than *faithful Christians*. It is important to remember this in reading early Celtic documents."

English Translation: *The early cultus of the Blessed Sacrament* in *The Month* (1907) v. 109, p. 377; Fr. Thurston acknowledges his version's debt to Dr. Neale's translation in *Mediaeval Hymns and Sequences* (1851) p. 13.

Melody: Orlando Gibbons (d. 1625), organist at Westminster Abbey.

M. Source: *Catholic Hymn Book* (London Oratory, 1998) p. 189; cf. *The Hymnes and Songs of the Church* (1623) p. 77, originally used for "How sad and solitary now (alas!)" from the Lamentations of Jeremias.

10 10 10 10

Tune: Song 24

474 Sancti Venite, Christi Corpus Sumite (640AD)

Fifth Tune – *Trns: Fr. Herbert Thurston (d. 1939) after Neale*

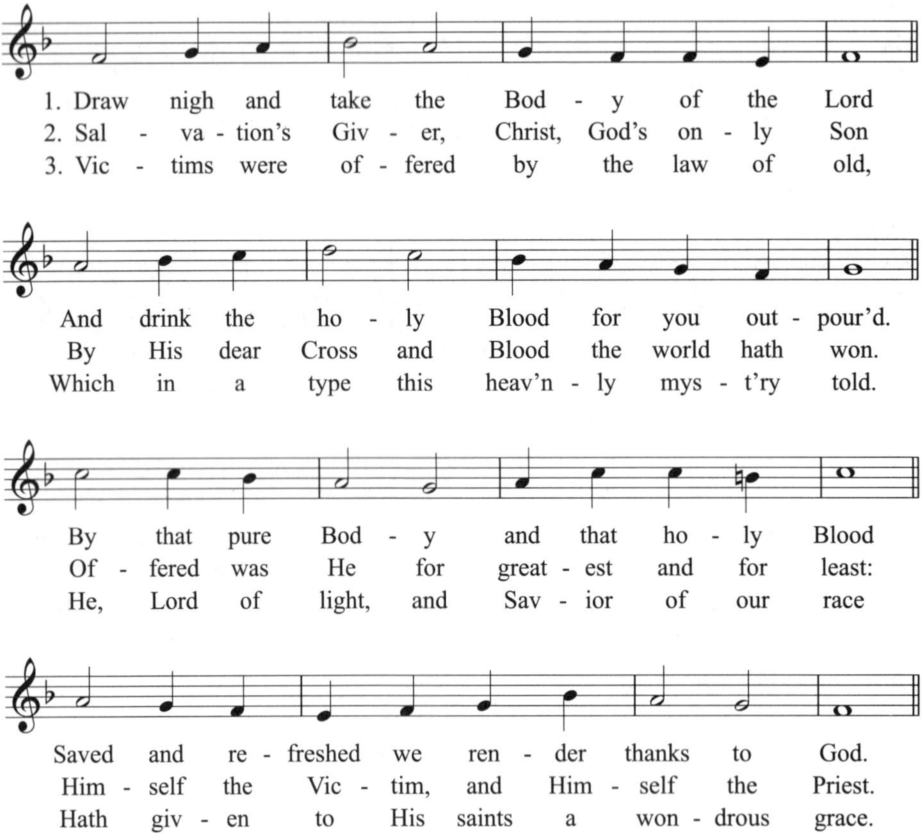

4. Approach ye then with faithful hearts sincere,
And take the safeguard of salvation here.
He that His saints in this world rules and shields
To all believers life eternal yields.

5. He feeds the hungry with the Bread of Heav'n,
And living streams to those who thirst are giv'n.
Alpha and Omega—to whom shall bow
All nations at the Doom—is with us now.

* The first line in Thurston's version was "Come saints and take the Body of the Lord," which is more faithful to the Latin original, to which he added: "By the word *saints*, as used in the first line and twice afterwards, the Celtic writer probably meant no more than *faithful Christians*. It is important to remember this in reading early Celtic documents."
English Translation: *The early cultus of the Blessed Sacrament* in *The Month* (1907) v. 109, p. 377; Fr. Thurston acknowledges his version's debt to Dr. Neale's translation in *Mediaeval Hymns and Sequences* (1851) p. 13.
Melody: Louis Bourgeois (d. 1559) in the *Genevan Psalter* (1551); also called "Old 124th."
M. Source: *People's Mass Book* (1964) p. 226; *New Saint Basil Hymnal* (1958) p. 80.

10 10 10 10

Tune:
Toulon

Sancti Venite, Christi Corpus Sumite (640AD) 475

Sixth Tune – *Trns: Fr. Herbert Thurston (d. 1939) after Neale*

1. Draw nigh and take the Bod - y of the Lord
2. Sal - va - tion's Giv - er, Christ, God's on - ly Son
3. Vic - tims were of - fered by the law of old,

And drink the ho - ly Blood for you out - pour'd.
By His dear Cross and Blood the world hath won.
Which in a type this heav'n - ly mys - t'ry told.

By that pure Bod - y and that ho - ly Blood
Of - fered was He for great - est and for least:
He, Lord of light, and Sav - ior of our race

Saved and re - freshed we ren - der thanks to God.
Him - self the Vic - tim, and Him - self the Priest.
Hath giv - en to His saints a won - drous grace.

4. Approach ye then with faithful hearts sincere,
And take the safeguard of salvation here.
He that His saints in this world rules and shields
To all believers life eternal yields.

5. He feeds the hungry with the Bread of Heav'n,
And living streams to those who thirst are giv'n.
Alpha and Omega—to whom shall bow
All nations at the Doom—is with us now.

* The first line in Thurston's version was "Come saints and take the Body of the Lord," which is more faithful to the Latin original, to which he added: "By the word *saints*, as used in the first line and twice afterwards, the Celtic writer probably meant no more than *faithful Christians*. It is important to remember this in reading early Celtic documents."
English Translation: *The early cultus of the Blessed Sacrament* in *The Month* (1907) v. 109, p. 377; Fr. Thurston acknowledges his version's debt to Dr. Neale's translation in *Mediaeval Hymns and Sequences* (1851) p. 13.
Melody: Henry Lawes (d. 1662), whose compositions John Milton (d. 1674) praised in a famous sonnet.
M. Source: *New Westminster Hymnal* (1939) p. 234; *Catholic Hymn Book* (London Oratory, 1998) p. 250.

10 10 10 10

Tune:
Farley Castle

476 Stabat Mater Dolorosa (13th century)

"Now there stood by the cross of Jesus, his mother..."—St. John 19.25

To sing in Latin,
use any 887 887 tune.

STABAT Mater dolorósa
Juxta Crucem lacrimósa,
Dum pendébat Fílius.

2. Cujus ánimam geméntem,
Contristátam et doléntem
Pertransívit gládius.

3. O quam tristis et afflícta
Fuit illa benedícta
Mater unigéniti! *n1*

4. Quae maerébat et dolébat,
Pia Mater, dum vidébat
Nati poenas íncliti.

5. Quis est homo qui non fleret,
Matrem Christi si vidéret
In tanto supplício?

6. Quis non posset contristári,
Christi Matrem contemplári
Doléntem cum Fílio?

7. Pro peccátis suae gentis, *n2*
Vidit Jesum in torméntis,
Et flagéllis súbditum.

8. Vidit suum dulcem natum
Moriéndo desolátum,
Dum emísit spíritum.

9. Eja Mater, fons amóris
Me sentíre vim dolóris
Fac, ut tecum lúgeam.

10. Fac ut árdeat cor meum
In amándo Christum Deum,
Ut sibi compláceam.

887 887

Tune:
VARIOUS

T. Source: *Paroissien Romain contenant la Messe et l'Office pour tous les dimanches et les fêtes doubles* (Dom André Mocquereau, 1903) p. 1223.

Assistance for comprehension

THE sorrowful Mother was standing,
tearful, near the Cross, *cf. Jn 19.25*
while her Son was hanging there.

2. She whose repining soul,
saddened and sorrowing,
a sword pierced. *cf. Lk 2.35*

3. O how sad and oppressed
was that blessed
Mother of an only Son! *n1*

4. She who was grieving and sorrowing,
tender Mother, while she saw
the pangs of her redoubtable Child.

5. What man is there who would not weep,
if he saw Christ's Mother
in such great torment?

6. Who would be incapable of sadness
if he were to consider Christ's Mother
as she sorrowed with her Son?

7. For the sins of her nation, *n2*
she saw Jesus in tortures
and subjected to scourges.

8. She saw her sweet Child
forsaken in dying, *cf. Mt 26.56*
while he sent forth his spirit. *cf. Mt 27.50*

9. Come then, Mother, spring of love,
cause me to feel the force of thy sorrow,
that I may mourn with thee.

10. Cause that my heart may burn
with loving Christ my God,
that I may please him.

[1] Both the Only-begotten of the Father and the Only-begotten of the Virgin.

[2] "His" is also a possible translation of *suae* (cf. Mt 1.21).

11. Sancta Mater, istud agas,
Crucifíxi fige plagas
Cordi meo válide.

12. Tui nati vulneráti,
Tam dignáti pro me pati,
Poenas mecum dívide.

13. Fac me tecum pie flere,
Crucifíxo condolére,
Donec ego víxero.

14. Juxta Crucem tecum stare,
Et me tibi sociáre
In planctu desídero.

15. Virgo vírginum praeclára,
Mihi jam non sis amára: *n3*
Fac me tecum plángere.

16. Fac ut portem Christi mortem
Passiónis fac consórtem,
Et plagas recólere.

17. Fac me plagis vulnerári,
Fac me cruc*e* inebriári,
Et cruóre Fílii.

18. Flammis ne urar succénsus,
Per te, Vírgo, sim defénsus
In die judícii.

19. Christe, cum sit hinc exíre,
Da per Matrem me veníre
Ad palmam victóriae.

20. Quando corpus moriétur,
Fac ut ánimae donétur
Paradísi glória.

11. Holy Mother, mayest thou do this:
stamp the injuries of the Crucified
strongly on my heart.

12. Divide with me the pangs
of thy wounded Child
who vouchsafed to suffer so much for me.

13. Cause me tenderly to weep with thee,
to suffer with the Crucified,
while I live.

14. To stand with thee near the Cross,
and ally myself with thee
in lament do I long.

15. O illustrious Virgin of virgins,
mayest thou not be unkind to me: *n3*
cause me to lament with thee.

16. Cause that I may bear the death of Christ, *cf. Gal 6.17, II Cor 4.11*
cause me to be a partner of his passion, *cf. Phil 3.10, Col 1.24*
and to contemplate his injuries.

17. Cause me to be wounded with his injuries,
cause me to be exhilarated
by the Cross and blood of thy Son.

18. Lest I be set on fire and burned by flames,
O Virgin, let me be protected by thee
on the day of judgment.

19. O Christ, when it is my hour to depart hence
grant by thy Mother for me to come
to the palm of conquest. *cf. Ap 7.9*

20. When my body dies,
cause that to my soul may be given
the glory of paradise.

[3] Literally "mayest thou not be bitter to me."

480 Stabat Mater Dolorosa (13th century)

First Tune – *Traditional Plainsong*

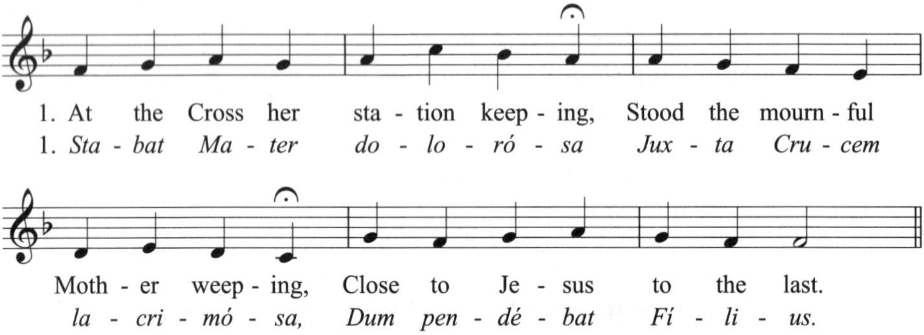

2. *Cujus ánimam geméntem,* *Contristátam et doléntem* *Pertransívit gládius.*	2. Through her heart, His sorrow sharing, All His bitter anguish bearing, Now at length the sword had pass'd.
3. *O quam tristis et afflícta* *Fuit illa benedícta* *Mater unigéniti!*	3. Oh, how sad, how heavy laden, Was that meek and blessèd Maiden, God's true Mother undefiled.
4. *Quae maerébat et dolébat,* *Pia Mater, dum vidébat* *Nati poenas íncliti.*	4. Deep the well of her affliction When she saw the Crucifixion Of her well belovèd Son.
5. *Quis est homo qui non fleret,* *Matrem Christi si vidéret* *In tanto supplício?*	5. What man is there so unfeeling, Who, his heart to pity steeling, Could behold that sight unmoved?
6. *Quis non posset contristári,* *Christi Matrem contemplári* *Doléntem cum Fílio?*	6. Lives there one whose heart with anguish Fills not, thus to see her languish, Agonizing with her Son?
7. *Pro peccátis suae gentis,* *Vidit Jesum in torméntis,* *Et flagéllis súbditum.*	7. For the guilt that doomed his nation Saw she Jesus in prostration 'Neath the scourges meekly bent;
8. *Vidit suum dulcem natum* *Moriéndo desolátum,* *Dum emísit spíritum.*	8. Saw the Lord's Anointed taken; Saw her Child in death forsaken; Heard his last expiring cry.
9. *Eja Mater, fons amóris* *Me sentíre vim dolóris* *Fac, ut tecum lúgeam.*	9. Mother, fount whence love flows truest, Let me know the pain thou knewest, Let me weep as thou hast wept;

Tune: Stabat Mater

Melody: *Hymni de Tempore et de Sanctis in Textu Antiquo et Novo* (Solesmes, 1885) p. 72.
English Translation: Fr. Edward Caswall (d. 1878); Very Rev'd Dominic Aylward (d. 1872); Denis Florence MacCarthy (d. 1882); Athanasius Diedrich Wackerbarth (d. 1884); Aubrey Thomas de Vere (d. 1902); Fr. John Fitzpatrick (d. 1929); Hon. Daniel Joseph Donahoe (d. 1930); Msgr. Hugh T. Henry (d. 1946); Msgr. Ronald A. Knox (d. 1957).

10. *Fac ut árdeat cor meum* *In amándo Christum Deum,* *Ut sibi compláceam.*	10. Make me, loving Christ, so love Him That now, setting naught above Him, To His Will my will may cleave.
11. *Sancta Mater, istud agas,* *Crucifíxi fige plagas* *Cordi meo válide.*	11. Mother, every wound and tremor Of the crucified Redeemer, Firmly fasten in my soul;
12. *Tui nati vulneráti,* *Tam dignáti pro me pati,* *Poenas mecum dívide.*	12. Since He deigns that all the merit Of His wounds I should inherit All His pain with me divide.
13. *Fac me tecum pie flere,* *Crucifíxo condolére,* *Donec ego víxero.*	13. Make me thy co-mourner truly, For His crucifixion duly Sorr'wing till my life is o'er:
14. *Juxta Crucem tecum stare,* *Et me tibi sociáre* *In planctu desídero.*	14. Mine with thee be that sad station, There to watch the great salvation Wrought upon th'Atoning Tree.
15. *Virgo vírginum praeclára,* *Mihi jam non sis amára:* *Fac me tecum plángere.*	15. Virgin of all virgins fairest, Share with me the pains thou bearest, Be thy crushing sorrows mine.
16. *Fac ut portem Christi mortem* *Passiónis fac consórtem,* *Et plagas recólere.*	16. Let me, mindful of His Passion Die in Christ, and, in some fashion, Bear the wounds He bore for me.
17. *Fac me plagis vulnerári,* *Fac me cruce‿inebriári,* *Et cruóre Fílii.*	17. All His bitter torments feeling, In the cross my spirit reeling, In His blood my senses drown.
18. *Flammis ne urar succénsus,* *Per te, Virgo, sim defénsus* *In die judícii.*	18. Lest I burn in fires unending, Sinless Maid, my cause befriending, Shield me at the judgment day.
19. *Christe, cum sit hinc exíre,* *Da per Matrem me veníre* *Ad palmam victóriae.*	19. Jesus, when earth's shadows leave me, Through Thy Mother's prayers receive me With the palm of victory.
20. *Quando corpus moriétur,* *Fac ut ánimae donétur* *Paradísi glória.*	20. When my body lies forsaken Let my ransomed soul awaken Safe, in Paradise, with Thee.

482 Stabat Mater Dolorosa (13th century)

Second Tune – *Paroissien Romain Melody*

2. *Cujus ánimam geméntem,* *Contristátam et doléntem* *Pertransívit gládius.*	2. Through her heart, His sorrow sharing, All His bitter anguish bearing, Now at length the sword had pass'd.
3. *O quam tristis et afflícta* *Fuit illa benedícta* *Mater unigéniti!*	3. Oh, how sad, how heavy laden, Was that meek and blessèd Maiden, God's true Mother undefiled.
4. *Quae maerébat et dolébat,* *Pia Mater, dum vidébat* *Nati poenas íncliti.*	4. Deep the well of her affliction When she saw the Crucifixion Of her well belovèd Son.
5. *Quis est homo qui non fleret,* *Matrem Christi si vidéret* *In tanto supplício?*	5. What man is there so unfeeling, Who, his heart to pity steeling, Could behold that sight unmoved?
6. *Quis non posset contristári,* *Christi Matrem contemplári* *Doléntem cum Fílio?*	6. Lives there one whose heart with anguish Fills not, thus to see her languish, Agonizing with her Son?
7. *Pro peccátis suae gentis,* *Vidit Jesum in torméntis,* *Et flagéllis súbditum.*	7. For the guilt that doomed his nation Saw she Jesus in prostration 'Neath the scourges meekly bent;
8. *Vidit suum dulcem natum* *Moriéndo desolátum,* *Dum emísit spíritum.*	8. Saw the Lord's Anointed taken; Saw her Child in death forsaken; Heard his last expiring cry.
9. *Eja Mater, fons amóris* *Me sentíre vim dolóris* *Fac, ut tecum lúgeam.*	9. Mother, fount whence love flows truest, Let me know the pain thou knewest, Let me weep as thou hast wept;

Tune: Couture

M. Source: *The Vatican II Hymnal* (Texas: Corpus Christi Watershed, 2011) p. 342.
English Translation: Fr. Edward Caswall (d. 1878); Very Rev'd Dominic Aylward (d. 1872); Denis Florence MacCarthy (d. 1882); Athanasius Diedrich Wackerbarth (d. 1884); Aubrey Thomas de Vere (d. 1902); Fr. John Fitzpatrick (d. 1929); Hon. Daniel Joseph Donahoe (d. 1930); Msgr. Hugh T. Henry (d. 1946); Msgr. Ronald A. Knox (d. 1957).

10. *Fac ut árdeat cor meum*
In amándo Christum Deum,
Ut sibi compláceam.

10. Make me, loving Christ, so love Him
That now, setting naught above Him,
To His Will my will may cleave.

11. *Sancta Mater, istud agas,*
Crucifíxi fige plagas
Cordi meo válide.

11. Mother, every wound and tremor
Of the crucified Redeemer,
Firmly fasten in my soul;

12. *Tui nati vulneráti,*
Tam dignáti pro me pati,
Poenas mecum dívide.

12. Since He deigns that all the merit
Of His wounds I should inherit
All His pain with me divide.

13. *Fac me tecum pie flere,*
Crucifíxo condolére,
Donec ego víxero.

13. Make me thy co-mourner truly,
For His crucifixion duly
Sorr'wing till my life is o'er:

14. *Juxta Crucem tecum stare,*
Et me tibi sociáre
In planctu desídero.

14. Mine with thee be that sad station,
There to watch the great salvation
Wrought upon th'Atoning Tree.

15. *Virgo vírginum praeclára,*
Mihi jam non sis amára:
Fac me tecum plángere.

15. Virgin of all virgins fairest,
Share with me the pains thou bearest,
Be thy crushing sorrows mine.

16. *Fac ut portem Christi mortem*
Passiónis fac consórtem,
Et plagas recólere.

16. Let me, mindful of His Passion
Die in Christ, and, in some fashion,
Bear the wounds He bore for me.

17. *Fac me plagis vulnerári,*
Fac me cruce‿inebriári,
Et cruóre Fílii.

17. All His bitter torments feeling,
In the cross my spirit reeling,
In His blood my senses drown.

18. *Flammis ne urar succénsus,*
Per te, Vírgo, sim defénsus
In die judícii.

18. Lest I burn in fires unending,
Sinless Maid, my cause befriending,
Shield me at the judgment day.

19. *Christe, cum sit hinc exíre,*
Da per Matrem me veníre
Ad palmam victóriae.

19. Jesus, when earth's shadows leave me,
Through Thy Mother's prayers receive me
With the palm of victory.

20. *Quando corpus moriétur,*
Fac ut ánimae donétur
Paradísi glória.

20. When my body lies forsaken
Let my ransomed soul awaken
Safe, in Paradise, with Thee.

484 Stabat Mater Dolorosa (13th century)

1687AD – Historic Roman Catholic Translation *

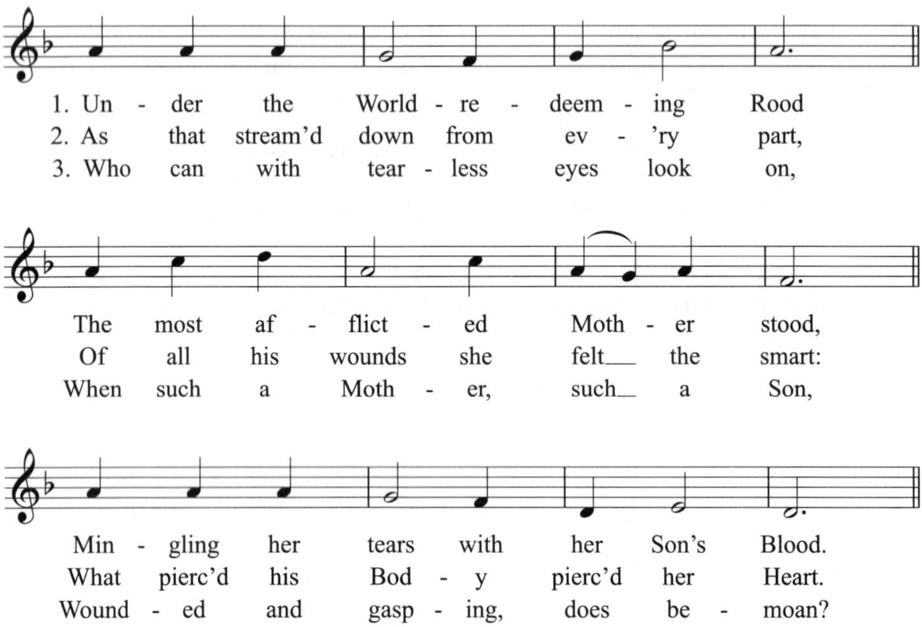

4. O harder hearts than stone that could
Unmov'd behold the double Flood
Of Mary's Tears, of Jesu's Blood.

5. Alas! Our sins, they were not His,
In this atoning Sacrifice,
For which he bleeds, for which he dies.

6. When Graves did open, Rocks were rent,
When Nature, and each Element,
His Torments, and Her Grief resent:

7. Shall Man, the Cause of all His Pain,
And all Her Grief; shall sinful Man,
Only insensible remain?

8. Ah! pious Mother, teach my Heart
Of Sighs and Tears the holy Art;
And in thy Grief to bear a part.

Melody: Peter Lejeune (b. 1991), after "O Mensch, sieh wie hie auf Erdreich."
M. Source: *Saint Jean de Brébeuf Hymnal* (2018).
T. Source: *The Office of the B. V. Mary in English, to which is added the Vespers in Latin and English, as it is sung in the Catholic Church upon all Sundays and principal Holy-days throughout the whole Year* (London: Printed by Henry Hills, Printer to the King's Most Excellent Majesty for his Household and Chappel; And are to be sold at his Printing-house on the Ditch-side in Black-Fryers, 1687) p. 393.

887

Tune:
BAYEUX

9. That sword of Grief which did pass through
Thy very soul, O may it now
One kind wound on my heart bestow!

10. Great Queen of Sorrows! in thy train
Let me a Mourner's place obtain,
With tears to cleanse all sinful stain.

11. To heal the Leprosy of sin,
We must the cure with tears begin;
All flesh corrupt without their brine.

12. Refuge of sinners, grant that we
May tread thy steps, and let it be
Our sorrow not to grieve like thee.

13. O! may the wounds of thy dear Son,
Our contrite Hearts possess alone,
And all terrene affections drown!

14. Those Wounds, which now the stars outshine,
Those Furnaces of Love-Divine,
May they our drossy souls refine:

15. And on us such Impression make,
That we, of suff'ring, for his sake,
May joyfully our Portion take.

16. Let us his proper Badge put on;
Let's glory in the Cross alone:
By which he marks us for his own.

17. That when the last Assizes come,
For ev'ry man to hear his Doom,
On his right hand we may find room.

18. O! hear us, Mary! Jesus, hear,
Our humble pray'rs, secure our fear,
When thou in judgment shalt appear.

19. Now give us sorrow, give us love;
That so prepar'd we may remove,
When call'd to the blest World above.

---

* This translation was allowed to be printed in London since it appeared during the reign of James II of England, a Catholic. He had converted from Anglicanism secretly in 1667, and refused to take a mandatory oath (1673 "Test Act") denouncing the doctrine of Transubstantiation, instead choosing to relinquish the post of Lord High Admiral. A devout man, he once said: "If occasion were, I hope God would give me his grace to suffer death for the true Catholic religion as well as banishment." His brother, who reigned as King of England until 1685, became a Catholic on his deathbed.

486 Stabat Mater Dolorosa (13th century)

1599AD – Historic Roman Catholic Translation *

Tune:
STABAT MATER

Melody: *Hymni de Tempore et de Sanctis in Textu Antiquo et Novo* (Solesmes, 1885) p. 72.
T. Source: *Primer, or, Office of the Blessed Virgin Marie in Latin and English, according to the reformed Latin, and with Lyke Graces Privileged* (Antwerp, 1599) p. 220. The Catholic Encyclopedia of 1912 attributes the hymn translations to the book's editor, Richard Verstegan (d. 1636), a Catholic publisher.

3. That would not wail, what wight is he,
if Christ his Mother he should see
in such torments to be done?
Who would not here condole the pain
the pious Mother doth sustain,
doleful with her doleful Son?

4. For his own people's only sin
such torments she saw Jesus in,
subject unto scourging smart;
her sweet Son there before her eye,
all desolate, she saw to die
while his spirit did depart.

5. O Mother, of true love the spring,
of dolor let me feel the sting:
make that I may wail with thee!
Make that my ardent heart accord
unto the love of Christ our Lord,
pleasing that to him I be!

6. Yield, holy Mother, my request,
and fix the hurts within my breast,
deeply, of the Crucified;
the pains thy wounded Son did deign
for me to suffer and sustain
vouchsafe with me to divide.

7. Make me to weep with thee indeed,
to sorrow with the Crucified,
and until my life expire;
beside the Cross to stand by thee
and gladly keep thee company,
dolefully, I do desire.

8. O Maid of maids, of most esteem,
do thou not bitter to me seem:
make me to lament with thee;
the death of Christ make me sustain:
his passion, anguish, and his pain
let me keep in memory.

9. And wounded with his wounds make me,
and with his Cross o'ercome to be
for the love of this thy Son:
that therewith being set on fire,
thou, Virgin, may'st me save from ire
when the judgment must be done.

10. The Cross, let it me keep and save,
by Christ his death defense to have,
nourished by his grace make me;
when as to die my body is,
grant that of paradise the bliss
to my soul may given be.

[1f] "Quite" means "fully."

[2d] "Complain" means "lament."

[3a] "Wail" means "grieve" — "Wight" means "man"

[3b] "Christ his Mother" means "The Mother of Christ."

[4c] "Smart" means "pain."

[10b] "Christ his death" means "the death of Christ."

* In the 1599 Preface, Richard Verstegan says: "Notwithstanding the difficulty, these hymns have been so turned into English meter that they may be sung unto the same tunes in English that they bear in Latin." For this particular translation, the harmonic rhythm must be that of Solesmes Abbey. See the following: (1) *Daily Hymn Book* (Westminster, 1949) p. 64, by Henri Potiron (d. 1972), Maître de Chapelle de la Basilique du Sacré Cœur et Professeur a l'Institut Grégorien; (2) *Liber Cantualis Comitante Organo* (Solesmes, 1981) p. 37, by Abbé Ferdinand Portier; (3) *Accompaniment to the Music of Holy Week* (Gregorian Institute of America, 1957) p. 83, by Dr. Eugene Lapierre, organist at Saint-Alphonse-d'Youville in Montréal.

488 Urbs Jerusalem Beata (6th century)

In Hebrew, the word "Jerusalem" means "City of Peace"

To sing in Latin,
use any 87 87 87 tune.

URBS Jerúsalem beáta,
Dicta pacis vísio,
Quae constrúitur in caelis
Vivis ex lapídibus,
Et Ángelis coronáta,
Ut sponsáta cómite.

2. Nova véniens e caelo,
Nuptiáli thálamo
Praeparáta, ut sponsáta
Copulétur Dómino:
Platéae et muri ejus
Ex auro puríssimo.

3. Portae nitent margarítis
Ádytis paténtibus;
Et virtúte meritórum
Illuc introdúcitur
Omnis, qui ob Christi nomen
Hic in mundo prémitur.

4. Tunsiónibus, pressúris
Expolíti lápides,
Suis coaptántur locis
Per manus artíficis,
Disponúntur permansúri
Sacris aedifíciis.

5. Gloria et honor Deo
Usquequáqu*e* altíssimo,
Una Patri, Filióque,
Ínclyto Paráclito,
Cui laus est et potéstas
Per aetérna saécula.

87 87 87

Tune:
VARIOUS

T. Surce: *Hymnal for the Church of Saint Hugh* (Letchworth: Fr. Adrian Fortescue, 1913) p. 122.

[1f] "Many thousands of angels" cf. Heb 12.22.

[2abcd] "And I, John, saw the holy city, the new Jerusalem, coming down out of heaven from God, prepared as a bride adorned for her husband" (Apoc 21.2).

[2ef] "The fashioning of its wall was of jasper, but the city itself was pure gold, that seemed to have the purity of glass" (Apoc 21.18).

Assistance for comprehension

THE blessed city of Jerusalem,
dubbed "vision of peace,"
which is raised in heaven
from living stones
and crowned like a bride
with an escort of Angels.

2. Which comes from heaven,
her bridal chamber, new,
made ready in order to be wed
as a bride to the Lord:
and whose streets and walls
are of purest gold.

3. Her gates gleam with pearls,
while her vaults lie open;
and by dint of merits
is brought there
every one who for Christ's name
is harried here in this world.

4. Polished through pounding
and crushing, her stones
are prepared for their sites
by the craftsman's hands,
and are set to endure
within her sacred buildings.

5. One glory and honor
be in every place to God
the most high, Father and Son
and illustrious Paraclete,
who commands praise
and might forevermore.

[3a] "And the foundations of the wall of the city were adorned with all manner of precious stones…" (Apoc 21.19); "And the twelve gates were twelve single pearls, one pearl for each gate; and the street of the city was of pure gold, that seemed like transparent glass." (Apoc 21.19).

[3b] "And the gates thereof shall not be shut by day: for there shall be no night there" (Apoc 21.25).

[3cdef] Every one who suffers persecution for the name of CHRIST in this world attains to the heavenly city through the merits of that suffering; cf. Mt 5.10; cf. also Eph 2.5, "it is his grace that has saved you."

[4b] "Be you also as living stones built up, a spiritual house" (I Pet 2.5).

490 Urbs Jerusalem Beata (6th century)

First Tune – *Trns: Fr. John Wilfrid Wallace, OSB (d. 1896)*

4. Stones which will form thy fearsome walls
Stroke upon stroke the chisel hews,
The workman's frequent hammer falls
To make them fitting for his use;
Then deftly joins them each to each,
Until thy tow'rs their summit reach.

5. To God the Father, God Most High,
Let all the world give honor meet;
And praise the Son with ceaseless cry,
And Holy Ghost, the Paraclete,
To whom be power, glory, praise,
Through lapse of everlasting days.

88 88 88

Tune:
St Catherine

Final Verses: Noel Rawsthorne (2011) #290.
Melody: Henri Frederick Hemy (d. 1888), a Catholic organist and publisher of hymnals who once taught in Tynemouth—and this tune is sometimes called "Tynemouth."
M. Source: *New Westminster Hymnal* (1939) p. 114; *Mediator Dei Hymnal* (1955) p. 106; *Hymns, Psalms, and Spiritual Canticles* (Massachusetts: Theodore Marier, 1983) p. 241.
T. Source: *Hymns of the Church* (London: Burns & Oates, 1874) p. 159.

Urbs Jerusalem Beata (6th century) 491

Second Tune – *Trns: Fr. John Wilfrid Wallace, OSB (d. 1896)*

1. Cit - y Ce - les - tial, Sa - lem blest, Thy peace - ful
2. How hap - p'ly thou art wed - ded now,_ The Fa - ther's
3. Thy gates, a - dorned with jew - els fair,_ Stand o - pen—

vi - sion greets___ our eyes,__ Thy walls on
glo - ry is______ thy dow'r,_ The Bride - groom's
all may en - ter in;___ 'Tis vir - tue

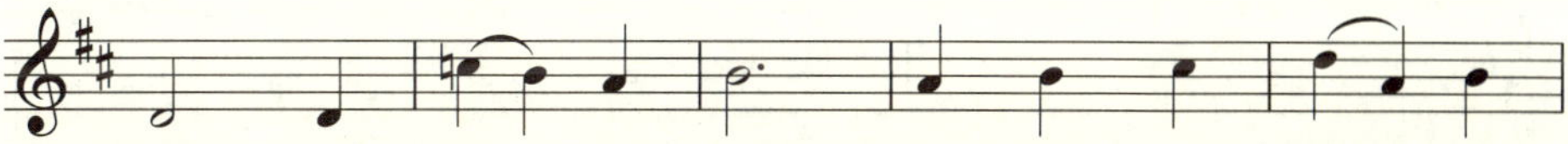

Christ's foun - da - tion rest, Thy tow'rs sur - mount the
grace is on___ thy brow; A queen in beau - ty,
must the heart_ pre - pare Of him who seeks_ thy

star - ry skies; All like a bride en - gir - dled round
rank, and pow'r, Bound fast to Christ by nup - tial ties,
courts to win, Who for the love of Christ sus - tains

With An - gels, who thy courts sur - round.
A shin - ing tem - ple of the skies.
Tor - ments His Ho - ly Will or - dains.

4. Stones which will form thy fearsome walls
Stroke upon stroke the chisel hews,
The workman's frequent hammer falls
To make them fitting for his use;
Then deftly joins them each to each,
Until thy tow'rs their summit reach.

5. To God the Father, God Most High,
Let all the world give honor meet;
And praise the Son with ceaseless cry,
And Holy Ghost, the Paraclete,
To whom be power, glory, praise,
Through lapse of everlasting days.

Melody: George Herbert (d. 1906).
M. Source: *New Westminster Hymnal* (1939) p. 242;
Mediator Dei Hymnal (1955) pp. 58, 107;
Catholic Hymn Book (London Oratory, 1998) p. 336.
T. Source: *Hymns of the Church* (London: Burns & Oates, 1874) p. 159.

88 88 88

Tune:
St Philip

492 Urbs Jerusalem Beata (6th century)

Third Tune – *Trns: Fr. John Wilfrid Wallace, OSB (d. 1896)*

4. Stones which will form thy fearsome walls
Stroke upon stroke the chisel hews,
The workman's frequent hammer falls
To make them fitting for his use;
Then deftly joins them each to each,
Until thy tow'rs their summit reach.

5. To God the Father, God Most High,
Let all the world give honor meet;
And praise the Son with ceaseless cry,
And Holy Ghost, the Paraclete,
To whom be power, glory, praise,
Through lapse of everlasting days.

88 88 88

Tune:
Vater Unser

Melody: Schumann's *Gesangbuch* (1539); this melody is sometimes called "Old 112th."
M. Source: *New Westminster Hymnal* (1939) p. 86; *Book of Hymns with Tunes* (Fr. Gregory Ould, 1913) p. 94; *Christ the King Hymnal for Congregational Singing* (Fr. Aloysius Knauff, 1955) p. 41.
T. Source: *Hymns of the Church* (London: Burns & Oates, 1874) p. 159.

Urbs Jerusalem Beata (6th century)

Fourth Tune – *Trns: Fr. John Wilfrid Wallace, OSB (d. 1896)*

4. Stones which will form thy fearsome walls
Stroke upon stroke the chisel hews,
The workman's frequent hammer falls
To make them fitting for his use;
Then deftly joins them each to each,
Until thy tow'rs their summit reach.

5. To God the Father, God Most High,
Let all the world give honor meet;
And praise the Son with ceaseless cry,
And Holy Ghost, the Paraclete,
To whom be power, glory, praise,
Through lapse of everlasting days.

T. Source: *Hymns of the Church* (London: Burns & Oates, 1874) p. 159.
Melody: Orlando Gibbons (d. 1625), organist at Westminster Abbey.
M. Source: *The Hymnes and Songs of the Church* (1623) p. 114; originally sung to "Thus Angells sung, and thus sing we." We have adopted the most commonly used rhythm, as on page 136 of the *New Saint Basil Hymnal* (1958). For 88 88 88 version, cf. *Songs of Syon* (Woodward, 1910) p. 524; *New English Hymnal* (1986) p. 676.

88 88 88

Tune: Angels' Song 8e

494 Urbs Jerusalem Beata (6th century)

FIFTH TUNE – *Trns: Fr. John Wilfrid Wallace, OSB (d. 1896)*

4. Stones which will form thy fearsome walls
Stroke upon stroke the chisel hews,
The workman's frequent hammer falls
To make them fitting for his use;
Then deftly joins them each to each,
Until thy tow'rs their summit reach.

5. To God the Father, God Most High,
Let all the world give honor meet;
And praise the Son with ceaseless cry,
And Holy Ghost, the Paraclete,
To whom be power, glory, praise,
Through lapse of everlasting days.

88 88 88

Tune:
STELLA

T. Source: *Hymns of the Church* (London: Burns & Oates, 1874) p. 159.
Melody: Henri Frederick Hemi (d. 1888), organist at St. Andrew's Catholic Church in Newcastle. As a professor and hymn editor, Hemi had great influence on Catholic hymn singing. He first heard this tune in the village of Stella, near his childhood home.
M. Source: *Catholic Hymn Book* (London Oratory, 1998) p. 246; *New Saint Basil Hymnal* (1958) p. 151.

Urbs Jerusalem Beata (6th century) 495

Trns: Fr. John Wilfrid Wallace, OSB (d. 1896)

Can be sung with any 88 88 88 meter, such as REGINA CAELORUM, ST MATTHIAS, SUSSEX CAROL, ST CHRYSOSTOM, COLCHESTER, etc.

CELESTIAL City, Salem blest,
Thy peaceful vision greets our eyes,
Thy walls on Christ's foundation rest,
Thy tow'rs surmount the starry skies;
All like a bride engirdled round
With Angels, who thy courts surround.

2. How happ'ly thou art wedded now,
The Father's glory is thy dow'r,
The Bridegroom's grace is on thy brow;
A queen in beauty, rank, and pow'r,
Bound fast to Christ by nuptial ties,
A shining temple of the skies.

3. Thy gates, adorned with jewels fair,
Stand open—all may enter in;
'Tis virtue must the heart prepare
Of him who seeks thy courts to win,
Who for the love of Christ sustains
Torments His Holy Will ordains.

4. Stones which will form thy fearsome walls
Stroke upon stroke the chisel hews,
The workman's frequent hammer falls
To make them fitting for his use;
Then deftly joins them each to each,
Until thy tow'rs their summit reach.

5. To God the Father, God Most High,
Let all the world give honor meet;
And praise the Son with ceaseless cry,
And Holy Ghost, the Paraclete,
To whom be power, glory, praise,
Through lapse of everlasting days.

88 88 88

Tune: VARIOUS

T. Source: *Hymns of the Church* (London: Burns & Oates, 1874) p. 159.

496 Urbs Jerusalem Beata (6th century)

1599AD – Historic Roman Catholic Translation

This translation, although 87 87 87, is more suited to plainsong, owing to the placement of accents. The same can be said about some of the other 1599AD translations.

JERUSALEM o city blest,
That of peace the vision hight: *n1*
Which framed art amid the heavens
And of lively stones ydight, *n2*
And as one that is espousèd,
Crownèd with the Angels bright.

2. From the heavens new descending,
As a wedding chamber fro,
And with our Lord as to be matched,
Like a bride so doth she go:
Whose walls and streets so brave *ap*pearing,
Of the purest gold do show.

3. The gates with pearls clearly glister,
To the which the paths appear,
Where by virtue of their merits
All are brought with joyful cheer,
Which for Christ have been afflicted,
While on earth they livèd here.

4. Both with beating, and with hewing,
Are the polished stones addressed,
As unto this holy building,
They may fit their places best:
By the workman's handy working,
So disposèd for to rest.

5. All glory and all honor due,
Unto God the highest be,
The father jointly and the son,
*Th'*Holy ghost of high degree:
Unto whom be praise, and power,
To endure eternally.

Urbs Jerúsalem beáta,
Dicta pacis vísio,
Quae constrúitur in caelis
Vivus ex lapídibus,
Et Ángelis coronáta,
Ut sponsáta cómite.

Nova véniens e caelo,
Nuptiáli thálamo
Praeparáta, ut sponsáta
Copulétur Dómino:
Platéae et muri ejus
Ex auro puríssimo.

Portae nitent margarítis
Ádytis paténtibus;
Et virtúte meritórum
Illuc introdúcitur
Omnis, qui ob Christi nomen
Hic in mundo prémitur.

Tunsiónibus, pressúris
Expolíti lápides,
Suis coaptántur locis
Per manus artíficis,
Disponúntur permansúri
Sacris aedifíciis.

Gloria et honor Deo
Usquequáqu*e* altíssimo,
Una Patri, Filióque,
Ínclyto Paráclito,
Cui laus est et potéstas
Per aetérna saécula.

[1] *Hight* is an archaic word meaning "named."

[2] *Ydight* is an archaic word meaning "built" or "clothed."

87 87 87

Tune: VARIOUS

T. Source: *Primer, or, Office of the Blessed Virgin Marie in Latin and English, according to the reformed Latin, and with Lyke Graces Privileged* (Antwerp, 1599) p. 25. The Catholic Encyclopedia of 1912 attributes the hymn translations to the book's editor, Richard Verstegan (d. 1636), a Catholic publisher. In the 1599 Preface, Verstegan says: "Notwithstanding the difficulty, these hymns have been so turned into English meter that they may be sung unto the same tunes in English that they bear in Latin." However, his accentual treatment is sometimes peculiar.

1719AD – Historic Roman Catholic Translation

English translation can be sung with any 88 88 88 meter, such as COLCHESTER, REGINA CAELORUM, ST MATTHIAS, SUSSEX CAROL, ST CHRYSOSTOM, etc.

Caeléstis urbs Jerúsalem,
Beáta pacis vísio,
Quae celsa de vivéntibus
Saxis ad astra tólleris,
Sponsaéque ritu cíngeris
Mill*e* Angelórum míllibus.

JERUSALEM, whose Name contains
That heav'nly Peace which in thee reigns,
Thy living stones raise thee so high,
That stars beneath thy Pavement lie;
Attended like a Bride in state,
Millions of Angels on thee wait.

O sorte nupta próspera,
Dotáta Patris glória,
Respérsa Sponsi grátia,
Regína formosíssima,
Christo jugáta Príncipi,
Caeli corúsca Cívitas.

2. O happy Bride, whose Dowry is
The Glory of the Father's Bliss!
Thrice beautiful and charming Queen,
In whom thy Spouse's Grace is seen!
City of Heaven shining bright,
Govern'd by Christ the Prince of Light!

Hic margarítis émicant,
Paténtque cunctis óstia:
Virtúte namque praévia
Mortális illuc dúcitur,
Amóre Christi pércitus
Torménta quisquis sústinet.

3. Thy Gates, with Orient Pearl array'd,
For all stand open and display'd:
Who follows close th'unerring Guide
Of Virtue, and by Torments try'd
Suffers with Patience for his Lord,
Finds here a plentiful Reward.

Scalpri salúbris íctibus,
Et tunsióne plúrima,
Fabri políta málleo
Hanc saxa molem cónstruunt,
Aptísque juncta néxibus
Locántur in fastígio.

4. The wholesome Chizel often went,
Many a saving Stroke was spent,
And th'Architect dealt heavy Blows,
The stones to polish which compose
This Pile, and join'd with fit Cement
Render its Roof magnificent.

Decus Parénti débitum,
Sit usquequáqu*e* Altíssimo,
Natóque Patris único,
Et ínclyto Paráclito,
C*ui* laus, potéstas, glória
Aetérna sit per saécula.

5. Let ev'ry Tongue and Place proclaim
Of God most high the holy Name,
Of God the Father, and his Son,
And holy Spirit, Three in One,
To whom be Power, Glory, Praise,
For an eternal Age of Days.

T. Source: *The Evening-Office of the Church in Latin and English, containing the Vespers for all Sundays and Festivals of Obligation, with the Addition of the Old Hymns* (1719) pp. 170-172.

NOTE : Pope Urban VIII changed this hymn so drastically that even the meter was altered. Fr. Adrian Fortescue (d. 1923) succinctly describes the reform in the following way:

> In the seventeenth century came the crushing blow which destroyed the beauty of all Breviary hymns. In a fatal moment, Pope Urban VIII (d. 1644) noticed that the hymns do not all conform to the rules of classical prosody. Attempts to reform them had been made before, but so far they had been spared. Urban VIII was destined to succeed in destroying them. He appointed four Jesuits to reform the hymns, so that they should no longer offend Renaissance ears. […] They slashed and tinkered, they rewrote lines and altered words, they changed the sense, and were not ashamed to lay their hands on Sedulius, on Prudentius, on St. Ambrose himself. Only in one or two cases does some sense of shame seem to have stopped their nefarious work. They left *Ave Maris Stella*, *Jam Lucis Orto Sidere*, and the hymns of St. Thomas Aquinas alone. In 1629, their mangled remnants were published.

All later hymnologists have condemned this reform: Abbé Pimont, Fr. Batiffol, Fr. Byrnes, Dom Baudot, etc.

88 88 88

Tune:
VARIOUS

498 Veni Creator Spiritus (9th century)

Rhabanus Maurus (d. 856AD), Archbishop of Mainz

To sing in Latin,
use any 88 88 (LM) tune.

VENI Creátor Spíritus:
Mentes tuórum vísita, *n1*
Imple supérna grátia,
Quae tu creásti péctora.

2. Qui Paráclitus díceris
Donum Dei altíssimi,
Fons vivus, ignis, cáritas,
Et spiritális únctio. *n2*

3. Tu septifórmis múnere,
Dextrae Dei tu dígitus,
Tu rite promíssum Patris,
Sermóne ditans gúttura. *n3*

4. Accénde lumen sénsibus,
Infúnd*e* amórem córdibus,
Infírma nostri córporis
Virtúte firmans pérpeti. *n4*

5. Hostem repéllas lóngius,
Pacémque dones prótinus;
Ductóre sic te praévio
Vitémus omne nóxium.

6. Per te sciámus da Patrem,
Noscámus atque Fílium,
Te utriúsque Spíritum,
Credámus omni témpore. *n5*

7. Glória Patri Dómino,
Natóque, qui a mórtuis
Surréxit, ac Paráclito,
In saeculórum saécula.

88 88 (LM)

Tune:
VARIOUS

[1] "Visitare" also means "assist."

[2] "Paraclitus" is from the Greek word, "advocate" (cf. Jn 14.16, 26; 15.26; 16.7); "gift" cf. Jn 4.10; "living spring" cf. ibid., Jn 7.38; "fire" cf. Ac 2.3; "charity" cf. Rom 5.5; "anointing" cf. Ac 10.38.

Assistance for comprehension

COME, thou Creator, thou Spirit:
visit the minds of those who are thine, *n1*
and fill with grace from above
the hearts that thou hast created.

2. Thou who art called the Paraclete,
the gift of God most high,
the living spring, fire, charity
and spiritual anointing. *n2*

3. Thou art sevenfold in favor,
thou the finger of God's right hand,
thou, duly promised by the Father,
enriching throats with speech. *n3*

4. Kindle light in our feelings,
pour love into our hearts,
steadying with continual power
the unsteadiness of our bodies. *n4*

5. Mayest thou drive the foe yet further
and grant peace continually;
thus with thee as the guide that leads the way
we will avoid whatever is harmful.

6. Grant us to know the Father by thee,
and let us recognize the Son also,
and at all times believe thee,
the Spirit of them both. *n5*

7. Glory be to the Father, who is Lord,
and to the Son, who rose from the dead,
and to the Paraclete,
for ever and ever.

[3] "Sevenfold in favor" are the seven gifts of the Holy Spirit, cf. Is 11.2-3; "finger" cf. Lk 11.20; "promised" cf. Lk 24.49, Ac 1.4; "enriching throats" cf. Ac 2.4.

[4] "Unsteadiness" could also be rendered "unsteady things."

[5] "Of them both" cf. Jn 14.26; 15.26; 16.7.

500 Veni Creator Spiritus (9th century)

Trns: Fr. John Fitzpatrick, Oblate of Mary (d. 1929)

1. Come, O Cre - a - tor - Spir - it, deign
2. The gift of God who reigns a - bove,
3. Fin - ger of God's right hand art Thou;

Our minds to vis - it, which are Thine;
Thou, who art called the Par - a - clete;
Thou dost a sev'n - fold gift im - part;

Fill with Thy heav'n - ly grace a - gain
His liv - ing fount, His fire, His love,
The Fa - ther's prom - ise, du - ly now

Our hearts, which are Thy work di - vine.
His unc - tion to the spir - it sweet.
En - rich - ing fal - t'ring tongues, Thou art.

4. Illumine Thou these minds of ours;
Upon our hearts Thy love outpour,
Strengthen with Thine immortal pow'rs
Our mortal weakness evermore.

5. Our enemy drive far away;
On us forthwith Thy peace bestow,
If Thou but lead us day by day,
No evil paths our feet shall go.

6. The Father unto us make known,
Make known His only Son, no less,
And let us ever Thee alone
The spirit of Them both confess.

7. To God the Father glory be,
And to the Son, who from the dead
Arose; likewise eternally
The Paraclete be hallowèd.

88 88 (LM)

Tune:
CUPERTINO

Melody: Kevin Allen (b. 1965), choirmaster at the Monastery of the Holy Cross in Chicago.
M. Source: *Saint Edmund Campion Missal and Hymnal* (2013) p. 882.
T. Source: *The Breviary and Missal Hymns* (London: Sands & Co, 1931) p. 84.

Veni Creator Spiritus (9th century)

Trns: Fr. John Fitzpatrick, Oblate of Mary (d. 1929)

Can be sung with any 88 88 meter, such as FULDA, SYMPHONIACAE, CUPERTINO, MEIN SEEL O GOTT, SONG 34, GONFALON ROYAL, WINCHESTER NEW, etc.

COME, O Creator-Spirit, deign
Our minds to visit, which are Thine;
Fill with Thy heav'nly grace again
Our hearts, which are Thy work divine.

2. The gift of God who reigns above,
Thou, who art called the Paraclete;
His living fount, His fire, His love,
His unction to the spirit sweet.

3. Finger of God's right hand art Thou;
Thou dost a sev'nfold gift impart;
The Father's promise, duly now
Enriching falt'ring tongues, Thou art.

4. Illumine Thou these minds of ours;
Upon our hearts Thy love outpour,
Strengthen with Thine immortal pow'rs
Our mortal weakness evermore.

5. Our enemy drive far away;
On us forthwith Thy peace bestow,
If Thou but lead us day by day,
No evil paths our feet shall go.

6. The Father unto us make known,
Make known His only Son, no less,
And let us ever Thee alone
The spirit of Them both confess.

7. To God the Father glory be,
And to the Son, who from the dead
Arose; likewise eternally
The Paraclete be hallowèd.

88 88 (LM)

Tune: VARIOUS

T. Source: *The Breviary and Missal Hymns* (London: Sands & Co, 1931) p. 84.

502 Veni Creator Spiritus (9th century)

First Tune – *Trns: Robert Campbell of Skerrington (d. 1868)*

4. Then to our souls Thy light impart,
And give Thy love to ev'ry heart;
Turn all our weakness into might,
O Thou the source of life and light.

5. Far from us keep our cruel foe,
And peace from Thine own hand bestow;
Upheld by Thee, our strength and guide,
No evil can our steps betide.

6. Spirit of faith, on us bestow
The Father and the Son to know;
And of the Twain, the Spirit, Thee—
Eternal One, eternal Three.

7. To God the Father let us sing;
To God the Son, our Risen King;
And equally with these adore
The Spirit, God for evermore.

88 88 (LM)

Tune:
Gonfalon Royal

Final Verses: Richard Lloyd (1993) #80; Noel Rawsthorne (2011) #136.
Melody: Sir Percy Carter Buck (d. 1947); first published in *Fourteen Hymn Tunes* (1913).
M. Source: *Catholic Hymn Book* (London Oratory, 1998) p. 140. The tune was originally paired with *Vexilla Regis* ("Flag of the King"). A *gonfalon* ("flag") was traditionally carried during Catholic processions.
T. Source: *Mediator Dei Hymnal* (1955) p. 40.
English Translation: Robert Campbell, a Scottish attorney who published *Hymns and Anthems for Use in the Holy Service of the Church* (1850). He converted to the Catholic Church in 1852, but was never a priest—despite the claim made in the *American Catholic Hymnal according to the Motu Proprio of His Holiness Pope Pius X* (1913) on page 251.

Veni Creator Spiritus (9th century) 503

Second Tune – *Trns: Robert Campbell of Skerrington (d. 1868)*

4. Then to our souls Thy light impart,
And give Thy love to ev'ry heart;
Turn all our weakness into might,
O Thou the source of life and light.

5. Far from us keep our cruel foe,
And peace from Thine own hand bestow;
Upheld by Thee, our strength and guide,
No evil can our steps betide.

6. Spirit of faith, on us bestow
The Father and the Son to know;
And of the Twain, the Spirit, Thee—
Eternal One, eternal Three.

7. To God the Father let us sing;
To God the Son, our Risen King;
And equally with these adore
The Spirit, God for evermore.

* This melody at a lower key is on page 248.

M. Source: Cento from *The Parochial Hymn Book, Words and Melodies; containing Vespers, Compline, and all the Liturgical Hymns for the Year both in Latin and English* (London, 1883), edited by Fr. Anatole Police; Imprimatur by Henry Edward Cardinal Manning (d. 1892), who in 1851 converted from Anglicanism and was appointed Archbishop of Westminster in 1865.
English Translation: Robert Campbell, a Scottish attorney who published *Hymns and Anthems for Use in the Holy Service of the Church* (1850). He converted to the Catholic Church in 1852, but was never a priest—despite the claim made in the *American Catholic Hymnal according to the Motu Proprio of His Holiness Pope Pius X* (1913) on page 251. T. Source: *Mediator Dei Hymnal* (1955) p. 40.

88 88 (LM)

Tune: Ioannes

504 Veni Creator Spiritus (9th century)

Third Tune – *Trns: Robert Campbell of Skerrington (d. 1868)*

1. Cre - a - tor - Spir - it, Lord__ of grace, Make
2. Come from the Throne of God__ a - bove, O
3. O Fin - ger of the Hand__ di - vine, The

Thou our hearts Thy dwell - ing - place, And with__ Thy
Par - a - clete, O ho - ly Dove; Come, oil__ of
sev'n - fold gifts of grace are Thine, And touched by

might__ ce - les - tial, aid The souls of those whom
glad - ness, cleans - ing fire And liv - ing spring of
Thee__ the lips pro - claim All praise to God's most

Thou hast made. *Al - le - lu - ia.*
pure de - sire. *Al - le - lu - ia.*
ho - ly name. *Al - le - lu - ia.*

4. Then to our souls Thy light impart,
And give Thy love to ev'ry heart;
Turn all our weakness into might,
O Thou the source of life and light.
Alleluia.

5. Far from us keep our cruel foe,
And peace from Thine own hand bestow;
Upheld by Thee, our strength and guide,
No evil can our steps betide.
Alleluia.

6. Spirit of faith, on us bestow
The Father and the Son to know;
And of the Twain, the Spirit, Thee—
Eternal One, eternal Three.
Alleluia.

7. To God the Father let us sing;
To God the Son, our Risen King;
And equally with these adore
The Spirit, God for evermore.
Alleluia.

88 88 A

Tune:
Erschienen Ist

T. Source: *Mediator Dei Hymnal* (1955) p. 40.
English Translation: Robert Campbell, a Scottish attorney who published *Hymns and Anthems for Use in the Holy Service of the Church* (1850). He converted to the Catholic Church in 1852, but was never a priest—despite the claim made in the *American Catholic Hymnal according to the Motu Proprio of His Holiness Pope Pius X* (1913) on page 251.
Melody: Nikolaus Hermann (d. 1561), organist at Joachimsthal, Bohemia.
M. Source: *Hymns Ancient and Modern* (1972) p. 832; cf. "Erschienen ist der herrlich Tag" in *The Four-Part Chorals of J. S. Bach with the German Text of the Hymns and English Translations* (Charles Sanford Terry, 1964) p. 87.

Veni Creator Spiritus (9th century)

Fourth Tune – *Trns: Robert Campbell of Skerrington (d. 1868)*

4. Then to our souls Thy light impart,
And give Thy love to ev'ry heart;
Turn all our weakness into might,
O Thou the source of life and light.

5. Far from us keep our cruel foe,
And peace from Thine own hand bestow;
Upheld by Thee, our strength and guide,
No evil can our steps betide.

6. Spirit of faith, on us bestow
The Father and the Son to know;
And of the Twain, the Spirit, Thee—
Eternal One, eternal Three.

7. To God the Father let us sing;
To God the Son, our Risen King;
And equally with these adore
The Spirit, God for evermore.

Final Verses: Richard Lloyd (1993) #64; Noel Rawsthorne (2011) #108.
Melody: Bartholomäus Gesius (d. 1613); adapted by Johann H. Schein (d. 1630).
M. Source: *New Saint Basil Hymnal* (1958) p. 120; *The Catholic Vesper Hymn Book set to Music either for Unison or Four Voices with Accompaniment* (Charles Lewis, 1877) p. 34; *Pope Pius XII Hymnal* (Ohio: Gregorian Institute of America, 1959) p. 13.
English Translation: Robert Campbell, a Scottish attorney who published *Hymns and Anthems for Use in the Holy Service of the Church* (1850). He converted to the Catholic Church in 1852, but was never a priest—despite the claim made in the *American Catholic Hymnal according to the Motu Proprio of His Holiness Pope Pius X* (1913) on page 251.
T. Source: *Mediator Dei Hymnal* (1955) p. 40.

88 88 (LM)

Tune: Eisenach

506 Veni Creator Spiritus (9th century)

Fifth Tune – *Trns: Robert Campbell of Skerrington (d. 1868)*

4. Then to our souls Thy light impart,
And give Thy love to ev'ry heart;
Turn all our weakness into might,
O Thou the source of life and light.

5. Far from us keep our cruel foe,
And peace from Thine own hand bestow;
Upheld by Thee, our strength and guide,
No evil can our steps betide.

6. Spirit of faith, on us bestow
The Father and the Son to know;
And of the Twain, the Spirit, Thee—
Eternal One, eternal Three.

7. To God the Father let us sing;
To God the Son, our Risen King;
And equally with these adore
The Spirit, God for evermore.

88 88 (LM)

Tune:
Rogers Park

Melody: Kevin Allen (b. 1965), choirmaster at the Monastery of the Holy Cross in Chicago.
M. Source: *Saint Jean de Brébeuf Hymnal* (2018). T. Source: *Mediator Dei Hymnal* (1955) p. 40.
English Translation: Robert Campbell, a Scottish attorney who published *Hymns and Anthems for Use in the Holy Service of the Church* (1850). He converted to the Catholic Church in 1852, but was never a priest—despite the claim made in the *American Catholic Hymnal according to the Motu Proprio of His Holiness Pope Pius X* (1913) on page 251.

Veni Creator Spiritus (9th century) 507

Sixth Tune – *Trns: Robert Campbell of Skerrington (d. 1868)*

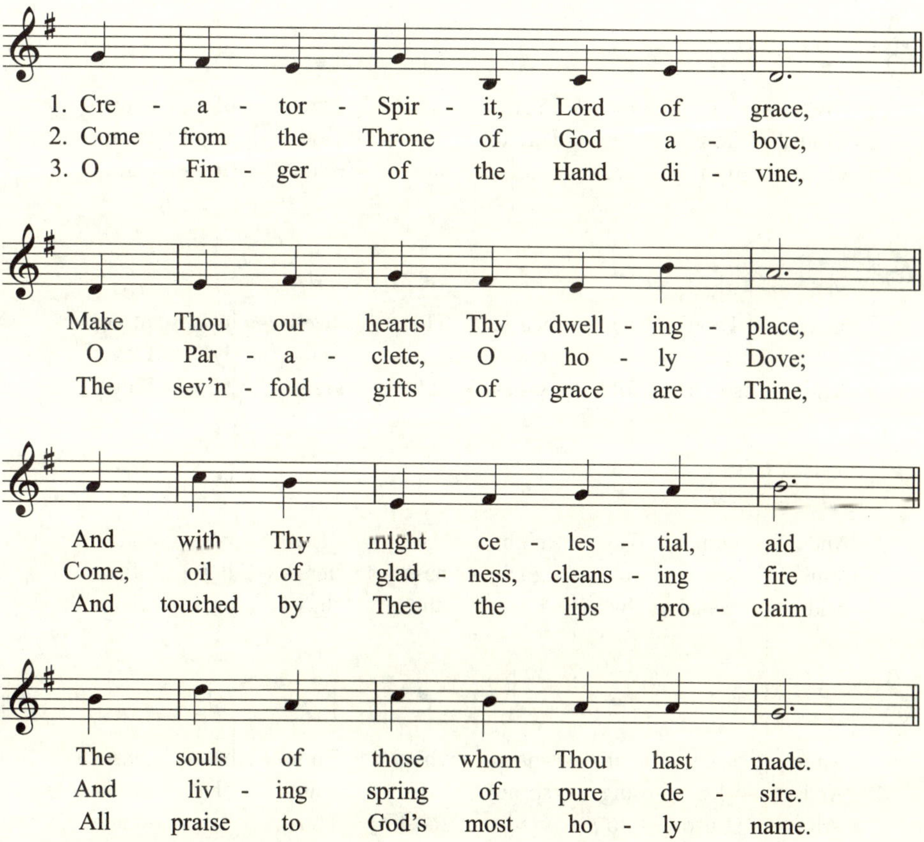

4. Then to our souls Thy light impart,
And give Thy love to ev'ry heart;
Turn all our weakness into might,
O Thou the source of life and light.

5. Far from us keep our cruel foe,
And peace from Thine own hand bestow;
Upheld by Thee, our strength and guide,
No evil can our steps betide.

6. Spirit of faith, on us bestow
The Father and the Son to know;
And of the Twain, the Spirit, Thee—
Eternal One, eternal Three.

7. To God the Father let us sing;
To God the Son, our Risen King;
And equally with these adore
The Spirit, God for evermore.

Melody: Henry Lawes (d. 1662).
M. Source: *Saint Edmund Campion Missal and Hymnal* (2013) p. 888.
English Translation: Robert Campbell, a Scottish attorney who published *Hymns and Anthems for Use in the Holy Service of the Church* (1850). He converted to the Catholic Church in 1852, but was never a priest—despite the claim made in the *American Catholic Hymnal according to the Motu Proprio of His Holiness Pope Pius X* (1913) on page 251. T. Source: *Mediator Dei Hymnal* (1955) p. 40.

88 88 (LM)

Tune: Whitehall

508 Veni Creator Spiritus (9th century)

Seventh Tune – *Trns: Robert Campbell of Skerrington (d. 1868)*

4. Then to our souls Thy light impart,
   And give Thy love to ev'ry heart;
   Turn all our weakness into might,
   O Thou the source of life and light.

5. Far from us keep our cruel foe,
   And peace from Thine own hand bestow;
   Upheld by Thee, our strength and guide,
   No evil can our steps betide.

6. Spirit of faith, on us bestow
   The Father and the Son to know;
   And of the Twain, the Spirit, Thee—
   Eternal One, eternal Three.

7. To God the Father let us sing;
   To God the Son, our Risen King;
   And equally with these adore
   The Spirit, God for evermore.

88 88 (LM)

Tune: Woolmer's

Melody: Frederick A. G. Ouseley (d. 1889), professor of music at Oxford.
M. Source: *Riverdale Hymn Book* (Chicago: Fleming H. Revell, 1912) p. 172.
English Translation: Robert Campbell, a Scottish attorney who published *Hymns and Anthems for Use in the Holy Service of the Church* (1850). He converted to the Catholic Church in 1852, but was never a priest—despite the claim made in the *American Catholic Hymnal according to the Motu Proprio of His Holiness Pope Pius X* (1913) on page 251. T. Source: *Mediator Dei Hymnal* (1955) p. 40.

Veni Creator Spiritus (9th century)

Trns: Robert Campbell of Skerrington (d. 1868)

Can be sung with any 88 88 meter, such as EISENACH, ROGERS PARK, BRESSANI, LA ROCHELLE, KEMPEN, BESSEMER, TALLIS CANON, WINCHESTER NEW, etc.

CREATOR-SPIRIT, Lord of grace,
Make Thou our hearts Thy dwelling-place,
And with Thy might celestial, aid
The souls of those whom Thou hast made.

2. Come from the Throne of God above,
O Paraclete, O holy Dove;
Come, oil of gladness, cleansing fire
And living spring of pure desire.

3. O Finger of the Hand divine,
The sev'n-fold gifts of grace are Thine,
And touched by Thee the lips proclaim
All praise to God's most holy name.

4. Then to our souls Thy light impart,
And give Thy love to ev'ry heart;
Turn all our weakness into might,
O Thou the source of life and light.

5. Far from us keep our cruel foe,
And peace from Thine own hand bestow;
Upheld by Thee, our strength and guide,
No evil can our steps betide.

6. Spirit of faith, on us bestow
The Father and the Son to know;
And of the Twain, the Spirit, Thee—
Eternal One, eternal Three.

7. To God the Father let us sing;
To God the Son, our Risen King;
And equally with these adore
The Spirit, God for evermore.

T. Source: *Mediator Dei Hymnal* (1955) p. 40.

ENGLISH TRANSLATION: Robert Campbell, a Scottish attorney who published *Hymns and Anthems for Use in the Holy Service of the Church* (1850). He converted to the Catholic Church in 1852, but was never a priest—despite the claim made in the *American Catholic Hymnal according to the Motu Proprio of His Holiness Pope Pius X* (1913) on page 251.

88 88 (LM)

Tune: VARIOUS

510 Veni Creator Spiritus (9th century)

Abridged Version – *Trns: Fr. Edward Caswall, Oratorian (d. 1878)*

4. Praise we the Lord, Father and Son,
And Holy Spirit, with them one;
And may the Son on us bestow
All gifts that from the Spirit flow,
All gifts that from the Spirit flow.

88 88 (LM)

Tune:
Lambillotte

T. Source: *New Saint Basil Hymnal* (1958) p. 135; *Mediator Dei Hymnal* (1955) p. 39. The original text by Fr. Caswall has been altered and shortened in this traditional version.

Melody: Fr. Louis Lambillotte (d. 1855), a Belgian Jesuit who, in addition to writing many popular melodies, generated interest in the restoration of Gregorian chant, eventually completed by Dom Pothier. For this reason, Lambillotte's tombstone reads: *Qui cecinit Jesum et Mariam, eripuitque tenebris Gregorium, hunc superis insere, Christe, choris.* (Receive, into Thy choirs above, O Christ, one who sang the praises of Jesus and Mary and rescued the music of Gregory from the darkness of ages.)

M. Source: *The Parochial Hymn Book, Words and Melodies; containing Vespers, Compline, and all the Liturgical Hymns for the Year both in Latin and English* (London, 1883) p. 422; *Saint Edmund Campion Missal and Hymnal* (2013) #883.

Veni Creator Spiritus (9th century)

Trns: Fr. Edward Caswall, Oratorian (d. 1878)

Can be sung with any 88 88 meter, such as FULDA, SYMPHONIACAE, CUPERTINO, MEIN SEEL O GOTT, SONG 34, GONFALON ROYAL, WINCHESTER NEW, etc.

COME, O Creator Spirit blest,
And in our souls take up Thy rest;
Come, with Thy grace and heav'nly aid,
To fill the hearts which Thou hast made.

2. Great Paraclete, to Thee we cry,
O highest gift of God most high,
O font of life, O fire of love,
And sweet Anointing from above.

3. Thou in Thy sev'nfold gifts art known,
The Finger of God's hand we own;
The promise of the Father Thou,
Who dost the tongue with pow'r endow.

4. Kindle our senses from above,
And make our hearts o'erflow with love;
With patience firm and virtue high
The weakness of our flesh supply.

5. Far from us drive the foe we dread,
And grant us Thy true peace instead;
So shall we not, with Thee for guide,
Turn from the path of life aside.

6. Oh, may Thy grace on us bestow,
The Father and the Son to know,
And Thee through endless times confess'd
Of Both th'Eternal Spirit blest.

7. All glory while the ages run,
Be to the Father, and the Son
Who rose from death; the same to Thee,
O Holy Ghost, eternally.

T. Source: Pages 176-177 of *The Parochial Hymn Book, Words and Melodies; containing Vespers, Compline, and all the Liturgical Hymns for the Year both in Latin and English* (London, 1883), edited by Marist Fr. Anatole Police; IMPRIMATUR by Henry Edward Cardinal Manning (d. 1892), who in 1851 converted from Anglicanism and was appointed Archbishop of Westminster in 1865.

88 88 (LM)

Tune: VARIOUS

512 Veni Creator Spiritus (9th century)

1599AD – Historic Roman Catholic Translation

Can be sung with any 88 88 meter, such as Hilderstone, Duguet, Breslau, Melcombe, Wareham, Old Hundredth, Mein Seel, Trinity College, etc.

COME holy Ghost that us hath made,
Thy servants' minds vouchsafe to see,
And fill the hearts with heav'nly grace,
Which have created been by thee.

2. Thou that the Comforter art high,
The gift of God excelling all,
The well of life, the fire and love,
The unction which we ghostly call.

3. Thou art in gifts full sevenfold,
The finger eke of God's right hand; *n1*
Thou art thy father's promised plight,
By thee to speak we understand.

4. Our senses with thy light enflame,
Thy love into our hearts distill,
Restore our bodies' strength decayed,
By virtue that endureth still.

5. Right far from us repel our foe,
Us with thy present peace endue;
So that thy self become our guide,
Each noisome thing we may eschew.

6. The Father let us know by thee,
The Son vouchsafe we likewise know,
And thee the Spirit from them both,
And that our faith be ever so.

7. To God the father glory be,
And to the son that rose again,
As also to the comforter,
All endless ages to remain.

Veni Creátor Spíritus:
Mentes tuórum vísita,
Imple supérna grátia,
Quae tu creásti péctora.

Qui Paráclitus díceris
Donum Dei altíssimi,
Fons vivus, ignis, cáritas,
Et spiritális únctio.

Tu septifórmis múnere,
Dextrae Dei tu dígitus,
Tu rite promíssum Patris,
Sermóne ditans gúttura.

Accénde lumen sénsibus,
Infúnd*e* amórem córdibus,
Infírma nostri córporis
Virtúte firmans pérpeti.

Hostem repéllas lóngius,
Pacémque dones prótinus;
Ductóre sic te praévio
Vitémus omne nóxium.

Per te sciámus da Patrem,
Noscámus atque Fílium,
Te utriúsque Spíritum,
Credámus omni témpore.

Glória Patri Dómino,
Natóque, qui a mórtuis
Surréxit, ac Paráclito,
In saeculórum saécula.

[1] "Eke" is an archaic word meaning *also*, *even*, or *moreover*.

88 88 (LM)

Tune: Various

T. Source: *Primer, or, Office of the Blessed Virgin Marie in Latin and English, according to the reformed Latin, and with Lyke Graces Privileged* (Antwerp, 1599) p. 13. The Catholic Encyclopedia of 1912 attributes the hymn translations to the book's editor, Richard Verstegan (d. 1636), a Catholic publisher. In the 1599 Preface, Verstegan says: "Notwithstanding the difficulty, these hymns have been so turned into English meter that they may be sung unto the same tunes in English that they bear in Latin." However, his accentual treatment is sometimes peculiar.

1651AD – Historic Roman Catholic Translation

English Translation can be sung with any 77 77 meter, such as SAVANNAH, UNIVERSITY COLLEGE, ORIENTIS PARTIBUS, LLANFAIR, CULBACH, MONKLAND, GOTT SEI DANK, etc.

Veni Creátor Spíritus,
Mentes tuórum vísita:
Imple supérna grátia
Quae tu creásti péctora.

COME Creator, Spir't divine,
Visit now the souls of Thine,
Fill with Grace distill'd from Heav'n,
Hearts to which thou life hast giv'n.

Qui díceris Paráclitus,
Altíssimi donum Dei,
Fons vivus, ignis, cáritas,
Et spiritális únctio.

2. Whom the Comforter we call,
Gift of God transcending all,
Living spring, fire, fervent love,
Ghostly unction from above.

Tu septifórmis múnere,
Dígitus patérnae déxterae,
Tu rite promíssum Patris,
Sermóne ditans gúttura.

3. Sev'n-fold Grace thou dost impart,
And God's right-hand-finger art;
Thou the Father's promise, which
Tongues with language doth enrich.

Accénde lumen sénsibus,
Infúnd*e* amórem córdibus,
Infírma nostri córporis
Virtúte firmans pérpeti.

4. Kindle light in ev'ry sense;
Love into our hearts dispense,
Strengthen what in flesh is frail,
With a virtue cannot fail.

Hostem repéllas lóngius,
Pacémque dones prótinus:
Ductóre sic te praévio,
Vitémus omne nóxium.

5. Drive away our mortal Foe,
Peace upon us soon bestow:
As a guide before us shine,
That all vice we may decline.

Per te sciámus da Patrem,
Noscámus atque Fílium,
Teq*ue* utriúsque Spíritum,
Credámus omni témpore.

6. By thee may it so be done,
That we Father know, and Son;
And in thee believe that dost
Flow from both, the Holy Ghost.

Deo Patri sit glória,
Et Fílio, qu*i* a mórtuis
Surréxit, ac Paráclito,
In saeculórum saécula.

7. Glorious may the Father reign,
And the Son, who rose again;
So the holy Paraclete,
During ages infinite.

77 77

T. Source: *The Primer or Office of the Blessed Virgin Mary In English: Exactly revised, and the new Hymnes and Prayers added, according to the Reformation of Pope Urban 8* (1651) p. 376.

Tune: VARIOUS

514 Veni Redemptor Gentium (4th century)

Saint Ambrose, Bishop of Milan (d. 397AD)

To sing in Latin,
use any 88 88 tune.

VENI, Redémptor gentium,
Osténde partum Vírginis;
Mirétur omne saéculum:
Talis decet partus Deum.

2. Non ex viríli sémine,
Sed mýstico spirámine
Verbum Dei factum caro
Fructúsque ventris flóruit.

3. Alvus tuméscit Vírginis,
Claustra pudóris pérmanent,
Vexílla virtútum micant,
Versátur in templo Deus. *n1*

4. Procédens de thál*a*mo suo, *n2*
Pudóris aula régia,
Góm*i*nae gigas substántiae,
Álacris ut currat viam. *n3*

5. Egréssus ejus a Patre,
Regréssus ejus ad Patrem:
Excúrsus usqu*e* ad ínferos,
Recúrsus ad sedem Dei.

6. Aequális aetérno Patri,
Carnis trophaéo cíngere, *n4*
Infírma nostri córporis
Virtúte firmans pérpeti.

7. Praesépe jam fulget tuum
Luménque nox spirat novum,
Quod nulla nox intérpolet,
Fidéque jugi lúceat.

88 88 (LM)

Tune:
VARIOUS

T. Source: *Breviarium Juxta Ritum Sacri Ordinis Praedicatorum Auctoritate Apostolica Approbatum Et Reverendissimi Patris Andreas Frühwirth Ejusdem Ordinis Generalis Magistri Permissu Editum* (Tournay: Desclée, 1894) p. 171; *Liber Hymnarius* (Solesmes: Saint Peter's Abbey, 1983) p. 11.

Veni Redemptor Gentium (4th century)

Literal translation by Fr. Joseph Aquinas Byrnes (d. 1961)

COME, Redeemer of the nations,
show thy birth of the Virgin;
let every age marvel:
such a birth befits God.

2. Not from the seed of man,
but by the mystic breath,
the Word of God was made flesh
and the fruit of the womb did blossom.

3. The womb of the Virgin inflates;
the cloisters of her purity remain;
the banners of her virtues gleam;
God dwells in his temple. *n1*

4. Proceeding from his bridal chamber, *n2*
the royal court of chastity,
the Giant of twofold nature
is eager to run his course. *n3*

5. His coming forth from the Father,
his going back to the Father,
his going into hell,
his return to the throne of God.

6. O thou, equal to the eternal Father,
gird thyself with the trophy of flesh, *n4*
making strong with thine eternal strength
the weakness of our body.

7. Now doth thy manger gleam
and the night breathe forth a new light,
which light may no night impede
and may it shine with undying faith.

[1] Saint John Damascene (d. 749AD): "The holy and animated Ark of the living God, which held within it its own Maker." The Little Office of the Blessed Virgin: "Thou gavest birth to Him that made thee and still remainest a Virgin always."

[2] This stanza adapts the words of the psalmist to the virgin birth. "And he, as a bridegroom coming out of his bride chamber, hath rejoiced as a giant to run the way" (Ps 18.6). Monsignor Knox translates "gigas" as *Great Runner*.

[3] The "course" (*via*) mentioned in the preceding stanza is here summarized. "I came forth from the Father and am come into the world; again I leave the world, and I go to the Father" (Jn 16.28); "Coming he preached to those spirits that were in prison" (I Pet 3.19); "And the Lord Jesus, after he had spoken to them, was taken up into heaven and sitteth on the right hand of God" (Mk 16.19).

[4] How Christ triumphed in the human flesh he assumed is the theme of the *Pange Lingua* by Bishop Fortunatus; cf. page 308.

516 Veni Redemptor Gentium (4th century)

Trns: William Morton Reynolds (d. 1876)

1. Sav - ior of the na - tions, come; Vir - gin's Son, here
2. Not by hu - man flesh_ and blood, By the Spir - it
3. Won - drous birth! O won - drous Child Of the Vir - gin

make Thy home! Mar - vel now, O heav'n and_ earth,
of our God Was the Word of God made flesh—
un - de - filed! Though by all the world dis - owned,

That the Lord chose such_ a birth.
Wom - an's Off - spring, pure_ and fresh.
Still to be in heav'n en - throned.

4. From the Father forth He came
And returneth to the same,
Captive leading death and hell—
High the song of triumph swell!

5. Thou, the Father's only Son,
Hast o'er sin the victory won.
Boundless shall Thy kingdom be;
When shall we its glories see?

6. Brightly doth Thy manger shine,
Glorious is its light divine.
Let not sin o'er cloud this light;
Ever be our faith thus bright.

7. Praise to God the Father sing,
Praise to God the Son, our King,
Praise to God the Spirit be
Ever and eternally.

N.B. This melody is excellent for use during Advent.

77 77

Tune:
NUN KOMM DER HEIDEN HEILAND

Text: This version omits the verse beginning "Procédens de thálamo suo."
T. Source: *Adoremus Hymnal* (1997) #302; *Summit Choirbook* (Dominican Monastery of Our Lady of the Rosary, 1983) #25;
Melody: Based on "Veni Redemptor Gentium"; for plainsong score, cf. *Liber Hymnarius* (Solesmes: Saint Peter's Abbey, 1983) p. 11.
M. Source: *New Westminster Hymnal* (1939) p. 146; *Catholic Hymn Book* (1998) p. 278; *Saint Andrew Hymnal, authorized by the Archbishops and Bishops of Scotland for use in the Scottish Dioceses* (1964) p. 203.

Veni Redemptor Gentium (4th century) 517

Trns: Dr. John M. Neale (d. 1866)

4. Forth from His chamber goeth He,
That royal home of purity,
A giant in two-fold substance one,
Rejoicing now His course to run.

5. From God the Father He proceeds,
To God the Father back He speeds;
His course He runs to death and hell,
Returning on God's throne to dwell.

6. To God the Father equal, Word,
Thy mortal vesture on Thee gird;
The weakness of our flesh at length
Sustaining by Thy changeless strength.

7. Thy cradle here shall glitter bright,
And darkness breathe a newer light,
Where endless faith shall shine serene,
And twilight never intervene.

8. All honor, laud and glory be,
O Jesus, Virgin-born, to Thee:
All honor, as is ever meet,
To Father and to Paraclete.

N.B. This melody is excellent for use during Advent.

T. Source: *Hymns of the Dominican Missal and Breviary* (Fr. Aquinas Byrnes, 1943) p. 57; *Hymnal for the Hours* (San Francisco: Benedict XVI Institute, 2014) p. 23.
Melody: *Rheinfelsisches Deutsches Catholisches Gesangbuch* (1666).
M. Source: *Gotteslob; Katholisches Gebet- und Gesangbuch Ausgabe für das Bistum Trier* (1975) p. 186; *The Parish Hymnal* (Sister Catherine Cecilia, 1957) p. 1; *Pope Pius XII Hymnal* (Ohio: Gregorian Institute of America, 1959) p. 10.

88 88 (LM)

Tune:
O Heiland Reiss

518 Veni Sancte Spiritus (12th century)

Literal translation by Fr. Adrian Fortescue (d. 1923)

The Latin can be sung to AMYOT (777 D) or the traditional plainsong.

VENI Sancte Spíritus,
Et emítte caélitus
Lucis tuae rádium.

COME Holy Ghost,
and send down from heaven
the ray of thy light.

2. Veni pater páuperum,
Veni dator múnerum,
Veni lumen córdium.

2. Come father of the poor,
come giver of gifts,
come light of hearts.

3. Consolátor óptime,
Dulcis hospes ánimae,
Dulce refrigérium.

3. Best comforter,
sweet guest of the soul,
sweet refreshment.

4. In labóre réquies,
In aestu tempéries,
In fletu solátium.

4. Rest in labor,
shade in the heat,
comfort in sorrow.

5. O lux beatíssima,
Reple cordis íntima
Tuórum fidélium.

5. O most blessed light,
fill the depth of the hearts
of thy faithful.

6. Sine tuo númine,
Nihil est in hómine,
Nihil est innóxium.

6. Without thy grace
there is nothing in man,
nothing not harmful.

7. Lava quod est sórdidum,
Riga quod est áridum,
Sana quod est sáucium.

7. Cleanse what is unclean,
water what is dry,
heal what is sick.

8. Flecte quod est rígidum,
Fove quod est frígidum,
Rege quod est dévium.

8. Bend what is hard,
warm what is cold,
straighten what is crooked.

9. Da tuis fidélibus,
In te confidéntibus,
Sacrum septenárium.

9. Give to the faithful
who trust in thee
thy holy sevenfold gift.

10. Da virtútis méritum,
Da salútis éxitum,
Da perénne gáudium.

10. Give reward of merit,
give salvation at last,
give eternal joy.

777 D

Tune:
VARIOUS

Literal English Translation: *Hymnal for the Church of Saint Hugh* (Letchworth: Fr. Adrian Fortescue, 1913) p. 55.
Latin Text: *Graduale Sacrosanctae Romanae Ecclesiae* (Schwann, 1958) p. 322; edited by Abbot Urbanus Bomm, Karl G. Fellerer, and Msgr. Johannes Overath.

Veni Sancte Spiritus (12th century) 519

Trns: Fr. Edward Caswall, Oratorian (d. 1878)

4. Heal our wounds; our strength renew;
On our dryness pour thy dew;
Wash the stains of guilt away:
Bend the stubborn heart and will;
Melt the frozen, warm the chill;
Guide the steps that go astray.

5. Thou, on those who evermore
Thee confess and Thee adore,
In Thy sev'nfold gifts descend:
Give them comfort when they die;
Give them life with Thee on high;
Give them joys that never end.

T. Source: *Hymns and Poems by Edward Caswall of the Oratory* (London, 1873) p. 123.
Melody: Samuel Webbe, the Elder (d. 1816), choirmaster of the Chapel of the Portuguese Embassy in Lincoln's Inn Fields (a public square), the only place in London where the Catholic liturgy could be publicly celebrated.
M. Source: *The Popular Hymn and Tune Book* (New York: Catholic Publication Society, 1868) #233; Mediator Dei Hymnal (1955) #38; *Catholic Hymn Book* (London Oratory, 1998) p. 150.

777 D

Tune: AMYOT

520 Veni Sancte Spiritus (12th century)

Trns: Fr. Edward Caswall, Oratorian (d. 1878)

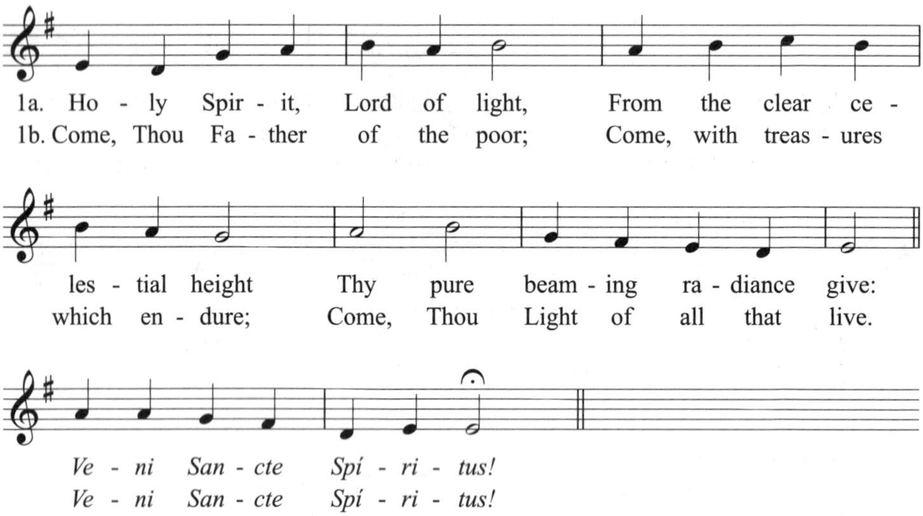

2a. Thou, of all consolers best,
Thou, the soul's delightsome guest,
Dost refreshing peace bestow;
Veni Sancte Spíritus!

2b. Thou in toil art comfort sweet;
Pleasant coolness in the heat,
Solace in the midst of woe.
Veni Sancte Spíritus!

3a. Light immortal, light divine,
Visit Thou these hearts of thine,
And our inmost being fill.
Veni Sancte Spíritus!

3b. If Thou take thy grace away,
Nothing pure in man will stay;
All his good is turn'd to ill.
Veni Sancte Spíritus!

4a. Heal our wounds; our strength renew;
On our dryness pour thy dew;
Wash the stains of guilt away:
Veni Sancte Spíritus!

4b. Bend the stubborn heart and will;
Melt the frozen, warm the chill;
Guide the steps that go astray.
Veni Sancte Spíritus!

5a. Thou, on those who evermore
Thee confess and Thee adore,
In Thy sev'nfold gifts descend:
Veni Sancte Spíritus!

5b. Give them comfort when they die;
Give them life with Thee on high;
Give them joys that never end.
Veni Sancte Spíritus!

Tune: CHAMPLAIN

Melody: Peter Lejeune (b. 1991), organist at Saint John Vianney Catholic Church in Springfield.
M. Source: Based on "Angelus Emittitur" in *Piae Cantiones* (1582);
cf. also the setting by Sir Richard Runciman Terry (d. 1938).
T. Source: *Hymns and Poems by Edward Caswall of the Oratory* (London, 1873) p. 123.

Veni Sancte Spiritus (12th century)

1651AD – Historic Roman Catholic Translation

Both English and Latin can be sung Amyot (777 D) or the traditional plainsong.

Veni Sancte Spíritus,
Et emítte caélitus
Lucis tuae rádium.

Veni pater páuperum,
Veni dator múnerum,
Veni lumen córdium.

Consolátor óptime,
Dulcis hospes ánimae,
Dulce refrigérium.

In labóre réquies,
In aestu tempéries,
In fletu solátium.

O lux beatíssima,
Reple cordis íntima
Tuórum fidélium.

Sine tuo númine,
Nihil est in hómine,
Nihil est innóxium.

Lava quod est sórdidum,
Riga quod est áridum,
Sana quod est sáucium.

Flecte quod est rígidum,
Fove quod est frígidum,
Rege quod est dévium.

Da tuis fidélibus,
In te confidéntibus,
Sacrum septenárium.

Da virtútis méritum,
Da salútis éxitum,
Da perénne gáudium.

COME into us, Holy Ghost;
From thy bright Celestial Coast
Send us a resplendent Beam.

2. Come thou Father of the Poor,
Come thou willing Gift bestow'r,
Come thou heart reviving Gleam,

3. Thou, of Comforters the best,
Thou the Soul's delightful Guest,
A refreshing sweet Relief,

4. Thou, in toil a resting Seat,
Temper in excessive heat,
Solace to a Soul in grief.

5. O thou blessèdest of Lights!
Those that love t'observe thy Rites,
With thy self their Bosoms fill.

6. While Th*ou art* absent, nothing can
Be regardable in Man,
Nothing can he act but ill.

7. What is sordid purify,
Moisten also what is dry,
What is Wounded, render Sound,

8. Pliant make what's hard to yield,
Cherish what with cold is chill'd,
Govern what is Vagabond.

9. In the Faithful that confide
In thy Mercies, cause reside
All thy Train of Sev'n-fold Grace;

10. Give what Virtue's merit is,
Give th' accomplishment of Bliss,
Joys of an Eternal Race.

T. Source: *The Primer or Office of the Blessed Virgin Mary In English: Exactly revised, and the new Hymnes and Prayers added, according to the Reformation of Pope Urban 8* (1651) p. 267; *A Manual of Prayers and other Christian Devotions; Printed by Henry Hills, Printer to the King's Most Excellent Majesty for his Household and Chapel* (London, 1686) p. 308; *The Primer or Office of the Blessed Virgin Mary* (1699) p. 246.

777 D
Tune:
VARIOUS

522 Verbum Supernum Prodiens (1264 AD)

St. Thomas Aquinas, Dominican Priest (d. 1274 AD)

To sing in Latin,
use any 88 88 (LM) tune.

VERBUM supérnum pródiens,
Nec Patris linquens déxteram,
Ad opus suum éxiens,
Venit ad vitae vésperam.

2. In mortem a discípulo
Suis tradéndus aémulis, *n1*
Prius in vitae férculo
Se trádidit discípulis.

3. Quibus sub bina spécie
Carnem dedit, et sánguinem,
Ut dúplicis substántiae
Totum cibáret hóminem.

4. Se nascens dedit sócium, *n2*
Convéscens in edúlium,
Se móriens in prétium,
Se regnans dat in praémium. *n1*

O SALUTÁRIS HÓSTIA,
Quae caeli pandis óstium:
Bella premunt hostília,
Da robur, fer auxílium.

6. Uni trinóque Dómino
Sit sempitérna glória:
Qui vitam sine término
Nobis donet in pátria. *n3*

88 88 (LM)

Tune:
VARIOUS

T. Source: *Hymni de Tempore et de Sanctis in Textu Antiquo et Novo* (Solesmes, 1885) p. 61.

Assistance for comprehension

THE sovereign Word, setting out,
though not leaving the right hand of the Father,
going forth to his work,
came to the evening of his life.

2. Yet to be delivered to his adversaries
unto death by a disciple, *n1*
he delivered himself to the disciples
beforehand in the food of life. *cf. Jn 6.35*

3. Under two appearances
he gave them his flesh and blood,
so as to feed the entire man
of twofold substance.

4. Being born, he gave himself as our ally, *n2*
sharing food, as our fare,
dying, as our ransom,
reigning, he gives himself as our recompense.

O SAVING VICTIM,
who unfoldest the portal of heaven,
the aggressions of the foe beset us:
give us hardiness, bring us aid.

6. To the Lord one and three
be glory everlasting,
and may be grant us life
without limit in the homeland. *n3*

[1] Christ is delivered by a disciple (*discipulo traditur*), but delivers himself to the disciples (*se discipulis tradit*). If we wish to follow the Savior, we must imitate him by loving our enemies. In this, we have been given a powerful example by the Jesuit martyrs of North America, led by St. Jean de Brébeuf, who—out of love for Jesus Christ—showed a most tender love in return for being treated with unspeakable and merciless cruelty.

[2] Christ is our ally through the INCARNATION, our food through the EUCHARIST, our ransom through the CROSS, and our recompense through the BEATIFIC VISION. This stanza presents an admirable example of perfect form and condensed meaning. Jean Baptiste Rousseau (d. 1741) is reported to have said that he would have given all his poetry to be this stanza's author. Abbot Guéranger (d. 1875) has written: "The *Verbum Supernum* is celebrated for its fourth strophe, which, in its graceful brevity, resumes the mystery of our Jesus, who is our companion, food, ransom, and recompense. Let us sing it with gratitude, confidence, and love."

[3] Heaven is our homeland: cf. Phil 3.20; Heb 13.14.

524 Verbum Supernum Prodiens (1264 AD)

Trns: Fr. Dylan Schrader (b. 1985)

4. Himself at birth he makes our kin,
Our friend at table and our fare,
Himself, in death the price for sin,
Himself, our king and our reward!

O SAVING VICTIM, op'ning wide
The gate of Heav'n to man below,
Our foes press on from every side,
Thine aid supply, Thy strength bestow.

6. To Thy great Name be endless praise,
Immortal Godhead, One in Three;
O grant us endless length of days
In our true native land, with Thee.

88 88 (LM)

Tune:
DUGUET

Melody: Dieudonné Duguet (d. 1849), organist at the Catholic Cathedral in Liège, Belgium, and teacher of César Franck.
M. Source: *Mediator Dei Hymnal* (1955) p. 66; *New Saint Basil Hymnal* (1958) p. 93; *Arundel Catholic Hymnal* (1905) p. 26; *Hymnal and Vesperal* (Archdiocese of Baltimore, 1878) p. 168; *Catholic Vesper Hymn Book set to Music for Unison or Four Voices* (Charles Lewis, 1877) p. 6.
T. Source: *Saint Jean de Brébeuf Hymnal* (2018).

Trns: Fr. Dylan Schrader (b. 1985)

Can be sung with any 88 88 meter, such as HILDERSTONE, DUGUET, BRESLAU, MELCOMBE, WAREHAM, OLD HUNDREDTH, MEIN SEEL, TRINITY COLLEGE, etc.

THE Word proceeding from above,
Yet leaving not the Father's side,
Goes forth unto his work of love
And comes to life's great eventide.

2. A member of his chosen band
Would hand him over to his foes:
Before his death, himself he hands
As food of life to whom he chose.

3. To them beneath two forms he gave
His flesh and blood, complete and whole,
That man, of twofold substance made,
Be fed in body and in soul.

4. Himself at birth he makes our kin,
Our friend at table and our fare,
Himself, in death the price for sin,
Himself, our king and our reward!

O SAVING VICTIM, op'ning wide
The gate of Heav'n to man below,
Our foes press on from every side,
Thine aid supply, Thy strength bestow.

6. To Thy great Name be endless praise,
Immortal Godhead, One in Three;
O grant us endless length of days
In our true native land, with Thee.

88 88 (LM)

Tune: VARIOUS

T. Source: *Saint Jean de Brébeuf Hymnal* (2018).

526 Vexilla Regis Prodeunt (6th century)

Venantius Fortunatus, Bishop of Poitiers (d. 609AD)

To sing in Latin,
use any 88 88 (LM) tune.

VEXÍLLA Regis pródeunt:
Fulget Crucis mystérium,
Quo carne carnis Cónditor
Suspénsus est patíbulo. *n1*

2. Quo vulnerátus ínsuper *n2*
Mucróne diro lánceae,
Ut nos laváret crímine,
Manávit und*a* et sánguine.

3. Impléta sunt quae cóncinit *n3*
David fidéli cármine,
Dicens: In natiónibus
Regnávit a ligno Deus.

4. Arbor decór*a* et fúlgida,
Ornáta Regis púrpura, *n4*
Elécta digno stípite
Tam sancta membra tángere.

5. Beáta, cujus bráchiis *n5*
Saecli pepéndit prétium,
Statéra facta córporis,
Praedámque tulit tártari.

6. O Crux, ave, spes única, *n6*
Hoc Passiónis témpore,
Auge piis justítiam,
Reísque dona véniam.

7. Te summa, Deus, Trínitas,
Colláudet omnis spíritus: *n7*
Quos per Crucis mystérium
Salvas, rege per saécula.

88 88 (LM)

Tune:
VARIOUS

T. Source: *Hymni de Tempore et de Sanctis in Textu Antiquo et Novo* (Solesmes, 1885) p. 40; Fr. Adrian Fortescue (d. 1923) called the *Vexilla Regis* "perhaps the greatest of all hymns."

[1] The banner (that is, flag or standard) of Christ is the Cross. *Vexilla* is plural, but here seems to be used poetically for the singular. "Through which," i.e. through which mystery. Regarding *Quo carne carnis Cónditor* ("Christ as Creator") cf. second footnote on page 421.

[2] "Insuper" can also mean "overhead."

[3] "Concinit" also means "prophesies."

[4] Cf. Mt 27.28; Mk 15.17; Jn 19.2, 5, in which "scarlet" and "purple" are interchangeable; dye derived from the purple-fish (*Murex*) or the cochineal insect (*Kermes quercus*).

Assistance for comprehension

THE standard of the King appears:
there gleams the mystery of the Cross,
through which the Founder of our flesh
was hung up on a gibbet. *n1*

2. Through which, moreover, wounded *n2*
by the dreadful point of a spear,
that he might cleanse us of wrongdoing,
he streamed with water and blood.

3. Fulfilled are the things that David *n3*
sings in a song of faith,
saying, Amid the nations
God has reigned from the wood.

4. O lovely and resplendent tree,
adorned with the scarlet of the King, *n4*
chosen with a worthy trunk
to touch limbs so holy!

5. Blessed, from whose branches *n5*
hung the ransom of the world,
made the balance of his body,
which bore the plunder of hell.

6. Hail, O Cross, our only hope! *n6*
In this Passiontide
increase the righteousness of the godly
and grant pardon to the guilty.

7. Thee, O God, highest Trinity,
let every spirit praise: *n7*
those whom by the mystery of the Cross
thou savest, rule for ever.

[5] "Blessed," i.e. *blessed tree*. A balance, or set of scales, has an upright and a crossbeam, and thus resembles a cross: Christ's body, the precious gold that has purchased the world, was weighed on the balance of the cross; the devil tried to seize this wealth and melt it down: but, paradoxically, these efforts only served to destroy his own power.

[6] The sixth and seventh verses are not by Fortunatus, but replace his original lines: *Fundis aroma cortice,* | *Vincis sapore nectare,* | *Jucunda fructu fertili* | *Plaudis triumpho nobili.* | *Salve ara, salve victima* | *De passionis gloria,* | *Qua vita mortem pertulit* | *Et morte vitam reddidit.* The other stanza by Fortunatus omitted in the Breviary version is: *Confixa clavis viscera* | *Tendens manus, vestigia,* | *Redemptionis gratia* | *Hic immolata est hostia.* Interestingly, when the reformers of Pope Urban VIII eliminated one of the authentic lines, they replaced it with "Qua vita mortem pertulit."

[7] Cf. Ps 150.6, *Omnis spiritus laudet Dominum:* "Let every spirit praise the Lord," i.e. let every creature that breathes praise the Lord.

528 Vexilla Regis Prodeunt (6th century)

First Tune – *Trns: Fr. Frederick C. Husenbeth (d. 1872)*

4. O beauteous tree, thy branches shine,
   Empurpled by our King divine,
   Preferred his sacred limbs to bear,
   Such honor worthiest deemed to share.

5. Blest Cross, to grateful souls endeared,
   Our ransom on thine arms was reared,
   And when thy balance proved its worth,
   It snatched from hell the sons of earth.

6. O Cross, with hope the Christian prays,
   Rejoicing in these paschal days,
   Grace for the guilty and the just,
   Through Christ, our sole resource and trust.

7. Blest Trinity, salvation's spring,
   Thy praise may every spirit sing;
   And where the Cross's triumphs glow,
   The Cross's glorious crown bestow.

* [6b] During Lent: "In these most solemn Passion days"

88 88 (LM)

Tune:
Gonfalon Royal

Final Verses: Richard Lloyd (1993) #80; Noel Rawsthorne (2011) #136.
T. Source: *Vespers Book for the Use of the Laity* (1841) p. 191; Rev. Frederick C. Husenbeth, a Catholic priest, also edited *The Roman Missal for the Use of the Laity* (1848).
Melody: Sir Percy Carter Buck (d. 1947); first published in *Fourteen Hymn Tunes* (1913).
M. Source: *Catholic Hymn Book* (London Oratory, 1998) p. 140. A *gonfalon* ("flag") was traditionally carried during Catholic processions; hence the tune name, since it was originally paired with *Vexilla Regis* ("Flag of the King") as it is above.

Vexilla Regis Prodeunt (6th century) 529

Second Tune – *Trns: Fr. Frederick C. Husenbeth* (*d. 1872*)

1. The King's bright ban - ner gleams a - bove,
2. The spear's sharp point laid o - pen wide
3. Ful - filled was that by Da - vid's tongue,

Re - ful - gent mys - t'ry of his love,
That source of grace,__ his sa - cred side,
Pro - phet - ic, once__ to na - tions sung:

The Cross, where Life him - self would die,
When forth with wa - ter streamed his blood
That God in af - ter - ag - es should

Our life,__ thus dy - ing, to sup - ply.
To wash_ our souls, a sav - ing flood.
Reign Mon - arch from the Cross - 's wood.

4. O beauteous tree, thy branches shine,
Empurpled by our King divine,
Preferred his sacred limbs to bear,
Such honor worthiest deemed to share.

5. Blest Cross, to grateful souls endeared,
Our ransom on thine arms was reared,
And when thy balance proved its worth,
It snatched from hell the sons of earth.

6. O Cross, with hope the Christian prays,
Rejoicing in these paschal days,
Grace for the guilty and the just,
Through Christ, our sole resource and trust.

7. Blest Trinity, salvation's spring,
Thy praise may every spirit sing;
And where the Cross's triumphs glow,
The Cross's glorious crown bestow.

* [6b] During Lent: "In these most solemn Passion days"

T. Source: *Vespers Book for the Use of the Laity* (1841) p. 191; Rev. Frederick C. Husenbeth, a Catholic priest, also edited *The Roman Missal for the Use of the Laity* (1848).
Melody: Traditional French air, sometimes sung with "O amor quam exstaticus."
M. Source: cf. *New Saint Basil Hymnal* (1958) p. 184; cf. *New Westminster Hymnal* (1939) p. 238.

88 88 (LM)
Tune: Notre Dame

530 Vexilla Regis Prodeunt (6th century)

THIRD TUNE – *Trns: Fr. Frederick C. Husenbeth (d. 1872)*

4. O beauteous tree, thy branches shine,
Empurpled by our King divine,
Preferred his sacred limbs to bear,
Such honor worthiest deemed to share.

5. Blest Cross, to grateful souls endeared,
Our ransom on thine arms was reared,
And when thy balance proved its worth,
It snatched from hell the sons of earth.

6. O Cross, with hope the Christian prays,
Rejoicing in these paschal days,
Grace for the guilty and the just,
Through Christ, our sole resource and trust.

7. Blest Trinity, salvation's spring,
Thy praise may every spirit sing;
And where the Cross's triumphs glow,
The Cross's glorious crown bestow.

* This melody at a lower key is on page 436.

* [6b] During Lent: "In these most solemn Passion days"

88 88 (LM)

Tune: TRINITY COLLEGE

Melody: John Bacchus Dykes (d. 1876).
M. Source: *Hymns Ancient and Modern* (1972) p. 64.
T. Source: *Vespers Book for the Use of the Laity* (1841) p. 191; Rev. Frederick C. Husenbeth, a Catholic priest, also edited *The Roman Missal for the Use of the Laity* (1848).

Vexilla Regis Prodeunt (6th century) 531

Fourth Tune – *Trns: Fr. Frederick C. Husenbeth (d. 1872)*

4. O beauteous tree, thy branches shine,
Empurpled by our King divine,
Preferred his sacred limbs to bear,
Such honor worthiest deemed to share.

5. Blest Cross, to grateful souls endeared,
Our ransom on thine arms was reared,
And when thy balance proved its worth,
It snatched from hell the sons of earth.

6. O Cross, with hope the Christian prays,
Rejoicing in these paschal days,
Grace for the guilty and the just,
Through Christ, our sole resource and trust.

7. Blest Trinity, salvation's spring,
Thy praise may every spirit sing;
And where the Cross's triumphs glow,
The Cross's glorious crown bestow.

* [6b] During Lent: "In these most solemn Passion days"

T. Source: *Vespers Book for the Use of the Laity* (1841) p. 191; Rev. Frederick C. Husenbeth, a Catholic priest, also edited *The Roman Missal for the Use of the Laity* (1848).
M. Source: Cento from *The Parochial Hymn Book, Words and Melodies; containing Vespers, Compline, and all the Liturgical Hymns for the Year both in Latin and English* (London, 1883), edited by Fr. Anatole Police; Imprimatur by Henry Edward Cardinal Manning (d. 1892), who in 1851 converted from Anglicanism and was appointed Archbishop of Westminster in 1865.

88 88 (LM)

Tune: Ioannes

532 Vexilla Regis Prodeunt (6th century)

Fifth Tune – *Trns: Fr. Frederick C. Husenbeth (d. 1872)*

4. O beauteous tree, thy branches shine,
Empurpled by our King divine,
Preferred his sacred limbs to bear,
Such honor worthiest deemed to share.

5. Blest Cross, to grateful souls endeared,
Our ransom on thine arms was reared,
And when thy balance proved its worth,
It snatched from hell the sons of earth.

6. O Cross, with hope the Christian prays,
Rejoicing in these paschal days,
Grace for the guilty and the just,
Through Christ, our sole resource and trust.

7. Blest Trinity, salvation's spring,
Thy praise may every spirit sing;
And where the Cross's triumphs glow,
The Cross's glorious crown bestow.

* [6b] During Lent: "In these most solemn Passion days"

88 88 (LM)

Tune: Woolmer's

Melody: Frederick A. G. Ouseley (d. 1889), professor of music at Oxford.
M. Source: *Riverdale Hymn Book* (Chicago: Fleming H. Revell, 1912) p. 172.
T. Source: *Vespers Book for the Use of the Laity* (1841) p. 191; Rev. Frederick C. Husenbeth, a Catholic priest, also edited *The Roman Missal for the Use of the Laity* (1848).

Vexilla Regis Prodeunt (6th century) 533

Sixth Tune – *Trns: Fr. Frederick C. Husenbeth (d. 1872)*

4. O beauteous tree, thy branches shine,
Empurpled by our King divine,
Preferred his sacred limbs to bear,
Such honor worthiest deemed to share.

5. Blest Cross, to grateful souls endeared,
Our ransom on thine arms was reared,
And when thy balance proved its worth,
It snatched from hell the sons of earth.

6. O Cross, with hope the Christian prays,
Rejoicing in these paschal days,
Grace for the guilty and the just,
Through Christ, our sole resource and trust.

7. Blest Trinity, salvation's spring,
Thy praise may every spirit sing;
And where the Cross's triumphs glow,
The Cross's glorious crown bestow.

* [6b] During Lent: "In these most solemn Passion days"

Final Verses: Richard Lloyd (1993) #239; Noel Rawsthorne (2011) #382.
Melody: William Knapp (d. 1768), church organist for the town of Wareham, in Dorset.
M. Source: *Catholic Hymn Book* (London Oratory, 1998) p. 218; *Hymns, Psalms, and Spiritual Canticles* (Massachusetts: Theodore Marier, 1983) p. 488.
T. Source: *Vespers Book for the Use of the Laity* (1841) p. 191; Rev. Frederick C. Husenbeth, a Catholic priest, also edited *The Roman Missal for the Use of the Laity* (1848).

88 88 (LM)

Tune: Wareham

534 Vexilla Regis Prodeunt (6th century)

Seventh Tune – *Trns: Fr. Frederick C. Husenbeth (d. 1872)*

1. The King's bright ban - ner gleams a - bove,
2. The spear's sharp point laid o - pen wide
3. Ful - filled was that by Da - vid's tongue,

Re - ful - gent mys - t'ry of__ his love,
That source of grace, his sa - cred side,
Pro - phet - ic, once to na - tions sung:

The Cross, where Life him - self would die,
When forth with wa - ter streamed his blood
That God in af - ter - ag - es should

Our life,__ thus dy - ing,__ to sup - ply.
To wash__ our souls, a__ sav - ing flood.
Reign Mon - arch from the__ Cross - 's wood.

4. O beauteous tree, thy branches shine,
Empurpled by our King divine,
Preferred his sacred limbs to bear,
Such honor worthiest deemed to share.

5. Blest Cross, to grateful souls endeared,
Our ransom on thine arms was reared,
And when thy balance proved its worth,
It snatched from hell the sons of earth.

6. O Cross, with hope the Christian prays,
Rejoicing in these paschal days,
Grace for the guilty and the just,
Through Christ, our sole resource and trust.

7. Blest Trinity, salvation's spring,
Thy praise may every spirit sing;
And where the Cross's triumphs glow,
The Cross's glorious crown bestow.

* [6b] During Lent: "In these most solemn Passion days"

88 88 (LM)

Tune:
Das Walt' Gott Vater

T. Source: *Vespers Book for the Use of the Laity* (1841) p. 191; Rev. Frederick C. Husenbeth, a Catholic priest, also edited *The Roman Missal for the Use of the Laity* (1848).
Melody: Daniel Vetter (d. 1721), organist at the church of St. Nicolas, Leipzig.
M. Source: *Songs of Syon* (Woodward, 1910) p. 41; *Hymns Ancient and Modern* (1972) p. 515.

Trns: Fr. Frederick C. Husenbeth (d. 1872)

Can be sung with any 88 88 meter, such as EISENACH, ROGERS PARK, BRESSANI, LA ROCHELLE, KEMPEN, BESSEMER, TALLIS CANON, WINCHESTER NEW, etc.

THE King's bright banner gleams above,
Refulgent myst'ry of his love,
The Cross, where Life himself would die,
Our life, thus dying, to supply.

2. The spear's sharp point laid open wide
That source of grace, his sacred side,
When forth with water streamed his blood
To wash our souls, a saving flood.

3. Fulfilled was that by David's tongue,
Prophetic, once to nations sung:
That God in after-ages should
Reign Monarch from the Cross's wood.

4. O beauteous tree, thy branches shine,
Empurpled by our King divine,
Preferred his sacred limbs to bear,
Such honor worthiest deemed to share.

5. Blest Cross, to grateful souls endeared,
Our ransom on thine arms was reared,
And when thy balance proved its worth,
It snatched from hell the sons of earth.

6. O Cross, with hope the Christian prays,
Rejoicing in these paschal days,
Grace for the guilty and the just,
Through Christ, our sole resource and trust.

7. Blest Trinity, salvation's spring,
Thy praise may every spirit sing;
And where the Cross's triumphs glow,
The Cross's glorious crown bestow.

* [6b] During Lent: "In these most solemn Passion days"

88 88 (LM)

T. Source: *Vespers Book for the Use of the Laity* (1841) p. 191; Rev. Frederick C. Husenbeth, a Catholic priest, also edited *The Roman Missal for the Use of the Laity* (1848).

Tune: VARIOUS

536 Vexilla Regis Prodeunt (6th century)

Trns: Robert Campbell of Skerrington (d. 1868)

4. O honored cross, O beauteous tree,
In Eden's bow'rs was none like thee;
What glory may with thine compare
The Lord, the King of kings to bear?

5. Blest balance, on whose arms is weighed
The price for our redemption paid—
The ransom dear of sinful men,
To bring us back to God again.

6. To thee, O Christ, for man betrayed,
Be endless praise and glory paid;
The Father equally adore,
And Holy Spirit evermore.

88 88 (LM)

Tune:
AGINCOURT

Melody: From a 15th century English manuscript.
M. Source: *Hymns, Psalms, and Spiritual Canticles* (Massachusetts: Theodore Marier, 1983) p. 450.
T. Source: Orby Shipley's *Annus Sanctus: Hymns of the Church for the Ecclesiastical Year; Translated from the Sacred Offices by various Authors, with Modern, Original, and other Hymns, and an Appendix of Earlier Versions* (London: Burns and Oates, 1884) p. 104.

Trns: Robert Campbell of Skerrington (d. 1868)

Can be sung with any 88 88 meter, such as EISENACH, ROGERS PARK, BRESSANI, LA ROCHELLE, KEMPEN, BESSEMER, TALLIS CANON, WINCHESTER NEW, etc.

THE King of kings his banner rears,
The mystery of love appears,
The Lord of life resigns his breath,
And dying ransoms all from death.

2. Though bowed his head and closed his eyes,
The love he bears us never dies;
And mingled now, more living flows
The stream that life on all bestows.

3. What prophets sang in heav'nly strain,
A king who should for ever reign,
Behold upon his purple throne,
Let all the earth his sceptre own.

4. O honored cross, O beauteous tree,
In Eden's bowers was none like thee;
What glory may with thine compare
The Lord, the King of kings to bear?

5. Blest balance, on whose arms is weighed
The price for our redemption paid—
The ransom dear of sinful men,
To bring us back to God again.

6. To thee, O Christ, for man betrayed,
Be endless praise and glory paid;
The Father equally adore,
And Holy Spirit evermore.

T. Source: Orby Shipley's *Annus Sanctus: Hymns of the Church for the Ecclesiastical Year; Translated from the Sacred Offices by various Authors, with Modern, Original, and other Hymns, and an Appendix of Earlier Versions* (London: Burns and Oates, 1884) p. 104.

88 88 (LM)
Tune: VARIOUS

538 **Vexilla Regis Prodeunt** (6th century)

First Tune – *Trns: Edward Arthur Dayman* (*d. 1890*)

4. Fulfilled is all that saints of old
In true prophetic song foretold,
Th'accursèd Tree becomes a Throne,
Whence reigns our King, the Lord alone.

5. True Tree of Life! O Tree most fair,
Ordained those holy limbs to bear,
In royal majesty it stood,
Empurpled with a Savior's Blood.

6. Upon its arms, extended wide,
The sinless One for sinners died,
The ransom of the world to pay,
He spoils the spoiler of his prey.

7. Pris'ners of hope, Thy Cross we hail,
Christ, by this sign may we prevail,
Saints find Thy glory here reveal'd,
And penitents their pardon seal'd.

8. To Thee, Eternal Three in One,
By all that breathe be homage done,
By that mysterious Cross restore,
And guide us, safe for evermore.

* For verse 7, cf. Zech 9.12.

88 88 (LM)

Tune:
Rogers Park

T. Source: *The Sarum Hymnal* (London, 1868) p. 56. Edward Dayman was Examiner for the Latin Scholarship at Exeter College (Oxford).
Melody: Kevin Allen (b. 1965), choirmaster at the Monastery of the Holy Cross in Chicago.
M. Source: *Saint Jean de Brébeuf Hymnal* (2018).

Vexilla Regis Prodeunt (6th century) 539

Second Tune – *Trns: Edward Arthur Dayman (d. 1890)*

1. The King's bright ban - ners for - ward go
2. With out - stretch'd hands, trans - fix'd and torn
3. Pierc'd by the spear His sa - cred side

The mys - t'ry of the Cross to show,
With bleed - ing brow and crown of thorn,
For us sent forth a min - gled tide,

Where God - In - car - nate death en - dured,
The One, the will - ing Vic - tim_ see,
A cleans - ing and a sav - ing_ flood,

And life by death for man pro - cured.
Self - sac - ri - ficed, man - kind to free.
Thence flowed the Wa - ter and the Blood.

4. Fulfilled is all that saints of old
In true prophetic song foretold,
Th'accursèd Tree becomes a Throne,
Whence reigns our King, the Lord alone.

5. True Tree of Life! O Tree most fair,
Ordained those holy limbs to bear,
In royal majesty it stood,
Empurpled with a Savior's Blood.

6. Upon its arms, extended wide,
The sinless One for sinners died,
The ransom of the world to pay,
He spoils the spoiler of his prey.

7. Pris'ners of hope, Thy Cross we hail,
Christ, by this sign may we prevail,
Saints find Thy glory here reveal'd,
And penitents their pardon seal'd.

8. To Thee, Eternal Three in One,
By all that breathe be homage done,
By that mysterious Cross restore,
And guide us, safe for evermore.

* For verse 7, cf. Zech 9.12.

T. Source: *The Sarum Hymnal* (London, 1868) p. 56. Edward Dayman was Examiner for the Latin Scholarship at Exeter College (Oxford).
Melody: Dieudonné Duguet (d. 1849), organist at the Catholic Cathedral in Liège, and teacher of César Franck.
M. Source: *Mediator Dei Hymnal* (1955) p. 66; *New Saint Basil Hymnal* (1958) p. 93; *Arundel Catholic Hymnal* (1905) p. 26; *Hymnal and Vesperal* (Archdiocese of Baltimore, 1878) p. 168; *Catholic Vesper Hymn Book set to Music either for Unison or Four Voices with Accompaniment* (Charles Lewis, 1877) p. 6.

88 88 (LM)

Tune: Duguet

540 Vexilla Regis Prodeunt (6th century)

THIRD TUNE – *Trns: Edward Arthur Dayman (d. 1890)*

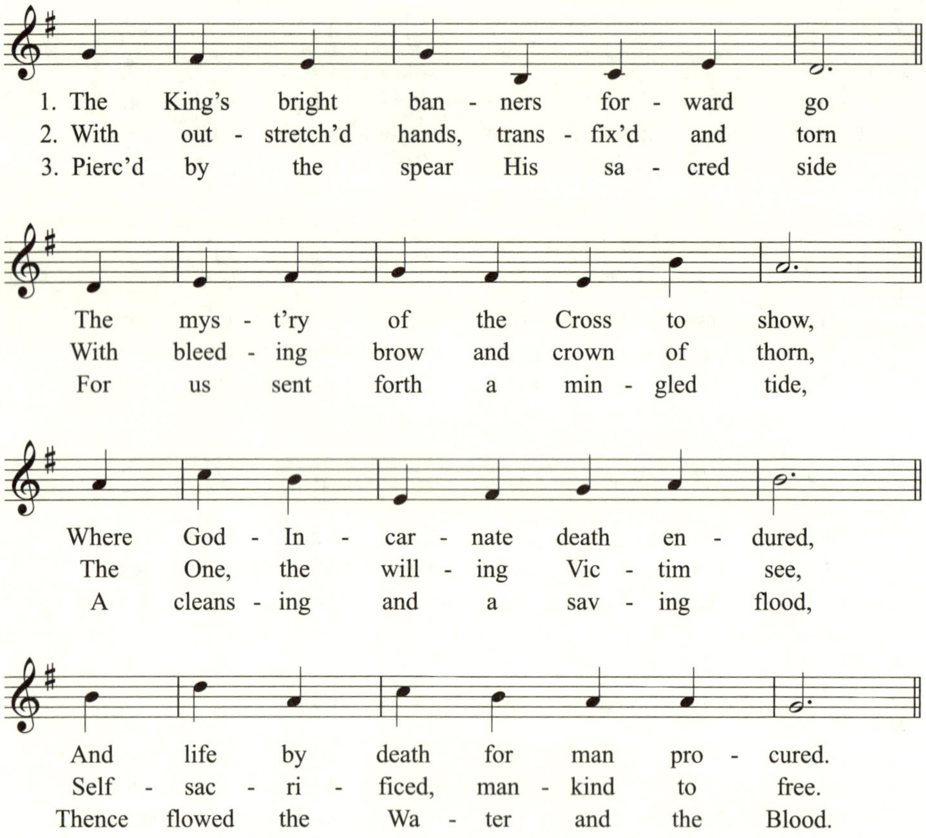

4. Fulfilled is all that saints of old
In true prophetic song foretold,
Th'accursèd Tree becomes a Throne,
Whence reigns our King, the Lord alone.

5. True Tree of Life! O Tree most fair,
Ordained those holy limbs to bear,
In royal majesty it stood,
Empurpled with a Savior's Blood.

6. Upon its arms, extended wide,
The sinless One for sinners died,
The ransom of the world to pay,
He spoils the spoiler of his prey.

7. Pris'ners of hope, Thy Cross we hail,
Christ, by this sign may we prevail,
Saints find Thy glory here reveal'd,
And penitents their pardon seal'd.

8. To Thee, Eternal Three in One,
By all that breathe be homage done,
By that mysterious Cross restore,
And guide us, safe for evermore.

* For verse 7, cf. Zech 9.12.

88 88 (LM)

Tune:
WHITEHALL

T. Source: *The Sarum Hymnal* (London, 1868) p. 56. Edward Dayman was Examiner for the Latin Scholarship at Exeter College (Oxford).
Melody: Henry Lawes (d. 1662).
M. Source: *Saint Edmund Campion Missal and Hymnal* (2013) p. 888.

Fourth Tune – *Trns: Edward Arthur Dayman (d. 1890)*

4. Fulfilled is all that saints of old
In true prophetic song foretold,
Th'accursèd Tree becomes a Throne,
Whence reigns our King, the Lord alone.

5. True Tree of Life! O Tree most fair,
Ordained those holy limbs to bear,
In royal majesty it stood,
Empurpled with a Savior's Blood.

6. Upon its arms, extended wide,
The sinless One for sinners died,
The ransom of the world to pay,
He spoils the spoiler of his prey.

7. Pris'ners of hope, Thy Cross we hail,
Christ, by this sign may we prevail,
Saints find Thy glory here reveal'd,
And penitents their pardon seal'd.

8. To Thee, Eternal Three in One,
By all that breathe be homage done,
By that mysterious Cross restore,
And guide us, safe for evermore.

* For verse 7, cf. Zech 9.12.

Final Verses: Richard Lloyd (1993) #64; Noel Rawsthorne (2011) #108.
T. Source: *The Sarum Hymnal* (London, 1868) p. 56. Edward Dayman was Examiner for the Latin Scholarship at Exeter College (Oxford).
Melody: Bartholomäus Gesius (d. 1613); adapted by Johann H. Schein (d. 1630).
M. Source: *New Saint Basil Hymnal* (1958) p. 120; *Pope Pius XII Hymnal* (Ohio: Gregorian Institute of America, 1959) p. 13.

88 88 (LM)
Tune: Eisenach

542 Vexilla Regis Prodeunt (6th century)

Fifth Tune – *Trns: Edward Arthur Dayman (d. 1890)*

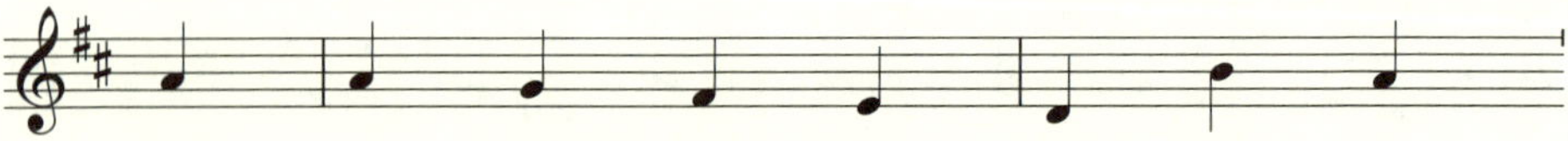

1. The King's bright ban - ners for - ward go
2. With out - stretch'd hands, trans - fix'd and torn
3. Pierc'd by the spear His sa - cred side

The mys - t'ry of the Cross to show,
With bleed - ing brow and crown of thorn,
For us sent forth a min - gled tide,

Where God - In - car - nate death en - dured,
The One, the will - ing Vic - tim see,
A cleans - ing and a sav - ing flood,

And life by death for man pro - cured.
Self - sac - ri - ficed, man - kind to free.
Thence flowed the Wa - ter and the Blood.

4. Fulfilled is all that saints of old
In true prophetic song foretold,
Th'accursèd Tree becomes a Throne,
Whence reigns our King, the Lord alone.

5. True Tree of Life! O Tree most fair,
Ordained those holy limbs to bear,
In royal majesty it stood,
Empurpled with a Savior's Blood.

6. Upon its arms, extended wide,
The sinless One for sinners died,
The ransom of the world to pay,
He spoils the spoiler of his prey.

7. Pris'ners of hope, Thy Cross we hail,
Christ, by this sign may we prevail,
Saints find Thy glory here reveal'd,
And penitents their pardon seal'd.

8. To Thee, Eternal Three in One,
By all that breathe be homage done,
By that mysterious Cross restore,
And guide us, safe for evermore.

* For verse 7, cf. Zech 9.12.

88 88 (LM)

Tune:
Melcombe

Final Verses: Richard Lloyd (1993) #133; Noel Rawsthorne (2011) #205.
T. Source: *The Sarum Hymnal* (London, 1868) p. 56. Edward Dayman was Examiner for the Latin Scholarship at Exeter College (Oxford).
Melody: Samuel Webbe, the elder (d. 1816).
M. Source: *Veritas Hymnal* (Dublin: Irish Church Music Association, 1974) p. 96; *Cantate Omnes: Hymnal of the Catholic Choirmasters' Guild* (1952) #78.

Vexilla Regis Prodeunt (6th century) 543

Sixth Tune – *Trns: Edward Arthur Dayman* (*d.* 1890)

4. Fulfilled is all that saints of old
In true prophetic song foretold,
Th'accursèd Tree becomes a Throne,
Whence reigns our King, the Lord alone.

5. True Tree of Life! O Tree most fair,
Ordained those holy limbs to bear,
In royal majesty it stood,
Empurpled with a Savior's Blood.

6. Upon its arms, extended wide,
The sinless One for sinners died,
The ransom of the world to pay,
He spoils the spoiler of his prey.

7. Pris'ners of hope, Thy Cross we hail,
Christ, by this sign may we prevail,
Saints find Thy glory here reveal'd,
And penitents their pardon seal'd.

8. To Thee, Eternal Three in One,
By all that breathe be homage done,
By that mysterious Cross restore,
And guide us, safe for evermore.

* For verse 7, cf. Zech 9.12.

Melody: Flor Peeters (d. 1986), organist at the Catholic Cathedral of Mechelen, Belgium, was made a Baron by King Baudouin.
M. Source: *People's Mass Book* (Omer Westendorf, 1964) p. 218.
T. Source: *The Sarum Hymnal* (London, 1868) p. 56. Edward Dayman was Examiner for the Latin Scholarship at Exeter College (Oxford).

88 88 (LM)

Tune: Kempen

544 Vexilla Regis Prodeunt (6th century)

Seventh Tune – *Trns: Edward Arthur Dayman (d. 1890)*

4. Fulfilled is all that saints of old
In true prophetic song foretold,
Th'accursèd Tree becomes a Throne,
Whence reigns our King, the Lord alone.

5. True Tree of Life! O Tree most fair,
Ordained those holy limbs to bear,
In royal majesty it stood,
Empurpled with a Savior's Blood.

6. Upon its arms, extended wide,
The sinless One for sinners died,
The ransom of the world to pay,
He spoils the spoiler of his prey.

7. Pris'ners of hope, Thy Cross we hail,
Christ, by this sign may we prevail,
Saints find Thy glory here reveal'd,
And penitents their pardon seal'd.

8. To Thee, Eternal Three in One,
By all that breathe be homage done,
By that mysterious Cross restore,
And guide us, safe for evermore.

* For verse 7, cf. Zech 9.12.

88 88 (LM)

Tune:
Bressani

T. Source: *The Sarum Hymnal* (London, 1868) p. 56. Edward Dayman was Examiner for the Latin Scholarship at Exeter College (Oxford).
Melody: From a hymn book published by Fr. Melchior Ludolf Herold (d. 1810).
M. Source: *New Westminster Hymnal* (1939) p. 173.

EIGHTH TUNE – *Trns: Edward Arthur Dayman (d. 1890)*

4. Fulfilled is all that saints of old
In true prophetic song foretold,
Th'accursèd Tree becomes a Throne,
Whence reigns our King, the Lord alone.

5. True Tree of Life! O Tree most fair,
Ordained those holy limbs to bear,
In royal majesty it stood,
Empurpled with a Savior's Blood.

6. Upon its arms, extended wide,
The sinless One for sinners died,
The ransom of the world to pay,
He spoils the spoiler of his prey.

7. Pris'ners of hope, Thy Cross we hail,
Christ, by this sign may we prevail,
Saints find Thy glory here reveal'd,
And penitents their pardon seal'd.

8. To Thee, Eternal Three in One,
By all that breathe be homage done,
By that mysterious Cross restore,
And guide us, safe for evermore.

* For verse 7, cf. Zech 9.12.

Final Verses: Richard Lloyd (1993) #244; Noel Rawsthorne (2011) #392.
Melody: Georg Wittwe's *Musikalisches Handbuch der Geistlichen Melodien* (Hamburg, 1690).
M. Source: *Episcopal Hymnal* (1940) ABAB #548; *New Saint Basil Hymnal* (1958) p. 1.
T. Source: *The Sarum Hymnal* (London, 1868) p. 56. Edward Dayman was Examiner for the Latin Scholarship at Exeter College (Oxford).

88 88 (LM)
Tune: WINCHESTER NEW

546 Vexilla Regis Prodeunt (6th century)

Ninth Tune – *Trns: Edward Arthur Dayman (d. 1890)*

4. Fulfilled is all that saints of old
In true prophetic song foretold,
Th'accursèd Tree becomes a Throne,
Whence reigns our King, the Lord alone.

5. True Tree of Life! O Tree most fair,
Ordained those holy limbs to bear,
In royal majesty it stood,
Empurpled with a Savior's Blood.

6. Upon its arms, extended wide,
The sinless One for sinners died,
The ransom of the world to pay,
He spoils the spoiler of his prey.

7. Pris'ners of hope, Thy Cross we hail,
Christ, by this sign may we prevail,
Saints find Thy glory here reveal'd,
And penitents their pardon seal'd.

8. To Thee, Eternal Three in One,
By all that breathe be homage done,
By that mysterious Cross restore,
And guide us, safe for evermore.

* For verse 7, cf. Zech 9.12.

88 88 (LM)

Tune:
Altona

Final Verses: Noel Rawsthorne (2011) #378; one note altered.
T. Source: *The Sarum Hymnal* (London, 1868) p. 56. Edward Dayman was Examiner for the Latin Scholarship at Exeter College (Oxford).
Melody: Schumann's *Geistliche Lieder* (1539); an adaptation by Fr. Stephan Lück (d. 1883) in his hymnal, *Gesang- und Gebetbuch für die Diözese Trier* (1847) p. 19. Called by various names (Vom Himmel Hoch, Erfurt, etc.) this melody has been set by such composers as Hassler, Gesius, Praetorius, and Bach.
M. Source: *Hosanna Catholic Hymn Book* (1914) p. 17; *New Westminster Hymnal* (1939) p. 8.

Vexilla Regis Prodeunt (6th century)

Trns: Edward Arthur Dayman (d. 1890)

Can be sung with any 88 88 meter, such as EISENACH, ROGERS PARK, BRESSANI, LA ROCHELLE, KEMPEN, BESSEMER, TALLIS CANON, WINCHESTER NEW, etc.

THE King's bright banners forward go
The myst'ry of the Cross to show,
Where God-Incarnate death endured,
And life by death for man procured.

2. With outstretch'd hands, transfix'd and torn
With bleeding brow and crown of thorn,
The One, the willing Victim see,
Self-sacrificed, mankind to free.

3. Pierc'd by the spear His sacred side
For us sent forth a mingled tide,
A cleansing and a saving flood,
Thence flowed the Water and the Blood.

4. Fulfilled is all that saints of old
In true prophetic song foretold,
Th'accursèd Tree becomes a Throne,
Whence reigns our King, the Lord alone.

5. True Tree of Life! O Tree most fair,
Ordained those holy limbs to bear,
In royal majesty it stood,
Empurpled with a Savior's Blood.

6. Upon its arms, extended wide,
The sinless One for sinners died,
The ransom of the world to pay,
He spoils the spoiler of his prey.

7. Pris'ners of hope, Thy Cross we hail,
Christ, by this sign may we prevail,
Saints find Thy glory here reveal'd,
And penitents their pardon seal'd.

8. To Thee, Eternal Three in One,
By all that breathe be homage done,
By that mysterious Cross restore,
And guide us, safe for evermore.

* For verse 7, cf. Zech 9.12.

T. Source: *The Sarum Hymnal* (London, 1868) p. 56. Edward Dayman was Examiner for the Latin Scholarship at Exeter College (Oxford).

88 88 (LM)

Tune: VARIOUS

548 Vexilla Regis Prodeunt (6th century)

1599AD – Historic Roman Catholic Translation

Can be sung with any 88 88 meter, such as Hilderstone, Duguet, Breslau, Melcombe, Wareham, Old Hundredth, Mein Seel, Trinity College, etc.

THE banners of the King come forth,
The myst'ry of the Cross displayed:
Whereon in flesh, as on a tree
He hangèd was, that flesh hath made.

2. And when, with sharp and piercing spear,
Thereon his body wounded was,
Then, that he might us wash from sin,
From him did blood and water pass.

3. What faithful David spoke in verse,
The same was now fulfillèd plain:
How God, amidst the race of men,
Should on a tree possess his reign.

4. O thou right fair and comely tree,
Whose worthy chosen stock was such,
As kingly purple did adorn,
And did so holy members touch.

5. Blest be the tree upon whose boughs
This worldès value did depend:
His body, made the price so just
To free from hell, it did extend.

6. All hail, O Cross, our special hope,
Now at this present Passion time:
Uprightness in the good increase,
And quit the guilty of their crime.

7. O God, the supreme Trinity,
Let thee each ghost with praise adore,
Whom by thy Cross's sign thou sav'st
Direct and govern evermore.

Vexílla Regis pródeunt:
Fulget Crucis mystérium,
Quo carne carnis Cónditor
Suspénsus est patíbulo.

Quo vulnerátus ínsuper
Mucróne diro lánceae,
Ut nos laváret crímine,
Manávit und*a* et sánguine.

Impléta sunt quae cóncinit
David fidéli cármine,
Dicens: In natiónibus
Regnávit a ligno Deus.

Arbor decór*a* et fúlgida,
Ornáta Regis púrpura,
Elécta digno stípite
Tam sancta membra tángere.

Beáta, cujus bráchiis
Saecli pepéndit prétium,
Statéra facta córporis,
Praedámque tulit tártari.

O Crux, ave, spes única,
Hoc Passiónis témpore,
Auge piis justítiam,
Reísque dona véniam.

Te summa, Deus, Trínitas,
Colláudet omnis spíritus:
Quos per Crucis mystérium
Salvas, rege per saécula.

[5b] "This worldès value"; that is, *the value of this world.* "Depend"; that is, *hang.*

[6d] "Quit"; that is, *acquit.*

88 88 (LM)

Tune:
Various

T. Source: *Primer, or, Office of the Blessed Virgin Marie in Latin and English, according to the reformed Latin, and with Lyke Graces Privileged* (Antwerp, 1599) p. 10. The Catholic Encyclopedia of 1912 attributes the hymn translations to the book's editor, Richard Verstegan (d. 1636), a Catholic publisher. In the 1599 Preface, Verstegan says: "Notwithstanding the difficulty, these hymns have been so turned into English meter that they may be sung unto the same tunes in English that they bear in Latin." However, his accentual treatment is sometimes peculiar.

1651AD – Historic Roman Catholic Translation

Can be sung with any 88 88 meter, such as EISENACH, ROGERS PARK, BRESSANI, LA ROCHELLE, KEMPEN, BESSEMER, TALLIS CANON, WINCHESTER NEW, etc.

Vexílla Regis pródeunt:
Fulget Crucis mystérium,
Qua vita mortem pértulit
Et morte vitam prótulit.

Quae vulneráta lánceae
Mucróne diro, críminum
Ut nos laváret sórdibus,
Manávit und*a* et sánguine.

Impléta sunt quae cóncinit
David fidéli cármine,
Dicendo natiónibus:
Regnávit a ligno Deus.

Arbor decór*a* et fúlgida,
Ornáta Regis púrpura,
Elécta digno stípite
Tam sancta membra tángere.

Beáta, cujus bráchiis
Prét*i*um pependit saéculi,
Statéra facta córporis,
Tulítque praedam tártari.

O Crux, ave, spes única,
Hoc Passiónis témpore
Piis adáuge grátiam,
Reísque dele crímina.

Te, fons salútis Trínitas,
Colláudet omnis spíritus:
Quibus Crucis victóriam
Largíris, adde praémium.

ABROAD the Regal Banners fly,
Now shines the Cross's mystery;
Upon it Life did death endure,
And yet by death did life procure.

2. Who, wounded with a direful Spear,
Did, purposely to wash us clear
From stain of Sin, pour out a flood
Of precious water mixed with Blood.

3. That which the Prophet-King of old
Hath in mysterious Verse foretold,
Is now accomplished, whilst we see
God Ruling Nations from a Tree.

4. O lovely and refulgent Tree,
Adorned with purpled Majesty;
Culled from a worthy stock, to bear
Those limbs which sanctifièd were.

5. Blest Tree, whose happy Branches bore
The wealth that did the world restore;
The Beam, that did that Body weigh
Which raised up Hell's expected prey.

6. Hail Cross, of Hopes the most sublime,
Now in this mourning Passion time;
Improve religious Souls in Grace,
The Sins of Criminals efface.

7. Blest Trinity, Salvation's Spring,
May Every Soul thy praises sing;
To those, thou grantest conquest by
The holy Cross, rewards apply.

T. Source: *The Office of the Holy Week according to the Missall and Roman Breviary; Translated out of French with a new and ample explication taken out of the Holy Fathers, of the Mysteries, Ceremonies, Gospels, Lessons, Psalms, and of all that belongs to this Office; enriched with many figures.* (Paris: Widow Chrestien, 1670) p. 354; edited by Sir William Kirkham Blount (d. 1717). Verse 3 uses a variant on Blount, taken from a 1687 Roman Catholic Primer printed in London by Henry Hills (d. 1713). Blount's original reads: "Fully accomplished are the Things | David, in faithful Meter, sings: | Where he to Nations does attest, | God on a Tree his reign possest."

88 88 (LM)

Tune: VARIOUS

550 Victis Sibi Cognomina (Holy Name of Jesus)

"If you ask the Father any thing in my name, he will give it you."—Jn 16.23

To sing in Latin, use any 88 88 (LM) tune.

VICTIS sibi cognómina
Sumant tyránni géntibus:
Tu, Christe, quanto dígnius
Ab his capis quos líberas!

2. Non álterum mortálibus
Aegris quod ínvocent datum,
Resúrgerent quo mórtui,
Perénne per quod víverent.

3. Tanti quod illi cónstitit,
Toto quod emptum sánguine,
Nostróne rursum crímine
Insána gens delébimus?

4. Sacro pati pro Nómine,
Summi sit instar múneris:
Amára non mors ámplius,
Fit mors per hoc amábilis.

5. Tu qui vocári sústines,
Jesu, salus mortálium,
Audi vocántes nos, tuo
Qui gloriámur Nómine.

6. Qui natus es de Vírgine,
Jesu, tibi sit glória,
Cum Patre, cumque Spíritu,
In sempitérna saécula.

88 88 (LM)

Tune:
VARIOUS

T. Source: Bl. John Henry Cardinal Newman's *Hymni Ecclesiae* (London, 1865), p. 47.

Assistance for comprehension

DESPOTS assume surnames for themselves
from nations they have conquered:
thou, O Christ, much more worthily
takest one from those whom thou settest free.

2. No other name has been given
to sick mortals on which they may call,
through which the dead might arise,
by which they might live unendingly.

3. That which accords with one so great,
which was bought by all his blood,
shall we through our wrongdoing,
a senseless folk, blot out again?

4. To suffer for the holy name,
let it be worth the highest gift:
bitter no more is death,
by it death becomes lovable.

5. Thou who consentest to be called,
O Jesus, the salvation of mortals,
hear us who call thee,
whose boast is thy name.

6. Thou who wast born of the Virgin,
O Jesus, to thee be glory,
with the Father and with the Spirit,
for ever and ever.

* Fr. George W. Rutler (b. 1945) attributes this Latin hymn to "an unknown medieval hand" (cf. *Stories of Hymns*, p. 178). The earliest known modern transcription is the 1736 *Paris Breviary*. See also *Breviarium ad usum Provinciae Viennensis, Pars Hiemalis* (Lyon, 1830) p. 315; *Breviarium Sanctae Lugdunensis Ecclesiae, Primae Galliarum Sedis, Pars Hiemalis* (Paris, 1780) p. 272.

552 Victis Sibi Cognomina (Holy Name of Jesus)

First Tune – *Trns: John David Chambers (d. 1893)*

4. No higher honor can we claim
Than suff'ring for that sacred Name;
By it death shall not bitter be,
But precious, when endured for Thee!

5. O Thou, whom we delight to call
Our Savior, Jesus, Lord of all;
O hearken, as with thankful voice
We in Thy glorious Name rejoice.

6. Jesus, to Thee the Virgin's Son,
Be everlasting homage done;
To God the Father we repeat
The same, and to the Paraclete.

88 88 (LM)

Tune:
Gonfalon Royal

Final Verses: Richard Lloyd (1993) #80; Noel Rawsthorne (2011) #136.
T. Source: *Lauda Syon: Ancient Latin Hymns* (London, 1857) p. 102; with several verses altered.
Melody: Sir Percy Carter Buck (d. 1947); first published in *Fourteen Hymn Tunes* (1913).
M. Source: *Catholic Hymn Book* (London Oratory, 1998) p. 140. The tune was originally paired with *Vexilla Regis* ("Flag of the King"). A *gonfalon* ("flag") was traditionally carried during Catholic processions.

Victis Sibi Cognomina (Holy Name of Jesus) 553

Second Tune – *Trns: John David Chambers (d. 1893)*

1. From con - quered realms let ty - rants claim
2. To none but Thine can man ap - peal
3. With blood that Name at first was bought,

The hon - ors of__ an earth - ly name;
His fa - tal mal - a - dies to heal;
With blood was our__ re - demp - tion wrought;

A bet - ter ti - tle, Christ, to Thee,
Naught else can dy - ing souls re - store,
Shall e - vil to such mad - ness grow

Is drawn from those whom Thou dost free.
And life__ im - part for ev - er - more.
This price - less treas - ure to fore - go?

4. No higher honor can we claim
Than suff'ring for that sacred Name;
By it death shall not bitter be,
But precious, when endured for Thee!

5. O Thou, whom we delight to call
Our Savior, Jesus, Lord of all;
O hearken, as with thankful voice
We in Thy glorious Name rejoice.

6. Jesus, to Thee the Virgin's Son,
Be everlasting homage done;
To God the Father we repeat
The same, and to the Paraclete.

88 88 (LM)

T. Source: *Lauda Syon: Ancient Latin Hymns* (London, 1857) p. 102; with several verses altered.
Melody: Traditional French air, sometimes sung with "O amor quam exstaticus."
M. Source: cf. *New Saint Basil Hymnal* (1958) p. 184; cf. *New Westminster Hymnal* (1939) p. 238.

Tune: Notre Dame

554 Victis Sibi Cognomina (Holy Name of Jesus)

Third Tune – *Trns: John David Chambers (d. 1893)*

4. No higher honor can we claim
Than suff'ring for that sacred Name;
By it death shall not bitter be,
But precious, when endured for Thee!

5. O Thou, whom we delight to call
Our Savior, Jesus, Lord of all;
O hearken, as with thankful voice
We in Thy glorious Name rejoice.

6. Jesus, to Thee the Virgin's Son,
Be everlasting homage done;
To God the Father we repeat
The same, and to the Paraclete.

88 88 (LM)

Tune:
Altona

Final Verses: Noel Rawsthorne (2011) #378; one note altered.
T. Source: *Lauda Syon: Ancient Latin Hymns* (London, 1857) p. 102; with several verses altered.
Melody: Schumann's *Geistliche Lieder* (1539); an adaptation by Fr. Stephan Lück (d. 1883) in his hymnal, *Gesang- und Gebetbuch für die Diözese Trier* (1847) p. 19. Called by various names (Vom Himmel Hoch, Erfurt, etc.) this melody has been set by such composers as Hassler, Gesius, Praetorius, and Bach.
M. Source: *Hosanna Catholic Hymn Book* (1914) p. 17; *New Westminster Hymnal* (1939) p. 8.

FOURTH TUNE – *Trns: John David Chambers (d. 1893)*

1. From con - quered realms let ty - rants claim
2. To none but Thine can man_ ap - peal
3. With blood that Name at first_ was bought,

The hon - ors of_ an earth - ly name;
His fa - tal mal - a - dies to heal;
With blood was our_ re - demp - tion wrought;

A bet - ter ti - tle, Christ,_ to Thee,_
Naught else can dy - ing souls_ re - store,_
Shall e - vil to_ such mad - ness grow_

Is drawn from those_ whom Thou_ dost free.
And life im - part_ for ev - er - more.
This price - less treas - ure to_ fore - go?

4. No higher honor can we claim
Than suff'ring for that sacred Name;
By it death shall not bitter be,
But precious, when endured for Thee!

5. O Thou, whom we delight to call
Our Savior, Jesus, Lord of all;
O hearken, as with thankful voice
We in Thy glorious Name rejoice.

6. Jesus, to Thee the Virgin's Son,
Be everlasting homage done;
To God the Father we repeat
The same, and to the Paraclete.

* This melody at a lower key is on page 248.

T. Source: *Lauda Syon: Ancient Latin Hymns* (London, 1857) p. 102; with several verses altered.
M. Source: Cento from *The Parochial Hymn Book, Words and Melodies; containing Vespers, Compline, and all the Liturgical Hymns for the Year both in Latin and English* (London, 1883), edited by Fr. Anatole Police; IMPRIMATUR by Henry Edward Cardinal Manning (d. 1892), who in 1851 converted from Anglicanism and was appointed Archbishop of Westminster in 1865.

88 88 (LM)

Tune: IOANNES

556 Victis Sibi Cognomina (Holy Name of Jesus)

Fifth Tune – *Trns: John David Chambers (d. 1893)*

4. No higher honor can we claim
Than suff'ring for that sacred Name;
By it death shall not bitter be,
But precious, when endured for Thee!

5. O Thou, whom we delight to call
Our Savior, Jesus, Lord of all;
O hearken, as with thankful voice
We in Thy glorious Name rejoice.

6. Jesus, to Thee the Virgin's Son,
Be everlasting homage done;
To God the Father we repeat
The same, and to the Paraclete.

88 88 (LM)

Tune:
Winchester New

Final Verses: Richard Lloyd (1993) #244; Noel Rawsthorne (2011) #392.
Melody: Georg Wittwe's *Musikalisches Handbuch der Geistlichen Melodien* (Hamburg, 1690).
M. Source: *Episcopal Hymnal* (1940) ABAB #548; *New Saint Basil Hymnal* (1958) p. 1.
T. Source: *Lauda Syon: Ancient Latin Hymns* (London, 1857) p. 102; with several verses altered.

Victis Sibi Cognomina (Holy Name of Jesus)

Trns: John David Chambers (d. 1893)

Can be sung with any 88 88 meter, such as EISENACH, ROGERS PARK, BRESSANI, LA ROCHELLE, KEMPEN, BESSEMER, TALLIS CANON, WINCHESTER NEW, etc.

FROM conquered realms let tyrants claim
The honors of an earthly name;
A better title, Christ, to Thee,
Is drawn from those whom Thou dost free.

2. To none but Thine can man appeal
His fatal maladies to heal;
Naught else can dying souls restore,
And life impart for evermore.

3. With blood that Name at first was bought,
With blood was our redemption wrought;
Shall evil to such madness grow
This priceless treasure to forego?

4. No higher honor can we claim
Than suff'ring for that sacred Name;
By it death shall not bitter be,
But precious, when endured for Thee!

5. O Thou, whom we delight to call
Our Savior, Jesus, Lord of all;
O hearken, as with thankful voice
We in Thy glorious Name rejoice.

6. Jesus, to Thee the Virgin's Son,
Be everlasting homage done;
To God the Father we repeat
The same, and to the Paraclete.

88 88 (LM)

Tune: VARIOUS

T. Source: *Lauda Syon: Ancient Latin Hymns* (London, 1857) p. 102; with several verses altered.

558 Victis Sibi Cognomina (Holy Name of Jesus)

First Tune – *Trns: John Chandler (d. 1876)*

77 77 D

Tune:
Paschal Lamb

Melody: Würth's *Katholisches Gesangbuch* (1859).
M. Source: *Cantate Omnes: Hymnal of the Catholic Choirmasters' Guild* (1952) #46.
T. Source: *Hymns of the Primitive Church* (London, 1837) p. 55.

Victis Sibi Cognomina (Holy Name of Jesus) 559

SECOND TUNE – *Trns: John Chandler (d. 1876)*

Final Verses: Richard Lloyd (1993) #197; Noel Rawsthorne (2011) #303.
Melody: George J. Elvey (d. 1893), organist at St George's Chapel at Windsor Castle.
M. Source: *Catholic Hymn Book* (1998) p. 120; *New Westminster Hymnal* (1939) p. 88; *Hymns, Psalms, and Spiritual Canticles* (Massachusetts: Theodore Marier, 1983) p. 230.
T. Source: *Hymns of the Primitive Church* (London, 1837) p. 55.

77 77 D

Tune: ST GEORGE

560 Victis Sibi Cognomina (Holy Name of Jesus)

THIRD TUNE – *Trns: John Chandler (d. 1876)*

77 77 D

Tune:
SALZBURG

Final Verses: Richard Lloyd (1993) #207; Noel Rawsthorne (2011) #325.
T. Source: *Hymns of the Primitive Church* (London, 1837) p. 55.
Melody: Jacob Hintze (d. 1702), court musician to the Elector of Brandenburg at Berlin.
M. Source: *Catholic Hymn Book* (London Oratory, 1998) p. 116.

Fourth Tune – *Trns: John Chandler (d. 1876)*

1. Con - qu'ring kings their ti - tles take From the foes they
2. For no oth - er Name is giv'n Un - to an - y
3. That which Christ so hard - ly wrought, That which he so

cap - tive make; Je - sus, by a nobl - er deed,
un - der heav'n Where - by souls in mor - tal strife
dear - ly bought, That sal - va - tion, mor - tals, say,

From the thou - sands he hath freed. *Al - le - lu - ia.*
Rise to gain e - ter - nal life. *Al - le - lu - ia.*
Will you mad - ly cast a - way? *Al - le - lu - ia.*

4. Rather gladly for that name
Bear the cross, endure the shame;
Suffer with him joyfully,
Death, through him, is victory.
Alleluia.

5. Dost thou, Jesus, condescend
To be called the sinners' friend?
Ours then it shall always be
Thus to make our boast of thee.
Alleluia.

6. Glory to the Father be;
Glory, Virgin-born, to thee;
Glory to the Holy Ghost,
Ever from the heav'nly host.
Alleluia.

Melody: *attr.* Pierre de Corbeil (d. 1222), Archbishop of Sens.
M. Source: *Mediator Dei Hymnal* (1955) #77; *American Catholic Hymnal according to the Motu Proprio of His Holiness Pope Pius X compiled by the Marist Brothers* (New York: Kenedy & Sons, 1913) p. 185.
T. Source: *Hymns of the Primitive Church* (London, 1837) p. 55.

77 77
Tune:
Orientis Partibus

562 Victis Sibi Cognomina (Holy Name of Jesus)

Fifth Tune – *Trns: John Chandler (d. 1876)*

4. Rather gladly for that name
Bear the cross, endure the shame;
Suffer with him joyfully,
Death, through him, is victory.
Alleluia.

5. Dost thou, Jesus, condescend
To be called the sinners' friend?
Ours then it shall always be
Thus to make our boast of thee.
Alleluia.

6. Glory to the Father be;
Glory, Virgin-born, to thee;
Glory to the Holy Ghost,
Ever from the heav'nly host.
Alleluia.

77 77 A

Tune:
Gott Sei Dank

Final Verses: Richard Lloyd (1993) #83; Noel Rawsthorne (2011) #192.
T. Source: *Hymns of the Primitive Church* (London, 1837) p. 55.
Melody: Adapted by Johann Anastasius Freylinghausen (d. 1739) in his *Geist-reiches Gesang-Buch, den Kern alter und neuer Lieder* (Halle, 1704); also called Lübeck.
M. Source: *New Westminster Hymnal* (1939) p. 249; *New Saint Basil Hymnal* (1958) p. 229.

Victis Sibi Cognomina (Holy Name of Jesus)

Sixth Tune – *Trns: John Chandler (d. 1876)*

77 77 D

Melody: Kevin Allen (b. 1965), choirmaster at the Monastery of the Holy Cross in Chicago.
Source of Text & Melody: *Saint Jean de Brébeuf Hymnal* (2018).
T. Source: *Hymns of the Primitive Church* (London, 1837) p. 55.

Tune: Heustis

564 Victis Sibi Cognomina (Holy Name of Jesus)

Seventh Tune – *Trns: John Chandler (d. 1876)*

4. Rather gladly for that name
Bear the cross, endure the shame;
Suffer with him joyfully,
Death, through him, is victory.

5. Dost thou, Jesus, condescend
To be called the sinners' friend?
Ours then it shall always be
Thus to make our boast of thee.

6. Glory to the Father be;
Glory, Virgin-born, to thee;
Glory to the Holy Ghost,
Ever from the heav'nly host.

77 77

Tune:
Song 13

Final Verses: Noel Rawsthorne (2011) #339.
T. Source: *Hymns of the Primitive Church* (London, 1837) p. 55.
Melody: Orlando Gibbons (d. 1625), organist at Westminster Abbey.
M. Source: *Catholic Hymn Book* (1986) p. 223; *New Westminster Hymnal* (1939) p. 120.

Trns: John Chandler (d. 1876)

Can be sung with any 77 77 meter, such as SAVANNAH, UNIVERSITY COLLEGE, ORIENTIS PARTIBUS, LLANFAIR, CULBACH, MONKLAND, GOTT SEI DANK, etc.

CONQU'RING kings their titles take
From the foes they captive make;
Jesus, by a nobler deed,
From the thousands he hath freed.

2. For no other Name is giv'n
Unto any under heav'n
Whereby souls in mortal strife
Rise to gain eternal life.

3. That which Christ so hardly wrought,
That which he so dearly bought,
That salvation, mortals, say,
Will you madly cast away?

4. Rather gladly for that name
Bear the cross, endure the shame;
Suffer with him joyfully,
Death, through him, is victory.

5. Dost thou, Jesus, condescend
To be called the sinners' friend?
Ours then it shall always be
Thus to make our boast of thee.

6. Glory to the Father be;
Glory, Virgin-born, to thee;
Glory to the Holy Ghost,
Ever from the heav'nly host.

77 77

Tune: VARIOUS

T. Source: *Hymns of the Primitive Church* (London, 1837) p. 55.

Textual Copyrights in the Brébeuf Hymnal

THE TEXTS in our hymnal—all of them—have undergone editorial revision, ranging from minimal to substantial, and as such are under copyright.[1] However, we have been profuse in providing the source of each text, including even the page number (something no other hymnal does), making it easy for those who wish to consult the original texts.

Modification of hymn texts for publication is standard practice. For example, John Mason Neale wrote "Draw nigh, draw nigh Emmanuel" in 1851; but when published, it became *O come, O come, Emmanuel*—and even the refrain was altered.[2] Nowhere can textual modification be seen more clearly than in the historic Roman Catholic primers:

Roman Catholic Primer (1706 AD)

2. Born from above, and **Born for Man,**
From Virgin's Womb **his Life began:**
He liv'd on Earth, **and Preach'd, to sow**
The Seeds of Heav'nly Truth below:
Then seal'd his Mission from above
With strange Effects of Pow'r and Love.

4. **The Word made Flesh** for Love of Man,
With words, of Bread, made Flesh again:
Turn'd Wine to Blood unseen by sense
By Virtue of Omnipotence;
And here the Faithful rest secure
Whilst God can Vouch, and Faith ensure.

5. **To this mysterious Table now**
Our Knees, our Hearts and Sense we **bow;**
Let Ancient Rites resign their Place
To nobler Elements of Grace;
And Faith for all Defects supply,
Whilst Sense is lost in Mystery.

Roman Catholic Primer (1738 AD)

2. For Man he came, was **born for Man;**
From a chaste Maid **his Life began;**
On Earth he liv'd **and preach'd, to sow—**
The Seeds of heav'nly Truth below;
And then with lasting Love to close
His Life, this wond'rous Way he chose.

4. **The Word made Flesh,** by Words he said,
Turns into Flesh substantial Bread;
Wine too he makes his Blood divine,
Tho' sense cry out, 'Tis Bread and Wine:
But Hearts sincere are here secur'd,
By Faith in Words of Truth assur'd.

5. **To this mysterious Table now**
Let Knees, and Heart, and Senses **bow:**
Let ancient Rites resign their Place
To nobler Elements of Grace:
What our weak senses can't descry,
Let stronger Faith the Want supply.

Nothing would have been easier than reproducing all texts unaltered, including archaic expressions unacceptable today.[3] Such a tempting course of action—deemed valid by several recent publications—would have significantly reduced our hymnal's production time; but we renounced such an approach because hymn texts must be received well by the faithful. Our textual changes always match the *style* of the poet, even when doing so necessitated adoption of highly idiosyncratic[4] capitalization conventions, and under no circumstances were theological truths diluted or obscured. Moreover, the notion of "change for the sake of change" was fiercely rejected, especially vis-à-vis hymns which are known and loved.

---

1 Even the historic Roman Catholic primers from centuries ago have been carefully edited. While the exact words, punctuation, and capitalization have been preserved, we have updated spelling where appropriate; for example, "sinne abyde" becomes *sin abide*, and so forth.

2 Consider, too, Dr. Neale's famous translation of *Quem Terra, Pontus, Sydera* ("The God whom earth, and sea, and sky"), first published in 1851. When placed into *Hymns Ancient and Modern* (1861), every verse was altered considerably. For the 1972 edition of *Hymns Ancient and Modern*, it was again severely modified, and the second verse was inexplicably deleted.

3 A very popular translation of *O Salutaris Hostia* (early 19th century) translated *bella premunt hostilia* as "intestine wars invade our breast."

4 Fr. Caswall unfailingly capitalizes "Thee" and "He" when referring to Christ, yet does not capitalize "thy" and "his."

OUR HYMNAL is dedicated to Saint Jean de Brébeuf because our society desperately needs the intercession of this shining example of Catholic virtue and bravery; but that is not the only reason. We look to Brébeuf as one unafraid to embrace unusual methods—such as becoming the world's pioneer of Iroquoian and Algonquian languages—to win souls for Christ. Imitating Brébeuf, we spared no effort when it came to revising hymn texts to make them accessible to today's Catholics, while being scrupulous never to dilute the theological meaning of these hymns. Yet Brébeuf is important for still another reason: his life coincided with a hymn revision that had sweeping consequences.

In 1625, the young Jesuit began his missionary work in "New France" (Canada). Just four years later, Pope Urban VIII began a revision of the breviary hymns, assisted by four Jesuits: Fathers Strada, Galluzzi, Sarbiewski, and Petrucci. While a few hymns were left intact, most were completely rewritten.[1] In 1631, their "mangled remnants"—as Fortescue dubbed them—were officially added to the breviary, although certain groups (such as religious orders who *sang* the hymns) never adopted the "corrected" version. Even a hundred years later, those who *sang* the hymns retained the ancient texts. It goes without saying that the Urbanite reform had an enormous impact on Catholic hymnody, both in Latin and in the vernacular. Our hymnal employs the ancient texts: those Brébeuf knew.

In 1644, five years before Brébeuf was martyred, Urban VIII died. During his papacy, the dramatic story of the Jesuit martyrs of North America unfolded, and it was Pope Urban VIII who, upon the request of Queen Anne of France (d. 1666), granted a special dispensation to Brébeuf's companion, Father Isaac Jogues, allowing him to offer the holy sacrifice of the Mass in spite of missing fingers, which had been sawn off as part of the brutal torment he suffered after falling into the hands of the Iroquois.

---

1 Sometimes only the first word of each stanza was kept, everything else being changed. Hymnologists have universally condemned this reform, and struggle to outdo one another in their harsh denunciations. The Second Vatican Council attempted to restore the ancient texts, but with mixed results. In fairness, Pope Urban VIII was not the first pope to consider revising the breviary hymns. For example, Pope Leo X (d. 1521) was involved in a similar reform—even more drastic—but his was ultimately abandoned.

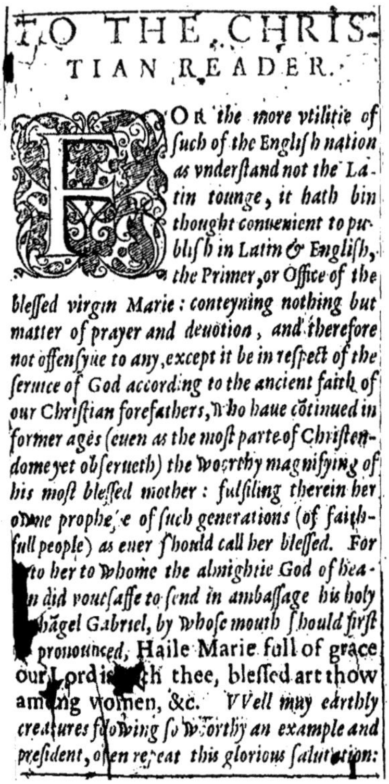

TO THE CHRISTIAN READER.

FOr the more vtilitie of such of the English nation as vnderstand not the Latin tounge, it hath bin thought conuenient to publish in Latin & English, the Primer, or Office of the blessed virgin Marie: conteyning nothing but matter of prayer and deuotion, and therefore not offensyue to any, except it be in respect of the seruice of God according to the ancient faith of our Christian forefathers, who haue cōtinued in former ages (euen as the most parte of Christendome yet obserueth) the worthy magnifying of his most blessed mother: fulfiling therein her owne prophesie of such generations (of faithfull people) as euer should call her blessed. For to her to whome the almightie God of heauen did voutsaffe to send in ambassage his holy Angel Gabriel, by whose mouth should first be pronounced, Haile Marie full of grace our Lord is with thee, blessed art thow among women, &c. Well may earthly creatures folowing so worthy an example and president, often repeat this glorious salutation:

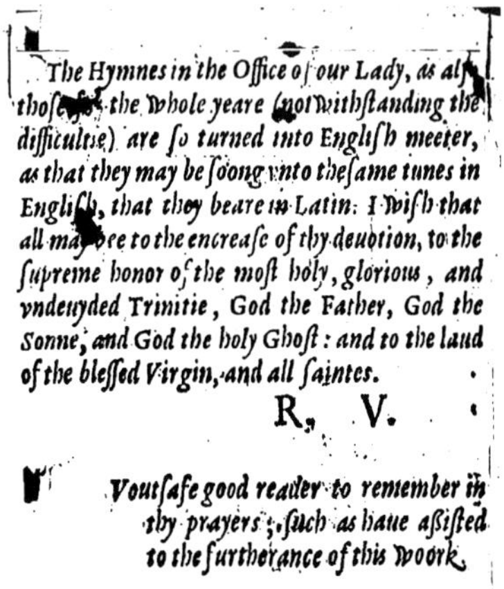

The Hymnes in the Office of our Lady, as also those of the whole yeare (notwithstanding the difficultie) are so turned into English meeter, as that they may be soong vnto the same tunes in English, that they beare in Latin. I wish that all may bee to the encrease of thy deuotion, to the supreme honor of the most holy, glorious, and vndeuyded Trinitie, God the Father, God the Sonne, and God the holy Ghost: and to the laud of the blessed Virgin, and all saintes.

R. V.

Voutsafe good reader to remember in thy prayers, such as haue assisted to the furtherance of this worke.

Image: First and last pages from the Preface to the *Primer, or, Office of the Blessed Virgin Marie in Latin and English, according to the reformed Latin, and with Lyke Graces Privileged* (Antwerp, 1599).
The Catholic Encyclopedia of 1912 attributes the hymn translations to the book's editor, Richard Verstegan a Roman Catholic who died in 1636.

THE 1599 ROMAN CATHOLIC PRIMER was published six years after Brébeuf was born and forty-one years after England permanently broke away from the Church. Richard Verstegan (d. 1636) begins the book:

> For the more utility of such of the English nation as understand not the Latin tongue, it hath been thought convenient to publish, in Latin & English, the Primer, or Office of the blessed virgin Mary; containing nothing but matter of prayer and devotion, and therefore not offensive to any, except it be in respect of the service of God according to the ancient faith of our Christian forefathers, who have continued in former ages (even as the most part of Christendom yet observeth) the worthy magnifying of his most blessed mother: fulfilling therein her own prophesy of such generations (of faithful people) as ever should call her blessèd. [etc.]

A most striking and significant sentence occurs on the final page: [2]

> Notwithstanding the difficulty, these hymns have been so turned into English meter that they may be sung unto the same tunes in English that they bear in Latin.

2 Verstegan's incontrovertible statement contradicts what was formerly believed. For example, Professor Walter H. Shewring wrote in 1938: "The hymns of the Primer are translations of liturgical texts, meant to interpret the Latin original and not to be sung congregationally."

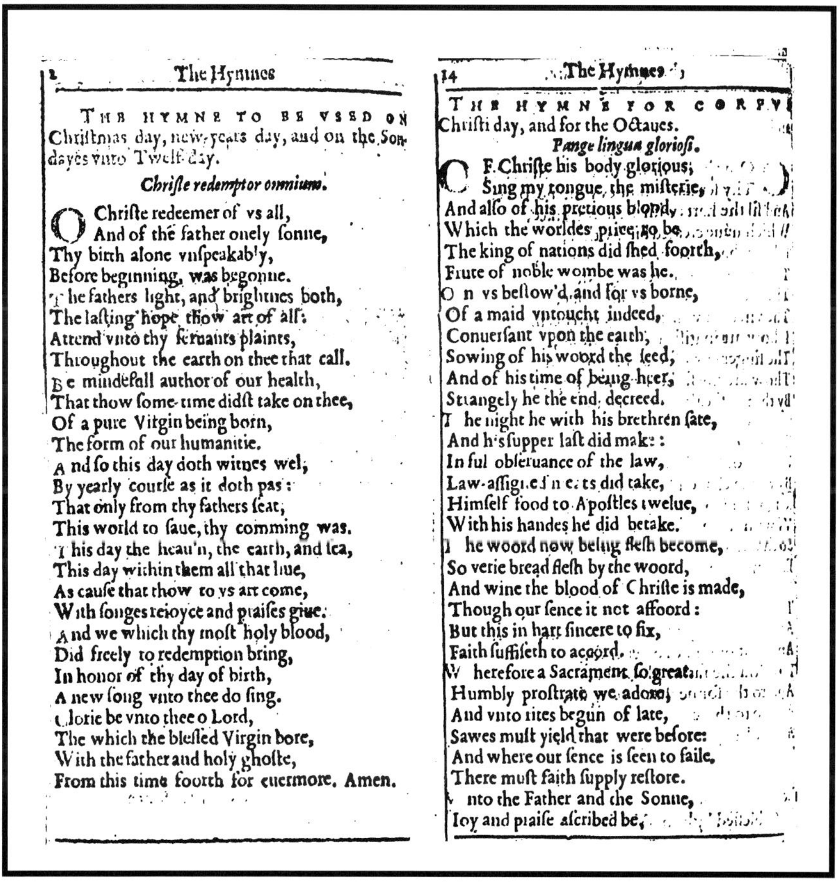

2 The Hymnes

THE HYMNE TO BE VSED ON Chriſtmas day, new-yeares day, and on the Sondayes vnto Twelf-day.

Chriſte redemptor omnium.

O Chriſte redeemer of vs all,
And of the father onely ſonne,
Thy birth alone vnſpeakably,
Before beginning, was begonne.
The fathers light, and brightnes both,
The laſting hope thow art of all:
Attend vnto thy ſeruants plaints,
Throughout the earth on thee that call.
Be mindefull author of our health,
That thow ſome-time didſt take on thee,
Of a pure Virgin being born,
The form of our humanitie.
And ſo this day doth witnes wel,
By yearly courſe as it doth pas:
That only from thy fathers ſeat,
This world to ſaue, thy comming was.
This day the heav'n, the earth, and ſea,
This day within them all that liue,
As cauſe that thow to vs art come,
With ſonges reioyce and praiſes giue.
And we which thy moſt holy blood,
Did freely to redemption bring,
In honor of thy day of birth,
A new ſong vnto thee do ſing.
Glorie be vnto thee o Lord,
The which the bleſſed Virgin bore,
With the father and holy ghoſte,
From this time foorth for euermore. Amen.

14 The Hymnes

THE HYMNE FOR CORPVS Chriſti day, and for the Octaues.

Pange lingua glorioſi.

Of Chriſte his body glorious,
Sing my tongue, the miſterie,
And alſo of his precious blood,
Which the worldes price, ſo be,
The king of nations did ſhed foorth,
Frute of noble wombe was he.
On vs beſtow'd, and for vs borne,
Of a maid vntoucht indeed,
Conuerſant vpon the earth,
Sowing of his woord the ſeed,
And of his time of being heer,
Strangely he the end decreed.
The night he with his brethren ſate,
And his ſupper laſt did make:
In ful obſeruance of the law,
Law-aſſigned meats did take,
Himſelf food to Apoſtles twelue,
With his handes he did betake.
The woord now being fleſh become,
So verie bread fleſh by the woord,
And wine the blood of Chriſte is made,
Though our ſence it not affoord:
But this in hart ſincere to fix,
Faith ſuffiſeth to accord.
Wherefore a Sacrament ſo great,
Humbly proſtrate we adore,
And vnto rites begun of late,
Sawes muſt yield that were before:
And where our ſence is ſeen to faile,
There muſt faith ſupply reſtore.
Vnto the Father and the Sonne,
Ioy and praiſe aſcribed be,

THESE TWO PAGES (above) from the 1599 Roman Catholic Primer show English translations of breviary hymns. Notice the use of capitalization—so different from today: "With the father and holy ghoste." Throughout our hymnal, we have been faithful to the conventions of each era.[3] Notice, too, the 1599 Primer's careful spelling of the word *heav'n*—"This day the heav'n, the earth, and sea"—something appreciated by singers.

Richard Verstegan claimed these hymns "have been so turned into English meter that they may be sung unto the same tunes in English that they bear in Latin"; and both hymns demonstrate this. The first example (*Christe Redemptor*) could be sung with any 88 88 melody—including plainsong—but the second example (*Pange Lingua*) seems suitable for the Gregorian setting only.

The 1631 Urbanite reform left unscathed the hymns of St. Thomas Aquinas (and *Pange Lingua* falls into this category), but *Christe Redemptor* was henceforth known as *Jesu Redemptor*. Throughout our hymnal, we have placed the Urbanite versions alongside the ancient texts, making comparison easy. In such instances, the 1599 Primer was often chosen to represent the ancient version, because its translations are so faithful to the Latin.

3 Indeed, capitalization conventions in religious poetry shift every fifty years or so.

Image: Ave Maris Stella • *Antiphonale* (circa 1342AD) from Soest, Germany.

Our hymnal emphasizes all of the major Catholic breviary hymns, such as the *Ave Maris Stella*. This manuscript page is remarkable because the music is fully written out—whereas normally the melodies were not provided because everyone knew them by heart. Our hymnal gently pushes congregations to sing from words without the melody, something which is (historically) quite Catholic.

Atsite8anon8ene Niio
Roniha nok Roienha,
Nok tehiatatenon8esta
Rotkon Roiatatokenti. Ethonaia8en.

AVE MARIS STELLA.

Tokenske tsiatakon
Niio onk8e rotonhon,
Tsi hiari8a8ire
Raronhiakehronon.

Onka aiek8eni
Aionte8eienton
Aiesasennaien,
Saiatatokenti?

Tsini tsiatanoron,
Seiatohetstenni
Eronhiakehronon
Nok ak8ekon nonk8e.

Ionk8atsennonniaton
Ionk8ari8iioston;
Hiaiatanoronston
Ne sonk8a8enniio.

Asak8isron, 8ari,
Ask8aiatakennha;
Tosa ionk8asenni
Ne noneshonhronon.

Ask8anikonhrata
Tsinaiak8aiere;
Asak8anakeren
Iesos ne hetsienha

Ahon8asennaien
Reniha, Roienha,
Niio oni Rotkon
Roiatatokenti. Ethonaia8en.

Image: Ave Maris Stella • *Paroissien Iroquois* (1865).

The Hurons spoke an Iroquoian dialect. Saint Brébeuf and his companions concentrated their efforts on the Hurons, yet had constant dealings with other tribes. Eventually, after the Iroquois annihilated the Hurons, they did allow Catholic missionaries into their villages. This page (above) is a plainsong version of the *Ave Maris Stella* in Iroquois (Mohawk). Ever since the Jesuit missionaries first started to evangelize the natives, such vernacular adaptations were used—a truly noteworthy situation. Even more unbelievable was the high quality of such books, which rivalled the best European editions.

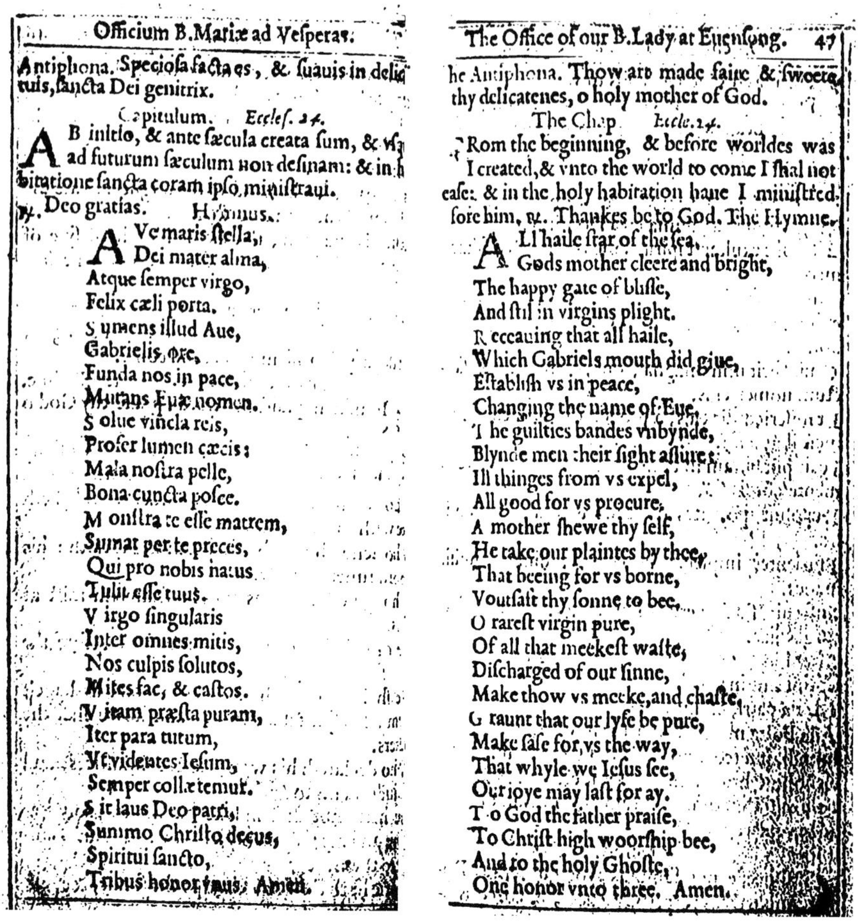

Officium B. Mariæ ad Vesperas.

Antiphona. Speciosa facta es, & suauis in delicijs tuis, sancta Dei genitrix.

Capitulum. *Eccles. 24.*

Ab initio, & ante sæcula creata sum, & vsque ad futurum sæculum non desinam: & in habitatione sancta coram ipso ministraui.

℟. Deo gratias. Hymnus.

Aue maris stella,
Dei mater alma,
Atque semper virgo,
Felix cæli porta.
Sumens illud Aue,
Gabrielis ore,
Funda nos in pace,
Mutans Euæ nomen.
Solue vincla reis,
Profer lumen cæcis:
Mala nostra pelle,
Bona cuncta posce.
Monstra te esse matrem,
Sumat per te preces,
Qui pro nobis natus
Tulit esse tuus.
Virgo singularis
Inter omnes mitis,
Nos culpis solutos,
Mites fac, & castos.
Vitam præsta puram,
Iter para tutum,
Vt videntes Iesum,
Semper collætemur.
Sit laus Deo patri,
Summo Christo decus,
Spiritui sancto,
Tribus honor vnus. Amen.

The Office of our B. Lady at Euensong. 47

The Antiphona. Thow art made faire & sweete in thy delicatenes, o holy mother of God.

The Chap. *Eccle. 24.*

From the beginning, & before worldes was I created, & vnto the world to come I shal not ease: & in the holy habitation haue I ministred before him. ℟. Thankes be to God. The Hymne.

All haile star of the sea,
Gods mother cleere and bright,
The happy gate of blisse,
And stil in virgins plight.
Receauing that all haile,
Which Gabriels mouth did giue,
Establish vs in peace,
Changing the name of Eue.
The guilties bandes vnbynde,
Blynde men their sight assure,
Ill thinges from vs expel,
All good for vs procure.
A mother shewe thy self,
He take our plaintes by thee,
That beeing for vs borne,
Voutsafe thy sonne to bee.
O rarest virgin pure,
Of all that meekest waste,
Discharged of our sinne,
Make thow vs meeke, and chaste.
Graunt that our lyfe be pure,
Make safe for vs the way,
That whyle we Iesus see,
Our ioye may last for ay.
To God the father praise,
To Christ high woorship bee,
And to the holy Ghoste,
One honor vnto three. Amen.

Image : Facing pages from a Roman Catholic Primer published in 1599AD.

Latin / English Layout: Our hymnal follows a noble Catholic tradition by providing Latin alongside the English. Notice the 1599 Primer (above) which painstakingly made sure each line of Latin corresponded perfectly across the page with each line of English.

[Facing page] Similarly, Sir Walter Kirkham Blount (d. 1717) took great pains in 1670 to place the Latin alongside the English. Indeed, the entire book—611 pages!—is awe-inspiring from the typesetter's point of view; and the English translations Sir Walter composed are also excellent. His version of *Vexilla Regis*, for example, was adopted in numerous Catholic hymnals well into the 20th century.

Our hymnal is unique in providing not only metrical ("singable") versions of the breviary hymns, but also the literal translation. First of all, this helps the congregation understand these theologically-rich texts. Secondly, it brings to light the artistry of the translators, who seek to convey the meaning and "character" of the Latin text while constrained by rhyme and meter.

354 ON GOOD

Purificatory; and the adoration being ended, he places the Croſs upon the altar. The Subdeacon takes the Miſſall from the Epiſtle, and carries it to the Goſpell ſide. Then a Proceſſion is made, to the place, where the bleſſed Sacrament is reſerved. The Subdeacon goes firſt with the Croſs, between two Acolytes, they carrying Candleſticks with lighted tapers: and the Clergie follows in order; the Prieſt laſt: with thoſe that Officiate.

when they are come unto the place, where the bleſſed Sacrament is the tapers are lighted, and not put out till after the Communion. The Prieſt kneels, and prayes a while: the Deacon in the meane time opens the Tabernacle, wherein the bleſſed Sacrament is. Then the Prieſt, riſing up putts incenſe into the cenſoires, without bleſſing it: then kneeling againe, he takes one of the Cenſoires, and incenſeth the Holy Sacrament. Then the Deacon, taking the Chalice, wherein the bleſſed Sacrament is, out of the Tabernacle, he puts it into the Prieſts hands; who covers it with the ends of the vaile, that is upon his shoulders; and ſo they go in order as they came: the Prieſt, with the bleſſed Sacrament, under the canopy; the two Acolytes incenſing; and all the people ſinging this Hymne:

ABroad the Regal Banners flie;	*VExilla Regis prodeunt,*
Now shines the Croſses myſterie:	*Fulget Crucis myſterium,*
Vpon it life did death endure,	*Quo carne carnis conditor;*
And yet by death did life procure.	*Suſpenſus eſt patibulo.*
Who wounded with a direfull Spear,	*Quo vulneratus inſuper,*
Did purpoſely to wash us cleare	*Mucrone diro lanceæ,*
From ſtaine of Sin, powr out a floud	*Vt nos lavaret crimine,*
Of precious water: mixed Bloud.	*Manavit unda & ſanguine.*

Image : Page from *The Office of the Holy Week according to the Missall and Roman Breviary* (Paris, 1670 AD).

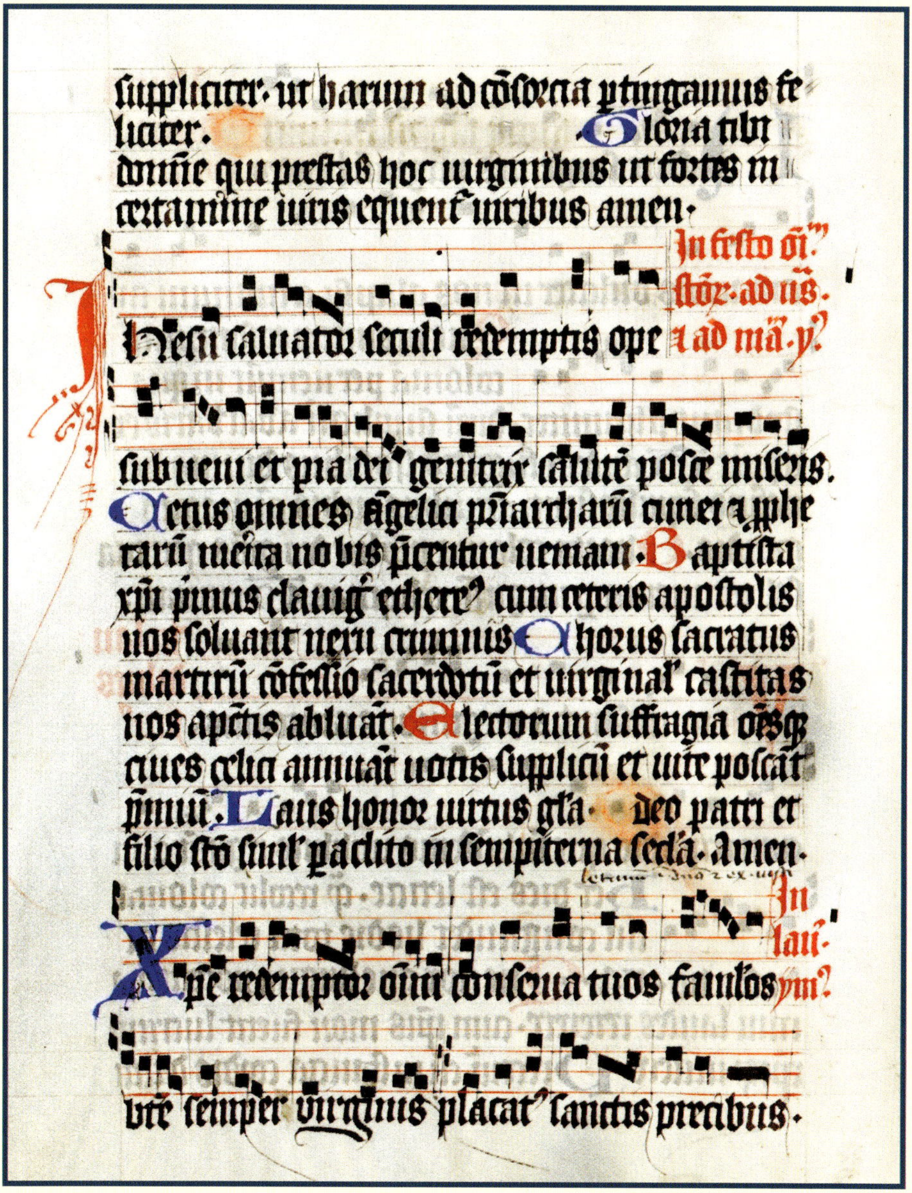

Image: Hymns for All Saints • *Dominican Hymnal* (circa 1422AD) from Bohemia.

Our hymnal provides several melodies for the hymn texts, to help choirmasters choose tunes familiar to each congregation. Throughout history, Catholic hymn texts have been sung to various tunes—for multifarious reasons. In the example above, from the 15th century, what is today known as "the Christmas tune" was married to hymn texts for the feast of All Saints.

On the one hand, singing a text with various melodies adds a freshness, and helps us consider the text in new ways. On the other hand, certain melodies have become associated with certain texts in a powerful way, and should never be altered. Good sense must rule the day.

2 Proceſſio in Bethlehem.

tui ſacra myſtéria veneràri; vt redemptiônis tuæ fructum in nobis iúgiter ſentiâmus. Qui viuis & regnas in ſæcula ſæculôrum. Amen.

Poſteà omnes Religioſi cum candelis accenſis in manibus, deuotè cantando Hymnum, procedunt ád locum, vbi Chriſtus Dominus noſter de Virgine Maria naſci dignatus eſt, & ad alia ſancta loca; quæ omnia Sacerdos incenſat.

Hymnus.

CHriſte Redémptor ómnium,
Ex Patre Patris vnice,
Solus ante princípium
Natus ineffabíliter.
Tu lumen, tu ſplendor Patris,
Tu ſpes perénnis ómnium,
Inténde quas fundunt preces
Tui per orbem fámuli.
Meménto ſalûtis Auctor,
Quòd noſtri quondam córporis,
Ex illibáta vírgine
Naſcéndo, formam ſúmpſeris.
Sic præſens teſtâtur locus,
Ad quem deuóti pérgimus,
Quòd ſolus à ſede Patris,
Mundi ſalus aduéneris.

Image: HYMN FOR CHRISTMAS • *Processionale* (1670AD) printed in Antwerp.

Although the Urbanite hymn "corrections" were officially promulgated in 1631, many groups did not adopt them for hundreds of years—and some never did. Most of the religious orders, for example, never used the Urbanite hymns. The example above, printed 39 years after the reform, still uses the ancient text (*Christe Redemptor Omnium*) and not the Urbanite text (*Jesu Redemptor Omnium*).

"Christe Redemptor Omnium" is the title for two completely different texts: a hymn for Christmas (5th century) and a hymn for All Saints (9th century). To avoid confusion, our book employs the Urbanite title—*Jesu Redemptor Omnium*—for the Christmas hymn.

Image: Ad Cenam Agni Providi • *Hymnarium* (circa 1364AD) from Soest, Germany.

This tune for *Ad Cenam Agni* will surprise some musicians—but we must remember that many of the ancient hymn melodies were "married" to hymn texts in a way that was not rigid. The 1962 Divine Office retains remnants of this: certain texts change melodies depending upon the liturgical season.

Image: Ad Cenam Agni Providi • *Hymnarium* (circa 1471AD) from Bödingen, Germany.

The above example is quite typical, whereas it is somewhat rare to encounter hymn melodies written out (as on the facing page) because everyone knew the melodies by heart. Indeed, the hymn texts themselves were frequently omitted, as well. Only the first few words were provided—and that was sufficient.

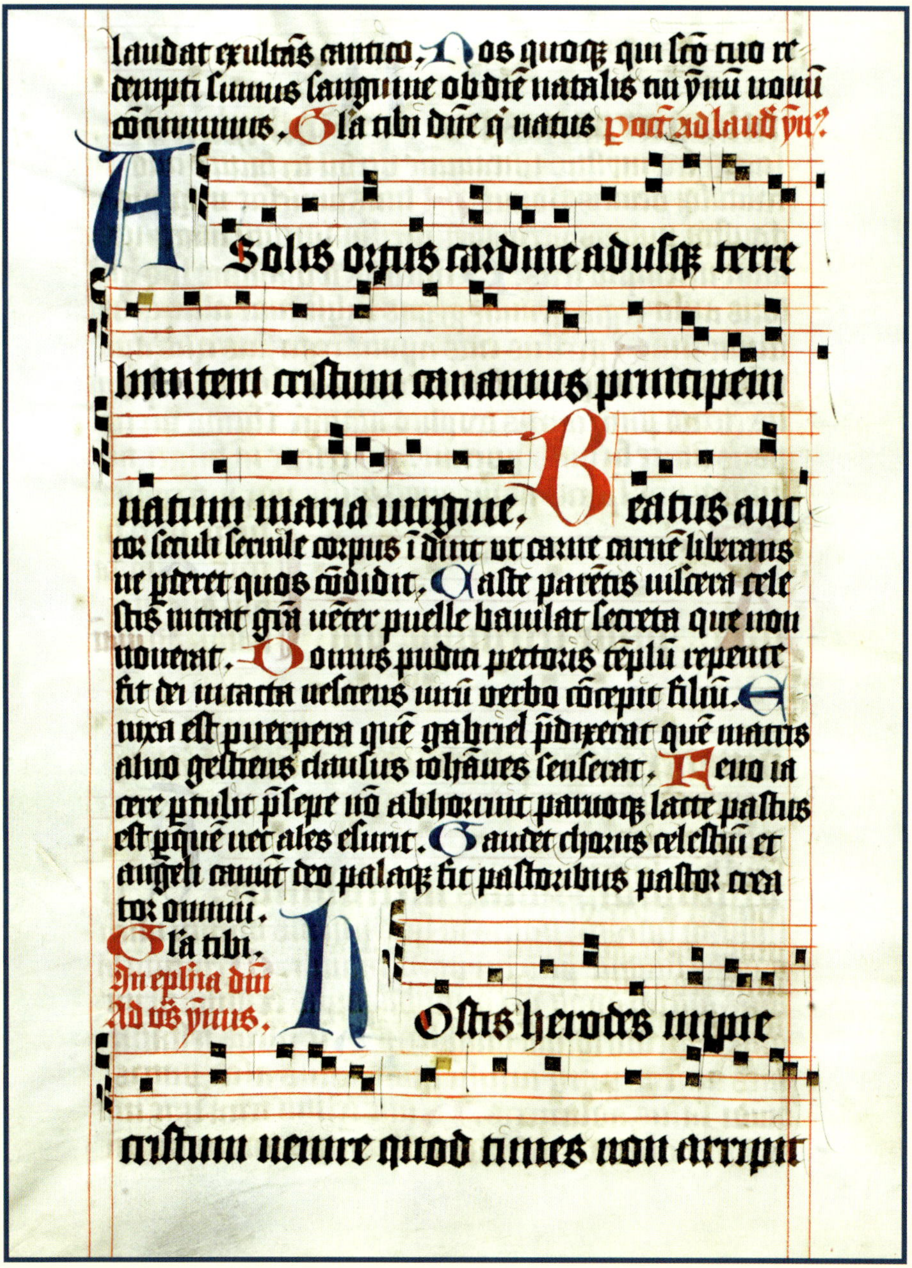

Image: A Solis Ortus Cardine • *Liber Antiphonarius* (circa 1484AD) from Switzerland.

Known as the "Abecedarius," this is an alphabetical hymn by Caelius Sedulius, a 5th-century poet. The colorful fonts of this manuscript make it easy to see the progression of each verse: A-B-C-D-E, etc. When Pope Urban VIII revised the hymns in 1631, he did violence to this progression; for example, *Crudelis Herodes* does not start with an "H," as it should.

Image: Crux Fidelis • *Graduale Romanum* (Düsseldorf: Schwann, 1953).

When Pope Saint Pius X (d. 1914) restored the Graduale Romanum in 1908, the ancient hymns—not the Urbanite versions—were restored: *Vexilla Regis, Jesu Nostra Redemptio*, and so forth. Inexplicably, the Antiphonale Romanum of 1912 used the Urbanite hymns. Editions of the *Graduale* then began to mix both versions in a haphazard way. Notice how the 1953 Schwann (edited by Karl Gustav Fellerer, Msgr. Johannes Overath, and Abbot Urbanus Bomm) includes both versions.

†

JESU, REDEMPTOR OMNIUM.

Jezos anamika8ata
Nongom patc ag8aciminang;
Bethleeming daje niki,
Manin o pininotagon.

Anjeni8ak nikamo8ak
O 8aseckana8a tibik.
Kijikong pas8e8ecinok,
Ikito8ak : Jezos niki.

Songa modjikenindanda,
Ikitota : Jezos nose,
Songa ki nakominimin
Pa iji ca8enimiiang.

Jezos ki 8i tebiimin
Aking e8akajiiiamintc
Ki cagodjitama8imin
Tci 8itc mina8asiminang.

Jezos, ki nakominimin,
Ki mamoia8aminimin,
Ki pakitinamonimin
Ni pimatisi8ininan.

Mani, 8itoka8icinam,
Gaganotama8icinam
Tci 8itapimangitc 8ak8ing
Jezos eg8acimiiiamintc

Kin, ketcit8a kikango8in,
Kin, 8enidjanisindaman
Jezos ot ag8acinge8in,
Gaganotama8icinam.

Kitcit8a8enindagosi
Jezos Mani o k8isisan
8ak8ing kitci tebiinang
Nongom kekona ki ingi.

AUDI BENIGNE CONDITOR.

Enabigis, k8enatc nose,
Kin ondjita ce8eningen,
Ca8enindamita8icin,
Ondjita ni gitimagis.

Onzam animak endian,
Nanengim ki ki nickiin;
Maneton ni patato8in,
Ni kitci agatenindis.

Image: Jesu Redemptor Omnium • *Aiamie Masinaigan* (1854) in Algonquin.

The first language Brébeuf learned was not Huron; it was the Montagnais language in the Algonquian family. This was in 1626, when he composed a small dictionary of that language. Although the greatest effort by the missionaries was spent on the Hurons, they constantly dealt with other tribes. It is not generally known that for centuries the Native Americans were allowed to sing parts of the Mass in the vernacular. The pioneer of this effort was Brébeuf's confrère: Saint Antoine Daniel (d. 1648).

CHRISTMAS HYMNS. 79

42 *HYMN FOR CHRISTMAS, AT VESPERS.* 43

Vesper. Ratisbon.

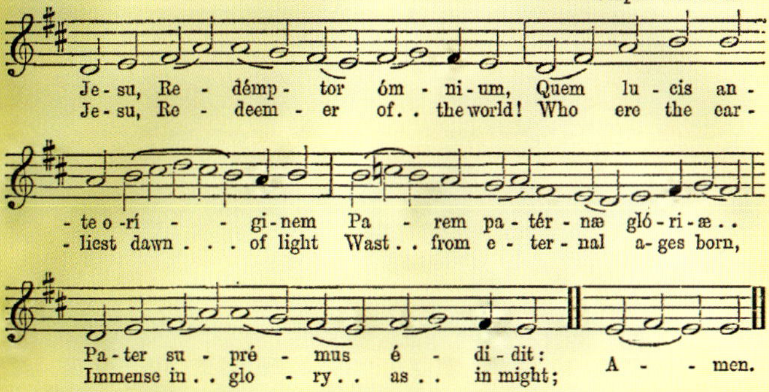

Tu lumen et splendor Patris,
Tu spes perénnis ómnium,
Inténde quas fundunt preces
Tui per orbem sérvuli.

Meménto, rerum Cónditor,
Nostri quod olim córporis,
Sacráta ab alvo Vírginis
Nascéndo, formam súmpseris.

Testátur hoc præsens dies,
Currens per anni círculum,
Quod solus e sinu Patris
Mundi salus advéneris.

Hunc astra, tellus, aéquora,
Hunc omne, quod cœlo subest,
Salútis Auctórem novæ
Novo salútat cántico.

Et nos, beáta quos sacri
Rigávit unda sánguinis,
Natális ob diem tui
Hymni tribútum sólvimus.

Jesu, tibi sit glória,
Qui natus es de Vírgine,
Cum Patre, et almo Spíritu,
In sempitérna saécula.
Amen.

2 Immortal Hope of all mankind!
In Whom the Father's face we see,
Hear Thou the prayers Thy people pour
This day throughout the world to Thee.

3 Remember, O Creator Lord!
That in the Virgin's sacred womb
Thou wast conceived, and of her flesh
Didst our mortality assume.

4 This ever-blest recurring day
Its witness bears, that all alone
From Thy own Father's bosom forth,
To save the world, Thou camest down.

5 O Day! to which the seas and sky,
And earth and Heaven glad welcome sing;
O Day! which healed our misery,
And brought on earth salvation's King.

6 We too, O Lord, who have been cleansed
In Thy own fount of Blood divine,
Offer the tribute of sweet song
On this blest natal day of Thine.

7 O Jesu! born of Virgin bright,
Immortal glory be to Thee;
Praise to the Father infinite,
And Holy Ghost eternally.
Amen.

FIRST VESPERS.

℣. Crastína die delébitur iníquitas terræ.
℟. Et regnávit super nos Salvátor mundi.

℣. To-morrow the iniquity of the earth shall be blotted out.
℟. And the Saviour of the world shall reign over us.

SECOND VESPERS.

℣. Notum fecit Dóminus. Allelúia.
℟. Salutáre suum. Allelúia.

℣. The Lord hath made known. Alleluia.
℟. His salvation. Alleluia.

Image: JESU REDEMPTOR OMNIUM • *Parochial Hymn Book* (London, 1883).

Published by Fr. Anatole Police, the "Parochial Hymn Book" bore an IMPRIMATUR by Henry Cardinal Manning (d. 1892), who converted from Anglicanism in 1851 and was appointed Archbishop of Westminster in 1865. Notice the careful placement of English translations alongside the Latin hymns. Our book follows this Catholic tradition, which stretches back to the 16th century. Moreover, when a choir sings in Latin, it is praiseworthy for the congregation to follow an English translation.

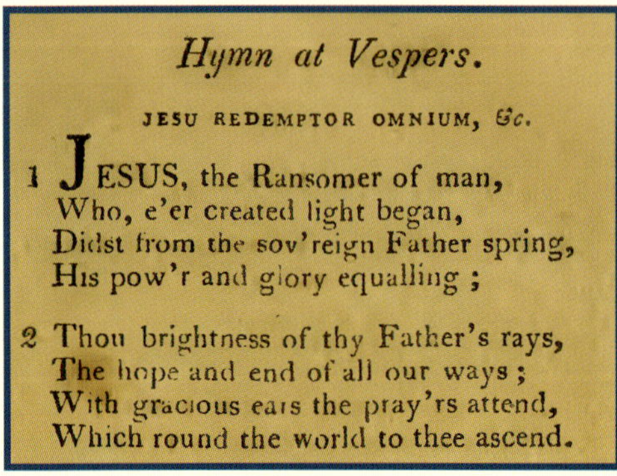

Hymn at Vespers.

JESU REDEMPTOR OMNIUM, &c.

1 JESUS, the Ransomer of man,
Who, e'er created light began,
Didst from the sov'reign Father spring,
His pow'r and glory equalling;

2 Thou brightness of thy Father's rays,
The hope and end of all our ways;
With gracious ears the pray'rs attend,
Which round the world to thee ascend.

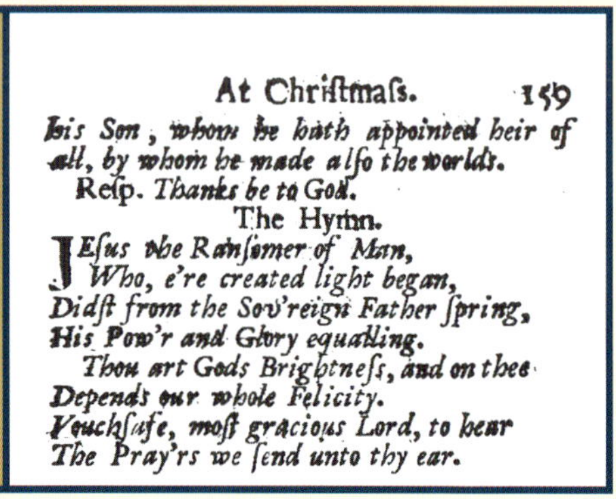

At Chriſtmaſs. 159

his Son, whom he hath appointed heir of all, by whom he made alſo the worlds.
Reſp. *Thanks be to God.*

The Hymn.

*JEſus the Ranſomer of Man,
Who, e're created light began,
Didſt from the Sov'reign Father ſpring,
His Pow'r and Glory equalling.
Thou art Gods Brightneſs, and on thee
Depends our whole Felicity.
Vouchſafe, moſt gracious Lord, to hear
The Pray'rs we ſend unto thy ear.*

Image: Baltimore "Hymns" (1807) **Image:** Roman Catholic Primer (1687)

ORBY SHIPLEY was the preëminent Catholic hymnologist of his time. A convert from Anglicanism, his books include *Lyra Eucharistica* (1863), *Lyra Messianica* (1864), *Lyra Mystica* (1865), and the mighty *Annus Sanctus* (1884). Regarding the Roman Catholic primers, he wrote:

> Of their historical and literary and what may be called their sentimental value, too high an estimate in the eyes of Catholics can hardly be made. Yet, the fact remains that not many persons are conscious of the existence of these hymns; none, with but one exception of those who have been consulted, proved otherwise than vague in their knowledge of them; and none, without an exception, knew the extent of the class.

Shipley is correct that too few know of the existence of these primers. Indeed, our hymnal contains breviary translations unknown to even the (otherwise infallible) Dr. John Julian. However, the editors[4] of a most remarkable book—*Hymns for the Use of the Catholic Church in the United States of America* (1807)—certainly knew of the primers:

Baltimore "Hymns" (1807)	**Catholic "Primer" (1687)**
Jesus, the Ransomer of man,	Jesus the Ransomer of Man,
Who, e're created light began,	Who, e're created light began,
Didst from the sov'reign Father spring,	Didst from the Sov'reign Father spring,
His pow'r and glory equalling.	His Pow'r and Glory equalling.

Whoever edited the 1807 book was incredibly meticulous in the modification of hymn texts—carefully improving a phrase here, a phrase there—demonstrating the value placed on singing in the vernacular. The book's introduction is singular:

> Next to the offering of the Eucharistical Sacrifice, which is the most sublime and the more essential act of divine worship, the singing of the praises of God and of the Lamb is unquestionably the noblest employment of a Christian. [...] It cannot be doubted but that the most proper time for this holy exercise is when the faithful meet together in Church...

4 This book was undoubtedly supported by a fascinating and influential figure in America: Most Rev'd John Carroll, the Archbishop of Baltimore from 1789-1815. Carroll, a Jesuit, never tired of promoting liturgical understanding on the part of lay people and was an early supporter of having certain parts of the Mass proclaimed in the vernacular. His older brother signed both the Articles of Confederation and the Constitution.

272 *In Feſto Circumciſionis Domini.*

AD NONAM.

Ant. 3. a. Omnes Prophétæ.

CAPITULUM. *Rom.* 10.

OMnis qui credit in illum, non confundétur ; Non enim eſt diſtínctio Judæi, & Græci : nam idem Dóminus ómnium, dives in omnes qui ínvocant illum ; Omnis enim quicumque invocáverit nomen Dómini : ſalvus erit.

℟. *br.* Sperent in te * qui novérunt nomen tuum. * Allelúia, allelúia. Sperent. ℣. Quóniam non dereliquiſti * quærentes te, Dómine. * Allelúia. Glória Patri. Sperent. *Pſ.* 9.

℣. Propter glóriam nóminis tui, Dómine, líbera nos, ℟. Et propítius eſto peccátis noſtris, propter nomen tuum. *Pſ.* 78.

AD II. VESPERAS.

Pſalmi de Dominica : loco ultimi, dicitur Pſ. Confitébor ... quóniam. 98.

Ant. 1. D. CHriſtum Jeſum propóſuit Deus propitiatiónem per fidem in ſánguine ipſíus. *Rom.* 3.

Ant. 2. D. Redémit nos de maledícto legis, ut in géntibus benedíctio Abrahæ fíeret in Chriſto Jeſu. *Galat.* 3.

Ant. 3. a. Ipſe eſt pax noſtra, legem mandatórum decrétis evácuans, ut duos condat in ſemetipſo in unum novum hóminem. *Epheſ.* 2.

Ant. 4. D. Cognóvit Dóminus qui ſunt ejus ; & diſcédat ab iniquitáte, omnis qui nóminat nomen Dómini. 2. *Tim.* 2.

Ant. 5. C. Nemo poteſt dícere Dóminus Jeſus, niſi in Spíritu ſancto. 1. *Cor.* 12.

CAPITULUM. *Coloſſ.* 3.

OMne quodcumque fácitis in verbo aut in ópere; ómnia in nómine Dómini Jeſu Chriſti : grátias agentes Deo & Patri per ipſum.

HYMNUS.

VIctis ſibi cognómina
Sumant tyranni géntibus :
Tu, Chriſte, quantò dígnius
Ab his capis quos líberas?

NON álterum mortálibus
Ægris quod ínvocent datum,
Reſúrgerent quo mórtui,
Perennè per quod víverent.

TANTI quod illi cónſtitit,
Toto quod emptum ſánguine,
Noſtro-ne rurſum crímine
Insána gens delébimus?

SACRO pati pro nómine,
Summi ſit inſtar múneris :
Amára non mors ámpliùs,
Fit mors per hoc amábilis.

TU qui vocári ſúſtines,
Jeſu, ſalus mortálium,
Audi vocantes nos, tuo
Qui gloriámur nómine.

QUI natus es de Vírgine,
Jeſu, tibi ſit glória
Cum Patre, cumque Spíritu,
In ſempiterna ſécula.
Amen.

℣. Salvávit eos propter nomen ſuum ; ℟. Ut notam fáceret poténtiam ſuam. *Pſ.* 105.

Ad Magníficat. *Ant.* 7. G. Vitam æternam dedit nobis Deus : & hæc vita in Fílio ejus eſt; ut ſciátis quóniam vitam habétis æternam, qui créditis in nómine Fílii Dei. 1. *Joan.* 5.

Oratio, ut ſuprà ad Laudes.

Image: VICTIS SIBI COGNOMINA • *Breviarium Sanctae Lugdunensis Ecclesia* (1780).

While it is undeniable that the Roman breviary forms the core of our hymnal, we did not exclude other beautiful expressions of the Catholic faith. *Victis Sibi Cognomina*, for example, ceased to be used once the Paris breviary was discarded in favor of the Roman—yet this prayer extolling the Holy Name is quite moving and we have included it.

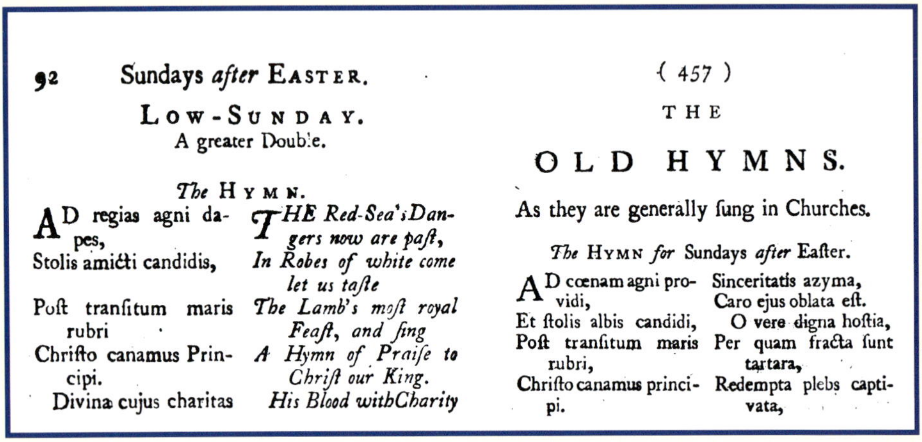

92 Sundays *after* EASTER.

LOW-SUNDAY.
A greater Double.

The HYMN.

AD regias agni dapes,
Stolis amicti candidis,
Poſt tranſitum maris rubri
Chriſto canamus Principi.
Divinæ cujus charitas

THE Red-Sea's Dangers now are paſt,
In Robes of white come let us taſte
The Lamb's moſt royal Feaſt, and ſing
A Hymn of Praiſe to Chriſt our King.
His Blood with Charity

(457)

THE

OLD HYMNS.

As they are generally ſung in Churches.

The HYMN *for* Sundays *after* Eaſter.

AD cœnam agni providi,
Et ſtolis albis candidi,
Poſt tranſitum maris rubri,
Chriſto canamus principi.

Sinceritatis azyma,
Caro ejus oblata eſt.
O vere digna hoſtia,
Per quam fracta ſunt tartara,
Redempta plebs captivata,

Image: *The Evening-Office of the Church in Latin and English* (1738).

IN CATHOLIC BOOKS, even hundreds of years after Pope Urban VIII promulgated his hymn revisions in 1631, the ancient texts continued to be printed and sung. Notice the terminology in the example shown above. The main book has the Urbanite hymns (e.g. *Ad regias agni dapes*), but the back of the book contains a section called:

> "THE OLD HYMNS. As they are generally sung in Churches."

On the other hand, some publications bragged about their inclusion of the "corrected" Latin of Pope Urban VIII. The preface to the 1651 Primer notes that it has been:

> ...thoroughly reformed according to the last corrected Latin of Pope Urban the VIII, now generally used in the Church; wherein you shall find all the Hymns put into a true divine Poetic strain, yet keeping close to the literal sense, of which there are some new ones, and many prayers, which did never before speak English...

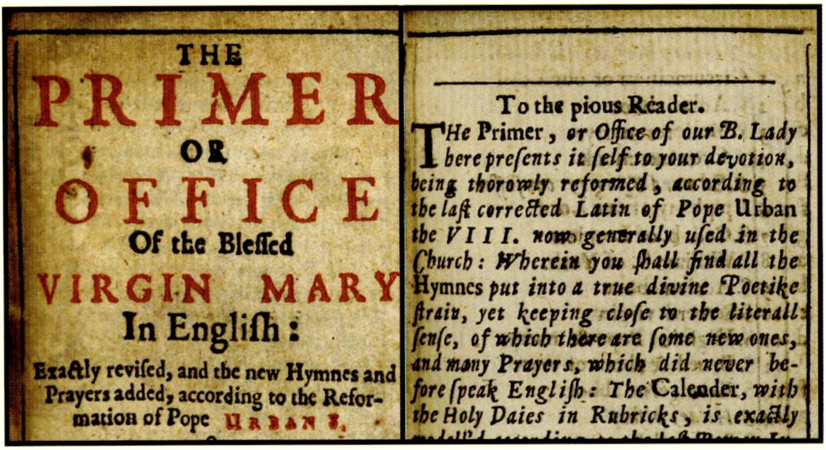

THE
PRIMER
OR
OFFICE
Of the Bleſſed
VIRGIN MARY
In Engliſh:
Exactly reviſed, and the new Hymnes and Prayers added, according to the Reformation of Pope URBAN 8.

To the pious Reader.

THe Primer, or Office of our B. Lady here preſents it ſelf to your devotion, being thorowly reformed, according to the laſt corrected Latin of Pope Urban the VIII. now generally uſed in the Church: Wherein you ſhall find all the Hymnes put into a true divine Poetike ſtrain, yet keeping cloſe to the literall ſenſe, of which there are ſome new ones, and many Prayers, which did never before ſpeak Engliſh: The Calender, with the Holy Daies in Rubricks, is exactly

Image: *The Primer or Office of the Blessed Virgin Mary in English; Exactly revised, and the new Hymnes and Prayers added, according to the Reformation of Pope Urban 8* (1651).

THE coexistence of the Urbanite and ancient hymns made it almost inevitable that translators would begin to blend the meanings of both into a single translation. The 1688 Primer demonstrates this phenomenon:

Conditor Alme Siderum (verse 2)
Who, lest the fraud of Hell's black King
Should all Men to destruction bring,
Did'st by a strong impulse of Love,
The fainting World's Physician prove.

A "strong impulse of love" is not found in the ancient version of *Conditor Alme Siderum* :

2. Who, sorrowing that the world should dissolve through the havoc of death, didst save the fainting earth, granting redress to the guilty.

It is clearly borrowed from *Creator Alme Siderum*, the Urbanite version:

2. Thou wert impelled by the power of love to become a remedy for the languid world, lest mankind should perish through the cunning of the devil.

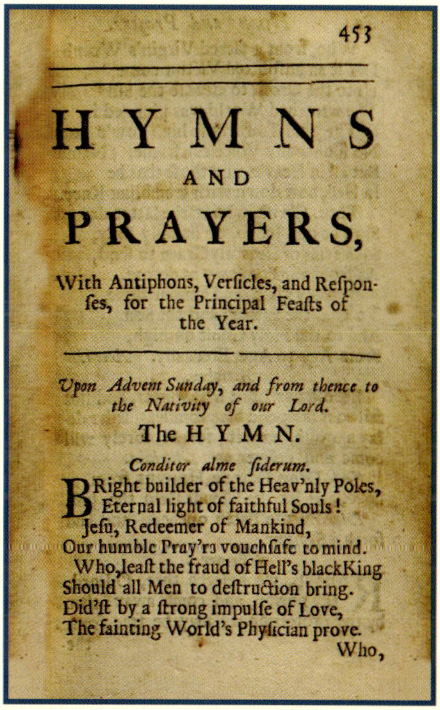

453

HYMNS
AND
PRAYERS,

With Antiphons, Verſicles, and Reſponſes, for the Principal Feaſts of the Year.

Upon Advent Sunday, and from thence to the Nativity of our Lord.

The HYMN.

Conditor alme ſiderum.

BRight builder of the Heav'nly Poles,
Eternal light of faithful Souls!
Jeſu, Redeemer of Mankind,
Our humble Pray'rs vouchſafe to mind.
Who, leaſt the fraud of Hell's black King
Should all Men to deſtruction bring.
Did'ſt by a ſtrong impulſe of Love,
The fainting World's Phyſician prove.
Who,

Image: Roman Catholic Primer (1688).

When Msgr. Knox translated this same hymn for the *New Westminster Hymnal* (1939), he did the opposite. He claimed to be translating *Creator Alme Siderum*, the Urbanite version:

Creator Alme Siderum (verse 3)
So, at the eventide of earth,
From that bridechamber of thy birth
Our mortal flesh thou didst assume
Born of a spotless Virgin's womb.

...yet he took the "bridechamber" idea from *Conditor Alme Siderum*, the ancient text:

3. Who, when the world's evening befell,
like a bridegroom from his chamber,
came forth from the most honorable
enclosure of thy Maiden Mother.

This meant eliminating the Urbanite version's reference to the Cross ("ad Crucem"):

3. To expiate the common guilt of mankind,
Thou, a spotless Victim,
didst go forth to the Cross
from the sacred womb of a Virgin.

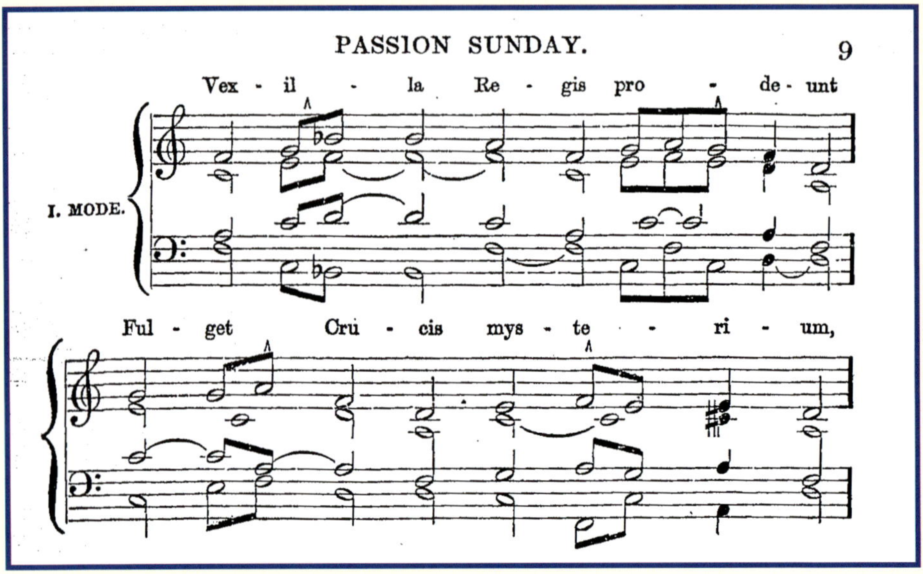

Image: Vexilla Regis • *Hymnarium Vesperale* (London: John Lambert, 1851).

Based on publications appearing in recent times, one could perhaps be forgiven for thinking that the Catholic Church has done a poor job fostering appreciation for the ancient breviary hymns. However, research has shown that Catholics in former times—going back at least as far as the 16th century—absolutely did strive to make such treasures accessible to the faithful.

Indeed, there was a constant desire to do better. Consider the progress made between Lambert's 1851 attempt (shown above) and that of Monsignor Jules Van Nuffel (d. 1953) in the *Nova Organi Harmonia* collection, which numbered among its composers such luminaries as Maestro Flor Peeters (d. 1986), Father Jules Vyverman (d. 1989), and Marinus de Jong (d. 1984).

Image: Vexilla Regis • *Nova Organi Harmonia* (Mechlin: Msgr. Van Nuffel, 1942).

VEXILLA REGIS PRODEUNT

***Venantius Fortunatus*, 530-609**

PASSION SUNDAY, AT VESPERS

THE King's own standard is unfurled :
The Cross in mystic splendour glows,
Whereon Life died, and for the world
Won life, through death's immortal throes.

There, wounded by the woeful spear,
Life has both blood and water shed,
To wash our souls from soilure clear,
And make them white as snow instead.

Now is fulfilled ere eventide,
What David's faithful psalm made known,
When to all lands he prophesied :
Lo ! God has made a tree His throne.

O beautiful, resplendent Tree !
That dost the King's own purple wear ;
Thy stock was chosen worthily
To touch such holy limbs, and bear.

Thou blessèd Tree ! whose arms were made
The ransom of this world to hold ;
Thou balance which that Body weighed,
From hell thus taking spoils untold.

O Cross, our only hope, all hail !
Now, ere the Passiontide is o'er,
Let grace to purge out sin avail,
And pious hearts fill, more and more.

61

Image: VEXILLA REGIS • *Breviary and Missal Hymns* (Fr. John Fitzpatrick, 1931).

Ours is the first Catholic hymnal to include the sublime translations of Fr. John Fitzpatrick (d. 1929). His magnificent collection of breviary hymns—218 pages!—was completed just before his death and published posthumously, according to his stated desires. An earlier version had appeared in 1924.

THERE WERE NOW eleven Frenchmen in the village: six priests, four workmen, and Jean Amyot. Father Jean de Brébeuf, the superior and the veteran missionary among the Hurons, addressed Jogues and two other recent arrivals, Fathers Garnier and Chastellain, concerning the mission. "Instead of being a great master and a great theologian, as in France," he said, "you must reckon on being here a humble scholar. The Huron language will be your Saint Thomas and your Aristotle. Clever men as you are, and speaking glibly among learned and capable persons, you must make up your minds to be mute for a long time among the forest dwellers. You will have accomplished much if you begin to stammer a little at the end of a considerable time."

Leaning over to them, and speaking very earnestly, Father Brébeuf continued: "You must realize that our lives depend upon a single thread. We are told to expect death every hour and be prepared for it, no matter where we are in the world; that applies here particularly…"

He then described the continual discomforts in store for them: piercing cold; smoke that would so inflame their eyes they could read no more than a few lines of their breviary at a time; coarse and unpalatable food; and the ever-present danger of death. He warned them of the mischievous sorcerers—jealous, resentful and treacherous—who might at any moment incite the natives against them.

"It is to souls like yours that God has appointed the conquest of many other souls… Fear no difficulties; there will be none for you, since it is your whole consolation to see yourself crucified with the Son of God."

—From *The Life of Saint Jean de Brébeuf*

SAINT JEAN DE BRÉBEUF

ONE OF THE EIGHT JESUIT MARTYRS OF NORTH AMERICA

"The Crucifixion" (1438AD) — *Missal for Saint Ursus Cathedral*, Switzerland, folio 103.

BRÉBEUF, in his spiritual notes, testifies that in May he again cloistered himself for spiritual retreat. His notebook reveals: "Beginning the Exercises on 12 May 1630. Lord Jesus Christ, my Redeemer, You have redeemed me by Your blood and most precious death. That is why I promise to serve You all my life in the Society of Jesus and never to serve any other. This I have subscribed with my own blood and my own hand, being ready to sacrifice it all for You as willingly as this drop."

English Titles • Alphabetical

Foreign Titles • Alphabetical

Italic titles are those modified by Pope Urban VIII in his 1631 reform

Hymn Tunes • Alphabetical

Hymn Tunes • Metrical

Tunes with a Peculiar Meter

57 57

65 65 D

66 66 Trochaic

66 66 Iambic

66 86 (SM)

S. M. D.

76 76 Trochaic

76 76 D Trochaic

Part I • Ancient Hymns

AD CENAM (cont'd)

PANGE LINGUA (cont'd)

Part II • Additional Hymns

Advent (Additional Hymns)

Christmas (Additional Hymns)

Christmas and Epiphany (Additional Hymns)

Epiphany and Baptism of the Lord (Additional Hymns)

Lent and Passiontide (Additional Hymns)

Lent and Passiontide (cont'd)

Easter (Additional Hymns)

Ascension (Additional Hymns)

Holy Ghost (Additional Hymns)

Holy Trinity (Additional Hymns)

Holy Eucharist (Additional Hymns)

Blessed Virgin (cont'd)

The Saints (Additional Hymns)

Faithful Departed (Additional Hymns)

General Use (Additional Hymns)

OPERAM NON PERDIT
QUI DEO LABORAT.

652 Veni Veni Emmanuel (The "O" Antiphons)

Old Testament titles for the Messiah

(23 December)
O Emmanuel, our King and our Law-Giver, the Expectation and the Savior of Nations! come to our Salvation, O Lord our God.

O EMMÁNUEL,
Rex et légifer noster, exspectátio
géntium, et salvátor eárum:
veni ad salvándum nos
Dómine Deus noster.

(22 December)
O King of the Gentiles, the Desired of Nations, the Corner Stone that unitest both in one! come, to the Salvation of Man, whom thou hast fram'd of Earth.
[i.e. God made man from slime of the earth]

O REX GÉNTIUM,
et desiderátus eárum,
lapísque anguláris, qui facis
útraque unum: veni, et salva hóminem,
quem de limo formásti.

(21 December)
O Orient ("Dawn"), the Splendor of Eternal Light, and Son of Justice! come and enlighten those that sit in the Dark, and in the Shades of Death.

O ÓRIENS,
splendor lucis aetérnae,
et sol justítiae: veni,
et illúmina sedéntes in ténebris,
et umbra mortis.

(20 December)
O Key of David, and Scepter of the House of Israel! who openest, and no one shuts, shuttest, and no one opens; come and bring forth from their Prisons, those that are in Chains, sitting in the Dark, and in the Shades of Death.

O CLAVIS DAVID,
et sceptrum domus Israël; qui áperis, et
nemo claudit; claudis, et nemo áperit:
veni, et educ vinctum de domo cárceris,
sedéntem in ténebris, et umbra mortis.

(19 December)
O Root of Jesse! who standest for a Sign to Nations, before whom Kings shall restrain their Mouths: Thou, whom the Gentiles shall Address, come to our Deliverance and now delay no more.

O RADIX JESSE,
qui stas in signum populórum,
super quem continébunt reges os suum,
quem Gentes deprecabúntur: veni
ad liberándum nos, jam noli tardáre.

(18 December)
O Adonai ("Lord"), and Leader of the House of Israel! who appeared'st to Moses in the Flaming Bush, and gavest to him the Law in Sinai, come and redeem us with thy strong Arm.

O ADONÁÏ,
et Dux domus Israël, qui Móysi
in igne flammae rubi apparuísti,
et ei in Sina legem dedísti: veni
ad rediméndum nos in bráchio exténto.

(17 December)
O Wisdom! who camest forth from the Mouth of the Most High; powerfully extending from End to End, and sweetly disposing all Things; come, and instruct us in the Ways of Prudence.

O SAPIÉNTIA,
quae ex ore Altíssimi prodísti,
attíngens a fine usque ad finem,
fórtiter suáviter disponénsque ómnia:
veni ad docéndum nos viam prudéntiae.

The deeply scriptural "O Antiphons" are quite ancient; e.g. Boethius (d. 525AD) refers to them. Liturgically, they are used as the Magnificat anthems for Vespers during the final days of Advent, and form an Advent acrostic—ERO CRAS—which means: "I will be there tomorrow." Because of the acrostic, they are normally sung in reverse: Emmanuel ("God with us"); Rex ("King of the Gentiles"); Oriens ("Sunrise"); Clavis ("Key of David"); Radix ("Root of Jesse"); Adonáï (Hebrew substitute for ineffable name of YHWH—"Lord"); Sapientia ("Wisdom").

Trns: Msgr. Ronald A. Knox (d. 1957)

O COME, O come, Emmanuel,
And ransom captive Israel,
That mourns in lonely exile here,
Until the Son of God appear.
R. *Rejoice, rejoice! Emmanuel shall come to thee, O Israel.*

O COME, of Gentile hearts the King,
A world that needs thee ransoming,
And save thy servants, who confess
With humbled hearts their faithlessness. R.

O COME, thou Daystar seen on high,
With healing for our hearts draw nigh;
Do thou the mists of night dispel,
And death's foreboding darkness quell. R.

O COME, thou Key of David's store,
Unlock the heav'nly gates once more;
Safe journey to thy courts bestow,
And shut the way that leads below. R.

O COME, thou Rod of Jesse, free
Thine own from Satan's tyranny;
From depths of hell thy people save,
And give them vict'ry o'er the grave. R.

O COME, thou everlasting Lord,
Who once by Israel's host adored
Thy ten commandments madest known,
In majesty of glory shown. R.

O COME, thou Wisdom whose decree
Doth govern all things peacefully;
The way of prudence here below
And life hereafter deign to show. R.

Final Verses: Richard Lloyd (1993) #234; Noel Rawsthorne (2011) #374.

Veni Veni Emmanuel (Latin) is a paraphrase of the "O Antiphons" created in 1710 by German Jesuits. The English translation is based on that of Msgr. Ronald Knox, as the famous 1851 translation by John Mason Neale (originally "Draw nigh, draw nigh, Emmanuel") omits two verses. The traditional melody dates from the 15th century. The literal translation is historical; cf. *Primer, or Office of the B. Virgin Mary* (Thomas Meighan, 1732) p. 426.

88 88 R

Tune:
VENI VENI EMMANUEL

654 Jordanis Oras Praevia (1736 AD)

Fr. Charles Coffin (d. 1749)

4. To heal the sick stretch out Thy hand,
And bid the fallen sinner stand;
Shine forth, and let Thy light restore
Earth's own true loveliness once more.

5. All praise, eternal Son, to Thee,
Whose advent sets Thy people free,
Whom with the Father we adore
And Holy Ghost forevermore.

88 88 (LM)

Tune:
Winchester New

Final Verses: Richard Lloyd (1993) #244; Noel Rawsthorne (2011) #392.
Melody: Georg Wittwe's *Musikalisches Handbuch der Geistlichen Melodien* (Hamburg, 1690).
M. Source: *Episcopal Hymnal* (1940) ABAB #548; *New Saint Basil Hymnal* (1958) p. 1.
English Translation: John Chandler (d. 1876); cf. *Hymns of the Primitive Church: now first collected, translated, and arranged* (London, 1837) p. 40.
T. Source: *Catholic Hymn Book* (London Oratory, 1998) p. 15; *Hymns, Psalms, and Spiritual Canticles* (Massachusetts: Theodore Marier, 1983) p. 391; *New Saint Basil Hymnal* (1958) p. 1.

En Clara Vox Redarguit (5th century) 655

Trns: Fr. John Fitzpatrick, Oblate of Mary (d. 1929)

4. And when next He comes, refulgent,
Girdling all the world with fear,
May He, as a Judge indulgent,
Shield us, though our guilt is clear.

5. Glory, pow'r, and praise unending
To the Father and the Son,
And the Paraclete, ascending
While eternal ages run.

Literal Translation:

1. The Baptist's message of rebuke rings loud and clear through all the world of darkness:
Away with dreams of darkness. Jesus, the light, is shining in the sky.

2. Let the slothful soul now arise and no longer lie earth-bound,
for a new sun is now shining, Christ, Who will take away every sin.

3. Behold the Lamb is sent to us to pay freely the debt we owe.
Therefore let all of us together, with tears of sorrow, ask for His pardon…

4. So that, when for the second time He comes resplendent and girdles the world with fear,
He will not then punish us, as our sins deserve, but in His pity be our protector.

5. Praise, honor, power, and glory be to God the Father, and to the Son,
and likewise to the Holy Paraclete, forever.

This hymn's title before 1631AD was *Vox Clara Ecce Intonat*. The revisers under Pope Urban VIII did not alter this hymn's meaning in any significant way. The use of "girdle" in verse 4 (*Mundúmque horror cinxerit*) simply means: "causes fear in all hearts."

Final Verses: Richard Lloyd (1993) #138; Noel Rawsthorne (2011) #210.
Melody: William H. Monk (d. 1889), organist at King's College London.
M. Source: *Hymns, Psalms, and Spiritual Canticles* (1983) p. 278; *New Westminster Hymnal* (1939) p. 3.
T. Source: *The Breviary and Missal Hymns* (London: Sands & Co, 1931) p. 40.

87 87
Tune: Merton

656 Instantis Adventum Dei (1736 AD)

Fr. Charles Coffin (d. 1749)

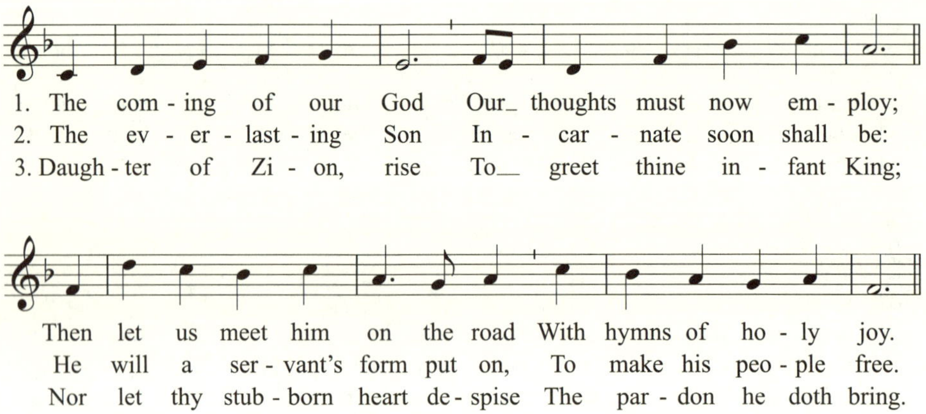

4. In glory from his throne
Again will Christ descend,
And summon all that are his own
To joys that never end.

5. Before that dreadful day
May all our sin be gone;
May the old man be put away,
And the new man put on.

6. Our joyful praises sing
To Christ, who set us free;
Like tribute to the Father bring,
And, Holy Ghost, to thee.

Can be sung with any 66 86 meter: Festal Song, Allington, Seán 8M, Dominica, Southwell, St Michael, Song 20, Potsdam, etc.

THE coming of our God
Our thoughts must now employ;
Then let us meet him on the road
With hymns of holy joy.

2. The everlasting Son
Incarnate soon shall be:
He will a servant's form put on,
To make his people free.

3. Daughter of Zion, rise
To greet thine infant King;
Nor let thy stubborn heart despise
The pardon he doth bring.

4. In glory from his throne
Again will Christ descend,
And summon all that are his own
To joys that never end.

5. Before that dreadful day
May all our sin be gone;
May the old man be put away,
And the new man put on.

6. Our joyful praises sing
To Christ, who set us free;
Like tribute to the Father bring,
And, Holy Ghost, to thee.

66 86 (SM)

Tune: Seán 8M

Melody: Richard J. Clark (b. 1969), choirmaster at the Cathedral of the Holy Cross in Boston.
M. Source: *Saint Jean de Brébeuf Hymnal* (2018).
English Translation: Based on a work by Robert Campbell of Skerrington (d. 1868).
T. Source: *Saint Andrew Hymnal, authorized by the Archbishops and Bishops of Scotland for use in the Scottish Dioceses* (1964) p. 8; *Summit Choirbook* (Dominican Monastery of Our Lady of the Rosary, 1983) #17; *Book of Hymns with Tunes* (Father Gregory Ould, 1910) p. 3.

Venez Divin Messie (18th century) 657

Trns: Sister Mary of Saint Philip (d. 1904)

Text: Abbé Simon-Joseph Pellegrin (d. 1745), a monk quite involved with writing opera libretti, frequently collaborating with Jean-Philippe Rameau (d. 1764), a French composer and theorist.
T. Source: *De La Salle Hymnal for Catholic Schools and Choirs* (New York, 1913) p. 3; *Book of Hymns with Tunes* (Father Gregory Ould, 1910) p. 4.
Melody: French Noël, 16th century.
Melody Source: *New Saint Basil Hymnal* (1958) p. 8; *Saint Michael Hymnal* (2003) #440.

78 76 R

Tune:
VENEZ, DIVIN MESSIE

658 Lo! He Comes With Clouds Descending

"Behold, he cometh with the clouds, and every eye shall see him, and they also that pierced him. And all the tribes of the earth shall bewail themselves because of him."—Apocalypse 1.7

4. Yea, Amen! let all adore thee, | High on thine eternal throne;
Savior, take the pow'r and glory: | Claim the kingdom for thine own:
O come quickly! (3x) | Alleluia! Come, Lord, come!

87 87 47

Tune:
HELMSLEY

Final Verses: Richard Lloyd (1993) #90; Noel Rawsthorne (2011) #149.
Melody: Thomas Olivers (d. 1799). M. Source: *New English Hymnal* (1906) p. 10.
Text: John Cennick (d. 1755). T. Source: *Catholic Hymn Book* (London Oratory, 1998) p. 11.

O Heiland Reiss Die Himmel Auf (Advent)

"You skies, pour down upon us the rain we long for: the Just One."—Isaias 45.8

4. The only store of hope worldwide,
and the one balm, where dost thou bide?
Yea, from the highest hall remove,
balm in this vale of tears to prove.

5. Thou sun and star, O fair and bright,
gladly would we enjoy thy sight!
Rise up, O sun: thy glow withdrawn,
all of us sit in gloom forlorn.

6. Here we endure the gravest want:
unending death doth us confront.
Come, lead us with a mighty hand
from wretchedness to our homeland!

Text: German text based on Isaias by Fr. Father Friedrich Spee von Langenfeld, SJ (d. 1635); English translation by Fr. Dominic Popplewell (b. 1973).
T. Source: *Saint Jean de Brébeuf Hymnal* (2018).
Melody: *Rheinfelsisches Deutsches Catholisches Gesangbuch* (1666).
M. Source: *Gotteslob; Katholisches Gebet- und Gesangbuch Ausgabe für das Bistum Trier* (1975) p. 186; *The Parish Hymnal* (Sister Catherine Cecilia, 1957) p. 1; *Pope Pius XII Hymnal* (Ohio: Gregorian Institute of America, 1959) p. 10.

88 88 (LM)

Tune:
O Heiland Reiss

660 Gabriel Saluting, Heaven Thee Recruiting

Fr. Dominic Popplewell (b. 1973)

4. Now and at life's ending,
help thy children lending,
by thy prayer, beyond compare,
thy ward with might endue. R.

66 76 R

Tune:
Reginald

Melody: Fr. Dominic Popplewell (b. 1973).
Text and Melody Source: *Saint Jean de Brébeuf Hymnal* (2018).

"And the desired of all nations shall come: and I will fill this house with glory."—Aggeus 2.8

4. Honor, glory, virtue, merit,
To the Father and the Son,
With the co-eternal Spirit,
While eternal ages run.

Can be sung with any 87 87 meter: Stuttgart, Halton Holgate, Redhead #46, Batty, Waltham, Vatican, Merton, Cross of Jesus, Marching, Bronzeville, etc.

COME, thou long-expected Jesus,
Born to set thy people free,
From our fears and sins release us,
Let us find our rest in thee.

2. Israel's strength and consolation,
Hope of all the earth thou art,
Dear Desire of every nation,
Joy of every longing heart.

3. Born thy people to deliver,
Born a Child and yet a King,
Born to reign in us for ever,
Now thy gracious kingdom bring.

4. Honor, glory, virtue, merit,
To the Father and the Son,
With the co-eternal Spirit,
While eternal ages run.

Final Verses: Richard Lloyd (1993) #47; Noel Rawsthorne (2011) #80.
Melody: John Stainer (d. 1901), organist at Magdalen College, Oxford, and St. Paul's Cathedral, London.
M. Source: *Catholic Hymn Book* (London Oratory, 1998) p. 98.
Text: Charles Wesley (d. 1788), who wrote more than 6,500 hymns. His son was Samuel Wesley (d. 1837), who converted to Catholicism and as a composer was dubbed "the English Mozart."
Text Source: *Catholic Hymn Book* (London Oratory, 1998) p. 1.

87 87
Tune:
Cross of Jesus

662 "Huron Carol" of Saint Jean de Brébeuf (d. 1649)

Trns: Fr. Dominic Popplewell (b. 1973)

* "Jesous ahatonnia" means "Jesus is born" in the language of the Hurons.

86 86 88 R

Tune:
Une Jeune Pucelle

This famous Christmas carol was possibly written around 1642, when Saint Brébeuf was in Quebec, recuperating from a broken collarbone, which had left him in excruciating pain for many months.
T. Source: *Saint Jean de Brébeuf Hymnal* (2018).
Melody: French Carol, first published in 1557.
M. Source: *New Saint Basil Hymnal* (1958) p. 18; *Summit Choirbook* (Dominican Monastery of Our Lady of the Rosary, 1983) #455.

Hark! The Herald Angels Sing 663

"And suddenly there was with the angel a multitude of the heavenly army, praising God, saying: Glory to God in the highest; and on earth peace to men of good will."—Lk 2.13-14

Final Verses: Richard Lloyd (1993) #136; Noel Rawsthorne (2011) #208.

Text: Charles Wesley (d. 1788), who wrote more than 6,500 hymns. His son was Samuel Wesley (d. 1837), who converted to Catholicism and as a composer was dubbed "the English Mozart."

Text Source: *Catholic Hymn Book* (London Oratory, 1998) p. 35; *Adoremus Hymnal* (1997) #325.

Melody: Adapted by William H. Cummings (d. 1915) from the second section ("Vaterland, in deinen Gauen") of the GUTENBERG CANTATA by Felix Mendelssohn (d. 1847). The fourth section harmonizes the hymn tune "Nun Danket," as Mendelssohn also did in the ninth section of his *Symphony No. 2.*

M. Source: *St. Mark's Hymnal for Use in the Catholic Church in the United States* (Peoria, Illinois: 1910) p. 45.

77 77d R

Tune: MENDELSSOHN

664 Joy To The World

"Rejoice, heaven, and let earth be glad; let the sea, and all the sea contains, give thunderous applause."—Ps 95.11

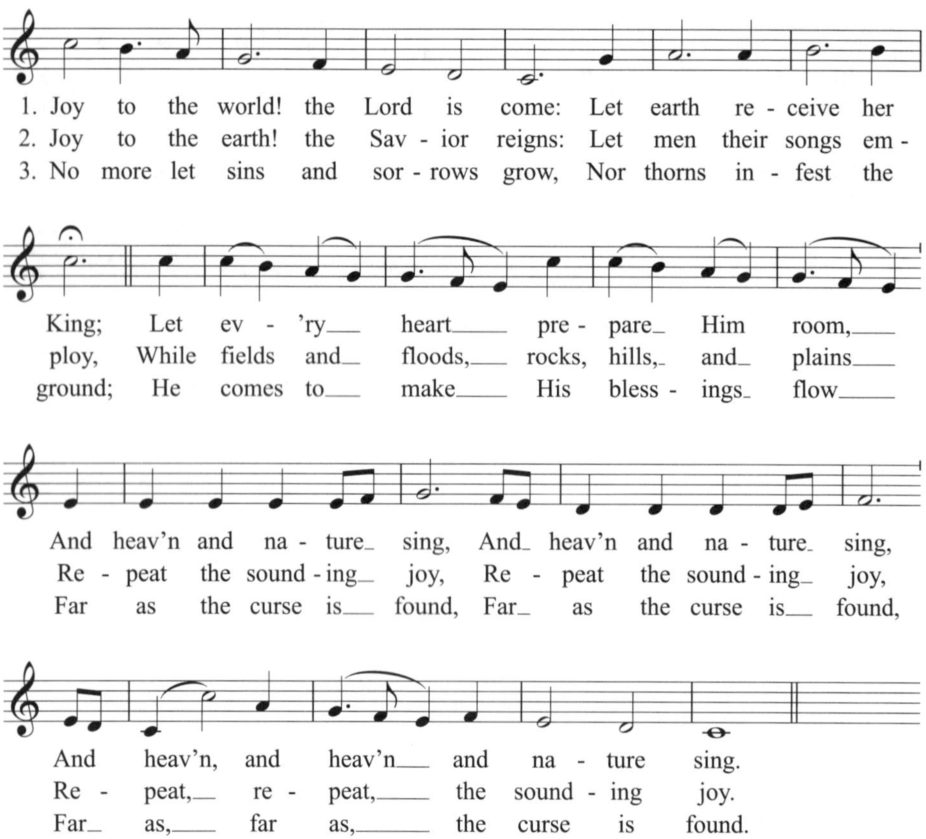

4. He rules the world with truth and grace,
And makes the nations prove
The glories of His righteousness,
And wonders of His love,
And wonders of His love,
And wonders, wonders of His love.

5. His name shall be the Prince of Peace,
The everlasting Lord,
The Wonderful, the Counsellor,
The God by all adored,
The God by all adored,
The God, the God by all adored.

86 86 (CM)

Tune:
Antioch

Text: Isaac Watts (d. 1748), based on Psalm 97.
T. Source: *Hymns, Psalms, and Spiritual Canticles* (Massachusetts: Theodore Marier, 1983) p. 311.
Melody: Lowell Mason (d. 1872), who composed more than 1,600 hymn tunes.
M. Source: *Saint Michael Hymnal* (St. Boniface Parish, 2003) #387.

In Dulci Jubilo (14th century) 665

attr. Bl. Henry Suso, Dominican Priest (*d.* 1366AD)

1. Good Chris - tian men, re - joice___ With heart and soul and voice;___
2. Good Chris - tian men, re - joice___ With heart and soul and voice;___
3. Good Chris - tian men, re - joice___ With heart and soul and voice;___

Give ye heed to what we say: Je - sus Christ is born to - day!
Now ye hear of end - less bliss: Je - sus Christ was born for this!
Now ye need not fear the grave: Je - sus Christ was born to save!

Ox and ass be - fore him bow, And he is in the man - ger
He has o - pened heav - en's door, And man is blest for - ev - er -
Calls you one and calls you all, To gain his ev - er - last - ing

now. Christ is born to - day!___ Christ is born to - day!
more. Christ was born for this!___ Christ was born for this!
hall. Christ was born to save!___ Christ was born to save!

Final Verses: Noel Rawsthorne (2011) #162.
Text and Melody: Both were written in the 14th century; the original text is macaronic, mixing Latin with German. The English translation is by Dr. John M. Neale (d. 1866), but without the exclamations— "News! News!" etc.—as they were due to an erroneous transcription of mensural notation.
T. Source: *Saint Michael Hymnal* (St. Boniface Parish, 2003)#322.
M. Source: *Cantate Omnes: Hymnal of the Catholic Choirmasters' Guild* (1952) #21; *St. Rose Hymnal* (1938) p. 15; *O Christ Hie Merk!* (Fr. Guido M. Dreves, 1885) p. 15.

66 77 78 55

Tune:
IN DULCI JUBILO

666 Once In Royal David's City

"And Joseph also went up from Galilee, out of the city of Nazareth into Judea, to the city of David, which is called Bethlehem: because he was of the house and family of David."—Mt 2.4

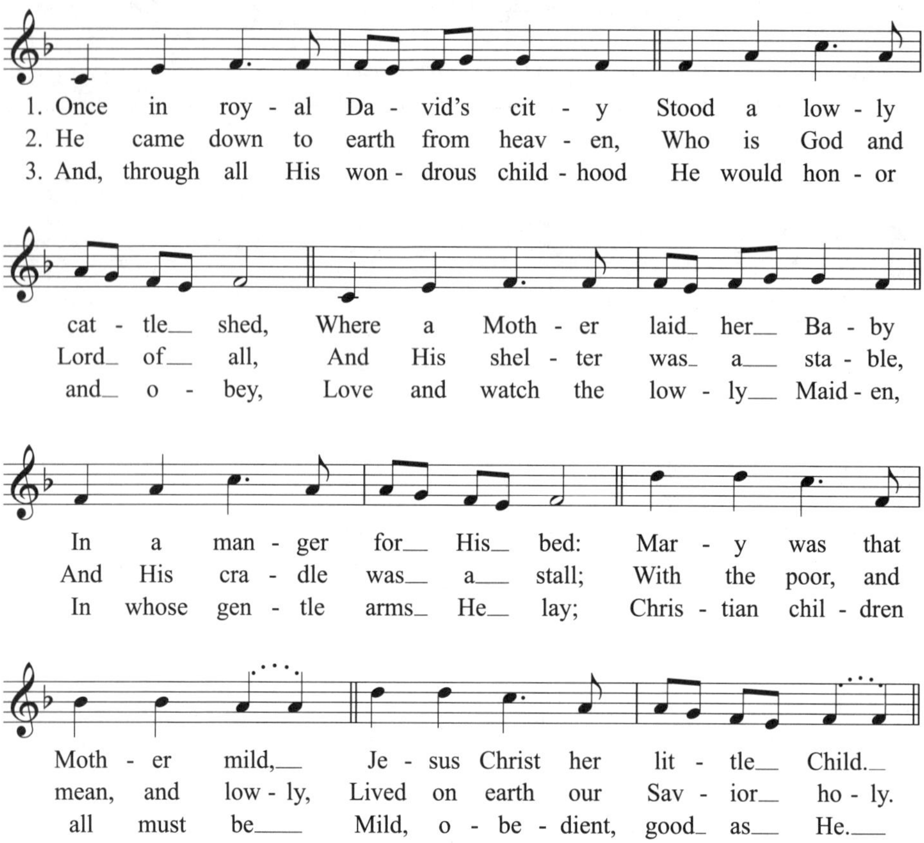

4. For He is our childhood's pattern, | Day by day like us He grew,
He was little, weak, and helpless, | Tears and smiles like us He knew;
And He feeleth for our sadness, | And He shareth in our gladness.

5. And our eyes at last shall see Him, | Through His own redeeming love,
For that Child so dear and gentle | Is our Lord in heav'n above;
And He leads His children on | To the place where He is gone.

6. Not in that poor lowly stable, | With the oxen standing by,
We shall see Him; but in heaven, | Set at God's right hand on high;
Where like stars His children crowned | All in white shall wait around.

87 87 77

Tune:
IRBY

Final Verses: Richard Lloyd (1993) #104; Noel Rawsthorne (2011) #166.
Melody: Henry John Gauntlett (d. 1876), an organist admired by Felix Mendelssohn.
M. Source: *250 Hymns in the Public Domain* (International Commission on English in the Liturgy, 1981) *#27.*
Text: Cecil Frances Alexander (d. 1895), who wrote more than 400 hymns.
T. Source: *Catholic Hymn Book* (London Oratory, 1998) p. 52; *Saint Michael Hymnal* (2003) #482.

Quem Vidistis Pastores? Dicite 667

Trns: Most Rev'd James Chadwick, Bishop of Hexham (*d.* 1882)

Text and Melody: "Les Anges Dans Nos Campagnes," an 18th century French Christmas carol.
M. Source: *Mediator Dei Hymnal* (1955) p. 8; *Catholic Hymn Book* (London Oratory, 1998) p. 24.
T. Source: *Catholic Hymns* (Baltimore: Fr. John Selner, 1954) p. 55.

77 77 R
Tune: Gloria

668 Corde Natus Ex Parentis (4th century)

Aurelius Prudentius (d. 413AD), Christian Poet

4. O ye heights of heav'n adore him;
Angel hosts, his praises sing;
Pow'rs, dominions, bow before him,
And extol our God and King;
Let no tongue on earth be silent,
Every voice in concert ring,
Evermore and evermore!

5. Laud and honor to the Father;
Laud and honor to the Son;
Laud and honor to the Spirit;
Ever Three and ever One:
Consubstantial, co-eternal,
While unending ages run,
Evermore and evermore.

Aurelius Clemens Prudentius (348-413), born in northern Spain, was successively an advocate, judge, and holder of an important military position at court. At the age of fifty-seven he retired from active life and devoted the remainder of his days to the service of God and to the writing of sacred poetry. He has been called the "Virgil and Horace of the Christians." Erasmus said of him *unum inter Christianos vere facundum poetam*. The two pervading influences in his work were the example of his contemporary, St. Ambrose, and the Christian art of the Catacombs.

87 87 87 R

Tune:
Divinum Mysterium

Final Verses: Richard Lloyd (1993) #55; Noel Rawsthorne (2011) #75.

Corde Natus Ex Parentis was excerpted from the ninth poem in the *Cathemerinon* of Prudentius; the complete poem is quite long. The translation is a Cento by the editors. The melody ("Divinum Mysterium") is an 11th century *Sanctus* trope, later adapted for *Piae Cantiones* (1582). English translations appear in many Catholic hymnals.

God Rest You Merry, Gentlemen 669

"And this shall be a sign unto you. You shall find the infant wrapped in swaddling clothes, and laid in a manger."—Lk 2.12

1. God rest you mer - ry, Gen-tle-men, Let noth-ing you dis - may,
2. From God our heav'n - ly Fa - ther A bless-èd an - gel came,
3. "Fear not," then said the an - gel, "Let noth-ing you af - fright,

For Je - sus Christ our Sav - ior Was born up - on this day,
And un - to cer - tain shep-herds Brought tid - ings of the same,
This day is born a Sav - ior, Of a pure Vir - gin bright,

To save us all from Sa - tan's pow'r When we were
How that in Beth - le - hem was born The Son of
To free all those who trust in him From Sa - tan's

gone a - stray. R. O___ tid - ings of com - fort and joy,
God by name.
pow'r and might."

com-fort and joy; O___ tid - ings of com - fort and joy!

4. And when to Bethlehem they came,
Whereat this infant lay,
They found him in a manger,
Where oxen feed on hay;
His mother Mary kneeling,
Unto the Lord did pray.

5. Now to the Lord sing praises,
All you within this place,
And with true love and brotherhood
Each other now embrace;
This holy tide of Christmas
Doth bring redeeming grace.

Final Verses: Richard Lloyd (1993) #78; Noel Rawsthorne (2011) #134.
Text: *Christmas Carols, Ancient and Modern; including the most popular in the West of England, and the Airs to which they are sung; also, specimens of French Provincial Carols* (London: William Sandys, 1833) p. 102.
Text Source: *Catholic Hymn Book* (London Oratory, 1998) p. 33; *Adoremus Hymnal* (1997) #326.
The meaning of "God rest you merry" is "God keep you merry." Note the archaic use of the word *rest* ("keep")—indeed, this carol probably dates from the 16th century.
Melody: Traditional 19th-century English tune; cf. *The Oxford Book of Carols* (London, 1928) p. 24.

86 86 86 R

Tune: God Rest You Merry

672 Puer Natus Est Nobis (Isaias 9.6)

"And he hath on his garment, and on his thigh written: King of kings, *and* Lord of lords.*"—Apocalypse 19.16*

1st Tune

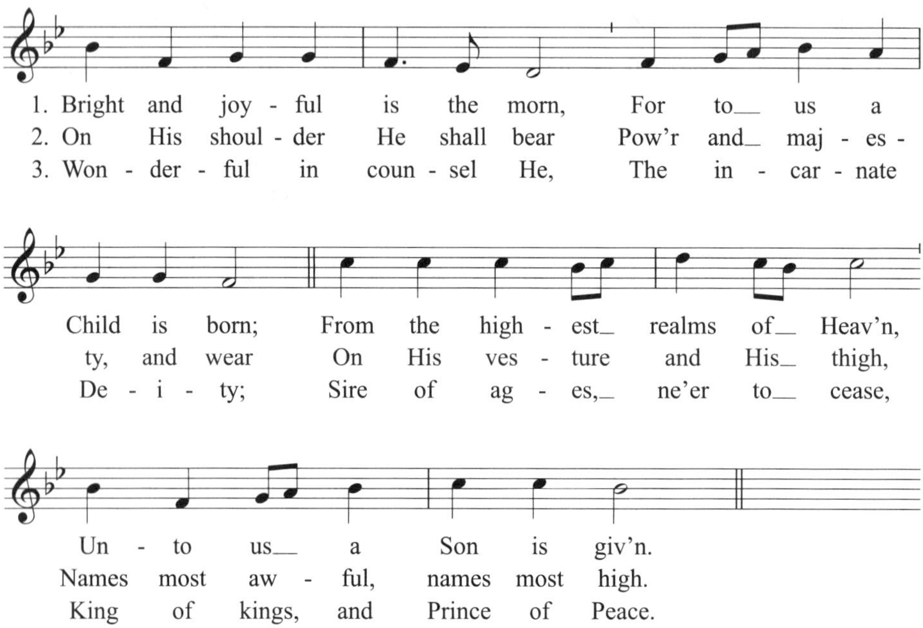

4. Come and worship at His feet;
Yield to Christ the homage meet;
From His manger to His throne,
Homage due to God alone.

5. Glory be to God on high;
Earth, uplift the joyful cry!
Praise Him, all ye heav'nly host,
Father, Son, and Holy Ghost.

This hymn is based on the Introit for the Christmas Daytime Mass ("Puer Natus Est Nobis"), which comes from Isaias 9.6:

> For a child is born to us, and a son is given to us,
> and the government is upon his shoulder:
> and his name shall be called,
> Wonderful, Counsellor, God the Mighty,
> the Father of the world to come, the Prince of Peace.

The verse attached to the Christmas Introit is Psalm 97—and ideas from it have been incorporated as well.

77 77

Tune:
All Saints 8B

T. Source: *The Church Hymnary; a Collection of Hymns and Tunes* (Edwin A. Bedell, 1893) p. 89.
Melody: *Geistreiches Gesangbuch* (Darmstadt, 1698).
M. Source: *New Saint Basil Hymnal* (1958) p. 203; *Catholic Hymn Book* (London Oratory, 1998) p. 290.
The rhythmical modification occurs in many hymnals; cf. *The Anglican Hymn Book* (London, 1871) #*56*.

Puer Natus Est Nobis (Isaias 9.6) 673

"And he hath on his garment, and on his thigh written: King of kings, *and* Lord of lords.*"—Apocalypse 19.16*

2nd Tune

1. Bright and joy - ful is the_ morn, Al - le - lu - ia.
2. On His shoul - der He shall_ bear Al - le - lu - ia.
3. Won - der - ful in coun - sel_ He, Al - le - lu - ia.

For to us a Child is_ born; Al - le - lu - ia.
Pow'r and maj - es - ty, and_ wear Al - le - lu - ia.
The in - car - nate De - i - ty; Al - le - lu - ia.

From the high - est realms of_ Heav'n, Al - le - lu - ia.
On His ves - ture and_ His_ thigh, Al - le - lu - ia.
Sire of ag - es, ne'er_ to_ cease, Al - le - lu - ia.

Un - to us a Son is_ giv'n. Al - le - lu - ia.
Names most aw - ful, names most_ high. Al - le - lu - ia.
King of kings, and Prince of_ Peace. Al - le - lu - ia.

The word "Alleluia" is sung after each line:

4. Come and worship at His feet;
Yield to Christ the homage meet;
From His manger to His throne,
Homage due to God alone.

5. Glory be to God on high;
Earth, uplift the joyful cry!
Praise Him, all ye heav'nly host,
Father, Son, and Holy Ghost.

This hymn is based on the Introit for the Christmas Daytime Mass ("Puer Natus Est Nobis"), which comes from Isaias 9.6:

> For a child is born to us, and a son is given to us,
> and the government is upon his shoulder:
> and his name shall be called,
> Wonderful, Counsellor, God the Mighty,
> the Father of the world to come, the Prince of Peace.

The verse attached to the Christmas Introit is Psalm 97—and ideas from it have been incorporated as well.

Final Verses: Lloyd (1993) #118; Noel Rawsthorne (2011) #186.
Melody: Robert Williams (d. 1821), a blind composer born in Wales.
M. Source: *Catholic Hymn Book* (London Oratory, 1998) p. 138.
T. Source: *The Church Hymnary; a Collection of Hymns and Tunes* (Edwin A. Bedell, 1893) p. 89.

77 77 A

Tune: Llanfair

674 Puer Natus Est Nobis (Isaias 9.6)

"And he hath on his garment, and on his thigh written: King of kings, *and* Lord of lords.*"—Apocalypse 19.16*

3rd Tune

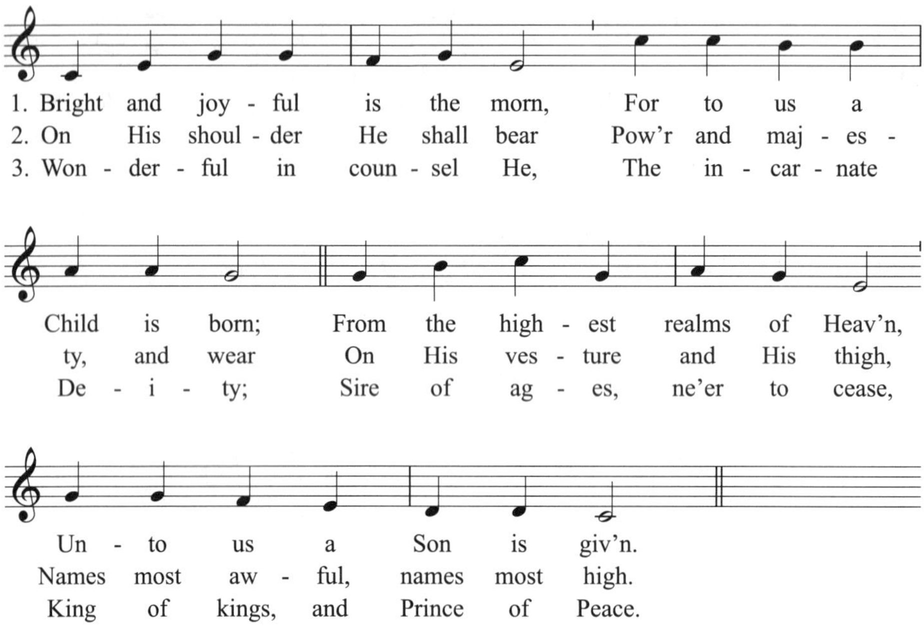

4. Come and worship at His feet;
Yield to Christ the homage meet;
From His manger to His throne,
Homage due to God alone.

5. Glory be to God on high;
Earth, uplift the joyful cry!
Praise Him, all ye heav'nly host,
Father, Son, and Holy Ghost.

This hymn is based on the Introit for the Christmas Daytime Mass ("Puer Natus Est Nobis"), which comes from Isaias 9.6:

> For a child is born to us, and a son is given to us,
> and the government is upon his shoulder:
> and his name shall be called,
> Wonderful, Counsellor, God the Mighty,
> the Father of the world to come, the Prince of Peace.

The verse attached to the Christmas Introit is Psalm 97—and ideas from it have been incorporated as well.

77 77

Tune: Culbach

Final Verses: Richard Lloyd (1993) #49; Noel Rawsthorne (2011) #82.
Melody: From a Chorale in Johann Scheffler's *Heilige Seelenlust* (1657).
M. Source: *New Saint Basil Hymnal* (1958) p. 218; *Mediator Dei Hymnal* (1955) p. 83.
T. Source: *The Church Hymnary; a Collection of Hymns and Tunes* (Edwin A. Bedell, 1893) p. 89.

Puer Natus Est Nobis (Isaias 9.6) 675

"And he hath on his garment, and on his thigh written: KING OF KINGS, and LORD OF LORDS."—Apocalypse 19.16

Can be sung with any 77 77 meter, such as SAVANNAH, UNIVERSITY COLLEGE, ORIENTIS PARTIBUS, LLANFAIR, CULBACH, MONKLAND, GOTT SEI DANK, etc.

BRIGHT and joyful is the morn,
For to us a Child is born;
From the highest realms of Heav'n,
Unto us a Son is giv'n.

2. On His shoulder He shall bear
Pow'r and majesty, and wear
On His vesture and His thigh,
Names most awful, names most high.

3. Wonderful in counsel He,
The incarnate Deity;
Sire of ages, ne'er to cease,
King of kings, and Prince of Peace.

4. Come and worship at His feet;
Yield to Christ the homage meet;
From His manger to His throne,
Homage due to God alone.

5. Glory be to God on high;
Earth, uplift the joyful cry!
Praise Him, all ye heav'nly host,
Father, Son, and Holy Ghost.

This hymn is based on the INTROIT for the Christmas Daytime Mass ("Puer Natus Est Nobis"), which comes from Isaias 9.6:

> For a CHILD IS BORN TO US, and a son is given to us,
> and the government is upon his shoulder:
> and his name shall be called,
> Wonderful, Counsellor, God the Mighty,
> the Father of the world to come, the Prince of Peace.

77 77

The verse attached to the Christmas INTROIT is Psalm 97—and ideas from it have been incorporated as well.

Tune: VARIOUS

T. Source: *The Church Hymnary; a Collection of Hymns and Tunes* (Edwin A. Bedell, 1893) p. 89.

676 The First Noël The Angel Did Say

"The angel said to the shepherds: Fear not; for, behold, I bring you good tidings of great joy."—Lk 2.10

1. The first Noël the Angel did say
2. They look-èd up and saw a Star
3. And by the light of that same Star,

Was to certain poor Shepherds in fields as they lay;
Shining in the East beyond them far,
Three Wise Men came from country far;

In fields where they lay keeping their sheep
And to the earth it gave great light,
To seek for a King was their intent,

On a cold winter's night that was so deep. R. No-
And so it continued both day and night.
And to follow the Star wherever it went.

ël, Noël, Noël, Noël, Born is the King of Israel.

4. This Star drew nigh
to the North West,
Over Bethlehem
it took its rest;
And there it did
both stop and stay,
Right over the place
where Jesus lay.
R. *Noël, Noël...*

5. Then enter'd in
those Wise Men three
Most rev'rently
upon their knee,
And offer'd there,
in his presénce,
Both gold, and myrrh,
and frankincense.
R. *Noël, Noël...*

6. Then let us all
with one accord
Sing praises to
our heavenly Lord;
That hath made heav'n
and earth of nought,
And with his blood
mankind hath bought.
R. *Noël, Noël...*

88 88 R

Tune: The First Nowell

Final Verses: Richard Lloyd (1993) #227; Noel Rawsthorne (2011) #363.
Text and Melody Source: *Christmas Carols, Ancient and Modern; including the most popular in the West of England, and the Airs to which they are sung; also, specimens of French Provincial Carols* (London: William Sandys, 1833). The text is given on page 74, the melody on page 192. Cf. also *The Oxford Book of Carols* (London, 1928) p. 59.

What Child Is This? 677

"And she brought forth her firstborn son, and wrapped him up in swaddling clothes, and laid him in a manger; because there was no room for them in the inn."—Lk 2.7

1. What child is this,__ who, laid to rest__ On
2. Why lies He in__ such mean es - tate__ Where
3. So bring Him in - cense, gold and myrrh,_ Come,

Mar - y's lap__ is sleep - ing? Whom an - gels
ox and ass__ are feed - ing? Good Chris - tian,
peas - ant, king__ to own__ Him; The King of

greet__ with an - thems sweet,_ While shep - herds watch__ are
fear:__ for sin - ners here__ The si - lent Word__ is
kings__ sal - va - tion brings,_ Let lov - ing hearts__ en -

keep - ing? This, this__ is Christ the King,__ Whom
plead - ing. OPT. *Nails, spear__ shall pierce Him through,_ The*
throne Him. OPT. *Raise, raise__ the song on high,__ The*

shep - herds guard__ and an - gels sing; Haste, haste,__ to
cross be borne,_ for me, for you: Hail, hail__ the
Vir - gin sings__ her lull - a - by: Joy, joy,__ for

bring Him laud,__ The Babe,_ the son__ of Mar - y.
Word made flesh,__ The Babe,_ the son__ of Mar - y.
Christ is born,__ The Babe,_ the son__ of Mar - y.

* *In some editions, all C-naturals are sung as C-sharp.*

87 87 R

Final Verses: Richard Lloyd (1993) #84; Noel Rawsthorne (2011) #139.
Text: William Chatterton Dix (d. 1898). Text and Melody Source: *Saint Michael Hymnal* (2003) #604.
Melody: Traditional English Melody; the first known printing was in 1580.

Tune: GREENSLEEVES

678 Silent Night, Holy Night

"And there were in the same country shepherds watching, and keeping the night watches over their flock."—Lk 2.8

The following verses may be used for the Epiphany:

1. Silent night, holy night,
Guiding Star, lend thy light;
See the eastern wise men bring
Gifts and homage to our King!
Christ the Savior is here,
Christ the Savior is here!

2. Silent night, holy night,
Wondrous Star, lend thy light;
With the angels let us sing
Alleluia to our King!
Christ the Savior is here,
Christ the Savior is here!

66 88 66

Tune:
STILLE NACHT

Final Verses: Richard Lloyd (1993) #217; Noel Rawsthorne (2011) #347.
Melody: Franz Xaver Gruber (d. 1863), organist at St. Nicholas Church in Oberndorf, Austria.
Melody and Text Source: *Catholic Hymns* (Baltimore: Fr. John Selner, 1954) p. 55.
Text: "Stille Nacht" was composed by Fr. Josef Mohr, a Catholic priest who died in 1848. He should not be confused with a Jesuit priest, Fr. Josef Hermann Mohr (d. 1892), who published many German hymnals. The English translation ("Silent Night") was composed by John Freeman Young (d. 1885).

Brightest And Best (Epiphany)

"Upon what are its bases grounded? or who laid the corner stone thereof, when the morning stars praised me together, and all the sons of God made a joyful melody?"—Job 38.6-7

1. Bright - est and best of the sons of the morn - ing,
2. Cold on his cra - dle the dew - drops are shin - ing,
3. Say, shall we yield him, in cost - ly de - vo - tion,

Dawn on our dark - ness and lend us thine aid;
Low lies his head with the beasts of the stall:
O - dors of E - dom and of - f'rings di - vine?

Star of the East,_ the ho - ri - zon a - dorn - ing,
An - gels a - dore_ him in slum - ber re - clin - ing,
Gems of the moun - tain and pearls of the o - cean,

Guide where our in - fant Re - deem - er is laid.
Mak - er and Mon - arch and Sav - ior of all.
Myrrh from the for - est or gold from the mine?

4. Vainly we offer each ample oblation,
Vainly with gifts would his favor secure;
Richer by far is the heart's adoration,
Dearer to God are the prayers of the poor.

5. Brightest and best of the sons of the morning,
Dawn on our darkness and lend us thine aid;
Star of the East, the horizon adorning,
Guide where our infant Redeemer is laid.

Final Verses: Noel Rawsthorne (2011) #114.
Text: Reginald Heber (d. 1826).
T. Source: *Stories of Hymns* (Fr. George W. Rutler, 2016) p. 210.
Melody: John Francis Thrupp (d. 1867).
M. Source: *Catholic Hymn Book* (London Oratory, 1998) p. 72.

11 10 11 10

Tune:
EPIPHANY

680 As With Gladness, Men Of Old

"Then, summoning the wise men in secret, Herod questioned them closely upon the time of the star's appearing."—Mt 2.7

4. Holy Jesus, every day
Keep us in the narrow way;
And, when earthly things are past,
Bring our ransomed souls at last
Where they need no star to guide,
Where no clouds Thy glory hide.

5. In the heav'nly country bright,
Need they no created light;
Thou its Light, its Joy, its Crown,
Thou its Sun which goes not down:
There forever may we sing
Alleluias to our King!

77 77 77

Tune:
Dix

Final Verses: Richard Lloyd (1993) #56; Noel Rawsthorne (2011) #96.
Melody: Dr. Conrad Kocher (d. 1872), founder of the School of Sacred Song in Stuttgart.
M. Source: *Catholic Hymn Book* (London Oratory, 1998) p. 70.
Text: William Chatterton Dix (d. 1898). T. Source: *Adoremus Hymnal* (1997) #353.

Songs Of Thankfulness And Praise 681

"The Epiphany–a cardinal feast–commemorates three manifestations of Christ's divinity: the visit of the Wise men, our Lord's Baptism, and the miracle at Cana."—Fr. Fortescue

4. Grant us grace to see Thee, Lord, | Mirrored in Thy holy Word;
May we imitate Thee now, | And be pure, as pure art Thou;
That we like to Thee may be | At Thy great Epiphany;
And may praise Thee, ever blest, | God in man made manifest.

Final Verses: Richard Lloyd (1993) #197; Noel Rawsthorne (2011) #303.
Melody: George J. Elvey (d. 1893), organist at St George's Chapel at Windsor Castle.
M. Source: *Catholic Hymn Book* (1998) p. 120; *New Westminster Hymnal* (1939) p. 88; *Hymns, Psalms, and Spiritual Canticles* (Massachusetts: Theodore Marier, 1983) p. 230.
Text: Christopher Wordsworth (d. 1885); a Greek scholar and nephew of the famous poet.
T. Source: *Saint Michael Hymnal* (St. Boniface Parish, 2003) #534; *Adoremus Hymnal* (1997) #351.

77 77 D
Tune:
St George

682 Summi Largitor Praemii (13th century)

Trns: Alan Gordon McDougall (d. 1965)

4. Therefore accept, O Lord, this tide
Of fast which thou hast sanctified,
That we may reach by mystic ways
The sacraments of Paschal days.

5. May he who is the threefold Lord
On us confer this high reward,
In whom so long as worlds abide
One only God is glorified.

88 88 (LM)

Tune:
Oakwood

Melody: Kevin Allen (b. 1965), choirmaster at the Monastery of the Holy Cross in Chicago.
M. Source: *Saint Edmund Campion Missal and Hymnal* (2013) p. 823.
T. Source: *Pange Lingua: Breviary Hymns of Old Uses with an English Rendering by Alan G. McDougall and an Introduction by Adrian Fortescue* (London: Burns & Oates, 1916) p. 23.

Clarum Decus Jejunii (6th century) 683

Saint Gregory the Great (d. 604AD)

Can be sung with any 88 88 meter, such as WHITEHALL, GONFALON ROYAL, TRINITY COLLEGE, ROGERS PARK, NOTRE DAME, BRESSANI, EISENACH, etc.

THE glory of these forty days
We celebrate with songs of praise;
For Christ, by Whom all things were made,
Himself has fasted and has prayed.

2. Alone and fasting Moses saw
The loving God who gave the law;
And to Elijah, fasting, came
The steeds and chariots of flame.

3. So Daniel trained his mystic sight,
Delivered from the lions' might;
And John, the Bridegroom's friend, became
The herald of Messiah's Name.

4. Then grant us, Lord, like them to be
Full oft in fast and prayer with Thee;
Our spirits strengthen with Thy grace,
And give us joy to see Thy face.

5. O Father, Son, and Spirit blest,
To Thee be every prayer addressed,
Who art in threefold Name adored,
From age to age, the only Lord.

N.B. This text is usually sung to SPIRES ("ERHALT UNS HERR"), which has many variants. Let the congregation, therefore, follow the choir.

Latin Text: *Historical Companion to Hymns Ancient and Modern* (London: Cambridge University Press, 1903) p. 57.
ENGLISH TRANSLATION: Maurice Frederick Bell (d. 1947).
T. Source: *Adoremus Hymnal* (1997) #363; *Saint Michael Hymnal* (St. Boniface Parish, 2003) #559.
Melody: SPIRES ("ERHALT UNS HERR") appears to have a well established association with Lent in the Catholic Church. Cf. the melody for "Audi Benigne" in *Catholic Vesper Hymn Book set to Music either for Unison or Four Voices with Accompaniment* (Charles Lewis, 1877) p. 20.

88 88 (LM)

Tune: VARIOUS

684 Forty Days And Forty Nights

"And when he had fasted forty days and forty nights,
afterwards he was hungry."—Mt 4.2

1. For - ty days and for - ty nights Thou wert
2. Should not we Thy sor - row share, And from
3. Then if Sa - tan on us press, Flesh or

fast - ing in the wild; For - ty days and
earth - ly joys ab - stain, Fast - ing with un -
spir - it to as - sail, Vic - tor in the

for - ty nights Tempt - ed, and yet un - de - filed.
ceas - ing prayer, Glad with Thee to suf - fer pain?
wil - der - ness, Grant we may not faint nor fail.

4. So shall we have peace divine;
Holier gladness ours shall be;
Round us, too, shall angels shine,
Such as ministered to Thee.

5. Keep, O keep us, Savior dear,
Ever constant by Thy side;
That with Thee we may appear
At th' eternal Eastertide.

77 77

Tune:
Aus Der Tiefe

Final Verses: Richard Lloyd (1993) #13; Noel Rawsthorne (2011) #29.
Text: George Hunt Smyttan (d. 1870).
T. Source: *Saint Michael Hymnal* (St. Boniface Parish, 2003) #300.
Melody: Martin Herbst (d. 1681); first published in *Nürnbergerisches Gesangbuch* (1676).
M. Source: *New Westminster Hymnal* (1939) p. 60; *Catholic Hymn Book* (London Oratory, 1998) p. 82.

Lord, Who Throughout These Forty Days 685

"Lord Jesus, who hast consecrated fasting, accept our fast, that we may mystically enjoy the Paschal sacraments."—Summi Largitor Praemii, v4

4. And through these days of penitence,
And through Thy Passiontide,
Forevermore, in life and death,
O Lord, with us abide.

5. Abide with us that when this life
Of suffering is past,
An Easter of unending joy
We may attain at last.

Final Verses: Richard Lloyd (1993) #194; Noel Rawsthorne (2011) #125.
Text: Claudia Frances Hernaman (d. 1898).
T. Source: *Saint Michael Hymnal* (St. Boniface Parish, 2003) #407.
Melody: *The Whole Booke of Psalmes collected into Englishe metre* (London: John Daye, 1584) p. 367. The texts for this book were composed by Thomas Sternhold (d. 1549), a special servant to King Henry VIII, in charge of bringing forward ceremonial clothing during the monarch's coronation.
M. Source: *New Westminster Hymnal* (1939) p. 93; *Adoremus Hymnal* (1997) #360; A version from 1621 has the melody in the Tenor voice; cf. *Hymns Ancient and Modern* (1972) p. 202.

86 86 (CM)

Tune:
St Flavian

686 O Amor Quam Ecstaticus (15th century)

Fr. Thomas à Kempis, Subprior of Mount St. Agnes (d. 1471)

4. For us to wicked men betrayed,
   Scourged, mocked, in crown of thorn arrayed;
   For us he bore the Cross's death;
   For us at length gave up his breath.

5. For us he rose from death again,
   For us he went on high to reign,
   For us he sent his Spirit here
   To guide, to strengthen, and to cheer.

88 88 (LM)

Tune:
Agincourt

English Translation: Benjamin Webb (d. 1885).
Text: Excerpted from *Apparuit Benignitas*, a Christmas poem by Fr. Thomas à Kempis.
T. Source: *Catholic Hymn Book* (London Oratory, 1998) p. 434.
Melody: From a 15th century English manuscript.
M. Source: *Hymns, Psalms, and Spiritual Canticles* (Massachusetts: Theodore Marier, 1983) p. 450.

When I Survey The Wondrous Cross 687

"But God forbid that I should glory, save in the cross of our Lord Jesus Christ; by whom the world is crucified to me, and I to the world."—Gal 6.14

1. When I__ sur - vey the won - drous Cross,
2. For - bid__ it, Lord, that I should boast
3. See from__ his head, his hands, his feet,

On which the Prince of glo - ry died,_
Save in the death of Christ_ my God;_
Sor - row and love flow min - gled down;

My rich - est gain I count_ but loss,
All the vain things that charm_ me most,
Did e'er such love and sor - row meet

And pour con - tempt on all__ my pride.
I sac - ri - fice them to__ his Blood.
Or thorns com - pose so rich__ a crown?

4. His dying crimson like a robe,
Spreads o'er his body on the Tree;
Then am I dead to all the globe,
And all the globe is dead to me.

5. Were the whole realm of nature mine,
That were a present far too small;
Love so amazing, so divine,
Demands my soul, my life, my all.

Final Verses: Richard Lloyd (1993) #181; Noel Rawsthorne (2011) #276.
Melody: Dr. Edward Miller (d. 1807), organist of Doncaster Parish Church; originally published in *Psalms of David for the Use of Parish Churches* (1790) p. 12; based on TUNBRIDGE (an older tune).
M. Source: *Catholic Hymn Book* (London Oratory, 1998) p. 115; *Church Hymns with Tunes* (1885) p. 44.
T. Source: *Saint Michael Hymnal* (St. Boniface Parish, 2003) #609. Text: Isaac Watts (d. 1748).

88 88 (LM)
Tune: ROCKINGHAM

688 O Come And Mourn With Me Awhile

Fr. Frederick William Faber, Oratorian (d. 1863)

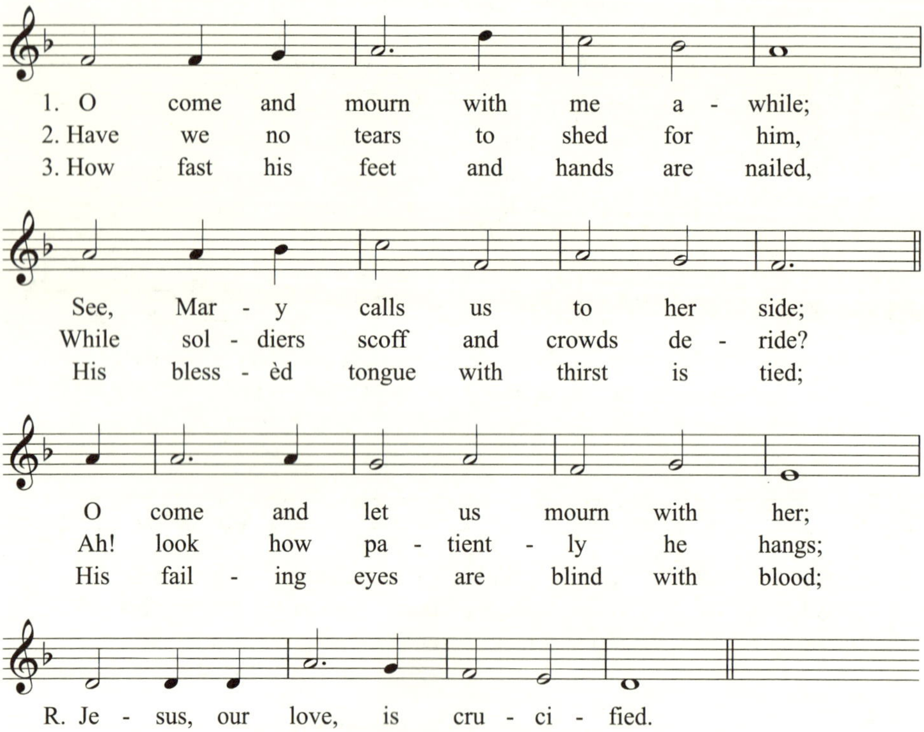

4. Sev'n times he spoke, sev'n words of love,
And all three hours his silence cried
For mercy on the souls of men; R.

5. O break, O break, hard heart of mine.
Thy weak self-love and guilty pride
His Pilate and his Judas were; R.

6. A broken heart, a fount of tears,
Ask, and they will not be denied;
A broken heart love's cradle is; R.

7. O love of God! O sin of man!
In this dread act your strength is tried;
And victory remains with love; R.

88 88 (LM)

Tune:
ST CROSS

Melody: John Bacchus Dykes (d. 1876).
M. Source: *New Westminster Hymnal* (1939) p. 53.
T. Source: *Catholic Hymn Book* (London Oratory, 1998) p. 105.

My Song Is Love Unknown 689

Samuel Crossman (d. 1683)

4. They rise, and needs will have
My dear Lord made away;
A murderer they save,
The Prince of Life they slay,
  Yet cheerful he
    To suff'ring goes,
    That he his foes
  From thence might free.

5. In life, no house, no home,
My Lord on earth might have;
In death no friendly tomb
But what a stranger gave.
  What may I say?
    Heav'n was his home;
    But mine the tomb
  Wherein he lay.

6. Here might I stay and sing,
No story so divine;
Never was love, dear King,
Never was grief like thine.
  This is my Friend,
    In Whose sweet praise
    I all my days
  Could gladly spend.

Final Verses: Richard Lloyd (1993) #123; Noel Rawsthorne (2011) #191.
T. Source: *Catholic Hymn Book* (London Oratory, 1998) p. 102.
Melody: John Ireland (d. 1962), organist at Saint Luke's Church, London.
Melody Source: *The Public School Hymn Book* (1919).

66 66 44 44

Tune:
LOVE UNKNOWN

690 The Painful Cross Of Christ (16th century)

Saint Thomas More, Lord Chancellor of England (d. 1535)

1. Who - e'er to vir - tue think - eth hard the way,
2. Con - sid - er well, how fool - ish 'tis and vain,
3. What - e'er good work thou dost, with la - bor do:

Be - cause we must have war con - tin - u - al
To look for heav'n through pleas - ure and de - light,
The la - bor goes, the good - ness doth re - main;

A - gainst the world, the flesh, the dev'l, that aye
Since Christ, our lead - er and our sov - er - eign,
If thou do ill, with pleas - ure join'd there - to,

Would force our souls in - to their bond and thrall;
As - cend - ed thith - er but by man - ly fight,
The pleas - ure which thine e - vil works con - tain

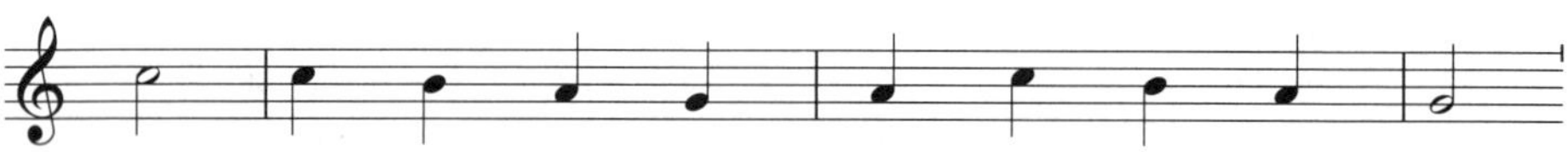

Let him re - mem - ber— choose what way he shall,
And bit - ter pas - sion: say, would it be right,
Gli - deth a - way— thou mayst it not re - tain:

E'en from the world it - self he must sus - tain
Your - selves his faith - ful foll - 'wers to re - cord,
Deep in thy soul the e - vil cleaves be - hind,

10 10 10 10 10 10 10

Tune:
LINCOLN'S INN

Melody: Kevin Allen (b. 1965), choirmaster at the Monastery of the Holy Cross in Chicago.
M. Source: *Saint Jean de Brébeuf Hymnal* (2018).

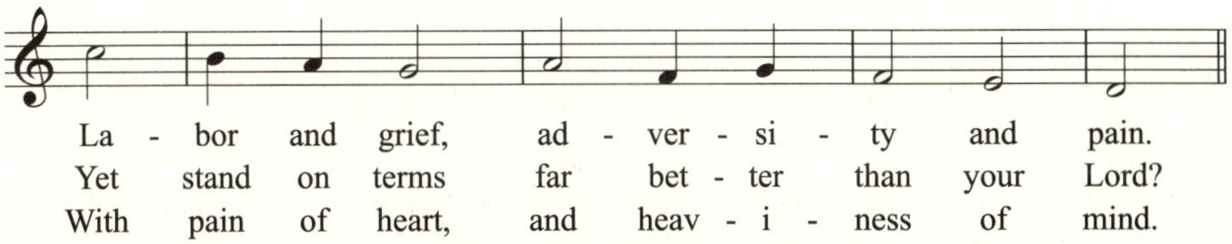

4. Consider well, that, both by night and day,
While we so busily provide and care
For our disport, our revel, and our play,
For pleasant melody and dainty fare,
Death stealeth on full slily; unaware
He lieth at hand, and shall us all surprise,
We know not when, nor where, nor in what wise.

5. When fierce temptations threat thy soul with loss,
Think on his Passion and the bitter pain,
Think on the mortal anguish of the Cross,
Think on Christ's blood let out at every vein,
Think of his precious heart all rent in twain:
For thy redemption think all this was wrought;
Nor be that lost which He so dearly bought!

T. Source: *Sir Thomas More; Selections From His Works* (Baltimore, 1841) p. 359; these verses come from a publication by St. Thomas More (d. 1535) called "The Life of John Picus," originally published circa 1510 AD. This work presents biographical information about Giovanni Pico della Mirandola (d. 1494), along with his literary creations, "translated out of Latin into English by Master Thomas More."

When it comes to Pico's *Duodecim Regulae* ("Twelve Rules"), Sir Thomas created a rhythmical paraphrase. We reproduce here the First Rule, Third Rule, and sections from the postscript: *The Followers Grief and Happiness*; *Death at our Hand and Unaware*; and *The Painful Cross of Christ*. The full title is: "Twelve Rules of John Picus, Earl of Mirandula, Partly Exciting, Partly Directing a Man in Spiritual Battle." Some authors refer to the postscript as: "The Twelve Weapons of Spiritual Battle, Which Every Man Should Have at Hand When the Pleasure of a Sinful Temptation Cometh to Mind." The postscript is not a translation of Pico, but was written by St. Thomas More.

692 Ah, Holy Jesus, How Hast Thou Offended?

"Jesus is condemned to death. His death warrant is signed, and who signed it but I, when I committed my first mortal sins?"—John Henry Cardinal Newman

1. Ah, ho - ly Je - sus, how hast thou of - fend - ed,
2. Who was the guilt - y? Who brought this up - on thee?
3. Lo, the good Shep - herd for the sheep is of - fered;

That man to judge thee hath in hate pre - tend - ed?
A - las! my trea - son, Je - sus, hath un - done thee.
The slave hath sin - nèd, and the Son hath suf - fered;

By foes de - rid - ed, by thine own re - ject - ed,
'Twas I, Lord Je - sus, I it was de - nied thee:
For man's a - tone - ment, while he noth - ing heed - eth,

O most af - flict - ed.
I cru - ci - fied thee.
God in - ter - ced - eth.

4. For me, kind Jesus, was thine incarnation,
Thy mortal sorrow, and thy life's oblation;
Thy death of anguish and thy bitter Passion,
For my salvation.

5. Therefore, kind Jesus, since I cannot pay thee,
I do adore thee, and will ever pray thee,
Think on thy pity and thy love unswerving,
Not my deserving.

11 11 11 5

Tune:
Herzliebster Jesu

Text: Johann Heermann (d. 1647) composed the German text, "Herzliebster Jesu," which is based on passages from *Meditationes Divi Augustini* by John of Fécamp (d. 1097), a Benedictine Abbot.
English Translation: Robert Bridges (d. 1930), a close friend of Fr. Gerard Manley Hopkins, SJ.
T. Source: *Adoremus Hymnal* (1997) #402.
Melody: Johann Crüger (d. 1662), choirmaster of St. Nicholas' Church, Berlin.
M. Source: *Catholic Hymn Book* (London Oratory, 1998) p. 92.

Lift High The Cross 693

"And he said to all: If any man will come after me, let him deny himself, and take up his cross daily, and follow me."—Lk 9.23

4. O Lord, once lifted on the glorious tree,
As thou hast promised, draw men unto thee. R.

5. Let every race and every language tell
Of him who saves our souls from death and hell. R.

6. Set up thy throne, that earth's despair may cease
Beneath the shadow of its healing peace. R.

Melody: Sydney Hugo Nicholson (d. 1947), organist at Westminster Abbey.
M. Source: *Saint Michael Hymnal* (St. Boniface Parish, 2003) #398.
Text: George Kitchin (d. 1912); originally published in 1887. The text was revised by Michael Robert Newbolt (d. 1956) when it appeared in the *Supplement to Hymns Ancient and Modern* (1916).
T. Source: *Adoremus Hymnal* (1997) #606.

10 10 R

Tune: CRUCIFER

694 Gloria, Laus, Et Honor Tibi Sit (9th century)

Saint Theodulf, Bishop of Orléans (*d.* 821AD)

4. To Thee before Thy passion,
They sang their hymns of praise;
To Thee now high exalted
Our melody we raise. R.

5. Thou didst accept their praises;
Accept the prayers we bring,
Who in all good delightest,
Thou good and gracious King. R.

76 76 R

Tune:
St Theodulph

English Translation: Dr. John M. Neale (d. 1866), who matches the Latin original admirably; cf. *Mass and Vespers with Gregorian Chant* (Paris: Solesmes, 1957) p. 516.
T. Source: *Parochial Hymnal* (Rev. Carlo Rossini, 1951) p. 30.
Melody: Melchior Teschner (d. 1635).
M. Source: *Hymns, Psalms, and Spiritual Canticles* (Massachusetts: Theodore Marier, 1983) p. 184.

Jesus, Meek And Lowly 695

Fr. Henry Augustine Collins, Cistercian (d. 1919)

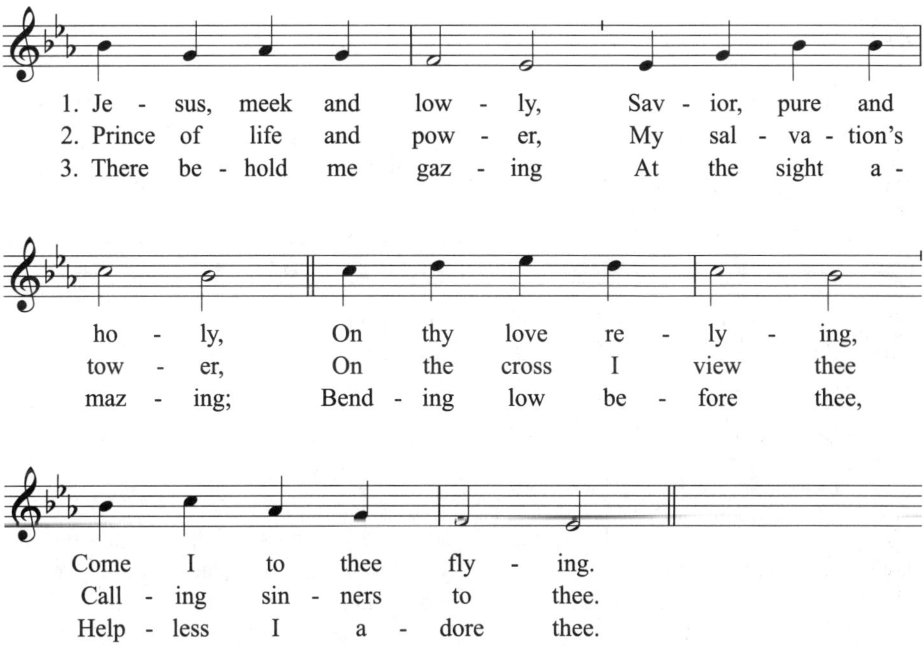

4. See the red wounds streaming,
With Christ's life-blood gleaming,
Blood for sinners flowing,
Pardon free bestowing.

5. Fountain rich in blessing,
Christ's fond love expressing,
Thou my aching sadness
Turnest into gladness.

6. Lord, in mercy guide me,
Be thou e'er beside me;
In thy ways direct me,
'Neath thy wings protect me.

Melody: Caspar Ett's *Cantica Sacra* (1840).
M. Source: *Arundel Catholic Hymnal* (1905) p. 326; *Catholic Hymn Book* (1998) p. 272; *Catholic Vesper Hymn Book set to Music either for Unison or Four Voices with Accompaniment* (Charles Lewis, 1877) p. 3.
T. Source: *Book of Hymns with Tunes* (Fr. Gregory Ould, 1910) p. 161; *Saint Andrew Hymnal, authorized by the Bishops of Scotland for use in the Scottish Dioceses* (1964) p. 79.

66 66 Trochaic
Tune: St Martin

696 Vita Sanctorum, Decus Angelorum (9th century)

Trns: Alan Gordon McDougall (d. 1965)

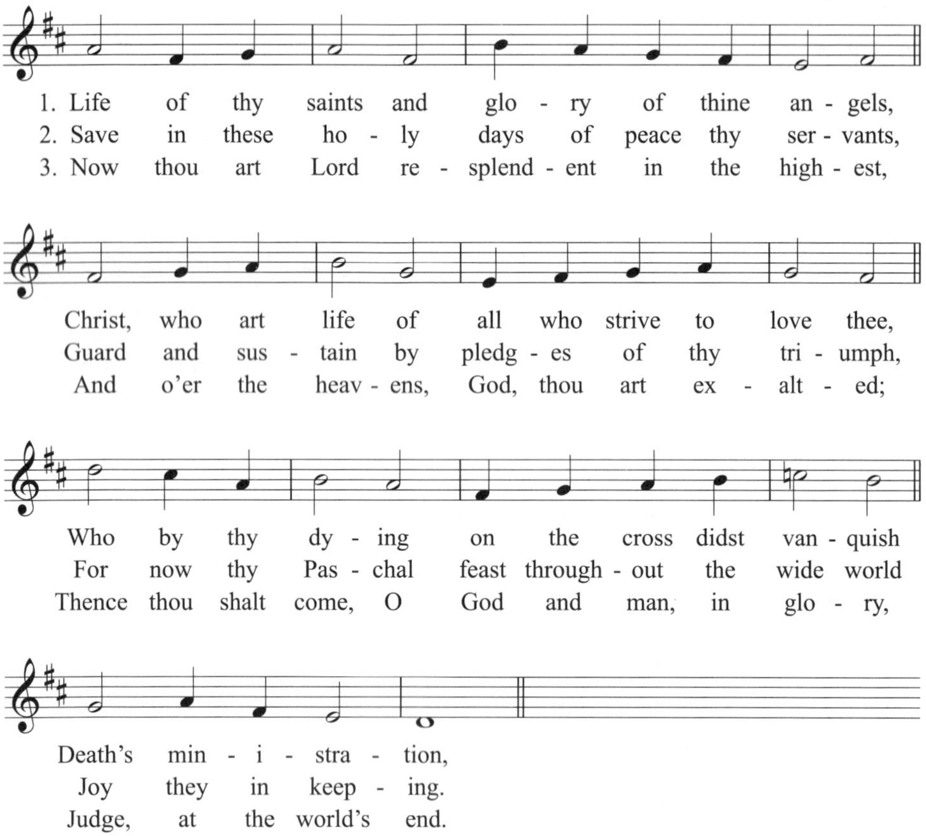

4. Raise thou our hearts to know thee in thy beauty
Where thou dost sit at the high Father's right hand,
Lest though we rise thy perfect justice cast us
Into the darkness.

5. This may the Father grant us, Holy Savior;
This may he grant who is of both the Spirit,
With whom thou reignest, one in perfect Godhead,
Unto all ages.

11 11 11 5

Tune:
Kenmore

Melody: Kevin Allen (b. 1965), choirmaster at the Monastery of the Holy Cross in Chicago.
M. Source: *Saint Edmund Campion Missal and Hymnal* (2013) p. 842.
Text: Neither the author nor the date of composition is known; some sources say "before the 9th century." Mr. McDougall says it is "found in many old Gallic and German breviaries."
T. Source: *Pange Lingua: Breviary Hymns of Old Uses with an English Rendering by Alan G. McDougall and an Introduction by Adrian Fortescue* (London: Burns & Oates, 1916) p. 31.

Victimae Paschali Laudes (11th century)

Wipo of Burgundy (d. 1048AD), Chaplain to Emperor Conrad II

4. Christ, who once for sinners bled, | Now the firstborn from the dead,
Thron'd in endless might and pow'r | Lives and reigns for evermore.
Hail, eternal Hope on high! | Hail, thou King of victory!
Hail, thou Prince of Life adored! | Help and save us, gracious Lord!

English Translation: Jane Elizabeth Leeson (d. 1882); nothing is known of her. As Samuel W. Duffield put it: "the particulars of her personal history are withheld." Her fine translation appeared on page 19 of *Roman Catholic Hymns* (1853), published by Fr. Henry Formby—a disciple of Cardinal Newman—who converted from Anglicanism in 1846 and was ordained a Catholic priest the following year.

T. Source: *A Daily Hymn Book* (Westminster: Desclée & Company, 1948) p. 99; *Laudate Hymnal and Choir Book* (Diocese of Leavenworth, 1942) p. 126; *De La Salle Hymnal* (1913) p. 27.

Melody: Würth's *Katholisches Gesangbuch* (1859).

M. Source: *Cantate Omnes: Hymnal of the Catholic Choirmasters' Guild* (1952) #46.

77 77 D

Tune: Paschal Lamb

698 Come, Ye Faithful, Raise The Strain (8th century)

Saint John Damascene (d. 749AD)

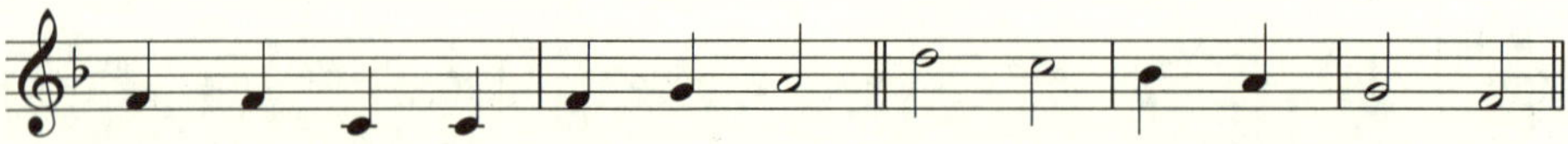

1. Come, ye faith - ful, raise the strain Of tri - um - phant glad - ness;
2. 'Tis the spring of souls to - day; Christ hath burst his pris - on,
3. Now the queen of sea - sons, bright With the day of splen - dor,

God hath brought his Is - ra - el In - to joy from sad - ness;
And from three days' sleep in death As a sun hath ris - en;
With the roy - al feast of feasts, Comes its joy to ren - der;

Loosed from Phar - aoh's bit - ter yoke Ja - cob's sons and daugh - ters;
All the win - ter of our sins, Long and dark, is fly - ing
Comes to glad Je - ru - sa - lem, Who with true af - fec - tion

Led them with un - mois - tened foot Through the Red Sea wa - ters.
From his light, to whom we give Laud and praise un - dy - ing.
Wel - comes in un - wea - ried strains Je - sus' res - ur - rec - tion.

4. Neither might the gates of death,
Nor the tomb's dark portal,
Nor the watchers, nor the seal
Hold thee as a mortal;
But today amidst the twelve
Thou didst stand, bestowing
That thy peace which evermore
Passeth human knowing.

76 76 D

Tune:
Ave Virgo Virginum

Final Verses: Richard Lloyd (1993) #15; Noel Rawsthorne (2011) #31.
Melody: Medieval melody arranged by Johann Roh (d. 1547).
M. Source: Printed in *Catholicum Hymnologium Germanicum* (Leisentritt, 1584).
English Translation: Dr. John M. Neale (d. 1866) from Greek.
T. Source: *Catholic Hymn Book* (London Oratory, 1998) p. 123; *Mediator Dei Hymnal* (1955) p. 34; *St. Mark's Hymnal for Use in the Catholic Church in the United States* (Peoria, Illinois: 1910) p. 47.

Aurora Caelum Purpurat (4th century)

Trns: Robert Campbell of Skerrington (d. 1868)

4. With Christ we died, with Christ we rose, | When at the font His name we chose;
Oh, nevermore let sin deface | Our souls enrobed in paschal grace.

5. To God the Father let us sing, | To God the Son, our risen king,
And equally let us adore | The Spirit, God for evermore.

Can be sung with any 88 88 meter: WHITEHALL, ROCKINGHAM, GONFALON ROYAL, etc.

THE morn had spread her crimson rays,
When rang the skies with shouts of praise;
Earth joined the joyful hymn to swell,
That brought despair to vanquished hell.

2. He comes victorious from the grave,
Who died our sinful souls to save;
He brings with Him to light of day
The saints who long imprisoned lay.

3. Let hymns of joy to grief succeed:
We know that Christ is ris'n indeed;
We hear his white-robed angel's voice,
And in our risen Lord rejoice.

4. With Christ we died, with Christ we rose,
When at the font His name we chose;
Oh, nevermore let sin deface
Our souls enrobed in paschal grace.

5. To God the Father let us sing,
To God the Son, our risen king,
And equally let us adore
The Spirit, God for evermore.

Text: Anonymous; originally *Aurora Lucis Rutilat*.
T. Source: *Catholic Hymnal* (Fr. John G. Hacker, 1920) p. 103.

88 88 (LM)

Tune: LA ROCHELLE

Melody: James W. Elliott (d. 1915) M. Source: *Hymns Ancient and Modern* (1972) p. 320.

702 Love's Redeeming Work Is Done

"For we are buried together with him by baptism into death; that as Christ is risen from the dead by the glory of the Father, so we also may walk in newness of life."—Romans 6.4

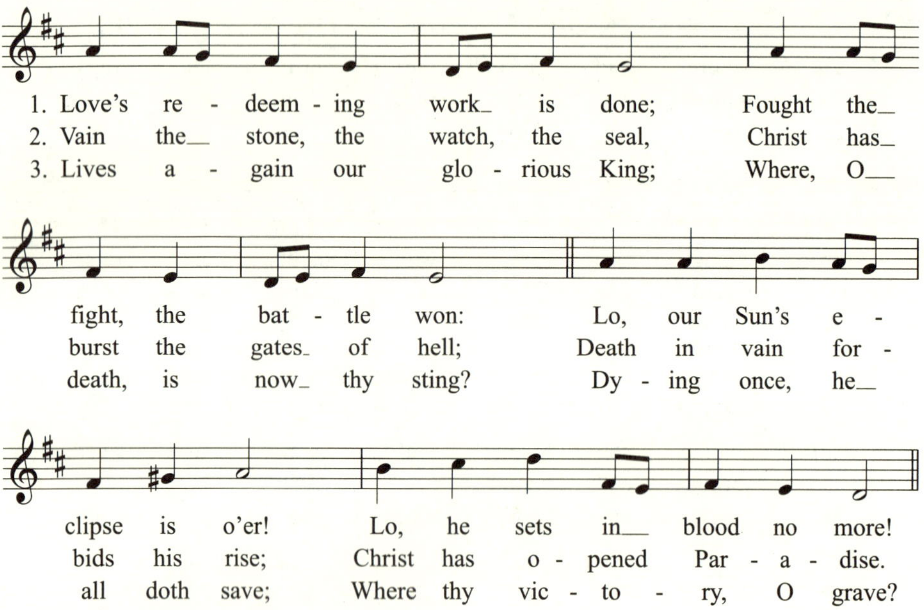

4. Soar we now where Christ has led,
Foll'wing our exalted Head;
Made like him, like him we rise;
Ours the Cross, the grave, the skies.

5. Hail the Lord of earth and heav'n!
Praise to thee by both be giv'n:
Thee we greet triumphant now;
Hail, the Resurrection thou!

77 77

Tune: Savannah

Melody: Herrnhut *Choralbuch* (1735).
M. Source: *Catholic Hymn Book* (London Oratory, 1998) p. 459.
Text: Charles Wesley (d. 1788), who wrote more than 6,500 hymns. His son was Samuel Wesley (d. 1837), who converted to Catholicism and as a composer was dubbed "the English Mozart."
T. Source: *Catholic Hymn Book* (London Oratory, 1998) p. 128.

O Filii Et Filiae (15th century) 703

Trns: Fr. Edward Caswall, Oratorian (d. 1878)

R. ALLELUIA, alleluia, alleluia.

The melody varies according to each region and parish.
Let congregations follow the lead of the choir.

O FÍLII et fíliae,
Rex caeléstis, Rex glóriae,
Morte surréxit hódie.

Alleluia. R. (*after each verse*)

2. Et mane prima sábbati,
Ad óstium monuménti
Accessérunt discípuli.

3. In albis sedens Ángelus
Praedíxit muliéribus:
In Galilaé*a* est Dóminus.

4. Discípulis adstántibus,
In médio stetit Chrístus,
Dicens: "Pax vobis omnibus."

5. Ut intelléxit Dídymus,
Quia surréxerat Jesus,
Remánsit fere dúbius

6. Vide, Thoma, vide latus,
Vide pedes, vide manus,
Noli esse incrédulus.

7. Quando Thomas Christi latus,
Pedes vidit atque manus,
Dixit: "Tu es Deus meus."

8. Beati qui non vidérunt,
Et fírmiter credidérunt,
Vitam aetérnam habébunt.

9. In hoc festo sanctíssimo
Sit laus et jubilátio,
Benedicámus Dómino.

YE sons and daughters of the Lord!
The King of glory, King ador'd,
This day Himself from death restor'd.

Alleluia. R. (*after each verse*)

2. All in the early morning grey,
Went holy women on their way,
To see the tomb where Jesus lay.

3. An angel clad in white they see,
Who sat, and spoke unto the three:
"Your Lord hath gone to Galilee."

4. That night th' apostles met in fear,
But Christ did in the midst appear:
"My peace," He saith, "be on all here!"

5. But Thomas, when of this he heard,
Was doubtful of his brethren's word;
Wherefore again there came the Lord.

6. "My piercèd Side, O Thomas, see;
My Hands, My Feet, I show to thee;
And doubt not, but believe in Me."

7. When Thomas saw that wounded Side,
The truth no longer he denied;
"Thou art my Lord and God!" he cried.

8. Oh, blest are they who have not seen
Their Lord, and yet believe in Him;
Eternal life awaiteth them.

9. On this most holy Day of days,
To God your hearts and voices raise
In laud and jubilee and praise.

Latin Text: *Crown Hymnal* (Boston, 1912) p. 524; edited by Fr. Leslie J. Kavanagh, Superintendent of Catholic Schools (New Orleans), and James M. McLaughlin, organist at St. Mary's Church (Boston, Massachusetts). Professor Amédée Gastoué (d. 1943), who served as consultor to the Pontifical Commission which created the *Editio Vaticana*, attributes this text to Jean Tisserand (d. 1494) a Franciscan monk.
English Text: *The Parochial Hymn Book* (London: Burns and Oates, 1881) #119; IMPRIMATUR by Henry Edward Cardinal Manning (d. 1892), who in 1851 converted from Anglicanism and was appointed Archbishop of Westminster in 1865.

888 A
Tune:
O FILII ET FILIAE

704 Hail The Day That Sees Him Rise (Ascension)

"And even as he blessed them he parted from them, and was carried up into heaven."—Lk 24.51

1. Hail the day that sees him_ rise, Al - le - lu - ia.
2. There the glo - rious tri - umph waits; Al - le - lu - ia.
3. See! the heav'n its Lord re - ceives, Al - le - lu - ia.

To the throne be - yond the_ skies. Al - le - lu - ia.
Lift your heads, e - ter - nal_ gates! Al - le - lu - ia.
Yet he loves the earth he_ leaves; Al - le - lu - ia.

Pas - chal Lamb for sin - ners_ giv'n Al - le - lu - ia.
He has van - quished death and_ sin; Al - le - lu - ia.
Though re - turn - ing to_ his_ throne, Al - le - lu - ia.

En - ters now the high - est_ heav'n. Al - le - lu - ia.
Take the King of glo - ry_ in. Al - le - lu - ia.
Still he calls man - kind his_ own. Al - le - lu - ia.

The word "ALLELUIA" is sung after each line:

4. See! he lifts his hands above;
   See! he shows the prints of love:
   Hark! his gracious lips bestow
   Blessings on his Church below.

5. Still for us he intercedes;
   His prevailing death he pleads;
   Near himself prepares our place,
   Harbinger of human race.

6. Lord, though parted from our sight,
   Far above yon azure height,
   Grant our hearts may thither rise,
   Seeking thee beyond the skies.

7. There we shall with thee remain,
   Partners of thine endless reign;
   There thy face unclouded see,
   Find our heav'n of heav'ns in thee.

77 77 A

Tune: LLANFAIR

Final Verses: Lloyd (1993) #118; Noel Rawsthorne (2011) #186.
Melody: Robert Williams (d. 1821), a blind composer born in Wales.
M. Source: *Catholic Hymn Book* (London Oratory, 1998) p. 138.
Text: After Charles Wesley (d. 1788) and Thomas Cotterill (d. 1823).
T. Source: *Catholic Hymn Book* (London Oratory, 1998) p. 139; *St. Mark's Hymnal for Use in the Catholic Church in the United States* (Peoria, Illinois: 1910) p. 55.

Aeterne Rex Altissime, Redemptor (5th century) 705

Trns: Fr. John Fitzpatrick, Oblate of Mary (d. 1929)

4. The Angels tremble as they see
Our mortal lot reversed again:
Flesh sinned; now flesh from sin doth free;
As God the flesh of God doth reign.

5. Be here our joy, until we find
That Thou above art our reward,
Beyond earth's joys of any kind,
Who art the earth's one only Lord.

6. To Thee we therefore humbly cry
Our sins in mercy to forgive,
To raise our hearts to Thee on high,
Which by Thy lofty graces live.

7. That when as Judge, the clouds being rent,
Thou com'st, a sudden dawn, once more,
Thou may'st remit our punishment,
And even our lost crowns restore.

Text: Anonymous; many alterations have been made over the centuries.
T. Source: *The Breviary and Missal Hymns* (London: Sands & Co, 1931) p. 80.
Melody: From a hymn book published by Fr. Melchior Ludolf Herold (d. 1810).
M. Source: *New Westminster Hymnal* (1939) p. 173.

88 88 (LM)
Tune: BRESSANI

706 Hymnum Canamus Gloriae (8th century)

Saint Bede the Venerable, Doctor of the Church (d. 735AD)

4. "Again ye shall behold Him so
As ye today have seen Him go,"
Alleluia, alleluia.
"In glorious pomp ascending high,
Up to the portals of the sky." R.

5. Be Thou our joy and strong defense,
Who art our future recompense:
Alleluia, alleluia.
So shall the light that springs from Thee
Be ours through all eternity. R.

6. O risen Christ, ascended Lord,
All praise to Thee let earth accord,
Alleluia, alleluia.
Who art, while endless ages run,
With Father and with Spirit One. R.

88 88 A

Tune:
Lasst Uns Erfreuen

Final Verses: Richard Lloyd (1993) #111; Noel Rawsthorne (2011) #178.
English Translation: After Benjamin Webb (d. 1885) and Elizabeth R. Charles (d. 1896).
Melody: From a Jesuit collection (Cologne, 1623).
M. Source: *Catholic Hymn Book* (1998) p. 478; *Hymns, Psalms, & Spiritual Canticles* (Marier, 1983) p. 328.

Hymnum Canamus Gloriae (8th century) 707

Saint Bede the Venerable, Doctor of the Church (d. 735AD)

Can be sung with any 88 88 meter, such as GONFALON ROYAL, TRINITY COLLEGE, ROGERS PARK, MELCOMBE, NOTRE DAME, BRESSANI, EISENACH, etc.

A HYMN of glory let us sing;
New songs throughout the world shall ring;
Christ, by a road before untrod,
Ascendeth to the throne of God.

2. The holy apostolic band
Upon the Mount of Olives stand,
And, with the Virgin-mother, see
Their Lord's resplendent majesty.

3. To whom the angels, drawing nigh:
"Why stand and gaze upon the sky?"
"This is the Savior," thus they say.
"This is His noble triumph day!"

4. "Again ye shall behold Him so
As ye today have seen Him go;
In glorious pomp ascending high,
Up to the portals of the sky."

5. Be Thou our joy and strong defense,
Who art our future recompense:
So shall the light that springs from Thee
Be ours through all eternity.

6. O risen Christ, ascended Lord,
All praise to Thee let earth accord,
Who art, while endless ages run,
With Father and with Spirit One.

* Saint Bede's second verse follows an ancient tradition which holds that Our Blessed Mother was present at Our Lord's Ascension:

> Apostoli tunc mystico
> In monte stantes chrismatis,
> Cum matre clara Virgine,
> Jesu videbant gloriam.

Saint Bede's hymn is an excellent choice for parishes which normally replace the *Introit* (Entrance Antiphon) with a hymn, as the official Ascension *Introit* is: "Men of Galilee, why are you gazing in astonishment at the sky? alleluia; just as you have seen him ascend into heaven, so, in like manner, shall he return, alleluia, alleluia, alleluia."

ENGLISH TRANSLATION: After Benjamin Webb (d. 1885) and Elizabeth R. Charles (d. 1896).

88 88 (LM)

Tune:
VARIOUS

708 Nunc Sancte Nobis Spiritus (4th century)

Trns: Bl. John Henry Cardinal Newman, Oratorian (d. 1890)

Can be sung with any 88 88 meter, such as Eisenach, Rogers Park, Bressani, La Rochelle, Kempen, Bessemer, Tallis Canon, Winchester New, etc.

COME, Holy Ghost, who ever One
Art with the Father and the Son;
Come, Holy Ghost, our souls possess
With Thy full flood of holiness.

2. Let flesh, and heart, and lips, and mind,
Sound forth our witness to mankind;
And love light up our mortal frame,
Till others catch the living flame.

3. Thou ever-blessèd Three in One,
O Father and Coequal Son,
O Holy Ghost the Comforter,
Thy grace on Thy redeemed confer.

88 88 (LM)

Tune:
Whitehall

Text: Saint Ambrose, Bishop of Milan (d. 397).
English Translation: *Tracts for the Times: On the Roman Breviary as embodying the substance of the devotional services of the Church Catholic* (London, 1837) p. 64.
Melody: Henry Lawes (d. 1662). M. Source: *Saint Edmund Campion Missal and Hymnal* (2013) p. 888.

Bianco da Siena (d. 1434)

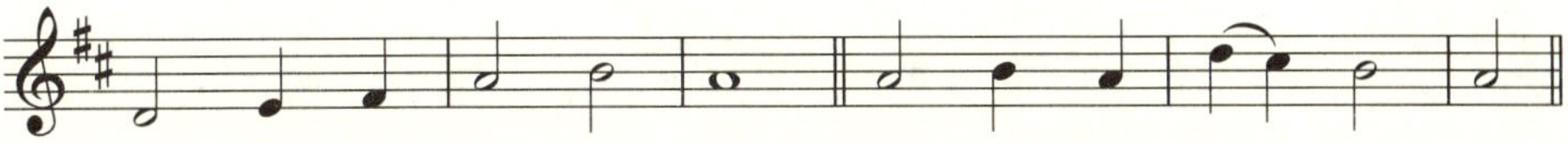

1. Come down, O love di - vine, Seek Thou this soul_ of mine,
2. O let it free - ly burn, Till earth - ly pas - sions turn
3. Let ho - ly char - i - ty Mine out - ward ves - ture be,

And vis - it it with Thine own ar - dor_ glow - ing.
To dust and ash - es in its heat con - sum - ing;
And low - li - ness be - come mine in - ner_ cloth - ing;

O Com - fort - er, draw near, With - in my heart ap - pear,
And let Thy glo - rious light Shine ev - er on my sight,
True low - li - ness of heart, Which takes the hum - bler part,

And kin - dle it, Thy ho - ly flame be - stow - ing.
And clothe me round, the while my path il - lum - ing.
And o'er its own short - com - ings weeps with loath - ing.

4. And so the yearning strong,
With which the soul will long,
Shall far outpass the pow'r of human telling;
For none can guess its grace,
Till he become the place
Wherein the Holy Spirit makes His dwelling.

Text: Translation from Italian by Richard Frederick Littledale (d. 1890), a close friend of John Mason Neale (d. 1866).
T. Source: *Adoremus Hymnal* (1997) #440; *Catholic Hymn Book* (1998) p. 147.
Melody: Ralph Vaughan Williams (d. 1958), a student of Maurice Ravel (d. 1937).
M. Source: *The English Hymnal* (1906) p. 216.

6 6 11 D
Tune:
DOWN AMPNEY

710 # Qui Procedis Ab Utroque (12th century)

Trns: Msgr. Ronald A. Knox (d. 1957)

4. Thou, who camest down in olden
Time to comfort and embolden
Christ's apostles faint with fear,
Send on us, thy comfort needing,
Grace, our little worth exceeding,
Every faithful soul to cheer.

5. As the Father is, so thou art;
As before all worlds, so now art;
Praise to him, while ages live,
With the Son whose blood hath bought us,
With thyself, whose light hath taught us,
We thy earthly servants give.

887 D

Tune:
Alles Ist An Gottes Segen

Final Verses: Noel Rawsthorne (2011) #118.
Text: Adam of St. Victor (d. 1146), a prolific composer of hymns and sequences; this sequence was sung on Pentecost Thursday according to the Use of Paris.
T. Source: *New Westminster Hymnal* (1939) p. 91.
Melody: Johann Balthasar König (d. 1758).
M. Source: *New Westminster Hymnal* (1939) p. 90; due to the considerable involvement Msgr. Knox had in the creation of the *New Westminster Hymnal*, it can be assumed that he preferred this tune.

Gott Vater Sei Gepriesen (Holy Trinity)

Trns: Fr. John Ernest Rothensteiner (d. 1936)

Melody: Limburg Gesangbuch (1838).
M. Source: *New Saint Basil Hymnal* (1958) p. 65.
ENGLISH TRANSLATION: Fr. Rothensteiner served as pastor for various parishes in Missouri. Toward the end of his life served as the historian of the Archdiocese of St. Louis.
T. Source: *Saint Pius X Hymnal* (Boston, 1953) p. 303; *Adoremus Hymnal* (1997) #464.

76 76 R

Tune:
GOTT VATER SEI GEPRIESEN

712 To Thee, O Gracious Father

Fr. Christopher G. Phillips (b. 1949)

13 13 13 13 14 14

Tune:
THAXTED

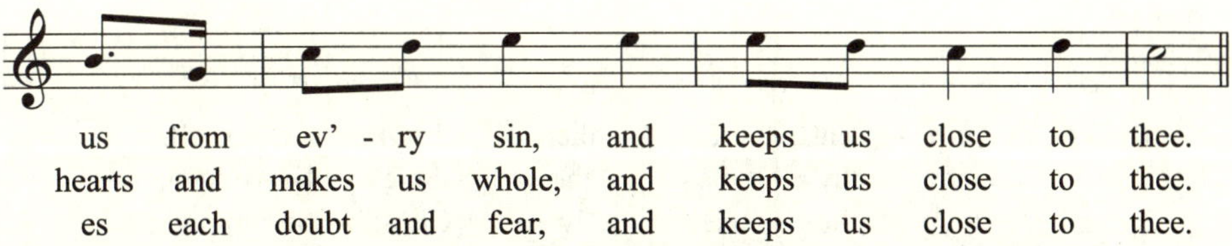

4. From thee, O Triune Godhead, salvation is come down;
Atonement now is given, mankind receives his crown.
In Sacrament tremendous we touch eternity;
We love thee, God our Savior: thou art our destiny.
O Father, Son, and Holy Ghost, our faith shall never cease!
In thee we have eternal life, and never-ending peace.

Melody: Gustav Holst (d. 1934) organist and choirmaster at Thaxted Parish Church (Essex, England).
M. Source: *Catholic Hymn Book* (London Oratory, 1998) p. 388.
T. Source: *Saint Jean de Brébeuf Hymnal* (2018).

714 Adesto Pater Domine (13th century)

First Tune – *Trns: Alan Gordon McDougall (d. 1965)*

4. O everlasting Trinity,
And ever perfect Unity,
Hear thou from heav'n thy suppliants' vows,
And cleanse from stains of sin their brows.

5. Laud, honor, might and praise be done
To God the Father and the Son,
And to the Holy Paraclete
Through endless ages, as is meet.

88 88 (LM)

Tune:
Cupertino

Melody: Kevin Allen (b. 1965), choirmaster at the Monastery of the Holy Cross in Chicago.
M. Source: *Saint Edmund Campion Missal and Hymnal* (2013) p. 882.
Text: From a 13th century Franciscan manuscript.
T. Source: *Pange Lingua: Breviary Hymns of Old Uses with an English Rendering by Alan G. McDougall and an Introduction by Adrian Fortescue* (London: Burns & Oates, 1916) p. 37.

Second Tune – *Trns: Alan Gordon McDougall (d. 1965)*

4. O everlasting Trinity,
And ever perfect Unity,
Hear thou from heav'n thy suppliants' vows,
And cleanse from stains of sin their brows.

5. Laud, honor, might and praise be done
To God the Father and the Son,
And to the Holy Paraclete
Through endless ages, as is meet.

Final Verses: Richard Lloyd (1993) #214; Noel Rawsthorne (2011) #342.
Melody: Orlando Gibbons (d. 1625), organist at Westminster Abbey.
M. Source: *The Hymnes and Songs of the Church* (1623) p. 114; originally sung to "Thus Angells sung, and thus sing we." We have adopted the most commonly used rhythm. Cf. *New Saint Basil Hymnal* (1958) p. 136.
Text: From a 13th century Franciscan manuscript.
T. Source: *Pange Lingua: Breviary Hymns of Old Uses with an English Rendering by Alan G. McDougall and an Introduction by Adrian Fortescue* (London: Burns & Oates, 1916) p. 37.

88 88 (LM)

Tune: Song 34

716 God Our Father, Lord Of Glory

First Tune – *Fr. Christopher G. Phillips* (*b.* 1949)

4. Loving mercy of the Father,
Sacrifice of Christ the Son,
Quick'ning power of the Spirit:
In us let Thy work be done!
May we rise to life eternal,
That our Paschal joy be won.

87 87 87

Tune:
Oriel

Final Verses: Richard Lloyd (1993) #162; Noel Rawsthorne (2011) #248.
Melody: Caspar Ett (d. 1847), Catholic composer and organist at St. Michael's in Munich.
M. Source: *Cantica Sacra Catholica* (Freiburg: Leopoldo Lumpp, 1859), p. 22; *Saint Basil's Hymnal* (1918) p. 281.
T. Source: *Saint Jean de Brébeuf Hymnal* (2018).

God Our Father, Lord Of Glory 717

SECOND TUNE – *Fr. Christopher G. Phillips (b. 1949)*

1. God our Fa - ther,_ Lord of glo - ry, Thanks and_ praise we
2. Je - sus Christ, our_ Ris - en Sav - ior, Of Thy_ sac - ri -
3. Ho - ly Spir - it,_ Breath from heav - en, We Thy_ pre - cious

give to Thee; In Thy mer - cy to our fa - thers,
fice we sing; As the lamb in an - cient mys - t'ry
gifts em - brace; At cre - a - tion all things liv - ing

Thou didst_ bring them through the sea. So by wa - ter_
To Thy_ peo - ple life didst bring, So in Eu - cha -
Thou didst_ sanc - ti - fy with grace. So may we, cre -

hast Thou saved us, Now from Ad - am's sin set free.
ris - tic glo - ry, Thou, God's Lamb,_ art made our King.
a - tion's glo - ry, Be for Thee_ a dwell - ing place.

4. Loving mercy of the Father,
Sacrifice of Christ the Son,
Quick'ning power of the Spirit:
In us let Thy work be done!
May we rise to life eternal,
That our Paschal joy be won.

87 87 87

Melody: Metrical Cento; cf. "Dum staret Abraham" (*Antiphonaire Monastique,* 13th century).
M. Source: *Paléographie musicale* (Volume XII), folio 81; *Cantus Selecti* (Solesmes, 1957) p. 245.
T. Source: *Saint Jean de Brébeuf Hymnal* (2018).

Tune:
BRETON

God Our Father, Lord Of Glory

THIRD TUNE – *Fr. Christopher G. Phillips (b. 1949)*

4. Loving mercy of the Father,
Sacrifice of Christ the Son,
Quick'ning power of the Spirit:
In us let Thy work be done!
May we rise to life eternal,
That our Paschal joy be won.

87 87 87

Tune:
REGENT SQUARE

Final Verses: Richard Lloyd (1993) #175; Noel Rawsthorne (2011) #265.
Melody: Henry Smart (d. 1879), organist at St. Philip's in London.
M. Source: *Catholic Hymn Book* (1998) p. 280; *Hymns, Psalms, and Spiritual Canticles* (1983) p. 213.
T. Source: *Saint Jean de Brébeuf Hymnal* (2018).

God Our Father, Lord Of Glory 719

Fourth Tune – *Fr. Christopher G. Phillips (b. 1949)*

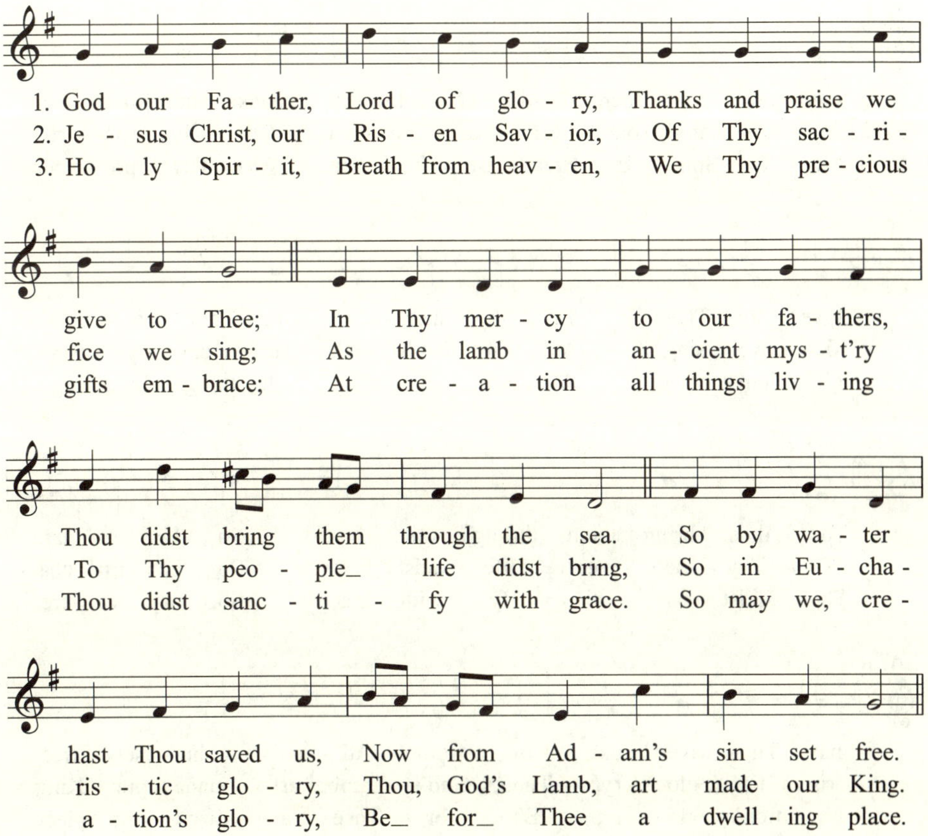

4. Loving mercy of the Father,
Sacrifice of Christ the Son,
Quick'ning power of the Spirit:
In us let Thy work be done!
May we rise to life eternal,
That our Paschal joy be won.

Melody: Samuel Webbe, the Elder (d. 1816), choirmaster of the Chapel of the Portuguese Embassy in Lincoln's Inn Fields (a public square), the only place in London where the Catholic liturgy could be publicly celebrated.

M. Source: *Essay on Church Plain-chant* (1782); *Mediator Dei Hymnal* (1955) #16; *St. Basil's Hymnal* (1918) p. 280; *St. Mark's Hymnal for Use in the Catholic Church in the United States* (Peoria, Illinois: 1910) p. 23, 66.

T. Source: *Saint Jean de Brébeuf Hymnal* (2018).

87 87 87

Tune: Dulce Carmen

720 God Our Father, Lord Of Glory

Fifth Tune – *Fr. Christopher G. Phillips (b. 1949)*

1. God our Fa - ther, Lord of glo - ry, Thanks and praise we
2. Je - sus Christ, our Ris - en Sav - ior, Of Thy sac - ri -
3. Ho - ly Spir - it, Breath from heav - en, We Thy pre - cious

give to Thee; In Thy mer - cy to our fa - thers,
fice we sing; As the lamb in an - cient mys - t'ry
gifts em - brace; At cre - a - tion all things liv - ing

Thou didst bring them through the sea. So by wa - ter
To Thy peo - ple life didst bring, So in Eu - cha -
Thou didst sanc - ti - fy with grace. So may we, cre -

hast Thou saved us, Now from Ad - am's sin set free.
ris - tic glo - ry, Thou, God's Lamb, art made our King.
a - tion's glo - ry, Be for Thee a dwell - ing place.

4. Loving mercy of the Father,
Sacrifice of Christ the Son,
Quick'ning power of the Spirit:
In us let Thy work be done!
May we rise to life eternal,
That our Paschal joy be won.

87 87 87

Tune:
Davost

Melody: Fr. Jules de Verneuil (d. 1938).
M. Source: Fr. Anatole Police, *The Parochial Hymn Book* (London: Burns & Oates, 1897).
T. Source: *Saint Jean de Brébeuf Hymnal* (2018).

God Our Father, Lord Of Glory

Fr. Christopher G. Phillips (b. 1949)

Can be sung with any 87 87 87 meter: RUNNELLS, MANNHEIM, DULCE CARMEN, BRETON, GAUFESTRE, LAUDA ANIMA, DAVOST, ST LEONARD, PICARDY, REGENT SQUARE, etc.

GOD our Father, Lord of glory,
Thanks and praise we give to Thee;
In Thy mercy to our fathers,
Thou didst bring them through the sea.
So by water hast Thou saved us,
Now from Adam's sin set free.

2. Jesus Christ, our Risen Savior,
Of Thy sacrifice we sing;
As the lamb in ancient myst'ry
To Thy people life didst bring,
So in Eucharistic glory,
Thou, God's Lamb, art made our King.

3. Holy Spirit, Breath from heaven,
We Thy precious gifts embrace;
At creation all things living
Thou didst sanctify with grace.
So may we, creation's glory,
Be for Thee a dwelling place.

4. Loving mercy of the Father,
Sacrifice of Christ the Son,
Quick'ning power of the Spirit:
In us let Thy work be done!
May we rise to life eternal,
That our Paschal joy be won.

87 87 87

Tune: VARIOUS

T. Source: *Saint Jean de Brébeuf Hymnal* (2018).

722 Almighty God, Majestic King

Fr. Christopher G. Phillips (b. 1949)

88 88 A

Tune:
Lasst Uns Erfreuen

Final Verses: Richard Lloyd (1993) #111; Noel Rawsthorne (2011) #178.
Melody: From a Jesuit collection (Cologne, 1623) entitled *Sacred Catholic Church Hymns, from Pentecost to Advent, Christmastide, Lenten Hymns, Paschal Hymns, Pilgrim songs, and all kinds to be sung throughout the whole year.* Two forms exist—placing "Alleluia" in various spots—and both are equally authentic.
M. Source: *Catholic Hymn Book* (1998) p. 478; *Hymns, Psalms, & Spiritual Canticles* (Marier, 1983) p. 328.
T. Source: *Saint Jean de Brébeuf Hymnal* (2018).

We Pray Thee, Heavenly Father 723

Hymn to the Father, Son, and Holy Ghost

Text: Based on a work by Vincent S. Coles (d. 1929).
T. Source: *Saint Edmund Campion Missal and Hymnal* (2013) p. 940.
Melody: Gustav Holst (d. 1934) organist and choirmaster at Thaxted Parish Church (Essex, England).
M. Source: *Catholic Hymn Book* (London Oratory, 1998) p. 388.

13 13 13 13 13 14
Tune:
THAXTED

724 O Pater Sancte, Mitis Atque Pie (10th century)

Trns: Msgr. Ronald A. Knox (d. 1957)

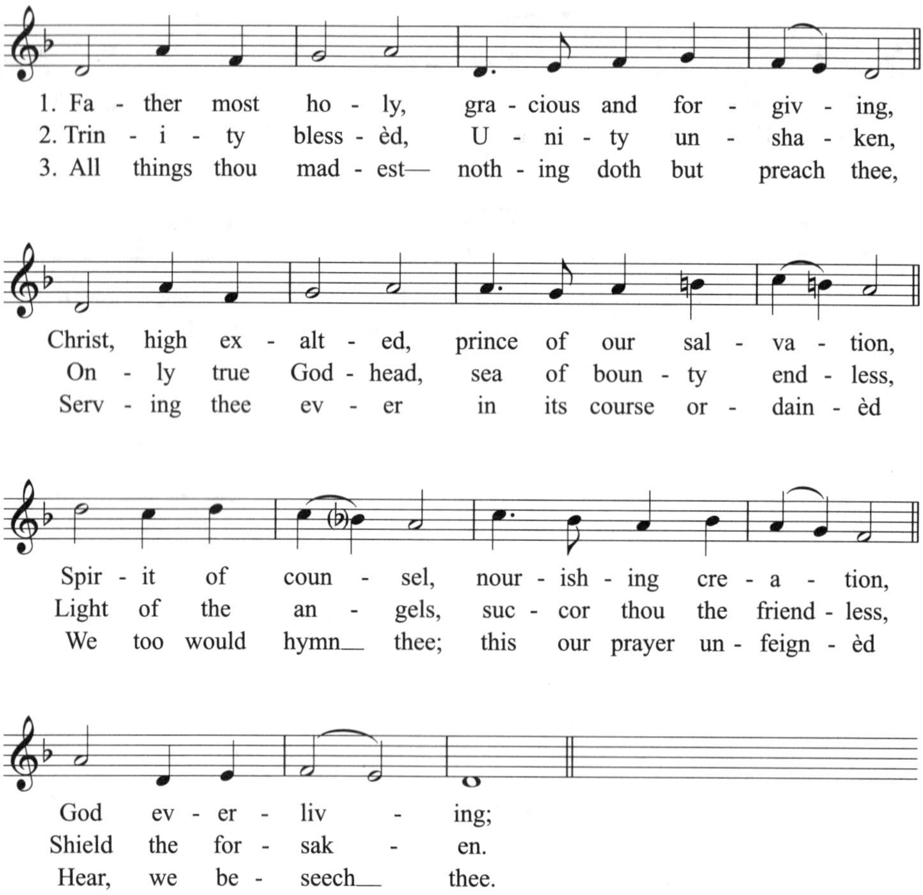

4. Boundless thy praise be, whom no limit boundeth,
God in three Persons, high in heaven living,
Where adoration, homage and thanksgiving
Ever resoundeth.

11 11 11 5

Tune:
Iste Confessor

Final Verses: Richard Lloyd (1993) #106; Noel Rawsthorne (2011) #168.
Melody: *Vesperale* (Poitiers, 1746).
M. Source: *Catholic Hymn Book* (London Oratory, 1998) p. 416; *Worship II Hymnal* (GIA, 1975) #221.
T. Source: *New Westminster Hymnal* (1939) p. 94.

O Lord, I Am Not Worthy 725

"The centurion said: Lord, I am not worthy that thou shouldst enter under my roof: but only say the word, and my servant shall be healed."—Mt 8.8

1. O__ Lord, I am not wor - thy That_ thou should'st
2. And hum - bly I'll re - ceive thee, The_ bride - groom
3. E - ter - nal Ho - ly Spir - it, Un - wor - thy

come to me: But__ speak the word of com - fort,
of my soul, No__ more by sin to grieve thee
though I be, Pre - pare me to re - ceive him

My spir - it healed shall be.
Or fly thy sweet con - trol.
And trust the Word to me.

4. Increase my faith, dear Jesus,
In thy Real Presence here,
And make me feel most deeply
That thou to me art near.

5. My hope in thee now strengthen,
O Savior of my soul,
Lest by temptation blinded,
I turn from my true goal.

6. O Sacrament most holy,
O Sacrament divine!
All praise and all thanksgiving
Be ev'ry moment Thine.

Melody: Anonymous; 19th century.
M. Source: *St. Michael Hymnal* (St. Boniface Parish, 2003) #458; *St. Basil's Hymnal* (1918) p. 57; *Eucharistic Hymnal, edited by Archbishop Joseph Schrembs* (1935) p. 4.
Text: Anonymous; possibly based on "O Herr, ich bin nicht würdig" (*Landshuter Gesangbuch*, 1777).
T. Source: *Adoremus Hymnal* (1997) #512; *The Parish Hymnal* (Sister Catherine Cecilia, 1957) p. 29.

76 76

Tune: Non Dignus

726 O Jesus, We Adore Thee

Fr. Irvin M. Udulutsch, Capuchin (d. 2010)

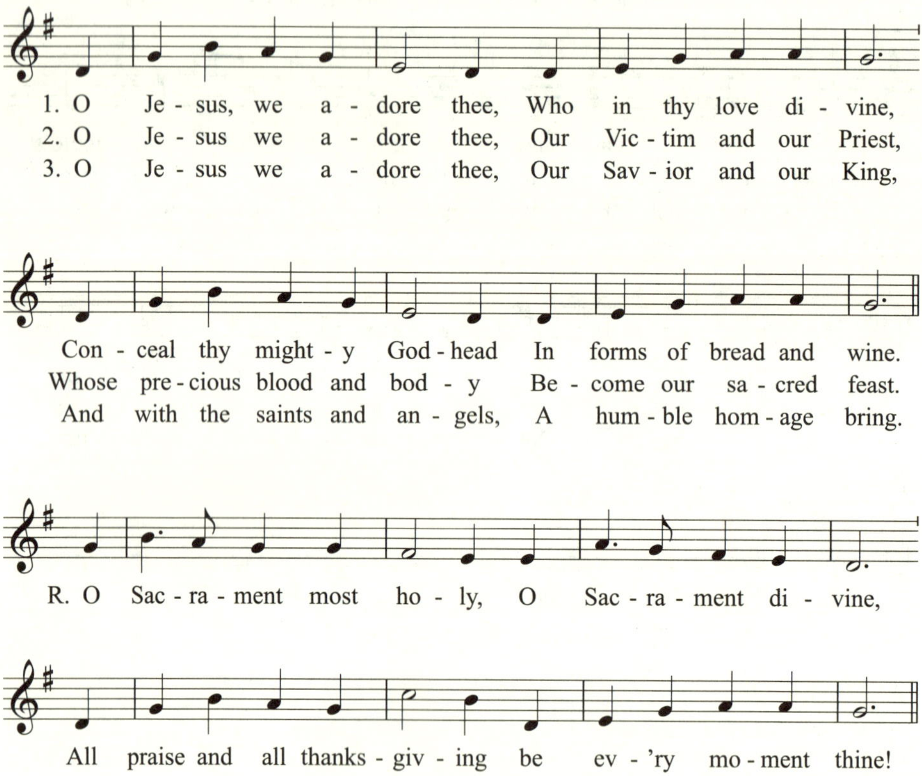

4. O Jesus, we adore thee;
Come, live in us, we pray,
That all our thoughts and actions
Be thine alone today. R.

5. O come, all you who labor
In sorrow and in pain;
Come, eat this bread from heaven,
Your peace and strength regain. R.

76 76 R

Tune:
UDULUTSCH

Text: Fr. Irvin M. Udulutsch was professor of music at the Seminary of St. Lawrence of Brindisi (Mount Calvary, Wisconsin) and a founding member of the Church Music Association of America.
T. Source: *Saint Michael Hymnal* (St. Boniface Parish, 2003) #452.
Melody: 1891 *Gesangbuch* from Fulda (Central Germany).
M. Source: *Adoremus Hymnal* (1997) #517.

Jesus, My Lord, My God, My All 727

Fr. Frederick William Faber, Oratorian (d. 1863)

4. Sound, sound His praises higher still,
And come, ye angels, to our aid;
'Tis God, 'tis God, the very God,
Whose pow'r both man and angels made. R.

5. Jesus, dear Pastor of the flock,
We crowd in love about Thy feet;
Our voices yearn to praise Thee, Lord,
And joyfully Thy presence greet. R.

Melody: Römisch-katholisches Gesangbüchlein (1826).
M. Source: *Mediator Dei Hymnal* (1955) p. 55; *Adoremus Hymnal* (1997) #516;
Eucharistic Hymnal, edited by Archbishop Joseph Schrembs (1935) p. 7.
Text: Father Faber, a disciple of Cardinal Newman, was the founder of the London Oratory. This text was published as #16 ("Corpus Christi") in *Oratory Hymns* (1954); the complete poem has nine verses.
T. Source: *Saint Andrew Hymnal, authorized by the Archbishops and Bishops of Scotland for use in the Scottish Dioceses* (1964) p. 185; *Pope Pius XII Hymnal* (Ohio: Gregorian Institute of America, 1959) p. 9.

88 88 R
Tune:
SWEET SACRAMENT

728 Let All Mortal Flesh Keep Silence

"But the Lord is in his holy temple: let all the earth keep silence before him."—Hab 2.20

4. At His feet the six-wingèd seraph;
Cherubim with sleepless eye,
Veil their faces to the Presence,
As with ceaseless voice they cry:
"Alleluia, alleluia,
Alleluia, Lord most high."

87 87 87

Tune:
PICARDY

Final Verses: Richard Lloyd (1993) #168; Noel Rawsthorne (2011) #257.
Text: English paraphrase (out of Greek) by Gerard Moultrie (d. 1885) of the *Cherubic Hymn*, from the Liturgy of Saint James; The text may have been written before 400 AD.
T. Source: *Hymns, Psalms, and Spiritual Canticles* (Massachusetts: Theodore Marier, 1983) p. 318.
Melody: 17th century French carol; cf. *Mélodies populaires des Provinces de France* (1848) #5, entitled *La Ballade de Jésus-Christ*. The name "Picardy" comes from the province of France from which it is believed to originate.
M. Source: *New English Hymnal* (1986) p. 1124.

O Jesus Christ, Remember 729

"Jesus said to him: I am. And you shall see the Son of man sitting on the right hand of the power of God, and coming with the clouds of heaven."—Mark 14.62

Final Verses: Richard Lloyd (1993) #12; Noel Rawsthorne (2011) #28.
Melody: Samuel Sebastian Wesley (d. 1876), organist at Hereford Cathedral.
M. Source: *Catholic Hymn Book* (London Oratory, 1998) p. 322. The tune name comes from *Urbs Sion Aurea*, as Wesley wrote it for Neale's famous translation: "Jerusalem the Golden." Cf. Wesley's *Collection of Hymn Tunes; Selected from British and Foreign Sources with Harmonies* (London: Novello, 1872) p. 341.
Text: Fr. Edward Caswall, Oratorian (d. 1878), a disciple of John Henry Cardinal Newman (d. 1890).
T. Source: *Lyra Eucharistica: Hymns and Verses on the Holy Communion* (London: Orby Shipley, 1863) p. 142.

76 76 D

Tune: Aurelia

730 In The Presence Of The Blessed Sacrament

"Then he took bread, and blessed and broke it, and gave it to them, saying, This is my body, given for you; do this for a commemoration of me."—Lk 22.19

1st Tune

1. Lord, en - throned in heav'n - ly splen - dor, First - be - got - ten
2. Here our humbl - est hom - age pay we; Here in lov - ing
3. Tho' the low - liest form doth veil thee As of old_ in

from the dead, Thou a - lone, our strong de - fend - er,
rev - 'rence bow; Here for faith's dis - cern - ment pray we,
Beth - le - hem, Here as there thine an - gels hail thee,

Lift - est up_ thy peo - ple's head. Al - le - lu - ia!
Lest we fail_ to know thee now. Al - le - lu - ia!
Branch and flow'r of Jes - se's stem. Al - le - lu - ia!

Al - le - lu - ia! Je - sus, true and liv - ing Bread.
Al - le - lu - ia! Thou art here, we ask not how.
Al - le - lu - ia! We in wor - ship join with them.

4. Paschal Lamb, thine off'ring, finished
Once for all when thou wert slain,
In its fullness undiminished
Shall for evermore remain,
Alleluia! Alleluia!
Cleansing souls from every stain.

5. Life-imparting heav'nly Manna,
Stricken Rock with streaming side,
Heav'n and earth with loud hosanna
Worship thee, the Lamb who died.
Alleluia! Alleluia!
Ris'n, ascended, glorified!

87 87 87

Tune:
Westminster Abbey F

Text: George Hugh Bourne (d. 1925). T. Source: *Catholic Hymn Book* (1998) p. 201.
Melody: Henry Purcell (d. 1695), organist at Westminster Abbey.
M. Source: cf. Final "Hallelujah" section of an anthem (1681), *O God, Thou Art My God.* Like many hymn tunes (Breslau, Old Hundredth, Bedford, Puer Nobis Nascitur, etc.) this melody can be sung in triple or quadruple meter; however, when sung in triple, it should follow Purcell's original rhythm and not what is commonly found in 20th century hymnals.

In The Presence Of The Blessed Sacrament

"Then he took bread, and blessed and broke it, and gave it to them, saying, This is my body, given for you; do this for a commemoration of me."—Lk 22.19

2nd Tune

4. Paschal Lamb, thine off'ring, finished
Once for all when thou wert slain,
In its fullness undiminished
Shall for evermore remain,
Alleluia! Alleluia!
Cleansing souls from every stain.

5. Life-imparting heav'nly Manna,
Stricken Rock with streaming side,
Heav'n and earth with loud hosanna
Worship thee, the Lamb who died.
Alleluia! Alleluia!
Ris'n, ascended, glorified!

Final Verses: Richard Lloyd (1993) #169; Noel Rawsthorne (2011) #258.
Text: George Hugh Bourne (d. 1925).
T. Source: *Catholic Hymn Book* (London Oratory, 1998) p. 201.
Melody: John Goss (d. 1880), Professor of Harmony at the Royal Academy of Music.
M. Source: *New Saint Basil Hymnal* (1958) p. 202; *Hymns, Psalms, and Spiritual Canticles* (1983) p. 294.

87 87 87
Tune:
Lauda Anima

732 In The Presence Of The Blessed Sacrament

"Then he took bread, and blessed and broke it, and gave it to them, saying, This is my body, given for you; do this for a commemoration of me."—Lk 22.19

3rd Tune

1. Lord, en - throned in heav'n - ly splen - dor, First - be - got - ten
2. Here our humbl - est hom - age pay we; Here in lov - ing
3. Tho' the low - liest form doth veil thee As of old in

from___ the dead, Thou a - lone, our strong de - fend - er,
rev - 'rence bow; Here for faith's dis - cern - ment pray we,
Beth - le - hem, Here as there thine an - gels hail thee,

Lift - est up thy peo - ple's head. Al - le - lu - ia!
Lest we fail to know___ thee now. Al - le - lu - ia!
Branch and flow'r of Jes - se's stem. Al - le - lu - ia!

Al - le - lu - ia! Je - sus, true and liv - ing Bread.
Al - le - lu - ia! Thou art here, we ask not how.
Al - le - lu - ia! We in wor - ship join with them.

4. Paschal Lamb, thine off'ring, finished
Once for all when thou wert slain,
In its fullness undiminished
Shall for evermore remain,
Alleluia! Alleluia!
Cleansing souls from every stain.

5. Life-imparting heav'nly Manna,
Stricken Rock with streaming side,
Heav'n and earth with loud hosanna
Worship thee, the Lamb who died.
Alleluia! Alleluia!
Ris'n, ascended, glorified!

87 87 87

Tune:
RUNNELLS

Text: George Hugh Bourne (d. 1925).
T. Source: *Catholic Hymn Book* (London Oratory, 1998) p. 201.
Melody: Kevin Allen (b. 1965), choirmaster at the Monastery of the Holy Cross in Chicago.
M. Source: *Saint Jean de Brébeuf Hymnal* (2018).

In The Presence Of The Blessed Sacrament 733

"Then he took bread, and blessed and broke it, and gave it to them, saying, This is my body, given for you; do this for a commemoration of me."—Lk 22.19

Can be sung with any 87 87 87 meter: RUNNELLS, MANNHEIM, DULCE CARMEN, BRETON, GAUFESTRE, LAUDA ANIMA, DAVOST, ST LEONARD, PICARDY, REGENT SQUARE, etc.

LORD, enthroned in heav'nly splendor,
First-begotten from the dead,
Thou alone, our strong defender,
Liftest up thy people's head.
Alleluia! Alleluia!
Jesus, true and living Bread.

2. Here our humblest homage pay we;
Here in loving rev'rence bow;
Here for faith's discernment pray we,
Lest we fail to know thee now.
Alleluia! Alleluia!
Thou art here, we ask not how.

3. Tho' the lowliest form doth veil thee
As of old in Bethlehem,
Here as there thine angels hail thee,
Branch and flow'r of Jesse's stem.
Alleluia! Alleluia!
We in worship join with them.

4. Paschal Lamb, thine off'ring, finished
Once for all when thou wert slain,
In its fullness undiminished
Shall for evermore remain,
Alleluia! Alleluia!
Cleansing souls from every stain.

5. Life-imparting heav'nly Manna,
Stricken Rock with streaming side,
Heav'n and earth with loud hosanna
Worship thee, the Lamb who died.
Alleluia! Alleluia!
Ris'n, ascended, glorified!

87 87 87

Text: George Hugh Bourne (d. 1925).
T. Source: *Catholic Hymn Book* (London Oratory, 1998) p. 201.

Tune:
VARIOUS

734 Panis Angelicus, Fit Panis Hominum (1264 AD)

Final Verses of "Sacris Solemniis," by St. Thomas Aquinas (d. 1274)

Literal Translation :

1. The bread of angels becomes man's bread;
the bread from heaven puts an end to the types.
What marvelous happening is this;
the poor, the servant, the lowly feeds upon his Lord.

2. We ask Thee, Godhead three and one,
to come to us even as we worship Thee.
Guide us along Thy paths to our journey's end—
to the light in which Thou dost dwell.

MANNA was the miraculous bread of the Israelites during their forty years' sojourn in the desert; it came down from heaven every morning, and it was consumed in the morning; it was small and white; and such was its nature that "neither had he more that had gathered more, nor did he find less that had provided less" (Ex 16.18).

Panis angelicus and *panis caelicus* are Scriptural allusions to the manna of old, which was a "type" of the Manna of the New Law. *Et pluit illis manna ad manducandum, et panem caeli dedit eis. Panem angelorum manducavit homo: cibaria misit eis in abundantia* (Ps 77.24-25).

12 12 12 8

Tune:
CHARLEROI

Melody: Fr. Louis Lambillotte (d. 1855), Jesuit music professor at colleges in Belgium, France, and Switzerland.
M. Source: *Adoremus Hymnal* (1997) #523; *Saint Michael Hymnal* (St. Boniface Parish, 2003) #490; *Cantate Omnes: Hymnal of the Catholic Choirmasters' Guild* (1952) #77.
T. Source: *Liber Usualis; with introduction and rubrics in English* (Solesmes Abbey, 1961) p. 922.

O Esca Viatorum (17th century) 735

"The bread of heaven was his gift to them; man should eat the food of angels, and so their want should be supplied abundantly."—Ps 77.24-25

1st Tune

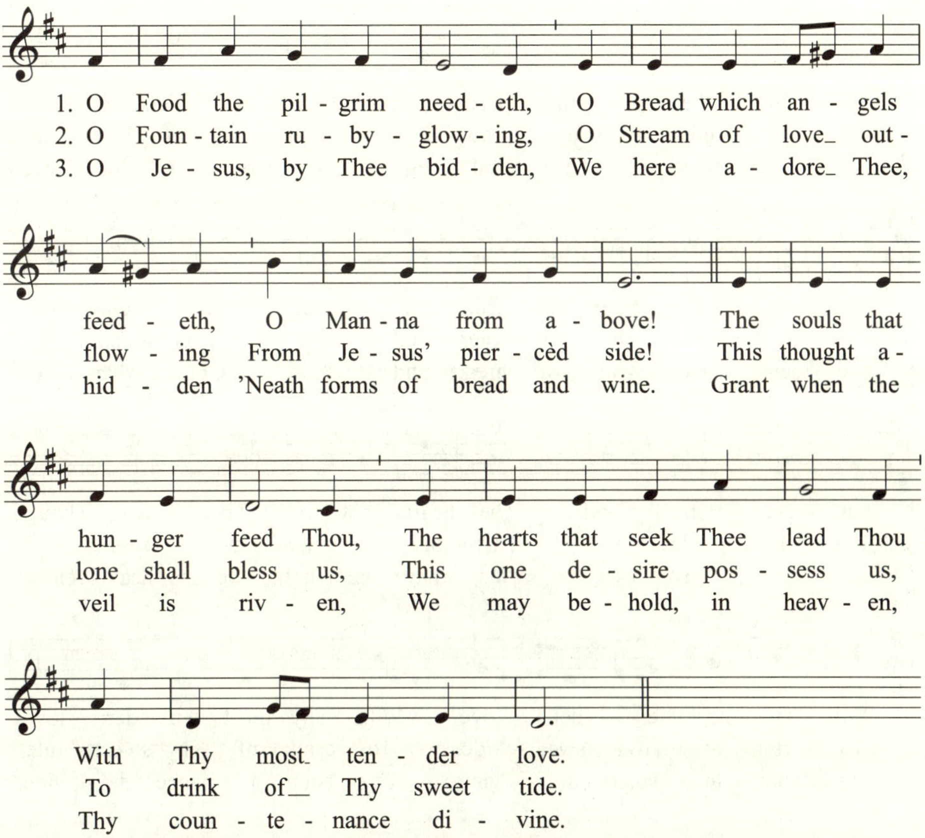

This hymn can be sung in Latin to the same tune :

1. O esca viatórum, | O panis angelórum | O manna caélitum!
   Esuriéntes ciba, | Dulcédine non priva | Corda quaeréntium.

2. O lympha, fons amóris, | Qui puro Salvatóris, | E corde prófluis!
   Te sitiéntes pota, | Haec sola nostra vota, | His una sûfficis.

3. O Jesu, tuum vultum, | Quem cólimus occúltum | Sub panis spécie,
   Fac, ut remóto velo, | Apérta nos in caelo | Cernámus ácie.

Melody: *Davidisches Harfen-und-Psalterspiel* (1749). M. Source: *Catholic Hymn Book* (1998) p. 204.
Text: From a Catholic hymnal (Mainz, 1661), given in Latin with German translation under the title "Hymn on the True Heavenly Bread."
English Translation: Cento; cf. *Laudate Hymnal and Choir Book* (Diocese of Leavenworth, 1942) p. 126; *Eucharistica: Verse & Prose in Honor of the Hidden God* (Msgr. Hugh T. Henry, 1912) p. 91; *Catholic Hymn Book* (London Oratory, 1998) p. 205.

776 D

Tune:
In Allen Meinen Thaten

736 O Esca Viatorum (17th century)

"The bread of heaven was his gift to them; man should eat the food of angels, and so their want should be supplied abundantly."–Ps 77.24-25

2nd Tune

1. O__ Food the pil - grim need - eth, O Bread which an - gels
2. O__ Foun - tain ru - by - glow - ing, O Stream of love out -
3. O__ Je - sus, by Thee bid - den, We here a - dore Thee,

feed - eth, O Man - na from a - bove! The souls that
flow - ing From Je - sus' pier - cèd side! This thought a -
hid - den 'Neath forms of bread and wine. Grant when the

hun - ger__ feed Thou, The hearts that seek Thee__ lead Thou
lone shall__ bless us, This one de - sire pos - sess us,
veil is__ riv - en, We may be - hold, in__ heav - en,

With Thy most ten - der__ love. With Thy most ten - der love.
To drink of Thy__ sweet tide. To drink of Thy sweet tide.
Thy coun - te - nance di - vine. Thy coun - te - nance di - vine.

This hymn can be sung in Latin to the same tune :

1. O esca viatórum, | O panis angelórum | O manna caélitum!
   Esuriéntes ciba, | Dulcédine non priva
   Corda quaeréntium, Corda quaeréntium.

2. O lympha, fons amóris, | Qui puro Salvatóris, | E corde prófluis!
   Te sitiéntes pota, | Haec sola nostra vota,
   His una súfficis, His una súfficis.

3. O Jesu, tuum vultum, | Quem cólimus occúltum | Sub panis spécie,
   Fac, ut remóto velo, | Apérta nos in caelo
   Cernámus ácie, Cernámus ácie.

Melody: Johann Michael Haydn (d. 1806), whose religious compositions were admired by his older brother, Franz Joseph Haydn (d. 1809).
M. Source: Mediator Dei Hymnal (1955) p. 44.
Text: From a Catholic hymnal (Mainz, 1661), given in Latin with German translation under the title "Hymn on the True Heavenly Bread."
English Translation: Cento; cf. *Laudate Hymnal and Choir Book* (Diocese of Leavenworth, 1942) p. 126; *Eucharistica: Verse & Prose in Honor of the Hidden God* (Msgr. Hugh T. Henry, 1912) p. 91; *Catholic Hymn Book* (London Oratory, 1998) p. 205.

776 D

Tune:
O Esca Viatorum

"The bread of heaven was his gift to them; man should eat the food of angels, and so their want should be supplied abundantly."—Ps 77.24-25

3rd Tune

1. O Food the pil - grim need - eth, O__ Bread which
2. O Foun - tain ru - by - glow - ing, O__ Stream of
3. O Je - sus, by__ Thee bid - den, We_ here a -

an - gels feed - eth, O Man - na from a - bove!
love out - flow - ing From Je - sus' pier - cèd side!
dore Thee, hid - den 'Neath forms of bread and wine.

The souls that hun - ger feed Thou, The__ hearts that
This thought a - lone_ shall bless us, This_ one de -
Grant when the veil_ is riv - en, We__ may be -

seek Thee lead Thou With Thy__ most ten - der love.
sire pos - sess us, To drink_ of Thy sweet tide.
hold, in heav - en, Thy coun - te - nance di - vine.

This hymn can be sung in Latin to the same tune :

1. O esca viatórum, | O panis angelórum | O manna caélitum!
Esuriéntes ciba, | Dulcédine non priva | Corda quaeréntium.

2. O lympha, fons amóris, | Qui puro Salvatóris, | E corde prófluis!
Te sitiéntes pota, | Haec sola nostra vota, | His una súfficis.

3. O Jesu, tuum vultum, | Quem cólimus occúltum | Sub panis spécie,
Fac, ut remóto velo, | Apérta nos in caelo | Cernámus ácie.

Melody: Heinrich Isaac (d. 1527); adapted by Sir Richard R. Terry (d. 1938) in the *Westminster Hymnal* (1912) p. 38. It occurs famously in J.S. Bach's *St. Matthew Passion* (1727).
Text: From a Catholic hymnal (Mainz, 1661), given in Latin with German translation under the title "Hymn on the True Heavenly Bread."
English Translation: Cento; cf. *Laudate Hymnal and Choir Book* (Diocese of Leavenworth, 1942) p. 126; *Eucharistica: Verse & Prose in Honor of the Hidden God* (Msgr. Hugh T. Henry, 1912) p. 91; *Catholic Hymn Book* (London Oratory, 1998) p. 205.

776 D

Tune: Innsbruck

738 O Precious Lord, Once Born For Us

Fr. Christopher G. Phillips (b. 1949)

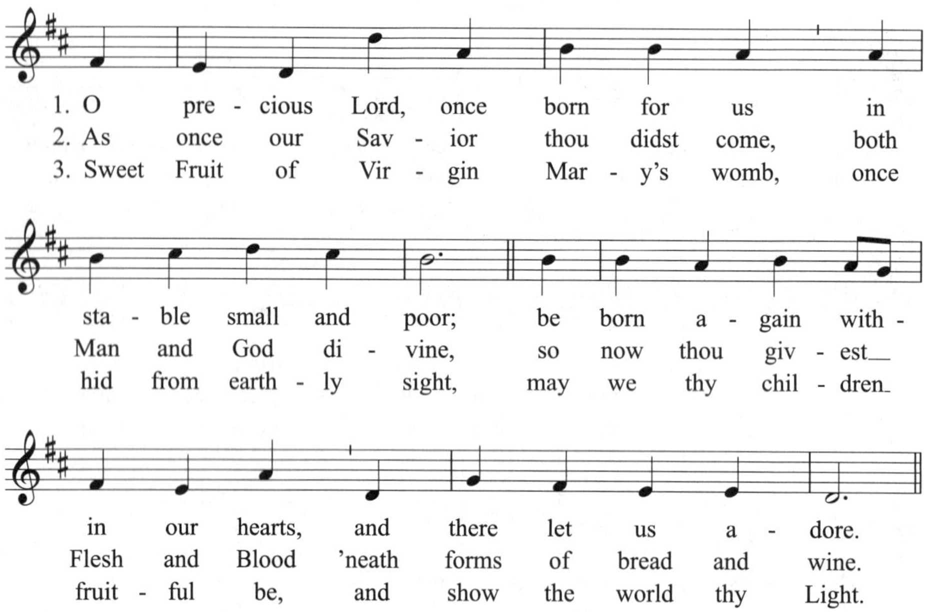

4. Now stay with us, Lord Jesus Christ,
in solemn Mystery,
that when our work on earth be done
thy glory we may see.

Can be sung with any 86 86 meter, such as St Magnus, Bedford, St Columba, Westminster, St Anne, St Hugh, Hereford, St Flavian, etc.

O PRECIOUS Lord, once born for us
in stable small and poor;
be born again within our hearts,
and there let us adore.

2. As once our Savior thou didst come,
both Man and God divine,
so now thou givest Flesh and Blood
'neath forms of bread and wine.

3. Sweet Fruit of Virgin Mary's womb,
once hid from earthly sight,
may we thy children fruitful be,
and show the world thy Light.

4. Now stay with us, Lord Jesus Christ,
in solemn Mystery,
that when our work on earth be done
thy glory we may see.

86 86 (CM)

Tune:
Metzler's Redhead

Final Verses: Richard Lloyd (1993) #139; Noel Rawsthorne (2011) #211.
Melody: Richard Redhead (d. 1901), organist at the church of St. Mary Magdalene, Paddington. Redhead collaborated with Frederick Oakeley (d. 1880) to create *Laudes Diurnae* (1843). Oakeley converted to Catholicism in 1845 and become a Canon of Westminster in 1852.
M. Source: *New Westminster Hymnal* (1939) p. 32; this tune first appeared in 1859.
T. Source: *Saint Jean de Brébeuf Hymnal* (2018).

"O Salutaris" and "Tantum Ergo"

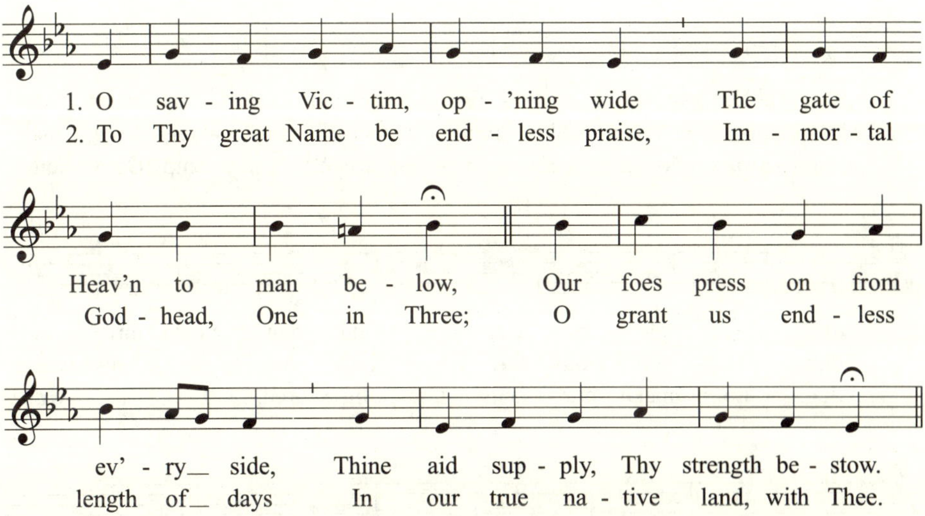

* Many other melodies and translations can be used, or this hymn may be sung in Latin. Search the index for *Verbum Supernum Prodiens* by St. Thomas Aquinas (d. 1274).

Shortly before the blessing with the Sanctissimum:

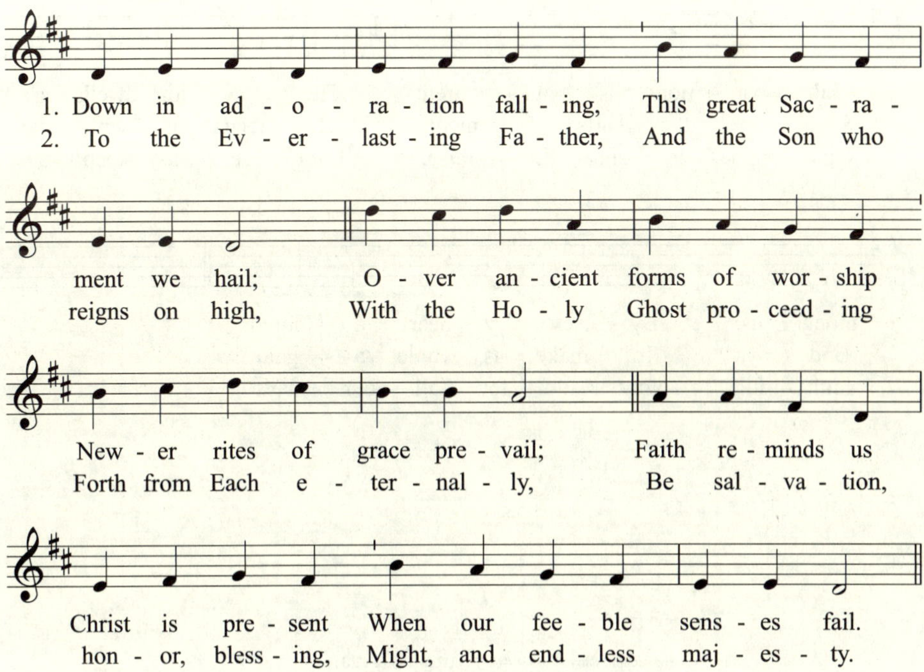

* Many other melodies and translations can be used, or this hymn may be sung in Latin. Search the index for *Pange Lingua Gloriosi* by St. Thomas Aquinas (d. 1274).

740 Behold Our Lord Transfigured

First Tune – *Fr. Christopher G. Phillips (b. 1949)*

1. Be - hold our Lord trans - fig - ured, In Sac - ra - ment Di -
2. No long - er on the moun - tain With Pe - ter, James and
3. With Mo - ses and E - li - jah, We wor - ship Christ our

vine; His glo - ry deep - ly hid - den, 'Neath forms of
John, Our pre - cious Sav - ior bids us To walk where
King; Lord, make our souls trans - fig - ured, Let us with

Bread and Wine. Our eyes of faith be - hold Him,
saints have gone. He has no last - ing dwell - ing,
an - gels sing. Lead us in paths of glo - ry,

Sal - va - tion is out - poured; The Sav - ior dwells a -
Save in the hearts of men; He feeds us with His
Give tongues to sing thy praise; Lord Je - sus, keep us

mong us, By ev - 'ry heart a - dored.
Bod - y, To make us whole a - gain.
faith - ful, Now and for all our days.

76 76 D

Tune:
Aurelia

Final Verses: Richard Lloyd (1993) #12; Noel Rawsthorne (2011) #28.
Melody: Samuel Sebastian Wesley (d. 1876), organist at Hereford Cathedral.
M. Source: *Catholic Hymn Book* (London Oratory, 1998) p. 322. The tune name comes from *Urbs Sion Aurea*, as Wesley wrote it for Neale's famous translation: "Jerusalem the Golden." Cf. Wesley's *Collection of Hymn Tunes; Selected from British and Foreign Sources with Harmonies* (London: Novello, 1872) p. 341.
T. Source: *Saint Jean de Brébeuf Hymnal* (2018).

Second Tune – *Fr. Christopher G. Phillips (b. 1949)*

Final Verses: Richard Lloyd (1993) #108; Noel Rawsthorne (2011) #175.
Melody: English Folk Tune.
M. Source: *Catholic Hymn Book* (London Oratory, 1998) p. 428.
T. Source: *Saint Jean de Brébeuf Hymnal* (2018).

76 76 D

Tune:
King's Lynn

742 Behold Our Lord Transfigured

Third Tune – *Fr. Christopher G. Phillips (b. 1949)*

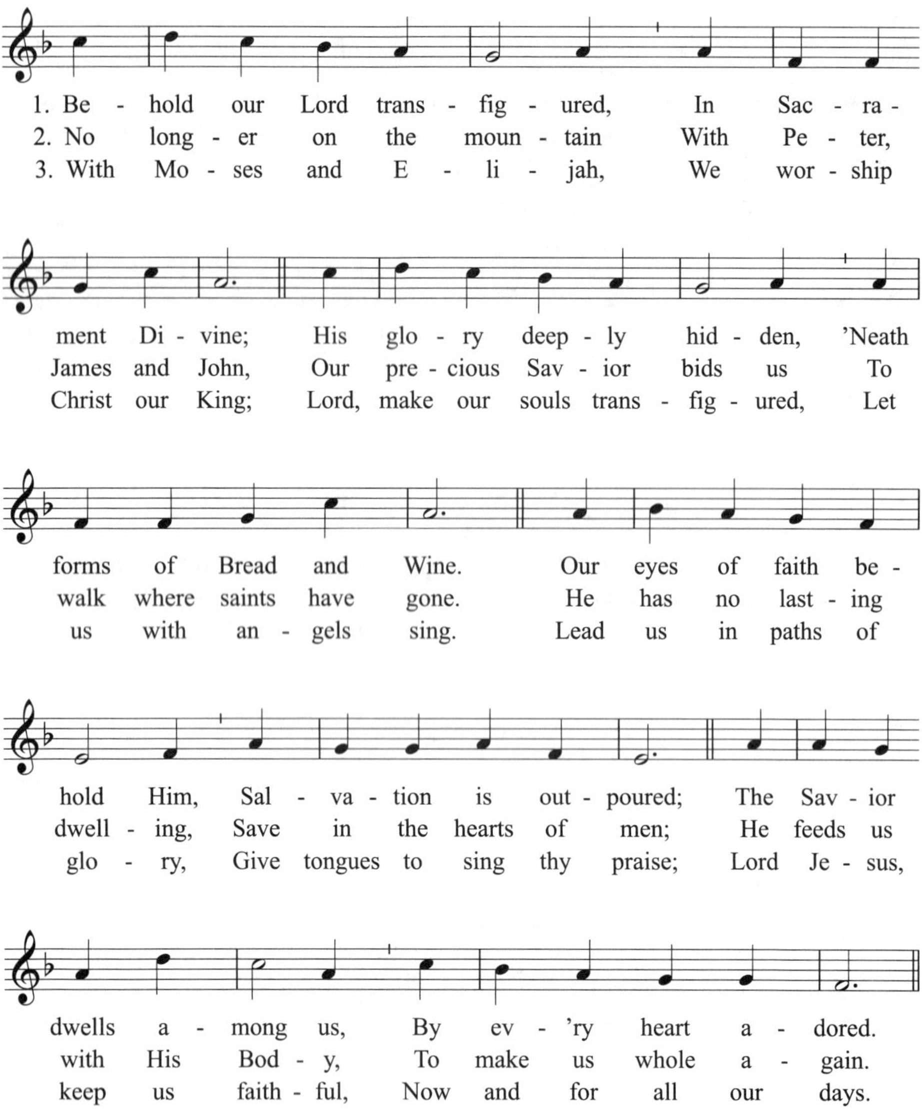

76 76 D

Tune:
Crüger

Final Verses: Richard Lloyd (1993) #48; Noel Rawsthorne (2011) #81.
Melody: Johann Crüger (d. 1662), choirmaster of St. Nicholas' Church, Berlin.
M. Source: *New Westminster Hymnal* (1939) p. 256; *Catholic Hymn Book* (London Oratory, 1998) p. 4.
T. Source: *Saint Jean de Brébeuf Hymnal* (2018).

Behold Our Lord Transfigured 743

Fr. Christopher G. Phillips (b. 1949)

Can be sung with any 76 76 D meter, such as: PEARSALL, PASSION CHORALE, EWING, KING'S LYNN, AURELIA, ST THEODULPH, CRÜGER, WOODBIRD, etc.

BEHOLD our Lord transfigured,
In Sacrament Divine;
His glory deeply hidden,
'Neath forms of Bread and Wine.
Our eyes of faith behold Him,
Salvation is outpoured;
The Savior dwells among us,
By ev'ry heart adored.

2. No longer on the mountain
With Peter, James and John,
Our precious Savior bids us
To walk where saints have gone.
He has no lasting dwelling,
Save in the hearts of men;
He feeds us with His Body,
To make us whole again.

3. With Moses and Elijah,
We worship Christ our King;
Lord, make our souls transfigured,
Let us with angels sing.
Lead us in paths of glory,
Give tongues to sing thy praise;
Lord Jesus, keep us faithful,
Now and for all our days.

* This text is excellent for use on the Second Sunday of Lent (Ordinary Form), when the Gospel recounts the Transfiguation, and can be sung to the tune of PASSION CHORALE.

T. Source: *Saint Jean de Brébeuf Hymnal* (2018).

76 76 D

Tune: VARIOUS

744 Quicumque Christum Quaeritis (4th century)

Trns: Fr. John Fitzpatrick, Oblate of Mary (d. 1929)

4. His witnesses the Prophets are,
And, therewithal, from Heav'n ajar,
His Father's witness we receive,
Who bids us hear Him and believe.

5. Be glory, Jesus, unto Thee,
Whom Thou dost let Thy children see,
Whom with the Father we adore
And Holy Ghost, for evermore.

This hymn is a CENTO from the twelfth poem in the *Cathemerinon* of Prudentius (d. 413AD). It was introduced by Pope Pius V (d. 1572) into the office of the Transfiguration. It originally referred to the Epiphany, which feast traditionally includes: (a) the Magi visit; (b) the miracle at Cana; and (c) our Lord's Baptism (Mt 3.17) where a voice from heaven says: "This is my beloved Son." A literal translation is as follows:

1. All you who look for Christ, lift up your eyes on high, for there you may see a sign of eternal glory.
2. We see a brilliant "Something" that knows no end, exalted, most high and boundless, older than the heavens or the primitive chaos.
3. This is the king of the nations and king of the Jewish race, who was promised to our father Abraham and to his seed for ever.
4. With the prophets as witnesses and signatories, the TESTATOR and FATHER bids us hear Him, and believe.

The Father is styled "Testator" in reference to Ps 2.8 and also the *testimony* (Mt 17.5) given vis-à-vis the Son at the Transfiguration: "a voice said to them out of the cloud, *This is my beloved Son, in whom I am well pleased; to him, then, listen.*"

88 88 (LM)

Tune: DUGUET

Melody: Dieudonné Duguet (d. 1849), organist at the Cathedral in Liège, Belgium, and teacher of César Franck.
M. Source: *Mediator Dei Hymnal* (1955) p. 66; *New Saint Basil Hymnal* (1958) p. 93; *Arundel Catholic Hymnal* (1905) p. 26; *Hymnal and Vesperal* (Archdiocese of Baltimore, 1878) p. 168; *Catholic Vesper Hymn Book set to Music for Unison or Four Voices* (Charles Lewis, 1877) p. 6.
T. Source: *The Breviary and Missal Hymns* (London: Sands & Co, 1931) p. 162.

Quicumque Christum Quaeritis (4th century)

Trns: Robert Campbell of Skerrington (d. 1868)

4. Prophets foretold his birth,
And witnessed when he came,
The Father speaks to all the earth
To hear, and fear his name.

5. To lowly hearts revealed,
Our Savior we adore,
Like tribute to the Father yield,
And Spirit evermore.

This hymn is a Cento from the twelfth poem in the *Cathemerinon* of Prudentius (d. 413AD). It was introduced by Pope Pius V (d. 1572) into the office of the Transfiguration. It originally referred to the Epiphany, which feast traditionally includes: (a) the Magi visit; (b) the miracle at Cana; and (c) our Lord's Baptism (Mt 3.17) where a voice from heaven says: "This is my beloved Son." A literal translation is as follows:

1. All you who look for Christ, lift up your eyes on high, for there you may see a sign of eternal glory.
2. We see a brilliant "Something" that knows no end, exalted, most high and boundless, older than the heavens or the primitive chaos.
3. This is the king of the nations and king of the Jewish race, who was promised to our father Abraham and to his seed for ever.
4. With the prophets as witnesses and signatories, the Testator and Father bids us hear Him, and believe.

The Father is styled "Testator" in reference to Ps 2.8 and also the *testimony* (Mt 17.5) given vis-à-vis the Son at the Transfiguration: "a voice said to them out of the cloud, *This is my beloved Son, in whom I am well pleased; to him, then, listen.*"

Melody: William Henry Walter (d. 1893), organist at Trinity Chapel in New York.
M. Source: *Episcopal Hymnal* (1940) #535.
English Translation: Robert Campbell was a Scottish attorney who published *Hymns and Anthems for Use in the Holy Service of the Church* (1850). He did become a Catholic in 1852, but was never a priest—in spite of the claim made on page 251 in the *American Catholic Hymnal according to the Motu Proprio of His Holiness Pope Pius X* (1913).
T. Source: *The Breviary and Missal Hymns* (London: Sands & Co, 1931) p. 162.

66 86 (SM)
Tune: Festal Song

746 Lux Alma, Jesu, Mentium (12th century)

Bl. John Henry Cardinal Newman, Oratorian (d. 1890)

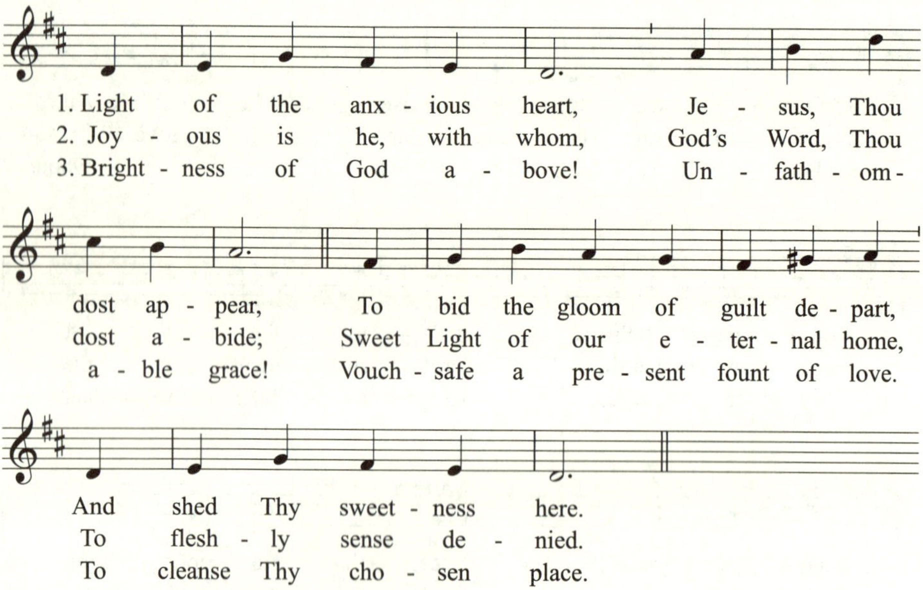

4. To Thee, whom children see,
The Father ever blest,
The Holy Spirit, One and Three,
Be endless praise addressed.

Can be sung with any 66 86 meter: Festal Song, Allington, Seán 8M, Dominica, Southwell, St Michael, Song 20, Potsdam, etc.

LIGHT of the anxious heart,
Jesus, Thou dost appear,
To bid the gloom of guilt depart,
And shed Thy sweetness here.

2. Joyous is he, with whom,
God's Word, Thou dost abide;
Sweet Light of our eternal home,
To fleshly sense denied.

3. Brightness of God above!
Unfathomable grace!
Vouchsafe a present fount of love.
To cleanse Thy chosen place.

4. To Thee, whom children see,
The Father ever blest,
The Holy Spirit, One and Three,
Be endless praise addressed.

Literal Translation: 1. O Jesus, kindly light of our souls, when You bring new life to our hearts, You drive away sin's gloom and fill us with consolation. 2. How happy the man that is host to You, for You are the companion of the Father at His right hand. You are the light that consoles heaven, but is unseen by man on earth. 3. Radiance of the Father's splendor and love unfathomable, bestow on us by Your presence an abundance of love.

66 86 (SM)

Tune: Potsdam

T. Source: *Hymns of the Breviary and Missal* (Fr. Matthew Britt, 1922) p. 285; this text—presumably a later version by Cardinal Newman—is radically different than the 1836 version published in "Tracts for the Times." Melody: Based on the magnificent Fugue in E, *Well-tempered Clavier*, Part II, No. 9, by J. S. Bach (d. 1750). M. Source: *Adoremus Hymnal* (1997) #471; *Songs of Syon* (Woodward, 1910) p. 51.

Blessed Lamb, On Calvary's Mountain

Matthew Bridges (d. 1894), a disciple of Cardinal Newman

Final Verses: Richard Lloyd (1993) #169; Noel Rawsthorne (2011) #258.
Melody: John Goss (d. 1880), Professor of Harmony at the Royal Academy of Music.
M. Source: *New Saint Basil Hymnal* (1958) p. 202; *Hymns, Psalms, and Spiritual Canticles* (1983) p. 294.
T. Source: *Lyra Catholica: Containing All the Hymns of the Roman Breviary and Missal* (New York, 1851) p. 369.

87 87 87
Tune:
LAUDA ANIMA

748 Quis Est Iste Qui Venit De Edom? (Isaias 63)

Fr. Dominic Popplewell (b. 1973)

87 87 87 87 87 87

Tune:
Ecclesia

T. Source: *Saint Jean de Brébeuf Hymnal* (2018).
Melody: Sir Richard R. Terry (d. 1938), choirmaster at Westminster Cathedral.
M. Source: *New Saint Basil Hymnal* (1958) p. 226; *New Westminster Hymnal* (1939) p. 298; *Our Parish Prays and Sings Hymnbook* (Minnesota: Order of Saint Benedict, 1966) #131.

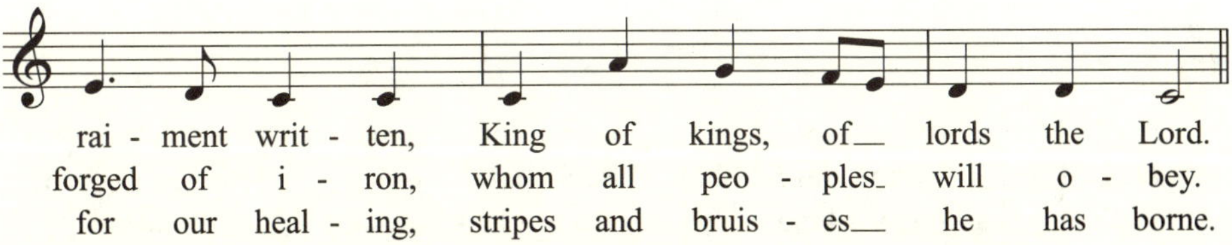

4. He was once devoid of beauty, all his comeliness grown dim,
naught appearing in his visage that would make us pleased with him.
He became a man of sorrows, deeply downcast and despised,
no respect to him accorded, heaven's arm unrecognized.
Like a lamb before the shearer, he contained his every cry,
all our ills and pangs he carried, led at his own will to die.

5. Now his face outshines the daystar, overthrows its blinding gaze;
now his wounds, five suns presenting, all created sight amaze;
now his blood, eternal ransom, testament for evermore,
peace bestowing, pardon bringing, gold and silver renders poor.
Light unbroached his habitation, like a robe that wraps him round,
Light is he, the world who made, in whom the world salvation found.

[1d] Is 63.1
[1f] Ap 19.11-16; Hb 4.12
[2d] Is 63.2-3; Ap 19.13-15
[2f] Ap 2.27, 12.5, 19.12, 15; Ps 2.9
[3f] Zc 13.6-7; Is 53.5-6
[4f] Is 53.1-4, 7
[5a] Ap 1.16
[5c] Eph 1.7; Hb 9.12, 12.24, 13.20
[5d] Col 1.14, 20; Hb 9.14, I Pt 1.18-19
[5e] I Tm 6.16; Ps 103.2
[5f] Jn 1.9-10, 4.42; I Jn 4.14

750 Quicumque Certum Quaeritis (18th century)

Trns: Fr. Edward Caswall, Oratorian (d. 1878)

1. All ye who seek a— com - fort sure In trou - ble
2. Je - sus, who gave him - self for you Up - on the
3. Ye hear how kind - ly— he in - vites; Ye hear his

and dis - tress, What - ev - er sor - rows vex the mind,
Cross to die, O - pens to you his Sa - cred Heart;
words so blest; "All ye that la - bor, come to me,

Or guilt the soul op - press:
Oh, to that Heart draw nigh.
And I will give you rest."

4. What meeker than the Savior's Heart?
As on the Cross he lay,
It did his murderers forgive
And for their pardon pray.

5. O Heart, thou joy of saints on high,
Thou hope of sinners here!
Attracted by those loving words,
To thee I lift my prayer.

6. Wash thou my wounds in that dear Blood
Which forth from thee doth flow;
New grace, new hope inspire; a new
And better heart bestow.

86 86 (CM)

Tune:
St Bernard

Text: Vespers hymn for the Sacred Heart.
T. Source: *Catholic Hymn Book* (London Oratory, 1998) p. 222.
Melody: Based on a tune in *Tochter Sion* (Cologne, 1741).
M. Source: *New Westminster Hymnal* (1939) p. 119.

Summi Parentis Filio (18th century) 751

Trns: Fr. Edward Caswall, Oratorian (d. 1878)

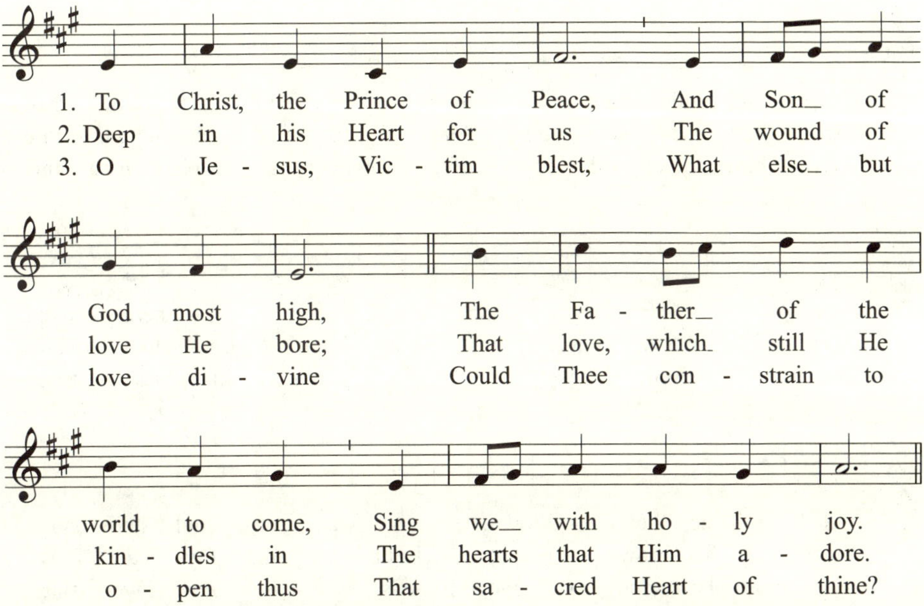

4. O Fount of endless life,
O Spring of waters clear,
O Flame celestial, cleansing all
Who unto Thee draw near!

5. Praise to the Father be;
Praise to his only Son;
Praise to the blessèd Paraclete,
While endless ages run.

Can be sung with any 66 86 meter: Festal Song, Allington, Seán 8M, Dominica, Southwell, St Michael, Song 20, Potsdam, etc.

To Christ, the Prince of Peace,
And Son of God most high,
The Father of the world to come,
Sing we with holy joy.

2. Deep in his Heart for us
The wound of love He bore;
That love, which still He kindles in
The hearts that Him adore.

3. O Jesus, Victim blest,
What else but love divine
Could Thee constrain to open thus
That sacred Heart of thine?

4. O Fount of endless life,
O Spring of waters clear,
O Flame celestial, cleansing all
Who unto Thee draw near!

5. Praise to the Father be;
Praise to his only Son;
Praise to the blessèd Paraclete,
While endless ages run.

66 86 (SM)

Text: Lauds hymn for the Sacred Heart. T. Source: *Adoremus Hymnal* (1998) #471.
Melody: William Henry Walter (d. 1893), organist at Trinity Chapel in New York.
M. Source: *Episcopal Hymnal* (1940) #535.

Tune:
Festal Song

752 Crown Him With Many Crowns

Matthew Bridges (d. 1894), a disciple of Cardinal Newman

4. Crown him the Lord of love,
Behold his hands and side,
Those wounds yet visible above
In beauty glorified:
No angel in the sky
Can fully bear that sight,
But downward bends his burning eye
At mysteries so bright.

5. Crown him the Lord of heav'n,
Enthroned in worlds above;
Crown him the King, to whom is giv'n
The wondrous name of Love;
Crown him with many crowns,
As thrones before him fall.
Crown him, ye kings, with many crowns,
For he is King of all.

S. M. D.

Tune:
Diademata

T. Source: *New Saint Basil Hymnal* (1958) p. 83.
Melody: George J. Elvey (d. 1893), organist at St George's Chapel at Windsor Castle.
M. Source: *Hymns, Psalms, and Spiritual Canticles* (Massachusetts: Theodore Marier, 1983) p. 232.

Te Saeculorum Principem (Christ the King)

Trns: Fr. John Fitzpatrick, Oblate of Mary (d. 1929)

4. For this, upon the grisly Tree | Thou hangest, with Thine arms outspread,
The spear-thrust showing cruelly | Thy Heart wherein love's fires are red.

5. For this, like bread and wine indeed, | Upon our altars Thou dost hide,
Outpouring, for Thy children's need, | Salvation from Thy wounded side.

6. With honors, public as the skies, | Let heads of nations Thee confess,
Let judge and statesman learn to prize, | And laws and all the arts express.

7. Let their insignia anew | Shine forth when kings to Thee submit,
And may Thy scepter meek subdue | Our country, and our homes, to it.

8. O'er every earthly mastery | 'Tis Thine, O Jesus, to preside:
With Father and with Spirit be | For endless ages glorified.

Fifth Verse • *Literally:* "For this, Thou art hidden on our altars under the form of bread and wine, and pour out on Thy children from Thy pierced side the grace of salvation."

Sixth Verse • *Literally:* "May the world's rulers publicly honor and extol Thee; may teachers and judges reverence Thee, may the laws express Thine order, and the arts reflect Thy beauty."

Text: Composed when the feast of Christ the King was instituted (12 December 1925) by Fr. Vittorio Genovési, (d. 1967), hymnographer of the Sacred Congregation of Rites from 1942 until his death.
T. Source: *The Breviary and Missal Hymns* (London: Sands & Co, 1931) p. 184.
Melody: Philip Hart (d. 1749), organist at St. Michael Church, Cornhill.
M. Source: *Hymns Ancient and Modern* (1972) p. 8; cf. *Church Hymns With Tunes* (1885) p. 230, edited by Sir Arthur Sullivan (d. 1900), organist at St. Peter Church, Kensington.

88 88 (LM)

Tune: Hilderstone

754 Hail Redeemer, King Divine

First Tune – *Fr. Patrick Brennan, Redemptorist* (*d.* 1951)

4. Crimson streams, O King of grace,
Drenched thy thorn-crowned head and face;
Floods of love's redeeming tide
Tore thy hands, thy feet, and side. *R. Angels, etc.*

5. Eucharistic King, what love
Draws thee daily from above,
Clad in signs of bread and wine:
Feed us, lead us, keep us thine! *R. Angels, etc.*

6. King, whose name creation thrills,
Rule our minds, our hearts, our wills,
Till in peace each nation rings
With thy praises, King of kings. *R. Angels, etc.*

77 77 D

Tune: St George

Final Verses: Richard Lloyd (1993) #197; Noel Rawsthorne (2011) #303.
Melody: George J. Elvey (d. 1893), organist at St George's Chapel at Windsor Castle.
M. Source: *Catholic Hymn Book* (1998) p. 120; *New Westminster Hymnal* (1939) p. 88; *Hymns, Psalms, and Spiritual Canticles* (Massachusetts: Theodore Marier, 1983) p. 230.
T. Source: *New Westminster Hymnal* (1939) p. 137.

Hail Redeemer, King Divine

Second Tune – *Fr. Patrick Brennan, Redemptorist* (*d.* 1951)

4. Crimson streams, O King of grace,
Drenched thy thorn-crowned head and face;
Floods of love's redeeming tide
Tore thy hands, thy feet, and side. *R. Angels, etc.*

5. Eucharistic King, what love
Draws thee daily from above,
Clad in signs of bread and wine:
Feed us, lead us, keep us thine! *R. Angels, etc.*

6. King, whose name creation thrills,
Rule our minds, our hearts, our wills,
Till in peace each nation rings
With thy praises, King of kings. *R. Angels, etc.*

Melody: Würth's *Katholisches Gesangbuch* (1859).
M. Source: *Cantate Omnes: Hymnal of the Catholic Choirmasters' Guild* (1952) #46.
T. Source: *New Westminster Hymnal* (1939) p. 137.

77 77 D
Tune:
Paschal Lamb

756 Christ Is King Of Earth And Heaven

"What David in his true hymn told to the nations is now fulfilled:
God reigns from the tree."—Vexilla Regis Prodeunt, v3

87 87 D

Tune:
Rustington

Final Verses: Noel Rawsthorne (2011) #278.
Melody: Sir Charles H. H. Parry (d. 1918).
M. Source: *Hymns, Psalms, and Spiritual Canticles* (Massachusetts: Theodore Marier, 1983) p. 439.
Text: Fr. Ivor Daniel (b. 1883), a Catholic priest who served as a military chaplain during the First World War. The date of his death is not known.
T. Source: *New Westminster Hymnal* (1939) p. 136.

Christ Is King Of Earth And Heaven 757

"What David in his true hymn told to the nations is now fulfilled:
God reigns from the tree."—Vexilla Regis Prodeunt, v3

Can be sung with any 87 87 meter: STUTTGART, HALTON HOLGATE, REDHEAD #46, BATTY, WALTHAM, VATICAN, MERTON, CROSS OF JESUS, MARCHING, BRONZEVILLE, etc.

CHRIST is King of earth and heaven,
Let his subjects all proclaim
In the splendor of his temple
Honor to his holy name.

2. Christ is King! No soul created
Can refuse to bend the knee
To the God made Man who reigneth,
As 'twas promised, from the tree.

3. Christ is King! Let humble sorrow
For our past neglect atone,
For the lack of faithful service
To the Master whom we own.

4. Christ is King! Let joy and gladness
Greet him; let his courts resound
With the praise of faithful subjects
To his love in honor bound.

5. Christ is King! In health and sickness,
Till we breathe our latest breath,
Till we greet in highest heaven
Christ the victor over death.

Text: Fr. Ivor Daniel (b. 1883), a Catholic priest who served as a military chaplain during the First World War. The date of his death is not known.
T. Source: *New Westminster Hymnal* (1939) p. 136.

87 87
Tune:
VARIOUS

758 Thee, O Christ, The Prince Of Ages

"If only I am lifted up from the earth, I will draw all men to myself."—Jn 12.32

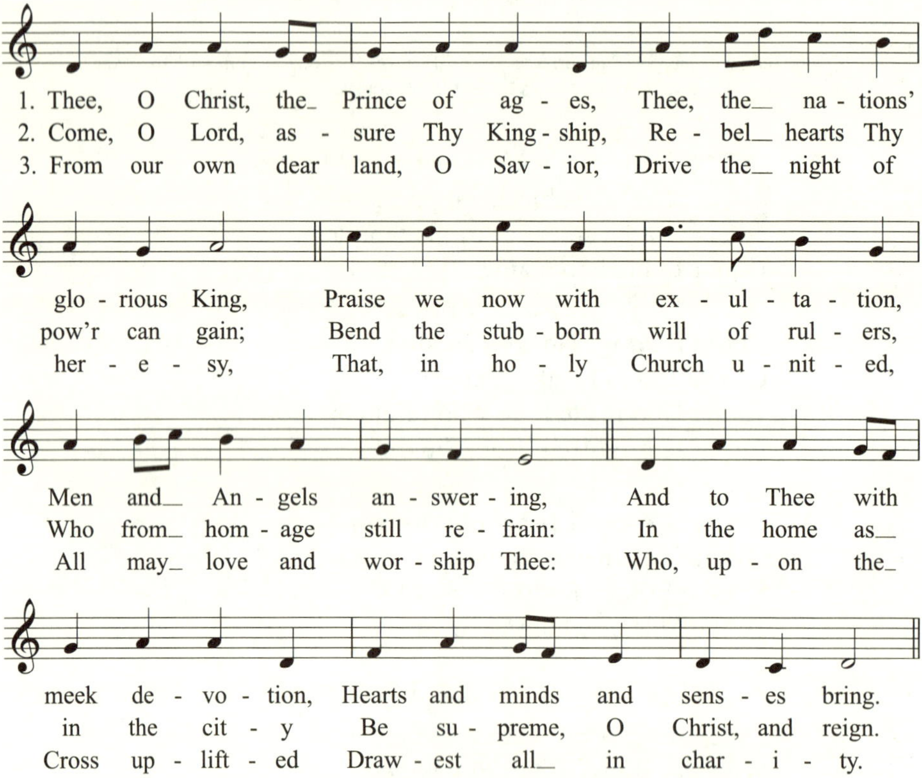

Can be sung with any 87 87 87 meter: RUNNELLS, MANNHEIM, DULCE CARMEN, BRETON, GAUFESTRE, LAUDA ANIMA, DAVOST, ST LEONARD, PICARDY, REGENT SQUARE, etc.

THEE, O Christ, the Prince of ages,
Thee, the nations' glorious King,
Praise we now with exultation,
Men and Angels answering,
And to Thee with meek devotion,
Hearts and minds and senses bring.

2. Come, O Lord, assure Thy Kingship,
Rebel hearts Thy pow'r can gain;
Bend the stubborn will of rulers,
Who from homage still refrain:
In the home as in the city
Be supreme, O Christ, and reign.

3. From our own dear land, O Savior,
Drive the night of heresy,
That, in holy Church united,
All may love and worship Thee:
Who, upon the Cross uplifted
Drawest all in charity.

87 87 87

Tune:
BRETON

Text: Anonymous; as found in the *St. Pius X Hymnal* (Melbourne, 1952) p. 80. This Australian publication—edited by Rev. Dr. Percival Jones (d. 1992), a priest and choirmaster—has nothing to do with the American *Pius X Hymnal*, which appeared a year later.
Melody: Metrical Cento; cf. "Dum staret Abraham" (*Antiphonaire Monastique,* 13th century).
M. Source: *Paléographie musicale* (Volume XII), folio 81; *Cantus Selecti* (Solesmes, 1957) p. 245.

To Jesus Christ, Our Sovereign King 759

Fr. Martin B. Hellriegel (d. 1981)

T. Source: *Saint Michael Hymnal* (St. Boniface Parish, 2011) #800.
Melody: *Mainzer Gesangbuch* (1870).
M. Source: *Traditional Roman Hymnal* (Society of Saint Pius X, 2000) p. 155.

87 87 R Iambic
Tune:
ICH GLAUB AN GOTT

760 Salve Mundi Domina

First Tune – *Trns: Fr. Dominic Popplewell (b. 1973)*

1a. Hail, the world and heav-en's Queen, Rul - ing and re - fin - ing;
2a. By the Lord be - yond all time Thou wert des - ig - nat - ed

Hail, O crown of maid - en - hood, Star at mor - row shin - ing;
Moth - er of his on - ly Word, By whom he cre - at - ed

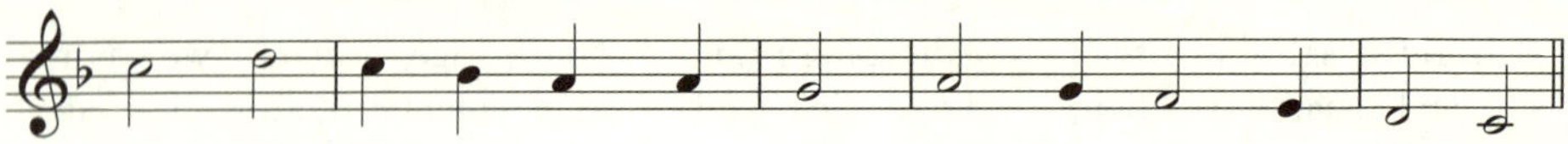

Hail, thou light di - vine - ly bright, Eve - ry grace com - bin - ing:
Land, sea, sky; his beau - teous bride, Whom he dec - o - rat - ed,

Has - ten, La - dy, bring - ing help To a world re - pin - ing.
So that Ad - am's crime to thee Nev - er was re - lat - ed.

The same hymn in the original Latin:

1b. Sal - ve, mun - di Dó - mi - na, Cae - ló - rum Re - gí - na:
2b. Ab ae - tér - no Dó - mi - nus Te prae - or - di - ná - vit

Sal - ve, Vir - go vír - gi - num, Stel - la ma - tu - tí - na.
Ma - trem u - ni - gé - ni - ti Ver - bi, quo cre - á - vit

Sal - ve, ple - na grá - ti - a, Cla - ra lux di - ví - na:
Ter - ram, pon - tum, aé - the - ra: Te pul - chram or - ná - vit

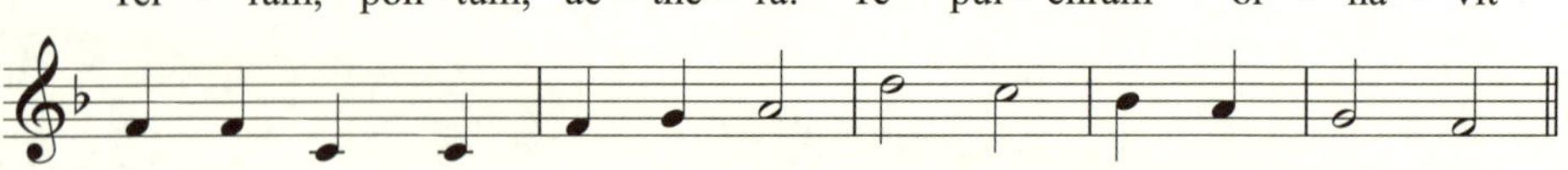

Mun - di in au - xí - li - um, Dó - mi - na, fe - stí - na.
Si - bi spon - sam, A - dá - mus In qua non pec - cá - vit.

76 76 D

Tune:
Ave Virgo Virginum

Final Verses: Richard Lloyd (1993) #15; Noel Rawsthorne (2011) #31.
T. Source: *Vetus Hymnarium Ecclesiasticum Hungariae* (Joseph Dankó, 1893) p. 319; from the Office of the Immaculate Conception of the Blessed Virgin Mary.
Melody: Medieval melody arranged by Johann Roh (d. 1547).
M. Source: Printed in *Catholicum Hymnologium Germanicum* (Leisentritt, 1584).

Salve Mundi Domina 761

SECOND TUNE – *Trns: Fr. Dominic Popplewell (b. 1973)*

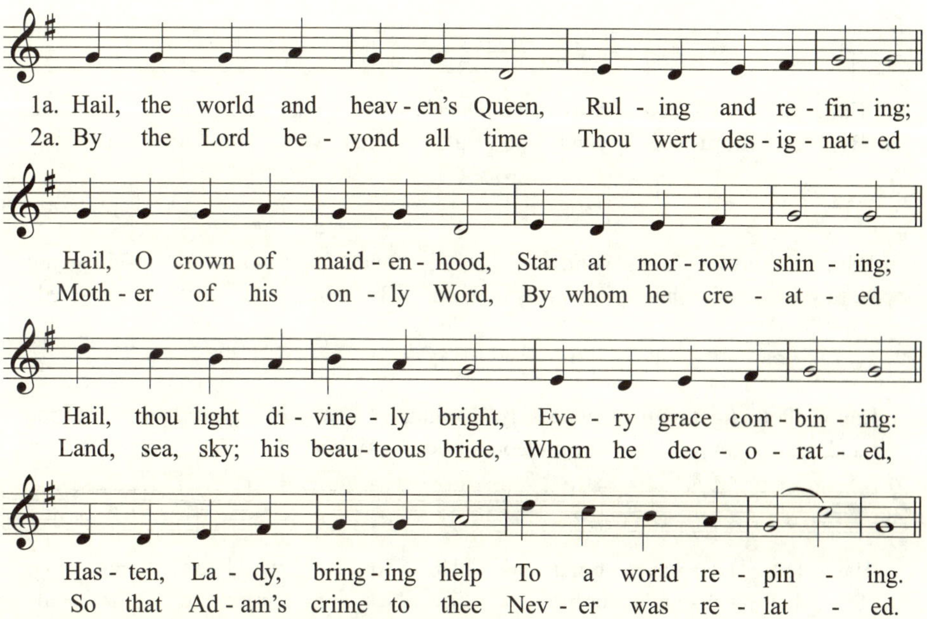

The same hymn in the original Latin:

T. Source: *Vetus Hymnarium Ecclesiasticum Hungariae* (Joseph Dankó, 1893) p. 319; from the Office of the Immaculate Conception of the Blessed Virgin Mary.
M. Source: 13th century Spring song, published in *Piae Cantiones* (Theodoric Petri, 1582); version as found in *The Hymnal* (1940) with a text for Martyrs.

76 76 D
Tune: TEMPUS ADEST FLORIDUM

762 Salve Mundi Domina

THIRD TUNE – *Trns: Fr. Dominic Popplewell (b. 1973)*

1a. Hail, the world and heav - en's Queen, Rul - ing and re - fin - ing;
2a. By the Lord be - yond all time Thou wert des - ig - nat - ed

Hail, O crown of maid - en - hood, Star at mor - row shin - ing;
Moth - er of his on - ly Word, By whom he cre - at - ed

Hail, thou light di - vine - ly bright, Eve - ry grace com - bin - ing:
Land, sea, sky; his beau - teous bride, Whom he dec - o - rat - ed,

Has - ten, La - dy, bring - ing help To a world re - pin - ing.
So that Ad - am's crime to thee Nev - er was re - lat - ed.

The same hymn in the original Latin:

1b. Sal - ve, mun - di Dó - mi - na, Cae - ló - rum Re - gí - na:
2b. Ab ae - tér - no Dó - mi - nus Te prae - or - di - ná - vit

Sal - ve, Vir - go vír - gi - num, Stel - la ma - tu - tí - na.
Ma - trem u - ni - gé - ni - ti Ver - bi, quo cre - á - vit

Sal - ve, ple - na grá - ti - a, Cla - ra lux di - ví - na:
Ter - ram, pon - tum, aé - the - ra: Te pul - chram or - ná - vit

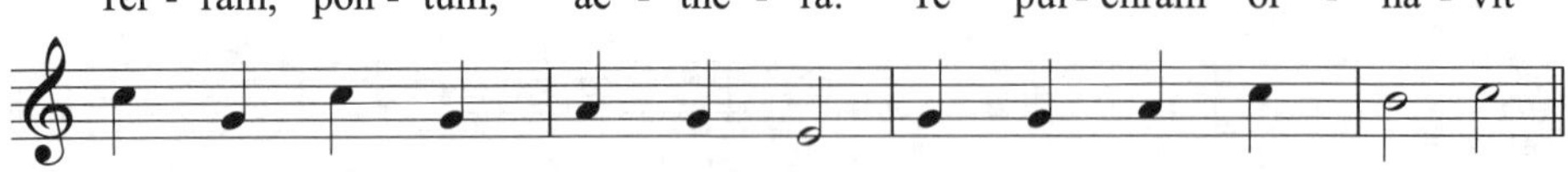

Mun - di in au - xí - li - um, Dó - mi - na, fe - stí - na.
Si - bi spon - sam, A - dá - mus In qua non pec - cá - vit.

76 76 D

Tune:
CHRISTUS CHRISTUS CHRISTUS IST

Melody: Peter Franck (d. 1675), first published in 1657.
M. Source: *Choral Harmony* (London: G. H. Davidson, 1854) #203.
T. Source: *Vetus Hymnarium Ecclesiasticum Hungariae* (Joseph Dankó, 1893) p. 319; from the Office of the Immaculate Conception of the Blessed Virgin Mary.

Fourth Tune – *Trns: Fr. Dominic Popplewell (b. 1973)*

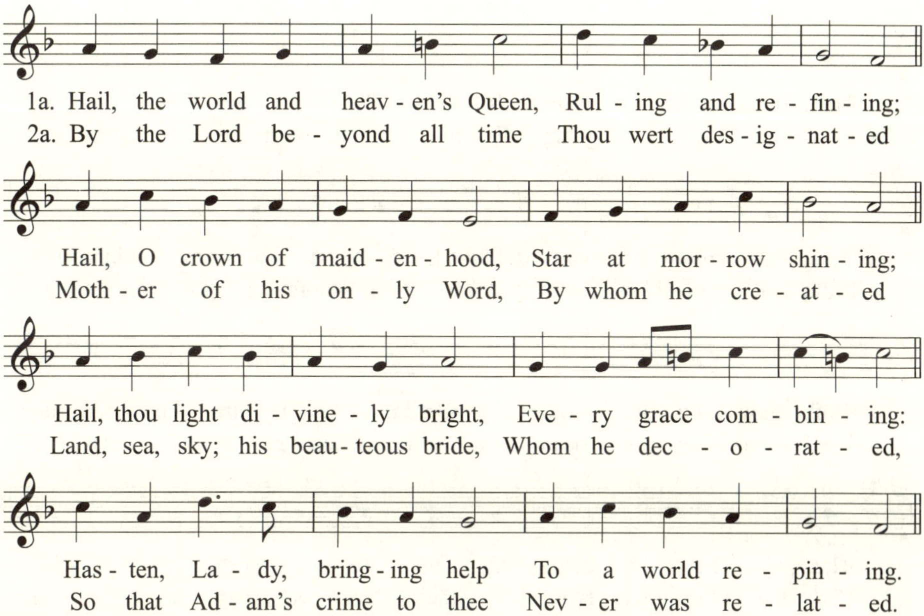

The same hymn in the original Latin:

Melody: Melchior Vulpius (d. 1615).
M. Source: *Songs of Syon* (Woodward, 1910) p. 567; cf. *Ein schön geistlich Gesangbuch* (1609).
T. Source: *Vetus Hymnarium Ecclesiasticum Hungariae* (Joseph Dankó, 1893) p. 319; from the Office of the Immaculate Conception of the Blessed Virgin Mary.

76 76 D

Tune:
Jesu Leiden Pein Und Tod

764 Salve Mundi Domina

Fifth Tune – *Trns: Fr. Dominic Popplewell (b. 1973)*

1a. Hail, the_ world and heav-en's Queen, Rul - ing and re - fin-ing;
2a. By the_ Lord be - yond all time Thou wert des - ig - nat-ed

Hail, O_ crown of maid-en-hood, Star at mor-row shin - ing;
Moth-er_ of his on - ly Word, By whom he cre - at - ed

Hail, thou light di - vine - ly bright, Eve - ry grace com-bin-ing:
Land, sea, sky; his beau-teous bride, Whom he dec - o - rat-ed,

Has-ten, La - dy, bring-ing help To a world re - pin-ing.
So that Ad-am's crime to thee Nev - er was re - lat-ed.

The same hymn in the original Latin:

1b. Sal-ve,_ mun-di Dó-mi-na, Cae - ló - rum Re - gí - na:
2b. Ab ae - tér - no Dó-mi-nus Te prae - or - di - ná - vit

Sal - ve,_ Vir - go vír - gi - num, Stel - la ma - tu - tí - na.
Ma-trem u - ni - gé - ni - ti Ver - bi, quo cre - á - vit

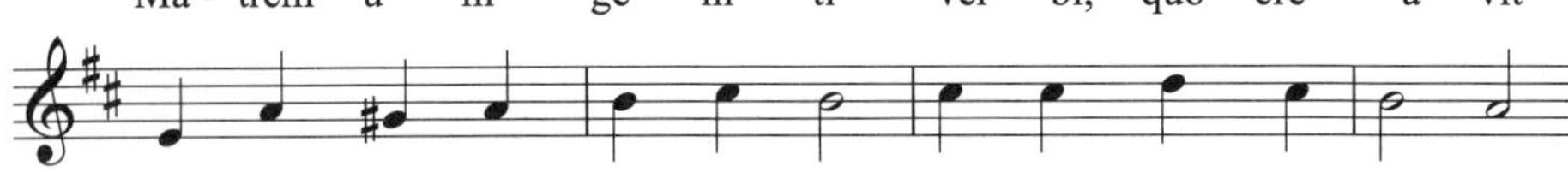

Sal - ve, ple - na grá - ti - a, Cla - ra lux di - ví - na:
Ter - ram, pon-tum, aé - the - ra: Te pul-chram or - ná - vit

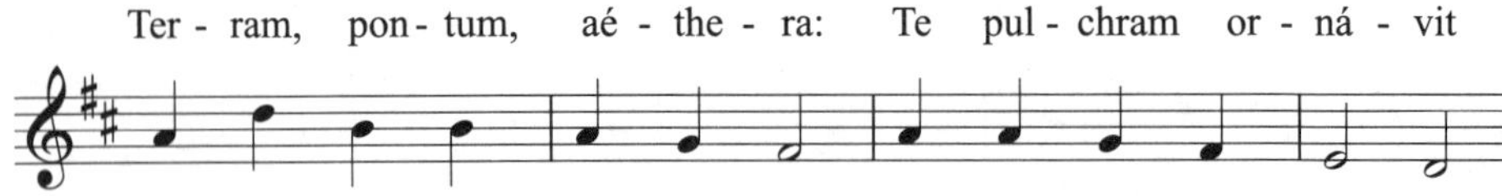

Mun-di in au - xí - li - um, Dó - mi - na, fe - stí - na.
Si - bi spon-sam, A - dá-mus In qua non pec - cá - vit.

76 76 D

Tune:
Ach Wie Kurz

Melody: J. H. Reiman, first published in 1747.
M. Source: *New Westminster Hymnal* (1939) p. 81.
T. Source: *Vetus Hymnarium Ecclesiasticum Hungariae* (Joseph Dankó, 1893) p. 319; from the Office of the Immaculate Conception of the Blessed Virgin Mary.

Pure Virgin, Hear Our Song Today

Fr. Dylan Schrader (b. 1985)

4. Your mystic Unicorn now lays
His Head upon your lap and sighs,
Dear Maiden, as with doleful gaze
He spies the huntsmen drawing nigh.

5. Unblemished Ewe, whose spotless Lamb
Was slain to spare a sinful race,
Guide freedmen to the promised land,
Where we shall see Him face to face.

Verse 1 • A golden urn held the manna from heaven (Heb 9:4) and is thus an image of Mary, who bore the true Bread from Heaven (Jn 6.32,35). Gideon's fleece (Jgs 6.36-40), which was miraculously covered with dew while all the ground was dry, is also an image of Mary, who conceived the Word from above (cf. Is 45.8; 55.10-11) while remaining a Virgin. The burning bush (Ex 3.2), on fire with God's presence but not itself burned up, is a symbol of Mary's virginity in childbirth.

Verse 2 • "The knot of Eve's disobedience was untied by Mary's obedience." -St. Irenaeus, *Against Heresies* III.22.4.

Verse 3 • *Turris draconi impervia* from the hymn *Praeclara custos virginum* of the Breviary for the Immaculate Conception. The tower rises up from the earth to show Mary's descent from Adam, but her resistance to the dragon bespeaks her sinlessness (Gen 3.15; Rev 12.13); "Where sin has abounded, grace has super-abounded" (Rom 5.20).

Verse 4 • Ancient lore held that unicorns were too fierce to be captured by force. If, however, a virgin awaited one in a forest or garden, the unicorn, taken by her beauty, would come and lay its head in her lap. Hunters could then kill it. Christians saw this as an allegory for Christ's Incarnation, when, drawn by love, the divine Word came to rest in the Virgin Mary's womb and let himself be slain by men.

Verse 5 • Melito of Sardis, in an Easter homily from the second century, refers to Mary as the "fair ewe." The rest of this verse applies imagery from the Passover to Christ's paschal mystery and our hope of eternal life.

Final Verses: Richard Lloyd (1993) #64; Noel Rawsthorne (2011) #108.
Melody: Bartholomäus Gesius (d. 1613); adapted by Johann H. Schein (d. 1630).
M. Source: *New Saint Basil Hymnal* (1958) p. 120; *Pope Pius XII Hymnal* (Ohio: Gregorian Institute of America, 1959) p. 13.
T. Source: *Saint Jean de Brébeuf Hymnal* (2018).

88 88 (LM)

Tune: EISENACH

766 Vergine Madre, Figlia Del Tuo Figlio (14th century)

Trns: Msgr. Ronald A. Knox (d. 1957)

1. Maid - en, yet a Moth - er, Daugh - ter of thy Son,
2. Thus his place pre - par - èd, He who all things made
3. Noon on Si - on's moun - tain Is thy char - i - ty;

High be - yond all oth - er— Low - li - er is none;
'Mid his crea - tures tar - ried, In thy bos - om laid;
Hope its liv - ing foun - tain Finds, on earth, in thee:

Thou the con - sum - ma - tion Planned by God's de - cree,
There his love he nour - ished,— Warmth that gave in - crease
La - dy, such thy pow - er, He, who grace would buy

When our lost cre - a - tion Nobl - er rose in thee!
To the Root whence flour - ished Our e - ter - nal peace.
Not as of thy dow - er, With - out wings would fly.

4. Nor alone thou hearest
When thy name we hail;
Often thou art nearest
When our voices fail;
Mirrored in thy fashion
All creation's good,
Mercy, might, compassion
Grace thy womanhood.

5. Lady, lest our vision,
Striving heav'nward, fail,
Still let thy petition
With thy Son prevail,
Unto whom all merit,
Pow'r and majesty
With the Holy Spirit
And the Father be.

Verse 3 • The charity of the Blessed Virgin shines like midday on Mount Sion; she is the living spring of faith on earth; her power is such that any one who sought grace through a channel other than herself would be like one trying to fly without wings. (The second part refers to Mary's role as Mediatrix of all graces.) Cf. Encyclical of Pope Leo XIII *Jucunda Semper Expectatione* (8 September 1894) para. 2.

65 65 D

Tune:
UNE VAINE CRAINTE

Melody: Traditional French Noël.
M. Source: *Adoremus Hymnal* (1997) #540; *New Westminster Hymnal* (1939) p. 156.
Text: Dante Alighieri (d. 1321); *Paradiso*, Canto XXXIII "Vergine Madre."
T. Source: *New Westminster Hymnal* (1939) p. 157; *Catholic Hymn Book* (1998) p. 262.

Vergine Madre, Figlia Del Tuo Figlio (14th century) 767

Trns: Msgr. Ronald A. Knox (d. 1957)

Can be sung with any 65 65 D meter: ANIMA CHRISTI, LAUDES, CUDDESDON, FIORILLO, SWAHILI, UNE VAINE CRAINTE, ADORO TE (Plainsong), KING'S WESTON, ST RITA, etc.

MAIDEN, yet a Mother,
Daughter of thy Son,
High beyond all other—
Lowlier is none;
Thou the consummation | Planned by God's decree,
When our lost creation | Nobler rose in thee!

2. Thus his place preparèd, | He who all things made
'Mid his creatures tarried, | In thy bosom laid;
There his love he nourished,— | Warmth that gave increase
To the Root whence flourished | Our eternal peace.

3. Noon on Sion's mountain | Is thy charity;
Hope its living fountain | Finds, on earth, in thee:
Lady, such thy power, | He, who grace would buy
Not as of thy dower, | Without wings would fly.

4. Nor alone thou hearest | When thy name we hail;
Often thou art nearest | When our voices fail;
Mirrored in thy fashion | All creation's good,
Mercy, might, compassion | Grace thy womanhood.

5. Lady, lest our vision, | Striving heav'nward, fail,
Still let thy petition | With thy Son prevail,
Unto whom all merit, | Pow'r and majesty
With the Holy Spirit | And the Father be.

Verse 3 • The charity of the Blessed Virgin shines like midday on Mount Sion; she is the living spring of faith on earth; her power is such that any one who sought grace through a channel other than herself would be like one trying to fly without wings. (The second part refers to Mary's role as Mediatrix of all graces.) Cf. Encyclical of Pope Leo XIII *Jucunda Semper Expectatione* (8 September 1894) para. 2.

65 65 D

Text: Dante Alighieri (d. 1321); *Paradiso*, Canto XXXIII "Vergine Madre."
T. Source: *New Westminster Hymnal* (1939) p. 157; *Catholic Hymn Book* (1998) p. 262.

Tune: VARIOUS

768 Omni Die, Dic Mariae (12th century)

Trns: Fr. Henry Bittleston, Oratorian (d. 1886)

4. All my senses, heart, affections,
Strive to sound her glory forth:
Spread abroad the sweet memorials
Of the Virgin's priceless worth.
Where the voice of music thrilling,
Where the tongue of eloquence,
That can utter hymns beseeming
All her matchless excellence?

5. All our graces flow from Mary;
All then join her praise to sing:
Fairest work of all creation,
Mother of creation's King.
Sing in songs of peace unending,
Call upon her lovingly:
Seat of wisdom, Gate of heaven,
Morning star upon the sea.

This Latin text (*Omni die, dic Mariae*) is known as the "Prayer of Saint Casimir" because it was found underneath St. Casimir's incorrupt body when his grave was opened in 1604; but it is attributed to Bernard of Cluny. Fr. Bittleston's translation was published as #35 in *Oratory Hymns* (1854) just four years after he joined the Oratory of St. Philip Neri at Birmingham. Many of Cardinal Newman's disciples (Fr. Oakeley, Fr. Caswall, Fr. Bittleston) attempted to translate sections of this Latin poem, which is quite lengthy. Some translators, such as Nicholas Cardinal Wiseman (d. 1865), kept the original meter—a daunting task!
Melody: Henri Frederick Hemy (d. 1888), a Catholic organist and publisher of hymnals.
M. Source: *Mediator Dei Hymnal* (1955) p. 72; *Saint Edmund Campion Missal and Hymnal* (2013) p. 912.

87 87 D

Tune:
Laudes Mariae

Omni Die, Dic Mariae (12th century) 769

Trns: Fr. Henry Bittleston, Oratorian (d. 1886)

Can be sung with any 87 87 D meter: Rustington, Domhnach Trionoide, Hyfrydol, Abbot's Leigh, Austria, Pleading Savior, Rex Gloriae, Hymn To Joy, etc.

DAILY, daily, sing to Mary,
Sing, my soul, her praises due;
All her feasts, her actions honor,
With the heart's devotion true.
Lost in wond'ring contemplation
Be her majesty confessed:
Call her Mother, call her Virgin,
Happy Mother, Virgin blest!

2. She is mighty in her pleading, | Tender in her loving care;
Ever watchful, understanding, | All our sorrows she will share.
Advocate and loving mother, | Mediatrix of all grace:
Heaven's blessings she dispenses | On our sinful human race.

3. Sing, my tongue, the Virgin's trophies, | Who for us our Maker bore;
For the curse of old inflicted, | Peace and blessing to restore.
Sing in songs of praise unending, | Sing the world's majestic Queen;
Weary not nor faint in telling | All the gifts she gives to men.

4. All my senses, heart, affections, | Strive to sound her glory forth:
Spread abroad the sweet memorials | Of the Virgin's priceless worth.
Where the voice of music thrilling, | Where the tongue of eloquence,
That can utter hymns beseeming | All her matchless excellence?

5. All our graces flow from Mary; | All then join her praise to sing:
Fairest work of all creation, | Mother of creation's King.
Sing in songs of peace unending, | Call upon her lovingly:
Seat of wisdom, Gate of heaven, | Morning star upon the sea.

This Latin text (*Omni die, dic Mariae*) is known as the "Prayer of Saint Casimir" because it was found underneath St. Casimir's incorrupt body when his grave was opened in 1604; but it is attributed to Bernard of Cluny. Fr. Bittleston's translation was published as #35 in *Oratory Hymns* (1854) just four years after he joined the Oratory of St. Philip Neri at Birmingham. Many of Cardinal Newman's disciples (Fr. Oakeley, Fr. Caswall, Fr. Bittleston) attempted to translate sections of this Latin poem, which is quite lengthy. Some translators, such as Nicholas Cardinal Wiseman (d. 1865), kept the original meter—a daunting task!

87 87 D

Tune: Various

770 Per Te Mundus Laetabundus (12th century)

Trns: Fr. Edward Caswall, Oratorian (d. 1878)

Text: Excerpt from the "Prayer of Saint Casimir," a Latin hymn of tremendous length attributed to Bernard of Cluny. A literal translation of the first section is:

Through you the world, full of joy, shines with new light, | Divested of the dark mist of ancient shadows.

Now the needy are powerful, as long ago you had said, | And they have become full, as you had prophesied.

The "Prayer of Saint Casimir" is also the source of *Omni die dic Mariae* and many other hymns.

87 87 D

Tune:
DOMHNACH TRIONOIDE

Melody: Traditional Gaelic. M. Source: *The Pius X Hymnal* (1953) p. 158.
T. Source: *Saint Edmund Campion Missal and Hymnal* (2013) p. 916.

Mater Facta, Sed Intacta (12th century)

"O happy Mother, O ever-stainless Virgin, thou art the glorious Queen of the world: intercede on our behalf with him who is the Lord of all."

Text: Bernard of Cluny, a 12th-century Benedictine monk. This short excerpt is from a long poem which employs a fascinating rhyme scheme. Consider the second stanza:

> *Per te mundus | laetabundus, | Novo fulget lumine, | Antiquarum | tenebrarum | Exutus caligine.*
> *Nunc potentes | sunt egentes, | Sicut olim dixeras: | Et egeni | fiunt pleni, | Ut tu prophetaveras.*

87 87 D

English Translation: By the editors, based on Thomas Isaac Ball (d. 1916).
Melody: Ludwig van Beethoven (d. 1827), composed for his *Ninth Symphony* (1824).
M. Source: *Hymns, Psalms, and Spiritual Canticles* (Massachusetts: Theodore Marier, 1983) p. 325.

Tune: Hymn To Joy

772 Maria Durch Ein' Dornwald Ging (Carol)

Trns: Fr. Dominic Popplewell (b. 1973)

4. Who has redeemed the world alone?
Kyrieleison!
The little Christ Child this has done,
he has redeemed the world alone:
Jesus Christ and Mary.

85 88 6

Tune:
MARIA DURCH

Text and Melody: Traditional German, c. 1850.
T. Source: *Saint Jean de Brébeuf Hymnal* (2018).

O Gloriosa Femina (6th century) 773

Venantius Fortunatus, Bishop of Poitiers (d. 609AD)

4. O Jesus, Virgin-born, to thee
Eternal praise and glory be,
Whom with the Father we adore
And Holy Spirit, evermore.

Final Verses: Richard Lloyd (1993) #244; Noel Rawsthorne (2011) #392.
Melody: Georg Wittwe's *Musikalisches Handbuch der Geistlichen Melodien* (Hamburg, 1690).
M. Source: *Episcopal Hymnal* (1940) ABAB #548; *New Saint Basil Hymnal* (1958) p. 1.
Text: *O Gloriosa Femina* was originally the second half of *Quem Terra, Pontus, Aethera*. The *Catholic Hymnal for the United States* (1807) includes the complete poem by Fortunatus; cf. page 392.
ENGLISH TRANSLATION: Percy Dearmer (d. 1936), who assisted in the compilation of *The English Hymnal With Tunes* (1906) and *The Oxford Book of Carols* (1928).
T. Source: *The English Hymnal With Tunes* (London, 1906) p. 313.

88 88 (LM)

Tune: WINCHESTER NEW

774 Te Gestientem Gaudiis (Most Holy Rosary)

Fr. Augustine Thomas Ricchini, Dominican (d. 1779)

4. Refulgent in His triumphing,
And in the Spirit's tongues of flame:
Lit with the splendors of the King,
All nations praise thy glorious name.

5. O come, ye nations, roses bring,
Culled from these mysteries divine,
And for the Mother of your King
With loving hands your chaplets twine.

6. We lay our homage at Thy feet,
Lord Jesus, Thou the Virgin's Son,
With Father and with Paraclete,
Reigning while endless ages run.

This hymn summarizes the traditional Rosary mysteries:

Verse 1 • *lit. translation*: "Virgin mother, we sing of the times when joy filled your soul or sorrow wounded your heart, and of the eternity that robes you with glory."

Verse 2 • (Joyful) *lit. translation*: "Hail, blessed mother; your joy knew no bounds when you conceived in your womb, visited Elizabeth, gave birth to your Son, offered Him in the temple, and found Him when lost."

Verse 3 • (Sorrowful) *lit. translation*: "Hail, queen of martyrs; full of sorrow, you suffered in your inmost heart all the anguish of the agony in the garden, the scourging, the crowning with thorns and your Son's cross." (Several translators substitute "Chief of martyrs" or even "Queen and Chief of martyrs.")

Verse 4 • (Glorious) *lit. translation*: "Hail, queen of shining glory, in your Son's triumphs, in the fires of Pentecost, and in the honor and light of the heavenly kingdom."

88 88 (LM)

Tune: Duguet

English Translation: Abbot Oswald Hunter-Blair (d. 1939); cf. *The Roman Breviary Translated out of Latin into English by John, Marquess of Bute* (1908) p. 1074.
M. Source: *Mediator Dei Hymnal* (1955) p. 66; *New Saint Basil Hymnal* (1958) p. 93; *Arundel Catholic Hymnal* (1905) p. 26; *Hymnal and Vesperal* (Archdiocese of Baltimore, 1878) p. 168.
Melody: Dieudonné Duguet (d. 1849), organist at the Cathedral in Liège, Belgium, and teacher of César Franck.

Pendens In Crucis Cornibus (Our Lady's Sorrows) 775

Trns: Alan Gordon McDougall (d. 1965)

4. Maiden, who weepest for thy son,
The blessèd Sole-begotten One,
Grant us the tears of love, we pray,
And wash our every stain away.

5. The God she bore within her womb
Is laid within the rock-hewn tomb;
Our souls enchained by death of yore,
Lord, at thy Mother's prayer restore.

6. Star of the sea most fair, we pray,
That guid'st us on life's narrow way,
No more by bonds of flesh oppress'd,
Grant us in Christ thy son to rest.

7. O Shepherd of the sheep, thy praise
A thousand bands of angels raise;
From all temptation thine elect
At thy blest mother's prayer protect.

8. Queen in the land of starshining
Whose praises every heart doth sing,
When all our earthly praise is done,
Reward us with thy benison.

9. Glory to thee through all the earth,
Lord Jesus, for thy virgin birth,
With Father and with Spirit One
While endless ages onward run.

Melody: Kevin Allen (b. 1965), choirmaster at the Monastery of the Holy Cross in Chicago.
M. Source: *Saint Edmund Campion Missal and Hymnal* (2013) p. 823.
Text: From a 14th century Polish hymnary.
T. Source: *Pange Lingua: Breviary Hymns of Old Uses with an English Rendering by Alan G. McDougall and an Introduction by Adrian Fortescue* (London: Burns & Oates, 1916) p. 42.

88 88 (LM)

Tune: St Peter Claver

776 Immaculate Mary, Thy Praises We Sing

"Elizabeth cried out with a loud voice, and said: Blessed art thou among women, and blessed is the fruit of thy womb."—Lk 1.42

1. Im - mac - u - late Mar - y, thy prais - es we_ sing;
2. In heav - en, the bless - èd thy glo - ry pro - claim;
3. Thy name is our pow - er, thy vir - tues our_ light,

Who reign - est in splen - dor with Je - sus our_ King.
On earth we, thy chil - dren, in - voke thy fair_ name.
Thy love is our com - fort, thy plead - ing our_ might.

R. A - ve, A - ve, A - ve Ma - rí - a!

A - ve, A - ve Ma - rí - a!

4. We pray for our Mother, the Church upon earth,
And bless, dearest Lady, the land of our birth.

The more traditional form of the refrain may also be used :

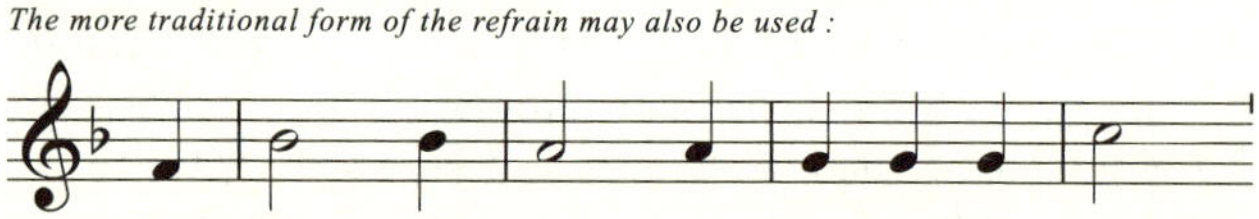

R. A - ve, A - ve, A - ve Ma - rí - a!

A - ve, A - ve, A - ve Ma - rí - a!

65 65 R

Tune:
LOURDES HYMN

Melody: Grenoble, 1882; cf. *Stories of Hymns* (Fr. George W. Rutler, 2016) p. 80.
M. Source: *New Westminster Hymnal* (1939) p. 322; *Hymns, Psalms, and Spiritual Canticles* (Theodore Marier, 1983) p. 291; *Parochial Hymn Book* (Fr. Anatole Police, 1897) p. 425.
T. Source: *Mediator Dei Hymnal* (1955) p. 80; *New Saint Basil Hymnal* (1958) p. 165.

The Immaculate Conception (1595 AD) 777

St. Robert Southwell, Martyr of Jesus Christ (d. 1595)

1. Our sec - ond Eve puts on her mor - tal shroud,
2. Both grace and na - ture did their force u - nite
3. Four on - ly wights bred with - out fault are named,

Earth breeds a heav'n for God's new dwell - ing - place;
To make this Babe the sum of all their best;
And all the rest con - ceiv - èd were in sin;

Now ris - eth up E - li - as' lit - tle cloud,
Our most, her least; our mil - lion, but her mite—
With - out both man and wife was Ad - am framed,

That grow - ing shall dis - til the show'rs of grace;
She was at eas - iest rate worth all the rest:
Of man, but not of wife, did Eve be - gin;

Her be - ing now be - gins, who, ere she end,
What grace to men, or an - gels, God did part,
Wife with - out touch of man Christ's Moth - er was,

Shall bring our good that shall our e - vil mend.
Was all u - nit - ed in this In - fant's heart.
Of man and wife this babe was bred in grace.

Melody: Kevin Allen (b. 1965), choirmaster at the Monastery of the Holy Cross in Chicago.
M. Source: *Saint Edmund Campion Missal and Hymnal* (2013) p. 907.
T. Source: *Carmina Mariana: an English anthology in verse in honour of or in relation to the Blessed Virgin Mary; collected and arranged by Orby Shipley* (London, 1893) pp. 358.

10 10 10 10 10 10

Tune: Quella

778 Our Lady's Salutation (1595 AD)

St. Robert Southwell, Martyr of Jesus Christ (d. 1595)

1. Spell E - va back and "A - ve" shall you find;
2. O vir - gin blest, the heav'ns to thee in - cline,
3. With haugh - ty mind to God - head man as - pired,

The first be - gan, the last re - versed our harms:
In thee their joy and sov - 'reign they ag - nize;
And was by pride from place of pleas - ure chased;

An an - gel's witch - ing words did E - va blind;
Too mean their glo - ry is to match with thine,
With lov - ing mind our man - hood God de - sired,

An an - gel's "A - ve" dis - en - chants the charms:
Whose chaste re - ceipt God more than heav'n did prize.
And as by love in great - er pleas - ure placed;

Death first by wom - an's weak - ness en - ter'd in,
Hail, fair - est Heav'n, that heav'n and earth did bless,
Man la - b'ring to as - cend pro - cured our fall;

In Wom - an's vir - tue life doth now be - gin.
Where vir - tue's star, God's sun of jus - tice is!
God yield - ing to de - scend cut off our thrall.

* Verse 2: *Agnize*: that is, "recognize."

10 10 10 10 10 10

Tune:
Enemond

Melody: Kevin Allen (b. 1965), choirmaster at the Monastery of the Holy Cross in Chicago.
M. Source: *Saint Jean de Brébeuf Hymnal* (2018).
T. Source: *American Ecclesiastical Review*, Vol. XXXII (Philadelphia, 1905) p. 155;
The Complete Works of R. Southwell, S.J. (London, 1876) p. 108.

The Assumption Of Our Lady (1595 AD) 779

St. Robert Southwell, Martyr of Jesus Christ (d. 1595)

1. If sin be cap - tive, grace must find re - lease;
2. The daz - zled eye doth dim - mèd light re - quire,
3. Gem to her worth, Spouse to her Love as - cends,

From curse of sin the in - no - cent is free;
And dy - ing sights re - pose in shroud - ing shades;
Prince to her throne, Queen to her heav'n - ly King,

Tomb, pris - on is for sin - ners that de - cease;
But, ea - gles' eyes to bright - est light as - pire,
Whose court with sol - emn pomp on her at - tends,

No tomb, but throne to guilt - less doth a - gree:
And liv - ing looks de - light in loft - y glades:
And choirs of saints with greet - ing notes do sing;

Though thralls of sin lie lin - g'ring in the grave.
Faint - wing - èd fowl by ground do faint - ly fly,
Earth ren - d'reth up her un - de - serv - èd prey;

Yet, fault - less corpse, with soul re - ward must have.
Our prince - ly Ea - gle mounts un - to the sky.
Heav'n claims the right, and bears the prize a - way.

Melody: Kevin Allen (b. 1965), choirmaster at the Monastery of the Holy Cross in Chicago.
M. Source: *Saint Jean de Brébeuf Hymnal* (2018).
T. Source: *Carmina Mariana: an English anthology in verse in honour of or in relation to the Blessed Virgin Mary; collected and arranged by Orby Shipley* (London, 1893) pp. 361-362.

10 10 10 10 10 10

Tune: ENEMOND

780 O Sanctissima, O Piissima (Blessed Virgin)

"Virgin Mother of God, He whom the whole world cannot contain was enclosed in thy womb, and was made man."—Virgo Dei Genitrix, vl

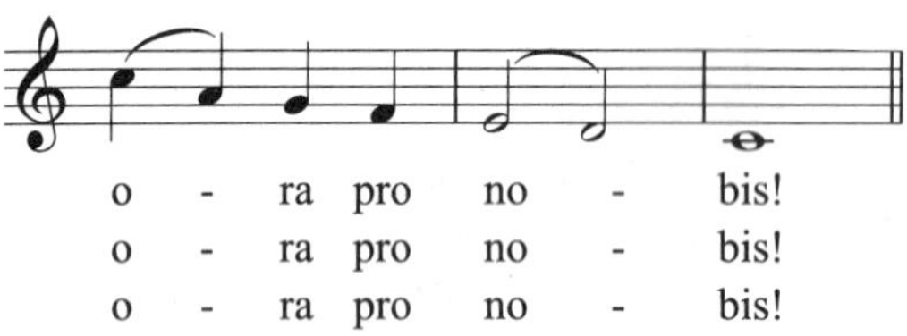

4. Virgo, réspice,
Mater, áspice,
Audi nos, O María!
Tu, medicínam,
Portas divínam;
Ora, ora pro nobis.

Literal Translation :

1. O most holy one
O most loving,
O sweet Virgin Mary!
Mother best beloved,
Mother undefiled,
Pray for us!

2. Thou art our comfort,
And our refuge,
Virgin Mother Mary!
All that we long for,
Through thee we hope for;
Pray for us!

3. See how weak we are,
Lost in tears,
Save us, O Mary!
Lighten our anguish,
Soothe our sorrows,
Pray for us!

4. Virgin, turn and look,
Mother, behold us;
Hear us, O Mary!
Thou art the bearer
Of health divine:
Pray for us!

10 7 10 7

Tune:
SICILIAN MARINERS

Latin Text: *Pius X Hymnal* (Boston, 1953) p. 115; *New Westminster Hymnal* (1939) p. 388.
Literal Translation: *Arundel Catholic Hymnal* (1905) p. 375.
Melody: Traditional; first printed in 1792. Haydn, Beethoven, and others have set this melody.
M. Source: *The People's Mass Book* (Cincinnati, 1964) p. 206.

Salve Regina, Mater Misericordiae (11th century) 781

1687AD – Historic Roman Catholic Translation

Can be sung with any 88 88 meter, such as GONFALON ROYAL, TRINITY COLLEGE, ROGERS PARK, MELCOMBE, NOTRE DAME, BRESSANI, EISENACH, etc.

HAIL to the Queen that reigns above,
Mother of Clemency and Love:
Hail, thou our Hope, Life, Sweetness: We,
Eve's banish'd Children, cry to Thee.

2. We, from this wretched Vale of Tears
Send Sighs and Groans unto thine ears.
O then, sweet Advocate, bestow
A pitying look on us below.

3. After this Exile, let us see
Our Blessèd Jesus, born of Thee,
O merciful, O pious Maid!
O gracious Mary! lend thine Aid.

T. Source: *The Office of the B. V. Mary in English; To which is added the Vespers, or Even-Song; In Latin and English, As it is Sung in the Catholic Church Upon all Sundays and principal Holy-days throughout the whole Year; With the Compline, Rosary, Hymn and Prayers that are sung at the Benediction of the B. Sacrament; The Ordinary of the Holy Mass; the Sequence, Dies irae, dies illa, that is sung at solemn Mass for the Dead: all in Latin and English; Together with several other Devout Prayers in English* (London, 1687) p. 130.
Melody: Henry Lawes (d. 1662). M. Source: *Saint Edmund Campion Missal and Hymnal* (2013) p. 888.

88 88 (LM)

Tune: WHITEHALL

782 Salve, Regina Caelitum (19th century)

Trns: Fr. Dominic Popplewell (b. 1973)

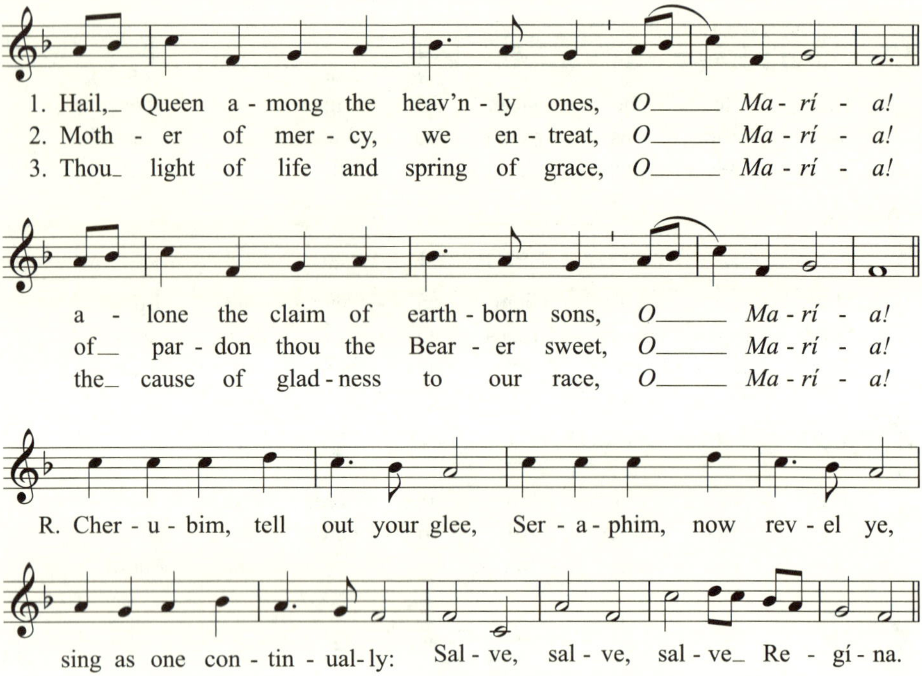

4. Our Lady, hail, our hope as well: *O María!*
   our wrongful undertakings quell, *R.*

5. Though banished, lo to thee we cry, *O María!*
   with thee our humble pleading ply, *R.*

6. List thou to us, Eve's progeny, *O María!*
   who wretched are but hope in thee, *R.*

7. So then, thy mien upon us train, *O María!*
   nor us thy servants yet disdain, *R.*

8. Thine eyes do thou vouchsafe to turn—*O María!*
   t'ward us who for thy guidance yearn, *R.*

9. Show him who is thy Son at last—*O María!*
   to us, this banishment once past, *R.*

88 R

Tune:
MAINZ

Melody: Mainz (1712).
M. Source: *Gotteslob; Katholisches Gebet- und Gesangbuch Ausgabe für das Bistum Trier* (1975) p. 548.
T. Source: *Saint Jean de Brébeuf Hymnal* (2018).

Salve Regina, Mater Misericordiae (11th century)

Hermann Contractus, Monk of Reichenau Abbey (d. 1054)

1. Hail, Ho - ly Queen en - throned a - bove, O Ma - ri - a!
2. Our life, our sweet - ness here be - low, O Ma - ri - a!
3. To thee we cry, poor sons of Eve, O Ma - ri - a!

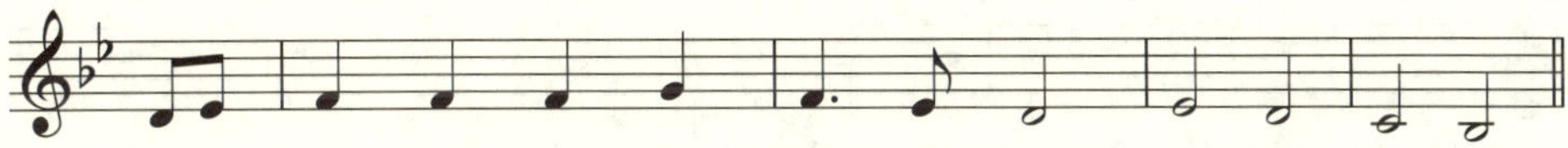

Hail, Mother of mer - cy and of love, O Ma - ri - a!
Our hope in sor - row and in woe, O Ma - ri - a!
To thee we sigh, we mourn, we grieve, O Ma - ri - a!

R. Tri - umph all ye cher - u - bim!
Final Verse: R. *An - gels, all your prais - es bring,*

Sing with us ye ser - a - phim! Heav'n and earth re -
Earth and heav - en, with us sing, All cre - a - tion

sound the hymn! Sal - ve, sal - ve, sal - ve Re - gi - na!
ech - o - ing: Sal - ve, sal - ve, sal - ve Re - gi - na!

4. This earth is but a vale of tears, O Maria!
A place of banishment and fears , O Maria! R.

5. Turn, then, most gracious Advocate, O Maria!
Toward us thine eyes compassionate, O Maria! R.

6. When this our exile is complete , O Maria!
Show us thy Son, our Jesus sweet , O Maria! R.

English Translation: *The Roman Hymnal: a complete manual of English hymns and Latin chants* (Fr. John B. Young, 1884) pp. 77-78.

Melody: German (1808); as reproduced in *Eucharistic Hymnal, edited by Archbishop Schrembs* (1935) p. 72. M. Source: *Crown Hymnal* (Boston, 1912) p. 122. This hymnal was edited by Fr. Leslie J. Kavanagh, Superintendent of Catholic Schools of the Archdiocese of New Orleans, and James M. McLaughlin, organist at St. Mary's Church (Charlestown) in Boston, Massachusetts.

88 R

Tune: Salve Regina Coelitum

784 Regina Caeli, Jubila (17th century)

Trns: Fr. Dominic Popplewell (b. 1973)

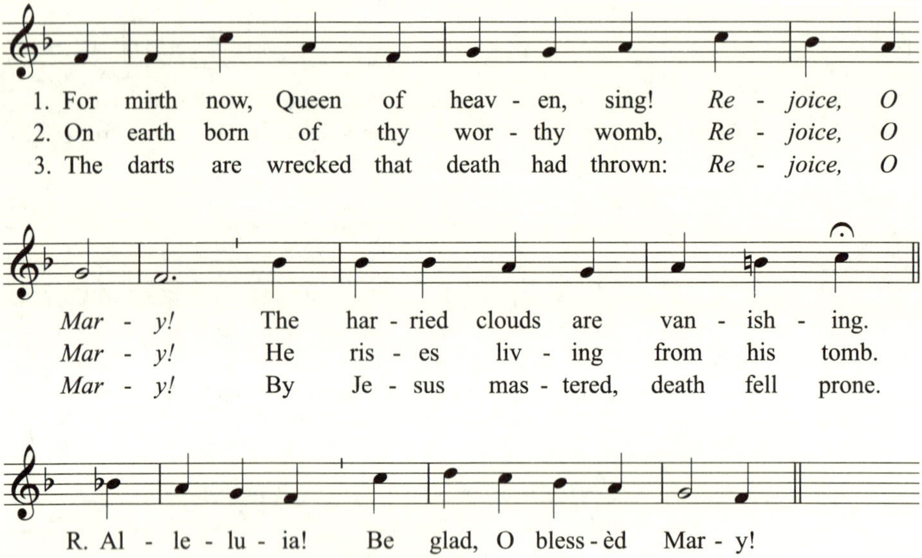

4. As bitterness and grief retreat, *Rejoice, O Mary!*
Relief and joy take up their seat. *R.*

5. His eyes, once foully spit upon, *Rejoice, O Mary!*
The daystar's glances render wan. *R.*

6. On hands and feet the wounds that show *Rejoice, O Mary!*
Are wellsprings whence his graces flow. *R.*

7. The crosswise timbers of the tree *Rejoice, O Mary!*
Are glinting staves of royalty. *R.*

8. The reed and purple cloak now glow *Rejoice, O Mary!*
Like molten flood of earth in throe. *R.*

9. The chain, the spear and nails, all three, *Rejoice, O Mary!*
Are badges of his victory. *R.*

10. Then Mary, be thy mirth displayed, *Rejoice, O Mary!*
To those who call on thee bring aid. *R.*

[5c] That is to say: "The eyes of the risen Lord are so bright that in comparison the light of the sun (Daystar) seems weak and pale." Original Latin: *Turbata sputis lumina* | *Phoebea vincunt fulgura.*

88 R

Tune:
Regina Caeli Jubila

Melody: Leisentritt's *Gesangbuch* (1584).
M. Source: *Saint Gregory Hymnal* (1920) p. 319; *New Saint Basil Hymnal* (1958) p. 55.
T. Source: *Das Gesangbuch der Diözese Rottenburg* (Adolf Zeller, 1871) p. 164.

Regina Caeli Laetare (12th century) 785

"With how glorious a light thou shinest, Princess of David's line; Mary the Virgin, thou dwellest in highest heaven above all the blessed"—O Quam Glorifica, v1

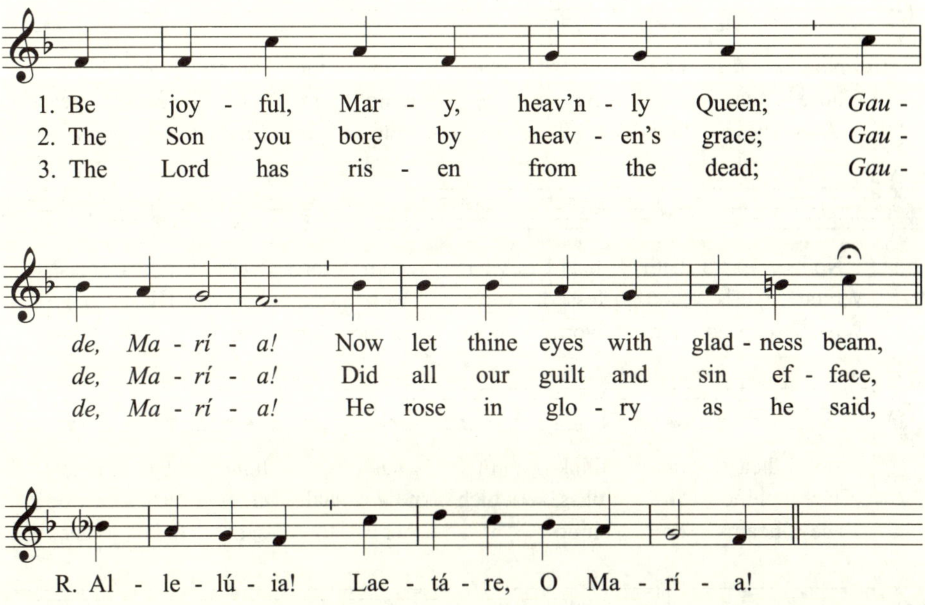

4. O pray to God, thou Virgin fair;
Gaude, María!
That he our souls to heaven bear,
R. Allelúia! Laetáre, O María!

Although now used during Eastertide, this text was adaptated from a 12th century Christmas antiphon:

Maria Virgo semper laetare
Quae meruisti Christum portare,
Caeli et terrae conditorem,
Quia de tuo utero protulisti mundi salvatorem.

ENGLISH TRANSLATION: Anonymous; cf. *Mediator Dei Hymnal* (1955) p. 87; cf. *Cantate Omnes: Hymnal of the Catholic Choirmasters' Guild* (1952) #49.
Melody: Leisentritt's *Gesangbuch* (1584).
M. Source: *Saint Gregory Hymnal* (1920) p. 319; *New Saint Basil Hymnal* (1958) p. 55.

88 R

Tune:
REGINA CAELI JUBILA

786 No Eye Hath Seen What Joys The Saints Obtain

Saint Philip Howard, Earl of Arundel (*d.* 1595)

4. Next above her, and on a higher throne, | Our Savior in His Manhood sitteth here;
From Whom proceeds all perfect joy alone, | And in Whose Face all glory doth appear:
The Saints' delight conceivèd cannot be | When they a Man the Lord of Angels see.

10 10 10 10 10 10

Tune:
ENEMOND

Melody: Kevin Allen (b. 1965), choirmaster at the Monastery of the Holy Cross in Chicago.
M. Source: *Saint Jean de Brébeuf Hymnal* (2018).
T. Source: *Arundel Catholic Hymnal* (1905) p. 488.

For All Thy Saints, O Lord 787

"These have come here out of the great affliction; they have washed their robes white in the blood of the Lamb."—Apoc 7.14

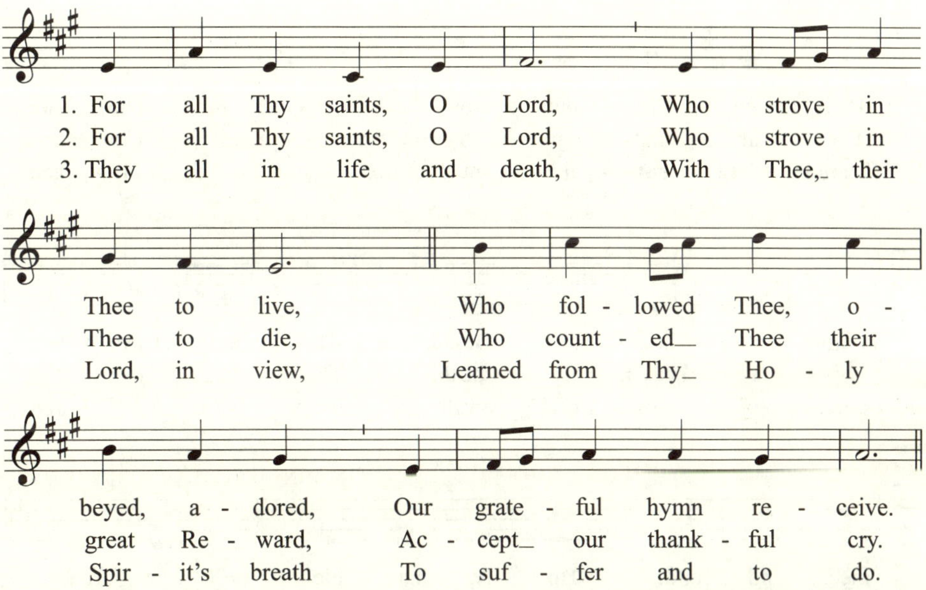

4. For this Thy name we bless
And humbly pray that we
May follow them in holiness
And live and die in Thee.

5. All might, all praise, be Thine,
Father, co-equal Son,
And Spirit, bond of love divine,
While endless ages run.

Can be sung with any 66 86 meter: FESTAL SONG, ALLINGTON, SEÁN 8M, DOMINICA, SOUTHWELL, ST MICHAEL, SONG 20, POTSDAM, etc.

FOR all Thy saints, O Lord,
Who strove in Thee to live,
Who followed Thee, obeyed, adored,
Our grateful hymn receive.

2. For all Thy saints, O Lord,
Who strove in Thee to die,
Who counted Thee their great Reward,
Accept our thankful cry.

3. They all in life and death,
With Thee, their Lord, in view,
Learned from Thy Holy Spirit's breath
To suffer and to do.

4. For this Thy name we bless
And humbly pray that we
May follow them in holiness
And live and die in Thee.

5. All might, all praise, be Thine, | Father, co-equal Son,
And Spirit, bond of love divine, | While endless ages run.

Text: Richard Mant (d. 1848), who, although not Catholic, translated all the Breviary hymns into English, publishing his collection in 1837.
T. Source: *Saint Edmund Campion Missal and Hymnal* (2013) p. 871.
Melody: William Henry Walter (d. 1893), organist at Trinity Chapel in New York.
M. Source: *Episcopal Hymnal* (1940) #535.

66 86 (SM)
Tune: FESTAL SONG

788 Blessed Are The Sons Of God

"See how the Father has shown his love towards us; that we should be counted as God's sons, should be his sons."—I John 3.1

77 77 77

Tune:
Dix

Final Verses: Richard Lloyd (1993) #56; Noel Rawsthorne (2011) #96.
Melody: Dr. Conrad Kocher (d. 1872), founder of the School of Sacred Song in Stuttgart.
M. Source: *Catholic Hymn Book* (London Oratory, 1998) p. 70.
Text: Cento; based on a work in a hymnal published by John Cennick (d. 1755).
T. Source: *Saint Edmund Campion Missal and Hymnal* (2013) p. 870.

Wer Sind Die Von Gottes Throne 789

"And one of the ancients answered, and said to me: These that are clothed in white robes, who are they? and whence came they?"—Apoc 7.13

1. Who are these, like stars ap - pear - ing, These be -
2. Who are these of daz - zling bright - ness, These in__
3. These are they who have con - tend - ed For their

fore God's throne who stand? Each a gold - en crown is wear - ing;
God's own truth ar - rayed, Clad in robes of pur - est white - ness,
Sav - ior's hon - or long, Wres - tling on till life was end - ed,

Who are_ all this glo - rious band? Al - le - lu - ia,__
Robes whose lus - ter ne'er shall fade, Ne'er be touched by__
Fol - l'wing not the sin - ful throng; These, who well the__

hark! they_ sing, Prais - ing loud_ their heav'n - ly king.
time's rude_ hand— Whence comes all_ this glo - rious band?
fight sus - tained, Tri - umph through the Lamb have gained.

4. These are they whose hearts were riven,
Sore with woe and anguish tried,
Who in pray'r full oft have striven
With the God they glorified;
Now, their painful conflict o'er,
God has bid them weep no more.

5. These like priests have watched and waited,
Off'ring up to Christ their will,
Soul and body consecrated,
Day and night to serve Him still:
Now in God's most holy place
Blest they stand before His face.

Final Verses: Richard Lloyd (1993) #7; Noel Rawsthorne (2011) #13.
Text: Meditation on Apocalypse 7.13-17 by Theobald H. Schenck (d. 1727); translation from German by Frances E. Cox (d. 1897).
T. Source: *Hosanna Catholic Hymn Book* (1914) p. 190. Melody: *Geistreiches Gesangbuch* (Darmstadt, 1698).
M. Source: *New Saint Basil Hymnal* (1958) p. 203; *Catholic Hymn Book* (London Oratory, 1998) p. 290.

87 87 77
Tune: ALL SAINTS

790 In Honor Of Saint Joseph

Fr. Dominic Popplewell (b. 1973)

4. This carpenter's reputed heir
were you, who built the cosmic frame,
and, since the foe attacked the same,
its damage ventured to repair.

5. His ancient namesake to prepare
against the famine wisely strove
and, precious grain preserved in trove,
he thus provided saving fare.

* Saint Joseph was chosen to be patron of the Hurons, as St. Jean de Brébeuf and his companions had a great devotion to him.

88 88 (LM)

Tune:
Song 34

Final Verses: Richard Lloyd (1993) #214; Noel Rawsthorne (2011) #342.
Melody: Orlando Gibbons (d. 1625), organist at Westminster Abbey.
M. Source: *The Hymnes and Songs of the Church* (1623) p. 114; originally sung to "Thus Angells sung, and thus sing we." We have adopted the most commonly used rhythm. Cf. *New Saint Basil Hymnal* (1958) p. 136.
T. Source: *Saint Jean de Brébeuf Hymnal (2018).*

6. The later Joseph kept the bread,
the manna true, divinely sent,
whose living flesh is nourishment
to those he rescues from the dead.

7. The Father's wisdom, in his house
his work you set about to do,
which brought both grief and gladness to
your foster-father and his spouse.

8. To Nazareth returning thence,
though nature hung upon your will
the natural law you honored still,
your parents paid obedience.

9. When came the hour to satisfy
the common debt of Adam's race,
then with your bearer, full of grace,
you helped her husband well to die.

10. In bliss and glory without end,
O Joseph, pray for those who here
yet bide, and dangers have to fear,
that heaven shield them and befriend.

11. Of families you are the stay,
the Church's patron, devils' dread:
on these your influence be shed,
to strengthen good and ill allay.

12. To him who is both one and three,
the spring of being, highest king,
let all he crafted praises ring
in splendor for eternity.

[1c] Heb 1.3
[1d] Wis 8.1
[2d] I Pt 1.18-19
[3b] Mt 1.18-24
[4b] Mt 13.55, Jn 6.42
[5d] Gen 41.45-47
[6d] Jn 6.33, 50-52
[7b] Wis 9.1-2, Mk 6.2
[7d] Lk 2.46-49
[8d] Lk 2.51

792 Holy Joseph, Intercessor

First Tune – *Fr. Christopher G. Phillips (b. 1949)*

4. Humble man in lofty station,
God has shed His grace on thee;
Pray such grace to us be given,
That we live eternally.

* Saint Joseph was chosen to be patron of the Hurons, as St. Jean de Brébeuf and his companions had a great devotion to him.

87 87

Tune: Stuttgart

Final Verses: Richard Lloyd (1993) #221; Noel Rawsthorne (2011) #353.
Melody: German tune adapted by Christian Friedrich Witt (d. 1716).
M. Source: *Mediator Dei Hymnal* (1955) #20; *New Saint Basil Hymnal* (1958) p. 28.
T. Source: *Saint Jean de Brébeuf Hymnal* (2018).

SECOND TUNE – *Fr. Christopher G. Phillips (b. 1949)*

4. Humble man in lofty station,
God has shed His grace on thee;
Pray such grace to us be given,
That we live eternally.

* Saint Joseph was chosen to be patron of the Hurons, as St. Jean de Brébeuf and his companions had a great devotion to him.

Final Verses: Richard Lloyd (1993) #138; Noel Rawsthorne (2011) #210.
Melody: William H. Monk (d. 1889), organist at King's College London.
M. Source: *Hymns, Psalms, and Spiritual Canticles* (1983) p. 278; *New Westminster Hymnal* (1939) p. 3.
T. Source: *Saint Jean de Brébeuf Hymnal* (2018).

87 87

Tune: MERTON

794 Holy Joseph, Intercessor

THIRD TUNE – *Fr. Christopher G. Phillips (b. 1949)*

1. Ho - ly Jo - seph, In - ter - ces - sor, Un - to
2. Faith - ful Spouse of faith - ful Vir - gin, Lov - er
3. Guard - ian of the Word In - car - nate, Si - lent

thee God's chil - dren sing; Be our Pa - tron and Pro -
of God's pu - ri - ty; From thy wor - thy place in
guide of God's own Son; Guard our hearts and lead us

tec - tor, To God's throne our prais - es bring.
heav - en, Pray that we may faith - ful be.
on - ward To the life that Christ has won.

4. Humble man in lofty station,
God has shed His grace on thee;
Pray such grace to us be given,
That we live eternally.

Can be sung with any 87 87 meter: STUTTGART, HALTON HOLGATE, REDHEAD #46, BATTY, WALTHAM, VATICAN, MERTON, CROSS OF JESUS, MARCHING, BRONZEVILLE, etc.

HOLY Joseph, Intercessor,
Unto thee God's children sing;
Be our Patron and Protector,
To God's throne our praises bring.

2. Faithful Spouse of faithful Virgin,
Lover of God's purity;
From thy worthy place in heaven,
Pray that we may faithful be.

3. Guardian of the Word Incarnate,
Silent guide of God's own Son;
Guard our hearts and lead us onward
To the life that Christ has won.

4. Humble man in lofty station,
God has shed His grace on thee;
Pray such grace to us be given,
That we live eternally.

* Saint Joseph was chosen to be patron of the Hurons, as St. Jean de Brébeuf and his companions had a great devotion to him.

87 87

Tune: VATICAN

Melody: Cento from *Collection of Hymn Tunes* (London: Novello, 1872).
M. Source: *The Vatican II Hymnal* (Texas: Corpus Christi Watershed, 2011) p. 342.
T. Source: *Saint Jean de Brébeuf Hymnal* (2018).

Blessed Joseph, Guardian Mild 795

Fr. Christopher G. Phillips (b. 1949)

* Saint Joseph was chosen to be patron of the Hurons, as St. Jean de Brébeuf and his companions had a great devotion to him.

Final Verses: Richard Lloyd (1993) #56; Noel Rawsthorne (2011) #96.
Melody: Dr. Conrad Kocher (d. 1872), founder of the School of Sacred Song in Stuttgart.
M. Source: *Catholic Hymn Book* (London Oratory, 1998) p. 70.
T. Source: *Saint Jean de Brébeuf Hymnal* (2018).

77 77 77

Tune: Dix

796 Hymn for Saint Mary MacKillop

Fr. Dominic Popplewell (b. 1973)

4. The lambs of Christ she saw bereft
of guidance and of nourishment:
his Cross to bear, all else she left,
his Heart to please made all her bent.

5. His Providence was all her fund,
his Foster-father all her ward;
all other maintenance she shunned:
her spirit, all unladen, soared.

6. The stroke of gladness or of woe,
when it befell, could never change
her purpose, sway her to forgo
her plighted faith, true love estrange.

7. O blessèd Mary, in the train
of that fair Bridegroom, that great Lord,
the spotless Lamb for sinners slain,
pray him for us, grace to afford.

8. May he from every fell design
the purchase of his pain defend,
where his device he bids to shine
amid the stars, his mercy send.

9. The land that owns thy mortal birth
be now the claimant of thy care,
and every clan of men on earth
the heirs of thy deserts and prayer.

10. Then to the bounteous One-and-Three
whence all things are, where all things tend,
true Godhead, sovereign mastery,
be praise and glory without end.

MARY MacKillop, the first Australian to be canonized, co-founded the *Josephites* (Sisters of St. Joseph of the Sacred Heart), a congregation living in dependence on Divine Providence and working for the education of poor children. She suffered misunderstanding and mistreatment from non-Catholics and Catholics alike, even some in the Church hierarchy, but bore all with fortitude and charity until her holy death on 8 August 1909.

88 88 (LM)

Tune:
ROGERS PARK

T. Source: *Saint Jean de Brébeuf Hymnal* (2018).
Melody: Kevin Allen (b. 1965), choirmaster at the Monastery of the Holy Cross in Chicago.
M. Source: *Saint Jean de Brébeuf Hymnal* (2018).

Simple Saint & Faithful Priest (St. Anthony)

Fr. Christopher G. Phillips (b. 1949)

77 77 77

Melody: Johann Georg Ebeling (d. 1676), choirmaster of St. Nicholas' Church, Berlin.
M. Source: *Songs of Syon* (Woodward, 1910) p. 348.
T. Source: *Saint Jean de Brébeuf Hymnal* (2018).

Tune: VOLLER WUNDER VOLLER KUNST

798 For The Dead

Bl. John Henry Cardinal Newman, Oratorian (d. 1890)

4. Oh, by their patience of delay,
Their hope amid their pain,
Their sacred zeal to burn away
Disfigurement and stain;

5. Oh, by their fire of love, not less
In keenness than the flame,
Oh, by their very helplessness,
Oh, by Thine own great Name,

6. Help, Lord, the souls which Thou hast made,
The souls to Thee so dear,
In prison for the debt unpaid
Of sins committed here.

86 86 (CM)

Tune:
St Flavian

Final Verses: Richard Lloyd (1993) #194; Noel Rawsthorne (2011) #125.
Text: Published in 1857; written at the request of his friend, Ambrose St. John (d. 1875), who, like Newman, converted and became a priest of the Oratory of St. Philip Neri.
T. Source: *Catholic Hymn Book* (1998) p. 311; *Sacred Heart Review*, Vol. 4, No. 23 (1890) p. 1.
Melody: *The Whole Booke of Psalmes collected into Englishe metre* (London: John Daye, 1584) p. 367. The texts for this book were composed by Thomas Sternhold (d. 1549), a special servant to King Henry VIII, in charge of bringing forward ceremonial clothing during the monarch's coronation.
M. Source: *New Westminster Hymnal* (1939) p. 93; *Adoremus Hymnal* (1997) #360; A version from 1621 has the melody in the Tenor voice; cf. *Hymns Ancient and Modern* (1972) p. 202.

The King Of Love My Shepherd Is (Psalm 22)

"For though I should walk in the midst of the shadow of death, I will fear no evils, for thou art with me."—Ps 22.4

4. In death's dark vale I fear no ill
With thee, dear Lord, beside me;
Thy rod and staff my comfort still,
Thy cross before to guide me.

5. Thou spread'st a table in my sight;
Thine unction, grace bestoweth;
And O what transport of delight
From thy pure chalice floweth!

6. And so through all the length of days
Thy goodness faileth never;
Good Shepherd, may I sing thy praise
Within thy house forever.

Final Verses: Richard Lloyd (1993) #190; Noel Rawsthorne (2011) #293.
Melody: Traditional Irish tune. M. Source: *Catholic Hymn Book* (1998) p. 462.
Text: Paraphrase of Psalm 22 by Sir Henry Williams Baker (d. 1877), who was the driving force behind *Hymns Ancient and Modern*, which appeared in 1861. Baker was not Catholic, but was sympathetic to Catholic theology. He came under attack from Protestants because of his inclusion of hymns honoring Our Lady and the Sanctissimum.
T. Source: *Hymns, Psalms, and Spiritual Canticles* (Massachusetts: Theodore Marier, 1983) p. 455.

87 87 Iambic
Tune:
ST COLUMBA 7M

800 De Profundis Exclamantes Audi (13th century)

"This the universal Church holds, by praying for the dead that they may be loosed from sins."—Saint Gregory of Nyssa (d. 386AD)

4. They are Thine, O take them quickly,
Thou their Hope, O raise them high;
Ever hoping, ever trusting,
Unto Thee they strive and cry;
Day and night, both morn and ev'ning,
Be, O Christ, their Guardian nigh.

5. Let Thy plenteous loving-kindness,
On them, as we pray, be poured;
Let them through Thy boundless mercy,
From all evil be restored;
Hearken to the gentle pleading
Of thy Mother, gracious Lord.

6. When, O kind and radiant Jesus,
Kneels the Queen thy throne before,
Let the court of Saints attending,
Mercy for the dead implore;
Hearken, loving Friend of sinners,
Whom the Cross exalted bore.

7. Hear and answer prayers devoutest,
Break, O Lord, each binding chain,
Dash the gates of death asunder,
Quell the devil and his train;
Bring the souls which Thou hast ransomed
Evermore in joy to reign.

Verse 2c ("Peccatores quamvis") and Stanza 3 ("Haec quam Patri obtulisti") speak of the value of the Sacrifice of the Mass for those who have died: "Although we are sinners and unable to endure if thou consider our vices: still, let the victim now offered by us avail for the dead. See, we offer the same as thou didst offer to the Father: may it be a succour to them; yea, be thou propitious to them, and in thy might, O Jesus, loose the bonds of the guilty."

87 87 87

Tune:
BRETON

Text: All Souls' day Sequence prior to the Council of Trent; for Latin text & literal translation cf. *The Liturgical Year by Abbot Guéranger*, Vol. 6 (Stanbrook Abbey, 1903) p. 223. Metrical English translation by Richard F. Littledale (d. 1890).
Melody: Metrical Cento; cf. "Dum staret Abraham" (*Antiphonaire Monastique,* 13th century).
M. Source: *Paléographie musicale* (Volume XII), folio 81; *Cantus Selecti* (Solesmes, 1957) p. 245.

Sing with any 87 87 87 meter: Runnells, Mannheim, Dulce Carmen, Regent Square, Lauda Anima, St Leonard, Gaufestre, Picardy, Breton, Davost, and so forth.

CHRIST, enthroned in highest Heaven,
Hear us crying from the deep,
For the faithful ones departed,
For the souls of all that sleep;
As Thy kneeling Church entreateth,
Hearken, Shepherd of the sheep.

2. King of Glory, hear our voices,
Grant Thy faithful rest, we pray;
We have sinned, and may not bide it,
If Thou mark our steps astray;
Yet we plead the saving Victim,
Which for them we bring today.

3. That which Thou Thyself hast offered
To Thy Father, offer we;
Let it win for them a blessing,
Bless them, Jesus, set them free;
They are Thine, they wait in patience;
Merciful and gracious be.

4. They are Thine, O take them quickly,
Thou their Hope, O raise them high;
Ever hoping, ever trusting,
Unto Thee they strive and cry;
Day and night, both morn and ev'ning,
Be, O Christ, their Guardian nigh.

5. Let Thy plenteous loving-kindness,
On them, as we pray, be poured;
Let them through Thy boundless mercy,
From all evil be restored;
Hearken to the gentle pleading
Of thy Mother, gracious Lord.

6. When, O kind and radiant Jesus,
Kneels the Queen thy throne before,
Let the court of Saints attending,
Mercy for the dead implore;
Hearken, loving Friend of sinners,
Whom the Cross exalted bore.

7. Hear and answer prayers devoutest,
Break, O Lord, each binding chain,
Dash the gates of death asunder,
Quell the devil and his train;
Bring the souls which Thou hast ransomed
Evermore in joy to reign.

87 87 87

Tune: Various

For notes, please see page 800.

802 Te Deum Laudamus, Te Dominum Confitemur

attr. Saint Nicetas, Bishop of Remesiana (d. 414AD)

4. Spare Thy people, Lord, we pray,
By a thousand snares surrounded:
Keep us free from sin today,
Never let us be confounded;
|| Lo, I put my trust in Thee—
Never, Lord, abandon me. || (2x)

78 78 77

Tune:
Grosser Gott

Final Verses: Richard Lloyd (1993) #99; Noel Rawsthorne (2011) #159.
Melody: *Katholisches Gesangbuch* (Vienna, 1774).
M. Source: *Saint Edmund Campion Missal and Hymnal* (2013) p. 881; *Hymns, Psalms, and Spiritual Canticles* (Massachusetts: Theodore Marier, 1983) p. 272.
Text: Paraphrase in English by Fr. Clarence Walworth (d. 1900), a Catholic priest.
T. Source: *Catholic Church Hymnal with Music* (A. Edmonds Tozer, 1905) p. 284; *Book of Hymns with Tunes* (Fr. Gregory Ould, 1910) p. 91.

Sing Praise To The Lord (Psalm 150) 803

"Praise him with timbrel and choir: praise him with strings and organs."—Ps 150.4

1. Sing praise to the Lord! praise God in the height;
2. Sing praise to the Lord! praise God on the earth,
3. Sing praise to the Lord! all things that give sound;

Re - joice in His Word, you an - gels of light.
In tune - ful ac - cord, all you of new birth;
Each ju - bi - lant chord, re - ech - o a - round;

O heav - ens, a - dore Him_ by_ whom you were made,
Praise Him who has brought you_ His_ grace from a - bove,
Loud or - gans, His glo - ry_ tell_ forth in deep tone,

And wor - ship be - fore_ Him in bright-ness ar - rayed.
Praise Him who has taught you to sing of His love.
And trum - pets, the sto - ry of what He has done.

4. Sing praise to the Lord! | thanksgiving and song
To Him be outpoured | all ages along;
For love in creation, | for heaven restored,
For grace of salvation, | sing praise to the Lord!

Final Verses: Richard Lloyd (1993) #112; Noel Rawsthorne (2011) #179.
Text: Sir Henry Williams Baker (d. 1877), who was the driving force behind *Hymns Ancient and Modern*, which appeared in 1861. Baker was not Catholic, but was sympathetic to Catholic theology. He came under attack from Protestants because of his inclusion of hymns honoring Our Lady and the Sanctissimum.
Text Source: *Saint Michael Hymnal* (St. Boniface Parish, 2003) #528.
Melody: Sir Charles H. H. Parry (d. 1918), professor at the Royal College of Music.
M. Source: *Hymns, Psalms, and Spiritual Canticles* (Massachusetts: Theodore Marier, 1983) p. 498.

10 10 11 11

Tune:
LAUDATE DOMINUM

804 In Principio Creavit Deus (Book of Genesis)

Fr. Dominic Popplewell (b. 1973)

98 98 D

Tune:
RENDEZ À DIEU

T. Source: *Saint Jean de Brébeuf Hymnal* (2018).
Melody: Louis Bourgeois (d. 1561), who helped produce the *Genevan Psalter* and was once imprisoned (3 December 1551) for changing the melodies of well-known psalms "without a license."
M. Source: *Adoremus Hymnal* (1997) #515; *Catholic Hymn Book* (London Oratory, 1998) p. 190.

4. Evening and morning alternating,
ocean and air were fraught with life,
down in the deep proliferating,
amid the lofty currents rife.
Those sick of sin, physician holy,
direct to penitence profound,
by virtue rising, ever lowly:
so let thy healing grace abound.

5. Cattle and savage beast were thriving
with those which crept along the land,
man, of thy making last arriving,
all else entrusted to his hand:
formed of the clay, thine image bearing,
a breath divine in vials of earth,
whose Prince, their vassal nature sharing,
paupered himself to mend their dearth.

6. Such was thy work, six days employment,
heaven and earth, with their array;
ending, their goodness thine enjoyment,
the seventh was thy resting day.
Let us, all toil and care discarding,
eternal sabbath entering,
thy face, whose sight is bliss, regarding,
thy praises never cease to sing.

[1a] Ex 3.14
[1g] Gen 1.1
[2d] Gen 1.3-5
[2g] I Cor 15.55
[3b] Gen 1.6-8
[3c] Gen 1.9-13
[3d] Gen 1.14-19
[3h] Ps 118.89-91, 152; Mt 24.35; I Pet 1.25
[4d] Gen 1.20-23
[5d] Gen 1.24-31
[5f] Gen 2.7; Eccl 12.9; II Cor 4.7
[5h] Phil 2.7; II Cor 8.9
[6d] Gen 2.1-2
[6g] I Cor 13.12; I Jn 3.2; Ap 22.4

806 Lead, Kindly Light

Bl. John Henry Cardinal Newman, Oratorian (d. 1890)

10 4 10 4 10 10

Tune:
ALLEN

Melody: Kevin Allen (b. 1965), choirmaster at the Monastery of the Holy Cross in Chicago.
M. Source: *Saint Edmund Campion Missal and Hymnal* (2013) p. 924.
T. Source: *Adoremus Hymnal* (1997) #578; *Arundel Catholic Hymnal* (1905) p. 538; *New Westminster Hymnal* (1939) p. 269; *Catholic Hymn Book* (London, 1998) p. 409; *Catholic Church Hymnal with Music* (A. Edmonds Tozer, 1905) p. 268.

O God, Our Help In Ages Past (Psalm 89) 807

"In thy sight, a thousand years are but as yesterday, that has come and gone, or as one of the night-watches."—Ps 89.4

4. A thousand ages in Thy sight
Are like an ev'ning gone;
Short as the watch that ends the night
Before the rising sun.

5. Time, like an ever rolling stream,
Bears all its sons away;
They fly, forgotten, as a dream
Dies at the op'ning day.

6. O God, our help in ages past,
Our hope for years to come,
Be Thou our guard while troubles last,
And our eternal home.

Final Verses: Richard Lloyd (1993) #186; Noel Rawsthorne (2011) #282.
Melody: William Croft (d. 1727), organist at Westminster Abbey.
M. Source: *Hymns, Psalms, and Spiritual Canticles* (Massachusetts: Theodore Marier, 1983) p. 507.
Text: Isaac Watts (d. 1748).
T. Source: *Saint Michael Hymnal* (St. Boniface Parish, 2003) #446; *Catholic Hymn Book* (London Oratory, 1998) p. 431.

86 86 (CM)

Tune: ST ANNE

808 Angularis Fundamentum (6th century)

"Behold I will lay in Sion a chief cornerstone, elect, precious. And he that shall believe in Him, shall not be confounded."—I Peter 2.6

4. Here vouchsafe to all Thy servants | What they ask of Thee to gain;
What they gain from Thee forever | With the blessèd to retain,
And hereafter in Thy glory | Evermore with Thee to reign.

5. Laud and honor to the Father, | Laud and honor to the Son,
Laud and honor to the Spirit, | Ever Three and ever One;
Consubstantial, co-eternal, | While unending ages run.

* *Angularis Fundamentum* (renamed *Alto Ex Olympi Vertice* in the Urbanite version) is the second half of *Urbs Jerusalem Beata*; cf. page 488.

Final Verses: Richard Lloyd (1993) #175; Noel Rawsthorne (2011) #265.
T. Source: *Hymns of the Dominican Missal and Breviary* (Fr. Aquinas Byrnes, 1943) p. 633.
English Translation: Dr. John M. Neale (d. 1866), author of *Mediaeval Hymns and Sequences translated in English* (1851).
Melody: Henry Smart (d. 1879), organist at St. Philip's in London.
M. Source: *Catholic Hymn Book* (1998) p. 280; *Hymns, Psalms, and Spiritual Canticles* (1983) p. 213.

87 87 87

Tune:
Regent Square

Urbs Sion Aurea, Patria Lactea (12th century) 809

Trns: Dr. John M. Neale (d. 1866)

4. O sweet and blessèd country, | The home of God's elect!
O sweet and blessèd country, | That eager hearts expect!
Jesus, in mercy bring us | To that dear land of rest;
Who art, with God the Father, | and Spirit, ever blest.

Final Verses: Richard Lloyd (1993) #71; Noel Rawsthorne (2011) #121.
Melody: Alexander Ewing (d. 1895).
M. Source: *Catholic Hymn Book* (London Oratory, 1998) p. 392.
Text: This is a Cento taken from a long poem of about 3,000 lines by Bernard of Cluny, who lived during the 12th century. The meter of the entire Latin hymn is most remarkable.
T. Source: *Arundel Catholic Hymnal* (1905) p.474.

76 76 D

Tune: Ewing

810 Lord Jesus Christ, Of Joys And Treasures Rarest

First Tune – *Fr. Dominic Popplewell (b. 1973)*

4. Drawing all things, who are of all the maker,
upon the cross uplifted, all to heal,
bearing a thirst that had one only slaker:
your precious blood outpoured to work our weal.

5. Goodness divine and kindness manifested,
you will not quench the flax that smoulders frail,
break not the reed that injury has wrested,
in whom the strong are shamed, the weak prevail.

11 10 11 10

Tune:
Cyriacus

T. Source: *Saint Jean de Brébeuf Hymnal* (2018).
Melody: Kevin Allen (b. 1965), choirmaster at the Monastery of the Holy Cross in Chicago.
M. Source: *Saint Jean de Brébeuf Hymnal* (2018).

6. There is no harm that lies beyond your mending,
nor any loss that you cannot restore:
hearts that are pure preserve in grace unending,
those sin has ravaged making whole once more.

7. Once, hidden God, a pilgrim people guiding,
your tabernacle told your presence true:
now too, Emmanuel, with us abiding,
you are the Word in flesh, nor yet in view.

8. Meal of the favored, wine whence maidens flourish,
vine that upholds its branches, lending life,
yielding itself to rear them, and to nourish,
that they would thrive, in fruitfulness be rife.

9. Honor and praise be offered without ceasing
to the almighty One, the holy Three,
Father, and Son, and Spirit, still increasing,
before the never-fading majesty.

[1b] Heb 1.3
[1c] Ps 44.3
[1d] Prv 8.31
[2b] Mt 28.20
[2d] Jn 13.1
[3b] Heb 2.14
[3d] Os 11.4
[4b] Jn 12.32
[4c] Jn 19.28
[5a] Tit 3.4
[5c] Mt 12.20; Is 42.3
[5d] I Cor 1.27; Lk 1.52
[7a] Is 45.15
[7b] Ex 40.32, 36; Nm 9.15-16
[7c] Mt 1.23; Is 7.14
[7d] Jn 1.14; Hb 8.2, 9.11
[8a] Zc 9.15
[8d] Jn 15.5

812 Lord Jesus Christ, Of Joys And Treasures Rarest

Second Tune – *Fr. Dominic Popplewell (b. 1973)*

1. Lord Je - sus Christ, of joys and treas - ures rar - est,
2. Al - ways to stay a - mong us is your pleas - ure,
3. Though our first fa - ther fell, his kin - dred leav - ing

glow of the Fa - ther's glo - ry, beam - ing bright,
un - til the world its fat - ed time should spend:
un - der the sway of death a fet - tered slave,

who have been made a child of men, the fair - est,__
ten - der - ness such as yours is, none could mea - sure,__
your bonds of mer - cy brought forth from their griev - ing__

__ for to be in their midst was your de - light.
__ lov - ing your own, and lov - ing to the end.
__ those whom by Ad - am's cords you came to save.

4. Drawing all things, who are of all the maker,
upon the cross uplifted, all to heal,
bearing a thirst that had one only slaker:
your precious blood outpoured to work our weal.

5. Goodness divine and kindness manifested,
you will not quench the flax that smoulders frail,
break not the reed that injury has wrested,
in whom the strong are shamed, the weak prevail.

11 10 11 10

Tune:
Highwood

Final Verses: Richard Lloyd (1993) #93; Noel Rawsthorne (2011) #152.
T. Source: *Saint Jean de Brébeuf Hymnal* (2018).
Melody: Sir Richard R. Terry (d. 1938), choirmaster at Westminster Cathedral.
M. Source: *Catholic Hymn Book* (London Oratory, 1998) p. 436.

6. There is no harm that lies beyond your mending,
nor any loss that you cannot restore:
hearts that are pure preserve in grace unending,
those sin has ravaged making whole once more.

7. Once, hidden God, a pilgrim people guiding,
your tabernacle told your presence true:
now too, Emmanuel, with us abiding,
you are the Word in flesh, nor yet in view.

8. Meal of the favored, wine whence maidens flourish,
vine that upholds its branches, lending life,
yielding itself to rear them, and to nourish,
that they would thrive, in fruitfulness be rife.

9. Honor and praise be offered without ceasing
to the almighty One, the holy Three,
Father, and Son, and Spirit, still increasing,
before the never-fading majesty.

[1b] Heb 1.3
[1c] Ps 44.3
[1d] Prv 8.31
[2b] Mt 28.20
[2d] Jn 13.1
[3b] Heb 2.14
[3d] Os 11.4
[4b] Jn 12.32
[4c] Jn 19.28
[5a] Tit 3.4
[5c] Mt 12.20; Is 42.3
[5d] I Cor 1.27; Lk 1.52
[7a] Is 45.15
[7b] Ex 40.32, 36; Nm 9.15-16
[7c] Mt 1.23; Is 7.14
[7d] Jn 1.14; Hb 8.2, 9.11
[8a] Zc 9.15
[8d] Jn 15.5

814 Lord Jesus Christ, Of Joys And Treasures Rarest

THIRD TUNE – *Fr. Dominic Popplewell* (*b.* 1973)

4. Drawing all things, who are of all the maker,
upon the cross uplifted, all to heal,
bearing a thirst that had one only slaker:
your precious blood outpoured to work our weal.

5. Goodness divine and kindness manifested,
you will not quench the flax that smoulders frail,
break not the reed that injury has wrested,
in whom the strong are shamed, the weak prevail.

11 10 11 10

Tune:
LAFITAU

T. Source: *Saint Jean de Brébeuf Hymnal* (2018).
Melody: Louis Bourgeois (d. 1561), who helped produce the *Genevan Psalter* and was once imprisoned (3 December 1551) for changing the melodies of well-known psalms "without a license."
M. Source: *Hymns Ancient and Modern* (1972) p. 122.

6. There is no harm that lies beyond your mending,
nor any loss that you cannot restore:
hearts that are pure preserve in grace unending,
those sin has ravaged making whole once more.

7. Once, hidden God, a pilgrim people guiding,
your tabernacle told your presence true:
now too, Emmanuel, with us abiding,
you are the Word in flesh, nor yet in view.

8. Meal of the favored, wine whence maidens flourish,
vine that upholds its branches, lending life,
yielding itself to rear them, and to nourish,
that they would thrive, in fruitfulness be rife.

9. Honor and praise be offered without ceasing
to the almighty One, the holy Three,
Father, and Son, and Spirit, still increasing,
before the never-fading majesty.

[1b] Heb 1.3
[1c] Ps 44.3
[1d] Prv 8.31
[2b] Mt 28.20
[2d] Jn 13.1
[3b] Heb 2.14
[3d] Os 11.4
[4b] Jn 12.32
[4c] Jn 19.28
[5a] Tit 3.4
[5c] Mt 12.20; Is 42.3
[5d] I Cor 1.27; Lk 1.52
[7a] Is 45.15
[7b] Ex 40.32, 36; Nm 9.15-16
[7c] Mt 1.23; Is 7.14
[7d] Jn 1.14; Hb 8.2, 9.11
[8a] Zc 9.15
[8d] Jn 15.5

816 Lord Jesus Christ, Of Joys And Treasures Rarest

ABRIDGED VERSION – *Fr. Dominic Popplewell (b. 1973)*

4. Once, hidden God, a pilgrim people guiding,
your tabernacle told your presence true:
now too, Emmanuel, with us abiding,
you are the Word in flesh, nor yet in view.

11 10 11 10

Tune:
RAYMBAULT

T. Source: *Saint Jean de Brébeuf Hymnal* (2018).
Melody: Peter Lejeune (b. 1991), organist at Saint John Vianney Catholic Church in Springfield.
M. Source: *Saint Jean de Brébeuf Hymnal* (2018).

The Earth Itself Declares 817

Saint Philip Howard, Earl of Arundel (d. 1595)

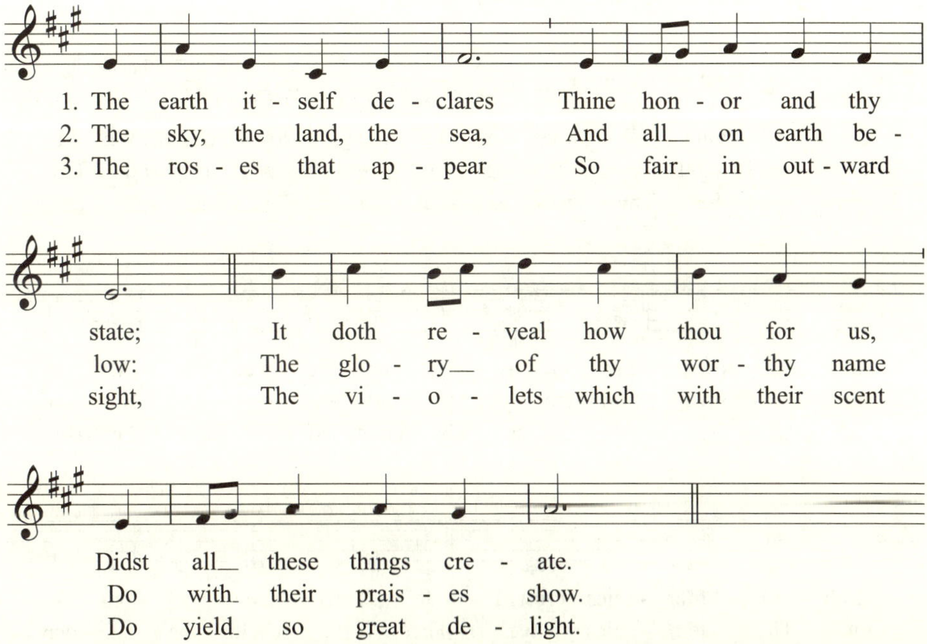

4. The winter yields thee praise
And summer doth the same:
The sun, the moon, the stars, and all
Do magnify thy name.

5. The thunder shows thy pow'r
And lightning which we see,
The snow and rain with wonder tell
That none is like to thee.

6. The pearls, the precious stones,
The birds thy praise do sing;
The woods, the wells, and all delights,
Which from this earth do spring.

7. Let us therefore with praise
Thy mighty works express,
With heart and hand, with mind and all
Which we from thee possess.

This text is part of a work written in the Tower of London by St. Philip Howard (d. 1595), Earl of Arundel, who in the Ordinary Form shares his 19 October Feastday with St. Jean de Brébeuf (d. 1649). St. Philip was a member of one of England's most powerful families. In 1581, he experienced a conversion after observing a "disputation" of St. Edmund Campion, wherein the pitiable Campion—given no time for preparation, no books, and still suffering greatly from the torture he had endured—publicly debated Anglicans at the Tower of London. In 1585, St. Philip was imprisoned at the Tower of London. Although he never met his fellow prisoner, St. Robert Southwell, they encouraged each other to remain faithful to Christ by means of St. Philip's dog, which secretly carried messages back and forth.

St. Philip desperately petitioned the Queen to allow him to see his wife and his son (born after his imprisonment), but she replied: "If he will but once attend the Protestant Service, he shall not only see his wife and children, but be restored to his honors and estates with every mark of my royal favor." St. Philip refused to attend the Anglican services and consequently died without ever seeing his family. Rather than betray Christ, St. Philip gave up everything—and we must follow his example. In 1873 Henry Fitzalan-Howard, a descendant of St. Philip, built the breathtaking Arundel Cathedral and in 1898 edited a very important Catholic hymnal called *Arundel Hymns*.

Melody: William Henry Walter (d. 1893), organist at Trinity Chapel in New York.

66 86 (SM)

Tune: Festal Song

818 Love Divine, All Loves Excelling

"Let us love one another; love springs from God; no one can love without being born of God, and knowing God."—I John 4.7

1st Tune

87 87 D

Tune: Rustington

Final Verses: Noel Rawsthorne (2011) #278.
Melody: Sir Charles H. H. Parry (d. 1918).
M. Source: *Hymns, Psalms, and Spiritual Canticles* (Massachusetts: Theodore Marier, 1983) p. 439.
Text: Charles Wesley (d. 1788), who wrote more than 6,500 hymns. His son was Samuel Wesley (d. 1837), who converted to Catholicism and as a composer was dubbed "the English Mozart."
T. Source: *Summit Choirbook* (Dominican Monastery of Our Lady of the Rosary, 1983) #455.

Love Divine, All Loves Excelling 819

"Let us love one another; love springs from God; no one can love without being born of God, and knowing God."—I John 4.7

2nd Tune

Final Verses: Richard Lloyd (1993) #100; Noel Rawsthorne (2011) #160.
Melody: Richard H. Pritchard (d. 1887); the tune name means "cheerful" in Welsh.
M. Source: *Catholic Hymn Book* (London Oratory, 1998) p. 182; *Hymns, Psalms, and Spiritual Canticles* (Massachusetts: Theodore Marier, 1983) pp. 192, 226, 404.
Text: Charles Wesley (d. 1788), who wrote more than 6,500 hymns. His son was Samuel Wesley (d. 1837), who converted to Catholicism and as a composer was dubbed "the English Mozart."
T. Source: *Summit Choirbook* (Dominican Monastery of Our Lady of the Rosary, 1983) #455.

87 87 D
Tune: HYFRYDOL

820 O Splendor Aeterni Patris (1736 AD)

Fr. Charles Coffin (d. 1749)

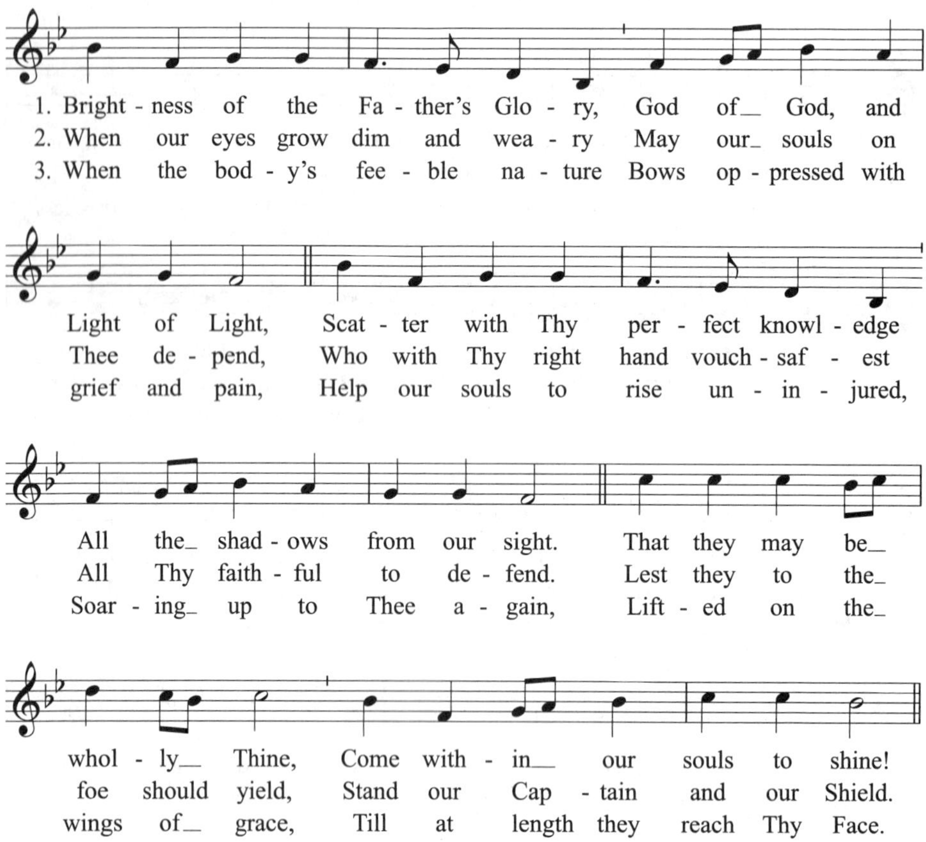

4. Only Hope of man's salvation!
Hear us—help us, when we pray;
Those, whom Thou by death hast purchased,
Cast not in Thy wrath away.
Grant Thy vengeance to subside,
Loving-kindness to provide.

5. Praise and worship to the Father,
Praise and worship to the Son,
Praise and worship to the Spirit,
Now and evermore be done:
Earth and Heaven join, their song,
Joyous, grateful, to prolong.

87 87 77

Tune:
All Saints

Final Verses: Richard Lloyd (1993) #7; Noel Rawsthorne (2011) #13.
Melody: *Geistreiches Gesangbuch* (Darmstadt, 1698).
M. Source: *New Saint Basil Hymnal* (1958) p. 203; *Catholic Hymn Book* (London Oratory, 1998) p. 290.
T. Source: The original Latin hymn was composed by Fr. Charles Coffin (d. 1749), and published in the *Paris Breviary* of 1736. The English translation was published in 1852 by James Russell Woodford (d. 1885).

O Splendor Aeterni Patris (1736 AD)

Fr. Charles Coffin (d. 1749)

Can be sung with any 87 87 77 meter, such as Coblenz, Westminster Abbey F7, Ich Begehr Nicht Mehr, Irby, Coelestia, etc.

BRIGHTNESS of the Father's Glory,
God of God, and Light of Light,
Scatter with Thy perfect knowledge
All the shadows from our sight.
That they may be wholly Thine,
Come within our souls to shine!

2. When our eyes grow dim and weary
May our souls on Thee depend,
Who with Thy right hand vouchsafest
All Thy faithful to defend.
Lest they to the foe should yield,
Stand our Captain and our Shield.

3. When the body's feeble nature
Bows oppressed with grief and pain,
Help our souls to rise uninjured,
Soaring up to Thee again,
Lifted on the wings of grace,
Till at length they reach Thy Face.

4. Only Hope of man's salvation!
Hear us—help us, when we pray;
Those, whom Thou by death hast purchased,
Cast not in Thy wrath away.
Grant Thy vengeance to subside,
Loving-kindness to provide.

5. Praise and worship to the Father,
Praise and worship to the Son,
Praise and worship to the Spirit,
Now and evermore be done:
Earth and Heaven join, their song,
Joyous, grateful, to prolong.

T. Source: The original Latin hymn was composed by Fr. Charles Coffin (d. 1749), and published in the *Paris Breviary* of 1736. The English translation was published in 1852 by James Russell Woodford (d. 1885).

87 87 77
Tune: Various

822 Praise To The Holiest In The Height

Bl. John Henry Cardinal Newman, Oratorian (d. 1890)

4. And that a higher gift than grace
Should flesh and blood refine,
God's Presence and His very Self,
And Essence all divine.

5. O gen'rous love! that He, who smote,
In man for man the foe,
The double agony in man
For man should undergo;

6. And in the garden secretly,
And on the Cross on high,
Should teach His brethren, and inspire
To suffer and to die.

7. Praise to the Holiest in the height,
And in the depth be praise;
In all His words most wonderful,
Most sure in all His ways.

86 86 (CM)

Tune:
BILLING

Final Verses: Richard Lloyd (1993) #19; Noel Rawsthorne (2011) #41.
Melody: Sir Richard R. Terry (d. 1938), choirmaster at Westminster Cathedral.
M. Source: *Catholic Hymn Book* (London Oratory, 1998) p. 454;
Saint Michael Hymnal (St. Boniface Parish, 2003) #496.
Text: From *The Dream of Gerontius* (1865). These verses ("Fifth Choir of Angelicals") are commonly used in Catholic hymnals, but the other four sections use the same meter and refrain.
T. Source: *Adoremus Hymnal* (1997) #615; *New Westminster Hymnal* (1939) p. 263.

Praise To The Holiest In The Height 823

Bl. John Henry Cardinal Newman, Oratorian (d. 1890)

Can be sung with any 86 86 meter, such as St Magnus, Bedford, St Columba, Westminster, St Anne, St Hugh, Hereford, St Flavian, etc.

PRAISE to the Holiest in the height,
And in the depth be praise;
In all His words most wonderful,
Most sure in all His ways.

2. O loving wisdom of our God!
When all was sin and shame,
A second Adam to the fight
And to the rescue came.

3. O wisest love! that flesh and blood,
Which did in Adam fail,
Should strive afresh against the foe,
Should strive and should prevail.

4. And that a higher gift than grace
Should flesh and blood refine,
God's Presence and His very Self,
And Essence all divine.

5. O gen'rous love! that He, who smote,
In man for man the foe,
The double agony in man
For man should undergo;

6. And in the garden secretly,
And on the Cross on high,
Should teach His brethren, and inspire
To suffer and to die.

7. Praise to the Holiest in the height,
And in the depth be praise;
In all His words most wonderful,
Most sure in all His ways.

86 86 (CM)

Text: From *The Dream of Gerontius* (1865). These verses ("Fifth Choir of Angelicals") are commonly used in Catholic hymnals, but the other four sections use the same meter and refrain.
T. Source: *Adoremus Hymnal* (1997) #615; *New Westminster Hymnal* (1939) p. 263.

Tune: Various

824 Schönster Herr Jesu (Jesuit Hymn)

Trns: Fr. Dominic Popplewell (b. 1973)

1. Lord Je - su fair - est, eve - ry lord who rul - est,
2. Thou who dost har - ness sole - ly all the fair - ness
3. Fair as the moon is, fair - er far the sun is,

God and Mar - y's_ Son who art, thee would I
that doth earth_ and_ heav'n en - dow, none else shall
fair the stars_ are_ e - qual - ly; nev - er was

cher - ish, hom - age would fur - nish, joy and rap - ture_
ev - er prove to me dear - er, Je - su dear - est_
an - gel fin - er than Je - sus, nor more pure_ could

of my heart.
mine, than thou.
be than he.

4. Fair find we silver,
pearls find even fairer,
fair indeed find gold agleam;
these now but glimmer
soon to grow dimmer:
evermore will Jesus beam.

5. Fair is each flower,
fairer still are childer
in men's fresh and early tide;
sure to fordo them,
death doth pursue them:
evermore will Jesus bide.

6. Lord Jesu dearest,
who yet here remainest
in the holiest Sacrament,
Jesu, I pray thee,
show us thy mercy
now and when our lives are spent.

[5b] "Childer" is an older form of "children."

567 557

Tune:
Schönster Herr Jesu

Text and Melody: From a Jesuit hymnal (1677) published in Münster, Germany.
T. Source: *Saint Jean de Brébeuf Hymnal* (2018).
M. Source: *Hymns, Psalms, and Spiritual Canticles* (Massachusetts: Theodore Marier, 1983) p. 225.

Gloriosi Salvatoris Nominis Praeconia (15th century) 825

Trns: Dr. John M. Neale (d. 1866)

4. Jesus, we thy name adoring,
Long to see thee as thou art:
Of thy clemency imploring
So to write it in our heart,
That hereafter, upward soaring,
We with angels may have part.

* FOURTH VERSE : Christians adore the name of JESUS because it is His name, and whatever belongs to God the Son is, by virtue of that same propriety, adorable. Cf. St. Thomas Aquinas, *Summa Theologiae*, 3rd part, Q. 25.

Final Verses: Richard Lloyd (1993) #175; Noel Rawsthorne (2011) #265.
T. Source: *Saint Michael Hymnal* (St. Boniface Parish, 2011) #801.
Melody: Henry Smart (d. 1879), organist at St. Philip's in London.
M. Source: *Catholic Hymn Book* (1998) p. 280; *Hymns, Psalms, and Spiritual Canticles* (1983) p. 213.

87 87 87
Tune:
REGENT SQUARE

826 Laudes Creaturarum (1224 AD)

Saint Francis of Assisi (d. 1226)

4. And thou most kind and gentle death,
Waiting to hush our latest breath:
O praise Him! Alleluia!
Thou leadest home the child of God,
And Christ our Lord the way hath trod: R.

5. Let all things their creator bless,
And worship Him in humbleness:
O praise Him! Alleluia!
Praise, praise the Father, praise the Son,
And praise the Spirit, Three in One: R.

88 88 A

Tune:
Lasst Uns Erfreuen

Final Verses: Richard Lloyd (1993) #111; Noel Rawsthorne (2011) #178.
Text: Based on Psalm 148; translated from Italian by William H. Draper (d. 1933). Sometimes called "The Canticle of the Sun," this text by St. Francis of Assisi is among the first works of literature written in the Italian language.
Melody: From a Jesuit collection (Cologne, 1623) entitled *Sacred Catholic Church Hymns, from Pentecost to Advent, Christmastide, Lenten Hymns, Paschal Hymns, Pilgrim songs, and all kinds to be sung throughout the whole year.* Two forms exist—placing "Alleluia" in various spots—and both are equally authentic.
M. Source: *Catholic Hymn Book* (1998) p. 478; *Hymns, Psalms, & Spiritual Canticles* (Marier, 1983) p. 328.

Trns: John Brownlie (d. 1925)

4. To Thee, Thou Three in One,
Ascend our songs divine;
One power, one kingdom without end,
And one dominion Thine.

5. O Christ, the source of light,
With light my soul inspire;
Come, make my heart the bright abode
Of Thy celestial fire.

Text: The provenance is not known, but the text is quite ancient.
T. Source: *Hymns of the Greek Church* (1900) p. 58.
Melody: William Henry Walter (d. 1893), organist at Trinity Chapel in New York.
M. Source: *Episcopal Hymnal* (1940) #535.

66 86 (SM)
Tune:
FESTAL SONG

828 Aeterna Caeli Gloria (5th century)

First Tune – *Trns: Msgr. Ronald A. Knox (d. 1957)*

4. Mysterious Trinity, be endless praise,
Father, and Son, and Holy Spirit, thine,
Long as time's star this twilight world displays,
And when outwearied suns no more shall shine.

* In this hymn, the Star is Christ (cf. II Pet 1.19; Ap 22.16).

Final Verses: Richard Lloyd (1993) #73; Noel Rawsthorne (2011) #123.
Text: Msgr. Ronald A. Knox (d. 1957); based on *Astre que l'Olympe revère* by Jean Racine (d. 1699) which is likewise based on *Aeterna Caeli Gloria* from Friday Lauds. The author of *Aeterna Caeli Gloria*—an alphabetical acrostic—is not known.
T. Source: *New Westminster Hymnal* (1939) p. 234.
M. Source: *New Westminster Hymnal* (1939) p. 234; *Catholic Hymn Book* (1998) p. 250.
Melody: Henry Lawes (d. 1662); due to the considerable involvement Msgr. Knox had in the creation of the *New Westminster Hymnal*, it can be assumed that he preferred this tune.

10 10 10 10

Tune:
Farley Castle

Second Tune – *Trns: Msgr. Ronald A. Knox (d. 1957)*

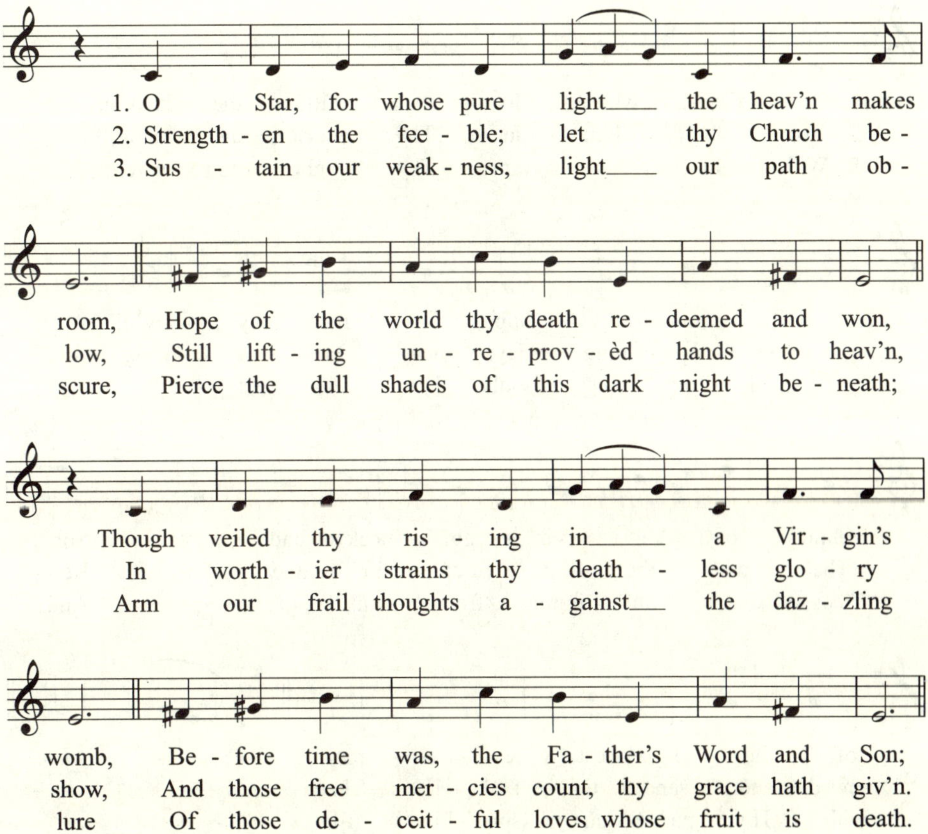

4. Mysterious Trinity, be endless praise,
Father, and Son, and Holy Spirit, thine,
Long as time's star this twilight world displays,
And when outwearied suns no more shall shine.

* In this hymn, the Star is Christ (cf. II Pet 1.19; Ap 22.16).

Text: Msgr. Ronald A. Knox (d. 1957); based on *Astre que l'Olympe revère* by Jean Racine (d. 1699) which is likewise based on *Aeterna Caeli Gloria* from Friday Lauds. The author of *Aeterna Caeli Gloria*—an alphabetical acrostic—is not known.
T. Source: *New Westminster Hymnal* (1939) p. 234.
Melody: Based on a work by Sir Percy Carter Buck (d. 1947) of the Royal College of Music.
M. Source: *New English Hymnal* (1986) p. 620.

10 10 10 10
Tune: Dublin

830 Aeterna Caeli Gloria (5th century)

Trns: Dr. John Julian (d. 1913)

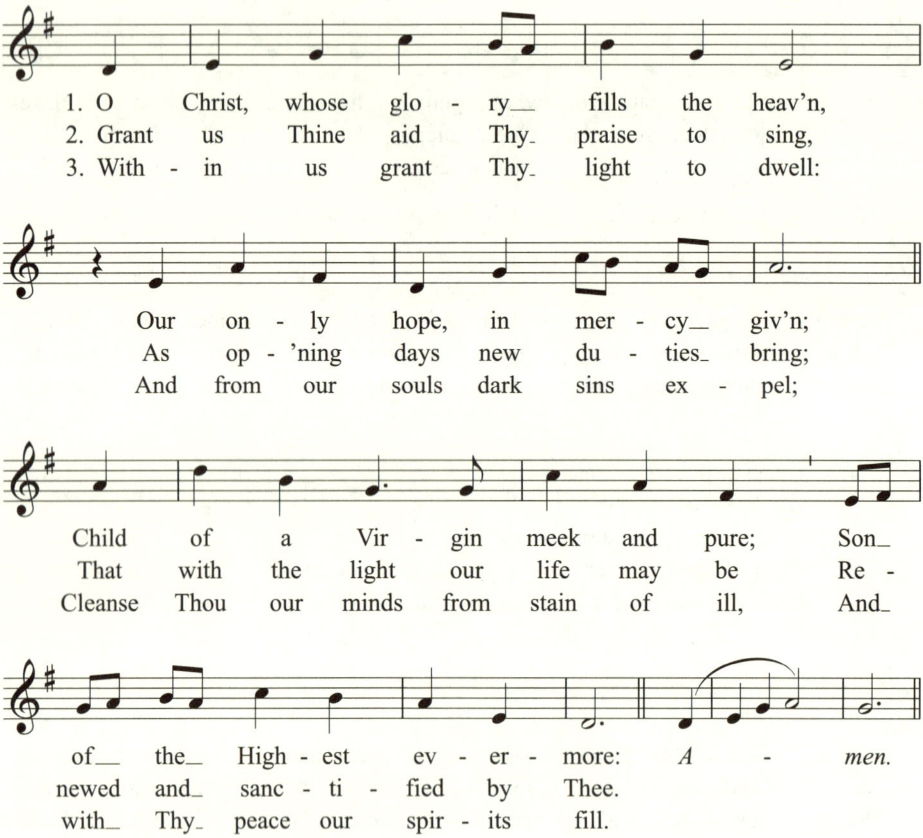

4. To us strong faith forever give,
With joyous hope, in Thee to live;
That life's rough way may ever be
Made strong and pure by charity.

5. All laud to God the Father be;
All praise, Eternal Son, to Thee;
All glory, as is ever meet,
To God the Holy Paraclete.

Final Verses: Richard Lloyd (1993) #80; Noel Rawsthorne (2011) #136.
Text: *Aeterna Caeli Gloria* is the Breviary hymn for Friday Lauds; an alphabetical acrostic whose author is not known.
T. Source: Fr. Matthew Britt, OSB, *Hymns of the Breviary and Missal* (1922) p. 68; courtesy of Dr. Julian's daughter.
Melody: Sir Percy Carter Buck (d. 1947); first published in *Fourteen Hymn Tunes* (1913).
M. Source: *Catholic Hymn Book* (London Oratory, 1998) p. 140. The tune was originally paired with *Vexilla Regis* ("Flag of the King"). A *gonfalon* ("flag") was traditionally carried during Catholic processions.

88 88 (LM)

Tune:
Gonfalon Royal

Trns: Dr. John Julian (d. 1913)

Can be sung with any 88 88 meter, such as EISENACH, ROGERS PARK, BRESSANI, LA ROCHELLE, KEMPEN, BESSEMER, TALLIS CANON, WINCHESTER NEW, etc.

O CHRIST, whose glory fills the heav'n,
Our only hope, in mercy giv'n;
Child of a Virgin meek and pure;
Son of the Highest evermore:

2. Grant us Thine aid Thy praise to sing,
As op'ning days new duties bring;
That with the light our life may be
Renewed and sanctified by Thee.

3. Within us grant Thy light to dwell:
And from our souls dark sins expel;
Cleanse Thou our minds from stain of ill,
And with Thy peace our spirits fill.

4. To us strong faith forever give,
With joyous hope, in Thee to live;
That life's rough way may ever be
Made strong and pure by charity.

5. All laud to God the Father be;
All praise, Eternal Son, to Thee;
All glory, as is ever meet,
To God the Holy Paraclete.

Text: *Aeterna Caeli Gloria* is the Breviary hymn for Friday Lauds.
It is an alphabetical acrostic whose author is not known.
T. Source: Fr. Matthew Britt, OSB, *Hymns of the Breviary and Missal* (1922) p. 68;
courtesy of Dr. Julian's daughter.

88 88 (LM)

Tune:
VARIOUS

832 Aeterna Caeli Gloria (5th century)

First Tune – *Trns: Robert Campbell of Skerrington (d. 1868)*

1. Christ, the glo - ry of the sky, Christ, of earth the
2. Help us now Thy praise to sing; Grant our souls to
3. Day that dawns be - fore our eyes But that ver - y

hope se - cure, On - ly Son of God most high,
know thy day: Light and life them let it bring,
Light de - clares Which the mind with strength sup - plies,

Off - spring of a Maid - en pure.
Clouds and dark - ness burn a - way.
World - ly night to brave pre - pares.

4. Purest Light, within us dwell,
Never from our souls depart;
Come, the shades of earth dispel,
Fill and purify the heart.

5. Faith in Him Whose name we bear
In our heart of hearts abound;
Hope, thy brightest torch prepare;
All with holy love be crowned.

6. Praise the Father, praise the Son,
Spirit blest, to Thee be praise;
To the Godhead Three in One
Glory be through endless days.

77 77

Tune:
Culbach

Final Verses: Richard Lloyd (1993) #49; Noel Rawsthorne (2011) #82.
T. Source: *American Catholic Hymnal according to the Motu Proprio of His Holiness Pope Pius X* (New York: Kenedy & Sons, 1913) p. 251.
Melody: From a Chorale in Johann Scheffler's *Heilige Seelenlust* (1657).
M. Source: *New Saint Basil Hymnal* (1958) p. 218; *Mediator Dei Hymnal* (1955) p. 83.

Aeterna Caeli Gloria (5th century) 833

Second Tune – *Trns: Robert Campbell of Skerrington (d. 1868)*

4. Purest Light, within us dwell,
Never from our souls depart;
Come, the shades of earth dispel,
Fill and purify the heart. *Alleluia.*

5. Faith in Him Whose name we bear
In our heart of hearts abound;
Hope, thy brightest torch prepare;
All with holy love be crowned. *Alleluia.*

6. Praise the Father, praise the Son,
Spirit blest, to Thee be praise;
To the Godhead Three in One
Glory be through endless days. *Alleluia.*

Melody: From *Hundert Arien* (Dresden, 1697), adapted by
William H. Monk (d. 1889), organist at King's College London.
M. Source: *Songs of Syon* (Woodward, 1910) p. 455; *New Westminster Hymnal* (1939) p. 80.
T. Source: *American Catholic Hymnal according to the Motu Proprio of His Holiness Pope Pius X* (New York: Kenedy & Sons, 1913) p. 251.

77 77 A

Tune: Würtemburg

834 Aeterna Caeli Gloria (5th century)

Third Tune – *Trns: Robert Campbell of Skerrington (d. 1868)*

4. Purest Light, within us dwell,
Never from our souls depart;
Come, the shades of earth dispel,
Fill and purify the heart.

5. Faith in Him Whose name we bear
In our heart of hearts abound;
Hope, thy brightest torch prepare;
All with holy love be crowned.

6. Praise the Father, praise the Son,
Spirit blest, to Thee be praise;
To the Godhead Three in One
Glory be through endless days.

N.B. This melody is excellent for use during Lent.

77 77

Tune:
Aus Der Tiefe

Final Verses: Richard Lloyd (1993) #13; Noel Rawsthorne (2011) #29.
Melody: Martin Herbst (d. 1681); first published in *Nürnbergerisches Gesangbuch* (1676).
M. Source: *New Westminster Hymnal* (1939) p. 60; *Catholic Hymn Book* (London Oratory, 1998) p. 82.
T. Source: *American Catholic Hymnal according to the Motu Proprio of His Holiness Pope Pius X* (New York: Kenedy & Sons, 1913) p. 251.

Aeterna Caeli Gloria (5th century) 835

Fourth Tune – *Trns: Robert Campbell of Skerrington (d. 1868)*

4. Purest Light, within us dwell,
Never from our souls depart;
Come, the shades of earth dispel,
Fill and purify the heart.
Alleluia.

5. Faith in Him Whose name we bear
In our heart of hearts abound;
Hope, thy brightest torch prepare;
All with holy love be crowned.
Alleluia.

6. Praise the Father, praise the Son,
Spirit blest, to Thee be praise;
To the Godhead Three in One
Glory be through endless days.
Alleluia.

Melody: From Johann Scheffler's *Heilige Seelenlust* (1657).
M. Source: *Songs of Syon* (Woodward, 1910) p. 428.
T. Source: *American Catholic Hymnal according to the Motu Proprio of His Holiness Pope Pius X* (New York: Kenedy & Sons, 1913) p. 251.

77 77 A

Tune:
Keine Schönheit Hat Die Welt

836 Aeterna Caeli Gloria (5th century)

Fifth Tune – *Trns: Robert Campbell of Skerrington (d. 1868)*

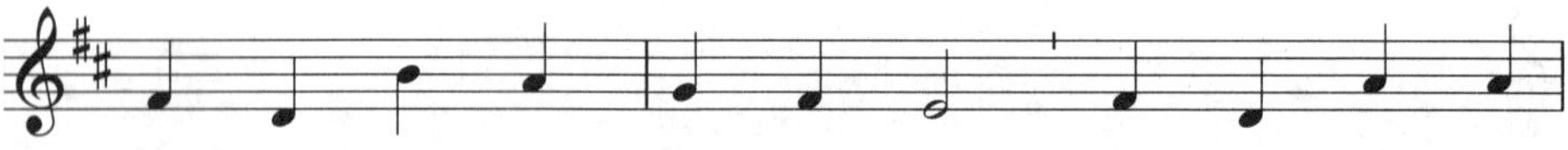

1. Christ, the glo - ry of the sky, Christ, of earth the
2. Help us now Thy praise to sing; Grant our souls to
3. Day that dawns be - fore our eyes But that ver - y

hope se - cure, On - ly Son of God most high,
know thy day: Light and life them let it bring,
Light de - clares Which the mind with strength sup - plies,

Off - spring of a Maid - en pure.
Clouds and dark - ness burn a - way.
World - ly night to brave pre - pares.

4. Purest Light, within us dwell,
Never from our souls depart;
Come, the shades of earth dispel,
Fill and purify the heart.

5. Faith in Him Whose name we bear
In our heart of hearts abound;
Hope, thy brightest torch prepare;
All with holy love be crowned.

6. Praise the Father, praise the Son,
Spirit blest, to Thee be praise;
To the Godhead Three in One
Glory be through endless days.

77 77

Tune:
University College

Final Verses: Richard Lloyd (1993) #233; Noel Rawsthorne (2011) #373.
Melody: Henry J. Gauntlett (d. 1876), organist at St. Olave's Church, London.
M. Source: *New English Hymnal* (1986) p. 916.
T. Source: *American Catholic Hymnal according to the Motu Proprio of His Holiness Pope Pius X* (New York: Kenedy & Sons, 1913) p. 251.

Aeterna Caeli Gloria (5th century)

Trns: Robert Campbell of Skerrington (d. 1868)

Can be sung with any 77 77 meter, such as SAVANNAH, UNIVERSITY COLLEGE, ORIENTIS PARTIBUS, LLANFAIR, CULBACH, MONKLAND, GOTT SEI DANK, etc.

CHRIST, the glory of the sky,
Christ, of earth the hope secure,
Only Son of God most high,
Offspring of a Maiden pure.

2. Help us now Thy praise to sing;
Grant our souls to know thy day:
Light and life them let it bring,
Clouds and darkness burn away.

3. Day that dawns before our eyes
But that very Light declares
Which the mind with strength supplies,
Worldly night to brave prepares.

4. Purest Light, within us dwell,
Never from our souls depart;
Come, the shades of earth dispel,
Fill and purify the heart.

5. Faith in Him Whose name we bear
In our heart of hearts abound;
Hope, thy brightest torch prepare;
All with holy love be crowned.

6. Praise the Father, praise the Son,
Spirit blest, to Thee be praise;
To the Godhead Three in One
Glory be through endless days.

77 77

T. Source: *American Catholic Hymnal according to the Motu Proprio of His Holiness Pope Pius X* (New York: Kenedy & Sons, 1913) p. 251.

Tune: VARIOUS

838 Anima Christi, Sanctifica Me (14th century)

Trns: Thomas I. Ball (d. 1916)

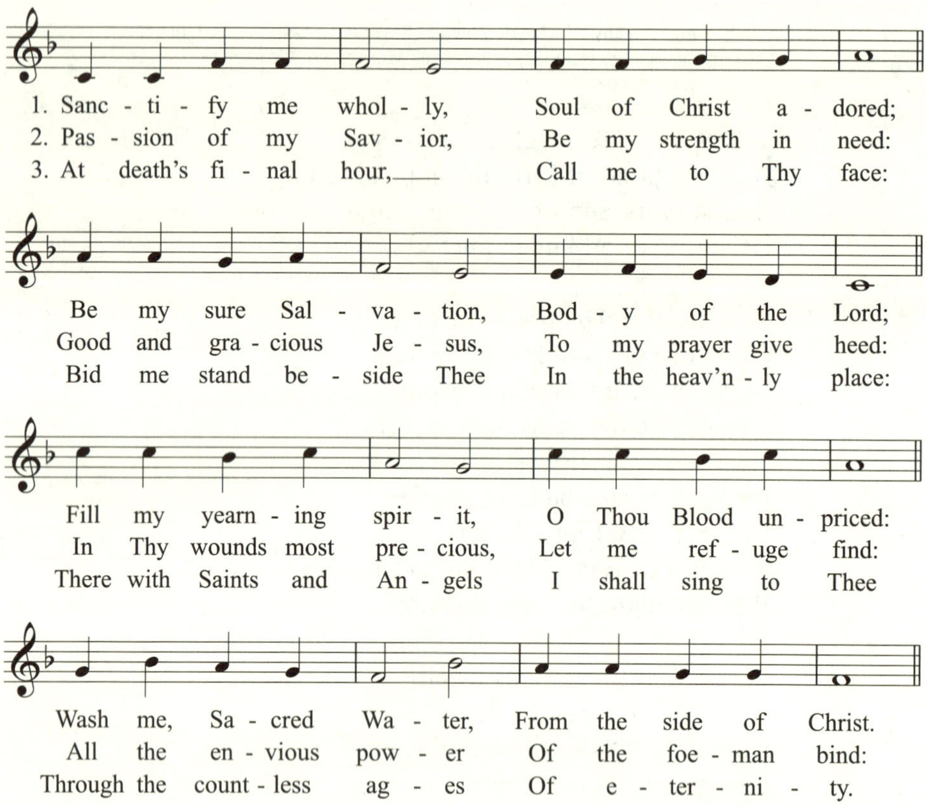

Another English translation from 1882 may also be sung to Anima Christi 10a:

Ánima Christi, sanctifíca me.
Corpus Christi, salva me.
Sanguis Christi, inébria me.
Aqua láteris Christi, lava me.

Pássio Christi, confórta me.
O bone Jesu, exáudi me.
Intra tua vúlnera abscónde me.
Ne permíttas me separári a te.

Ab hoste malígno defénde me.
In hora mortis meae voca me.
Et jube me veníre ad te.
Ut cum sanctis tuis laudem te.

SOUL of my Savior, sanctify my breast;
Body of Christ, be Thou my saving guest;
Blood of my Savior, bathe me in Thy tide;
Wash me, ye waters, flowing from His side.

2. Strength and protection may Thy Passion be;
O blessèd Jesus, hear and answer me;
Deep in Thy wounds, Lord, hide and shelter me;
So shall I never, never part from Thee.

3. Save me from evil, make me Thine alone;
In my last moments take me for Thine own;
Call me and bid me hasten to Thy side,
That I may see Thee praised and glorified.

65 65 D

Tune: Anima Christi

Final Verses: Noel Rawsthorne (2011) #22.
Melody: Fr. William J. Maher (d. 1877), editor of Trappes's *Hymns for the Liturgical Year* (1865).
M. Source: *New Saint Basil Hymnal* (1958) p. 119; *Catholic Hymn Book* (1998) p. 215.
T. Source: *New St. Basil Hymnal* (1958) p. 117; *Hymns of the Breviary and Missal* (Fr. Matthew Britt, 1922) p. 193.

Now Thank We All Our God

"Who hath done great things in all the earth, who hath increased our days from our mother's womb, and hath done with us according to his mercy."—Sirach 50.24

Final Verses: Richard Lloyd (1993) #154; Noel Rawsthorne (2011) #233.
Text: Martin Rinkart (d. 1649); based on Sirach 50.22-24. Original title in German: *Nun danket alle Gott.* English translation by Catherine Winkworth (d. 1878).
T. Source: *Saint Michael Hymnal* (St. Boniface Parish, 2003) #428.
Melody: Johann Crüger (d. 1662), choirmaster of St. Nicholas' Church, Berlin.
M. Source: *New Saint Basil Hymnal* (1958) p. 224; *New Westminster Hymnal* (1939) p. 265.

67 67 66 66

Tune:
NUN DANKET

840 Alleluia, Sing To Jesus

"Thou wert slain in sacrifice; out of every tribe, every language, every people, every nation thou hast ransomed us with thy blood and given us to God."—Apocalypse 5.9

1st Tune

4. Alleluia, King eternal, | Thee the Lord of lords we own;
Alleluia, born of Mary, | Earth Thy footstool, heav'n thy throne:
Thou within the veil hast entered, | Robed in flesh our great High Priest;
Thou on earth both Priest and Victim | In the Eucharistic Feast.

87 87 D

Tune: HYFRYDOL

Final Verses: Richard Lloyd (1993) #100; Noel Rawsthorne (2011) #160.
Melody: Richard H. Pritchard (d. 1887); the tune name means "cheerful" in Welsh.
M. Source: *Summit Choirbook* (Dominican Monastery of Our Lady of the Rosary, 1983) #466.
Text: William Chatterton Dix (d. 1898). T. Source: *Catholic Hymn Book* (1998) p. 183.

"Thou wert slain in sacrifice; out of every tribe, every language, every people, every nation thou hast ransomed us with thy blood and given us to God."—Apocalypse 5.9

2nd Tune

4. Alleluia, King eternal,
Thee the Lord of lords we own;
Alleluia, born of Mary,
Earth Thy footstool, heav'n thy throne:
Thou within the veil hast entered,
Robed in flesh our great High Priest;
Thou on earth both Priest and Victim
In the Eucharistic Feast.

87 87 D

Final Verses: Noel Rawsthorne (2011) #278. Melody: Sir Charles H. H. Parry (d. 1918).
M. Source: *Hymns, Psalms, and Spiritual Canticles* (Massachusetts: Theodore Marier, 1983) p. 439.
Text: William Chatterton Dix (d. 1898). T. Source: *Catholic Hymn Book* (1998) p. 183.

Tune: RUSTINGTON

842 Sing Praise To God Who Reigns Above

"A high God is the Lord, a king high above all the gods; beneath his hand lie the depths of earth, his are the mountain peaks; his the ocean..."—Ps 94.3-4

4. Let all who name Christ's holy Name
Give God all praise and glory;
Let all who own His pow'r proclaim
Aloud the wondrous story!
Cast each false idol from its throne,
For Christ is Lord, and Christ alone: R.

87 87 88 7

Tune:
Mit Freuden Zart

Final Verses: Richard Lloyd (1993) #141; Noel Rawsthorne (2011) #215.
Melody: *Kirchengeseng* (Böhmische Brüder, 1566); based on "Une pastourelle gentille," a chanson published by Pierre Attaingnant in 1529.
M. Source: *Saint Michael Hymnal* (St. Boniface Parish, 2003) #527.
Text: Johann Jakob Schütz (d. 1690); transl. from German by Frances Elizabeth Cox (d. 1897).
T. Source: *Hymns, Psalms, and Spiritual Canticles* (Massachusetts: Theodore Marier, 1983) #301.

Lift Up Your Heads, Ye Mighty Gates (Psalm 23) 843

"Lift up your gates, O ye princes, and be ye lifted up, O eternal gates: and the King of Glory shall enter in."—Ps 23.7

1. Lift up your heads, ye might - y gates;
2. O blest the land, the cit - y blest,
3. Fling wide the por - tals of your heart;

Be - hold, the King__ of__ glo - ry waits;
Where Christ the Rul - er__ is con - fessed!
Make it a tem - ple,__ set a - part

The King of kings is draw - ing__ near;
O hap - py hearts and hap - py__ homes
From earth - ly use for heav'n's em - ploy,

The Sav - ior of__ the__ world is here.
To whom this King__ in__ tri - umph comes!
A - dorned with prayer__ and__ love and joy.

4. So come, my Sovereign, enter in!
Let new and nobler life begin;
Thy Holy Spirit guide us on,
Until the glorious crown be won.

* This hymn is often sung in Advent as well as for feasts involving the Kingship of Christ.

Final Verses: Richard Lloyd (1993) #230; Noel Rawsthorne (2011) #370.
Melody: Anonymous; first published by a British hymnal (*Psalmodia Evangelica*) in 1789, paired with *Now To The Lord A Noble Song*, a text by Isaac Watts (d. 1748). Truro is an ancient city in Southwest England.
M. Source: *Hymns, Psalms, and Spiritual Canticles* (Massachusetts: Theodore Marier, 1983) p. 279.
Text: Georg Weissel (d. 1635); translation from German by Catherine Winkworth (d. 1878).
T. Source: *Saint Michael Hymnal* (St. Boniface Parish, 2003) #399.

88 88 (LM)
Tune:
TRURO

844 God Of Mercy, God Of Grace (Psalm 66)

"May God be merciful to us, and bless us; may he grant us the favor of his smile."—Ps 66.2

77 77 77

Tune:
Heathlands

Final Verses: Richard Lloyd (1993) #89; Noel Rawsthorne (2011) #148.
Melody: Henry Smart (d. 1879), organist at St. Philip's in London.
M. Source: *Hymns Ancient and Modern* (1972) p. 353.
Text: Henry Francis Lyte (d. 1847).
T. Source: *Summit Choirbook* (Dominican Monastery of Our Lady of the Rosary, 1983) #508.

I Sing The Mighty Power Of God 845

"The dry land God called Earth, and the water, where it had collected, he called the Sea. All this God saw, and found it good."—Genesis 1.10

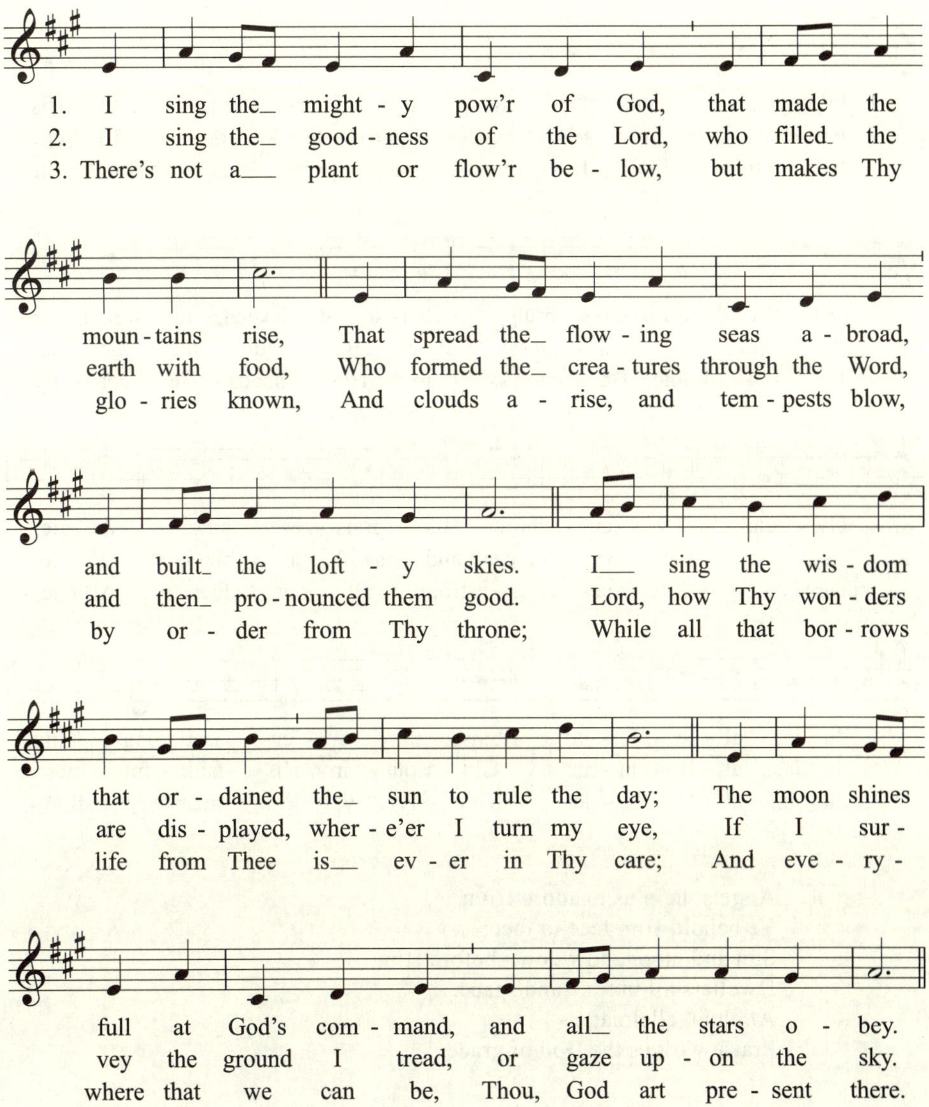

Final Verses: Richard Lloyd (1993) #65; Noel Rawsthorne (2011) #109.
Melody: Würtemburg *Gesangbuch* (1784).
M. Source: *Catholic Hymn Book* (London Oratory, 1998) p. 398; *New Westminster Hymnal* (1939) p. 270.
Text: Isaac Watts (d. 1748).
T. Source: *Hymns, Psalms, and Spiritual Canticles* (Massachusetts: Theodore Marier, 1983) #301.

86 86 D
Tune:
ELLACOMBE

846 Praise, My Soul, The King Of Heaven (Psalm 102)

"Bless the Lord, O my soul: and let all that is within me bless his holy name. Bless the Lord, O my soul, and never forget all he hath done for thee."—Ps 102.1-2

1. Praise, my soul, the King of Heav - en; To His
2. Praise Him for His grace and fa - vor To our
3. Fa - ther - like He tends and spares us; Well our

feet thy trib - ute bring. Ran - somed, healed, re - stored, for -
fa - thers in dis - tress; Praise Him still the same as
fee - ble frame He knows; In His hands He gen - tly

giv - en, Ev - er - more His prais - es sing: Al - le -
ev - er, Slow to chide, and swift to bless. Al - le -
bears us, Res - cues us from all our foes. Al - le -

lu - ia, al - le - lu - ia; Praise the ev - er - last - ing King.
lu - ia, al - le - lu - ia; Glo - rious in His faith - ful - ness.
lu - ia, al - le - lu - ia; Wide - ly yet His mer - cy flows.

4. Angels, help us to adore Him;
Ye behold Him face to face;
Sun and moon, bow down before Him,
Dwellers all in time and space.
Alleluia, alleluia;
Praise with us the God of grace.

87 87 87

Tune:
Lauda Anima

Final Verses: Richard Lloyd (1993) #169; Noel Rawsthorne (2011) #258.
Melody: John Goss (d. 1880), Professor of Harmony at the Royal Academy of Music.
M. Source: *New Saint Basil Hymnal* (1958) p. 202; *Hymns, Psalms, and Spiritual Canticles* (1983) p. 294.
Text: Henry Francis Lyte (d. 1847).
T. Source: *Saint Michael Hymnal* (St. Boniface Parish, 2003) #527; *Hymns, Psalms, and Spiritual Canticles* (Massachusetts: Theodore Marier, 1983) p. 400.

Praise, My Soul, The King Of Heaven (Psalm 102) 847

"Bless the Lord, O my soul: and let all that is within me bless his holy name. Bless the Lord, O my soul, and never forget all he hath done for thee."—Ps 102.1-2

Can be sung with any 87 87 87 meter: RUNNELLS, MANNHEIM, DULCE CARMEN, BRETON, GAUFESTRE, LAUDA ANIMA, DAVOST, ST LEONARD, PICARDY, REGENT SQUARE, etc.

PRAISE, my soul, the King of Heaven;
To His feet thy tribute bring.
Ransomed, healed, restored, forgiven,
Evermore His praises sing:
Alleluia, alleluia;
Praise the everlasting King.

2. Praise Him for His grace and favor
To our fathers in distress;
Praise Him still the same as ever,
Slow to chide, and swift to bless.
Alleluia, alleluia;
Glorious in His faithfulness.

3. Fatherlike He tends and spares us;
Well our feeble frame He knows;
In His hands He gently bears us,
Rescues us from all our foes.
Alleluia, alleluia;
Widely yet His mercy flows.

4. Angels, help us to adore Him;
Ye behold Him face to face;
Sun and moon, bow down before Him,
Dwellers all in time and space.
Alleluia, alleluia;
Praise with us the God of grace.

Text: Henry Francis Lyte (d. 1847).
T. Source: *Saint Michael Hymnal* (St. Boniface Parish, 2003) #527; *Hymns, Psalms, and Spiritual Canticles* (Massachusetts: Theodore Marier, 1983) p. 400.

87 87 87
Tune: VARIOUS

848 O Bello Dio, Signor Del Paradiso

Saint Alphonsus Liguori, Founder of the Redemptorists (d. 1787)

66 66 66 8

Tune:
St Elizabeth

Text: Most Rev'd Alphonsus Maria Liguori (d. 1787) named "Doctor of the Church" in 1871 by Pope Pius IX, was known during his lifetime for his solicitude for the poor, his theological writings, and the pains he took to assure his priests celebrated Mass with proper reverence. Toward the end of his life, he suffered greatly from an incurable neck injury that left him unable to lift his head.
English Translation: Fr. Edmund Vaughan (d. 1908), a Priest of the Congregation of the Most Holy Redeemer ("Redemptorists").
T. Source: *Mediator Dei Hymnal* (1955) p. 43; *Adoremus Hymnal* (1997) #608.
Melody: Henry Smart (d. 1879), organist at St. Philip's in London.
M. Source: *Traditional Roman Hymnal* (2003) p. 296; *St. Edmund Campion Hymnal* (2013) p. 930.

Holy, Holy, Holy! Lord God Almighty 849

"And they cried one to another, and said: Holy, holy, holy, the Lord God of hosts, all the earth is full of his glory."—Isaias 6.3

4. Holy, holy, holy! Lord God Almighty!
All Thy works shall praise Thy name,
in earth, and sky, and sea;
Holy, holy, holy; merciful and mighty!
God in three Persons, blessèd Trinity!

Final Verses: Richard Lloyd (1993) #152; Noel Rawsthorne (2011) #228.
Melody: John Bacchus Dykes (d. 1876).
M. Source: *Hymns, Psalms, and Spiritual Canticles* (Massachusetts: Theodore Marier, 1983) p. 280; *Adoremus Hymnal* (1997) #460.
Text: Reginald Heber (d. 1826); written for use on Trinity Sunday.
T. Source: *Saint Michael Hymnal* (St. Boniface Parish, 2003) #343.

11 12 12 10
Tune: NICAEA

850 Consors Paterni Luminis (5th century)

First Tune – *Trns: Fr. Dominic Popplewell (b. 1973)*

1. Our hope a - lone, thy sov - 'reign Fa - ther's peer,
2. Thy might - y grace as fire on us pour out;
3. Be gra - cious to a peo - ple who be - lieve,

Of earth and heav'n the ev - er - last - ing day,
Thy voice re - sound - ing rout the force of hell;
Now gath - ered, Christ, and thee to bless who yearn:

Thou Word, our in - ward eyes to thee we rear:
Thou of the soul, whose frail - ty sees her flout
Their hymns, raised to thy death - less fame, re - ceive,

O sav - ing God, look down on us, we pray.
Thy laws, the le - thal sense - less - ness dis - pel.
Then, with thy gifts re - plete, let them re - turn.

4. O Father, Son and Spirit, God alone,
The Holy One, the Word, their Bond divine,
Our fervent prayer attend, whose empires own
Nor rise nor term, and self-illumined shine.

T. Source: After Jean Racine (d. 1699), *Verbe, égal au Très-Haut*—based on the Breviary hymn *Consors Paterni luminis*. When sung for Vespers, the first verse should be altered to:

1. Our hope alone, thy sov'reign Father's peer,
Of earth and heav'n the everlasting day,
Thou Word, the still of peaceful night we shear:
O saving God, look down on us, we pray.

10 10 10 10

Tune:
Toulon

Melody: Louis Bourgeois (d. 1559) in the *Genevan Psalter* (1551); also called "Old 124th."
M. Source: *People's Mass Book* (1964) p. 226; *New Saint Basil Hymnal* (1958) p. 80.

Consors Paterni Luminis (5th century)

Second Tune – *Trns: Fr. Dominic Popplewell (b. 1973)*

4. O Father, Son and Spirit, God alone,
The Holy One, the Word, their Bond divine,
Our fervent prayer attend, whose empires own
Nor rise nor term, and self-illumined shine.

T. Source: After Jean Racine (d. 1699), *Verbe, égal au Très-Haut*—based on the Breviary hymn *Consors Paterni luminis*. When sung for Vespers, the first verse should be altered to:

1. Our hope alone, thy sov'reign Father's peer,
Of earth and heav'n the everlasting day,
Thou Word, the still of peaceful night we shear:
O saving God, look down on us, we pray.

10 10 10 10

Melody: Henry Lawes (d. 1662), whose compositions John Milton (d. 1674) praised in a famous sonnet.
M. Source: *New Westminster Hymnal* (1939) p. 234; *Catholic Hymn Book* (London Oratory, 1998) p. 250.

Tune: Farley Castle

852 Faith Of Our Fathers, Holy Faith

Fr. Frederick Faber, Founder of the London Oratory (d. 1863)

4. Faith of our fathers! We will love
Both friend and foe in all our strife;
And preach thee, too, as love knows how
By kindly words and virtuous life. R.

88 88 88

Tune:
ST CATHERINE

Final Verses: Noel Rawsthorne (2011) #290.
Melody: Henri Frederick Hemy (d. 1888), a Catholic organist and publisher of hymnals who once taught in Tynemouth—and this tune is sometimes called "Tynemouth."
M. Source: *New Westminster Hymnal* (1939) p. 114; *Mediator Dei Hymnal* (1955) p. 106; *Hymns, Psalms, and Spiritual Canticles* (Massachusetts: Theodore Marier, 1983) p. 241.
T. Source: *Saint Michael Hymnal* (St. Boniface Parish, 2003) #294; *Saint Edmund Campion Missal and Hymnal* (2013) p. 928; *Adoremus Hymnal* (1997) #603.

Praise To The Lord, The Almighty 853

"From them that resist thy right hand keep me, as the apple of thine eye. Protect me under the shadow of thy wings."—Ps 16.8

4. Praise to the Lord! Oh, let all that is in me adore Him.
All that hath life and breath, come now with praises before Him.
Let the "Amen"
sound from His people again,
Now as we worship before Him.

Final Verses: Richard Lloyd (1993) #119; Noel Rawsthorne (2011) #187.
Melody: *Erneuerten Gesangbuch* (Stralsund, 1665).
M. Source: *Catholic Hymn Book* (London Oratory, 1998) p. 178.
Text: Joachim Neander (d. 1680); translation from German by Catherine Winkworth (d. 1878).
T. Source: *Hymns, Psalms, and Spiritual Canticles* (Massachusetts: Theodore Marier, 1983) #407; *New Saint Basil Hymnal* (1958) p. 70; *Saint Michael Hymnal* (St. Boniface Parish, 2003) #498.

14 14 4 7 8

Tune:
LOBE DEN HERREN

856 Praise The Lord, Ye Heavens Adore Him

"Praise ye the Lord from the heavens: praise ye him in the high places. Praise ye him, all his angels, praise ye him, all his hosts."—Ps 148.1-2

87 87 D

Tune:
RUSTINGTON

Final Verses: Noel Rawsthorne (2011) #278. Melody: Sir Charles H. H. Parry (d. 1918).
M. Source: *Hymns, Psalms, and Spiritual Canticles* (Massachusetts: Theodore Marier, 1983) p. 439.
Text: *Psalms, Hymns, and Anthems of the Foundling Hospital, London* (1796);
final verse from *The Mitre Hymn Book* (1836), by Edward Osler (d. 1863).
T. Source: *Catholic Hymn Book* (1998) p. 453; *Catholic Hymns* (Baltimore: Fr. John Selner, 1954) p. 12.

Splendor Paternae Gloriae (4th century)

Trns: David T. Morgan (d. 1886)

1. O Thou, the Bright - ness of the Fa - ther's glo - ry,
2. O Thou, true Sun, shine down up - on Thy crea - tures,
3. And on the Fa - ther let us in - stant call - ing—

Who from that ra - diance bring - est us the light,
Thou shin - est ev - er, suff - 'rest no de - cay,
The Fa - ther of e - ter - nal glo - ry— pray

Thy - self the Light of Light, the Fount of clear - ness,
And all our sens - es, all our in - most na - ture
That He His all - po - ten - tial grace be - stow - ing,

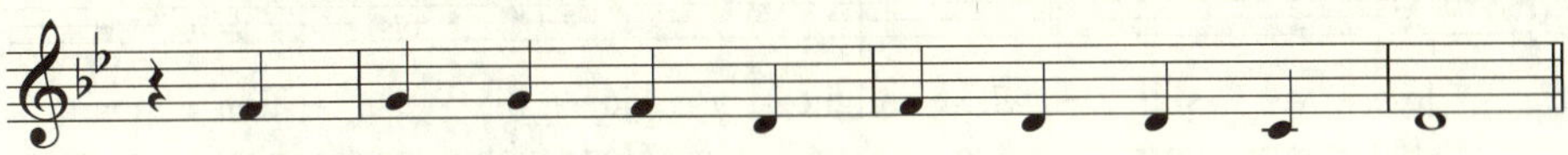

The Day of Days il - lu - min - ing our night.
Fill with the Ho - ly Spir - it's gra - cious ray:
De - ceit - ful sin will ban - ish far a - way;

4. Pray Him to brace us for our earthly combat,
To blunt the weapons of our envious foe,
Amidst the storms of life to raise us falling,
And grant us heav'nward on our path to go.

5. Pray Him our erring minds to rule and govern,
That soul and body pure and true may meet,
And let our faith, with warmest ardor glowing,
Know not the fraudful poison of deceit.

6. So this good day with holy gladness passing,
Our modesty as blushing dawn may be,
Our faith as glows the sun's meridian brightness,
And may our soul no dark'ning twilight see.

Text: Saint Ambrose, Bishop of Milan (d. 397AD).
T. Source: *Hymns of the Latin Church* (1871) p. 86.
Melody: Peter Lejeune (b. 1991), organist at Saint John Vianney Catholic Church in Springfield.
M. Source: *Saint Jean de Brébeuf Hymnal* (2018).

11 10 11 10
Tune: RAYMBAULT

858 The Living God, With Meekness Crowned

First Tune – *Fr. Dominic Popplewell (b. 1973)*

4. Glory to Christ above | and to the blessèd tree
on which he bled, compelled by love, | to set the fettered free!
For him creation waits: | he keeps his heav'nly seat,
his awesome retribution bates, | ere all lie at his feet.

[1d] Lk 19.40
[1f] Ps 23.7
[2f] Is 53.7; Jer 11.19; Acts 8.32
[2g] Zach 9.9; Mt 21.5
[2h] Job 41.16; Mt 26.53
[3b] Phil 2.7; Rom 8.3
[3d] Rom 5.8
[3h] Ez 37.26
[4e] Rom 8.22
[4h] Ps 109.1; I Cor 15.25

S. M. D.

Tune: Diademata

T. Source: *Saint Jean de Brébeuf Hymnal* (2018).
Melody: George J. Elvey (d. 1893), organist at St George's Chapel at Windsor Castle.
M. Source: *Hymns, Psalms, and Spiritual Canticles* (Massachusetts: Theodore Marier, 1983) p. 232.

The Living God, With Meekness Crowned

Second Tune – *Fr. Dominic Popplewell (b. 1973)*

4. Glory to Christ above | and to the blessèd tree
on which he bled, compelled by love, | to set the fettered free!
For him creation waits: | he keeps his heav'nly seat,
his awesome retribution bates, | ere all lie at his feet.

[1d] Lk 19.40
[1f] Ps 23.7
[2f] Is 53.7; Jer 11.19; Acts 8.32
[2g] Zach 9.9; Mt 21.5
[2h] Job 41.16; Mt 26.53
[3b] Phil 2.7; Rom 8.3
[3d] Rom 5.8
[3h] Ez 37.26
[4e] Rom 8.22
[4h] Ps 109.1; I Cor 15.25

S. M. D.

T. Source: *Saint Jean de Brébeuf Hymnal* (2018).
Melody: Sir Richard R. Terry (d. 1938), choirmaster at Westminster Cathedral.
M. Source: *New Saint Basil Hymnal* (1958) p. 83; *New Westminster Hymnal* (1939) p. 132.

Tune:
Corona

860 Glorious Things Of Thee Are Spoken (Isaias 33)

*"The Lord loveth the gates of Sion above all the tabernacles of Jacob.
Glorious things are said of thee, O city of God."—Ps 86.2-3*

1st Tune

87 87 D

Tune: Rustington

Final Verses: Noel Rawsthorne (2011) #278. Melody: Sir Charles H. H. Parry (d. 1918).
M. Source: *Hymns, Psalms, and Spiritual Canticles* (Massachusetts: Theodore Marier, 1983) p. 439.
Text: John Newton (d. 1807), who published 280 hymns in *Olney Hymns* (1779); text is based on Isaias 33.20-21.
T. Source: *Catholic Hymn Book* (London Oratory, 1998) p. 381; *Stories of Hymns* (Fr. George W. Rutler, 2016) p. 202.

Glorious Things Of Thee Are Spoken (Isaias 33) 861

"The Lord loveth the gates of Sion above all the tabernacles of Jacob. Glorious things are said of thee, O city of God."—Ps 86.2-3

2nd Tune

Final Verses: Richard Lloyd (1993) #14; Noel Rawsthorne (2011) #30.

Melody: Franz Joseph Haydn (d. 1809), a Catholic who often prayed the rosary when he encountered difficulties composing. The tune is based on "Stal se jesem," a Croatian folk song. The title of Haydn's version: "Gott erhalte Franz den Kaiser."

M. Source: *Saint Basil's Hymnal* (1918) p. 280; *Catholic Hymn Book* (1998) p. 453.

Text: John Newton (d. 1807), who published 280 hymns in *Olney Hymns* (1779); text is based on Isaias 33.20-21.

T. Source: *Catholic Hymn Book* (London Oratory, 1998) p. 381; *Stories of Hymns* (Fr. George W. Rutler, 2016) p. 202.

87 87 D

Tune: AUSTRIA

864 Rex Gloriose Martyrum (6th century)

Trns: Fr. Edward Caswall, Oratorian (d. 1878)

4. To God the Father glory be, | And to his sole-begotten Son;
The same, O Holy Ghost, to Thee, | While everlasting ages run.

Can be sung with any 88 88 meter, such as Hilderstone, Duguet, Breslau, Melcombe, Wareham, Old Hundredth, Mein Seel, Trinity College, etc.

O THOU, the Martyrs' glorious King,
Of Confessors the crown and prize;
Who dost to joys celestial bring
Those who the joys of earth despise.

2. By all the praise thy Saints have won;
By all their pains in days gone by;
By all the deeds which they have done;
Hear Thou thy suppliant people's cry.

3. Thou dost amid thy Martyrs fight;
Thy Confessors Thou dost forgive;
May we find mercy in thy sight,
And in thy sacred presence live.

4. To God the Father glory be,
And to his sole-begotten Son;
The same, O Holy Ghost, to Thee,
While everlasting ages run.

* Though brief, this hymn is potent. A literal translation: "Glorious king of martyrs, crown of those who confess Thee and leader to heaven of all who despise worldly pleasures, give a ready and gracious hearing to our hymn; our theme is the martyrs' holy triumph, our plea is for pardon of our sins. Thy might is displayed in the martyrs, and Thy mercy in those who confess Thee. Exert Thy mighty power over our sins and pour out Thy mercy on us."

88 88 (LM)

Tune:
Bressani

T. Source: *Catholic Church Hymnal with Music* (A. Edmonds Tozer, 1905) p. 208.
Melody: From a hymn book published by Fr. Melchior Ludolf Herold (d. 1810).
M. Source: *New Westminster Hymnal* (1939) p. 173.

Deus Judicium Tuum Regi Da (Psalm 71) 865

Paraphrase by James Montgomery (d. 1854)

13 13 13 13 13 13

T. Source: *Songs of Zion: Being Imitations of Psalms* (1823) p. 53.
Melody: Gustav Holst (d. 1934) organist and choirmaster at Thaxted Parish Church (Essex, England).
M. Source: *Catholic Hymn Book* (London Oratory, 1998) p. 388.

Tune:
Thaxted

872 Solemn Hymn To The Son Of God

Fifth Tune – *Fr. Dominic Popplewell (b. 1973)*

1. Of the Fa - ther born a - lone, Heir co - re - gent of his
2. Ev - er God, in time a man, Lim - it - ed, whom none may
3. Come for men to me - di - ate, Sov-'reign Priest and Ad - vo -

throne, Word he speaks e - ter - nal - ly, Mir - ror
span, Know - ing all, whose wis - dom grew, Pas - chal
cate, To your own who pledged to send, For their

of his maj - es - ty: Man to save, who man be - came,
Lamb and Shep - herd true: Who by yield - ing won the strife,
help, an - oth - er Friend: With the Fa - ther in - ter - cede,

Pleased his ser - vile form to claim, As a bless - èd
Who by dy - ing gar - nered life, Who de - part - ed,
Sin - less one, for sin - ners plead, That the way of

Maid - en's child Earth to heav - en rec - on - ciled.
but to bide With the Church, your cho - sen Bride.
life they tread, By your grace to glo - ry led.

4. God almighty, three in one, | Holy Father, holy Son,
With the holy Paraclete, | Let your works your praise repeat:
To your most exalted name | Let unfaltering acclaim
From created things ascend | Now and ever, without end.

[1b] Jn 1.18
[1c] Jn 1.3, Col 1.16
[1d] Wis 7.26, Col 1.15
[1f] Rom 8.3, Phil 2.6, Heb 2.17
[2c] Lk 2.52
[2d] Jn 1.29, 36; I Cor 5.7; I Pt 1.19; Jn 10.11, 14; I Pt 2.25
[2g] Mt 28.20
[2h] Eph 5.25-27; Ap 21.2, 9
[3a] I Tm 2.5; Heb 8.6, 9.15
[3b] Heb 4.14; I Jn 2.1; Heb 7.25
[3d] Jn 14.16, 15.26, 16.7
[3f] Heb 4.15
[3g] Mt 7.14

77 77 D

Tune:
Christus Christus Christus Ist 7E

Melody: Peter Franck (d. 1675), first published in 1657.
M. Source: *Choral Harmony* (London: G. H. Davidson, 1854) #203.
T. Source: *Saint Jean de Brébeuf Hymnal* (2018).

Solemn Hymn To The Son Of God

Sixth Tune – *Fr. Dominic Popplewell (b. 1973)*

4. Who by yielding won the strife,
Who by dying garnered life,
Who departed, but to bide
With the Church, your chosen Bride. *Alleluia.*

5. Come for men to mediate,
Sovereign Priest and Advocate,
To your own who pledged to send,
For their help, another Friend: *Alleluia.*

6. With the Father intercede,
Sinless one, for sinners plead,
That the way of life they tread,
By your grace to glory led. *Alleluia.*

7. God almighty, three in one,
Holy Father, holy Son,
With the holy Paraclete,
Let your works your praise repeat: *Alleluia.*

8. To your most exalted name
Let unfaltering acclaim
From created things ascend
Now and ever, without end. *Alleluia.*

* For Scripture references, please see page 868.

T. Source: *Saint Jean de Brébeuf Hymnal* (2018).
Melody: From *Hundert Arien* (Dresden, 1697), adapted by William H. Monk (d. 1889), organist at King's College London.
M. Source: *Songs of Syon* (Woodward, 1910) p. 455; *New Westminster Hymnal* (1939) p. 80.

77 77 A

Tune: Würtemburg

874 Solemn Hymn To The Son Of God

Seventh Tune – *Fr. Dominic Popplewell (b. 1973)*

4. Who by yielding won the strife,
   Who by dying garnered life,
   Who departed, but to bide
   With the Church, your chosen Bride.

5. Come for men to mediate,
   Sovereign Priest and Advocate,
   To your own who pledged to send,
   For their help, another Friend:

6. With the Father intercede,
   Sinless one, for sinners plead,
   That the way of life they tread,
   By your grace to glory led.

7. God almighty, three in one,
   Holy Father, holy Son,
   With the holy Paraclete,
   Let your works your praise repeat:

8. To your most exalted name
   Let unfaltering acclaim
   From created things ascend
   Now and ever, without end.

N.B. This melody is excellent for use during Advent.

77 77

Tune:
Nun Komm Der Heiden Heiland

* For Scripture references, please see page 868.

T. Source: *Saint Jean de Brébeuf Hymnal* (2018).
Melody: Based on "Veni Redemptor Gentium"; for plainsong score, cf. *Liber Hymnarius* (Solesmes: Saint Peter's Abbey, 1983) p. 11.
M. Source: *New Westminster Hymnal* (1939) p. 146; *Catholic Hymn Book* (1998) p. 278; *Summit Choirbook* (Dominican Monastery of Our Lady of the Rosary, 1983) #25; *Saint Andrew Hymnal, authorized by the Bishops of Scotland for use in the Scottish Dioceses* (1964) p. 203.

Solemn Hymn To The Son Of God 875

Eighth Tune – *Fr. Dominic Popplewell (b. 1973)*

4. Who by yielding won the strife,
   Who by dying garnered life,
   Who departed, but to bide
   With the Church, your chosen Bride. *Alleluia.*

5. Come for men to mediate,
   Sovereign Priest and Advocate,
   To your own who pledged to send,
   For their help, another Friend: *Alleluia.*

6. With the Father intercede,
   Sinless one, for sinners plead,
   That the way of life they tread,
   By your grace to glory led. *Alleluia.*

7. God almighty, three in one,
   Holy Father, holy Son,
   With the holy Paraclete,
   Let your works your praise repeat: *Alleluia.*

8. To your most exalted name
   Let unfaltering acclaim
   From created things ascend
   Now and ever, without end. *Alleluia.*

* For Scripture references, please see page 868.

T. Source: *Saint Jean de Brébeuf Hymnal* (2018).
Melody: Peter Lejeune (b. 1991), after "Louez Dieu tout hautement."
M. Source: *Saint Jean de Brébeuf Hymnal* (2018).

77 77 A
Tune: Coelestem Panem

876 Solemn Hymn To The Son Of God

Ninth Tune – *Fr. Dominic Popplewell (b. 1973)*

4. God almighty, three in one, | Holy Father, holy Son,
With the holy Paraclete, | Let your works your praise repeat:
To your most exalted name | Let unfaltering acclaim
From created things ascend | Now and ever, without end.

[1b] Jn 1.18
[1c] Jn 1.3, Col 1.16
[1d] Wis 7.26, Col 1.15
[1f] Rom 8.3, Phil 2.6, Heb 2.17
[2c] Lk 2.52
[2d] Jn 1.29, 36; I Cor 5.7; I Pt 1.19; Jn 10.11, 14; I Pt 2.25
[2g] Mt 28.20
[2h] Eph 5.25-27; Ap 21.2, 9
[3a] I Tm 2.5; Heb 8.6, 9.15
[3b] Heb 4.14; I Jn 2.1; Heb 7.25
[3d] Jn 14.16, 15.26, 16.7
[3f] Heb 4.15
[3g] Mt 7.14

77 77 D

Tune:
Ach Wie Kurz 7E

Melody: J. H. Reiman, first published in 1747.
M. Source: *New Westminster Hymnal* (1939) p. 81.
T. Source: *Saint Jean de Brébeuf Hymnal* (2018).

Solemn Hymn To The Son Of God 877

Fr. Dominic Popplewell (b. 1973)

Can be sung with any 77 77 meter, such as Savannah, University College, Orientis Partibus, Llanfair, Culbach, Monkland, Gott Sei Dank, etc.

OF the Father born alone,
Heir co-regent of his throne,
Word he speaks eternally,
Mirror of his majesty:

2. Man to save, who man became,
Pleased his servile form to claim,
As a blessèd Maiden's child
Earth to heaven reconciled.

3. Ever God, in time a man,
Limited, whom none may span,
Knowing all, whose wisdom grew,
Paschal Lamb and Shepherd true:

4. Who by yielding won the strife,
Who by dying garnered life,
Who departed, but to bide
With the Church, your chosen Bride.

5. Come for men to mediate,
Sovereign Priest and Advocate,
To your own who pledged to send,
For their help, another Friend:

6. With the Father intercede,
Sinless one, for sinners plead,
That the way of life they tread,
By your grace to glory led.

7. God almighty, three in one,
Holy Father, holy Son,
With the holy Paraclete,
Let your works your praise repeat:

8. To your most exalted name
Let unfaltering acclaim
From created things ascend
Now and ever, without end.

77 77

* For Scripture references, please see page 868.

Tune: Various

T. Source: *Saint Jean de Brébeuf Hymnal* (2018).

MELCHISEDECH, KING OF SALEM, BRINGING FORTH BREAD AND WINE, FOR HE WAS THE PRIEST OF THE MOST HIGH GOD, BLESSED HIM...

WHEN HE HAD BOUND ISAAC, HE LAID HIM ON THE ALTAR UPON THE PILE OF WOOD, AND PUT FORTH HIS HAND...TO SACRIFICE HIS SON.

WAY OF THE CROSS

Father Fulton J. Sheen *

At the Cross her station keeping,	Stabat Mater dolorósa
Stood the mournful Mother weeping,	Juxta Crucem lacrimósa,
Close to Jesus to the last.	Dum pendébat Fílius.

OPENING PRAYER *(Kneeling)*

THE CURTAIN is now about to go up on the awful and abiding drama of Thy Redemptive Love. And as I hear Thy words, "Take up thy Cross daily and follow Me," I stand fearful, lest its burden be too great and its shame too bitter. If I could but see that Thy command to follow Thee to Calvary was not just an iron law of cruel fate, but a condition of everlasting happiness, perhaps I could better make the journey—but I fear, dear Jesus, lest having Thee I must have naught else beside.

Let this fear be dispelled in seeing death as the condition of life. For through Thy apostle, Paul, Thou hast told us it is the joy at the end of the journey that makes us endure the Cross, and even Thou, in loving kindness, hast asked all who labor and are burdened to come unto Thee, where they will find rest for their souls.

"God forbid that I should glory, save in the cross of our Lord Jesus Christ; by whom the world is crucified to me, and I to the world." (Gal 6.14)

---

* IMPRIMATUR, 2 April 1933, by Patrick Cardinal Hayes (d. 1938), Archbishop of New York; 1932 © by the National Council of Catholic Men. At the time of publication, Fr. Sheen—later elevated to the Episcopacy—was listed as: "Reverend Doctor Fulton J. Sheen, Agrégé en Philosophie, University of Louvain, Belgium; Catholic University of America." These meditations were delivered on the radio seven days before being granted their first IMPRIMATUR by Bishop John F. Noll on 27 March 1932. The thirteenth station has been slightly modified to incorporate a later version. The original introduction is as follows: *The author of these Meditations on the Way of the Cross has a two-fold purpose in offering them in printed form. The first is that they may enkindle in souls a flaming love for the Crucified Savior Who through His Passion and Death revealed to us that it is only through the Cross that we are ever ushered into glory and eternal life. The second purpose is that those who meditate on the great love of Our Lord for sinners will be kind enough to say a prayer for the author that increase of years may bring increase of intimacy with the Love which is God.*

Through her heart, his sorrow sharing, *All his bitter anguish bearing,* *Now at length the sword had pass'd.*	Cujus ánimam geméntem, Contristátam et doléntem Pertransívit gládius.

THE FIRST STATION

Jesus is Condemned to Death

(Genuflect) *We adore Thee, O Christ, and we praise Thee.*

R. Because by Thy holy Cross Thou hast redeemed the world.

PILATE, the time-serving politician, stepped forward on his sunlit portico. On his right stood Christ, the Just One who came to give His life for the redemption of many; on his left stood Barabbas, the wicked one, who had incited a revolt and taken a life. Pilate asked the mob to choose between the two: "Whether you will that I release unto you Christ or Barabbas?"

How would I have answered that question, had I been in the courtyard that Good Friday morning? I cannot escape answering by saying that the question belongs only to the past, for it is as actual now as ever. My conscience is the tribunal of Pilate. Daily, hourly, and every minute of the day, Christ comes before that tribunal, as virtue, honesty and purity. Barabbas comes as vice, dishonesty and uncleanness. As often as I choose to speak the uncharitable word, do the dishonest action, or consent to the evil thought, I say in so many words, "Release unto me Barabbas"—and to choose Barabbas means to crucify Christ.

V. Pray for us, O Holy Mother of God.

R. That we may be made worthy of the promises of Christ.

PRAYER SAID BY ALL (*Kneeling*)

O JESUS, many times in my life
I have preferred Barabbas to Thee.

There is no way that I can undo that choice,
but to make my way to Thy feet,
and beg Thy forgiveness.

But that is so humiliating,
for Thou wearest the garment of a fool,
and Thou bearest in Thy hand
the reed sceptre of a mock king.

It is so hard to do penance
and admit that I am guilty!
It is so hard to be seen with Thee,
who art wearing Thy crown of thorns.
It is hard! But let me see, Jesus,
that it is harder to wear the crown of thorns!

Oh, how sad, how heavy laden,	O quam tristis et afflícta
Was that meek and blessèd Maiden,	Fuit illa benedícta
God's true Mother undefiled.	Mater unigéniti!

THE SECOND STATION

Jesus is Made to Bear His Cross

(Genuflect) *We adore Thee, O Christ, and we praise Thee.*
R. Because by Thy holy Cross Thou hast redeemed the world.

OUR Blessed Lord had been a visitor to our earth but forty days when Simeon, with prophetic vision, declared He would become a sign of contradiction. That day had now come, for "He came unto His own, and His own received Him not."

As a symbol of the world's contradiction of His life-giving message, they gave Him a Cross, in which one bar is at variance or contradiction with another. But by a Divine Act, He made the sign of contradiction the sign of Redemption. The circle is the symbol of selfishness, for it is continually circumscribed by self, never able to break out of the limits, but the cross is

What man is there so unfeeling,	Quis est homo qui non fleret,
Who, his heart to pity steeling,	Matrem Christi si vidéret
Could behold that sight unmoved?	In tanto supplício?

THE FOURTH STATION

Jesus Meets His Afflicted Mother

(Genuflect) *We adore Thee, O Christ, and we praise Thee.*

R. Because by Thy holy Cross Thou hast redeemed the world.

AT the marriage feast of Cana, when Mary first noted the embarrassment of the hosts, and asked Her Divine Son to work His first miracle, He answered: "My hour is not yet come." But at her solicitation He anticipated it, and changed the water into wine.

"His hour," He said, "was not yet come"—but His hour was her hour too, and now it had come! At Cana, He changed water into wine. On the road to Calvary, the wine is changed into blood. It is the solemn hour of consecration by which she unites herself with the sufferings of her Beloved Son, to save the world from the terrible embarrassment of sin, and the want of God's redemptive wine of love.

It was the hour of reversal of the world's estimate of love, for a Son is summoning His mother to suffer. Love, then, does not mean to have: it means to be had: it is the giving of oneself for another. No one ever loved Jesus like Mary; therefore, no one ever suffered for Jesus like Mary.

V. Pray for us, O Holy Mother of God.

R. That we may be made worthy of the promises of Christ.

PRAYER SAID BY ALL (*Kneeling*)

MARY, dear Mother,
in this, thy hour of sorrow,
thou art paying dearly for the privilege
of thy Immaculate Conception!

Thou art doing even more!
For thy present sorrows
are the pains of childbirth
by which thou dost become
the Mother of Mankind,
as in Bethlehem thou didst become
the Mother of Jesus, thy First Born.
Thou art, then, really my Mother,
not by the title of courtesy,
but by the pains of birth.

Teach me, Mother, to see
that Jesus calls to suffering
those whom He loves, and grant that
just as Jesus keeps the best wine of His love
for the hour when we need it most,
so too He may keep thee near us
when we need thee most—
in all trials and temptations,
and in particular at the hour of our death.

Lives there one whose heart with anguish
Fills not, thus to see her languish,
Agonizing with her Son?

Quis non posset contristári,
Christi Matrem contemplári
Doléntem cum Fílio?

THE FIFTH STATION

The Cyrenian Helps Jesus to Carry His Cross

(Genuflect) *We adore Thee, O Christ, and we praise Thee.*

R. Because by Thy holy Cross Thou hast redeemed the world.

IT WAS NOT MERELY death sinful men wished Our Blessed Savior; it was a particular kind of death upon the sign of contradiction. Lest exhaustion and weakness should rob them of unfurling Him as a banner of salvation upon the Cross of Calvary, they forced Simon of Cyrene to help Him with His task. Simon saw in the cross only the burden of wood, but not the burden of the world's sins, and hence became at first an unwilling aid and a constrained helper. A few minutes, however, in the sweet company of Jesus changed his outlook—slavery became freedom, constraint became love, and reluctance a sweet abandon.

I, too, am like Simon in his first moments: I know about Jesus, but I do not know Jesus. I have feared to be a sharer of His Cross, and hence have loved but little, because I have known only a little. I have too often insisted on beginning with pleasure, when it is with pleasure that I should have ended.

V. Pray for us, O Holy Mother of God.

R. That we may be made worthy of the promises of Christ.

PRAYER SAID BY ALL *(Kneeling)*

GIVE me, O Jesus,
an understanding of this great mystery:
that it is only at a distance
that the Cross frightens—
that its shadow is really more terrible
than its reality—
that its splinters are more terrifying
than its beams—
that the whole of it is more easy to carry
than a part.

Thou hast told us, dear Savior,
that we must take up our Cross daily
and follow Thee.

Grant, then, that when a Cross
comes between Thee and me,
as it did between Thee and Simon,
that I may be quite content
just to see Thy footsteps and follow them
as Simon did,
until at last I shall be forever more
an uncaught captive
in the hands of Thy Sweet Love.

For the guilt that doomed his nation	Pro peccátis suae gentis,
Saw she Jesus in prostration	Vidit Jesum in torméntis,
'Neath the scourges meekly bent;	Et flagéllis súbditum.

THE SIXTH STATION

Veronica Wipes the Face of Jesus

(Genuflect) *We adore Thee, O Christ, and we praise Thee.*

R. Because by Thy holy Cross Thou hast redeemed the world.

SIMON the Cyrenean helped Jesus with His burden as a reminder that man is called to the sublime vocation of carrying a Cross. But woman, too, has her role to play, and on that dread day Veronica, with a woman's own peculiar vision, looked out on a countenance bruised and stained with dust and blood, and saw in it the very Face of Divinity.

Braving human respect, she touched a towel to His visage, and —as if to remind us that the likeness between Christ and us is most perfect in suffering and sorrow—the Divine Savior, on His way not to Tabor but to Calvary, left the impression of His Divinely sorrowful face.

V. Pray for us, O Holy Mother of God.

R. That we may be made worthy of the promises of Christ.

PRAYER SAID BY ALL (*Kneeling*)

THE day, O Lord, I was born anew
of water and the Holy Ghost,
the image of Thy Cross
was stamped on my soul,
and the inscription of Thy sorrow
graven on my heart.

THE EIGHTH STATION

Jesus Speaks to the Women of Jerusalem

(Genuflect) *We adore Thee, O Christ, and we praise Thee.*

R. Because by Thy holy Cross Thou hast redeemed the world.

OF ALL THINGS on earth, that which we know least is our own self. We know the sins and defects of others a thousand times better than our own, and see forever the mote in our brother's eye, but not the beam in our own. That great truth, it seems, was unheeded on the journey to Calvary.

The pious women of Jerusalem, though quite unafraid to declare their loyalty before impious men, yet saw only the suffering Christ whom they loved; they did not see the loving Christ who suffered for them. They sympathized with the pain, but did not see themselves as the cause of that pain.

It was their own sins, and mine as well, which He took upon Himself, and as if to bring that truth home to us all there welled up from the depths of the Sacred Heart the plaintive words: "Weep not for Me, but weep for yourselves."

V. Pray for us, O Holy Mother of God.

R. That we may be made worthy of the promises of Christ.

PRAYER SAID BY ALL (*Kneeling*)

O JESUS, let me see the personal equation
between my sins and Calvary.

Let me weep not for Thee apart from me,
but for Thee on account of me.

Let me see that if I had been less proud,
the crown of thorns would have been less piercing;
that if I had been less self-willed,
the Cross would have been less heavy;

that if I had been less sinful,
the road would have been much shorter.

Give me the grace to weep for my sins,
and since sorrow and joy share the same source,
which is the fountain of tears,
give me also to understand
that my sorrows may one day,
through Thy Love,
be changed into everlasting joy.

Make me, loving Christ, so love Him
That now, setting naught above Him,
To His Will my will may cleave.

Fac ut árdeat cor meum
In amándo Christum Deum,
Ut sibi compláceam.

THE NINTH STATION

Jesus Falls the Third Time

(Genuflect) *We adore Thee, O Christ, and we praise Thee.*

R. Because by Thy holy Cross Thou hast redeemed the world.

THE THIRD temptation on the mount was the temptation, not of the flesh or the world, but of the devil himself, asking Our Blessed Lord to fall down and adore him, promising He would be given all the kingdoms of the earth. But Jesus said to him: "Begone, Satan, for it is written: *The Lord thy God shalt thou adore, and Him only shalt thou serve.*"

There have been countless occasions in my life when I exchanged the priceless treasure of Thy grace for the toy of some passing pleasure. Unlike Christ, I have believed the devil's lies, and bartered eternity for time, peace for remorse, and the freedom of the children of God for the terrible slavery of sin. And each time I have learned that whereas Satan promises the pleasure of his kingdom, he actually gives only his barren desert of unhappiness and pain.

V. Pray for us, O Holy Mother of God.

R. That we may be made worthy of the promises of Christ.

PRAYER SAID BY ALL (*Kneeling*)

MANY times, dear Jesus,
I promised Thee,
after having fallen by the flesh and the world,
I would never fall again.

This, Thy third fall, dear Jesus,
is a witness that I have fallen
by the snares of the devil,
but by rising again
Thou hast given me another pledge of hope.

Thou hast taught me now
that there are two classes of people in the world:
those who fall and stay down,
and those who fall and get up again.

By this third fall,
Thou hast purchased for me the grace of rising again.
Never let me fall again.
The devil would give the world to have my soul;
Thou art giving Thy very life to have it.
Therefore, dear Jesus, it must be worth saving!
O help me save it.

Mother, every wound and tremor	Sancta Mater, istud agas,
Of the crucified Redeemer,	Crucifíxi fige plagas
Firmly fasten in my soul;	Cordi meo válide.

THE TENTH STATION

Jesus is Stripped of His Garments

(Genuflect) *We adore Thee, O Christ, and we praise Thee.*

R. Because by Thy holy Cross Thou hast redeemed the world.

GOD'S dealing with man has been a continuous process of overflowing goodness. The first overflowing was giving things existence, and that was creation; the second was the over-flowing of the secrets of His love, and that was revelation.

Finally, love, which knows no limits, exhausted itself in the INCARNATION, for here in the language of Paul, "He emptied Himself," cast His glory into the background, and took upon Himself the form and habit of man. Now on the hill of Calvary, Jesus wills not only to empty Himself of His Divine glory, but even the least of His earthly possessions. The Heavenly Vagabond, who had nowhere to lay His head, is now stripped of His garments, so that in death He might have nothing but give all, and thus be utterly empty.

V. Pray for us, O Holy Mother of God.

R. That we may be made worthy of the promises of Christ.

PRAYER SAID BY ALL *(Kneeling)*

BUT, Jesus,
love is reciprocal,
and every emptying implies a filling.
If Thou hast emptied Thyself
by giving us divine life,
was it not because I should be filled by it?

Grant, then, dear Jesus,
that I may be emptied of selfishness,
and filled with Thy charity;
emptied of sins,
and filled with Thy grace;
emptied of earthliness,
and filled with heavenliness.

Strip me of the garments which are worldly,
and clothe me with the white robe of baptism,
so that through the poverty of earthly things,
I may become rich.

Strengthen me to repay
Thy life of emptying
by my love of sacrifice,
and by filling up in my body
the sufferings which are wanting
to Thy Passion, O Christ!

Since He deigns that all the merit	Tui nati vulneráti,
Of His wounds I should inherit	Tam dignáti pro me pati,
All His pain with me divide.	Poenas mecum dívide.

THE ELEVENTH STATION

Jesus is Nailed to the Cross

(Genuflect) *We adore Thee, O Christ, and we praise Thee.*

R. Because by Thy holy Cross Thou hast redeemed the world.

OUR Blessed Lord mounts His pulpit for the last time. This time it is not Peter's bark, nor Galilean hills, but the pulpit of the Cross which, like the words He shall utter, will itself be eloquent even when time shall be no more.

The Preacher is the Word of God; the congregation is made up of soldiers who shake dice for His garments; of unbelievers, whose mouths are craters of hate and volcanoes of blasphemy; and of the faithful ones: Mary, Magdalen, and John—innocence, penitence, and priesthood—the three types of souls forever to be found beneath the pulpit of the Cross.

The sermon is the Seven Last Words—words of love and forgiveness—first to enemies: "Forgive them, for they know not what they do"; then to sinners: "This day thou shalt be with Me in paradise"; then to saints: "Mother, behold thy son."

V. Pray for us, O Holy Mother of God.

R. That we may be made worthy of the promises of Christ.

PRAYER SAID BY ALL (*Kneeling*)

DEAR Jesus,
as I listen to Thy sermon,
which reveals Thy tremendous thirst for love,
I begin to discover what love really is,
and how many times I have crucified it:

Thy hands, so often raised to bless me,
I have nailed fast;
Thy feet, which so often sought me
in devious ways of sin,
I dug with steel;
Thy lips, which have so often summoned me
from paths of wickedness,
I blistered with dust.

And now I hear Thy word of love
which pardons and forgives,
and I begin to understand
that when I pierced Thy heart,
it was my own I slew.

To Thy Cross I now return
as the chalice of all common miseries
and the hope of forlorn sinners.

Ever beneath it, let me learn the lesson
that it does not require much time to make me a saint,
but only much love;
and that, if I had never sinned, O Jesus,
I never could call Thee "Savior."

Make me thy co-mourner truly,
For His crucifixion duly
Sorr'wing till my life is o'er:

Fac me tecum pie flere,
Crucifíxo condolére,
Donec ego víxero.

THE FIRST STATION

Jesus is Condemned to Death

(Genuflect) *We adore Thee, O Christ, and we praise Thee.*

R. Because by Thy holy Cross Thou hast redeemed the world.

CONSIDER HOW JESUS, after having been scourged and crowned with thorns, was unjustly condemned by Pilate to die on the Cross.

PRAYER SAID BY ALL *(Kneeling)*

MY ADORABLE JESUS,
it was not Pilate,
no, it was my sins
that condemned Thee to die.

I beseech Thee,
by the merits of this sorrowful journey,
to assist my soul in its journey towards eternity.

I love Thee, my beloved Jesus;
I repent with my whole heart
of having offended Thee.
Never permit me to separate myself from Thee again.

Grant that I may love Thee always;
and then do with me what Thou wilt.

All Recite: Our Father, Hail Mary, and Glory Be

Oh, how sad, how heavy laden,
Was that meek and blessèd Maiden,
God's true Mother undefiled.

O quam tristis et afflícta
Fuit illa benedícta
Mater unigéniti!

THE SECOND STATION

Jesus is Made to Bear His Cross

(Genuflect) *We adore Thee, O Christ, and we praise Thee.*

R. Because by Thy holy Cross Thou hast redeemed the world.

CONSIDER HOW JESUS, in making this journey with the Cross on His shoulders, thought of us, and for us offered to His Father the death He was about to undergo.

PRAYER SAID BY ALL (*Kneeling*)

MY MOST BELOVED JESUS,
I embrace all the tribulations
Thou hast destined for me until death.

I beseech Thee,
by the merits of the pain Thou didst suffer
in carrying Thy Cross,
to give me the necessary help
to carry mine with perfect patience and resignation.

I love Thee, Jesus my love;
I repent of having offended Thee.
Never permit me to separate myself from Thee again.

Grant that I may love Thee always;
and then do with me what Thou wilt.

All Recite: Our Father, Hail Mary, and Glory Be

Deep the well of her affliction
When she saw the Crucifixion
Of her well belovèd Son.

Quae maerébat et dolébat,
Pia Mater, dum vidébat
Nati poenas íncliti.

THE NINTH STATION

Jesus Falls the Third Time

(Genuflect) *We adore Thee, O Christ, and we praise Thee.*

R. Because by Thy holy Cross Thou hast redeemed the world.

CONSIDER THE THIRD FALL of Jesus Christ. His weakness was extreme, and the cruelty of His executioners was excessive, who tried to hasten His steps when He had scarcely strength to move.

PRAYER SAID BY ALL (*Kneeling*)

AH, MY OUTRAGED JESUS,
by the merits of the weakness
Thou didst suffer
in going to Calvary,
give me strength sufficient
to conquer all human respect,
and all my wicked passions,
which have led me to despise Thy friendship.

I love Thee, Jesus my love, with my whole heart;
I repent of having offended Thee.
Never permit me to offend Thee again.

Grant that I may love Thee always;
and then do with me what Thou wilt.

All Recite: Our Father, Hail Mary, and Glory Be

Mother, every wound and tremor	Sancta Mater, istud agas,
Of the crucified Redeemer,	Crucifíxi fige plagas
Firmly fasten in my soul;	Cordi meo válide.

THE TENTH STATION

Jesus is Stripped of His Garments

(Genuflect) *We adore Thee, O Christ, and we praise Thee.*

R. Because by Thy holy Cross Thou hast redeemed the world.

CONSIDER THE VIOLENCE with which the executioners stripped Jesus. His inner garments adhered to His torn flesh, and they dragged them off so roughly that the skin came with them. Have pity on your Savior thus cruelly treated, and say to Him:

PRAYER SAID BY ALL (*Kneeling*)

MY INNOCENT JESUS,
by the merits
of the torment Thou hast felt,
help me to strip myself
of all affection to things of earth,
in order that I may place all my love in Thee,
who art so worthy of my love.

I love Thee, O Jesus, with my whole heart;
I repent of having offended Thee.
Never permit me to offend Thee again.

Grant that I may love Thee always;
and then do with me what Thou wilt.

All Recite: Our Father, Hail Mary, and Glory Be

Since He deigns that all the merit	Tui nati vulneráti,
Of His wounds I should inherit	Tam dignáti pro me pati,
All His pain with me divide.	Poenas mecum dívide.

THE ELEVENTH STATION

Jesus is Nailed to the Cross

(Genuflect) *We adore Thee, O Christ, and we praise Thee.*

R. Because by Thy holy Cross Thou hast redeemed the world.

CONSIDER HOW JESUS, after being thrown on the Cross, extended His hands, and offered to His Eternal Father the sacrifice of His death for our salvation. These barbarians fastened Him with nails, and then, raising the Cross, allowed Him to die with anguish on this infamous gibbet.

PRAYER SAID BY ALL (*Kneeling*)

MY JESUS,
loaded with contempt,
nail my heart to Thy feet,
that it may ever remain there,
to love Thee, and never quit Thee again.

I love Thee more than myself;
I repent of having offended Thee.
Never permit me to offend Thee again.

Grant that I may love Thee always;
and then do with me what Thou wilt.

All Recite: Our Father, Hail Mary, and Glory Be

Make me thy co-mourner truly,	Fac me tecum pie flere,
For His crucifixion duly	Crucifíxo condolére,
Sorr'wing till my life is o'er:	Donec ego víxero.

THE TWELFTH STATION

Jesus Dies Upon the Cross

(Genuflect) *We adore Thee, O Christ, and we praise Thee.*

R. Because by Thy holy Cross Thou hast redeemed the world.

CONSIDER HOW thy Jesus, after three hours' Agony on the Cross, consumed at length with anguish, abandons Himself to the weight of His body, bows His head, and dies.

PRAYER SAID BY ALL (*Kneeling*)

O MY DYING JESUS,
I kiss devoutly the Cross
on which Thou didst die for love of me.
I have merited by my sins to die a miserable death;
but Thy death is my hope.

Ah, by the merits of Thy death,
give me grace to die, embracing Thy feet,
and burning with love for Thee.
I yield my soul into Thy hands.

I love Thee with my whole heart;
I repent of ever having offended Thee.
Never permit me to offend Thee again.

Grant that I may love Thee always;
and then do with me what Thou wilt.

All Recite: Our Father, Hail Mary, and Glory Be

Mine with thee be that sad station,	Juxta Crucem tecum stare,
There to watch the great salvation	Et me tibi sociáre
Wrought upon th'Atoning Tree.	In planctu desídero.

THE THIRTEENTH STATION

Jesus is Taken Down from the Cross

(Genuflect) *We adore Thee, O Christ, and we praise Thee.*

R. Because by Thy holy Cross Thou hast redeemed the world.

AFTER THE DEATH of our Lord, two of His disciples—Joseph and Nicodemus—took Him down from the Cross and placed Him into the arms of His afflicted Mother, who received Him with unutterable tenderness, and pressed Him close to her bosom.

PRAYER SAID BY ALL *(Kneeling)*

O MOTHER OF SORROW,
for the love of this Son,
accept me for thy servant,
and pray to Him for me.

And Thou, my Redeemer,
since Thou hast died for me,
permit me to love Thee;
for I wish but Thee, and nothing more.

I love Thee, my Jesus,
and I repent of ever having offended Thee.
Never permit me to offend Thee again.

Grant that I may love Thee always;
and then do with me what Thou wilt.

All Recite: Our Father, Hail Mary, and Glory Be

Virgin of all virgins fairest,	Virgo vírginum praeclára,
Share with me the pains thou bearest,	Mihi jam non sis amára:
Be thy crushing sorrows mine.	Fac me tecum plángere.

THE FOURTEENTH STATION

Jesus is Placed in the Tomb

(Genuflect) *We adore Thee, O Christ, and we praise Thee.*

R. Because by Thy holy Cross Thou hast redeemed the world.

CONSIDER HOW the disciples carried the body of Jesus to bury it, accompanied by His holy Mother, who arranged it in the sepulcher with her own hands. They then closed the tomb, and all withdrew.

PRAYER SAID BY ALL *(Kneeling)*

OH, MY BURIED JESUS,
I kiss the stone that encloses Thee.
But Thou didst rise again the third day.
I beseech Thee, by Thy Resurrection,
make me rise glorious with Thee at the last day,
to be always united with Thee in heaven,
to praise Thee and love Thee forever.

I love Thee,
and I repent of ever having offended Thee.
Never permit me to offend Thee again.

Grant that I may love Thee always;
and then do with me what Thou wilt.

All Recite: Our Father, Hail Mary, and Glory Be

Let me, mindful of His Passion	Fac ut portem Christi mortem
Die in Christ, and, in some fashion,	Passiónis fac consórtem,
Bear the wounds He bore for me.	Et plagas recólere.

FINAL PRAYER SAID BY ALL *(Kneeling)*

BEHOLD,
O kind and most sweet Jesus,
I cast myself upon my knees in Thy sight,
and with the most fervent desire of my soul
I pray and beseech Thee
that Thou wouldst impress upon my heart
lively sentiments of Faith, Hope, and Charity,
with true repentance for my sins,
and a most firm desire of amendment,
whilst with deep affection and grief of soul
I ponder within myself
and mentally contemplate
Thy five most precious Wounds;
having before my eyes
that which David spoke in prophecy
long ago concerning Thee:
"They have pierced My hands and My feet,
they have numbered all My bones."

"STABAT MATER" CONCLUSION

All His bitter torments feeling, *In the cross my spirit reeling,* *In His blood my senses drown.*	Fac me plagis vulnerári, Fac me cruce inebriári, Et cruóre Fílii.
Lest I burn in fires unending, *Sinless Maid, my cause befriending,* *Shield me at the judgment day.*	Flammis ne urar succénsus, Per te, Vírgo, sim defénsus In die judícii.
Jesus, when earth's shadows leave me, *Thru thy Mother's prayers receive me* *With the palm of victory.*	Christe, cum sit hinc exíre, Da per Matrem me veníre Ad palmam victóriae.
When my body lies forsaken *Let my ransomed soul awaken* *Safe, in Paradise, with thee.*	Quando corpus moriétur, Fac ut ánimae donétur Paradísi glória.

In the Presence of the Sanctissimum, the following may be added silently:

PRAYER OF ST. ALPHONSUS LIGUORI

LORD Jesus Christ, who—through the love which Thou bearest to men—dost remain with them, day and night, in this Sacrament, full of mercy and of love, expecting, inviting, and receiving all who come to visit Thee: I believe that Thou art present in the Sacrament of the Altar.

From the abyss of my nothingness I adore Thee, and I thank Thee for all the graces which Thou hast bestowed upon me, particularly for having given me Thyself in this Sacrament, for having given me for my advocate Thy most holy Mother, Mary, and for having called me to visit Thee in this church.

I pay my homage this day to Thy most loving Heart, and I do so, first, in thanksgiving for this great gift itself; secondly, as a reparation for all the injuries which Thou hast received from Thine enemies in this Sacrament; thirdly, I wish, by this visit, to adore Thee in all those places on earth where Thou art Sacramentally present, and in which Thou art the least honored and the most abandoned.

My Jesus, I love Thee with my whole heart. I am sorry for having hitherto so many times offended Thine infinite goodness. I intend, with the assistance of Thy grace, never more to offend Thee; and, at this moment, miserable as I am, I consecrate my whole being to Thee. I give Thee my entire will, all my affections and desires, and all that I have.

From this day forward, do what Thou wilt with me—and with everything that belongs to me. I ask and desire only Thy holy love, the gift of final perseverance, and the perfect fulfillment of Thy will. I commend to Thee the souls in purgatory, particularly those who were most devoted to the most Blessed Sacrament and to the Blessed Virgin Mary; and I also commend to Thee all poor sinners.

Finally, my dear Savior, I unite all my affections with the affections of Thy most loving Heart; and—thus united—I offer them to the Eternal Father, and I entreat Him, in Thy name and for Thy sake, to accept and answer them. AMEN.

IT WAS I WHO BROUGHT THEE OUT OF EGYPT AND DROWNED PHARAOH IN THE RED SEA : AND THOU HAST BETRAYED ME INTO THE HANDS OF THE CHIEF PRIESTS. FOR THY SAKE I STRUCK DOWN THE KINGS OF CANAAN : AND THOU HAST STRUCK MY HEAD WITH A REED.

THEY SAID : "LET HIM BE CRUCIFIED." THE GOVERNOR ASKED : "WHY, WHAT EVIL HATH HE DONE?" BUT THEY CRIED OUT THE MORE, SAYING : "LET HIM BE CRUCIFIED."

WAY OF THE CROSS

Joseph Cardinal Ratzinger *

At the Cross her station keeping,	Stabat Mater dolorósa
Stood the mournful Mother weeping,	Juxta Crucem lacrimósa,
Close to Jesus to the last.	Dum pendébat Fílius.

IN THE NAME of the Father, ✠ and of the Son, and of the Holy Spirit. R. AMEN.

OPENING PRAYER SAID BY ALL (*Kneeling*)

LORD JESUS CHRIST, for our sake you became like the grain of wheat that falls to the earth and dies, so that it may bear much fruit (John 12.24). You invited us to follow you along this path when you told us that "he who loves his life will lose it; he who is an enemy to his own life in this world will keep it, so as to live eternally." (John 12.25). Yet we are attached to our life. We do not want to abandon it; we want to keep it all for ourselves. We want to hold on to it, not to give it away.

But you go before us, showing us that it is only by giving away our life that we can save it. As we walk with you on the Way of the Cross, you lead us along the way of the grain of wheat, the way of a fruitfulness which leads to eternity. The cross—our self-offering—weighs heavily upon us. Along your own Way of the Cross you also carried my cross. Nor did you carry it just at one distant moment in the past, for your love continues to accompany every moment of my life.

Today you carry that cross with me and for me, and, amazingly, you want me, like Simon of Cyrene, to join you in carrying your Cross;

* These meditations by Joseph Aloisius Ratzinger (b. 1927) were first read by Camillo Cardinal Ruini (b. 1931) during the Colosseum "Way of the Cross" on GOOD FRIDAY, 25 March 2005. An ancient Christian tradition assigns the first Good Friday to 25 March—the day we celebrate the INCARNATION—and Catholics throughout history, especially the medieval artists, have explored the powerful connection between these two Events. The two feasts—that is to say, Good Friday and the Annunciation (25 March)—coincide but a few times each century. They did in 1622, the year St. Jean de Brébeuf was ordained, and he offered his first Mass on the (transferred) feast of the Annunciation at the College Church of Rouen.

you want me to walk at your side and place myself with you at the service of the world's redemption.

Grant that my Way of the Cross may not be just a moment of passing piety. Help all of us to accompany you—not only with noble thoughts, but with all our hearts and in every step we take each day of our lives. Help us resolutely to set out on the Way of the Cross and to persevere on your path. Free us from the fear of the Cross, from the fear of mockery, from the fear that our life may escape our grasp unless we cling possessively to everything it has to offer. Help us to unmask all those temptations that promise life, but whose enticements in the end leave us only empty and deluded. Help us not to take life, but to give it. As you accompany us on the path of the grain of wheat, help us to discover, in "losing our lives," the path of love, the path which gives us true life, and life in abundance (John 10.10).

Through her heart, his sorrow sharing,	Cujus ánimam geméntem,
All his bitter anguish bearing,	Contristátam et doléntem
Now at length the sword had pass'd.	Pertransívit gládius.

THE FIRST STATION

Jesus is Condemned to Death

(Genuflect) *We adore Thee, O Christ, and we praise Thee.*

R. Because by Thy holy Cross Thou hast redeemed the world.

Pilate said to them, "Then what should I do with Jesus who is called the Messiah?" All of them said, "Let him be crucified!" Then he asked, "Why, what evil has he done?" But they shouted all the more, "Let him be crucified!" So he released Barabbas for them; and after flogging Jesus, he handed him over to be crucified. (Mt 27.22-23,26)

THE JUDGE OF THE WORLD, who will come again to judge us all, stands there, dishonored and defenseless before the earthly judge. Pilate is not utterly evil. He knows the condemned man is innocent, and he looks for a way to free him. But his heart is divided. And in the end he lets his own position, his own self-interest, prevail over what is right. Nor are the men who are shouting and demanding the death of Jesus utterly evil. Many of them, on the day of Pentecost, will feel "cut to the heart" (Acts 2.37), when Peter will say to them: "Jesus of Nazareth, a man attested to you by God... you crucified and killed by the hands of those outside the law" (Acts 2.22ff). But at that moment they are caught up in the crowd. They are shouting because everyone else is shouting—and they are shouting the same thing that everyone else is shouting. And in this way, justice is trampled underfoot by weakness, cowardice and fear of the diktat of the ruling mindset. The quiet voice of conscience is drowned out by the cries of the crowd. Evil draws its power from indecision and concern for what other people think.

PRAYER SAID BY ALL (*Kneeling*)

LORD, you were condemned to death
because fear of what other people may think
suppressed the voice of conscience.
So too, throughout history,
the innocent have always been
maltreated, condemned and killed.

How many times have we ourselves
preferred success to the truth,
our reputation to justice?
Strengthen the quiet voice of our conscience,
your own voice, in our lives.
Look at me as you looked at Peter after his denial.
Let your gaze penetrate our hearts
and indicate the direction our lives must take.

On the day of Pentecost
you stirred the hearts of those who,
on Good Friday, clamoured for your death,
and you brought them to conversion.
In this way you gave hope to all.
Grant us, ever anew, the grace of conversion.

Oh, how sad, how heavy laden,	O quam tristis et afflícta
Was that meek and blessèd Maiden,	Fuit illa benedícta
God's true Mother undefiled.	Mater unigéniti!

THE SECOND STATION

Jesus is Made to Bear His Cross

(Genuflect) *We adore Thee, O Christ, and we praise Thee.*

R. Because by Thy holy Cross Thou hast redeemed the world.

After this, the governor's soldiers took Jesus into the palace, and gathered the whole of their company about him. And stripping him, they put a scarlet cloak about him. And platting a crown of thorns, they put it upon his head, and a reed in his right hand. And bowing the knee before him, they mocked him, saying: Hail, King of the Jews. And spitting upon him, they took the reed, and struck his head. And after they had mocked him, they took off the cloak from him, and put on him his own garments, and led him away to crucify him. (Mt 27.27-31)

OUR LORD, condemned as an imposter king, is mocked, but this very mockery lays bare a painful truth. How often are the symbols of power borne by the great ones of this world, an affront to truth, to justice, and to the dignity of man! How many times are their pomps and their lofty words nothing but grandiose lies, a parody of their solemn obligation to serve the common good!

It is because Jesus is mocked and wears the crown of suffering that he appears as the true King. His scepter is justice (cf. Ps 45:7). The price of justice in this world is suffering: Jesus, the true King, does not reign through violence, but through a love which suffers for us and with us. He takes up the Cross, our cross, the burden of being human, the burden of the world. And so he goes before us and points out to us the way which leads to true life.

PRAYER SAID BY ALL (*Kneeling*)

LORD, you willingly subjected yourself
to mockery and scorn.
Help us not to ally ourselves
with those who look down on the weak and suffering.

Help us to acknowledge your face
in the lowly and the outcast.
May we never lose heart
when faced with the contempt of this world,
which ridicules our obedience to your will.

You carried your own Cross
and you ask us to follow you on this path (cf. Mt 10:38).
Help us to take up the Cross,
and not to shun it.
May we never complain
or become discouraged by life's trials.
Help us to follow the path of love and—
in submitting to its demands—
to find true joy.

Deep the well of her affliction	Quae maerébat et dolébat,
When she saw the Crucifixion	Pia Mater, dum vidébat
Of her well belovèd Son.	Nati poenas íncliti.

THE THIRD STATION

Jesus Falls the First Time under His Cross

(Genuflect) *We adore Thee, O Christ, and we praise Thee.*

R. Because by Thy holy Cross Thou hast redeemed the world.

Surely he hath borne our infirmities and carried our sorrows: and we have thought him, as it were, a leper—and as one struck by God and afflicted. But he was wounded for our iniquities, and bruised for our sins: the chastisement of our peace was upon him, and by his bruises we are healed. All we like sheep have gone astray—every one hath turned aside into his own way: and the Lord hath laid on him the iniquity of us all. (Is 53.4-6)

MAN HAS FALLEN, and he continues to fall: often he becomes a caricature of himself, no longer the image of God, but a mockery of the Creator. Is not the man who—on the way from Jerusalem to Jericho—fell among robbers who stripped him and left him half-dead and bleeding beside the road, the image of humanity par excellence?

Our Lord's fall beneath the Cross is not just the fall of the man Jesus, exhausted from his scourging. There is a more profound meaning in this fall, as Paul tells us in the Letter to the Philippians: "His nature is, from the first, divine, and yet he did not see, in the rank of Godhead, a prize to be coveted; he dispossessed himself, and took the nature of a slave, fashioned in the likeness of men… and then he lowered his own dignity, accepting an obedience which brought him to death, even death on a cross" (Phil 2.6-8).

In our Lord's fall beneath the weight of the Cross, the meaning of his whole life is seen: his voluntary abasement, which lifts us up from the depths of our pride. The nature of our pride is also revealed: it is that arrogance which makes us want to be liberated from God and left alone to ourselves—the arrogance which makes us think we do not need his eternal love, but can be the masters of our own lives.

In this rebellion against truth—this attempt to be our own god, creator, and judge—we fall headlong and plunge into self-destruction. The humility of Jesus is the surmounting of our pride; by his abasement he lifts us up. Let us allow him to lift us up. Let us strip away our sense of self-sufficiency, our false illusions of independence, and learn from him, the One who humbled himself, to discover our true greatness by bending low before God and before our downtrodden brothers and sisters.

PRAYER SAID BY ALL (*Kneeling*)

LORD JESUS, the weight of the cross
made you fall to the ground.
The weight of our sin,
the weight of our pride, brought you down.
But your fall is not a tragedy, or mere human weakness.
You came to us when, in our pride, we were laid low.

The arrogance that makes us think
that we ourselves can create human beings
has turned man into a kind of merchandise,
to be bought and sold,
or stored to provide parts for experimentation.

In doing this,
we hope to conquer death by our own efforts,
yet in reality
we are profoundly debasing human dignity.

Lord help us; we have fallen.
Help us to abandon our destructive pride and,
by learning from your humility,
to rise again.

What man is there so unfeeling,	Quis est homo qui non fleret,
Who, his heart to pity steeling,	Matrem Christi si vidéret
Could behold that sight unmoved?	In tanto supplício?

THE FOURTH STATION

Jesus Meets His Afflicted Mother

(Genuflect) *We adore Thee, O Christ, and we praise Thee.*

R. Because by Thy holy Cross Thou hast redeemed the world.

Simeon blessed them, and said to his mother Mary, "Behold, this child is destined to bring about the fall of many and the rise of many in Israel; to be a sign which men will refuse to acknowledge; and so the thoughts of many hearts shall be made manifest. As for thy own soul, it shall have a sword to pierce it." And his mother kept in her heart the memory of all this. (Lk 2.34-35, 51)

ON OUR LORD'S Way of the Cross, we also find Mary, his Mother. During his public life she had to step aside, to make place for the birth of Jesus' new family: the family of his disciples.

She also had to hear the words: "Who is my mother and who are my brothers? [...] Whoever does the will of my Father in heaven is brother, and sister and mother" (Mt 12.48-50). Now we see her as the Mother of Jesus, not only physically, but also in her heart. Even before she conceived him bodily, through her obedience she conceived him in her heart.

It was said to Mary: "And behold, you will conceive in your womb and bear a son. He will be great and the Lord God will give to him the throne of his father David" (Lk 1.31ff). And she would hear from the mouth of the elderly Simeon: "A sword will pierce through your own soul" (Lk 2.35). She would then recall the words of the prophets, words like these: "He was oppressed, and he was afflicted, yet he opened not his mouth; he was like a lamb that is led to slaughter" (Is 54.7). Now it all takes place.

In her heart she had kept the words of the angel, spoken to her in the beginning: "Do not be afraid, Mary" (Lk 1.30). The disciples fled, yet she did not flee. She stayed there, with a Mother's courage, a Mother's fidelity, a Mother's goodness, and a faith which did not waver in the hour of darkness: "Blessed is she who believed" (Lk 1.45). "Nevertheless, when the Son of man comes, will he find faith on earth?" (Lk 18.8). Yes, in this moment Jesus knows: he will find faith. In this hour, this is his great consolation.

PRAYER SAID BY ALL *(Kneeling)*

HOLY MARY, Mother of the Lord,
you remained faithful when the disciples fled.
Just as you believed
the angel's incredible message—
that you would become the Mother of the Most High—
so, too, you believed
at the hour of his greatest abasement.

In this way, at the hour of the Cross,
at the hour of the world's darkest night,
you became the Mother of all believers,
the Mother of the Church.

We beg you: teach us to believe,
and grant that our faith
may bear fruit in courageous service
and be the sign of a love ever ready
to share suffering and to offer assistance.

Lives there one whose heart with anguish	Quis non posset contristári,
Fills not, thus to see her languish,	Christi Matrem contemplári
Agonizing with her Son?	Doléntem cum Fílio?

THE FIFTH STATION

The Cyrenian Helps Jesus to Carry His Cross

(Genuflect) *We adore Thee, O Christ, and we praise Thee.*

R. Because by Thy holy Cross Thou hast redeemed the world.

As for his cross, they forced a man of Cyrene, Simon by name, whom they met on their way out, to carry it. — Jesus said to his disciples: If any man will come after me, let him deny himself, and take up his cross, and follow me. (Mt 27.32, 16.24)

SIMON of Cyrene is on his way home, returning from work, when he comes upon the sad procession of those condemned—for him, perhaps, it was a common sight. The soldiers force this rugged man from the country to carry the Cross on his own shoulders. How annoying he must have thought it to be suddenly caught up in the fate of those condemned men!

He does what he must do, but reluctantly. Significantly, the Evangelist Mark does not only name him, but also his children, who were evidently known as Christians and as members of that community (cf. Mk 15.21). From this chance encounter, faith was born. The Cyrenian, walking beside Jesus and sharing the burden of the Cross, came to see that it was a grace to be able to accompany him to his crucifixion and to help him.The mystery of Jesus, silent and suffering, touched his heart.

Jesus, whose divine love alone can redeem all humanity, wants us to share his Cross so that we can complete what is still lacking in his suffering (cf. Col 1.24). Whenever we show kindness to the suffering, the persecuted and defenseless, and share in their sufferings, we help to carry that same Cross of Jesus. In this way we obtain salvation, and help contribute to the salvation of the world.

How often is the holy sacrament of his Presence abused; how often must he enter empty and evil hearts! How often do we celebrate only ourselves, without even realizing he is there! How often is his Word twisted and misused! What little faith is present behind so many theories, so many empty words! How much filth there is in the Church, and even among those who—in the priesthood—ought to belong entirely to him! How much pride, how much self-complacency! What little respect we pay to the Sacrament of Confession, where he waits for us, ready to raise us up whenever we fall!

All this is present in his Passion. His betrayal by his disciples, their unworthy reception of his Body and Blood, is certainly the greatest suffering endured by the Redeemer; it pierces his heart. We can only call to him from the depths of our hearts: *Kyrie eleison!* Save us, O Lord! (cf. Mt 8.25).

PRAYER SAID BY ALL (*Kneeling*)

LORD, your Church often seems
like a boat about to sink,
a boat taking in water on every side.

In your field, we see more weeds than wheat.
The soiled garments and face of your Church
throw us into confusion.
Yet it is we ourselves who have soiled them!

It is we who betray you time and time again,
after all our lofty words and grand gestures.
Have mercy on your Church;
within her too, Adam continues to fall.

When we fall,
we drag you down to earth,
and Satan laughs,
for he hopes that you will not be able
to rise from that fall;
he hopes that being dragged down
in the fall of your Church,
you will remain prostrate and overpowered.

But you will rise again.
You stood up, you arose
and you can also raise us up.
Save and sanctify your Church.
Save and sanctify us all.

Mother, every wound and tremor	Sancta Mater, istud agas,
Of the crucified Redeemer,	Crucifíxi fige plagas
Firmly fasten in my soul;	Cordi meo válide.

THE TENTH STATION

Jesus is Stripped of His Garments

(Genuflect) *We adore Thee, O Christ, and we praise Thee.*

R. Because by Thy holy Cross Thou hast redeemed the world.

And so they reached a place called Golgotha, that is, the place named after a skull. Here they offered him wine mixed with gall—which he tasted, but would not drink—and then crucified him, dividing his garments among them by casting lots. The prophecy must be fulfilled: *They divide my spoils among them, cast lots for my garments.* There, then, they sat, keeping guard over him. (Mt 27.33-36)

OUR REDEEMER is stripped of his garments. Clothing gives a man his social position; it gives him his place in society, it makes him someone. His public stripping means that Jesus is no longer anything at all—he is simply an outcast, despised by all alike. The moment of the stripping reminds us of the expulsion from Paradise: God's splendor has fallen away from man, who now stands naked and exposed, unclad and ashamed.

And so Jesus once more takes on the condition of fallen man. Stripped of his garments, he reminds us that we have all lost the "first garment" that is God's splendor. At the foot of the Cross, the soldiers draw lots to divide his paltry possessions, his clothes.

The Evangelists describe the scene with words drawn from Psalm 21: "They divided my garments among themselves; and for my vesture they cast lots." By doing so, they tell us the same thing that Jesus would tell his disciples on the road to Emmaus: that everything takes place "according to the Scriptures." Nothing is mere coincidence; everything that happens is contained in the Word of God and sustained by his divine plan.

The Lord passes through all the stages and steps of man's fall from grace—yet each step, for all its bitterness, becomes a step towards our redemption: this is how he carries home the lost sheep. Let us not forget how St. John says that lots were drawn for our Savior's tunic, "woven without seam from top to bottom" (Jn 19.23). We may consider this as a reference to the High Priest's robe, which was "woven from a single thread" without stitching (Fl. Josephus, a III, 161). For he, the Crucified One, is the true High Priest.

PRAYER SAID BY ALL (*Kneeling*)

LORD JESUS,
you were stripped of your garments,
exposed to shame, and cast out of society.
You took upon yourself the shame of Adam,
and you healed it.
You also take upon yourself
the sufferings and needs of the poor,
the outcasts of our world.
And in this very way
you fulfill the words of the prophets.

This is how you bring meaning
into apparent meaninglessness.
This is how you make us realize
that your Father holds you, us,
and the whole world in his hands.
Give us a profound respect for man
at every stage of his existence,
and in all the situations in which we encounter him.
Clothe us in the light of your grace.

Since He deigns that all the merit	Tui nati vulneráti,
Of His wounds I should inherit	Tam dignáti pro me pati,
All His pain with me divide.	Poenas mecum dívide.

THE ELEVENTH STATION

Jesus is Nailed to the Cross

(Genuflect) *We adore Thee, O Christ, and we praise Thee.*

R. Because by Thy holy Cross Thou hast redeemed the world.

Over his head they set a written proclamation of his offense: *This is Jesus, the king of the Jews*. And with him they crucified two thieves, one on his right and one on his left. Those passing by blasphemed against him, tossing their heads. "Come now," they said, "thou who wouldst destroy the temple and build it up in three days, rescue thyself; come down from that cross, if thou art the Son of God." The chief priests, with the scribes and elders, mocked him in the same way. "He saved others," they said, "himself he cannot save. If he is the king of Israel, he has but to come down from the cross, here and now, and we will believe in him." (Mt 27.37-42)

OUR LORD is nailed to the Cross. The shroud of Turin gives us an idea of the unbelievable cruelty of this procedure. Jesus does not drink the numbing gall offered to him: he deliberately takes upon himself all the pain of the Crucifixion. His whole body is racked; the words of the Psalm have come to pass: "But I am a worm, and no man: the reproach of men, and the outcast of the people" (Ps 21.7). "As one from whom men hide their faces, he was despised ... surely he has borne our infirmities and carried our sorrows" (Is 53.3-4).

Let us halt before this image of pain, before the suffering Son of God. Let us look upon him at times of presumptuousness and pleasure, in order to learn to respect limits and to see the superficiality of all merely material goods. Let us look upon him at times of trial and tribulation, and realize that it is then that we are closest to God. Let us try to see his face in the people we might look down upon.

As we stand before the condemned Lord—who did not use his power to come down from the Cross, but endured its suffering to the end—another thought comes to mind. Saint Ignatius of Antioch, a prisoner in chains for his faith in the Lord, praised the Christians of Smyrna for their invincible faith; saying they were, so to speak, *nailed with flesh and blood to the Cross of the Lord Jesus Christ* (Epistle to the Smyrnaeans 1.1). Let us nail ourselves to him, resisting the temptation to stand apart, or to join others in mocking him.

PRAYER SAID BY ALL *(Kneeling)*

LORD JESUS CHRIST,
you let yourself be nailed to the Cross,
accepting the terrible cruelty of this suffering,
the destruction of your body and your dignity.

You allowed yourself to be nailed fast;
you did not try to escape
or to lessen your suffering.
May we never flee
from what we are called to do.

Help us to remain faithful to you.
Help us to unmask the false freedom
which would distance us from you.
Help us to accept your "binding" freedom, and,
"bound" fast to you, to discover true freedom.

Make me thy co-mourner truly,	Fac me tecum pie flere,
For His crucifixion duly	Crucifíxo condolére,
Sorr'wing till my life is o'er:	Donec ego víxero.

THE TWELFTH STATION

Jesus Dies Upon the Cross

(Genuflect) *We adore Thee, O Christ, and we praise Thee.*

R. Because by Thy holy Cross Thou hast redeemed the world.

And Pilate wrote out a proclamation, which he put on the cross; and the writing was: *Jesus of Nazareth, the king of the Jews*. This proclamation was read by many of the Jews, since the place where Jesus was crucified was close to the city; and it was written in Hebrew, Greek, and Latin. (Jn 19.19-20)

IN GREEK AND LATIN, the two international languages of the time, and in Hebrew, the language of the Chosen People, a sign stood above the Cross of Jesus, indicating who he was: the King of the Jews, the promised Son of David. Pilate, the unjust judge, became a prophet despite himself. The kingship of Jesus was proclaimed before all the world.

Jesus himself had not accepted the title "Messiah" because it would have suggested a mistaken, human idea of power and deliverance. Yet now the title can remain publicly displayed above the Crucified Christ. He is indeed the king of the world.

Now he is truly "lifted up." In sinking to the depths, he rose to the heights. Now he has radically fulfilled the commandment of love; he has completed the offering of himself, and in this way he is now the revelation of the true God, the God who is love.

Now we know who God is. Now we know what true kingship is. Jesus prays Psalm 21, which begins with the words: "My God, my God, why have you forsaken me?" He takes to himself the whole suffering people of Israel, all of suffering humanity, the drama of God's darkness, and he makes God present in the very place where he seems definitively vanquished and absent.

The Cross of Jesus is a cosmic event. The world is darkened, when the Son of God is given up to death. The earth trembles. And on the Cross, the Church of the Gentiles is born. The Roman centurion understands this, and acknowledges Jesus as the Son of God. From the Cross he triumphs—ever anew.

PRAYER SAID BY ALL (*Kneeling*)

LORD JESUS CHRIST,
at the hour of your death
the sun was darkened.
Ever anew you are being nailed to the Cross.
At this present hour of history
we are living in God's darkness.

Through your great sufferings
and the wickedness of men,
the face of God—your face—
seems obscured, unrecognizable.
And yet, on the Cross,
you have revealed yourself.

Precisely by being the one
who suffers and loves,
you are exalted.
From the Cross on high, you have triumphed.

Help us to recognize your face
at this hour of darkness and tribulation.
Help us to believe in you
and to follow you in our hour
of darkness and need.
Show yourself once more
to the world, at this hour.
Reveal to us your salvation.

Mine with thee be that sad station,
There to watch the great salvation
Wrought upon th'Atoning Tree.

Juxta Crucem tecum stare,
Et me tibi sociáre
In planctu desídero.

THE THIRTEENTH STATION

Jesus is Taken Down from the Cross

(Genuflect) *We adore Thee, O Christ, and we praise Thee.*

R. Because by Thy holy Cross Thou hast redeemed the world.

The centurion and those who kept guard with him over Jesus, when they perceived the earthquake and all that befell, were overcome with fear. "No doubt," they said, "but this was the Son of God." There were also many women there, looking on from afar, who had followed Jesus from Galilee, ministering to him. (Mt 27.54-55)

JESUS IS DEAD. From his heart, pierced by the lance of the Roman soldier, blood and water flow: a mysterious image of the stream of the sacraments, Baptism and the Eucharist, by which the Church is constantly reborn from the opened heart of the Lord. Our Redeemer's legs are not broken, like those of the two men crucified with him. He is thus revealed as the true Paschal lamb, "not one of whose bones must be broken" (cf. Ex 12.46).

And now, at the end of his sufferings, it is clear that—for all the dismay which filled men's hearts, for all the power of hatred and cowardice—he was never alone. There are faithful ones who remain with him. Under the Cross stand: MARY, his Mother; Mary, the sister of his Mother; Mary Magdalen; and the disciple whom he loved. A wealthy man, Joseph of Arimathea, appears on the scene: a rich man is "able to pass through the eye of a needle," for God has given him the grace.

Joseph buries Jesus in his own empty tomb, in a garden. At the burial of Jesus, the cemetery becomes a garden: the garden from which Adam was cast out when he abandoned the fullness of life, his Creator. The garden tomb symbolizes that the dominion of death is about to end. A member of the Sanhedrin also comes along—Nicodemus, to whom Jesus had proclaimed the mystery of rebirth by water and the Spirit. Even in the Sanhedrin, which decreed his death, there is a believer; someone who knows and recognizes Jesus after his death.

In this hour of immense grief, of darkness and despair, the light of hope is mysteriously present. The hidden God continues to be the God of life, ever near. Even in the night of death, the Lord continues to be our Lord and Savior. The Church of Jesus Christ—his new family—begins to take shape.

PRAYER SAID BY ALL *(Kneeling)*

LORD, you descended
into the darkness of death.
But your body is placed in good hands
and wrapped in a white shroud (Mt 27.59).

Faith has not completely died;
the sun has not completely set.

How often does it appear that you are asleep!
How easy it is for us to step back
and say to ourselves: "God is dead."

In the hour of darkness,
help us to know that you are still there.
Do not abandon us
when we are tempted to lose heart.
Help us not to leave you alone.

Give us the fidelity
to withstand moments of confusion
and a love ready to embrace you
in your utter helplessness,
like your Mother,
who once more holds you in her arms.

Help us—the poor and rich,
simple and learnèd—
to look beyond all our fears and prejudices,
and to offer you our abilities,
our hearts and our time,
and thus to prepare a garden for the Resurrection.

Virgin of all virgins fairest,
Share with me the pains thou bearest,
Be thy crushing sorrows mine.

Virgo vírginum praeclára,
Mihi jam non sis amára:
Fac me tecum plángere.

THE FOURTEENTH STATION

Jesus is Placed in the Tomb

(Genuflect) *We adore Thee, O Christ, and we praise Thee.*

R. Because by Thy holy Cross Thou hast redeemed the world.

Joseph took possession of the body, and wrapped it in a clean winding-sheet; then he buried it in a new grave—which he had fashioned for himself out of the rock—and left it there, rolling a great stone against the grave-door. When he had gone, there were two who sat there opposite the tomb: Mary Magdalen and the other Mary with her. (Mt 27.59-60)

OUR REDEEMER, disgraced and mistreated, is honorably buried in a new tomb. Nicodemus brings a mixture of myrrh and aloes—about a hundred pounds' weight—which gives off a precious scent. In the Son's self-offering, as at his anointing in Bethany, we see an "excess" which evokes God's generous and superabundant love. God offers himself unstintingly. If God's measure is superabundance, then we for our part should consider nothing too much for God. This is the teaching of Jesus himself, in the Sermon on the Mount (Mt 5.20). But we should also remember the words of Saint Paul, who says that God "through us, spreads the fragrance of the knowledge of Christ everywhere. We are the aroma of Christ" (II Cor 2.14ff).

Amid the decay of ideologies, our faith needs once more to be the fragrance which returns us to the path of life. At the very moment of his burial, our Lord's words are fulfilled:

> "Believe me when I tell you this: A grain of wheat must fall into the ground and die, or else it remains nothing more than a grain of wheat—but if it dies, then it yields rich fruit." (Jn 12.24).

Jesus is the grain of wheat which dies. From that lifeless grain of wheat comes forth the great multiplication of bread which will endure until the end of the world. Jesus is the bread of life which can satisfy superabundantly the hunger of all humanity and provide its deepest nourishment. Through his Cross and Resurrection, the eternal Word of God became flesh and bread for us. The mystery of the Eucharist already shines forth in the burial of Jesus.

PRAYER SAID BY ALL *(Kneeling)*

LORD JESUS CHRIST,
in your burial you have taken on
the death of the grain of wheat.
You have become the lifeless grain of wheat
which produces abundant fruit
for every age and for all eternity.

From the tomb shines forth in every generation
the promise of the grain of wheat
which gives rise to the true manna,
the Bread of Life,
in which you offer us your very self.

The eternal Word,
through his Incarnation and death,
has become a Word which is close to us:
you put yourself into our hands
and into our hearts,
so that your word can grow within us
and bear fruit.

Through the death of the grain of wheat
you give us yourself,
so that we, too, can dare to lose our life
in order to find it,
so that we, too, can trust the promise
of the grain of wheat.

Help us grow in love and veneration
for the Eucharistic mystery—
to make you, the Bread of heaven,
the source of our life.
Help us to become your "fragrance,"
and to make known in this world
the mysterious traces of your life.

Like the grain of wheat which rises from the earth,
putting forth its stalk and then its ear,
you could not remain enclosed in the tomb:

the tomb is empty because he—the Father—
"did not abandon you to the nether world,
nor let your flesh see corruption" (Acts 2.31; Ps 15.10).

No, you did not see corruption.
You have risen,
and have made a place
for our transfigured flesh
in the very heart of God.

Help us to rejoice in this hope
and bring it joyfully to the world.
Help us to become witnesses of your resurrection.

Let me, mindful of His Passion
Die in Christ, and, in some fashion,
Bear the wounds He bore for me.

Fac ut portem Christi mortem
Passiónis fac consórtem,
Et plagas recólere.

IN THE NAME of the Father, ✠ and of the Son, and of the Holy Spirit. R. AMEN.

"STABAT MATER" CONCLUSION

All His bitter torments feeling,
In the cross my spirit reeling,
In His blood my senses drown.

Fac me plagis vulnerári,
Fac me cruce inebriári,
Et cruóre Fílii.

Lest I burn in fires unending,
Sinless Maid, my cause befriending,
Shield me at the judgment day.

Flammis ne urar succénsus,
Per te, Vírgo, sim defénsus
In die judícii.

Jesus, when earth's shadows leave me,
Thru thy Mother's prayers receive me
With the palm of victory.

Christe, cum sit hinc exíre,
Da per Matrem me veníre
Ad palmam victóriae.

When my body lies forsaken
Let my ransomed soul awaken
Safe, in Paradise, with thee.

Quando corpus moriétur,
Fac ut ánimae donétur
Paradísi glória.

Overview • Brébeuf Hymnal

Part I • Ancient Hymns of the Catholic Church

With literal translation, as well as numerous melodies and metrical translations.

Color Plates

Including facsimiles of Catholic hymnals with rhyming vernacular translations of breviary hymns reaching as far back as 1599AD.

Complete Indices

Located in the center of the book, immediately after the color pages.

Part II • Additional Hymns

Organized by the various seasons: Advent, Christmas, and so forth.

Stations of the Cross